DEBBIE MUMM'S PROJECT KIDS™

1116 E. Westview Ct.
Spokane, WA 99218-1384

Toll Free: (888) 819-2923
www.debbiemumm.com

CREDITS

Designed by Debbie Mumm®
Special thanks to my creative teams

QUILT TEAM

Pamela Mostek:
Publications Manager

Roberta Rose-Knauth &
Jean Van Bockel:
Quilt & Craft Designers

Janet Wickell: *Editor*

Darra Williamson: *Writer*

Candy Huddleston:
Seamstress & Machine Quilter

Shirley Porter: *Seamstress*

Nona King & Wanda Jeffries:
Machine Quilters

BOOK DESIGN TEAM

Marcia Smith: *Art Director*

Tom Harlow: *Production Manager*

Heather Hughes: *Production*

Sandy Ayars:
Pen & Ink Illustrations

J. Craig Sweat Photography

Revised ©2001 Debbie Mumm, Inc.

Printed in China

FIVE LITTLE MONKEYS

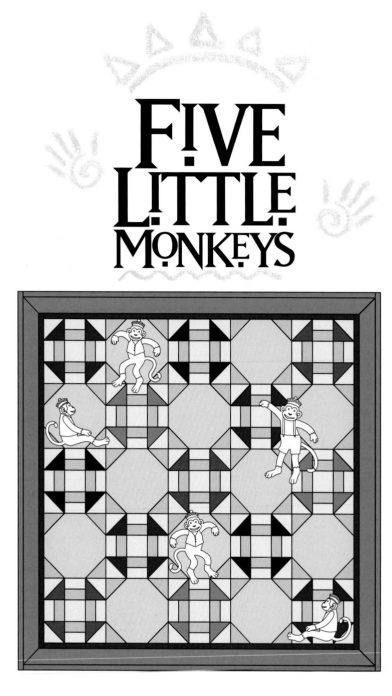

Quilt Layout
Finished Size: 71" square
Photo: page 26

What's "more fun than a barrel of monkeys?" Why, a quilt full of monkeys, of course! And what better partner for our five charming monkeys than the traditional Monkey Wrench block, combined with the so-simple Snowball block for a subtle—but super—secondary design. Quick corner triangles and quick-fuse appliqué make construction a breeze. Read all instructions before beginning and use $^1/_4$" seams throughout.

Fabric Requirements

Fabric A *(Monkey Wrench blocks)*
Gold background
$1^1/_2$ yards

Fabric B *(Snowball blocks)*
Gold star background
$1^1/_2$ yards

Fabric C *(Monkey Wrench and Snowball Blocks)*
Check fabric
$1^1/_4$ yards

Fabric D *(Monkey Wrench blocks)*
$^1/_3$ yard each of 4 fabrics (red, teal, blue, and navy)

Appliqué Monkey Bodies
$^1/_2$ yard

Appliqué Monkey Body Accent
$^1/_4$ yard

Appliqué Mouths, Hats, and Clothes
Assorted scraps

Accent Border - $^1/_3$ yard

Border - 1 yard

Binding - $^2/_3$ yard

Backing - $4^1/_4$ yards

Lightweight Batting
78" square

Sewable Fusible Web - 1 yard

Tear-away Stabilizer

Notions
Pom-poms, buttons, ric rac, and embroidery floss

CUTTING THE STRIPS AND PIECES

Pre-wash and press fabrics. Using rotary cutter, see-through ruler, and cutting mat, cut the following strips and pieces. If indicated, some will need to be cut again into smaller strips and pieces. The approximate width of the fabric is 42". Measurements for all the pieces include $1/4$" seam allowance.

Fabric A *(Monkey Wrench blocks)*
Gold background
  Eight $4^1/_2$" x 42" strips, cut into
    Sixty-five $4^1/_2$" squares
  Six $2^1/_2$" x 42" strips

Fabric B *(Snowball blocks)*
Gold star background
  Four $12^1/_2$" x 42" strips, cut into
    Twelve $12^1/_2$" squares

Fabric C *(Snowball blocks)*
Check fabric
  Six $4^1/_2$" x 42" strips, cut into
    Forty-eight $4^1/_2$" squares
(Monkey Wrench blocks)
Check fabric
  Six $2^1/_2$" x 42" strips

Fabric D *(Monkey Wrench blocks)*
Red, teal, blue, and navy fabric
  Two $4^1/_2$" x 42" strips of each
    fabric, cut into
      Sixteen $4^1/_2$" squares (red)
(Monkey Wrench blocks)
  Twelve $4^1/_2$" squares from teal,
    blue, and navy

Accent Border
  Six $1^1/_2$" x 42" strips

Border
  Seven $4^1/_2$" x 42" strips

Binding
  Eight $2^3/_4$" x 42" strips

MAKING THE BLOCKS

You will be making 13 Monkey Wrench blocks and 12 Snowball blocks. To use the assembly line method for each step, position pieces right sides together next to your sewing machine. Stitch first set together, then continue sewing others without breaking threads. When all units are sewn, clip threads to separate them. Press in direction of arrows in diagrams.

Monkey Wrench Blocks

1. Refer to Quick Corner Triangle directions on page 62. Sew each $4\frac{1}{2}$" Fabric D square to a $4\frac{1}{2}$" Fabric A square. Trim and press. Repeat to sew each $4\frac{1}{2}$" Fabric D squares to a $4\frac{1}{2}$" Fabric A square. Stack like units together. Red Fabric D will make 16 units; the others will make 12 each. You will have 13 Fabric A squares left over. Set these aside.

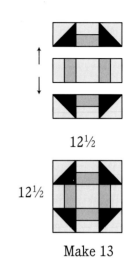

A/D= $4\frac{1}{2} \times 4\frac{1}{2}$

2. Sew $2\frac{1}{2}$" x 42" Fabric A and Fabric C strips in pairs to make six identical strip sets. Cut fifty-two $4\frac{1}{2}$" segments.

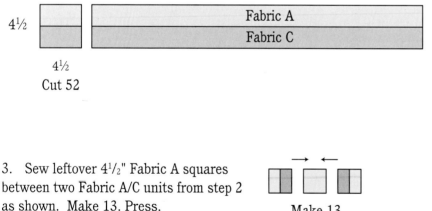

$4\frac{1}{2}$

Fabric A
Fabric C

$4\frac{1}{2}$

Cut 52

3. Sew leftover $4\frac{1}{2}$" Fabric A squares between two Fabric A/C units from step 2 as shown. Make 13. Press.

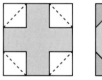

Make 13

4. Sew remaining Fabric A/C units between two matching Fabric A/D units from step 1 as shown. Make 26. Press.

Make 26

5. Sew units from step 3 between like units from step 4 as shown. Press.

$12\frac{1}{2}$

$12\frac{1}{2}$

$12\frac{1}{2}$

Make 13

Snowball Blocks

Refer to Quick Corner Triangle directions on page 62. Sew four $4\frac{1}{2}$" Fabric C squares to each $12\frac{1}{2}$" Fabric B square. Trim and press. Snowball blocks will now measure $12\frac{1}{2}$" square.

C= $4\frac{1}{2} \times 4\frac{1}{2}$
B= $12\frac{1}{2} \times 12\frac{1}{2}$

ASSEMBLY

1. Arrange blocks as shown in the layout on page 2. Press seams in adjoining rows in opposite directions. Join rows and press.

Accent Borders

1. Measure the quilt from side to side through its horizontal midpoint. Trim and piece the 1¹/₂" x 42" strips to obtain two borders that exact length. Fold crosswise to determine borders' midpoint, then match and pin midpoint to the midpoint on the top of the quilt, right sides together. Match and pin the ends, then continue matching and pinning along the entire top, easing in fullness if necessary. Sew together, then press the seam allowance toward the border. Repeat to add the bottom accent border.

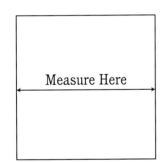

Measure Here

2. Measure the quilt through its vertical midpoint, including top and bottom borders. Trim and piece the remaining 1¹/₂" x 42" strips to obtain two borders that exact length. Pin each to one side of the quilt using the same technique as in step 2, matching midpoint and ends first, then pinning along the entire length. Sew to the quilt and press seam allowance toward the border.

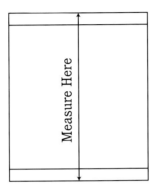

Measure Here

Mitered Borders

1. To add the mitered borders, measure the quilt again vertically and horizontally. Measurements should be the same. If they differ slightly, determine their average, then add 12 inches. Trim and piece together the 4¹/₂" x 42" strips to make four borders that exact length.

2. Fold crosswise to find borders' midpoint and mark with a pin. Using the quilt dimension measured in step 1, pin-mark border ends to show where edges of the quilt will be (do not match the border to the side of the quilt to determine length). Repeat with remaining borders.

3. Beginning at a marked end point, draw a 45° diagonal line to represent the mitered seam line. Repeat on the opposite end of the strip, drawing a mirror-image line, and on remaining borders.

4. Align a border to the quilt as for straight sewn borders, pinning midpoints and ends first, and then pinning along an entire side. Sew the border to the quilt, back-stitching at stop and start points. Do not sew past the pin marks at either end. Sew all borders to the sides in this way.

5. Fold quilt corners diagonally, right sides together. Match and pin the marked sewing lines at one corner. End points of adjacent seams should match. Begin sewing at the same spot where side seam ended. Backstitch at the beginning of the seam and continue sewing to the ends of strips. Trim excess border ¹/₄" from seam and press open. Repeat on remaining corners.

QUICK-FUSE APPLIQUÈ

1. Refer to Quick-Fuse Appliqué directions on page 63. Trace appliqué designs from pages 6-9 and 13. Fuse bodies, body accents, hats, and clothing to blocks, refering to color photo on page 26 for placement.

2. Finish edges using a machine blanket, satin, or small zigzag stitch. If desired, use tear-away stabilizer on wrong side of quilt for an even stitch.

3. Referring to face pattern on page 6-9 and 13 for placement, handstitch button eyes in place. Refer to Embroidery Stitch Guide on page 62 and use three strands of embroidery floss for satin stitch nose. Add ric rac, buttons, and pom-poms referring to color photo on page 26.

LAYERING AND FINISHING

1. Cut backing fabric crosswise into two equal pieces. Sew together to make one 76" x 84" (approximate) backing piece. Press seam open. Arrange and baste backing, batting, and top together referring to Layering the Quilt directions on page 63.

2. Machine or hand quilt as desired.

3. Sew eight $2^3/_4$" x 42" binding strips together in pairs. Refer to Binding the Quilt directions on page 63 to finish.

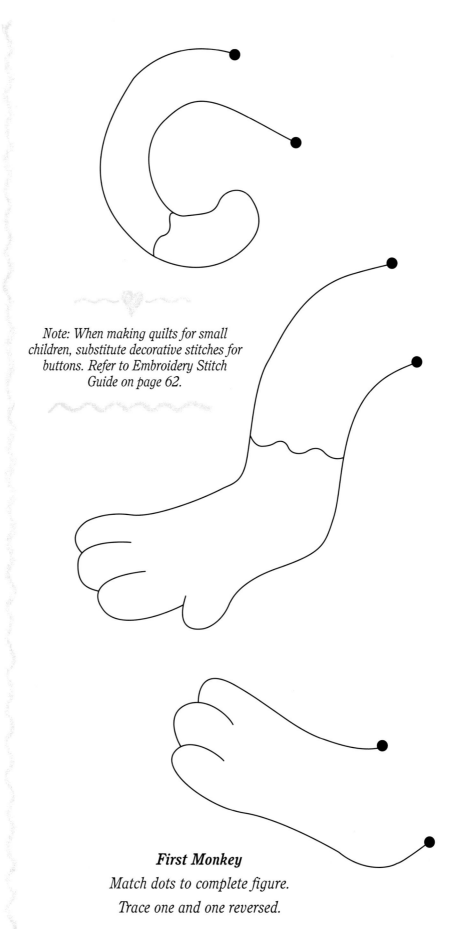

Note: When making quilts for small children, substitute decorative stitches for buttons. Refer to Embroidery Stitch Guide on page 62.

First Monkey
Match dots to complete figure.
Trace one and one reversed.

First Monkey

Match dots to complete figure.

Trace one and one reversed.

7

Second Monkey

Match dots to complete figure.

Trace one.

8

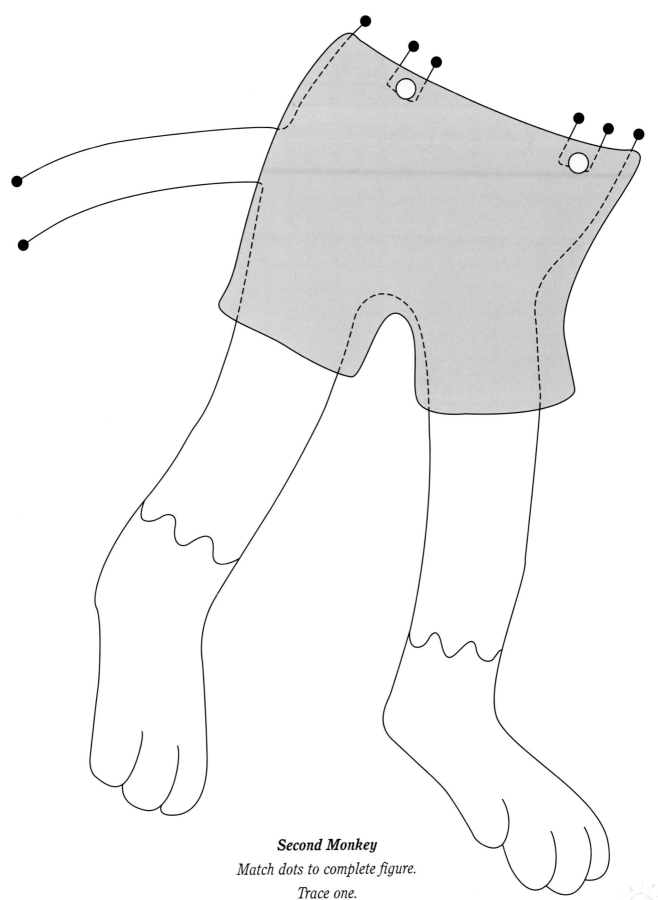

Second Monkey

Match dots to complete figure.

Trace one.

9

MONKEY PILLOW

Pillow Layout
Finished Size: 32" square
Photo: page 26

A frisky Mr. Monkey swings casually from his very own Monkey Wrench perch! Children everywhere will appreciate these comfy pillows, perfectly sized for TV watching...or just for snuggling. Read all instructions before beginning and use $^1/_4$" seams throughout.

Fabric Requirements

Fabric A *(Monkey Wrench background)*
$^5/_8$ yard

Fabric B *(Monkey Wrench strips)*
$^1/_6$ yard

Fabric C *(Monkey Wrench triangles)*
$^1/_3$ yard

Appliqués
Assorted scraps for body, face, hands, feet, hat, shorts, and suspenders

Accent Border - $^1/_6$ yard

Border - $^1/_2$ yard

Backing - $1^3/_8$ yards

Sewable Fusible Web - $^1/_3$ yard

Tear-away Stabilizer

Needlepunch Fleece
Two $32^1/_2$" squares

Polyester Fiberfill Stuffing

Notions
Hook and loop tape, embroidery floss, small buttons, decorative ric rac, small pom-pom

CUTTING THE STRIPS AND PIECES

Read first paragraph of *Cutting the Strips and Pieces* on page 3.

Fabric A *(Monkey Wrench background)*
  One 8½" square
  Two 8⅞" squares,
    cut diagonally
  One 4½" x 42" strip

Fabric B *(Monkey Wrench strips)*
  One 4½" x 42" strip

Fabric C *(Monkey Wrench triangles)*
  Two 8⅞" squares,
    cut diagonally

Accent Border
  Two 1½" x 24½" strips
  Two 1½" x 26½" strips

Border
  Two 3½" x 26½" strips
  Two 3½" x 32½" strips

Backing
  Two 22½" x 32½" pieces

MONKEY WRENCH BLOCK

Whenever possible, use assembly-line sewing. Position pieces right sides together and line up next to your sewing machine. Stitch first set together and continue without breaking your thread. Trim and press in direction of arrows in diagrams.

1. Sew 4½" x 42" Fabric A and Fabric B strips along one long side to make a strip set. Press seam toward darker fabric. Cut four 8½" square segments.

2. Pair Fabric A and Fabric C triangles right sides together and sew. Press seam toward darker fabric.

3. Sew 8½" Fabric A square between two Fabric A/B units from step 1 as shown. Press.

4. Sew Fabric A/B unit between two Fabric A/C units from step 2 as shown. Make two and press.

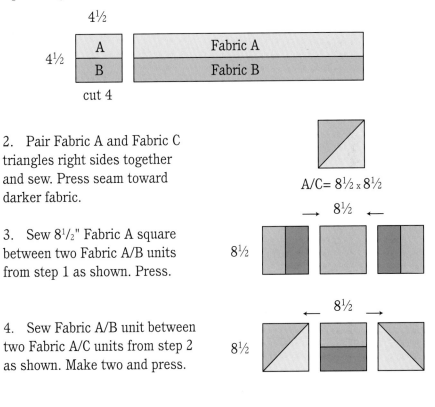

A/C = 8½ x 8½

5. Sew unit from step 3 between units from step 4 as shown. Press.

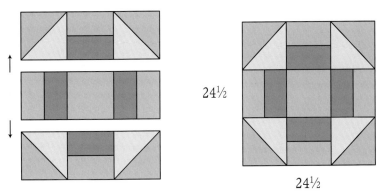

Borders
Sew short accent border strips to top and bottom of block. Press seams toward accent border. Sew long accent border strips to sides of block. Press. Repeat to add border strips to top and bottom and sides. Press.

QUICK-FUSE APPLIQUÉ

1. Refer to Quick-Fuse Appliqué directions on page 63. Trace body, face, hands, feet, shorts, suspenders, and hat from patterns on pages 8 and 9. Quick-fuse to pillow, referring to layout on page 10 and color photo on page 26 for placement.

2. Finish edges using a machine blanket, satin, or small zigzag stitch. If desired, use tear-away stabilizer on wrong side of block for an even stitch.

3. Referring to monkey pattern on page 8 for placement, hand stitch button eyes in place. Refer to Embroidery Stitch Guide on page 62 and use three strands of embroidery floss for satin stitch nose.

4. Add additional embellishments as desired. We added ric rac trim and pom-pom to monkey's hat, buttons to "fasten" his suspenders, and fabric bowtie.

Making Pillow Form

Place 32¹⁄₂" squares of needlepunch fleece together, aligning raw edges. Using ¹⁄₄" seam, sew around all edges, leaving 4" opening for turning. Trim corners and turn right-side out. Stuff to desired fullness with polyester fiberfill and hand stitch opening closed.

LAYERING AND FINISHING

1. Narrow hem one long edge of each 22¹⁄₂" x 32¹⁄₂" backing piece by folding under ¹⁄₄" to wrong side. Press. Fold again ¹⁄₄" to wrong side. Press. Topstitch along folded edge.

2. With right sides up, lay one backing piece over second piece so hemmed edges overlap, making single 32¹⁄₂" square backing panel. Baste pieces together at top and bottom where they overlap.

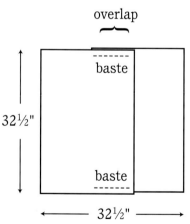

overlap

baste

32¹⁄₂"

baste

32¹⁄₂"

3. With right sides together, position and pin pillow top to backing. Using ¹⁄₄" seam, sew around edges. Trim corners, turn right side out, and press.

4. Insert pillow form in pillow cover. If desired, stitch hook and loop tape to overlapped hemmed edges to secure.

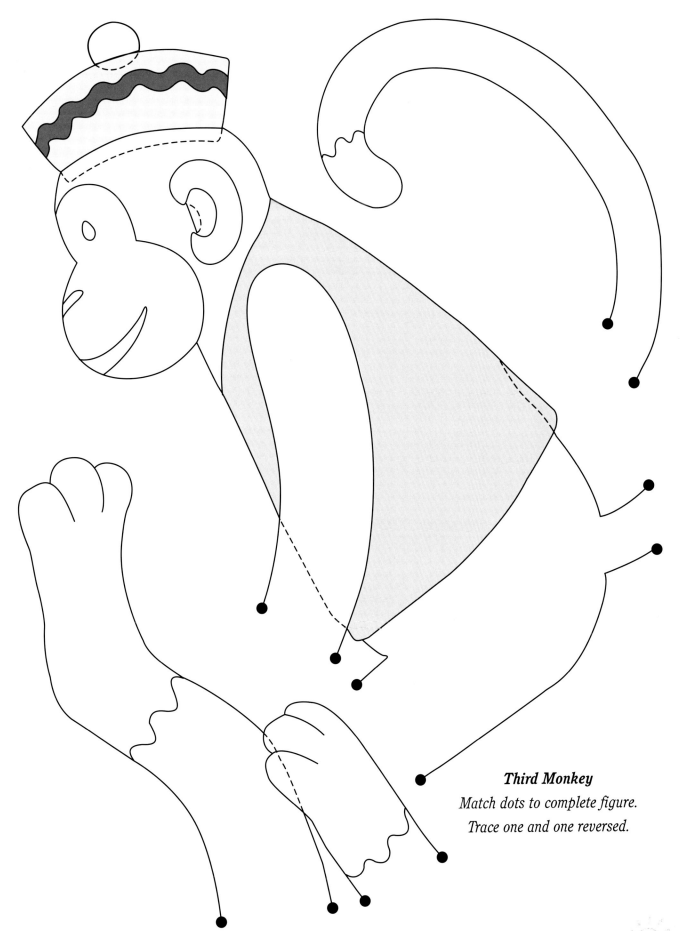

Third Monkey
Match dots to complete figure.
Trace one and one reversed.

RAFFLE QUILT

Quilt Layout
Finished Size: 89" x 111"
Photo: page 24

*Harvest a bounty of funds for your favorite children's charity!
Three simple blocks combine with luscious fruit and vine
appliqués in this stunning queen-sized quilt. Scrappy blocks and
border triangles are easily divided among various stitchers, and
just as easily group-assembled when individual efforts are
complete. Read all instructions before beginning and use
$1/4$" seam allowances throughout.*

Fabric Requirements

Fabric A *(background)*
Block 3
> Four 8$1/2$" squares of
> four fabrics

Fabric B *(assorted dark fabrics)*
Block 1 and 3
> 2$3/4$ yards

Fabric C *(assorted light fabrics)*
Block 1, 2, and 3
> 4$1/4$ yards

Fabric D *(assorted medium fabric
and setting triangles)*
Block 1, 2, and setting triangles
> 3$1/2$ yards

Fabric E *(setting border)*
> 2$7/8$ yards

**Berry, Grape, Stem, Tendril, and
Grape Leaf Appliqués**
> Assorted scraps

Leaf Appliqués - $1/2$ yard
Vine - 1 yard
Binding - 1 yard
Backing - 8$1/2$ yards
Lightweight Batting
> 96" x 118" piece

14

CUTTING THE STRIPS AND PIECES

Read first paragraph of *Cutting the Strips and Pieces* on page 3.

Fabric B *(assorted darks)*
Block 1 and 3
  Forty 9" squares
Fabric C *(assorted lights)*
Block 1 and 2
  Fifty-six 4" squares
Block 1 and 2
  Twenty 5³/₈" squares
Block 1
  Thirty-six 7" squares
Block 2 and 3
  Twenty-eight 9" squares
Fabric D *(assorted medium fabrics and setting triangles)*
Block 1 and 2
  Fifty-six 4" squares
Block 1 and 2
  Thirty-six 5³/₈" squares
Block 2
  Twenty 7" squares
Setting Triangles
  Fourteen 8¹/₂" squares
Fabric E *(setting border)*
  Four 24¹/₄" squares
Vine
  1⁵/₈" wide bias strips
    (approximately 450" total)
Binding
  Eleven 2³/₄" x 42" strips

MAKING THE BLOCKS

This quilt requires three different block variations. You will be making 18 of block 1 (dark outer triangles), 10 of block 2 (light outer triangles), and four of block 3 (center blocks for appliqué). Finished block size for all three is 16".

To use the assembly line method for each step, position pieces right sides together next to your sewing machine. Stitch first unit together, then continue sewing others without breaking threads. When all units are sewn, clip threads to separate them. Press units in opposite directions.

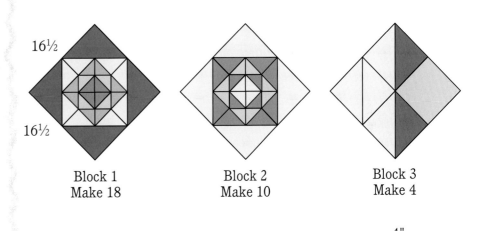

Block 1
Make 18

Block 2
Make 10

Block 3
Make 4

1. Use ruler to mark one diagonal on fifty-six 4" Fabric C squares on wrong side. Mark dashed diagonal line exactly ¹/₄" from both sides of original line as shown.

4"
4"
Make 56

2. Pair each marked Fabric C square with a 4" Fabric D square right sides together. With Fabric C facing you, sew directly on both dashed diagonal lines. Using rotary cutter and ruler, cut each stitched square into two units along solid diagonal line. (You'll have 112 light-medium units.) Press half of seams toward light triangles and half toward medium triangles. Trim pieced squares to 3 ³/₈", using the 45-degree line on a rotary ruler to make sure each half of the square is equal.

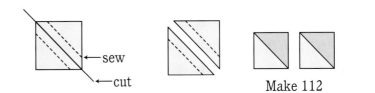

sew
cut

Make 112

3.   Arrange four pieced squares as shown to form 28 four-patch blocks. In 18 blocks, turn light Fabric C triangles to outside edge (block 1). In remaining 10, turn medium Fabric D triangles to outside edge (block 2). For best matching, arrange triangle squares so that adjoining units have diagonal seams pressed in opposite directions. Sew squares into pairs. Press new seams in opposite directions. Join pairs and press.

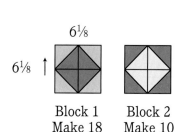

$6\frac{1}{8}$

$6\frac{1}{8}$

Block 1
Make 18

Block 2
Make 10

4.   Cut $5\frac{3}{8}$" Fabric D squares in half twice diagonally to make 144 triangles. Sew triangles together in scrappy pairs along one short side (block 1) to make 72 medium two-triangle units. Press carefully, since the stretchy bias is on the short edges. Repeat with $5\frac{3}{8}$" Fabric C squares to make a total of 40 light two-triangle units (block 2).

Make 72   Make 40

5.   Sew each block 1 square unit from step 3 between two block 1 triangle units from step 4. Press. Sew block 1 triangle units to remaining sides. Press. Repeat to sew block 2 triangle units to all sides of block 2 square units. Trim blocks to $8\frac{1}{2}$".

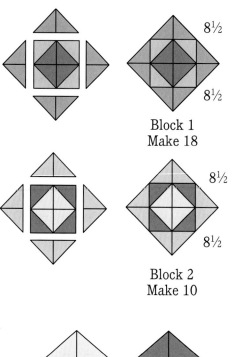

$8\frac{1}{2}$

$8\frac{1}{2}$

Block 1
Make 18

$8\frac{1}{2}$

$8\frac{1}{2}$

Block 2
Make 10

6.   Cut 7" Fabric C squares in half twice diagonally to make 144 triangles. Sew triangles together in scrappy pairs along one short side (block 1) to make 72 light two-triangle units. Press. Repeat with 7" Fabric D squares to make 40 medium two-triangle units (block 2).

Block 1
Make 72

Block 2
Make 40

7.   Sew block 1 triangle units from step 6 to all sides of a block 1 square from step five, matching seam intersections carefully. Press seams toward new unit after each addition. Repeat to sew block 2 triangle units to all sides of block 2 square units. Square-up blocks to $11\frac{3}{4}$".

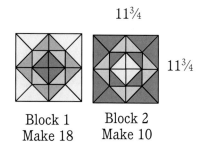

$11\frac{3}{4}$

$11\frac{3}{4}$

Block 1
Make 18

Block 2
Make 10

8.   Cut 9" Fabric B and Fabric C squares in half along one diagonal. Sew a Fabric B triangle to one side of a block 1 from step 7. Press seam toward new triangle. Sew Fabric B triangles to remaining sides, pressing after each addition. Sew Fabric C triangles to all sides of block 2 square units. You'll have some triangles left over. Square-up blocks to $16\frac{1}{2}$".

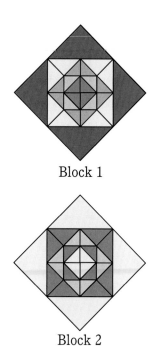

Block 1

Block 2

9. Sew eight of the leftover 9" Fabric C triangles right sides together in scrappy pairs along diagonal edge to make four units. Press. Pair remaining Fabric C triangles with remaining Fabric B triangles and sew long diagonal edge. Press. Square-up units to measure 8½" square, taking care to leave ¼" seam allowance around all edges.

C/C=8½" x 8½"
Make 4

B/C=8½" x 8½"
Make 8

10. Arrange Fabric A square, a Fabric C/C square from step 9, and two Fabric B/C squares from step 9 to layout a block 3 as shown. Sew squares into pairs. Press in opposite directions. Join pairs and press. Make a total of four.

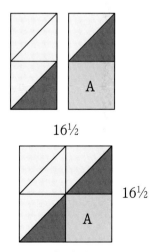

16½

16½

Block 3
Make 4

11. Arrange four block 3 units into single large block, rotating units so that Fabric A square is in center as shown. Sew block 3 units into pairs. Press seams in opposite directions. Join pairs and press.

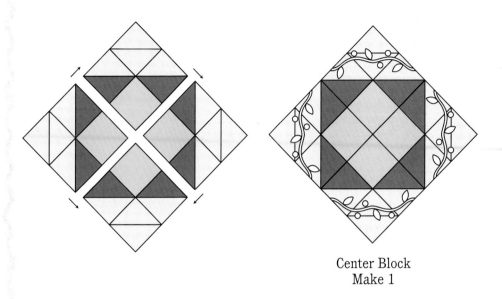

Center Block
Make 1

PREPARING FOR APPLIQUÉ

1. Trace appliqué designs from pages 18-19. Make templates and use assorted scraps to trace one each of pieces 2 (stem), 3,5,6, and 12 (grape leaves). Use leaf fabric to trace 54 vine leaves. Cut out appliqués, adding ¼" seam allowance around each piece.

2. For tendrils, fold one 1⅛" x 18" bias strip right sides together. Stitch down unfinished edge to make ⅛" bias tube. Cut piece in half for pieces one and four on page 18. Press with ⅛" bias bar.

3. Make template for 1½" circle (piece 28) on page 19. Use assorted scraps to trace 22 circles for grape cluster and 12 for vine berries. Cut out circles, adding ¼" seam allowance around each one.

4. Sew 1⅝" bias strips end to end to make one continuous strip. Cut into fourteen 1⅝" x 23" strips for border vines, and four 1⅝" x 25" strips for center vines. Fold strips right sides together. Stitch down unfinished edge to make ⅝" bias tube. Press with ⅝" bias bar.

5. Position stem, tendrils, grape leaves, and grapes in center of large block 3 unit, referring to color photo on page 24 for placement. Use preferred method to hand stitch appliqués in place.

6. Position one ⅝" x 25" vine, three vine leaves, and three berries on each corner of center panel as shown in step 11 above. Use preferred method to hand appliqué vines, leaves, and berries in place. Repeat for the other corners.

Grapes and Leaf Appliqué

Match grape numbers on page 19 to complete image.

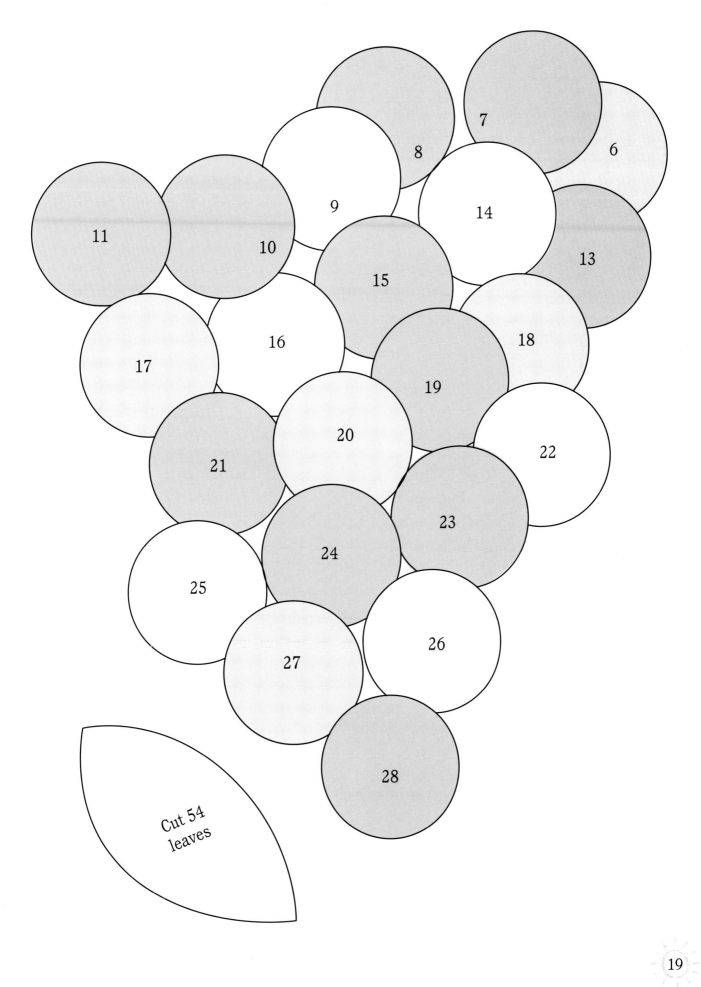

Cut 54 leaves

SETTING TRIANGLES

1. Cut the 24" Fabric E squares on both diagonals to make 16 setting triangles. You will need 14; set extras aside for another project.

2. Refer to Quick-Corner Triangle directions on page 62. Sew one 8½" Fabric D square to each setting triangle as shown.

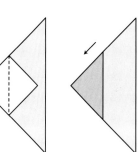

Setting Borders
Make 14

3. Position a ⅝" x 23" vine on each setting triangle, reversing curve of vine as shown. Place three leaves on each triangle. Leave seam allowance free of appliqué. Use preferred method to hand appliqué vines and leaves in place.

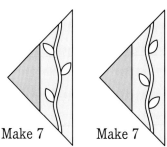

Make 7   Make 7

ASSEMBLY

1. The Raffle Quilt is assembled in diagonal rows. Referring to layout on page 14, arrange blocks in their proper position. Alternate block 1 and block 2 units, and insert appliquéd center panel in rows four and five as shown. Begin and end each diagonal row with an appliquéd setting border.

2. Keep track of layout while sewing blocks together into rows 1, 2, 3, 6, 7, and 8. Press seams in adjoining rows in opposite directions.

3. Assemble top left row segments of rows four and five. Press seams in opposite directions. Join row segments and press. Repeat to assemble and join lower right row segments. Press.

4. Sew top left and lower right segments of rows four and five to appliquéd center panel. Press.

5. Complete quilt top by sewing rows 1, 2, and 3 to upper right edge of row 4/5 strip. Sew rows 6, 7, and 8 to lower left edge. Press.

Rows 4 and 5
Make 2

FOR A GROUP PROJECT

With its scrappy good looks and block-to-block construction, The Raffle Quilt makes the perfect group project. Use the following guidelines when making individual block assignments.

Block 1 — make 18
For each block you will need:
  Fabric B (dark) four half-square triangles cut from 9" squares
  Fabric C (light) two 4" squares; eight scrappy quarter-square triangles cut from 7" squares
  Fabric D (medium) two 4" squares; eight scrappy quarter-square triangles cut from 5⅜" squares

Block 2 — make 10
For each block you will need:
  Fabric C (light) two 4" squares; eight quarter square triangles cut from 5⅜" four half-square triangles cut from 9" squares
  Fabric D (medium) two 4" squares; eight quarter-square triangles cut from 7" squares

Block 3 — make 4
  Fabric A (light) one 8½" square
  Fabric B (dark) two half-square triangles cut from 9" squares
  Fabric C (light) four half-square triangles cut from 9" squares

Setting Triangles — Make 14
For an assignment of four triangles:

  Fabric D *(medium)* four $8\frac{1}{2}$" squares

  Fabric E *(light)* one $24\frac{1}{4}$" square

Bias Stems For consistency, select one person to make all stems from bias strips

Appliqué Assignments
You probably have members who love to appliqué. Turn the pieced units over to them when its time to add the grapes and vines. Give each person yardage for grapes and leaves so she or he can cut pieces with their own preferred seam allowances.

Center Panel
  Four Block 3, sewn together
  Stem *(piece 2)*, cut one
  Tendrils *(pieces 1, 4)*
  Grape Leaves *(pieces 3, 5, 12)*, cut one each
  Grapes and Berries *(piece 28)*, cut 34 from assorted scraps, approximately $\frac{1}{3}$ yard total
  Vines - four $1\frac{5}{8}$" x 25" bias strips
  Vine Leaves, cut 12 from assorted scraps, approximately $\frac{1}{8}$ yard total

For Each Group of Four Setting Triangles
  Vines - Four $1\frac{5}{8}$" x 23" bias strips
  Leaves - cut 12 from assorted scraps (approximately $\frac{1}{8}$ yard total)

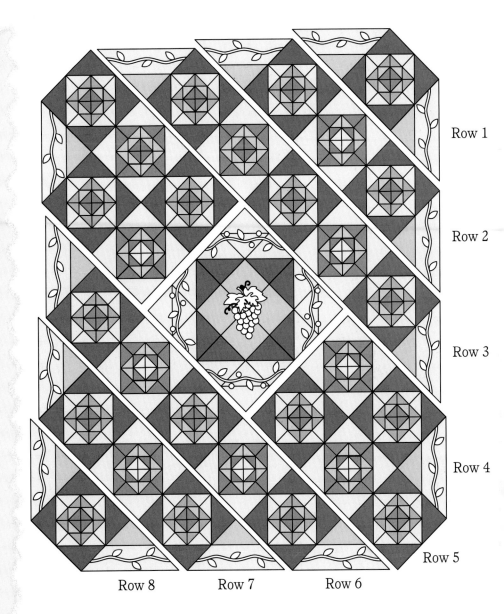

Row 1
Row 2
Row 3
Row 4
Row 5
Row 6
Row 7
Row 8

LAYERING AND FINISHING

1. Cut backing fabric crosswise into three equal pieces. Sew together to make one 100" x 124" (approximate) backing piece. Arrange and baste backing, batting, and top together, referring to Layering the Quilt directions on page 63.

2. Machine or hand quilt as desired.

3. Use $2\frac{3}{4}$" x 42" strips to make four binding strips, each approximately 18" long. Refer to Binding the Quilt directions on page 63. Sew these strips to the four corners of the quilt. Trim ends flush with quilt after sewing. Make two more binding strips for top and bottom, each 75" long. Sew the top and bottom strips to quilt, folding under where they meet corners. Make two more binding strips for sides, each 105" long. Sew side bindings to quilt in the same way.

CRAYON PATCH

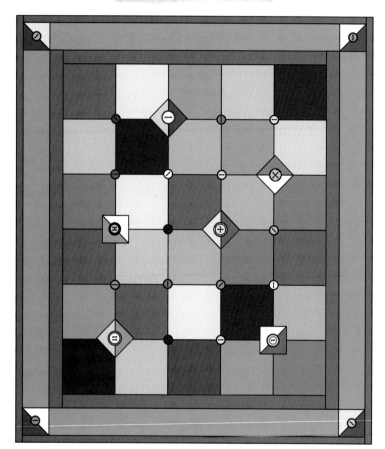

Quilt Layout
Finished Size: 51" x 59"
Photo: page 31

Crisp and colorful as a brand new box of crayons, this cheerful quilt is sure to brighten even the rainiest of days. Scrappy squares piece together in a flash, while quick-fuse appliqués add sparkle in a jiffy. Colorful buttons attach with matching floss to secure the layers for a quick-as-a-wink finish. Read all instructions before beginning and use $1/4$" seams throughout.

Fabric Requirements

Fabric *(blocks)*
Thirty $8^{1}/_{2}$" squares of
assorted scrappy fabrics

Fabric B *(corner patches)*
Twenty $4^{1}/_{2}$" squares of
assorted scrappy fabrics

Accent Border - $1/_{3}$ yard

Border - $5/_{8}$ yard

Faux Binding - $1/_{4}$ yard

Backing - $3^{1}/_{2}$ yards

High Loft Batting
56" x 64" piece

Sewable Fusible Web - $1/_{4}$ yard

Notions
24 assorted buttons,
embroidery floss

CUTTING THE STRIPS AND PIECES

Read first paragraph of *Cutting the Strips and Pieces* on page 3.

Accent Border
Five $1^{1}/_{2}$" x 42" strips

Border
Six $4^{1}/_{2}$" x 42" strips

Faux Binding
Seven 1" x 42" strips

ASSEMBLY

1. Arrange and sew 8½" Fabric A squares into six horizontal rows of five squares each. Press seam allowances in adjoining rows in opposite directions. Join rows and press.

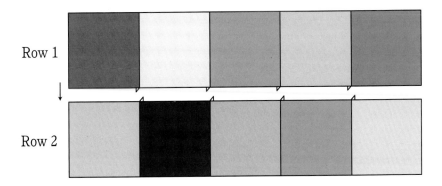

Row 1

Row 2

2. Refer to Quick Corner Triangle directions on page 62. Sew all 4½" squares in pairs to make 10 corner patches. Press.

3. Refer to Quick-Fuse Appliqué directions on page 63. Fuse six corner patches at block junctions. Refer to color photo on page 31 for placement. Referring to Embroidery Stitch Guide on page 62, use three strands of embroidery floss to blanket stitch around edges of corner patches.

Adding the Borders

1. Measure quilt through the center from side to side. Trim two 1½" accent border strips to this measurement. Sew to top and bottom. Press seams toward accent border.

2. Measure quilt through the center from top to bottom, including the accent borders. Use remaining 1½" accent border strips to make two borders this length. Sew to sides. Press.

3. Repeat measuring as described in step 1. Trim two 4½" border strips to make two borders this measurement. Sew to the top and bottom of the quilt. Press seams toward the borders.

4. Use the remaining 4½" border strips to make two side borders the same length determined for accent borders in step 2.

5. Sew a corner patch to each end of side borders. Press seams toward borders. Fit, pin, and sew border strips to each side of the quilt.

Faux Binding

1. Measure the quilt through the center from side-to-side. Trim one 1" x 42" faux binding strip in half. Sew halves together in pairs with one 1" binding strip. Trim binding strips to this measurement. Sew to top and bottom. Press seams toward binding.

2. Measure the quilt through the center from top-to-bottom. Sew remaining binding strips together and trim to this measurement. Sew to sides. Press.

LAYERING AND FINISHING

1. Cut backing fabric crosswise into two equal pieces. Sew together and trim to make one 60" x 82" (approximately) backing piece.

2. Center top on backing right sides together. Center both pieces on top of batting and pin through all layers. Using ¼" seam, sew around all edges, leaving a 9" opening for turning. Trim backing and batting to same size as quilt top. Trim corners and turn right side out. Turn under raw edges neatly and hand stitch opening closed. Press lightly.

3. Use matching embroidery floss to tie a colored button at each four-block junction and in each corner of accent border. Refer to color photo on page 31 for placement. Be sure to tie through all layers, and knot securely. Tie without buttons as desired throughout the quilt.

Note: When making tied quilts for small children, tie without buttons.

Raffle Quilt, p.14

Nursery Windows, p.32

Sleepy Time, p.58

Nighty Night Baby, p.60

Five Little Monkeys, p. 2
Monkey Pillow, p.10

Kid's Art, p. 42

Huggy Bear Quilt, p. 46 ● *Bear Hug Doll, p. 50*

Heavenly Baby Quilt ●
p.38

● *Heavenly Baby Quilt Variation, p.38*
For a different look, try this quick-and-easy quilt in Debbie's
traditional palette of blues, reds, and tans

Ric Rac, p. 36

Crayon Patch, p. 22 ◎ *Ragamumm Kids*, *p. 52*

MAKE IT SCRAPPY!

Nursery Windows can be a fun and easy group project and a perfect way to use those small pieces of favorite fabrics that you've been saving.

Divide the 30 blocks into 5 different colors and assign a color to each volunteer. For an even faster assembly, two or more quilters can create blocks from each color. A total of six blocks is needed from each of the five color schemes. When the blocks are sewn, put them together in an assembly line style. In no time at all you will have a delightful quilt that is ready to share with a child in need of a big hug!

NURSERY WINDOWS

Quilt Layout
Final Size: 48" x 40"
Photo: page 25

Create the feeling of dimension and depth with this clever use of light and dark fabrics. Strip sets are pieced in five different colorways, then cut apart and reassembled for a soothing sunshine-and-shadow effect. Prairie Points provide the perfect finishing touch. Read all instructions before beginning and use $1/4$" seam allowances throughout.

Fabric Requirements

Fabric A *(light window frames)*
  $1/4$ yard each of five different
    light colored fabrics

Fabric B *(dark window frames)*
  $1/4$ yard of darker shade of each
    Fabric A color

Fabric C *(window centers)*
  $2^{1}/_{8}$ yards of assorted fabrics

Prairie Points
  $3/4$ yard of assorted scraps

Backing
(minimum 44" wide)
  $1^{1}/_{2}$ yards

Lightweight Batting
  44" x 52" piece

Fabric A
Light window frames

Fabric B
Dark window frames

Fabric C
Window centers and
Prairie Points for borders

CUTTING THE STRIPS AND PIECES

Read first paragraph of *Cutting the Strips and Pieces* on page 3.

Fabric A *(light window frames)*
  Three $2^{1}/_{2}$" x 42" strips of
    each light fabric, cut each into
    Two $2^{1}/_{2}$" x 18" strips

Fabric B *(dark window frames)*
  Three $2^{1}/_{2}$" x 42" strips of
    each dark fabric, cut each into
    Two $2^{1}/_{2}$" x 18" strips

Fabric C *(window centers)*
  Thirty $2^{1}/_{2}$" x 42" strips total,
    cut into four $2^{1}/_{2}$" x 9" strips
    from each strip

Prairie Points
  Fifty-eight 4" scrappy squares

MAKING THE BLOCKS

You will be making 30 window blocks. To use the assembly line method for each step, position pieces right sides together next to your sewing machine. Stitch first unit together, and continue sewing others without breaking threads. When all units are sewn, clip threads to separate them. Press in direction of arrows in diagrams.

1.   Sort 2½" x 18" Fabric A and Fabric B strips by color. Choose one dark and one light shade of the same color.

2.   Select two different 2½" x 9" Fabric C strips. Sew lengthwise to a Fabric A strip, align short edges together where they meet at strip center. Clip the long seam allowance almost to the stitching where Fabric C strips meet together. Press the long seam allowance, reversing directions at the clip.

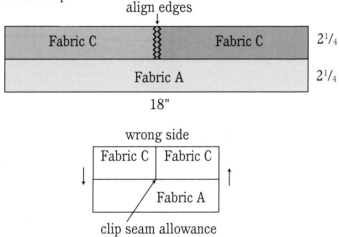

3.   Select another pair of the same two Fabric C strips used in step 2, sewing them lengthwise to the darker B strip. Butt short ends, clip seam, and press as before. Group strip sets together and set aside.

4.   Assemble remaining strip sets in the same way, keeping each pair of strips together. You will have 60 strip sets.

5.   Use the pattern on page 35 to make a triangle template. Align the longest edge of the template with the raw edge of Fabric A or Fabric B in each strip set as shown. Cut two triangles from each strip set, keeping groups together.

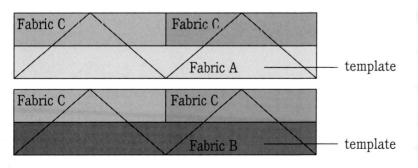

6.   Sew each group of four triangles into a block. Sew the two light-bottomed triangles together, then sew the two dark-bottomed triangles together, matching seams. Press new seams in opposite directions and join block halves, carefully matching center seams. Repeat with all groups to make a total of 30 blocks.

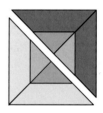

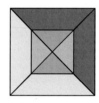

ASSEMBLY

Referring to layout on page 32, arrange blocks in a balanced color arrangement of six horizontal rows containing five blocks each. Keep track of layout while sewing blocks together into rows. Press seams in adjoining rows in opposite directions. Join rows and press.

LAYERING AND FINISHING

1. Use 4" assorted scrap squares to make 58 Prairie Points, folding each twice along the diagonal as shown.

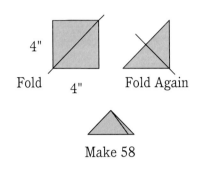

4"

Fold   4"   Fold Again

Make 58

2. Starting at the center and working outwards, align and pin raw edges of 13 Prairie Points along the top edge of quilt as shown, nesting one inside the folds of another if necessary to adjust total width. Repeat on the bottom edge of quilt.

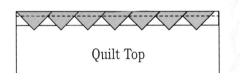

Quilt Top

3. Pin 16 Prairie Points to each side of the quilt in the same way. Triangle edges should meet at quilt corners.

4. When you are satisfied with the arrangement, sew all Prairie Points to the quilt with $1/4$" seams.

5. Arrange and baste backing, batting, and top together referring to Layering the Quilt directions on page 63. Machine or hand quilt as desired being careful not to quilt through Prairie Points. Leave 1" from all edges of quilt free from quilting.

6. Trim batting and backing to match quilt top, then trim an additional $1/4$" of batting from all sides.

7. Fold Prairie Points away from quilt, pointing them outward. Turn under $1/4$" of backing and hand stitch in place, covering seams that attached Prairie Points to quilt. Add more quilting around edges if desired.

match with seam line

Nursery Window Template
$1/4$" seam allowance included

Cut 120

RIC RAC

Quilt Layout
Finished Size: 50" x 66"
Photo: page 30

Ribbons of color streak top to bottom on this scrappy quilt! You'll piece the half-square triangle blocks lightning-quick with a simple two-for-one, cut-no-triangle method. Read all instructions before beginning and use 1/4" seam allowances throughout.

Fabric Requirements

Darks

  1 1/3 yards assorted scraps

Lights

  1 1/3 yards assorted scraps

First Accent Border - 1/3 yard

Second Accent Border - 1/3 yard

Border - 1 yard

Binding - 2/3 yard

Backing - 3 1/4 yards

Lightweight Batting

  54" x 70" piece

CUTTING THE STRIPS AND PIECES

Read first paragraph of *Cutting the Strips and Pieces* on page 3.

Darks

  Seventy 4 7/8" squares

Lights

  Seventy 4 7/8" squares

First Accent Border

  Six 1" x 42" strips

Second Accent Border

  Six 1" x 42" strips

Border

  Seven 4" x 42" strips

Binding

  Seven 2 3/4" x 42" strips

MAKING THE BLOCKS

The Fabric A and Fabric B squares are used to make 140 half square triangle units. The assembly line method will help you sew them together in record time.

1. Use a ruler to mark one diagonal on the wrong side of each $4^{7}/_{8}$" Fabric B square. Mark a dashed line exactly $^{1}/_{4}$" from both sides of the original line as shown or use $^{1}/_{4}$" presser foot.

2. Pair each Fabric A square with a Fabric B square, right sides together. Stack the pairs next to your sewing machine, light squares up. Sew a pair together directly on one dashed line. Continue feeding pairs through the machine without breaking the thread. When all pairs are sewn, cut the threads between them and feed through the machine again to sew a seam on the remaining dashed lines.

3. Cut threads between the units and press flat to set the seams. Use a rotary cutter and ruler to cut each square apart along its solid diagonal line. Press the triangle squares open, with seam allowances toward the dark sides.

A/B= $4^{1}/_{2}$ x $4^{1}/_{2}$

ASSEMBLY

1. Referring to the layout on page 36, arrange blocks as shown with 10 triangle squares in 14 horizontal rows. Press seams in adjoining rows in opposite directions. Join rows and press.

2. Measure quilt through the center from side to side. Cut one 1" x 42" accent border strip in half and sew a piece to each of two accent border strips. Trim strips to the measurement. Sew to top and bottom. Press toward border.

3. Measure quilt through the center from top to bottom. Sew two pairs of accent border strips together. Trim strips to this measurement. Sew to sides. Press. Repeat for second accent border.

4. Measure for and add the 4" borders to the quilt in the same manner.

LAYERING AND FINISHING

1. Cut backing fabric crosswise into two equal pieces. Sew pieces together on the long edges to make one 58" x 82" (approximate) backing piece. Arrange and baste backing, batting, and top together referring to Layering the Quilt directions on page 63.

2. Machine or hand quilt as desired.

3. Sew four $2^{3}/_{4}$" x 42" binding strips together in pairs. Cut one remaining $2^{3}/_{4}$" x 42" binding strip in half and sew halves to remaining $2^{3}/_{4}$" x 42" strips. Using shorter strips for top and bottom and longer strips for sides, refer to Binding the Quilt directions on page 63 to finish.

TIP

If you have an accurate $^{1}/_{4}$" presser foot, there is no need to mark the dashed lines. Just use the foot to gauge the distance.

HEAVENLY BABY QUILT

Quilt Layout
Finished Size: 40" x 52"
Photo: page 29

*Sweet dreams are all but guaranteed for the lucky little one
sleeping beneath this celestial confection. Best of all, assembly is
"heavenly" too! You'll layer, piece, and quilt all in one simple
step! What could be easier...or quicker? For a different look, try
it without the appliqué. See color photo on page 29. Read
all instructions before beginning and use
$^{1}/_{4}$" seam allowances throughout.*

Fabric Requirements

Fabric A *(appliqué background)*
  $^{1}/_{3}$ yard
Fabric B *(stripes and checkerboard border)*
  $^{2}/_{3}$ yard
Fabric C *(stripes and checkerboard border)*
  $^{2}/_{3}$ yard
Fabric D *(accent border)*
  $^{1}/_{3}$ yard
Fabric E *(checkerboard border)*
  $^{1}/_{6}$ yard
Fabric F *(checkerboard border)*
  $^{1}/_{6}$ yard
Fabric G *(checkerboard border)*
  $^{1}/_{6}$ yard
Appliqués
  Assorted 4" square scraps
Binding - $^{1}/_{2}$ yard
Backing - $1^{5}/_{8}$ yards
  (minimum 44" wide)
Lightweight Batting
  44" x 56" piece
Sewable Fusible Web - $^{1}/_{2}$ yard
Notions
Marking pencil or water
soluble pen, basting spray,
walking foot

CUTTING THE STRIPS AND PIECES

Read first paragraph of *Cutting the Strips and Pieces* on page 3.

Fabric A *(appliqué background)*
Two 4½" x 30½" strips

Fabric B *(stripes and checkerboard border)*
One 4½" x 42" strip
Five 3½" x 32½" strips

Fabric C *(stripes and checkerboard border)*
One 4½" x 42" strip
Five 3½" x 32½" strips

Fabric D *(accent border)*
Seven 1½" x 42" strips

Fabric E *(checkerboard border)*
One 4½" x 42" strip

Fabric F *(checkerboard border)*
One 4½" x 42" strip

Fabric G *(checkerboard border)*
One 4½" x 42" strip

Binding
Five 2¾" x 42" strips

ASSEMBLING THE STRIPES

1. Working on a clean, flat surface, open and smooth out batting. Use a chalk marker or water soluble pen to mark a horizontal line 12" from the top edge of the batting.

2. Beginning from the horizontal line, mark a 32" vertical line down the center of the batting. This line determines placement for your stripes, so be extra sure it is straight and accurate.

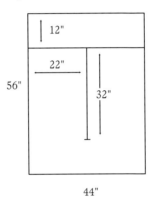

3. Spread backing fabric wrong side up on a clean, flat surface. Smooth out wrinkles and tape edges to surface to secure. Following the manufacturer's instructions, spray backing with basting spray. Center batting over backing with the marked side up.

4. Position a Fabric C strip right side up on the batting. Carefully match the long left edge of the strip with the vertical center line, aligning its short top edge with the horizontal marking.

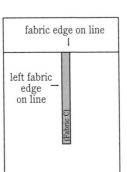

5. Place a Fabric B strip face down over the Fabric C strip and pin. Use a walking foot to machine stitch a seam exactly ¼" from the left edge of the layered strips. You'll be stitching through the strips, batting, and backing so you may want to lengthen your stitch a little.

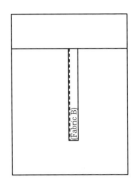

6. Flip and press the top strip (Fabric B). Cover it with a face down Fabric C strip, aligning the left, top, and bottom raw edges. Pin, stitch, flip, and press as before.

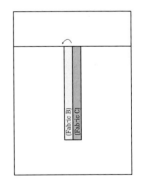

7. Continue adding strips, alternating Fabric B and Fabric C until you have five strips to the left of the center line. Then add alternating strips to the opposite side of the original strip until you have five strips to the right of the center line. Pin carefully to keep the strips straight and to be sure that the top and bottom edges of the strips remain aligned.

8. Trim two $1^1/2$" x 42" Fabric D accent border strips to $30^1/2$" each. Place one strip face down along the top edge of the pieced center stripes, carefully aligning the raw edges. Pin and stitch the top edge with an accurate $1/4$" seam, then flip and press. Repeat to add the bottom strip, this time stitching $1/4$" from the matched bottom raw edges.

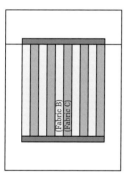

QUICK-FUSE APPLIQUÉ

1. Refer to Quick-Fuse Appliqué directions on page 63. Trace appliqué designs from page 41 onto 4" squares of appliqué fabric to make four of each shape. Quick-fuse two of each shape to a $4^1/2$" x $30^1/2$" Fabric A strip, referring to color photo on page 29 for placement.

2. Stitch around each shape with a blanket or satin stitch. Embroider or pin-stitch eyes, mouth, and cheek on moon.

3. Add an appliqué strip to top and bottom edges of the assembled quilt, matching raw edges carefully. In the same manner, add a $1^1/2$" x $30^1/2$" Fabric D accent border to the long edge of each appliqué strip.

4. Cut one $1^1/2$" x 42" Fabric D strip in half and sew halves to each remaining 42" long Fabric D strip. Trim to measure $1^1/2$" x $44^1/2$" and add to the sides of the assembled quilt as before.

CHECKERBOARD BORDER

1. Arrange the $4^1/2$" x 42" Fabric B, C, E, F, and G strips in a pleasing color arrangement. Sew the strips together to make one strip set, pressing seams toward the darker fabrics.

2. Using rotary cutter and ruler, cut the strip set into $4^1/2$" wide segments.

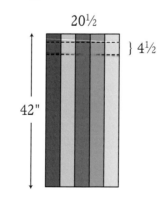

3. Stitch two five-block segments together side by side. Use seam ripper to remove two blocks from the strip. Repeat to make a second eight-block strip.

4. Compare strips to top and bottom edges of the pieced quilt. You many need to take in or let out a few seams ($1/16$" or less) to make them fit. Pin and sew an eight-block strip to top and bottom edges as before.

5. Stitch two-five block segments together side by side. Add three $4^1/2$" squares to the strip (use the strip set leftovers). Repeat to make a second 13-block strip. Adjust seams as necessary, then pin and sew a 13-block strip to each side of the quilt.

FINISHING

1. Hand or machine quilt in seam lines of checkerboard border. Outline appliqués by quilting $1/16$" away from edges. Add additional quilting as desired.

2. Cut one $2^3/4$" x 42" binding strip in half and sew halves to two remaining $2^3/4$" x 42" strips. Using the shorter strips for top and bottom, and the longer strips for sides, refer to Binding the Quilt directions on page 63.

Moon ~ trace four

Star ~ trace four

Saturn's Ring ~ trace four

Placement lines
for Saturn's ring

Saturn ~ trace four

K!DS ART

Quilt Layout
Finished Size: 62" x 75"
Photo: page 27

How better to celebrate children than to celebrate their precious artwork? Courthouse Step blocks create the ideal framework for colorful, childlike appliqués—either ours or the handiwork of your own special someone. Simple "strip 'n square" construction lends itself perfectly to a satisfying assembly-line sewing bee, so gather your friends and set those sewing machines humming! Read all instructions before beginning and use ¹/₄" seams throughout.

Fabric Requirements

Fabric A *(pale yellow block centers)*
¹/₂ yard

Fabric B *(blue and green inside and outside strips)*
1 yard of two different fabrics

Fabric C *(red middle strips)*
³/₄ yard

Fabric D *(check middle strips)*
³/₄ yard

Scraps for Appliqué

Accent Border - ¹/₃ yard

Border - 1 yard

Binding - ⁵/₈ yard

Backing - 4¹/₂ yards

Lightweight Batting
66" x 79" piece

Sewable Fusible Web - 1 yard

Tear-away Stablizer

Appliqué Pressing Sheet™
(see ordering information on page 63)

CUTTING THE STRIPS AND PIECES

Read first paragraph of *Cutting the Strips and Pieces* on page 3.

Fabric A *(block centers)*
Three 5½" x 42" strips,
cut into twenty 5½" squares

Fabric B *(inside and outside strips)*
Three 2½" x 42" strips of
each fabric, cut into
Twenty 2½" x 5½" pieces
Seven 2½" x 42" strips of
each fabric, cut into
Twenty 2½" x 13½" strips

Fabric C *(red middle strips)*
Ten 2½" x 42" strips, cut into
Forty 2½" x 9½" strips

Fabric D *(check middle strips)*
Ten 2½" x 42" strips, cut into
Forty 2½" x 9½" strips

Accent Borders
Six 1½" x 42" strips

Borders
Seven 4½" x 42" strips

Binding
Seven 2¾" x 42" strips

MAKING THE BLOCKS

You will be making 20 Courthouse Step blocks in two different fabric arrangements. Use the assembly line method to make Block A and Block B. Position pieces right sides together and line up next to your sewing machine. Stitch first set together then continue without breaking your thread, trim, and press in the direction of arrows in diagrams.

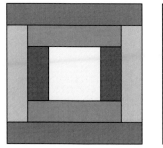 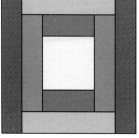

Block A
Make 10

Block B
Make 10

1. Sew matching 2½" x 5½" B strips to opposite sides of each 5½" square. Press.

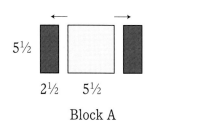 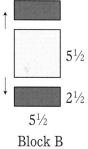

5½   2½   5½

2½   5½

Block A

Block B

2. Sew 2½" x 9½" C strips to top and bottom of units from step 1. Press.

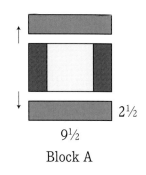 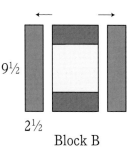

2½

9½

Block A

9½

2½

Block B

3. Sew ½" x 9½" Fabric D strips to opposite sides of units from step 2. Press.

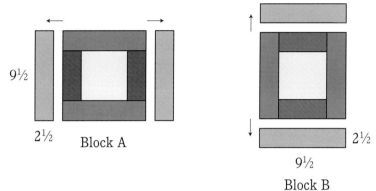

Block A

Block B

4. Sew matching 2½" x 13½" Fabric E strips in second Fabric B color to top and bottom of units from step 3. Press.

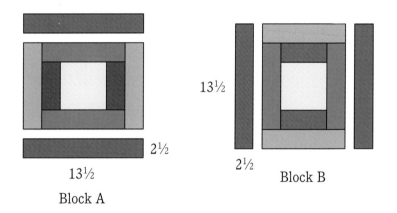

Block A

Block B

ASSEMBLY

Referring to layout on page 42, arrange Courthouse Step blocks in five horizontal rows of four blocks each alternating Block A and Block B. Keep track of layout while sewing blocks together into rows. Press seams in adjoining rows in opposite directions. Join rows and press.

QUICK-FUSE APPLIQUÉ

1. Refer to Quick-Fuse Appliqué directions on page 63. Trace appliqué designs from page 45. Quick-Fuse designs to background, referring to color photo on page 27 for placement. Hint: We found it very helpful to use the Appliqué Pressing Sheet™ by Bear Thread Designs to easily position and center these designs. To use the Appliqué Pressing Sheet™, trace appliqué design on a plain sheet of paper; then retrace onto back of paper. Use this reversed image as a guide for positioning and fusing. See page 63 for ordering information.

2. Finish edges using a machine blanket, satin, or small zigzag stitch. If desired, use tear-away stablizer on wrong side of quilt for an even stitch.

ADDING THE BORDERS

1. Sew four 1½" x 42" accent border strips in pairs and trim to 1½" x 67½". Sew one remaining piece to each 1½" x 42" strip. Sew shorter strips to top and bottom. Trim and press. Sew longer strips to sides. Press.

2. Sew four 4½" x 42" border strips together in pairs. Cut one 4½" x 42" border strip in half and sew halves to two remaining 4½" x 42" strips. Sew shorter strips to top and bottom. Trim and press. Sew longer strips to sides. Trim and press.

LAYERING AND FINISHING

1. Cut backing fabric crosswise into two equal pieces. Sew together to make one 81" x 84" (approximate) backing piece. Arrange and baste backing, batting, and top together, referring to Layering the Quilt directions on page 63.

2. Machine or hand quilt as desired.

3. Sew four 2¾" x 42" binding strips together in pairs. Cut one remaining 2¾" x 42" binding strip in half and sew halves to two remaining 2¾" x 42" strips. Using shorter strips for top and bottom and longer strips for sides, refer to Binding the Quilt directions on page 63 to finish.

Kids Art
Appliqué Shapes

HUGGY BEAR QUILT

Quilt Layout
Finished Size: 43" x 59"
Photo: page 28

*With his clever dimensional bow tie and ears, Huggy Bear is
bound to charm any child he meets! We've made our sample in a
variety of blues, greens, and tans, but you and your friends can
use any scrappy combination you choose. Read all instructions
before beginning and use $1/4$" seams throughout.*

Fabric Requirements

Fabric A *(blue Four-Patch blocks)*
$1/6$ yard of four fabrics

Fabric B *(tan Four-Patch blocks)*
$1/6$ yard of four tan fabrics

Fabric C *(green Four-Patch blocks)*
$1/6$ yard of four green fabrics

Appliqué Backgrounds
Twelve $8^1/2$" squares of
assorted fabrics

Appliqués
$1/6$ yard each of five fabrics

Bow Ties
Twelve $2^1/2$" x $4^1/2$" pieces of
assorted scraps

Accent Border - $1/4$ yard

Border - $3/4$ yard

Border Corner Squares
$1/8$ yard each of four fabrics

Binding - $1/2$ yard

Backing - $2^3/4$ yards

Lightweight Batting
47" x 63" piece

Sewable Fusible Web - $1^1/2$ yard

Appliqué Pressing Sheet™
(see ordering information on
page 63)

Embroidery Floss

Buttons - Twenty-four $1/2$" buttons

CUTTING THE STRIPS AND PIECES

Read first paragraph of *Cutting the Strips and Pieces* on page 3.

Fabric A, B, and C
(blue Four-Patch blocks, tan Four-Patch blocks, green Four-Patch blocks)
One $4^1/_2$" x 20" strip of each fabric (12 total strips)

Accent Border
Five $1^1/_2$" x 42" strips

Border
Five $4^1/_2$" x 42" strips

Border Corner Squares
One $2^1/_2$" x 24" strip of each fabric (4 total strips)

Binding
Five $2^3/_4$" x 42" strips

MAKING THE BLOCKS

You will be making 12 Huggy Bear blocks and 12 Four-Patch blocks. To use the assembly line method for each step, position pieces right sides together next to your sewing machine. Stitch first unit together, then continue sewing others without breaking threads. When all units are sewn, clip threads to separate them. Press in direction of arrows in diagrams.

Four-Patch Blocks
1. Sew $4^1/_2$" x 20" Fabric A, B, and C strips together in pairs to make six $8^1/_2$" x 20" strip sets. Press in opposite directions. Using rotary cutter and ruler, cut four $4^1/_2$" x $8^1/_2$" segments from each strip set.

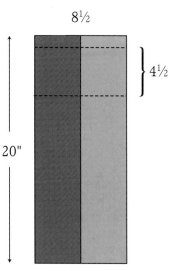

Make 6

2. Sew segments together in pairs to make 12 Four-Patch blocks. Press.

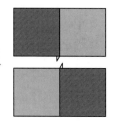

HUGGY BEAR BLOCKS

1. Refer to Quick-Fuse Appliqué directions on page 63. Trace 12 bear heads and bear bodies using pattern on page 49. Fuse heads and shoulders together using Appliqué Pressing Sheet™ by Bear Thread Designs. (see directions on page 44.)

2. Make template for bear ears using pattern on page 49. Layer ear fabrics with right sides together and trace two ears for each bear. Sew on the traced line, leaving bottom straight edges open for turning. Cut out ears $1/_4$" from stitched lines, clip curves, and turn right side out.

3. Line up bottom edge of bear with bottom edge of a background block. Leave ½" free on block sides for seam allowance and quilting.

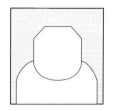

4. Insert ears between bear head and background square as shown. Fuse bear to background square. Referring to Embroidery Stitch Guide on page 62, hand or machine blanket stitch around edges of bear, leaving ears free. Satin stitch noses by hand or machine.

Border Corner Blocks

1. Sew 2½" x 24" strips together in pairs to make two 4½" x 24" strip sets. Press in opposite directions. Using rotary cutter and ruler, cut eight 2½" x 4½" segments from each strip set.

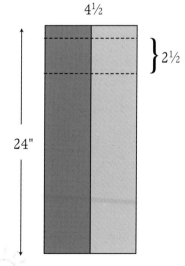

2. Sew segments from each strip set in pairs to make four corner Four-Patch blocks. Press.

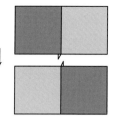

ASSEMBLY

1. Referring to layout on page 44, lay out blocks in a pleasing color arrangement, alternating Four-Patch and Huggy Bear blocks. Make five horizontal rows of four blocks each. Keep track of blocks while sewing together into rows. Press seams toward Huggy Bear blocks. Join rows and press.

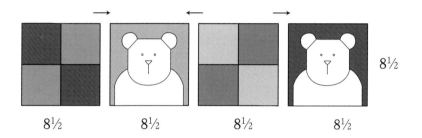

2. Measure quilt through the center from side to side. Trim two 1½" accent border strips to this measurement. Sew to top and bottom of quilt. Press toward accent border.

3. Measure quilt through the center from top to bottom. Trim one 1½" accent border strip in half. Sew halves to two remaining 1½" accent border strips. Trim strips to this measurement. Sew strips to sides of quilt. Press.

4. Measure quilt through the center from side to side. Trim two 4½" border strips to this measurement. Sew to top and bottom of quilt. Press toward border.

5. Use measurement of accent border strips from step 3 to cut remaining border strips for sides of quilt. Sew 4½" border corner squares to each end of strips. Press toward border. Fit, pin, and sew border strips to sides. Press.

Note: When making quilts for small children, substitute decorative stitches for buttons. Refer to Embroidery Stitch Guide on page 62.

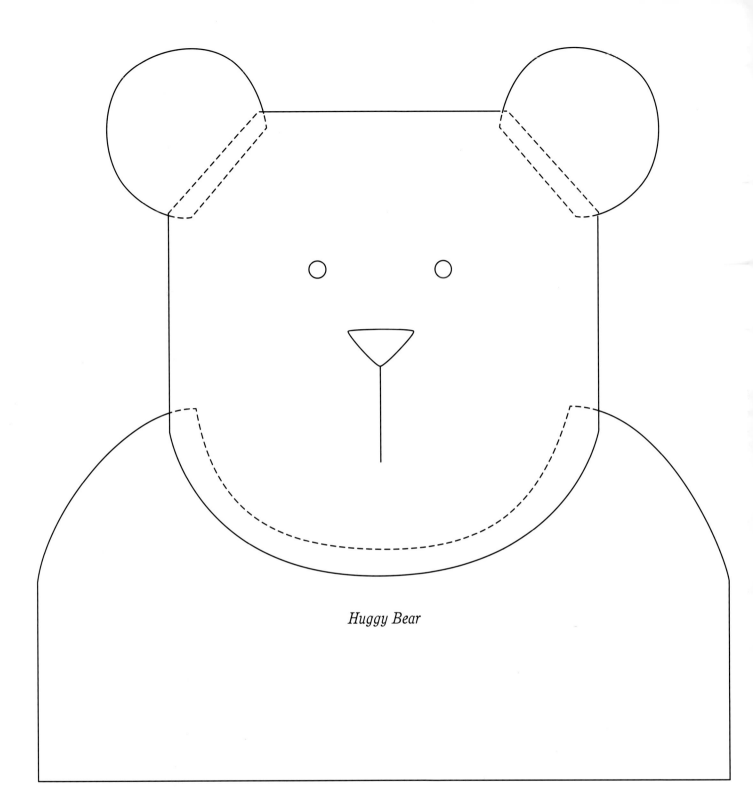

Huggy Bear

LAYERING AND FINISHING

1. Arrange and baste backing, batting, and top together referring to Layering the Quilt directions on page 63.

2. Hand or machine quilt as desired.

3. Use pinking shears to cut approximately $^1/_8$" from edges of $2^1/_2$" x $4^1/_2$" scrappy rectangles. Gather in center to make bow ties and stitch gather in place. Hand or machine stitch bow ties securely under each bear's chin.

4. Securely hand stitch two button eyes to each bear face.

5. Cut one $2^3/_4$" x 42" binding strip in half and sew halves to two remaining $2^3/_4$" x 42" strips. Using shorter strips for top and bottom and longer strips for sides, refer to Binding the Quilt directions on page 63 to finish.

BEAR HUG DOLL

Finished Size: 14" tall
Photo: page 28

Looking for a great project for your quilt group to donate to kids? This cuddly doll makes the perfect companion to our Huggy Bear Quilt...and the ideal project for a rainy day sew-a-thon! Read all instructions before beginning.

Materials List

Body - ³/₈ yard
Bow Tie
  One 2¹/₂" x 5" piece for bow
  One ³/₄" x 12" strip for neck tie
Front Trim
  One 10" length decorative trim
  Five ⁵/₈" diameter buttons
Polyester Fiberfil Stuffing
Plastic Pellet Beanbag Fill
Eyes
  Two ¹/₂" diameter buttons
Embroidery Floss

ASSEMBLY

1.   Make template for bear body from pattern on page 51. Join pattern halves at dots indicated on pattern. Fold body fabric in half with right sides together. Place template on fold and trace two bear body pieces. Cut out bear bodies on traced lines.

2.   Unfold bear body pieces, place right sides together and pin. Using ¹/₄" seam, sew bear body pieces together.

3.   Cut 2" opening in back side of body as indicated on pattern. Clip curves and turn body right side out.

4.   Stuff to desired fullness with polyester fiberfill. Hand stitch opening closed. Refer to Embroidery Stitch Guide on page 62 and use six strands of embroidery floss to blanket stitch around edge of bear.

Note: If using plastic pellet beanbag fill, blanket stitch around bear edges before adding fill. Fill lower body (including arms) first, capping off with polyester fiberfill. Stuff upper body with fiberfill. Hand stitch opening closed.

5.   Referring to color photo on page 28, hand stitch button eyes in place. Lightly mark nose placement with pencil. Referring to Embroidery Stitch Guide on page 62, use three strands of floss to satin stitch nose.

6.   Cut decorative trim to desired length. Space buttons evenly and sew them on trim. Referring to color photo for placement, hand stitch trim to bear front.

7.   Use pinking shears to trim edges of 2¹/₂" x 5" bow tie piece. Gather in center and stitch gather in place. Use ³/₄" x 12" strip to make bow tie "knot." Wrap ends of strip around bear's neck. Fit snuggly, overlap ends, and stitch in place. Make sure strip covers stitched opening. Trim excess.

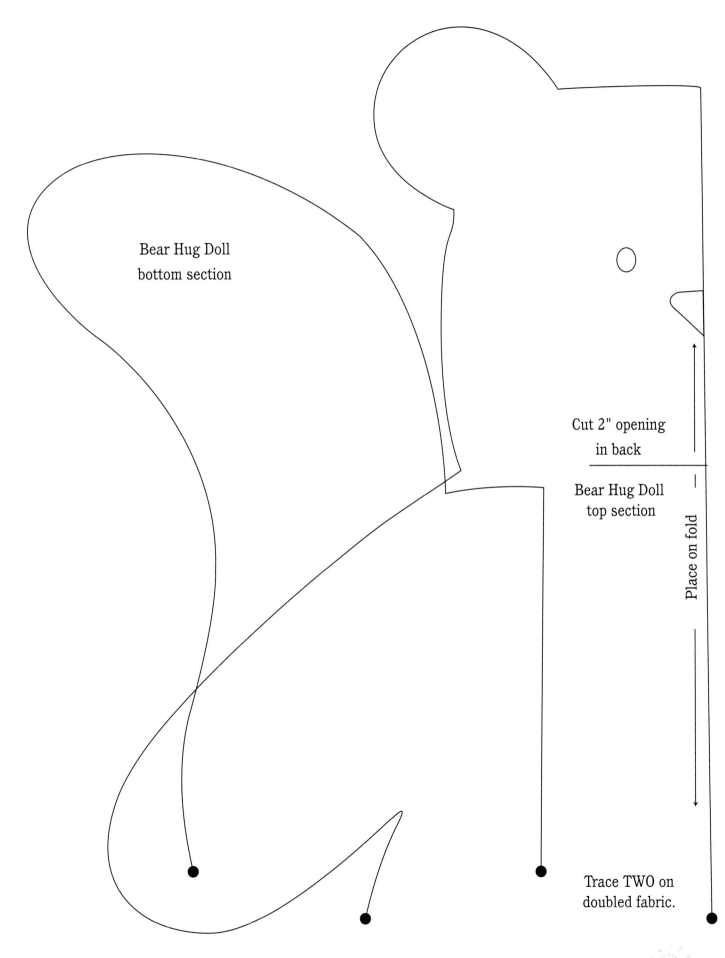

Bear Hug Doll
bottom section

Cut 2" opening
in back

Bear Hug Doll
top section

Place on fold

Trace TWO on
doubled fabric.

RAGAMUMM KiDS®

Quilt Layout
Finished Size: 30" x 26"
Photo: page 31

Feel "like a kid again" as you clutch your trusty Crayolas® and color the four fanciful vignettes that make up this darling wall quilt. Better still, share the fun with family or friends. Let each color a block, then gather together to assemble the results. Read all instructions before beginning and use ¹/₄" seam allowances throughout.

Fabric Requirements

Blocks - ¹/₃ yard
Lattice - ¹/₄ yard
Border - ¹/₂ yard
Binding - ³/₈ yard
Backing - 1 yard
Lightweight Batting
   34" x 30" piece
Notions
Plain white paper, Crayola®
crayons, fine-point permanent,
marking pen, Scotchguard®,
freezer paper (four 8¹/₂" x 10¹/₂"
pieces), buttons

CUTTING THE STRIPS AND PIECES

Read first paragraph of *Cutting the Strips and Pieces* on page 3.

Background Squares
   Four 8¹/₂" x 10¹/₂" squares
Lattice
   Two 1¹/₂" x 8¹/₂" strips
   Three 1¹/₂" x 21¹/₂" strips
   Two 1¹/₂" x 19¹/₂" strips
Border
   Two 3¹/₂" x 23¹/₂" strips
   Two 3¹/₂" x 25¹/₂" strips
Binding
   Four 2³/₄" x 42" strips

COLORING THE BACKGROUND SQUARES

1.   Press one 8½" x 10½" piece of freezer paper, shiny side down, onto back side of each 8½" x 10½" background square. Freezer paper helps stabilize fabric as you transfer and color designs.

2.   Spray right side of stabilized fabric pieces with Scotchguard® and allow to dry thoroughly before proceeding.

3.   Trace block designs on pages 54–57 onto plain white paper such as typing paper. Using light box, center background block fabric side up over traced design. Transfer design onto fabric block using fine point permanent marking pen.

4.   Color as desired with crayons. *Hint:* For bolder color, apply more crayon. Carefully brush crayon fragments or residue from background blocks.

5.   Place colored blocks face down on plain white paper and press with medium high heat to set. Do not drag iron over surface, but use up-and-down motion to avoid smearing crayon.

6.   Remove freezer paper from heat-set blocks. Spray lightly with Scotchguard® and allow to dry thoroughly before proceeding.

ASSEMBLY

1.   For each row, sew one 1½" x 8½" lattice strip between two 8½" x 10½" colored background squares. Press seams toward lattice.

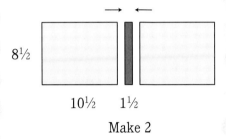

Make 2

2.   Pin and sew 1½" x 21½" lattice strip between two rows from step 1. Press.

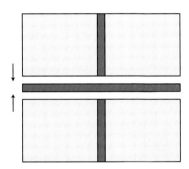

3.   Sew 1½" x 21½" lattice strips to top and bottom. Press seams toward lattice. Sew 1½" x 19½" lattice strips to sides. Press.

4.   Sew 3½" x 23½" border strips to top and bottom. Press seams toward borders. Sew 3½" x 25½" border strips to sides. Press.

LAYERING AND FINISHING

1.   Arrange and baste backing, batting, and top together referring to Layering the Quilt directions on page 63.

2.   Hand or machine quilt as desired.

3.   Using four 2¾" x 42" binding strips, refer to Binding the Quilt directions on page 63.

4.   Referring to color photo on page 31, sew assorted buttons to wall quilt.

Ragamumm Kids® Feed the Birds

color tracings

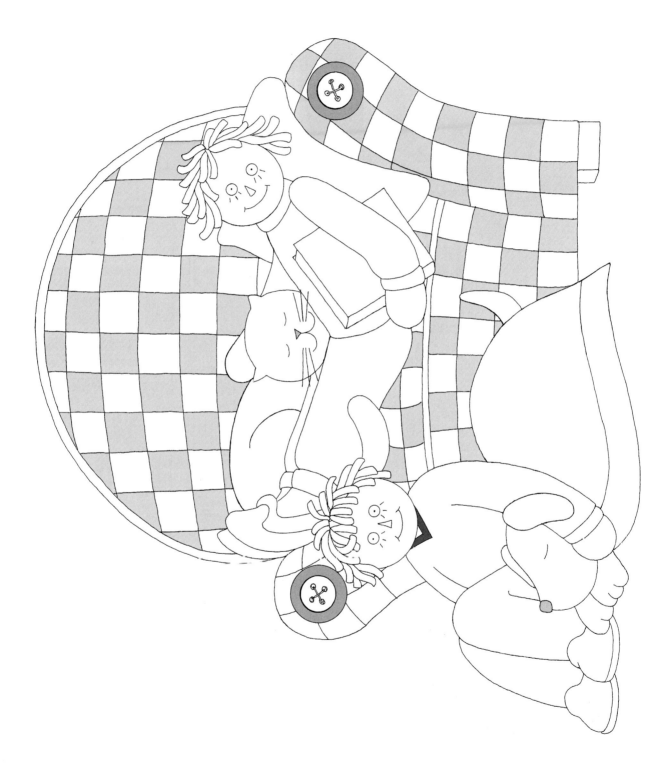

Ragamumm Kids® Bedtime

color tracings

Ragamumm Kids® Tend the Garden
color tracings

Ragamumm Kids® Go to School

color tracings

DICTIONARY

VOL II

SLEEPY TIME

Quilt Layout
Finished Size: 46" x 52"
(Finished size quilt will depend on measurements of panel used.)
Photo: page 25

Does your group need a quilt or two or ten in a hurry? Here's a solution that makes clever use of preprinted panels.
Choose a Debbie Mumm penguin panel or one with your favorite juvenile motif. Add borders, quilt, and embellish with whimsical trims and buttons. Read all instructions before beginning and use ¹/₄" seam allowances throughout.

Fabric Requirements

Note: Adjust yardage for borders, backing, and binding as necessary to fit your center panel.

Quilt Center
  One preprinted panel for this quilt, 36" x 42"
Accent Border - ¹/₄ yard
Border - ³/₄ yard
Corner Squares - ¹/₆ yard
Binding - ¹/₂ yard
Backing - 3 yards
Lightweight Batting
  50" x 56" piece
Quilter's Square Ruler
Decorative Trims
Assorted Buttons
Embroidery Floss

CUTTING THE STRIPS AND PIECES

Read first paragraph of *Cutting the Strips and Pieces* on page 3.

Accent Border
  Five 1¹/₂" x 42 strips
Border
  Five 4¹/₂" x 42" strips
Border Corner Squares
  Four 4¹/₂" squares
Binding
  Six 2³/₄" x 42" strips

ASSEMBLY

1. Use rotary cutter, long ruler, and quilter's square ruler (or T-square) to trim edges and square corners of preprinted panel. The outer edges of our panel included corner square motifs. Be sure to include $\frac{1}{4}$" seam allowance around all four sides.

2. Measure panel from side to side through center and trim two $1\frac{1}{2}$" x 42" border strips to this measurement. Sew to top and bottom of quilt. Press seams toward accent borders.

3. Measure quilt from top to bottom through center. Use remaining $1\frac{1}{2}$" x 42" strips to make two accent borders this length. Sew to sides of quilt. Press seams toward accent borders.

4. Measure quilt as in step 2. Make two borders this measurement from $4\frac{1}{2}$" x 42" border strips. Sew to top and bottom. Press seams toward borders.

5. Use remaining $4\frac{1}{2}$" x 42" border strips to make two side borders the same length determined for accent borders in step 3. Sew $4\frac{1}{2}$" border corner squares to each end of borders. Press seams toward borders. Fit, pin, and sew borders to sides of quilt. Press.

LAYERING AND FINISHING

1. Decorative stitch as desired, referring to Embroidery Stitch Guide on page 62.

2. Arrange and baste backing, batting, and quilt top together, referring to Layering the Quilt directions on page 63.

3. Machine or hand quilt as desired.

4. Use decorative trims and buttons to further embellish center panel as desired. We added decorative trim to the penguin's socks and securely attached colorful buttons.

5. Refer to Binding the Quilt directions on page 63. Cut one $2\frac{3}{4}$" x 42" binding strip in half, and sew halves to two $2\frac{3}{4}$" x 42" strips. Use shorter strips to bind top and bottom, and longer strips to bind sides.

Note: When making quilts for small children, substitute decorative stitches for buttons. Refer to Embroidery Stitch Guide on page 62.

NOTES

N!GHTY N!GHT B!BY

Quilt Layout
Finished Size of Sample: 39" x 45"
(Finished size of your quilt will vary depending
on measurements of panel used.)
Photo: page 25

*With a few minor modifications in color and embellishment, the
Sleepy Time Quilt on page 58 can be tailored for a special little
boy. Read all instructions before beginning and use
1/4" seam allowances throughout.*

Fabric Requirements

Note: Adjust yardages for borders,
backing, and binding as necessary
to fit your center panel.

Quilt Center
  One preprinted panel
    for this quilt, 36" x 42"
Border - 1/3 yard
Binding - 1/2 yard
Backing - 1 1/3 yards
Lightweight batting
  43" x 49" piece
Quilter's Square Ruler
Decorative Trims
Assorted Buttons
Embroidery Floss

CUTTING THE STRIPS AND PIECES

Read first paragraph of *Cutting
the Strips and Pieces* on page 3.

Border
  Four 2" x 42" strips
Binding
  Five 2 3/4" x 42" strips

ASSEMBLY

1. Use rotary cutter, long ruler, and quilter's square ruler (or T-square) to trim edges and square corners of preprinted panel. The outer edges of our panel included corner square motifs. Be sure to include $1/4$" seam allowance around all four sides.

2. Measure panel from side-to-side through center and trim two 2" x 42" border strips to this length. Sew to top and bottom of quilt. Press seams toward borders.

3. Measure quilt from top to bottom through center, including borders. Use remaining 2" x 42" strips to make two borders this length. Sew to sides of quilt. Press seams toward borders.

LAYERING AND FINISHING

1. Decorative stitch as desired, referring to Embroidery Stitch Guide on page 62.

2. Arrange and baste backing, batting, and quilt top together, referring to Layering the Quilt directions on page 63.

3. Machine or hand quilt as desired.

4. Use decorative trims and buttons to further embellish center panel as desired. We added decorative trim to the penguin's socks and securely attached colorful buttons. If your quilt is to be used by a baby or toddler, we do not recommend the use of buttons.

5. Refer to Binding the Quilt directions on page 63. Cut one $2^3/_4$" x 42" binding strip in half, and sew halves to two $2^3/_4$" x 42" strips. Use shorter strips to bind top and bottom, and longer strips to bind sides.

GENERAL DIRECTIONS

HAND APPLIQUÉ

Hand appliqué is easy when you start out with the right supplies. Cotton machine embroidery thread is easy to work with. Pick a color that matches the applique fabric as closely as possible. Use a long, thin needle like a sharp for stitching, and slender appliqué or silk pins for holding shapes in place.

1. Make a plastic template for every shape in the appliqué design. Use a dotted line to show where pieces overlap.

2. Place template on right side of appliqué fabric. Trace around template.

3. Cut out shapes 1/4" beyond traced line.

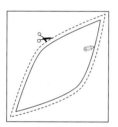

4. Position shapes on background fabric. For pieces that overlap, follow numbers on patterns. Pieces with lower numbers go underneath; pieces with higher numbers are layered on top. Pin shapes in place.

5. Stitch shapes in order following pattern numbers. Where shapes overlap, do not turn under and stitch edges of bottom pieces. Turn and stitch the edges of the piece on top.

6. Use the traced line as your turn-under guide. Entering from the wrong side of the appliqué shape, bring the needle up on the traced line. Using the tip of the needle, turn under the fabric along the traced line. Using a blind stitch, stitch along the folded edge to join the appliqué shape to the background fabric. Turn under and stitch only about 1/4" at a time.

7. Clip curves and V-shapes to help the fabric turn under smoothly. Clip to within a couple threads of the traced line.

8. When you're done stitching the entire block, press it face down on top of a thick towel and press.

QUICK CORNER TRIANGLES

Quick corner triangles are formed by simply sewing fabric squares to other squares and rectangles. The directions and diagrams with each project show you what size pieces to use and where to place each square on corresponding piece. See fabric key with each project for fabric identification. Follow steps 1–3 below to make corner triangle units.

1. With pencil and ruler, draw diagonal line on wrong side of fabric square that will form the triangle. See Diagram A. This will be your sewing line.

2. With right sides together, place square on corresponding piece. Matching raw edges, pin in place and sew ON drawn line.

3. Press seam in direction of arrow as shown in step-by-step project diagram. Trim off excess fabric leaving 1/4" seam allowance as shown in Diagram B. Measure completed corner triangle unit to ensure greatest accuracy.

A.

Sewing line

B.

Trim 1/4" away from sewing

C.

Finished corner

EMBROIDERY STITCH GUIDE

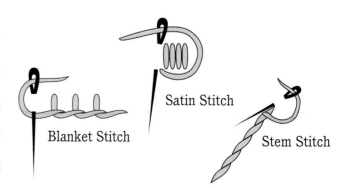

Satin Stitch

Blanket Stitch

Stem Stitch

LAYERING THE QUILT

1. Cut backing and batting 3" x 6" larger than quilt top.

2. Lay pressed backing on bottom (right side down), batting in middle, and pressed quilt top on top. Make sure everything is centered and that backing and batting are flat. Backing and batting will extend beyond quilt top.

3. Begin basting in center and work toward outer edges. Baste vertically and horizontally, forming a 3" – 4" grid. Baste or pin completely around edge of quilt top. Trim batting and backing to 1/4" from raw edge of quilt top.

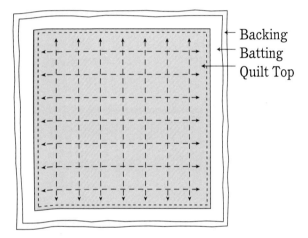

← Backing
← Batting
← Quilt Top

BINDING THE QUILT

1. Fold and press binding strips in half lengthwise with wrong sides together.

2. With raw edges even, lay binding strips on top and bottom edges of quilt top. Sew through all layers, 1/4" from quilt edge. Press binding away from quilt top. Trim excess length of binding.

3. Sew remaining two binding strips to quilt sides. Press and trim excess length.

4. Folding top and bottom first, fold binding around to back. Press and pin in position. Hand stitch binding in place.

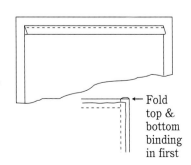

← Fold top & bottom binding in first

QUICK-FUSE APPLIQUÉ

Quick-fuse appliqué is a method of adhering appliqué pieces to a background with fusible web. For quick and easy results, simply quick-fuse appliqué pieces in place. Use sewable, lightweight fusible web, such as HeatnBond Lite®, for the projects in this book. Finishing raw edges with stitching is desirable. Laundering is not recommended unless edges are finished.

1. With paper side up, lay fusible web over appliqué design. Leaving 1/2" space between pieces, trace all elements of design. Cut around traced pieces, approximately 1/4" outside traced line. See Diagram A.

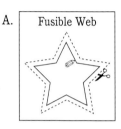

A. Fusible Web

2. With paper side up, position and iron fusible web to wrong side of selected fabrics. Follow manufacturer's directions for iron temperature and fusing time. Cut out each piece on traced line. See Diagram B.

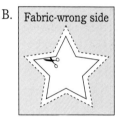

B. Fabric-wrong side

3. Remove paper backing from pieces. A thin film will remain on wrong side. Position and fuse all pieces of one appliqué design at a time onto background, referring to color photos for placement.

ORDERING INFORMATION

Appliqué Pressing Sheet™
Bear Thread Designs
Route 1, Box 1640
Belgrade, MO 63622
(573)766-5695

Potato Medley

page 248

Jolof Rice

page 289

Fresh Noodles Lo Mein

serves 6

With the help of the fresh pasta sold in supermarket refrigerator cases, this flavorful dish can be on the table in less than 10 minutes.

> 1 tablespoon dark sesame oil
>
> 1/2 pound firm tofu, cut into 1-inch cubes
>
> 4 vegetable bouillon cubes
>
> 4 cups cold water
>
> 1 tablespoon grated fresh ginger root
>
> 1/8 teaspoon cayenne pepper (optional)
>
> 3 tablespoons bottled teriyaki sauce
>
> 1 large clove garlic, minced
>
> One 8-ounce package fresh linguine
>
> One 16-ounce bag frozen Oriental-style vegetables
>
> 1 small onion, sliced lengthwise into "petals"
>
> 2 scallions (green and white parts), sliced finely

HEAT the sesame oil in a skillet over medium-high heat, and cook the tofu, stirring, until golden on all sides, about 2 to 3 minutes. In a large soup pot, bring the bouillon and water to a boil. Add the ginger, cayenne, teriyaki sauce, garlic and linguine. Simmer 2 minutes. Stir in the browned tofu, vegetables and onion, return to a boil and simmer 2 minutes more. Garnish with scallions.

Variation:

Use dried linguine or other pasta instead of fresh, and increase the boiling time to cook the pasta *al dente.*

> **PER SERVING:**
> 230 Cal.; 12g Prot.; 6g Fat; 30g Carb.;
> 62mg Chol.; 432mg Sod.; 4g Fiber.

Fajitas

serves 4

Robust chili teams with seitan to make this 15-minute dish taste like it took an hour to prepare. Set out a platter of the savory mixture and bowls of garnishes (such as guacamole, fresh tomato, grated cheese and salsa) and let diners fashion their own fajitas.

> Whole-wheat fajita wrappers, wrapped in foil
>
> 1 small red onion, chopped
>
> 2 medium cloves garlic, minced
>
> 2 bell peppers, seeded and sliced into strips
>
> 1 pound seitan, cut into thin shreds
>
> 1 tablespoon chili powder
>
> 2 tablespoons soy sauce, shoyu or tamari
>
> Guacamole (optional)
>
> 2 or 3 plum tomatoes, peeled and finely diced
>
> Garnishes: Low-fat grated cheddar cheese, salsa,
>   low-fat sour cream

PLACE the fajita wrappers in a 200°F toaster oven to heat while you prepare the filling. Spray a medium skillet with olive oil cooking spray, add the onion and cook, stirring, over medium-low heat until softened slightly. Add the minced garlic and bell peppers and cook, stirring frequently, 5 minutes more. Add the seitan, chili powder and soy sauce, shoyu or tamari. Lower the heat and simmer 5 minutes.

PLACE the fajita wrappers under a napkin to keep them warm, and arrange the fajita filling on a small platter. Spoon the guacamole, tomatoes, cheese, salsa and sour cream in small dishes.

> **PER SERVING**
> **WITHOUT GUACAMOLE:**
> 203 Cal.; 11g Prot.; 5g Fat; 29g Carb.;
> 0mg Chol.; 803mg Sod.; 3g Fiber.

Polenta and Pinto Bean Pizza

serves 6

Here's a different—and distinctly delicious—microwave entrée.

CRUST

- 2 1/2 cups hot water
- 1 1/4 cups cornmeal
- 1 tablespoon margarine
- 1/4 teaspoon garlic powder
- 1/8 teaspoon seasoned salt

SAUCE

- One 8-ounce can tomato sauce
- 1 clove garlic, minced
- 1/2 teaspoon dried Italian seasoning
- 1/2 teaspoon sugar

TOPPINGS

- 1/2 yellow bell pepper, seeded and cut into thin strips
- 1/2 green bell pepper, seeded and cut into thin strips
- 1 cup sliced white button mushrooms
- 1/2 cup sliced onion
- 1 teaspoon virgin olive oil (optional)
- 1 cup cooked pinto beans
- 1 tomato, cut into 1/4-inch slices
- 1 cup shredded low-fat mozzarella cheese
- 1 tablespoon chopped fresh parsley

CRUST: Place the water in a 2-quart casserole. Cover. Microwave at high power until boiling, about 6 to 8 minutes. Using a wire whisk, stir in the remaining crust ingredients. Microwave at high power, uncovered, until the mixture thickens, about 1 to 2 minutes, stirring once or twice.

SPOON the mixture onto a 12-inch round platter. With a rubber scrapper, spread it to within 1 inch of the edges, mounding slightly around the edges. Cover with plastic wrap; set aside.

SAUCE: In a 4-cup measure, combine all the sauce ingredients. Mix well. Microwave at high power, uncovered, until the sauce is hot and bubbly, about 3 to 5 minutes, stirring once or twice. Set aside.

TOPPINGS: In a 2-quart casserole dish, combine the peppers, mushrooms, onions and oil. Microwave at high power, uncovered, just until the vegetables are tender, about 3 to 5 minutes, stirring once or twice.

SPOON the sauce evenly over the crust. Top with the vegetable mixture and pinto beans. Arrange the tomato slices over the vegetables and beans. Sprinkle with the cheese and parsley. Microwave at high power until the pizza is hot and the cheese melts, about 3 to 4 minutes, rotating platter once or twice. Serve in wedges.

PER SERVING:
231 Cal.; 10g Prot.; 5g Fat; 37g Carb.;
11mg Chol.; 424mg Sod.; 6g Fiber.

Tofu with Fermented Black Beans and Ginger

serves 6

Accompany this exotic sauté with plenty of brown rice.

- 2 tablespoons canola oil
- 1 pound extra-firm tofu, pressed for at least 1 hour and cut into 1/2-inch cubes
- 1 tablespoon Chinese fermented black beans, rinsed, drained and mashed
- 3 drops Tabasco sauce, or to taste
- 3 medium cloves garlic, minced finely
- 3 thin slices fresh ginger root, minced finely
- Salt and freshly ground black pepper to taste
- 2 tablespoons Chinese rice wine or dry sherry
- 3 bell peppers, red or green (or both), cored, seeded and cut into 1-inch strips
- 4 scallions (green and white parts), cut into 1-inch lengths
- 3 tablespoons arrowroot or cornstarch dissolved in 3 tablespoons cold water
- 1/4 cup egg substitute
- 2 cups vegetable stock (page 178)

HEAT a large skillet or wok until very hot. Add the oil and tofu, and stir-fry until lightly golden on all sides, about 10 minutes. Add the black beans, Tabasco, garlic, ginger, salt, pepper, rice wine or sherry, bell peppers and scallions. Cook, stirring constantly, for 2 minutes.

COMBINE the dissolved arrowroot or cornstarch with the egg substitute; set aside. Add the stock to the skillet or wok and bring to a boil. Remove from the heat, push the mixture to one side of the skillet and add the arrowroot or cornstarch mixture, stirring constantly until the liquid is thick and smooth. Return to low heat, and distribute the sauce evenly through the tofu and vegetables. Serve hot.

PER SERVING:
199 Cal.; 12g Prot.; 10g Fat; 10g Carb.;
0mg Chol.; 224mg Sod.; 1g Fiber.

Cabbage Rolls with Seasoned Rice

serves 4

- 4 large outer cabbage leaves
- 1/3 cup chopped onion
- 1/2 teaspoon nutmeg
- 1/2 teaspoon salt
- One 8-ounce can low-sodium tomato sauce
- 2 cups cooked brown rice

BRING a pot of water to boil, drop in the cabbage leaves and cook 3 minutes; drain. In a skillet, cook the onion, stirring, in a small amount of water over medium heat until limp, 5 to 10 minutes. Stir in the nutmeg, salt, half of the tomato sauce and 1 cup rice. Divide the rice mixture among the cabbage leaves, roll up and fasten with toothpicks.

SPREAD the remaining rice in a lightly oiled casserole dish. Arrange the cabbage rolls on top of the rice and pour the remaining tomato sauce on top. Cover the dish, and microwave on medium-high power for 8 minutes. (Or preheat the oven to 375°F and bake 35 to 40 minutes.) Serve hot.

Helpful hint:

If you don't have cooked brown rice on hand, use packaged quick-cooking brown rice. Prepare as directed on the package.

> **PER SERVING:**
> 143 Cal.; 3g Prot.; 0.8g Fat; 31g Carb.;
> 0mg Chol.; 283mg Sod.; 4g Fiber.

Sesame-Crusted Tempeh with Fruited Barbecue Sauce

serves 6

Here's a quick and hearty burger with a peachy difference. In place of bread crumbs to coat the burgers, the coating of choice is sesame seeds and nutritional yeast, a delicious alternative found in natural food stores.

BARBECUE SAUCE

- 1/4 cup finely chopped onion
- 1/2 cup water
- 2 tablespoons cider vinegar
- 1 tablespoon vegetarian Worcestershire sauce
- 1/4 cup fresh lemon juice
- 2 tablespoons brown sugar or molasses
- 1 cup chili sauce or ketchup
- 1 1/2 cups diced fresh or frozen peaches
- 1/2 teaspoon salt
- 1/4 teaspoon freshly ground black pepper
- 1 teaspoon prepared mustard

BURGERS

- Six 4-ounce tempeh burgers
- 1/2 cup nutritional yeast
- 1/3 cup raw sesame seeds
- 1/2 teaspoon salt, or to taste
- 1/4 teaspoon freshly ground black pepper
- Nonstick cooking spray, plain or butter-flavored
- Whole-wheat burger rolls or pita pockets
- Finely shredded lettuce (optional)

SAUCE: In a saucepan, combine all the sauce ingredients. Simmer slowly, covered, for 20 minutes. Set aside, uncovered.

BURGERS: Rinse the tempeh burgers quickly in cold water and set aside without drying. If the label indicates that the burgers have not been presteamed, place them on a rack (set in a pot) above 1 to 2 inches of boiling water. Cover and steam 20 minutes.

IN A FLAT DISH, combine the nutritional yeast, sesame seeds, salt and pepper. Press the wet tempeh firmly into the sesame mixture, turning the burgers over repeatedly until both sides are completely coated. Place them in a single layer on a dish next to the stove.

PLACE a large nonstick griddle over medium-high heat. Spray the top exposed surface of the burgers with nonstick cooking spray and carefully place the burgers, sprayed side down, on the griddle. Cook until the bottom is golden and crisp, about 4 to 6 minutes. Spray the top surfaces with nonstick cooking spray, turn the burgers very carefully, and brown the other side for 4 minutes.

SERVE the burgers in warmed burger rolls or pita pockets with the reserved barbecue sauce and shredded lettuce.

> **PER SERVING:**
> 314 Cal.; 14g Prot.; 6g Fat; 50g Carb.;
> 0mg Chol.; 1,101mg Sod.; 7g Fiber.

Singapore Sling Seitan

serves 6

Don't let the number of ingredients scare you. This dish is easy to make and a joy to eat. Just be sure you make a trip to an Asian market or well-stocked natural foods store or supermarket to get everything you need. Serve it over brown rice.

3 large or 4 medium dried shiitake mushrooms

1 pound asparagus, cut diagonally into 1/2-inch pieces

1 pound seitan, cut into slices and then into 1-inch shreds

1 teaspoon cornstarch mixed with 1 teaspoon water

2 teaspoons canola or safflower oil

3 tablespoons rice wine or dry sherry

2 tablespoons soy sauce or tamari

1/2 teaspoon Chinese hot chili paste, or more to taste

1 teaspoon hoisin sauce

1 teaspoon dark sesame oil

1 teaspoon sugar

3 cloves garlic, minced finely

One 1-inch piece ginger root, minced finely

1 medium onion, sliced thinly from stem to root

3 cups frozen Oriental stir-fry vegetables, rinsed in hot water and drained

3 scallions (green and white parts), sliced thinly

SOAK the mushrooms in hot water until softened, about 20 minutes. Remove and discard the stems, and slice the caps into 1/4-inch strips. Blanch the asparagus: cook in salted boiling water for 30 seconds, drain, refresh in cold water and drain again. Set aside.

COMBINE the seitan with the dissolved cornstarch. Heat 1 teaspoon canola or safflower oil in a wok or nonstick skillet; add the seitan and cook, stirring, until golden, about 3 to 4 minutes. Remove the seitan mixture; set aside. Combine the rice wine or sherry, soy sauce or tamari, chili paste, hoisin sauce, sesame oil and sugar in a small bowl; set aside.

IN THE WOK or skillet, heat the remaining teaspoon of canola or safflower oil over high heat and cook the ginger, garlic and onion, stirring, for 2 minutes. Add the

Oriental stir-fry vegetables, mushrooms and blanched asparagus; cook, stirring, for 2 minutes more.

STIR in the soy sauce mixture, and cook, stirring constantly, until the sauce thickens. Return the seitan to the wok or skillet and cook 1 minute. Serve hot.

> **PER SERVING:**
> 172 Cal.; 7g Prot.; 7g Fat; 18g Carb.;
> 0mg Chol.; 707mg Sod.; 3g Fiber.

Fettuccine with Black Olive Pesto and Scallions

serves 6

Fresh pasta teams up deliciously with black olives and scallions. For extra appeal, we've added strands of lemon zest and lots of freshly ground black pepper.

- One 9-ounce can pitted black olives, rinsed
- 1/4 teaspoon cayenne pepper, or to taste
- 1 medium garlic clove
- 1 medium shallot or small onion
- 2 tablespoons fresh parsley leaves
- 1/2 teaspoon fresh thyme leaves
- 1 teaspoon red wine vinegar
- 1/4 teaspoon salt
- 1/3 cup virgin olive oil
- One 8-ounce package fresh fettuccine
- 1/4 teaspoon freshly ground black pepper
- 4 scallions (green and white parts), sliced finely on the diagonal
- Finely julienned zest from 1 small lemon

PLACE the olives in a food processor fitted with a steel blade and process until coarsely chopped. Add the cayenne, garlic, shallot or onion, parsley, thyme, vinegar and salt. While the machine is running, dribble in the oil in a thin, steady stream through the feed tube.

PREPARE the fettuccine according to the package directions; drain. Divide the pasta among 6 plates. Spoon some of the black olive pesto on each serving, then sprinkle with black pepper and scatter scallions and lemon zest on top.

> **PER SERVING:**
> 335 Cal.; 5g Prot.; 19g Fat; 33g Carb.;
> 0mg Chol.; 413 Sod.; 3g Fiber.

Brown Rice with Red Beans and Green Chilies

serves 6

- 3 to 4 cups cooked brown rice
- 1 can red kidney beans, rinsed
- 3 cloves garlic, minced finely
- 1 large onion, chopped
- Two 4-ounce cans diced mild green chilies (with liquid)
- 1 cup shredded, low-fat Monterey Jack cheese
- 1 cup fat-free ricotta cheese
- 1/2 cup low-fat cheddar cheese, grated

PREHEAT the oven to 350°F. Lightly spray a 1 1/2-quart baking dish with nonstick cooking spray; set aside. In a large bowl, mix the rice, beans, garlic, onion and chilies. In another dish combine the Monterey Jack and ricotta cheeses. Layer the rice-bean mixture into the baking dish alternately with the cheese mixture, starting and ending with the rice and beans. Bake 15 minutes; sprinkle the cheddar cheese over the top and bake 5 minutes more.

> **PER SERVING:**
> 329 Cal.; 17g Prot.; 11g Fat; 38g Carb.;
> 36mg Chol.; 366mg Sod.; 5g Fiber.

BRING to a boil the sun-dried tomatoes, onion, garlic, bouillon and water. Stir in the couscous and turmeric. Return to a simmer; then remove from the heat, cover and let sit 5 minutes. Sprinkle paprika on top.

> **PER SERVING:**
> 187 Cal.; 7g Prot.; 0.2g Fat; 21g Carb.;
> 0mg Chol.; 81mg Sod.; 7g Fiber.

Quick Couscous Pilaf with Sun-Dried Tomatoes

serves 2

Here's an easy dinner to make—whether you're at home or on the trail. It's versatile, too. In place of couscous, you may choose another quick-cooking grain, such as kasha or cracked wheat, with equally delicious results.

6 sun-dried tomatoes, cut into bite-sized pieces

1/2 cup dehydrated onion

1/4 tablespoon dehydrated garlic

6 low-sodium vegetable bouillon cubes

6 cups water

2 1/2 cups instant couscous

Dash turmeric

Dash paprika, for garnish (optional)

CHAPTER

20

side dishes

SIDE DISHES PLAY AN OFTEN UNAPPRECIATED YET INTEGRAL ROLE in making your lunch or dinner a real meal. Once you've selected your main dish, ask yourself what's missing. Maybe you need a side dish with a bright color, a chewy or creamy texture, a cooling or spicy flavor or a vitamin boost. It may seem at first that side dishes are secondary, but they can make or break a meal. For instance, which sounds better to you as a side dish with burritos: sauerkraut or herb-roasted corn? Undoubtedly, you selected the latter choice and are well on your way to the proper pairing of entrées and satisfying side dishes. If you're unsure of your meal-planning skills, turn to chapters 4 and 6.

Artichokes with Light Lemon Dipping Sauce

serves 2

Artichokes are perhaps the most sensuous of vegetables—always eaten with the fingers. Cooking them with lemon slices preserves their color.

SAUCE

- 2/3 cup plain nonfat yogurt
- 1/3 cup fresh lemon juice
- 1 tablespoon frozen apple juice concentrate, thawed (or apple juice)
- 1 tablespoon minced garlic
- 2 tablespoons Dijon mustard
- 1 teaspoon curry powder

ARTICHOKES

- 2 artichokes
- 3 quarts water
- 1 lemon, quartered

SAUCE: In a medium bowl, whisk together all the sauce ingredients. Let sit at room temperature.

ARTICHOKES: Trim the bases of the artichokes so that they stand upright. Using kitchen shears, clip the points from the artichoke leaves. Bring a pot of water to boil; add the artichokes and lemon. Boil, uncovered, until tender, about 25 minutes. Drain well. To serve, center each artichoke on a small plate. Spoon the sauce into its cavity or into a small bowl for dipping.

> **PER SERVING:**
> 185 Cal.; 8g Prot.; 3g Fat; 32g Carb.;
> 1mg Chol.; 332mg Sod.; 4g Fiber.

Artichokes with Green Herb Sauce

serves 6

- 6 large artichokes
- 6 tablespoons pine nuts
- 1 cup chopped fresh Italian flat-leaf parsley
- 1/2 cup chopped fresh basil leaves
- 1/4 cup chopped fresh marjoram or oregano leaves
- 2 cloves garlic, minced
- 2 tablespoons tiny capers, rinsed (optional)
- 1/2 to 1 cup virgin olive oil
- Zest and juice of 2 lemons
- 1/2 teaspoon salt
- Freshly ground pepper to taste

TRIM the bases of the artichokes so that they stand upright. Using kitchen shears, clip the points from the artichoke leaves. Turn the artichokes upside down in a steaming basket set in a pot of boiling water. Steam until a leaf can be easily plucked from an artichoke, about 25 to 30 minutes. Drain.

TOAST the pine nuts in a dry pan over medium heat until golden. (Watch carefully—the nuts burn easily.) Let cool, then chop finely. Place in a bowl with the parsley, basil, marjoram, garlic and capers. Stir in the oil. Just before serving, stir in the lemon zest and juice. Season with salt and pepper.

TO SERVE, center each artichoke on a small plate. Spoon the sauce into its cavity. Pour extra sauce into a serving bowl and pass at the table.

Helpful hint:

You may steam the artichokes and put together the sauce (except for the lemon zest and juice) the morning of your dinner. Wait until the last minute to add the lemon so that the sauce will taste fresh.

PER SERVING:
63 Cal.; 2g Prot.; 4g Fat; 5g Carb.;
0mg Chol.; 273mg Sod.; 2g Fiber.

**PER SERVING
(WITH 1 TABLESPOON SAUCE):**
212 Cal.; 4g Prot.; 17g Fat; 14g Carb.;
0mg Chol.; 262mg Sod.; 5g Fiber.

Orange-Scented Asparagus with Sweet Red Pepper and Kiwifruit

serves 2

The acid in the orange juice helps keep the grilled asparagus bright green, and the kiwifruit adds to the tang of the citrus.

> 1/3 pound fresh asparagus, trimmed
> 1/2 teaspoon virgin olive oil mixed with 1 teaspoon warm water
> 1/2 red bell pepper, seeded and julienned
> 1 teaspoon frozen orange juice concentrate, thawed
> Freshly ground black pepper to taste
> 1 kiwifruit, peeled and sliced thinly
> 1 teaspoon brown sugar (optional)

PREHEAT the broiler. In a steamer or large pot of boiling water, cook the asparagus until barely tender, about 7 minutes; drain. Meanwhile, heat the olive oil and water in a small skillet over medium-high heat, and cook the red bell pepper, stirring frequently, until slightly softened, about 5 minutes. Remove from the heat and gently stir in the orange juice concentrate and black pepper.

ARRANGE the asparagus spears on 2 gratin dishes with the kiwifruit. Spoon the bell pepper and sauce on top. Sprinkle with the brown sugar. Broil until lightly browned, about 2 to 3 minutes. Serve at once.

Roasted Asparagus with Sesame Seeds

serves 8

Roasting brings out extra flavor in this springtime vegetable. Serve warm or at room temperature.

> 1 tablespoon virgin olive oil
> 2 pounds fresh asparagus, trimmed
> 1 teaspoon coarse salt
> 3 to 4 tablespoons sesame seeds

PREHEAT the oven to 425°F. Lightly brush the oil over the asparagus spears, rolling them to distribute the oil evenly. Spread the spears in a single layer in a shallow pan and sprinkle with salt. Roast, uncovered, until the spears are just tender when pierced with the tip of a knife, about 10 minutes.

WHILE THE ASPARAGUS is roasting, toast the sesame seeds in a dry skillet over medium heat, stirring constantly, until the seeds are golden and aromatic, about 2 to 3 minutes. Arrange the asparagus on a serving plate and sprinkle with the toasted seeds.

Variation:

Substitute lemon juice for orange juice concentrate, and use lemon slices instead of kiwifruit.

> **PER SERVING:**
> 61 Cal.; 2g Prot.; 1g Fat; 10g Carb.;
> 0mg Chol.; 6mg Sod.; 3g Fiber.

Sesame Broccoli

serves 6

Sesame, ginger and lemon are delicious with almost any seasonal green. You may substitute kale, chard or bok choy for the broccoli.

> 1 teaspoon puréed fresh ginger root
>
> 1 tablespoon soy sauce
>
> 1 teaspoon sesame oil
>
> 1 tablespoon fresh lemon or orange juice
>
> 2 pounds broccoli florets and stalks
>
> 1 tablespoon sesame seeds, toasted (page 106)
>
> Freshly ground black pepper to taste

WHISK TOGETHER the ginger, soy sauce, oil and lemon juice or orange juice in a shallow serving bowl. Set aside. Trim, peel and cut the broccoli stalks diagonally into 1/2-inch slices. Steam the broccoli florets and stalks until tender-crisp. Transfer the broccoli to the serving bowl and toss it with the ginger sauce. Sprinkle with sesame seeds and pepper.

> **PER SERVING:**
> 60 Cal.; 3g Prot.; 2g Fat; 8g Carb.;
> 0mg Chol.; 209mg Sod.; 5g Fiber.

Steamed Broccoli with Garlic

serves 1

This simple side dish is quick to prepare. Double the recipe and eat it cold for lunch the next day.

> 2 cups broccoli florets
>
> 1 to 2 teaspoons oil
>
> 1 clove garlic, minced
>
> 1/2 red or yellow bell pepper, diced
>
> Salt and freshly ground black pepper to taste

IN A SAUCEPAN fitted with a steamer, steam the broccoli for 2 minutes. Set aside. Heat the oil in a medium skillet over medium heat. Add the garlic and pepper; cook, stirring, for 2 minutes. Add the broccoli and cook, stirring, 2 minutes more. Season with salt and pepper.

Variation:

For a main dish, toss broccoli with pasta or serve with rice.

> **PER SERVING:**
> 91 Cal.; 3g Prot.; 4g Fat; 9g Carb.;
> 0mg Chol.; 569mg Sod.; 6g Fiber.

Brussels Sprouts à la Grecque

serves 15

The unexpected tang of lemon offsets the sweetness of the Brussels sprouts, cooked until just barely tender.

4 cups water

3 pounds Brussels sprouts

3 teaspoons red wine vinegar

2 teaspoons lemon zest

Juice of 1 lemon

Salt and freshly ground black pepper to taste

1/3 cup chopped fresh parsley

1/4 cup pimiento (optional)

IN A LARGE POT, bring the water to a boil and add the Brussels sprouts. Cover and cook until just barely tender, about 7 minutes. While the Brussels sprouts are cooking, whisk together the vinegar, lemon zest, lemon juice, salt, pepper, parsley and pimiento in a small bowl. Drain the Brussels sprouts and transfer them to a serving dish. Toss with the lemon mixture.

PER SERVING:
36 Cal.; 1g Prot.; 0.3g Fat; 7g Carb.;
0mg Chol.; 91mg Sod.; 3g Fiber.

Braised Red Cabbage with Currants

serves 6

Vegetables are braised by sautéeing and then baking in a small amount of liquid. The result: a lot of flavor and little or no fat.

1 tablespoon whole caraway seeds or cumin seeds

2 teaspoons dry red wine

1 red or yellow onion, sliced thinly

1/4 to 1/2 teaspoon salt

1 small red cabbage, sliced thinly

1/2 cup currants

2 to 3 tablespoons red wine vinegar, cider vinegar or rice vinegar

2/3 cup water or apple juice

TOAST the caraway or cumin seeds in a dry skillet until aromatic, about 1 minute. In a large pot, heat the wine over medium heat. Add the onion and salt, and cook, stirring, until the onion softens and smells sweet, about 5 minutes. Add the red cabbage and cook, stirring, over medium-low heat until it wilts a little, about 5 minutes. (Add water as needed to prevent the vegetables from sticking.) Add the caraway or cumin seeds and currants. Combine the vinegar and water or apple juice, and pour the liquid over the cabbage and mix well. The cabbage should become bright red.

PREHEAT the oven to 375°F. Lightly oil a 2-quart baking dish and spoon the cabbage and liquid into it. Cover and bake for 45 to 60 minutes. Serve warm or at room temperature.

Variation:

Omit the currants and substitute 1/2 cup raisins or diced apple.

PER SERVING:
43 Cal.; 1g Prot.; 0.4g Fat; 8g Carb.;
0mg Chol.; 98mg Sod.; 2g Fiber.

Cinnamon-Glazed Carrots

serves 6

| 1 pound carrots, peeled and sliced into 1/4-inch-thick rounds
| 1/3 cup unsweetened apple juice concentrate, thawed
| 1/2 teaspoon ground cinnamon

COMBINE all the ingredients in a saucepan and stir well. Bring to a simmer, cover and cook over medium heat until the carrots are tender-crisp, about 15 to 20 minutes. Cook, uncovered, until the liquid is reduced to a glaze, about 3 to 5 minutes.

PER SERVING:
60 Cal.; 0.5g Prot.; 0.1g Fat; 14g Carb.;
0mg Chol.; 55mg Sod.; 3g Fiber.

Stir-Fried Collards

serves 4

If collards aren't available in your area, try kale. The recipe works just as well with either vegetable.

| 2 pounds collard leaves
| 1 to 2 tablespoons virgin olive or walnut oil
| 1/4 cup finely minced onion
| 1 clove garlic, crushed and minced
| Salt to taste
| Freshly ground pepper to taste

STRIP the collard leaves off the stems; discard the stems. Wash the leaves in several changes of cold water. Stack them about 4 to 6 high, then roll up tightly like cigars. Stand the rolls vertically in the feeding tube of a food processor and slice with an ultra-thin blade. (Or, with patience and scissors or a very sharp knife, slice paper-thin by hand.) Unfurl and fluff the strands with your fingers. Set aside.

IN A LARGE SKILLET, heat the oil and cook the onion, stirring, 1 minute. Add the garlic and cook 1 minute more. Add the collards and cook, stirring constantly, just until they turn bright green and limp. Season with a sprinkle of salt and pepper. Serve at once.

PER SERVING:
78 Cal.; 3g Prot.; 3g Fat; 8g Carb.;
0mg Chol.; 331mg Sod.; 8g Fiber.

Herb-Roasted Corn

serves 6

Cooking corn with herbs—basil in this version—gives it a wonderful aroma and taste.

| 6 ears corn (with husks)
| 24 fresh basil leaves
| Water for soaking

PEEL BACK the corn husks, leaving them attached to the ears; remove the corn silk. Place 4 basil leaves around the surface of each ear of corn. Put the husks back in place, tying the tops with string. Soak the corn in cold water for 10 minutes; drain. Grill the corn for 25 to 30 minutes over medium-hot coals, turning every 5 minutes to ensure even cooking. Remove the husks. Serve warm.

PER SERVING:
160 Cal.; 4g Prot.; 10g Fat; 33g Carb.;
0mg Chol.; 20mg Sod.; 4g Fiber.

Marinated Cucumber Fans

serves 6

| 2 regular cucumbers (or 1 long, seedless cucumber)
| 1 small white onion, sliced
| 1/2 teaspoon salt (optional)
| 1/4 cup white vinegar
| 1/4 cup water
| 1/4 cup superfine sugar

IF YOU'RE USING regular cucumbers, cut in half lengthwise and scoop out the seeds. Cut the cucumber halves, crosswise, as thinly as possible, slicing almost but not quite all the way through. Then cut all the way through every 3 inches. Place the cucumbers and onion in a non-aluminum bowl and sprinkle with salt.

IN A SMALL BOWL, stir together the vinegar, water and sugar until the sugar dissolves. Pour this mixture over the cucumbers and onion; let marinate at least 15 minutes. Lift the cucumbers out of the marinade, place on individual plates and garnish with the marinated onion.

PER SERVING:
51 Cal.; 0.5g Prot.; 0.1g Fat; 4g Carb.;
0mg Chol.; 3mg Sod.; 2g Fiber.

Teriyaki Grilled Corn

serves 6

Kids—and grownups, too—love this simple dish. The sauce can be prepared several days in advance and refrigerated until grilling time.

| 1 tablespoon brown sugar
| 1 tablespoon tomato paste or ketchup
| 1/4 teaspoon cornstarch
| 2 tablespoons water
| 1 to 2 teaspoons sesame seeds (optional)
| 6 ears fresh corn

COMBINE all the ingredients except the corn in a saucepan. Bring to a boil, stirring constantly. Lower the heat and simmer 1 minute. Remove from the heat.

PREPARE the grill. Remove the husks from the corn. Grill, covered, for 5 to 10 minutes. When almost done, baste the corn 2 or 3 times with the glaze.

PER SERVING:
70 Cal.; 1g Prot.; 1g Fat; 15g Carb.;
0mg Chol.; 6mg Sod.; 4g Fiber.

Sweet Stuffed Japanese Eggplants

serves 8

Serve these eggplants as a side dish or over rice for a great dinner.

> 8 Japanese eggplants
>
> Nonstick cooking spray
>
> 1 tablespoon canola oil
>
> 1 1/2 cups minced onion
>
> 1 medium red bell pepper, chopped
>
> 1 cup vegetable stock (page 178) or water
>
> 1 tablespoon minced fresh ginger root
>
> 2/3 cup tomato sauce
>
> 2 tablespoons dark brown sugar
>
> 2 tablespoons raisins
>
> 1/3 to 1/2 cup sliced, blanched almonds
>
> 1 teaspoon salt, or to taste
>
> 1 tablespoon curry powder, or to taste

PREHEAT the oven to 350°F. Spray a 9 × 13-inch baking pan with nonstick cooking spray. Make a deep lengthwise slit in each eggplant, but don't cut all the way through. Set aside. To make the stuffing, heat the oil in a large skillet, and cook the onion and bell pepper over medium-high heat, stirring, until soft, about 5 minutes. Add the remaining ingredients, stir and simmer 2 minutes.

SPREAD a thin layer of the stuffing on the bottom of the baking pan. Spoon the remaining stuffing into the cut of each eggplant and place the stuffed eggplants in the baking dish. Cover the pan with foil and bake 25 minutes. Uncover and bake until the eggplants are tender, about 20 to 25 minutes more.

> **PER SERVING:**
> 85 Cal.; 2g Prot.; 4g Fat; 12g Carb.;
> 0mg Chol.; 10mg Sod.; 2g Fiber.

Braised Greens with Vinegar and Sesame Seeds

serves 2

> 1/4 cup flavored vinegar (wine vinegar or blackberry vinegar is especially good)
>
> 1 clove garlic, minced
>
> 1 pound beet greens, chopped coarsely
>
> 1/4 cup water
>
> Pinch cayenne pepper
>
> 1 tablespoon sesame seeds

HEAT the vinegar and garlic in a saucepan. Add the greens and cook until wilted. Add the water, cover and simmer 2 minutes, adding more water as necessary to keep from sticking. Uncover, and cook until any remaining liquid evaporates. Sprinkle with cayenne and sesame seeds before serving.

> **PER SERVING:**
> 81 Cal.; 4g Prot.; 2g Fat; 12g Carb.;
> 0mg Chol.; 456mg Sod.; 8g Fiber.

Garlicky Greens Sauté

serves 4

Pick some greens for a hefty shot of iron and beta-carotene. Try this sauté with a rice or lentil pilaf and steamed carrots or squash.

> 4 to 6 cloves garlic, pressed or minced
>
> 1 large onion, minced
>
> 1 to 2 tablespoons virgin olive oil
>
> 1/4 cup sherry or white wine (optional)
>
> Salt and freshly ground black pepper to taste
>
> 1/4 teaspoon allspice
>
> 1/4 teaspoon dried oregano
>
> 1/4 teaspoon dried basil
>
> 8 cups dark leafy greens (spinach, chard, beet greens, kale)
>
> 1/4 cup grated Parmesan cheese

IN A LARGE, DEEP SKILLET, cook the garlic and onion in the oil, stirring, over medium-high heat for 5 minutes. Add the sherry or white wine, salt, pepper, allspice, oregano and basil. Stir in the greens, pressing them down with the back of a spoon as they wilt. Cook, stirring, until completely wilted, about 10 minutes. Sprinkle with Parmesan cheese.

Variation:

To make a Quick Greens Flan, preheat the oven to 350°F. Whisk 2 eggs and 2 cups skim milk into the wilted greens mixture. Spoon the mixture into a greased 9 × 13-inch baking dish and bake until firm, about 35 minutes. Cut into squares.

PER SERVING:
97 Cal.; 4g Prot.; 5g Fat; 9g Carb.;
4mg Chol.; 200mg Sod.; 4g Fiber.

Boiled Kale and Sauerkraut

serves 6

Simple and delicious, this peasant food is vitamin-rich.

> 2 bunches kale
>
> 1/4 to 1/2 cup finely chopped sauerkraut (according to your taste preference)

REMOVE the stems from the kale, chop them finely and set aside. Fill a large pot with a 1/4 inch of water and bring to a boil. Add the stems, cover and cook 3 minutes. Stir in the kale leaves, cover and simmer about 8 minutes. (The kale should be bright green and slightly crisp.) Mix in the sauerkraut. Serve warm.

PER SERVING:
29 Cal.; 1g Prot.; 0.7g Fat; 5g Carb.;
0mg Chol.; 85mg Sod.; 3g Fiber.

Stir-Fried Kale with Ginger

serves 1

Ginger root and soy sauce give this dish an Asian flair.

| 1 tablespoon minced fresh ginger root
| 1/2 tablespoon safflower oil
| 1/4 pound kale, chopped coarsely
| 1 teaspoon soy sauce
| 1/4 cup water
| 1 teaspoon toasted sesame seeds (page 106) (optional)

IN A MEDIUM SKILLET, cook the ginger root in oil, stirring, over medium heat for 1 minute. Add the kale and raise the heat to medium high. Add the soy sauce and water, and stir-fry until the kale is wilted but still slightly crunchy, about 3 minutes. Sprinkle with sesame seeds. Serve warm or cold.

Variation:

Substitute spinach or bok choy for the kale.

PER SERVING:
124 Cal.; 3g Prot.; 7g Fat; 11g Carb.;
0mg Chol.; 396mg Sod.; 7g Fiber.

Lima Beans with Fennel Seeds

serves 6

You may use almost any white bean and seasonal vegetables in this quick dish.

| 1 1/2 tablespoons virgin olive oil
| 1/2 tablespoon fennel seeds
| 1 clove garlic, chopped finely (or 1/4 teaspoon asafetida)
| 1 cup diced celery
| 1 1/2 cups diced red bell pepper
| Small bunch spinach leaves, trimmed
| 3 1/2 cups cooked lima beans, cannellini beans or white beans (or three 15-ounce cans white beans, rinsed)
| Salt and freshly ground black pepper to taste

WARM half of the oil in a large skillet over medium-low heat. Add the fennel seeds and garlic or asafetida and cook until the seeds darken slightly. Stir in the celery and bell pepper, and cook just until softened, about 4 to 5 minutes.

STACK the spinach leaves, roll into a tight cigar shape and cut crosswise into fine shreds. Add the shredded spinach and beans to the skillet and cook just until the beans are warm and the spinach is wilted. Season with salt and pepper. Drizzle with the remaining oil.

PER SERVING:
154 Cal.; 7g Prot.; 4g Fat.; 23g Carb.;
0mg Chol.; 260mg Sod.; 7g Fiber.

Baked Sweet Lima Beans

serves 6

| 2 cups dried baby lima beans, rinsed
| 1 teaspoon salt
| 2 tablespoons canola oil
| 1 tablespoon butter-flavored granules
| 1/2 cup honey

COVER the lima beans with water, bring to a boil and cook 5 minutes. Remove from the heat, cover and let sit 1 hour. Drain and rinse the beans, place in a large pot and cover with fresh cold water. Bring to a boil again, and cook, uncovered, until barely tender, about 1 to 1 1/2 hours. Add salt during the last few minutes of cooking.

PREHEAT the oven to 350°F. Drain the beans and place them in a 2-quart baking dish. Stir in the oil, butter-flavored granules and honey. Bake, stirring occasionally, for 1 hour.

> **PER SERVING:**
> 253 Cal.; 7g Prot.; 1g Fat; 45g Carb.;
> 0.1mg Chol.; 406mg Sod.; 6g Fiber.

Pickled Onions

Makes 2 cups

The redder the onion, the more intense the color will be after pickling. Pickled onions keep for several weeks in your refrigerator.

| 1 tablespoon sugar
| 1 teaspoon salt
| 1 cups white vinegar
| 1 cups cold water
| 2 teaspoons mixed peppercorns, crushed
| 3 bay leaves
| Sprigs of fresh thyme and marjoram (optional)
| 1 pound red onions, peeled and sliced into rings
| 4 cups boiling water

COMBINE the sugar, salt, vinegar and cold water in a large bowl. Stir to dissolve, then add the peppercorns, bay leaves and herbs. Set aside.

PLACE the onions in a colander and pour the boiling water over them. Shake off the excess moisture. Transfer the onions to the bowl and press the onions into the liquid. (If there isn't enough liquid to cover, add more vinegar and water in equal amounts until covered.) Refrigerate. The color will change after 20 minutes.

Serving suggestions:
- Dice and toss into a green salad.
- Combine with cooked beets and toasted peppers for a side salad.

> **PER 2-TABLESPOON SERVING:**
> 15 Cal.; 0.2g Prot.; 0.1g Fat; 3g Carb.;
> 0mg Chol.; 134mg Sod.; 0.6g Fiber.

Glazed Onions

serves 6

| 4 cups peeled pearl onions or peeled and quartered yellow onions
| 1 1/2 to 2 cups water
| 1 teaspoon virgin olive oil or butter
| 2 tablespoons maple syrup or honey
| Pinch salt (or 1 tablespoon soy sauce)
| 1 bunch watercress

IN A MEDIUM SKILLET, combine the onions, water (to nearly cover the onions), oil or butter, maple syrup or honey, and salt or soy sauce. Cover and bring to a boil. Uncover and continue boiling for 10 minutes. Lower the heat to medium and simmer until most of the water has evaporated, stirring frequently. Lower the heat to low and cook until the onions are golden brown and have a rich aroma. They may stick a little, but be careful not to let them burn.

CUT the thick stems off the watercress and trim to about 3-inch pieces. Place a bed of watercress on each plate and top with 1/2 cup or more glazed onions.

Helpful hint:

To peel pearl onions, place them in a pot of boiling water for 2 minutes, then drain and rinse with cold water. When cool enough to handle, squeeze the onions at the root end to pop them out of their skins.

> **PER SERVING:**
> 63 Cal.; 0.8g Prot.; 0.9g Fat; 9g Carb.;
> 0mg Chol.; 58mg Sod.; 2g Fiber.

Honey-Glazed Onions

serves 20

A nest of confetti-colored vegetables and a honey-mustard glaze elevates a simple onion to a lovely dish.

ONIONS AND FILLING

| 10 medium Spanish onions
| 1 cup seasoned bread crumbs
| 1 cup whole-kernel corn (frozen or canned)
| 1 cup diced zucchini
| 1 cup grated carrots
| 1 cup diced canned beets
| 1 cup water

GLAZE

| 1/2 cup honey
| 3 tablespoons Dijon mustard
| 2 tablespoons balsamic vinegar or red wine vinegar
| 2 teaspoons paprika
| 1/2 teaspoon ground ginger
| 1 1/2 teaspoons salt, or more to taste
| 1 teaspoon freshly ground black pepper, or more to taste

ONIONS AND FILLING: Preheat the oven to 350°F. Slice the onions in half on the equator. Remove the centers, leaving a "bowl" in the center of the onion halves. (Reserve the centers for another use.) In a bowl, stir together 1/2 cup bread crumbs, corn, zucchini, carrots and beets. Firmly pack the filling in the hollowed-out onion halves and arrange them in a shallow baking dish so that the onions fit snugly. Pour the water around base of the onions.

GLAZE: In a separate bowl, whisk together the glaze ingredients. Drizzle half of the mixture over the tops of the stuffed onions. Bake 30 minutes. Drizzle with the remaining glaze sauce. Bake 30 minutes more. Just before serving, sprinkle the onions with the remaining 1/2 cup bread crumbs and place the onions under the broiler until the crumbs are toasted and golden brown.

> **PER SERVING:**
> 92 Cal.; 2g Prot.; 1g Fat; 19g Carb.;
> 0mg Chol.; 303mg Sod.; 2g Fiber.

Fruited Parsnips

serves 4

> 6 small parsnips, peeled and sliced
> 1 orange, peeled and sliced
> 3 apples, peeled, cored and sliced
> 1/4 cup apple juice or water
> 2 tablespoons honey

PREHEAT the oven to 350°F. Mix together the parsnips, oranges and apples in a baking dish. Stir in the apple juice or water, and honey. Cover and bake 20 minutes, stirring several times. Uncover and bake 10 minutes more. Serve hot.

> **PER SERVING:**
> 193 Cal.; 2g Prot.; 0.4g Fat; 49g Carb.;
> 0mg Chol.; 11mg Sod.; 6g Fiber.

Braised Green Peas with Scallions

serves 6

Braising is the classic way to transform ordinary root vegetables into a deep-down sweetness. Luckily, the technique works just as well with other vegetables, especially green peas.

> Half a small head of Boston or bibb lettuce, rinsed
> 3 cups freshly shelled green peas (or two 10-ounce packages frozen green peas, thawed)
> 2 scallions (green and white parts), sliced
> 1/2 cup water
> 2 teaspoons butter
> 1/2 teaspoon salt
> 1/4 teaspoon white pepper

SLICE the lettuce leaves into thin shreds with water still clinging to them. In a medium saucepan, combine the lettuce with the remaining ingredients, and bring the mixture to a boil. Lower the heat, cover, and simmer until the peas are just tender, about 10 minutes. Uncover, raise the heat and rapidly boil away most of the liquid. Serve hot.

> **PER SERVING:**
> 76 Cal.; 4g Prot.; 1g Fat; 12g Carb.;
> 3mg Chol.; 261mg Sod.; 4g Fiber.

Green Pea Mousse with Carrot Garnish

serves 6

This dish has a brilliant color combination.

- 1 1/2 cups julienned carrots
- Mild vegetable stock (page 178) or water to cover carrots
- 1 teaspoon honey
- Salt to taste
- 1/2 onion, chopped
- 1 tablespoon water
- 1/2 pound fresh or frozen green peas
- 3/4 cup water or mild vegetable stock (page 178)
- 1 1/2 teaspoons honey
- 2 tablespoons dry white wine
- 1/3 cup soymilk or low-fat milk
- Salt to taste
- White pepper to taste
- 1 teaspoon powdered agar-agar (or 2 tablespoons flaked)
- 2/3 cup small cauliflower florets, steamed (optional)

COMBINE the carrots, stock or water, honey and salt in a pot, and cook over medium heat until the carrots are just tender, about 10 to 15 minutes; drain. Rinse the carrots under cold water to set their color. Drain again. Line the bottom and sides of a terrine or bread pan with carrots. (The ends of the pan do not have to be covered.)

IN A POT, cook the onion in 1 tablespoon water, stirring, over medium heat until tender. Add the peas, water or stock, honey and wine. Cook until the peas are just tender, about 3 to 5 minutes. (Do not overcook.) Drain, reserving the liquid. (You should have about 1/2 cup liquid. If you have much more, boil rapidly to reduce.)

PURÉE the peas in a blender or food processor with the milk until completely smooth. Season with salt and white pepper. Place the reserved cooking liquid in a small pot and whisk in the agar-agar. Bring to a boil, and boil for 1 minute to dissolve the agar completely. Add the agar mixture to the pea-soymilk mixture and blend again for 15 seconds. Pour into the carrot-lined pan. Press the steamed cauliflower florets into the mousse down the middle in a row. (It looks very pretty when sliced.) Chill the mousse until firm, at least 4 hours. To serve, unmold the mousse onto a large plate, slice into 1/2-inch-thick slices, and place 2 slices on each plate.

> **PER SERVING:**
> 66 Cal.: 3g Prot.: 0.2g Fat: 10g Carb.:
> 0mg Chol.: 194mg Sod.: 2g Fiber.

Roasted Peppers

serves 4

- 2 bell peppers
- 1 teaspoon virgin olive oil (optional)

PLACE the peppers on a gas burner, directly in the flame. Turn occasionally until the skin is charred all over. Transfer to a bowl at once and cover with a plate. Let steam at least 10 minutes. Remove the skins with a knife or your fingers. (Don't rinse the peppers under running water or you'll wash away much of the flavor.)

AFTER PEELING, slice open the peppers and remove the seeds and membranes. Slice into strips. Toss with olive oil and store in a jar, refrigerated, until needed. Peppers will keep a week but are best used within a few days.

Helpful hints:

- For roasting, choose heavy peppers, with thick flesh. Light, thin-walled peppers will burn before the skins char.

- If you don't have a gas stove, you can use your oven. First cut the peppers in half lengthwise and remove the seeds. Then brush with vegetable oil and broil until the skin is charred. Steam as directed, then remove the skin.

> **PER SERVING:**
> 10 Cal.; 5g Prot.; 0.1g Fat; 2g Carb.;
> 0mg Chol.; 1mg Sod.; 1g Fiber.

Grilled Plantains

serves 4

In different stages of ripeness, plantains are a starch, a vegetable or even a dessert. Try them grilled for an almost potato-like dish.

> 2 large plantains (see Note)
> Cayenne pepper to taste

CUT the plantains into fourths crosswise, then slice lengthwise to form rectangular pieces about 1/4-inch thick and about 2 inches long. Sprinkle with cayenne. Grill or broil until just tender, about 6 minutes. Serve warm.

Note:

The plantain looks like a banana, but it's a bit bigger and tastes more like a squash. You must cook it before eating. Wait until its skin is black; then it tastes sweet when cooked.

> **PER SERVING:**
> 109 Cal.; 1g Prot.; 0.3g Fat; 26g Carb.;
> 0mg Chol.; 4mg Sod.; 2g Fiber.

Plantains with Spices

serves 4

> 2 tablespoons butter or vegetable oil
> 2 yellow plantains, peeled and sliced 1/4 inch thick on the diagonal
> 1/4 teaspoon ground cloves
> 1/4 teaspoon ground nutmeg

IN A LARGE SKILLET, melt the butter or heat the oil over medium-high heat, and cook the plantains with half of the spices for 4 or 5 minutes. Turn the plantains, sprinkle with the remaining spices, and cook until golden brown, about 4 minutes more.

> **PER SERVING:**
> 161 Cal.; 1g Prot.; 6g Fat; 29g Carb.;
> 16mg Chol.; 62mg Sod.; 0.7g Fiber.

Scalloped Potatoes

serves 4

There's only 1 gram of fat in a serving, far lower than the fat content in the traditional version of this dish.

- 4 medium russet potatoes, sliced thinly
- 1/2 medium onion, sliced thinly
- 1/4 cup instant nonfat powdered milk
- 1 cup water or vegetable stock (page 178)
- 1 scant tablespoon virgin olive oil
- 1/4 teaspoon ground nutmeg

PREHEAT the oven to 375°F. Spray a 2-quart soufflé dish or other baking dish with nonstick cooking spray. Layer the potato and onion slices in the dish. In a small bowl or blender, whisk together the powdered milk, water or stock, oil and nutmeg until smooth. Pour over the vegetable slices. Cover the dish with foil. Bake until the potatoes have absorbed most of the liquid, about 1 hour; then remove the foil and bake until browned, about 15 minutes more.

> **PER SERVING:**
> 164 Cal.; 5g Prot.; 1g Fat; 33g Carb.;
> 0mg Chol.; 47mg Sod.; 3g Fiber.

Gratin of Potatoes and Garlic

serves 5

- 2 tablespoons minced garlic
- 1 teaspoon dried rosemary
- 2 tablespoons virgin olive oil
- 10 medium red potatoes, boiled and sliced thinly
- Salt and freshly ground black pepper to taste

PREHEAT the oven to 375°F. Spray a 9 × 12-inch baking dish with nonstick cooking spray. In a small bowl, stir together the garlic, rosemary and oil. Layer the potatoes, overlapping them slightly, on the bottom of the baking dish. Drizzle with the garlic mixture and sprinkle with salt and pepper. Bake until the potatoes are evenly browned and crisp, about 30 to 45 minutes.

> **PER SERVING:**
> 296 Cal.; 4g Prot.; 5g Fat; 58g Carb.;
> 0mg Chol.; 228mg Sod.; 5g Fiber.

Stuffed Baked Potatoes

serves 6

- 6 large baking potatoes
- 1 cup nonfat plain yogurt
- 4 tablespoons crumbled blue cheese
- 4 scallions (green and white parts), minced
- Paprika, for garnish

PREHEAT the oven to 425°F. Wash and dry the potatoes, then pierce them a few times with a fork. Place on an oven rack and bake until very soft, about 45 to 60 minutes. Remove from your oven; preheat the broiler.

LET THE POTATOES cool slightly, then cut a wedge equal to a third of the potato from the top of each, being careful not to break the skin of the rest of the potato. Remove enough of the interior to leave a 1/2-inch thickness of potato inside the skin, and mash in a bowl with the yogurt, blue cheese and scallions. Spoon this mixture back into the potato shells, mounding over the top. Sprinkle with the paprika. Broil until lightly browned, about 5 minutes.

Variation:

To serve the potatoes as a main dish, jazz them up by mixing chopped, cooked vegetables into the yogurt and cheese. Proceed with the recipe.

> **PER SERVING:**
> 265 Cal.; 7g Prot.; 2g Fat; 55g Carb.;
> 5mg Chol.; 127mg Sod.; 5g Fiber.

Roasted Potatoes with Thyme

serves 3

For the most color, use yellow-fleshed fingerling potatoes or purple Peruvians.

- **1 pound fingerling, purple (also called Peruvian or blue potatoes) or new red potatoes**
- **1 tablespoon virgin olive oil**
- **Salt and freshly ground black pepper to taste**
- **8 sprigs fresh thyme**

PREHEAT the oven to 375°F. Toss the potatoes with the olive oil, and season with salt and pepper. Place the potatoes in a baking dish and scatter thyme on top. Cover with foil and bake until tender when pierced with a knife, about 25 minutes for small potatoes, longer for larger ones. Once or twice during baking, give the pan a shake. When done, let the potatoes cool. Serve the small ones whole; slice the larger ones lengthwise.

> **PER SERVING:**
> 190 Cal.; 3g Prot.; 5g Fat; 34g Carb.;
> 0mg Chol.; 366mg Sod.; 3g Fiber.

Potato-Apple Torten

serves 6

This layered dish is a simple, satisfying mixture of apples, potatoes and onions.

- **2 large crisp, sweet apples**
- **2 pounds red or white potatoes**
- **2 to 3 teaspoons vegetable oil**
- **Salt and freshly ground black pepper to taste**
- **1 red onion, chopped**
- **Freshly grated nutmeg**

PREHEAT the oven to 350°F. Core and thinly slice the apples; thinly slice the potatoes. Oil the bottom and sides of a large, cast-iron skillet. As neatly as possible, place a layer of potatoes in the skillet. Sprinkle with salt, pepper and half of the onions. Place a layer of apples on top, using half of the apples. Repeat the layers, ending with a layer of apple slices. Sprinkle with nutmeg and press down the mixture with a plate. Remove the plate and bake until the apples are tender and the potatoes are crispy and brown, about 35 to 40 minutes. Let cool for 10 minutes before cutting into wedges.

Variation:

If you don't have a cast-iron skillet, use a casserole dish. Be sure to coat the inside of the dish with oil.

> **PER SERVING:**
> 208 Cal.; 3g Prot.; 2g Fat; 45g Carb.;
> 0mg Chol.; 190mg Sod.; 5g Fiber.

Potato Logs

serves 6

These orange-scented "logs" are low in fat.

| 3 pounds potatoes
| 2 tablespoons margarine
| 1/2 cup egg substitute
| 2 teaspoons grated orange zest
| 1/8 teaspoon ground nutmeg
| 2 teaspoons salt, or to taste
| 1/4 teaspoon ground white pepper
| Butter-flavored cooking spray

PEEL the potatoes, cut in half or quarters, and cook in boiling water until tender but still firm, about 15 to 20 minutes; drain. Put the potatoes through a food mill or potato ricer to make a smooth paste; transfer to a bowl. Add the margarine, egg substitute, orange zest, nutmeg, salt and white pepper. Beat until fluffy. Let cool. Spray a baking sheet with butter-flavored cooking spray. Set aside.

PILE the potato mixture into a pastry bag fitted with a large star tip or into a quart-size zipper-type plastic bag with one corner cut off and fitted with a star tip. Squeeze out rows of 3-inch-long logs onto the prepared baking sheet, refilling the bag as needed until all of the potato mixture is used.

TO KEEP a crust from forming, lightly spray the surface of the logs with butter-flavored spray. Preheat the broiler. Broil just until the ridges on the logs take on a deep brown color.

Variation:

To make sweet potato logs, cook 1 1/2 pounds white potato and 1 1/2 pounds sweet potatoes, then proceed with the recipe.

> **PER SERVING:**
> 292 Cal.; 6g Prot.; 4g Fat; 58g Carb.;
> 0mg Chol.; 789mg Sod.; 6g Fiber.

Canary Islands Potatoes with Mojo Sauce

serves 6

In the Canary Islands, off the northwest coast of Africa, the potatoes are cooked in seawater and liberally splashed with mojo sauce, a tart and fiery concoction.

12 medium red-skinned potatoes

1/2 cup red wine vinegar

2 tablespoons virgin olive oil

2 cloves garlic, pressed or minced

3/4 teaspoon paprika

3/4 teaspoon cumin seeds, toasted (page 106) and crushed slightly

1/8 teaspoon cayenne pepper, or to taste

1/2 teaspoon salt, or to taste

2 teaspoons minced fresh parsley

CUT the potatoes in half. Bring a large pot of salted water to a boil and add the potatoes. Cook until tender but not mushy, about 15 to 20 minutes; drain. Meanwhile, make a sauce by whisking together the remaining ingredients in a small bowl. Transfer the potatoes to a serving dish, and pour the sauce over them. Serve hot or at room temperature.

> **PER SERVING:**
> 203 Cal.; 4g Prot.; 5g Fat; 36g Carb.;
> 0mg Chol.; 184mg Sod.; 6g Fiber.

Paprika Mashed Potatoes

serves 6

These mashed potatoes have old-fashioned flavor, more color and less fat. Vary the flavor by adding 1/2 tablespoon of any dried herb.

6 medium potatoes, peeled and cubed

3/4 cup plain nonfat yogurt

1/4 cup evaporated skim milk or low-fat soymilk

1/2 tablespoon paprika

Salt to taste

1/2 teaspoon freshly ground black pepper

1 teaspoon melted unsalted butter or margarine

PLACE the potatoes in a saucepan, add cold water to cover and bring to a boil. Lower the heat, cover with the lid ajar and gently boil until tender, about 15 to 20 minutes; drain. Combine the potatoes with the yogurt, milk or soymilk, paprika, salt and pepper. Mash or beat with an electric mixer until smooth. Drizzle the potatoes with butter or margarine.

> **PER SERVING:**
> 142 Cal.; 3g Prot.; 1g Fat; 30g Carb.;
> 4mg Chol.; 412mg Sod.; 3g Fiber.

Pesto Mashed Potatoes

serves 6

Pesto-flavored mashed potatoes are a rich-tasting variation on the traditional milk-and-butter recipe.

> 6 medium potatoes, peeled and cubed
>
> 2 tablespoons instant nonfat powdered milk
>
> 1/2 cup firmly packed fresh basil leaves
>
> 1 tablespoon virgin olive oil
>
> 1 tablespoon grated Parmesan cheese
>
> 2 small cloves garlic
>
> White pepper to taste

PLACE the potatoes in a large pot, cover with water and bring to a boil. Lower the heat and simmer until the potatoes are soft enough to be mashed easily with a wooden spoon against the side of the pot, about 20 minutes. Drain and place in a large bowl. Using an electric beater, whip the potatoes, sprinkling the mixture every few minutes with milk powder, until light and fluffy. Set aside.

IN A BLENDER or food processor, blend the basil, oil, Parmesan and garlic until it becomes a paste. Stir the pesto into the potatoes, blending well. Season with white pepper. Serve hot.

> **PER SERVING:**
> 157 Cal.; 3g Prot.; 2g Fat; 30g Carb.;
> 1mg Chol.; 37mg Sod.; 3g Fiber.

Skinny French Fries

serves 2

If you crave french fries but can do without the grease, try these baked "skinnies."

> 1 teaspoon safflower or canola oil
>
> 1 large baking potato, unpeeled and cut into french-fry strips

PREHEAT the oven to 450°F. Measure half of the oil into the palm of your hand and rub half of the fries with the oil. Spread the fries in a single layer on a baking sheet. Repeat the process with the remaining oil and fries. Bake 15 minutes, then turn and bake until evenly browned, about 10 minutes more.

> **PER SERVING:**
> 93 Cal.; 1g Prot.; 2g Fat; 17g Carb.;
> 0mg Chol.; 4 mg Sod.; 2g Fiber.

Spicy New Potatoes

serves 4

> 2 pounds new potatoes
>
> 1 cup nonfat plain yogurt
>
> 3-inch piece fresh horseradish root, peeled and grated
>   (or 4 tablespoons bottled, grated white horseradish)
>
> 1/8 teaspoon sugar
>
> Salt to taste
>
> Ground white pepper to taste

GENTLY boil the potatoes until they can be pierced easily with a fork, about 15 to 20 minutes. Drain. Combine the remaining ingredients, and pour over the potatoes. Serve warm.

> **PER SERVING:**
> 213 Cal.; 6g Prot.; 0.3g Fat; 47g Carb.;
> 1mg Chol.; 77mg Sod.; 3g Fiber.

Oriental Acorn Squash

serves 2

| 1 acorn squash, halved, seeded and scraped to remove strings
| 3 tablespoons fresh lemon juice
| 2 tablespoons honey
| 1 tablespoon soy sauce
| 1 tablespoon grated ginger root

PREHEAT the oven to 400°F. Place the squash halves cut-side down in a baking dish filled with 1/2 inch of water. Bake for 30 minutes. Remove the dish from your oven and turn the squash halves cut side up. In a small bowl, stir together the lemon juice, honey, soy sauce and ginger root. Spoon this mixture into the squash halves. Return to your oven and bake 10 minutes more.

> **PER SERVING:**
> 162 Cal.; 3g Prot.; 0.3g Fat; 38g Carb.;
> 0mg Chol.; 523mg Sod.; 6g Fiber.

Fruited Squash

serves 4

This festive dish dresses up a holiday table.

| 2 acorn or delicata squashes, halved and seeded (see Note)
| 1/2 cup fresh cranberries
| 1 small apple, chopped
| 1/4 cup chopped raisins
| Juice and grated peel of 1 small orange
| 1 1/2 tablespoons honey
| Dash salt

PREHEAT the oven to 375°F. Place the squash in a baking dish; set aside. In a bowl, combine the remaining ingredients; pile this mixture into the squash cavities. Cover the dish and bake until squash is tender, about 25 to 45 minutes, depending on the variety. (Acorn cooks more quickly than delicata.) Transfer to a serving dish.

Note:

Delicata squash is a lightly ridged, oblong-shaped squash about 6 to 9 inches in length. Its skin is ivory and striped with dark green; the flesh is yellow.

> **PER SERVING:**
> 185 Cal.; 3g Prot.; 1g Fat; 45g Carb.;
> 0mg Chol.; 4mg Sod.; 11g Fiber.

Southern Crookneck Squash

serves 4

Yellow squash is a Southern favorite, but it's usually made with loads of fat. Here's a delicious, lighter approach.

> 2 tablespoons water
>
> 2 tablespoons minced onion
>
> 3 cups diced yellow crookneck (summer) squash
>
> 1/2 to 3/4 cup skim milk or soymilk
>
> 1/2 teaspoon salt
>
> 1/4 teaspoon ground white pepper
>
> 2 tablespoons finely minced fresh parsley (optional)

HEAT the water in a medium saucepan over medium-high heat; add the onion and lightly cook, stirring, until the water has evaporated, about 3 minutes. Add the squash, enough milk to almost cover, salt and pepper. Cook on very low heat until the squash is tender, about 5 or 6 minutes. Garnish with parsley. Serve at once.

> **PER SERVING:**
> 41 Cal.; 2g Prot.; 0.2g Fat; 7g Carb.;
> 1mg Chol.; 284mg Sod.; 2g Fiber.

Baked Sweet Potatoes with Yogurt-Rice Topping

serves 6

> 6 small sweet potatoes
>
> 3/4 cup plain nonfat yogurt
>
> 1/2 cup warm cooked rice
>
> Salt to taste
>
> White pepper to taste

PREHEAT the oven to 450°F. Score the surface of the sweet potatoes with a fork several times, and bake until tender, about 35 to 40 minutes. Slit each one down the middle and remove a couple of tablespoons of flesh to make room for the filling. (Reserve the flesh for another use.) Wrap the potatoes in foil and set aside.

IN A SEPARATE BOWL, combine the yogurt, rice, salt and pepper. Place the potatoes on a serving dish. Fold back foil to make a "boat" and spoon in the filling.

Variation:

Replace some of the rice with wild rice, add chopped herbs and dried apricots, and garnish with toasted pecans (page 106).

> **PER SERVING:**
> 148 Cal.; 4g Prot.; 0.2g Fat; 34g Carb.;
> 1mg Chol.; 122mg Sod.; 3g Fiber.

Cherry Tomatoes with Tomato Cream

serves 8

These tiny bright red cups are flavorful and pretty. You may make them in advance, and keep them chilled until serving time.

- 18 to 20 ripe cherry tomatoes
- 1/2 cup tomato juice
- 2 tablespoons celery leaves, minced
- 2 teaspoons fresh basil leaves (or 1/2 teaspoon dried)
- Salt and freshly ground black pepper to taste
- 1/2 cup fat-free cream cheese
- Parsley sprigs, for garnish

CUT the tops off the cherry tomatoes. Using a small spoon, carefully scoop out the centers into a saucepan, being careful not to pierce the outer skin. Salt the tomato cavities very lightly and turn them upside down on a towel to drain. Chill them while making the tomato cream.

ADD the tomato juice, celery leaves, basil, salt and pepper to the saucepan. Bring to a simmer and cook, stirring occasionally, for 15 minutes. Process the mixture in a blender or food processor; then pour it through a fine strainer set over a bowl to remove the seeds. Chill thoroughly. Add the cream cheese to the bowl and blend until smooth.

TURN the tomato cups right side up and arrange on a serving tray. Spoon or pipe the cream into each tomato, mounding it slightly. Garnish each one with a tiny sprig of fresh parsley. Chill before serving.

> **PER SERVING:**
> 33 Cal.; 1g Prot.; 1g Fat; 7g Carb.;
> 0mg Chol.; 136mg Sod.; 2g Fiber.

Fluffy Mashed Sweet Potatoes

serves 6

- 2 cups cooked and mashed sweet potatoes (cook in boiling water for 15 to 20 minutes)
- 3 bananas, mashed
- 1 1/2 cups soymilk or milk
- 1/2 cup prune juice
- 3 tablespoons honey
- 1 teaspoon allspice
- 2 teaspoons chopped candied ginger

PREHEAT the oven to 375°F. Combine all the ingredients except the ginger and beat until fluffy. Spoon into an oiled casserole and bake until golden brown, about 50 to 60 minutes. Sprinkle with candied ginger.

> **PER SERVING:**
> 236 Cal.; 3g Prot.; 1g Fat; 52g Carb.;
> 0mg Chol.; 24mg Sod.; 6g Fiber.

Sweet-Spicy Leeks, Cabbage and Onion

serves 8

| 3 cups water or vegetable stock (page 178)
| 1 head cabbage, cut into 8 wedges
| 1 large onion, chopped
| 3 leeks, washed well and chopped coarsely
| 3/4 teaspoon ground cinnamon
| 1/2 teaspoon ground cloves
| Salt to taste

IN A LARGE PAN, bring the liquid to a boil. Add the cabbage wedges and remaining ingredients. Cover. Simmer about 30 minutes, turning the cabbage once. Serve warm.

> **PER SERVING:**
> 21 Cal.; 1g Prot.; 0g Fat; 5g Carb.;
> 0mg Chol.; 147mg Sod.; 2g Fiber.

Sauté of Spaghetti Squash, Carrot and Daikon

serves 6

Cook the spaghetti squash a day ahead of time if you like, then store the pasta-like strands in a covered dish until you're ready to finish the dish.

| 4 cups spaghetti squash strands (1 large squash, see Note)
| 2 tablespoons canola oil
| 1 tablespoon butter or margarine
| 4 cups shredded carrots
| 2 cups shredded daikon radish
| 1 medium clove garlic, crushed and minced
| 1 teaspoon salt, or to taste
| 1/2 teaspoon freshly ground black pepper, or to taste
| 1 scant teaspoon dried thyme (or 1 tablespoon fresh, finely minced)
| Pinch sugar

IN A SAUCEPAN fitted with a steamer, steam the spaghetti squash strands in a small amount of water until heated through, about 5 minutes. Set aside. In a large skillet over medium heat, heat together the oil and butter or margarine until very hot. Add the spaghetti squash, carrots and daikon radish. Cook, stirring frequently, until the carrot shreds are tender, about 10 to 15 minutes.

ADD the remaining ingredients. Raise the heat to medium-high and stir-fry until the vegetables look crisp and golden, about 5 minutes more. Serve hot.

Note:

To cook a whole squash, submerge it in a large pot of boiling water. Cook for 1 hour. Remove from the pot and let cool. Cut squash in half lengthwise, remove seeds and scrape out stringy flesh. Separate the strands with a fork.

> **PER SERVING:**
> 127 Cal.; 1g Prot.; 7g Fat; 15g Carb.;
> 5mg Chol.; 425mg Sod.; 5g Fiber.

Baked Beans

serves 6

Homemade baked beans take a bit of effort to make, but the payoff is grand.

> 1 1/2 cups dry great northern beans (or 3 cups canned beans)
>
> 1/2 cup reserved bean-cooking liquid or water
>
> 1 tablespoon tomato paste
>
> 1 large onion, sliced thinly
>
> 1 tablespoon cider vinegar
>
> 2 tablespoons molasses or maple syrup
>
> 1 teaspoon dry mustard
>
> Pinch cayenne pepper or white pepper
>
> Salt to taste

IF YOU'RE USING DRY BEANS, let them soak overnight in water to cover; drain. Combine with 3 1/2 cups fresh water in a large saucepan. Bring to a boil, lower the heat and simmer for 2 to 2 1/2 hours. Drain, reserving the bean-cooking liquid. If you're using canned beans, drain them over a bowl and reserve the bean liquid.

PREHEAT the oven to 350°F. Combine all the ingredients in a baking dish and stir well. Cover and bake 30 minutes. Uncover and bake 30 minutes more.

> **PER SERVING:**
> 136 Cal.; 8g Prot.; 0.8g Fat; 26g Carb.;
> 0mg Chol.; 145mg Sod.; 8g Fiber.

Southern-Style Ranch Beans

serves 8

This sweet-sour dish takes advantage of two veteran convenience foods: canned beans and canned stewed tomatoes.

> 2 medium onions, chopped
>
> 2 tablespoons water
>
> 1 cup brown sugar
>
> 2 tablespoons prepared mustard
>
> One 16-ounce can stewed tomatoes
>
> 1 tablespoon cider vinegar
>
> Three 16-ounce cans vegetarian baked beans
>
> One 16-ounce can red kidney beans, rinsed

LIGHTLY GREASE a skillet with nonstick cooking spray or oil. Add the onions and water; cook, stirring, over medium-high heat until the water has evaporated and the onions are limp, about 5 minutes. Stir in the brown sugar, mustard, tomatoes and tomato liquid, vinegar, baked beans and drained kidney beans. Cover and simmer 20 minutes.

> **PER SERVING:**
> 345 Cal.; 11g Prot.; 0.8g Fat; 36g Carb.;
> 0mg Chol.; 1,127mg Sod.; 17g Fiber.

Vegetables with Far East Flair

serves 6

Stir-frying these vegetables in water makes them crisp while keeping fat content at zero.

- 2 cups sliced celery
- 3/4 cup sliced onion
- 3/4 cup sliced white button mushrooms
- 3/4 pound broccoli, sliced
- 1/4 cup sliced water chestnuts
- Water for stir-frying
- 3/4 cup water
- 1 tablespoon low-sodium soy sauce or tamari
- 1/2 teaspoon salt (optional)
- 3 tablespoons cornstarch dissolved in 3 tablespoons water

IN A WOK OR SKILLET, cook the vegetables, stirring, in a small amount of water for about 5 minutes. Add 3/4 cup water, soy sauce or tamari, and salt. Bring to a boil. Add the dissolved cornstarch to the vegetable mixture and combine thoroughly. Cook until the sauce thickens. Serve at once.

> **PER SERVING:**
> 45 Cal.; 2g Prot.; 0g Fat; 10g Carb.;
> 0mg Chol.; 212mg Sod.; 6g Fiber.

Roasted Vegetables

serves 6

As vegetables roast over high heat, their natural sugars caramelize and intensify the flavors.

- 2 yellow bell peppers, seeded
- 2 green bell peppers, seeded
- 1 pound carrots
- Olive oil cooking spray
- Salt to taste (optional)

PREHEAT the oven to 500°F. Cut each pepper into eighths. Cut the carrots on the diagonal into 1/4-inch slices. Arrange the peppers and carrots in a single layer on 2 baking sheets and mist lightly with olive oil cooking spray. Roast until well-cooked but not burned, about 12 to 15 minutes. Sprinkle with salt. Serve at once.

> **PER SERVING:**
> 45 Cal.; 0.8g Prot.; 0.1g Fat; 10g Carb.;
> 0mg Chol.; 289mg Sod.; 3g Fiber.

Feta-Pumpkin Casserole

serves 4

The tangy taste of feta cheese blends well with pumpkin in this interesting side dish.

1/4 cup dry sherry or apple juice

1 cup chopped onion

3 cloves garlic, minced

1 medium tomato, diced

1 small zucchini, sliced

2 cups peeled and cubed fresh pumpkin

1 whole egg plus 2 egg whites lightly beaten

1/2 cup low-fat buttermilk

1/2 cup nonfat plain yogurt

1/4 cup crumbled feta cheese

1/8 teaspoon cayenne pepper

1/2 teaspoon ground coriander

1/2 cup toasted bread crumbs (page 106)

PREHEAT the oven to 375°F. Lightly oil a 2-quart baking dish. In a nonstick skillet, heat the sherry or apple juice over medium-high heat. Add the onion and cook, stirring, until soft, about 2 minutes. Add the garlic, tomato, zucchini and pumpkin. Cook, stirring, 2 minutes more; set aside.

IN A MEDIUM BOWL, whisk together the egg and egg whites, buttermilk and yogurt. Add the feta, spices, bread crumbs and the sautéed vegetables. Mix well and spoon into the baking dish. Bake until firm, about 25 minutes. Serve hot.

PER SERVING:
198 Cal.; 12g Prot.; 4g Fat; 26g Carb.;
52mg Chol.; 300mg Sod.; 2g Fiber.

Ginger Applesauce

serves 10

Fresh ginger root and lemon zest give this applesauce a special zing.

10 Cortland apples

1 cup apple cider

2 cinnamon sticks

1 1/2 teaspoons lemon zest

1/4 cup brown sugar

1/4 teaspoon ground nutmeg

1 1/2 tablespoons finely chopped ginger root

PLACE the apples in a large saucepan and add the cider, cinnamon and lemon zest. Simmer over medium heat for 30 minutes, stirring occasionally. Remove the cinnamon sticks. Add the sugar, nutmeg and ginger, and cook until thick, about 10 minutes. Serve warm or chilled.

PER SERVING:
214 Cal.; 2g Prot.; 6g Fat; 41g Carb.;
0mg Chol.; 112mg Sod.; 1g Fiber.

Pasta with Asparagus and Strawberries

serves 4

The berries you choose for this delicious side dish don't have to be firm or pretty, but they must be ripe and sweet.

> 2 cups fresh asparagus tips
>
> 1/4 cup water
>
> 6 ounces uncooked bow-tie pasta
>
> 1 tablespoon fresh lemon juice
>
> 1 tablespoon mashed ripe avocado
>
> 2 tablespoons neufchâtel cheese or light cream cheese
>
> 1/4 cup finely diced Muenster or Monterey Jack cheese
>
> 1 cup sliced fresh strawberries

PLACE the asparagus tips and water in a shallow pan. Cover and bring to a boil. Simmer until the asparagus is bright green and barely cooked, about 2 minutes. Remove the asparagus and set aside to drain. Reserve 2 tablespoons cooking water.

PREPARE the pasta according to the package directions; drain, reserving about 2 tablespoons cooking water. Place the reserved pasta water in a large pot and, working quickly, add the asparagus water, lemon juice, avocado, neufchâtel cheese or cream cheese, and Muenster or Monterey Jack cheese. Blend until creamy. Add the pasta and toss with a wooden spoon. Add the asparagus and strawberries, and toss well. Serve at once.

> **PER SERVING:**
> 246 Cal.; 9g Prot.; 5g Fat; 39g Carb.;
> 13mg Chol.; 80mg Sod.; 3g Fiber.

Sweet Potato Stuffing

serves 8

This flavorful stuffing goes well with any gravy, but Chunky Tomato Gravy (page 484) is a sure bet.

> 1 1/2 pounds sweet potatoes, peeled and cut into chunks
>
> 3 to 4 tablespoons butter or margarine
>
> 8 scallions (green and white parts), chopped finely
>
> 2 eggs (or equivalent egg substitute)
>
> 1 cup plus 2 tablespoons fresh, whole-wheat bread crumbs
>
> 1/4 teaspoon freshly ground black pepper
>
> 1/2 teaspoon salt
>
> 1/2 teaspoon orange zest
>
> 3 tablespoons chopped fresh parsley

PLACE the sweet potatoes in a medium saucepan with enough water to cover. Cook over medium-high heat until tender, about 25 minutes; drain. Transfer to a food processor or blender, and purée with 1 tablespoon butter or margarine. Meanwhile, cook the scallions in 1 to 2 tablespoons butter or margarine, stirring, for 1 minute. In a medium bowl, combine the puréed potatoes, scallions, eggs or egg substitute, 1 cup bread crumbs, pepper, salt, zest and parsley. Mix well and set aside. In a small skillet, melt the remaining 1 tablespoon butter or margarine. Add the remaining 2 tablespoons bread crumbs and toast over medium-high heat.

PREHEAT the oven to 350°F. Spoon the stuffing mixture into an oval gratin dish or baking dish. Sprinkle the toasted bread crumbs over the stuffing and bake until set, about 20 minutes. Serve hot.

Wild Rice and Apricot Stuffing

serves 8

Here's an all-time, year-round favorite.

- 1 cup uncooked wild rice
- 3 cups water
- 1/2 teaspoon salt
- 2 to 4 tablespoons margarine or butter
- 2 shallots, minced
- 1 clove garlic, minced
- 1 cup dried apricots, chopped
- 1/4 cup chopped fresh parsley
- 1/4 teaspoon freshly ground black pepper

BRING THE WILD RICE with water and 1/4 teaspoon salt to a boil in a medium saucepan. Lower the heat; cover and simmer until the grain split open, about 1 hour. Drain and let cool. Melt the margarine or butter in a small skillet; add the shallots and garlic, and cook, stirring, 2 minutes. In a medium bowl, combine the cooked vegetables with the rice, apricots, parsley, pepper and remaining 1/4 teaspoon salt.

PREHEAT the oven to 350°F. Transfer the wild rice mixture to a medium baking dish, cover and bake 15 minutes. Serve hot or at room temperature.

Herbed Rice with Yogurt

serves 4

In southern India, this refreshing dish is pure comfort. It's the perfect accompaniment to spicy hot entrées.

- 1 tablespoon vegetable oil
- 2 teaspoons black mustard seeds
- 2 teaspoons finely minced fresh ginger root
- 1 small green chili, seeded and minced (optional)
- 4 cups cooked brown rice, cooled
- 1 1/2 cups nonfat yogurt, beaten smooth
- 1 teaspoon salt

HEAT the oil in a skillet over medium-high heat. As soon as the oil begins to ripple, add the mustard seeds and cover the skillet with a lid at once. When the popping of the seeds slows down, add the ginger, chili, rice, yogurt and salt. Cook gently for 5 minutes. Remove from the heat and chill. Serve cool.

Parslied Bulgur Pilaf

serves 1

If you soak the bulgur ahead of time and refrigerate it, this dish can be on the table in less than 5 minutes.

| 3/4 cup uncooked bulgur
| 1 cup hot water or vegetable broth
| 1/2 tablespoon virgin olive oil
| 2 tablespoons chopped fresh parsley
| 1/4 teaspoon salt
| 1/4 teaspoon freshly ground black pepper

COMBINE the bulgur and water or broth in a small bowl, cover and set aside until the liquid is absorbed, about 20 minutes; drain. Heat the olive oil in a medium skillet over medium heat. Add the bulgur and cook, stirring, 2 minutes. Add the parsley, salt and pepper. Serve hot.

Variation:

Substitute 1 1/2 cups cooked brown rice or basmati rice for the bulgur. Omit the soaking step and add cooked rice along with 1/2 onion, chopped and sautéed.

> **PER SERVING:**
> 257 Cal.; 7g Prot.; 5g Fat; 49g Carb.;
> 0mg Chol.; 271mg Sod.; 1g Fiber.

Ring of Rice with Parsley

serves 6

This method of serving rice turns a simple food into an elegant dish. If don't have a ring mold, you may use a bundt pan. Be sure the rice is on the sticky side so that it stays in its molded form.

| 2 cups uncooked white rice (such as basmati rice)
| 3 3/4 cups boiling water
| 1 bay leaf
| Pinch salt
| Pinch white pepper
| 1/3 cup minced fresh parsley
| Sprigs of fresh parsley or watercress, sautéed white button mushrooms and sliced olives, for garnish (optional)

PLACE the rice, boiling water, bay leaf, salt and white pepper in a pot. Stir and bring to a boil. Lower the heat, cover and simmer until the liquid is absorbed, about 15 minutes. If the rice isn't somewhat sticky, add 1/4 to 1/2 cup water and simmer until absorbed. Remove the bay leaf and fluff the rice with a fork. Stir in minced parsley.

SPOON the rice mixture into a lightly oiled 4-cup ring mold. Press lightly but don't pack. Cover the mold with a plate and keep it warm until serving time. Then invert the mold to remove the ring of rice onto a platter or plate. Top with garnishes. Serve at once.

> **PER SERVING:**
> 227 Cal.; 4g Prot.; 0.4g Fat; 50g Carb.;
> 0mg Chol.; 46mg Sod.; 1g Fiber.

Rice in a Lotus Leaf

serves 4

Lotus leaves make great wrappers because they contribute both aroma and flavor to dishes, but they're not meant to be eaten. If you can find only small leaves, divide the rice mixture in half and make two smaller packets. Parchment paper or foil may be used in place of lotus leaves.

> 4 dried shiitake mushrooms
>
> 2 large dried lotus leaves
>
> 1 tablespoon vegetable oil
>
> 2 shallots, chopped
>
> 1/4 cup diced celery
>
> 1/4 cup diced carrot
>
> 1 teaspoon chopped fresh cilantro leaves
>
> 2 tablespoons soy sauce
>
> 1 tablespoon sesame oil
>
> 3 cups cooked medium-grain white or brown rice

SOAK the mushrooms in warm water for 30 minutes; drain. Cut off and discard the stems and thinly dice the caps. Set aside. Plunge the lotus leaves into a large pot of boiling water, and cook until softened, about 15 minutes. Drain and set aside.

PLACE a wok or a wide skillet over high heat until hot. Add the vegetable oil, swirling to coat the sides. Add the shallots and cook, stirring, for 1 minute. Add the celery, carrot, cilantro and reserved mushrooms; stir-fry for 1 minute more. Stir in the soy sauce, sesame oil and rice. Remove from the heat.

SPREAD a lotus leaf on your work surface. Cover it with a second leaf. Place the rice mixture in the center of the lotus leaves. Fold the edges of the leaves over to make a square packet that encloses the mixture. Place a steaming rack in a wok (or use a steamer fitted in a large saucepan). Pour water to just below the level of the rack, and bring to a boil. Place the lotus leaf packet on a heatproof dish and set the dish on the rack. Cover the wok or saucepan and steam, adding additional water if necessary, for 30 minutes. Transfer the packet to a serving dish and unfold the leaves for a pretty presentation.

> **PER SERVING:**
> 305 Cal.: 6g Prot.; 7g Fat; 54g Carb.;
> 0mg Chol.: 530mg Sod.: 2g Fiber.

Kasha with Potatoes, Onion and Herbs

serves 4

Potatoes offset the strong flavor of kasha in this savory dish.

> 1 cup uncooked kasha
>
> 1/2 teaspoon salt
>
> 2 cups water
>
> 1 onion, diced
>
> 1 teaspoon vegetable oil plus 1/4 cup water
>
> 1 cup diced potato, steamed
>
> 1 teaspoon dillweed

LIGHTLY TOAST the kasha in a skillet over medium heat until fragrant. Set aside. In a saucepan, add the salt to the water and bring to a boil. Slowly stir in the toasted kasha. Cover, lower the heat and simmer for 15 minutes.

MEANWHILE, cook the onion in the oil and water, stirring, in a large skillet over medium heat. When the onion is tender, stir in potato, dillweed and kasha, and warm through.

> **PER SERVING:**
> 141 Cal.; 3g Prot.; 4g Fat; 24g Carb.;
> 0mg Chol.; 269mg Sod.; 6g Fiber.

Steamed Dumplings

Makes 30

These open-topped steamed dumplings are a favorite in Chinese teahouses. Serve them with soy sauce or Chinese hot mustard.

- 1 pound firm tofu, drained
- 2 scallions (green and white parts), chopped finely
- 1/4 cup coarsely chopped water chestnuts
- 1 1/2 tablespoons soy sauce
- 1 tablespoon rice wine or dry sherry
- 2 teaspoons cornstarch
- 2 teaspoons minced ginger root
- 1 1/2 teaspoons sesame oil
- 1 teaspoon sugar
- 1/4 teaspoon white pepper
- 30 wonton or siu mai wrappers, covered with a damp dishcloth to prevent drying (see Note)

IN A MEDIUM BOWL, mash the tofu with a fork until smooth. Mix in the remaining ingredients except the wrappers. Set aside for 30 minutes to allow the flavors to blend.

NEXT, if you're using wonton wrappers, trim edges to form circles. (Siu mai wrappers are circular.) Place 1 heaping teaspoon of filling in the center of a wrapper. Use your fingers to gather up and pleat the wrapper around the filling to form an open-topped pouch. Gently squeeze the middle to enclose the filling. Cover with a damp dishcloth while filling the remaining wrappers in the same manner.

PLACE a steaming rack in a wok (or use a steamer in a large saucepan). Fill with water to just below the rack and bring to a boil. Arrange the dumplings, filling side up, without letting them touch, in a lightly greased, heat-proof dish; set on the rack. (You'll probably need to cook the dumplings in batches.) Cover the wok or saucepan. Let the dumplings steam, adding more water if necessary, until the filling is heated through, about 12 minutes.

Note:

Both types of wrappers usually contain eggs, but you can find brands that don't. Check Asian markets.

> **PER DUMPLING:**
> 43 Cal.; 2g Prot.; 2g Fat; 6g Carb.;
> 18mg Chol.; 104mg Sod.; 0.5g Fiber.

Brown Rice and Poppy Seeds

serves 6

This simple dish combines rice and poppy seeds, a common ingredient in Hungarian cooking.

- 3 cups uncooked short-grain brown rice
- 4 cups water
- 3 to 6 tablespoons poppy seeds
- 1/8 to 1/4 teaspoon salt
- Chopped fresh parsley, for garnish

PLACE the rice and water in a pot. (If desired, soak the rice 4 to 8 hours to soften it.) Toast the poppy seeds in a covered, dry skillet over medium-high heat until they begin to pop. Let cool. Add the poppy seeds and salt to the rice. Cover the pot and bring to a boil over medium heat; then lower the heat and simmer 45 minutes. Remove from the heat and let sit 10 minutes. Stir gently. Transfer the mixture to a serving bowl, and garnish with parsley.

PER SERVING:
363 Cal.; 8g Prot.; 4g Fat; 72g Carb.;
0mg Chol.; 55mg Sod.; 5g Fiber.

Tabouli

serves 3

Tabouli, traditionally made with oil, is a Middle Eastern staple. After tasting this version, you'll be sold on oil-free.

- 1/2 cup uncooked bulgur
- 1 cup boiling water
- 1 tomato, chopped
- 1/2 cup chopped fresh parsley
- 2 tablespoons fresh lemon juice
- 1/8 teaspoon garlic powder
- 1/4 cup chopped scallions (green and white parts)
- 1/2 cup cooked chickpeas (page 102)

MEASURE the bulgur into a small mixing bowl. Pour in the boiling water and mix gently. Cover with a dishcloth and let sit 1 hour. Remove the excess water by pouring the bulgur into a fine mesh strainer. Press the bulgur with your hands to remove as much of the water as possible. Place the drained bulgur in a bowl. Add the remaining ingredients, tossing well to mix. Cover and refrigerate at least 2 hours before serving.

PER SERVING:
177 Cal.; 8g Prot.; 2g Fat; 35g Carb.;
0mg Chol.; 363 Sod.; 6g Fiber.

Black-Eyed Peas with Tomatoes and Herbs

serves 6

A long-time favorite, black-eyed peas traditionally have been a Southern food.

3 cups black-eyed peas

6 cups fresh water

1 large onion, chopped

1 cup chopped green bell pepper

2 bay leaves

1 teaspoon cumin

2 cups chopped fresh or canned tomatoes

1 tablespoon virgin olive oil

Dash cayenne pepper

1 teaspoon salt

SOAK the beans in water to cover for 8 hours or overnight; drain. Add 6 cups fresh water, cover and bring to a boil. Lower the heat to a simmer, and add the onion, green bell pepper, bay leaves and cumin. Return to a boil and simmer until the beans are tender, 45 minutes to 1 hour. Remove the bay leaves. Stir in the tomatoes, olive oil, cayenne and salt. Cook until heated through.

PER SERVING:
223 Cal.; 14g Prot.; 4g Fat; 35g Carb.;
0mg Chol.; 67mg Sod.; 22g Fiber.

21

desserts

DINNER JUST DOESN'T SEEM COMPLETE without an appropriate finale. That's especially true when you're entertaining company. But the word *dessert* conjures up a picture of something scrumptious that'll bust your buttons. These recipes—except for a few outrageously filling ones that we sneaked in—are light and tasty. Many of them are combinations of fruit. Others are creamy puddings and mousses or cooling ices. A few are fussy. When choosing a dessert to prepare, keep in mind the other dishes in your meal. If your main dish is heavy, go for a simple fruit dessert. But if your main dish is light—a pasta tossed with vegetables, for instance—then opt for a more substantial finale. Also, remember that desserts do add nutrition to your meal, so indulge with a clear conscience.

Baked Apples

serves 4

4 Rome Beauty apples
1/2 cup golden raisins
1/4 cup chopped pecans or walnuts
1/3 cup brown sugar
2 tablespoons fresh lemon juice
1 teaspoon ground cinnamon
1/4 teaspoon ground ginger
1/4 teaspoon ground nutmeg
Plain yogurt (optional)

PREHEAT the oven to 350°F. Using a corer or paring knife, remove the core from each apple without cutting through the bottom. Make the hole 1 inch larger in diameter to accommodate the filling. Pare a 1 1/2-inch strip of peel around the top of each apple. Combine the raisins, nuts, brown sugar, juice and spices in a small bowl, and spoon this mixture into the apples. Place in an 8-inch baking pan. Fill the pan halfway with water and bake until soft, about 1 hour. Cool slightly and serve with yogurt.

> **PER SERVING:**
> 236 Cal.; 1g Prot.; 5g Fat; 51g Carb.;
> 0mg Chol.; 10mg Sod.; 5g Fiber.

Baked Apples Filled with Chestnut Purée

serves 6

This dessert is especially good served with Maple Rum Rice Creme (page 404).

1 pound fresh chestnuts (or 1 1/2 cups canned or bottled chestnuts, or 4 ounces dried chestnuts, cooked)
1/3 cup soymilk
1/3 cup apple juice
5 to 6 tablespoons maple syrup or honey
1 teaspoon ground cinnamon
1/4 teaspoon ground nutmeg
1/3 cup currants or raisins
6 to 8 crisp, sweet apples (Granny Smith, gala or pippins)
2 to 3 tablespoons fresh lemon juice
Additional ground cinnamon
3/4 cup white wine
3 tablespoons margarine
1 cinnamon stick
Mint leaves and thin orange slices, for garnish (optional)

PREHEAT the oven to 350°F. To prepare fresh chestnuts, place them in large pot of water and cook, covered, until they've expanded and turned lighter in color, about 20 minutes. To prepare canned or bottled chestnuts, cook them in their liquid until heated through. To prepare dried chestnuts, follow package directions.

DRAIN and rinse the hot chestnuts under cold water. Cut off the flat part with a sharp knife, and scoop out the nut meal with a spoon. In a food processor, combine the chestnut meal with the soymilk, apple juice, 4 table-spoons maple syrup or honey, 1 teaspoon cinnamon and nutmeg. Fold in the currants or raisins.

PEEL the apples and remove the core from the top, leaving the bottom of the apples intact. Using a grapefruit spoon or measuring spoon, hollow out the apples, leaving a 1/2-inch shell. Brush the shells with the lemon juice to prevent discoloration. Sprinkle the inside with a little cinnamon. Chop the scooped-out apple and combine with the chestnut mixture.

FILL the apple shells with the chestnut-apple mixture. Arrange them in a greased baking dish. Pour the wine and remaining maple syrup or honey around the apples. Add the margarine and cinnamon stick to the pan. Bake until tender, about 30 to 40 minutes. (Baste occasionally with the wine-apple mixture.) The wine-apple mixture should cook down into a light syrup. If it is watery, drain it from baking dish into a saucepan and cook it on your stovetop over high heat until it thickens. Pour the syrup over apples. Garnish with mint leaves and orange slices.

> **PER SERVING:**
> 348 Cal.; 3g Prot.; 2g Fat; 74g Carb.;
> 0mg Chol.; 9mg Sod.; 14g Fiber.

Baked Pears

serves 4

If desired, serve baked pears with vanilla yogurt, frozen yogurt or ice cream.

> 4 ripe pears
> 1 teaspoon ground cinnamon
> 2 tablespoons wheat germ

PREHEAT the oven to 375°F. Cut the pears into quarters lengthwise. Remove the cores and slice each quarter into thinner slices. Place the slices in a small baking dish, sprinkle with the cinnamon and wheat germ, cover and bake until tender, about 15 to 20 minutes.

> **PER SERVING:**
> 113 Cal.; 2g Prot.; 0 Fat; 24g Carb.;
> 0mg Chol.; 1mg Sod.; 5g Fiber

Pears in Raspberry Sauce

serves 6

> 3 firm bosc or bartlett pears
> 1/4 cup raspberry jam or jelly
> Juice of 1 orange (or 1/2 cup orange juice)
> Pinch ground cinnamon or nutmeg
> Pinch salt
> 2 tablespoons mirin, white wine or fruit liqueur (optional)
> Fresh raspberries, strawberries and fresh mint leaves, for garnish

PREHEAT oven to 350°F. Slice the pears in half and scoop out the seeds with a spoon. Place the pears sliced side down in a baking dish. Combine jam or jelly, juice, cinnamon or nutmeg, salt, and mirin, wine or liqueur, and pour over the pears. Cover the dish with foil or a lid, and bake until the pears are soft when pierced with a fork, about 30 minutes. To serve, turn the pears over and spoon some raspberry sauce over them. Garnish with berries and mint.

> **PER SERVING:**
> 98 Cal.; 0.6g Prot.; 0.5g Fat; 24g Carb.;
> 0mg Chol.; 46mg Sod.; 3g Fiber.

Lemon Meringue Melon

serves 6

3 cantaloupes

18 strawberries, sliced (or 2/3 cup any other berries)

3 peaches, peeled and sliced (or 1 1/2 bananas, sliced)

1 1/2 cups lemon-flavored yogurt

3 large egg whites

3 tablespoons sugar or honey

Dash cream of tartar

1 tablespoon vanilla extract

PREHEAT the oven to 450°F. Cut the cantaloupes in half crosswise, and slice off the rounded ends so each half can stand upright on a plate. Remove the seeds. Widen the cavities by carving out 1/2 inch of fruit. Chop and set aside.

IN A SMALL BOWL, stir together the fruit and lemon yogurt. In a separate bowl, combine the egg whites and sugar or honey, and beat to form soft peaks. Add the cream of tartar and beat until stiff peaks form. Fold in the vanilla. Fill the melon cavities with the yogurt mixture, and spoon the egg whites on top. Bake until browned, about 3 to 5 minutes. Serve at once.

> **PER SERVING:**
> 208 Cal.; 7g Prot.; 2g Fat; 44g Carb.;
> 2mg Chol.; 69mg Sod.; 5g Fiber.

Pineapple-Yogurt Ambrosia

serves 4

One 1-pound can diced unsweetened pineapple, drained

2 cups vanilla yogurt

1/4 cup raisins

2 small oranges, peeled and sectioned

COMBINE all the ingredients in a medium bowl. Chill. Spoon the mixture into dessert cups and serve.

> **PER SERVING:**
> 239 Cal.; 7g Prot.; 4g Fat; 42g Carb.;
> 22mg Chol.; 75mg Sod.; 3g Fiber.

Layered Berry Parfaits in Champagne Glasses

serves 4

1 cup fresh blueberries

1 cup sliced fresh strawberries

1 cup fresh blackberries

1 cup red currants

1/3 cup sweet dessert wine (such as sauténe) or apple juice

1 1/2 cups fresh raspberries

3 tablespoons maple syrup, or to taste

2 cups crumbled vanilla wafers

4 sprigs fresh mint leaves, for garnish

IN A LARGE BOWL, combine the berries (except raspberries), currants and wine or apple juice. Let marinate 30 minutes, stirring occasionally. Meanwhile, purée the raspberries and maple syrup in a blender or food processor to make a sauce.

TO ASSEMBLE the dessert, spoon a layer of mixed berries into the bottom of four champagne or wine glasses. Top with a drizzle of raspberry sauce, then a light layer of wafer crumbs. Repeat until all the ingredients are used up, ending with the raspberry sauce. Refrigerate until chilled, about 1 hour. Garnish with mint.

PER SERVING:
303 Cal.; 3g Prot.; 7g Fat; 55g Carb.;
19mg Chol.; 120mg Sod.; 11g Fiber.

Fresh Fruit with Honey-Lime Dressing

serves 6

DRESSING
3/4 cup mild honey or barley syrup
1/3 cup fresh lime juice, preferably from key limes
6 tablespoons crushed pineapple (with juice)
Pinch salt

FRUIT
2 cups fresh or frozen peaches, diced
1 tablespoon fresh lemon juice
2 cups seedless red grapes
2 cups seeded or seedless watermelon, diced
2 cups diced honeydew melon
2 bananas
1 cup fresh or frozen raspberries

DRESSING: Combine the honey, lime juice, pineapple and salt in a blender or food processor; process until the mixture is well-blended, about 15 seconds. Set aside.

FRUIT: If you're using fresh peaches, remove the pits and cut the fruit into 1-inch cubes; sprinkle the cubes with the lemon juice to prevent them from darkening. Place in a bowl. Pile the grapes on top, then the watermelon and honeydew melon. Spoon 1/2 cup dressing over all. Cover and refrigerate.

JUST BEFORE SERVING, slice the bananas and arrange them in a circle around the edge of the bowl. Last, pile the raspberries in the middle. Dribble with a little more dressing and pass the remaining dressing separately.

PER SERVING:
248 Cal.; 1g Prot.; 0 Fat; 60g Carb.;
0mg Chol.; 54mg Sod.; 3g Fiber.

Lemony Orange Slices

serves 4

| 4 oranges, peeled, with white part removed
| 3 tablespoons fresh lemon juice
| 2 tablespoons honey

Slice the oranges thinly and place in a serving dish. Whisk together the lemon juice and honey, and pour over the oranges. Cover and chill before serving.

Variation:

Substitute 3 cups sliced fresh peaches or strawberries for the oranges.

> **PER SERVING:**
> 95 Cal.; 1g Prot.; 0 Fat; 25g Carb.;
> 0mg Chol.; 1mg Sod.; 2g Fiber.

Summer Peaches with Raspberries

serves 6

| 2 pounds firm, unblemished peaches, peeled, pitted
| and sliced
| 2 tablespoons fresh lemon juice
| 2 tablespoons fresh orange juice
| 2 tablespoons maple sugar or syrup
| 1 cup raspberries or other fresh berries

SPRINKLE the peaches with the juices and sweetener. Spoon into stemmed glasses and top with berries.

> **PER SERVING:**
> 55 Cal.; 1g Prot.; 1g Fat; 14g Carb.;
> 0mg Chol.; 2mg Sod.; 3g Fiber.

Sweet Sesame Bananas

serves 4

In Thailand, bananas come in several varieties and are turned into wonderful desserts like this one.

| 1/4 cup sesame seeds
| Juice of 2 limes
| 4 fresh, firm bananas, peeled and sliced diagonally
| 1 cup sugar
| 1/2 cup water

IN A DRY SKILLET, toast the sesame seeds until golden. Set aside. Squeeze the lime juice over the banana slices and set aside. In a heavy saucepan, heat the sugar and water over a slow, even heat until the temperature reaches about 235°F on a candy thermometer and the mixture forms threads. The syrup should be thick and bubbling. Remove from the heat. Butter a sheet of waxed paper. Dip the banana slices into the syrup, place them on the waxed paper and sprinkle them with the sesame seeds. Serve at once.

> **PER SERVING:**
> 222 Cal.; 3g Prot.; 4g Fat; 28g Carb.;
> 0mg Chol.; 2mg Sod.; 3g Fiber.

Banana-Pineapple Kabobs

serves 6

The caramel glaze complements many fresh fruits: If pineapple is unavailable, try apples, orange sections or apricots.

1 whole vanilla bean
1/3 cup brown sugar
1/4 cup water
1 to 2 teaspoons margarine (optional)
Pinch salt (optional)
3 to 4 bananas
1/2 small pineapple (or 1/2 to 1 pound other fruits)

SLIT THE VANILLA BEAN lengthwise and scrape out the seeds with a knife. Place the seeds and pod in a small saucepan along with the remaining ingredients except the fruit. Bring to a boil, stirring constantly. Lower the heat and simmer, stirring, until all of the sugar has dissolved, about 3 minutes. Remove from the heat. If the glaze hardens, reheat before using.

PREPARE THE GRILL. Peel the bananas; peel and core the pineapple. Cut the fruit into bite-sized chunks. Alternate the bananas and pineapple on skewers. Place the skewers on a hot grill and cook for 5 to 10 minutes, turning once. When the fruit is hot, baste 2 to 3 times with the glaze. Turn and baste again.

PER SERVING:
139 Cal.; 0.8 Prot.; 0.4g Fat; 33g Carb.;
0mg Chol.; 6mg Sod.; 2g Fiber.

Bananas with Lime

serves 4

4 firm bananas, peeled
1 to 2 tablespoons butter or margarine
3 to 4 heaping tablespoons dark-brown sugar
Juice of 2 limes
Toasted coconut, for garnish (optional)

CUT the bananas in half crosswise; then cut in half lengthwise. Set aside. Melt the butter or margarine in a skillet. Fry the bananas until golden and softened slightly. Sprinkle the brown sugar on top and cook over medium heat until the sugar becomes a syrup.

ARRANGE the bananas on 4 small serving plates. Squeeze 1/2 lime over each plate of fruit, and garnish with toasted coconut. Serve at once.

PER SERVING:
172 Cal.; 1g Prot.; 3g Fat; 25g Carb.;
8mg Chol.; 34mg Sod.; 2g Fiber.

Warm Pear Charlotte

serves 6

This dessert looks like you fussed over it, but it's a breeze to make. For a different flavor, use McIntosh apples instead of pears. You may use a traditional 1-quart metal charlotte mold, glass soufflé dish or oven-proof saucepan or casserole.

> 4 pounds ripe bartlett or anjou pears
>
> 1 tablespoon fresh lemon juice
>
> 1/3 cup granulated sugar cane juice or brown sugar
>
> One 2-inch piece vanilla bean (or 1/2 teaspoon vanilla extract)
>
> 1/4 teaspoon ground cardamom
>
> About 10 slices very thin white bread
>
> 3/4 cup softened nonfat vanilla frozen yogurt or soy ice cream
>
> 1 tablespoon chopped walnuts or pecans

PREHEAT the oven to 375°F. Coat the inside of a baking dish with nonstick cooking spray; line the bottom with cooking parchment or waxed paper. Peel, core and slice all the pears but one. Set aside. Peel the remaining pear; cut in half lengthwise. From the middle, cut a full slice of pear about 1/8-inch thick; place it on the bottom of the baking dish. Slice the remainder of the pear and add to the others.

IN A SKILLET, briefly warm the lemon juice, sweetener, vanilla bean or vanilla and cardamom over medium-low heat. Add the pears and stir gently. Cook, with lid ajar, for 15 minutes, stirring occasionally. Uncover the skillet, and cook 5 minutes more. Drain the pears, reserving liquid.

IN A SMALL PAN, cook the reserved pear liquid until it's reduced to about 1/2 cup syrup; set aside. (The procedure up to this point may be done 1 or 2 days ahead; cover the pears and pear liquid and refrigerate. Continue with the recipe about 1 1/2 hours before serving.)

TO PREPARE THE CRUST, slice the crusts off bread and discard. Place 1 slice of bread on top of the pear slice on the bottom of the baking dish. Cut another slice of bread into shapes to fit around the bottom bread slice, covering the bottom of the pan completely.

CUT 5 or 6 bread slices into 1-inch strips. Stand the bread strips vertically in the baking pan to line the sides. They should overlap slightly.

PREHEAT the oven to 375°F. Spoon the pears into the prepared mold to within 1/4-inch of top. Pack gently with the back of a spoon. With scissors, trim the tops of the bread strips even with the level of the pears or the top of the baking dish. Cut the bread slices to cover the top. Spray with nonstick cooking spray and top with a circle of parchment or waxed paper. Cover tightly with foil; cut eight 1-inch slits in the foil to vent steam.

BAKE until the bread is crisp and lightly browned, about 45 minutes. Uncover and unmold at once onto a serving plate. Let cool 1 hour.

TO SERVE, slice the dessert into 6 pieces. Swirl about half of the reserved thickened pear syrup into softened frozen yogurt or soy ice cream. Stir the nuts into the remaining pear sauce. Serve a wedge of charlotte drizzled with syrup and some frozen yogurt or soy ice cream on the side.

> **PER SERVING:**
> 333 Cal.; 5g Prot.; 3g Fat; 70g Carb.;
> 2mg Chol.; 193mg Sod.; 8g Fiber.

Caribbean Bananas

serves 6

1 tablespoon freshly grated lemon zest

1 tablespoon freshly grated orange zest

1 tablespoon fresh lemon juice

3 tablespoons fresh orange juice

3 cups banana chunks

2 eggs (or equivalent egg substitute)

1/4 cup date sugar (or 1/3 cup brown sugar)

3 tablespoons pineapple juice

1 cup soymilk or milk

1 cup bread crumbs

2 tablespoons margarine, melted and cooled

Boiling water

PREHEAT the oven to 300°F. Oil a 1 1/2-quart mold. Combine the lemon and orange zests, lemon and orange juices, and banana. Set aside.

PLACE the eggs or egg substitute, date sugar or brown sugar and pineapple juice in a food proccessor and pulse until blended. Add the soymilk or milk and bread crumbs and pulse a few more times. Spoon the bread crumb mixture over the banana mixture. Add the melted margarine and mix well. Pour into the prepared mold.

PLACE the mold in large pan, and pour enough boiling water into the pan to reach halfway up the sides of the mold. Bake until a knife inserted in the center comes out clean, about 80 minutes. (You may have to add boiling water to the pan as the dessert bakes to keep it at the desired level.) Cool 20 to 30 minutes. Unmold. Refrigerate at least 2 hours before serving.

PER SERVING:
214 Cal.; 5g Prot.; 6g Fat; 35g Carb.;
56mg Chol.; 99mg Sod.; 2g Fiber

Crepes Suzette Updated

serves 6

The classic dessert is loaded with butter and sugar. Not this one!

12 No-Cholesterol Dessert Crepes (page 412)

1/3 cup margarine

1/3 cup honey

1/2 to 3/4 cup fresh orange juice

1 teaspoon orange zest

1 teaspoon vanilla extract

1/4 cup orange liqueur

2 to 3 tablespoons brandy or rum

FOLD the crepes in half and then again in half to make quarters. Place them next to each other in a shallow chafing dish or attractive skillet. Set aside.

IN A SMALL SKILLET, heat the margarine and honey until melted. Add the remaining ingredients except the brandy or rum and cook for a couple of minutes over low heat. Pour over the crepes. Cook the crepes over low heat until the sauce is slightly thickened. Remove from the heat. Just before serving, pour the brandy or rum over the crepes and light with a match, taking care to stand clear of the flames. Use caution. When the flames die down, portion servings onto dessert plates.

PER SERVING:
427 Cal.; 4g Prot.; 10g Fat; 50g Carb.;
0mg Chol.; 345mg Sod.; 4g Fiber.

Fruit-and-Crepe Bombe

serves 8

Artfully presented, this bombe is as beautiful as it is delicious—and only 6 grams of fat per serving.

    2 cups soymilk

    1/2 cup honey

    2 teaspoons powdered agar-agar (or 1/4 cup flaked
        agar-agar), dissolved in 2 tablespoons water

    1/4 cup cornstarch dissolved in 3 tablespoons water

    2 teaspoons vanilla extract

    10 ounces soft tofu

    2 tablespoons orange liqueur

    12 No-Cholesterol Dessert Crepes (page 412)

    4 cups chopped or sliced fruit in season (such as straw-
        berries, bananas, kiwi, pears, papayas, mangoes,
        oranges)

    Raspberry Sauce (page 490) or Chocolate Sauce (page
        490)(optional)

IN A MEDIUM SAUCEPAN, combine the soymilk and honey, and cook the mixture over low heat until hot. Blend in the dissolved agar-agar, and stir until the mixture boils for a couple of minutes. Add the dissolved cornstarch and cook until thickened. Whisk in the vanilla extract. Set aside.

IN A BLENDER or food processor, purée the tofu and orange liqueur until smooth. Stir in the soymilk mixture. Pour it into to a bowl and let cool in the refrigerator until set and chilled, about 2 hours. The texture will be very much like custard.

TO ASSEMBLE the bombe once the custard has set, place a crepe on the bottom of a 2-quart glass bowl. Then place 3 or 4 crepes around the side of the bowl so that it is completely covered. Spread about 1/2 cup custard on the bottom and place a layer of fruit on top. Place a crepe on top and spread more custard over it. Top with another layer of fruit. Continue layering until all the ingredients are used up. End with a crepe. If the edges of some crepes are jutting out on the side of the bowl, fold them over. Place a plate on top of the bombe to hold it down. Refrigerate at least 2 hours.

JUST BEFORE SERVING, invert the bombe onto a platter. Decorate with more fruit, or drizzle with Raspberry Sauce or Chocolate Sauce. To serve, cut the bombe into wedges.

> **PER SERVING WITHOUT SAUCE:**
> 310 Cal.; 8g Prot.; 6g Fat; 56g Carb.;
> 0mg Chol.; 167mg Sod.; 5g Fiber.

Quince, Pear and Persimmon Compote

serves 6

A compote is fruit that has been stewed or cooked in syrup. This one highlights quince, a golden fruit that turns pink when cooked for hours.

2 pounds yellow quinces

4 cups water

3/4 cup sugar

1/2 vanilla bean, split lengthwise

One 3-inch piece cinnamon stick

5 whole cloves

1/4 teaspoon cardamom seeds

2 strips orange peel, 1/2 inch wide

1/3 cup currants

2 fuyu persimmons

2 ripe comice or bartlett pears

CUT each quince into sections 1/2 inch wide. Using a sharp knife, remove the peel and core, taking care not to break the brittle fruit. In a large saucepan, bring the water to a boil. Add the sugar, spices and orange peel. Stir to dissolve the sugar, then add the quinces. Lower the heat and simmer, with the lid ajar, until the quinces have turned deep pink, about 2 or 3 hours. When done, add the currants. Chill.

ASSEMBLE the compote in six shallow soup dishes. Arrange five slices of quince in each, along with some of the syrup. Wash the persimmons, cut into thin rounds and add to the quince. Peel and quarter the pears, remove the seeds and slice the fruit into 1/2-inch pieces. Divide the pear chunks among the dishes. Scatter the currants on top.

> **PER SERVING:**
> 187 Cal.; 2g Prot.; 0.5g Fat; 47g Carb.;
> 0mg Chol.; 5mg Sod.; 2g Fiber.

Dried Fruit Compote

serves 12

Dried apricots, currants, green raisins and prunes are flavorful choices for this compote.

2 pounds mixed dried fruit

1 cup apple juice or water

1/4 cup sugar, or to taste

Juice of 1 lemon

1 cinnamon stick, broken in half

COMBINE all the ingredients in a medium saucepan. Bring to a boil, lower the heat and simmer, uncovered, stirring occasionally until the fruit is tender, about 10 to 15 minutes. Remove from the heat, let cool and refrigerate overnight. Remove the cinnamon stick before serving.

> **PER SERVING:**
> 210 Cal.; 2g Prot.; 0.1g Fat; 50g Carb.;
> 0mg Chol.; 13mg Sod.; 7g Fiber.

Citrus Compote

serves 4

Navel and valencia oranges work well in this compote, but you can also try a mixture of tangelos, tangerines, blood oranges, pomelos or clementines.

| 6 to 8 citrus fruits
| 1/3 cup honey or other liquid sweetener
| 2 tablespoons rose or orange flower water (see Note)
| 1/4 teaspoon cardamom
| 1 tablespoon chopped or slivered pistachio nuts

PEEL THE FRUIT and remove the white pith. Slice crosswise into 1/4-inch slices. Layer the slices on individual plates or on a shallow platter. Drizzle the fruit with the sweetener and sprinkle with the remaining ingredients.

Note:

Rose water and orange flower water are flavorings available in specialty shops or Middle Eastern grocery stores.

PER SERVING:
104 Cal.; 0.8g Prot.; 0.6g Fat; 26g Carb.;
0mg Chol.; 2mg Sod.; 1g Fiber.

Low-Fat Chocolate Mousse

serves 6

| 1/2 cup brown rice syrup
| 2 teaspoons vanilla
| 1 pound soft tofu, cut into chunks
| 1/4 cup unsweetened cocoa powder
| 1/2 teaspoon grated orange zest
| Water as needed

PLACE the rice syrup and vanilla in a food processor or blender. Process, adding the tofu a few chunks at a time, then add the cocoa and orange zest. Add the water to thin if needed. Pour the mousse into serving dishes. Chill.

PER SERVING:
154 Cal.; 6g Prot.; 4g Fat; 25g Carb.;
0mg Chol.; 9mg Sod.; 0.5g Fiber.

Almost-Traditional Chocolate Mousse

serves 6

| 3/4 cup low-fat milk
| 6 ounces semisweet chocolate chips
| 1/2 cup egg substitute
| 2 tablespoons butter or margarine, at room
| temperature
| 1 tablespoon grated orange zest
| 1/4 cup strong coffee
| 2 tablespoons orange liqueur
| Nondairy topping or whipped cream, for garnish
| (optional)

IN A MEDIUM SAUCEPAN, heat the milk until almost boiling. Combine the remaining ingredients except the nondairy topping or whipped cream in a blender or food processor. Add the hot milk and whip at high speed until smooth and creamy, about 2 minutes. Pour into a medium bowl or individual custard cups, and chill for at least 2 hours before serving. Garnish with a rosette of nondairy topping or whipped cream.

PER SERVING:
230 Cal.; 5g Prot.; 12g Fat; 8g Carb.;
12mg Chol.; 84mg Sod.; 2g Fiber.

Grand Marnier Soufflé

serves 6

A soufflé without eggs? You bet. And it puffs just like a real dessert soufflé. (It also will collapse like a real soufflé, although not as fast.) Inside it is light, airy, rich and creamy and should be devoured joyfully within minutes of coming out of the oven. Although delicious by itself, try it with vanilla ice cream or Raspberry Sauce (page 490).

1 cup chocolate or carob chips

1 pound firm tofu (water-packed, not aseptic)

1/2 cup unsweetened cocoa powder or carob powder

3/4 to 1 cup honey

3 to 4 tablespoons Grand Marnier or other liqueur

1 teaspoon vanilla extract

1/2 cup soymilk

1/2 cup unbleached white flour

1 teaspoon baking powder

PREHEAT the oven to 350°F. Place the chocolate or carob chips in a bowl. Place over boiling water to melt, stirring with a spoon. Place the remaining ingredients in a food processor, and process until smooth and creamy. Add the melted chocolate and process a few more moments. Pour into a lightly oiled 1-quart soufflé mold or glass baking dish. Bake until completely puffed up, about 45 minutes. Cool 5 minutes, then serve at once.

PER SERVING:
499 Cal.; 16g Prot.; 16g Fat; 68g Carb.;
6mg Chol.; 110mg Sod.; 5g Fiber.

Chocolate Ricotta Cream

serves 6

This chocolate dessert is light, luscious and barely sweet. Serve with dried or fresh fruit—perhaps grapes, pineapple, oranges or kiwi.

One 15-ounce container part-skim ricotta cheese

2 tablespoons sifted unsweetened cocoa powder

5 tablespoons fructose or honey

1/4 teaspoon ground cinnamon

1/2 teaspoon vanilla extract

1 tablespoon toasted sliced almonds, for garnish (page 106)

IN A FOOD PROCESSOR or blender, process the ricotta 1 minute. Add the cocoa, fructose or honey, cinnamon and vanilla, and process until creamy smooth. Adjust sweetness. Spoon into martini glasses or onto dessert plates. Garnish with almonds. Serve at once.

Maple Rum Rice Creme with Chocolate Sauce

s e r v e s   6

If you like custards, flans and cremes, try this delicious dessert, with only 3 grams of fat in a serving. Serve it in bowls or in wine glasses layered with chocolate sauce.

MAPLE RICE CREME

- 1 cup white medium or short-grain rice
- 2 1/2 cups water
- 2 cups soymilk or rice milk
- 1/2 cup maple syrup
- 1 teaspoon vanilla extract
- 2 tablespoons gold or dark rum

CHOCOLATE SAUCE

- 1/2 cup unsweetened cocoa powder
- 1 cup water
- 1/2 to 3/4 cup honey (use a light-flavored one)
- 1 teaspoon vanilla extract

MAPLE RICE CREME: In a large saucepan, cook the rice with water, soymilk or rice milk and maple syrup, covered, until the rice is very soft and most of the liquid has been absorbed, about 1 1/4 hours. In a food processor or blender, purée the cooked rice mixture with the vanilla and rum until very smooth. Transfer to a bowl, cover tightly and chill for several hours.

CHOCOLATE SAUCE: Combine alll the ingredients in a saucepan and mix well with a whisk. Bring to a boil, lower the heat and simmer gently, stirring often, until the sauce has thickened and is reduced to 1 cup, about 15 to 20 minutes. Let cool.

AT SERVING TIME, serve the maple rice creme with the chocolate sauce.

Spiced Pumpkin Custard

s e r v e s   8

Instead of a high-fat pie, serve this low-fat pumpkin custard.

- 3/4 cup pumpkin purée (canned or fresh)
- 1 tablespoon molasses
- 1 tablespoon honey
- 2/3 cup maple syrup
- 3 tablespoons ground cinnamon
- 1 teaspoon ground ginger
- 1/2 teaspoon ground cloves
- 1 teaspoon ground nutmeg
- 2 3/4 cups skim milk
- 2 tablespoons arrowroot powder or cornstarch
- 4 eggs, beaten (or 2 tablespoons egg substitute and 1/2 cup water)
- 1 cup nonfat vanilla yogurt

PREHEAT the oven to 350°F. Lightly oil eight 1-cup soufflé or custard dishes and place them on a baking sheet.

IN A LARGE SAUCEPAN, combine the pumpkin, honey, molasses, maple syrup, cinnamon, ginger, cloves and nutmeg. Mix 1/4 cup milk in a small bowl with the arrowroot or cornstarch. Add the remaining 2 1/2 cups milk, then pour the milk-arrowroot mixture into the saucepan. Stir well. Bring to a boil over medium heat, whisking frequently, and cook until thickened to the consistency of heavy cream. Remove from the heat. Stir in the beaten eggs or egg substitute and water. Pour into the baking dishes. Bake until firm, about 30 minutes. Let cool slightly, then serve with a dollop of nonfat yogurt.

> **PER SERVING:**
> 180 Cal.; 8g Prot.; 3g Fat; 31g Carb.;
> 108mg Chol.; 109mg Sod.; 0.2g Fiber.

Spiced Carrot Pudding

serves 15

1/2 cup margarine or butter, plus extra for mold

1 cup sugar, plus extra for mold

2 cups raisins

1 cup grated, unpeeled tart green apples (such as Granny Smith)

1 cup chopped, toasted pecans or walnuts (page 106)

1 cup grated, unpeeled carrots

1 cup grated, peeled potatoes

3/4 cup unbleached white flour

1 teaspoon baking soda

1/2 teaspoon ground cinnamon

1/2 teaspoon ground nutmeg

1/2 teaspoon ground allspice

Pinch ground cloves

GREASE an 8-cup mold with the margarine or butter and dust lightly with sugar. In a bowl, stir together the fruit, nuts and vegetables; set aside. In a separate bowl, stir together flour, baking soda and spices; set aside. In the bowl of an electric mixer, cream the margarine and sugar. Stir in the carrot mixture by hand, then the flour mixture, blending thoroughly. Spoon the batter into the mold. The mold should not be more than 2/3 full. Run a knife through the batter to release any air pockets. Cover the mold with its lid or with a double-thickness of foil pressed tightly to the sides and tied with string.

POUR 1 inch of water into the bottom of a pot a little larger than the mold. Set a trivet, inverted heatproof bowl or custard cups in the bottom of the pot to create a platform. Bring the water to a boil. Set the mold on the platform, cover the pot and steam until the center springs back slightly when touched, about 2 1/2 hours. Remove the mold from the pot and uncover. Let the pudding set 10 minutes before unmolding. Slice and serve.

> **PER SERVING:**
> 222 Cal.; 2g Prot.; 7g Fat.; 34g Carb.;
> 0mg Chol.; 97mg Sod.; 2g Fiber.

Lemon Pudding Updated

serves 8

Traditional puddings are loaded with eggs and milk. This zesty update has neither.

> 2 cups unsweetened pineapple juice
>
> 3/4 cup cornstarch
>
> 2 1/2 cups apricot nectar
>
> 3/4 cup honey
>
> 1/2 cup fresh lemon juice
>
> 2 tablespoons vanilla extract
>
> 1 1/2 tablespoons lemon zest

IN A BOWL, stir together 3/4 cup pineapple juice and cornstarch. Set aside. In a saucepan, combine the remaining 1 1/4 cups pineapple juice, apricot nectar and honey. Bring to a boil. Pour in the cornstarch mixture and stir until thickened. Lower the heat. Add the remaining ingredients, and stir until blended. Raise the heat and boil 1 minute. Transfer the pudding to a large bowl or eight small bowls. Chill before serving.

> **PER SERVING:**
> 222 Cal.; 1g Prot.; 0.1g Fat; 57g Carb.;
> 0mg Chol.; 8mg Sod.; 0.6g Fiber.

Apple-Blueberry Rice Pudding

> 2 cups cooked brown rice
>
> 3/4 cup low-fat milk
>
> 1/4 cup light brown sugar
>
> 1 tablespoon margarine, melted
>
> 1 teaspoon ground cinnamon
>
> 2 Granny Smith apples, cored and diced
>
> 2 cups fresh or frozen blueberries
>
> 1 tablespoon toasted wheat germ

PREHEAT the oven to 350°F. Combine the rice, milk, brown sugar, margarine, cinnamon and apples in a medium bowl. Stir well. Gently fold in the blueberries, taking care not to crush them.

TRANSFER the mixture to an 8-inch baking pan. Sprinkle with wheat germ, cover with foil and bake 30 minutes. Serve warm or at room temperature.

> **PER SERVING:**
> 204 Cal.; 4g Prot.; 3g Fat; 42g Carb.;
> 1mg Chol.; 48mg Sod.; 5g Fiber.

Rice Pudding with Dates

serves 6

This Middle Eastern recipe isn't as sweet as American rice pudding. Dates serve as the primary sweetener—a nutritious change. The pudding is delicious warm or cold.

2 cups cooked white rice

15 pitted dates, chopped finely

2 cups low-fat milk

3 tablespoons sugar

IN A FOOD PROCESSOR or blender, process the rice until coarse. Transfer the rice to a large saucepan. Add the dates, milk and sugar. Cook, covered, on low heat, until the dates are tender, about 15 to 20 minutes.

PER SERVING:
188 Cal.; 5g Prot.; 1g Fat; 42g Carb.;
3mg Chol.; 42mg Sod.; 1g Fiber.

Rice Cream with Berries

serves 6

Choose raspberries or blueberries to sweeten and add a touch of color to this pudding-like dessert.

1 1/4 cups water

Pinch salt (optional)

1 cup uncooked quick-cooking brown rice

1/2 cup unsweetened shredded coconut (optional)

1/3 cup chopped walnuts or pecans (optional)

1 1/2 cups nondairy topping

1/2 teaspoon vanilla extract

1 1/2 cups frozen berries, thawed and drained

BRING the water to a boil in a small saucepan and add the salt. Add the rice, lower the heat, cover and simmer until tender, about 10 minutes. Uncover and let cool to room temperature.

PLACE the rice in a large bowl. Add the coconut and nuts. Stir in the topping and vanilla. Gently fold in the berries.

PER SERVING:
151 Cal.; 2g Prot.; 5g Fat; 18g Carb.;
0mg Chol.; 143mg Sod.; 2g Fiber.

Banana Dream

serves 4

Top this cold dessert with Chocolate Sauce (page 490) or serve as is.

1 vanilla bean (or 1 teaspoon vanilla extract)

1 large banana

2 cups plain or vanilla soymilk or skim milk

1 tablespoon nonfat powdered milk (optional) (see Note)

2 tablespoons honey

1/4 teaspoon almond extract

SPLIT the vanilla bean lengthwise and scrape the inside of one half with a knife. (Reserve other half for another use.) Combine the scrapings or vanilla extract and remaining ingredients in a blender. Process until smooth. Freeze in an ice cream maker according to directions on your machine.

Note:

Adding nonfat powdered milk lends a richer flavor.

PER SERVING:
99 Cal.; 4g Prot.; 2g Fat; 18g Carb.;
0mg Chol.; 1mg Sod.; 1g Fiber.

Three-Fruit Sorbet

serves 6

| 1 cup pineapple juice
| 1 frozen banana, sliced
| 1/2 to 1 cup frozen blueberries or strawberries, sliced
| 2 cups frozen pineapple, sliced

POUR the pineapple juice in a blender; cover. While the blender is at medium speed, add the frozen fruit through the feed opening in the blender lid. Blend the mixture until it has a "soft serve" consistency. Pour this sorbet into a serving dish. Serve at once or store it in freezer for a short time before serving.

PER SERVING:
99 Cal.; 0.8g Prot.; 0.6g Fat; 25g Carb.;
0mg Chol.; 2mg Sod.; 2g Fiber.

Key Lime Italian Ice

serves 6

When you have a hankering for something sweet and absolutely fat-free, make Italian ice with Floridian flair.

| 1 key lime, washed
| 1 cup sugar
| 4 cups water
| Dash salt
| 1/2 cup freshly squeezed key lime juice mixed with 1/8 cup water

WITH A VEGETABLE PEELER, remove the zest from the lime (be careful not to include the bitter white pith); cut the zest into small pieces. Place the zest and sugar in a blender or food processor fitted with a steel blade, and process until very finely chopped. Empty the mixture into a large saucepan. Add the water and salt to the pan, and heat until the sugar dissolves. Cool.

ADD the lime juice combination (made fom the key lime) to the cooled sugar-water mixture. Pour into divided ice cube trays and freeze until hard. Place the frozen cubes in a blender; cover and blend until the cubes become a slush. Serve at once with a straw or spoon.

PER SERVING:
128 Cal.; 3g Prot.; 0 Fat; 34g Carb.;
0mg Chol.; 45mg Sod.; 0 Fiber

Peach Yogurt Freeze

serves 4

| 1 pound fresh or frozen unsweetened peaches
| 1/2 teaspoon vitamin C powder or Fruit Fresh (optional)
| 1/2 cup sugar, or to taste
| 1/2 teaspoon vanilla extract
| 1/2 cup plain nonfat yogurt

IF YOU'RE USING fresh peaches, remove their skins by immersing the fruit in boiling water for 30 to 60 seconds. The skins will then slip off under cool running water.

PIT the peaches and cut them into 1-inch chunks. Place them on a cookie sheet and sprinkle with vitamin C powder or Fruit Fresh to prevent darkening. Freeze until firm (a minimum of 5 hours).

ABOUT 15 MINUTES before serving remove the fruit chunks from your freezer and combine with the sugar in a food processor fitted with a steel blade. Process until finely chopped. Remove the cover, taste and add additional sugar, if desired. With the machine running, pour the vanilla and yogurt through the feed tube. Continue processing the mixture until smooth and fluffy, about 1 minute more. Serve at once.

Variation:

Store the dessert in a covered container in the freezer. (Remove from the freezer 10 minutes before serving and whip again in processor until creamy-smooth.)

> **PER SERVING:**
> 157 Cal.; 3g Prot.; 0 Fat; 14g Carb.;
> 1mg Chol.; 24mg Sod.; 2g Fiber.

Pumpkin Freeze

serves 6

You may make this tasty "ice cream" several days ahead of time. Just store the frozen cubes in freezer bags until you're ready to serve.

- 8 ripe but firm bananas, peeled and cut into pieces
- 1/3 cup maple syrup, honey, frozen apple juice concentrate, apricot jam or other sweetener
- 1/2 to 1 tablespoon pumpkin pie spice
- 2 cups pumpkin purée or canned pumpkin
- 2 tablespoons finely chopped candied ginger, for garnish (optional)

IN A FOOD PROCESSOR, purée the bananas, sweetener and pumpkin pie spice. Add the pumpkin and process until

blended. Spoon the mixture into 3 or 4 divided ice cube trays (mini-ice-cube trays work best) and freeze until solid.

ABOUT 10 MINUTES before serving remove the frozen cubes from the trays and place them in the food processor to thaw a bit. (If you're using large ice cubes, chop the cubes before processing.) Process until creamy. Spoon the mixture into chilled dessert dishes and sprinkle with candied ginger.

> **PER SERVING:**
> 213 Cal.; 2g Prot.; 0.5g Fat; 49g Carb.;
> 0mg Chol.; 7mg Sod.; 5g Fiber.

Grape Ice

serves 6

This light and refreshing frozen dessert takes only minutes to prepare and is even more delicious made with a distinctive grape juice such as muscat or Chardonnay.

- 1 cup grape juice, chilled
- 3 tablespoons honey or other liquid sweetener to taste
- 2 tablespoons fresh lemon juice
- 2/3 cup frozen grape juice concentrate
- 2 1/3 cups ice cubes
- 30 red and green grapes, frozen overnight
- 2 tablespoons chopped pistachios

COMBINE the grape juice, sweetener and lemon juice in a food processor; pulse briefly. Add the ice cubes, and process until the mixture has an icy consistency. Spoon into chilled goblets with frozen grapes. Sprinkle with pistachios. Serve at once.

Strawberry-Banana Glace

serves 6

This light dessert is the perfect finale to a hearty meal. Serve in champagne or wine glasses or in Lacy Maple Cups (right).

| 5 very ripe bananas, frozen
| 1/2 to 1 cup frozen strawberries
| 1 teaspoon vanilla extract
| 1/4 to 1/2 cup soymilk or low-fat milk

CUT the bananas into 1/2-inch-thick slices. Break up the strawberries if they're clumped together. Place the fruit, vanilla and about 1/4 cup milk in a food processor. Blend, adding more milk as necessary until the mixture is smooth and creamy. Do not overblend or it will become runny. Spoon into serving glasses. Serve at once.

Helpful hint:

To freeze bananas, peel them, wrap them in plastic and place them in your freezer for at least 4 hours.

Variation:

Substitute frozen raspberries, blueberries or mangoes for the strawberries.

Lacy Maple Cups

makes 8

These thin wafers can be shaped into cups and then filled with a sorbet or other type of frozen dessert. Be sure to cook them until they are a medium brown, not a light or golden brown, or they will not hold their shape.

| 1/2 cup maple syrup
| 2 1/2 tablespoons margarine or butter
| 1 teaspoon vanilla extract
| 1/2 teaspoon ground cinnamon
| 1/2 cup unbleached white flour or whole wheat pastry flour

PREHEAT the oven to 350°F. Place the maple syrup and margarine or butter in a small pot and bring to a rapid boil. Continue boiling for 1 minute. Remove from the heat. Add the vanilla, cinnamon and flour, mixing well. (The mixture will be runny.) Drop the mixture, 2 tablespoons at a time, several inches apart, on a lightly greased cookie sheet. (The wafers will double or triple in size, so you may be able to bake only 2 to 4 at a time.) Place the cookie sheet in your oven at once, and bake until the wafers are lacy and medium brown, about 8 to 9 minutes.

REMOVE the sheet from your oven; let cool for 20 to 30 seconds. Place a warm and still pliable wafer in a small bowl or cup with steep sides and mold into shape. Let the wafer cool and set. Repeat procedure to use up all of the batter.

Variation:

Instead of cups, you can form the wafers into other shapes. To make baskets, take opposite ends of the wafer and curl each side upward with your fingers. To make cylinders, roll each wafer around the handle of a wooden spoon. Pipe in the frozen dessert with a pastry bag.

> **PER WAFER:**
> 108 Cal.; 0.8g Prot.; 4g Fat; 6g Carb.;
> 0mg Chol.; 2mg Sod.; 0 Fiber.

Berry-Banana Bars

makes 16

This is the master recipe for frozen bars that are very low in calories and are cholesterol-free. We provide three methods of preparation—one requiring a pan, a second requiring an ice-cream maker, and the third only plastic molds.

> 1 1/4 cups fresh (or frozen, unsweetened) strawberries
> 1 1/2 cups vanilla-flavored soymilk
> 1 small banana, cut into chunks
> 1/4 teaspoon almond extract

STEP ONE: Chill the ingredients thoroughly. Place them in a blender or food processor. Blend until very smooth. Then choose one of the following methods to produce the bars.

METHOD 1: Pour the blended mixture into a shallow pan and freeze until somewhat frozen but not rock hard. With an ice cream scoop or metal spoon, transfer chunks of the frozen mixture into a blender or food processor fitted with a metal blade; process until smooth. Spoon the mixture into the plastic molds (or small paper cups) at once, and proceed with step two.

METHOD 2: Pour the blended mixture into a small ice cream maker (which holds about 5 cups). Follow the manufacturer's directions until the mixture is somewhat frozen but still very soft. Then spoon the mixture into plastic molds (or small paper cups) and proceed with step two.

METHOD 3: When you're short on time (or if you like icier bars), pour the unfrozen mixture from the food processor or blender directly into plastic molds (or small paper cups). Then proceed with step two.

STEP TWO: When spooning the mixture into the molds, press down to remove air pockets and leave 1/8 to 1/4 inch of head room. Place a wooden or plastic stick in the center of each one. Freeze for several hours. At serving time, run hot water over the mold to dislodge the bar.

Note:

If you have more mixture than molds, freeze the extra in another container and eat it like ice cream before it gets too hard.

> **PER BAR:**
> 23 Cal.; 0.5g Prot.; 0.3g Fat; 4g Carb.;
> 0mg Chol.; 2mg Sod.; 0.5g Fiber.

Fudgey Peanut Butter Bars

makes 16

Are you a health-minded chocoholic? Try these bars, which combine chocolate and peanut butter.

| 1 liter (about 4 cups) carob-flavored soymilk
| 2 tablespoons smooth peanut butter
| 3 tablespoons unsweetened cocoa powder
| 1 1/4 teaspoons almond extract

FOLLOW the instructions in Berry-Banana Bars (page 411), using these ingredients.

> **PER BAR:**
> 64 Cal.; 2g Prot.; 2g Fat; 8g Carb.;
> 0mg Chol.; 17mg Sod.; 0.5g Fiber.

Strawberry Bars

makes 16

| 1 1/4 cups fresh (or frozen, unsweetened) strawberries
| 1 1/2 cups vanilla-flavored soymilk
| 1 tablespoon fresh lemon juice
| 1/4 teaspoon almond extract
| 1/4 cup thawed, unsweetened apple juice concentrate

FOLLOW the instructions in Berry-Banana Bars (page 411), using these ingredients.

> **PER BEAR:**
> 23 Cal.; 0.5g Prot.; 0.3g Fat; 5g Carb.;
> 0mg Chol.; 3mg Sod.; 0.5g Fiber.

No-Cholesterol Dessert Crepes

makes 10

These sweetened crepes are just right for desserts. The surprise is they contain neither eggs nor dairy products and taste great.

| 1 1/2 cups plus 2 tablespoons water
| 1/4 cup granulated sugarcane juice or sugar
| 2 tablespoons egg substitute (or 1/2 beaten egg)
| 1/2 cup whole-wheat pastry flour
| 1/2 cup unbleached white flour
| 1/3 cup chickpea flour (available in natural food stores)
| 1/2 teaspoon salt

IN A LARGE BOWL, whisk together the water, sugarcane juice or sugar, and egg substitute. Stir in the remaining ingredients and whisk until smooth. (Or, process all the ingredients in a blender or food processor.)

TO COOK the crepes, place a crepe pan or a nonstick 8-inch skillet over low heat. Brush it lightly with oil. Let the pan heat on low for a few minutes. Remove from the heat and pour in 3 or 4 tablespoons of batter and tilt the pan so that the batter coats the bottom of the pan lightly. Cook for a few minutes over medium-low heat. The crepe will become lightly browned. Flip the crepe using a spatula and cook the other side for 30 seconds. Slide it onto a plate. Repeat with the remaining batter, stacking the crepes on the plate. Use them at once or wrap them in plastic and refrigerate them up to one week.

> **PER CREPE:**
> 74 Cal.; 2g Prot.; 0.2g Fat; 16g Carb.;
> 0mg Chol.; 107mg Sod.; 2g Fiber.

Very Berry Good Treats

makes 16

These slightly sticky cookie bars are rich with red berries. And they have less than a gram of fat per bar.

- 1 3/4 cups rolled oats
- 4 cups fresh of frozen unsweetened boysenberries or other berries
- 2 teaspoons ground cinnamon, or to taste
- 1 teaspoon ground cloves
- 1/4 cup arrowroot
- 1/4 cup apple juice concentrate
- 16 whole berries, for garnish

PREHEAT the oven to 350°F. Lightly oil an 8-inch square baking pan. In a blender or food processor, grind the oats into a course powder. Combine the ground oats and remaining ingredients (except the berries for garnish) in a large bowl and mix well. Spread the batter into the pan. Decorate the surface with 16 evenly spaced berries. Bake until firm, about 35 to 45 minutes. Let cool, then cut into 16 squares with one berry topping each.

> **PER SERVING:**
> 54 Cal.; 1g Prot.; 0.7g Fat; 12g Carb.;
> 0mg Chol.; 4mg Sod.; 3g Fiber.

Not Too Rich Brownies

makes 16

- Nonstick cooking spray
- 2 cups sugar
- 3/4 cup unsweetened cocoa
- 1 1/4 cups unbleached flour
- 1/4 teaspoon salt
- 1 egg plus 1 egg white, lightly beaten
- 1 teaspoon vanilla extract
- 1/2 cup reduced-fat margarine, melted
- 1/2 cup low-fat vanilla yogurt

PREHEAT the oven to 350°F. Lightly grease an 8-inch square pan with nonstick cooking spray. Combine the dry ingredients in a mixing bowl. Make a well in the center and add the egg mixture and vanilla. Stir. Add the melted margarine and mix well. Stir in the yogurt. Spread the mixture in the pan. Bake just until the brownies begin to pull away from the sides of the pan, about 30 minutes. Let cool before cutting into squares.

Variation:

For an even lower-fat brownie, use nonfat plain yogurt in place of the vanilla yogurt. For an extra special flavor in the plain yogurt brownie, stir in 2 tablespoons of kahlua and increase the vanilla extract from 1 to 2 teaspoons before adding margarine.

> **PER SERVING:**
> 180 Cal.; 3g Prot.; 5g Fat; 9g Carb.;
> 11mg Chol.; 96mg Sod.; 2g Fiber.

Cinnamon Oatmeal-Apple Cookies

makes 36

3 cups rolled oats

1 cup unbleached white flour

4 teaspoons ground cinnamon

2 teaspoons baking powder

2 teaspoons baking soda

1/4 teaspoon ground nutmeg

1/2 cup brown sugar or date sugar

1/2 cup apple juice concentrate or honey

2 teaspoons vanilla extract

1 cup grated, peeled apple

3/4 cup raisins

4 egg whites, stiffly beaten

PREHEAT the oven to 400°F. In a food processor or blender, combine 1 cup oats with the flour, ground cinnamon, baking powder, baking soda, nutmeg, and browm sugar or date sugar. Process until the oats are coursely ground and the ingredients are well mixed. Stir in the remaining oats.

IN A BOWL, combine the apple juice concentrate or honey, vanilla, apple and raisins. Combine the oat mixture and apple mixture, then fold in the egg whites. Drop the batter by heaping tablespoonfuls onto nonstick baking sheet. Bake 12 to 15 minutes. Let the cookies cool slightly on the baking sheets before transferring them to a wire rack.

> **PER SERVING:**
> 75 Cal.; 2g Prot.; 0.5g Fat; 15g Carb.;
> 0mg Chol.; 52mg Sod.; 1g Fiber.

No Toll Cookies

makes 48

Typical chocolate chip cookies are loaded with fat, sugar and calories. Not these taste-alikes. They contain almost no fat, are sweetened with honey instead of sugar and have only 55 calories per cookie.

3 cups whole-wheat flour

1 teaspoons baking soda

3/4 cup unsweetened applesauce

3/4 cup honey

2 teaspoons vanilla extract

3/4 cup unsweetened carob chips or semisweet chocolate chips

1/2 cup chopped nuts or sunflower seeds (optional)

PREHEAT the oven to 350°F. In a large bowl, combine the flour and baking soda. Stir together the applesauce, honey and vanilla in a separate bowl. Add to the dry ingredients and stir well. Fold in the carob chips or chocolate chips and nuts.

DROP the batter by the tablespoonfuls onto a nonstick or lightly oiled cookie sheet. Flatten with fork. Bake until lightly browned, about 12 minutes.

> **PER SERVING:**
> 55 Cal.; 1g Prot.; 0.9g Fat; 12g Carb.;
> 0mg Chol.; 18mg Sod.; 0g Fiber.

CHAPTER

22

cakes, tarts and pies

IN THIS SELECTION, YOU'LL FIND DELICIOUS LOWER-FAT VERSIONS of traditionally high-caloric goodies as well as terribly rich cakes, tarts and pies that we just couldn't pass up. In the spotlight, however, are remakes: High-calorie, high-fat recipes that our recipe developers turned into treats with an acceptable nutritional profile (and with great taste!). We're not suggesting that you make cakes and the like a part of your daily feasting, but when the mood strikes, pull out your baking pans.

415

Chocolate Layer Cake

serves 24

This egg- and dairy-free cake is the most deliciously moist chocolate layer cake you can imagine. You may serve it as a layer cake or fashion it into fun shapes— such as a heart, a bear face or a rocket spaceship for a birthday or holiday. To make a smaller cake, cut all ingredients by half and make only one layer.

CAKE

- 5 cups unbleached white flour
- 1 1/3 cups unsweetened cocoa powder, sifted
- 4 cups sugar
- 4 teaspoons baking soda
- 1 teaspoon salt
- 3/4 cup canola oil
- 4 3/4 cups water
- 2 teaspoons vanilla extract
- 1/4 cup cider vinegar, white vinegar or rice vinegar

ICING

- 2/3 cup unbleached white flour
- 2 cups plain "lite" soymilk or skim milk
- 2 cups sugar
- 6 tablespoons margarine or butter
- 2 teaspoons vanilla extract
- 1/4 teaspoon salt

CAKE: In a large bowl, whisk together the dry ingredients. In a separate bowl, combine the liquid ingredients. Add the liquid ingredients to the dry ingredients and stir only until blended.

PREHEAT the oven to 350°F. Grease and flour two 9 × 12-inch cake pans and line with parchment paper cut about 2 inches larger than the pans. Pour the batter into the pans. Bake until a toothpick inserted in the center comes out clean, about 45 minutes. Place the pans on racks to cool for 15 minutes. Pick up the parchment to lift the cakes out of the pans and invert them onto cookie sheets lined with wax paper. Peel off the parchment paper. Place the cookie sheets in your refrigerator and let the cakes cool for several hours.

ICING: In a medium saucepan, whisk together the flour and soymilk or milk. Cook over medium heat, stirring and scraping the bottom and sides of the pan with a rubber spatula, until the mixture is thick and smooth. Remove from the heat. Place the pan in a pot of cold water to cool. Meanwhile, in a separate bowl, combine the sugar, margarine or butter, vanilla and salt until light and fluffy. When the flour mixture is completely cool, stir it into the sugar mixture and blend well. To assemble the cake, stack and ice the cake layers or make them into a fun shape.

Helpful hint:

For a smooth surface of frosting, first frost the cake with a thin layer of icing. Let sit for 30 minutes, then add the remainder of frosting.

Variation:

For a chocolate cake with sophisticated style, sift a small amount of unsweetened cocoa over the top of the cake after the cake has been frosted. Then cut a stencil out of posterboard and sift 1 1/4 cups confectioners sugar in a design of your choice on top. Cut out another stencil and repeat with 2 tablespoons ground cinnamon. In a decorative arrangement, add orange slices and chocolate-covered almonds.

PER SERVING:
388 Cal.; 5g Prot.; 11g Fat; 68g Carb.;
0mg Chol.; 281mg Sod.; 3g Fiber.

Black Forest Cake

serves 12

Here's a cholesterol-free version of the traditional favorite.

CAKE

- 1 cup water
- 1 cup honey
- 1/2 cup applesauce
- 1 teaspoon vanilla extract
- 1 teaspoon vinegar
- 2 cups whole-wheat pastry flour or unbleached white flour
- 3/4 cup unsweetened cocoa powder
- 1 tablespoon baking powder
- 1 teaspoon baking soda

SYRUP

- 1/2 cup water
- 1/4 cup honey
- 2 thin lemon or orange slices
- 1/3 cup kirsch (cherry liqueur), or light or gold rum

ICING

- 3/4 cup raw cashews
- 3/4 cup water
- 2 teaspoons vanilla extract
- 1/2 cup honey
- 10 ounces firm tofu
- 3 ounces semi-sweet chocolate, melted
- 16-ounce jar or can pitted cherries, drained (not maraschino)

CAKE: Preheat the oven to 350°F. Combine the liquid ingredients in a large bowl and whisk well. Sift together the dry ingredients and whisk into the liquid ingredients. Pour into a greased and floured 9-inch cake pan and bake until springy to the touch, about 35 minutes. Cool the cake completely, and remove it from the pan. With a serrated knife, cut the cake horizontally to make 3 thin layers.

SYRUP: Combine the water, honey, and lemon or orange slices in a small pan and boil 3 minutes. Let cool, then add the kirsch or rum. Set aside.

ICING: In a blender, combine the cashews, water and vanilla. Blend until smooth and creamy. Add the honey and tofu, and blend again. Set aside 2 cups of this mixture for the vanilla icing for the top and sides of the cake. To the mixture in blender, add the melted chocolate and 3 tablespoons syrup. Blend again until smooth. Chill both icings before using.

TO ASSEMBLE, carefully remove the two top layers of the cake. Brush some syrup onto the bottom layer, and spread half of the chocolate icing on it. Place the middle cake layer on top. Brush with more syrup, and spread the rest of the chocolate icing on it. Put down a layer of cherries, and dot with a little of the vanilla icing to help the top layer stick. Place the top layer on the cherries, and brush again with the syrup. Frost the top and sides of the cake with the vanilla icing and decorate with the cherries.

CHILL several hours before serving. The cake may be kept covered if you're not serving it until the following day. After three days, the frosting tends to discolor.

PER SERVING:
419 Cal.; 9g Prot.; 9g Fat; 72g Carb.; 0mg Chol.; 188mg Sod.; 6g Fiber.

Chocolate-Espresso Cake with Espresso Sauce

serves 8

CAKE

- 7 ounces soft tofu
- 1/2 cup mild honey
- 1 teaspoon vanilla extract
- 1/2 cup espresso or very strong coffee
- 1/2 cup unsweetened cocoa powder
- 1 1/4 cups unbleached white flour or whole-wheat pastry flour
- 1 tablespoon baking powder
- 1 teaspoon baking soda

SAUCE

- 10 ounces soft tofu
- 1/2 cup honey
- 1 teaspoon vanilla extract
- 3/4 cup espresso or very strong coffee
- 1 to 2 tablespoons brandy or cognac

OPTIONAL GARNISHES

- Fresh or frozen berries of choice
- Mint sprigs
- Confectioners sugar

CAKE: Preheat the oven to 350°F. Purée the tofu with the honey and vanilla in a blender or food processor. Add the espresso or coffee, and cocoa. Sift the flour with the baking powder and baking soda. If you're using a food processor, add the flour mixture to the tofu mixture, and process until smooth. If you're using a blender, transfer the tofu mixture to a bowl, add the flour mixture and beat well. Pour the combined mixture into a lightly oiled

8 1/2-inch bundt pan and bake until firm to the touch, about 25 minutes. Let cool.

SAUCE: Combine the sauce ingredients in a blender or food processor, and blend until creamy. Chill at least 1 hour. (The sauce will thicken as it cools; dilute with more espresso if necessary.)

REMOVE the cake from the bundt pan and place it on a serving platter; cut it into 8 to 10 slices. Spoon 1/4 to 1/3 cup sauce on 8 to 10 dessert plates and top each plate with a slice of cake. Garnish with berries, sprigs of mint and a light dusting of confectioners sugar.

> **PER SERVING WITH SAUCE:**
> 196 Cal.; 6g Prot.; 2g Fat; 17g Carb.;
> 0mg Chol.; 268mg Sod.; 3g Fiber

Banana Cake with Chocolate Glaze

serves 12

CAKE

- 2 1/2 cups unbleached white flour
- 1 to 1 1/4 cups sugar
- 1 1/2 teaspoon baking powder
- 1 teaspoon baking soda
- 1 teaspoon salt
- 6 tablespoons margarine or butter, at room temperature
- 1 1/8 cups mashed ripe banana
- 2/3 cup nonfat yogurt or buttermilk
- 2 eggs
- 1 teaspoon vanilla extract

GLAZE

1 cup confectioners sugar

3 to 4 tablespoons unsweetened cocoa powder

2 to 3 tablespoons skim milk

CAKE: Preheat the oven to 350°F. Grease and lightly flour two 9-inch round baking pans. In a mixing bowl, combine the flour, sugar, baking powder, baking soda and salt. Add the margarine or butter and banana; blend at low speed of an electric mixer until combined. Add the yogurt or buttermilk, eggs and vanilla; beat 2 minutes on medium speed. Pour the batter into the prepared pans. Bake until a toothpick inserted in the center comes out clean, about 30 minutes. Cool 10 minutes on wire racks. Remove from the pans and cool thoroughly.

GLAZE: In a small bowl, combine the sugar and cocoa. Using a fork, mix in the skim milk, a little at a time. The glaze should be just thin enough to pour. Place 1 layer of cake on a cake stand or platter. Spread a thin layer of glaze on top, then top with the second layer of cake. Drizzle with the remaining glaze, letting it drip down the sides, or spread the glaze thinly over the top and sides of the cake.

Helpful hint:

For an easy mess-free way to mash bananas, place the bananas in a tightly sealed zipper-type plastic baggie and squish with your hands until the bananas are no longer lumpy.

PER SERVING:
274 Cal.; 5g Prot.; 6g Fat; 23g Carb.;
32mg Chol.; 322mg Sod.; 3g Fiber.

Chocolate Cupcakes

makes 12

Kids gobble up these delicious cupcakes, made with neither eggs nor dairy products. You'll love them, too.

CUPCAKES

2 1/2 cups unbleached white flour

2/3 cups unsweetened cocoa powder, sifted

2 cups sugar

2 teaspoons baking soda

1/2 teaspoon salt

6 tablespoons vegetable oil

2 1/4 cups plus 2 tablespoons water

1 teaspoon vanilla extract

2 tablespoons cider vinegar, white vinegar or rice vinegar

ICING

1 1/3 cups unsweetened cocoa powder, sifted

1 1/2 cups sugar

2/3 cup cornstarch

2 cups plain "lite" soymilk or skim milk

1/2 teaspoon vanilla extract

OPTIONAL DECORATIONS

12 small cookies

Finely shredded unsweetened coconut

Colored sprinkles

CUPCAKES: In a large bowl, whisk together the dry ingredients. In a separate bowl, combine the liquid ingredients. Stir the liquid ingredients into the dry ingredients only until blended.

PREHEAT the oven to 375°F. Line a 12-cup muffin tin with baking cups. Fill with the batter. Bake until a toothpick inserted in the cupcakes comes out clean, about 20 to 25 minutes. Remove the cupcakes and place on a rack to cool.

ICING: In a medium saucepan, whisk together the cocoa and sugar. In a bowl, combine the cornstarch and milk until no lumps remain. Whisk the cornstarch mixture into the cocoa-sugar mixture. Cook over medium heat, stirring constantly and scraping the bottom and sides of the pan with a rubber spatula, until the mixture is glossy, about 7 minutes. Remove from the heat and add the vanilla. Beat to remove any lumps (strain through a fine sieve if necessary). Cool completely, stirring occasionally.

WHEN THE CUPCAKES ARE COOL, spread with the icing. For decoration, place a small cookie in the center while the icing is still sticky. Top the icing with coconut or colored sprinkles.

> **PER CUPCAKE:**
> 406 cal.. 7g Prot.; 4g Fat; 86g Carb.;
> 240mg Sod.; 0mg Chol.; 7g Fiber.

Pumpkin Spice Cake

serves 12

If you like fruitcakes and sweetened breads, you'll love this low-fat pumpkin spice cake. Slice and serve it with dollops of Mock Whipped Cream (page 436).

3 1/2 cups whole-wheat pastry flour

1 tablespoon baking powder

1 teaspoon baking soda

1 teaspoon salt (optional)

1/4 cup chopped walnuts or pecans

1/2 cup raisins or chopped dates

2 cups puréed cooked or canned pumpkin

1 tablespoon fresh lemon juice

1/4 cup safflower oil

1 cup maple syrup

2 eggs, separated

1/4 cup nonfat buttermilk or yogurt

LIGHTLY OIL AND FLOUR a 9 × 5-inch loaf pan. Preheat the oven to 350°F. In a large bowl, sift together the flour, baking powder, baking soda and salt. Stir in the nuts and raisins or dates. In another bowl, combine the puréed pumpkin, lemon juice, oil, maple syrup, egg yolks, and buttermilk or yogurt.

COMBINE the contents of the two bowls. In a clean bowl, beat the egg whites to form soft peaks, then fold into the batter. Pour into the prepared baking pan, and bake until lightly browned and springy to the touch, 45 minutes to 1 hour. Let cool completely, then remove from the pan.

> **PER SERVING:**
> 279 Cal.; 6g Prot.; 7g Fat; 30g Carb.;
> 28mg Chol.; 91mg Sod.; 6g Fiber.

Honey-Yogurt Cake with Syrup

serves 12 to 16

This rich Grecian dessert is a delicious treat, not everyday fare.

CAKE

- 3 cups uncooked farina
- 1/2 cup unbleached white flour
- 2 teaspoons baking powder
- 1 teaspoon baking soda
- 1 1/2 cups honey
- 2 cups plain yogurt
- 1/2 cup coarsely chopped blanched almonds
- 2 tablespoons frozen orange juice concentrate

SYRUP

- 3 cups honey
- 2 1/2 cups water
- 1 thin slice of orange

CAKE: Preheat the oven to 350°F. Sift together the farina, flour, baking powder and baking soda. Stir in the honey, yogurt, almonds and orange juice concentrate. Pour the batter into a well-greased, 9 × 13-inch baking pan. Bake until top is golden brown, about 45 minutes.

SYRUP: Combine the honey, water and orange slice in a saucepan. Bring to a boil, lower the heat and simmer 5 minutes. Remove and discard the froth and orange slice.

WHEN THE CAKE IS DONE, pour the syrup mixture over it. Gently poke the cake surface with a toothpick. Let cool, and allow all of the syrup to be absorbed. Cut and serve.

> **PER SERVING:**
> 501 Cal.; 4g Prot.; 4g Fat; 120g Carb.;
> 5mg Chol.; 148mg Sod.; 1g Fiber.

Simple Honey Cake

serves 16

Here's a lightened-up version of a traditional Jewish dish.

- 1 cup sugar
- 4 large eggs
- 1/4 cup canola oil
- 1 cup honey
- 1/2 cup fresh orange juice
- 1/2 cup applesauce
- 3 cups sifted all-purpose flour
- 1/2 teaspoon ground cinnamon
- 1/2 teaspoon ground ginger
- 1/2 teaspoon salt
- 1/2 teaspoon baking soda
- 3 teaspoons baking powder
- 3/4 cup coarsely chopped walnuts, divided

PREHEAT the oven to 350°F. Line a 9 × 13-inch baking pan with waxed paper. Set aside. In the large bowl of an electric mixer, beat the sugar and eggs until light, about 10 minutes. Add the oil and beat 1 or 2 minutes more. Add the honey and beat another minute. Add the orange juice and applesauce, and beat 1 minute more. Set aside.

IN A SEPARATE BOWL, sift together the flour, cinnamon, ginger, salt, baking soda and baking powder. Add to the egg-honey mixture and beat until well-blended and fluffy, about 1 to 2 minutes. With a spoon or spatula, gently fold 1/2 cup chopped walnuts into the batter.

POUR the batter into the prepared pan and smooth the top. Sprinkle the remaining 1/4 cup walnuts on top and bake until a toothpick inserted in center comes out clean, about 50 minutes. Let the cake cool in the pan on a rack. Cut it into squares and serve.

PER SERVING:
281 Cal.; 5g Prot.; 8g Fat; 47g Carb.;
53mg Chol.; 192mg Sod.; 1g Fiber.

Three-Berry Shortcake

serves 8

- 2 cups fresh blackberries
- 2 cups fresh raspberries
- 2 cups fresh strawberries
- 4 teaspoons fresh lemon juice
- 1/3 cup maple syrup or honey
- 2 cups unbleached white flour or whole-wheat pastry flour
- 1 tablespoon plus 2 teaspoons baking powder
- 1/2 teaspoon ground cinnamon
- 1 teaspoon salt (optional)
- 3 tablespoons honey, warmed
- 1/4 cup unsalted butter or vegetable oil
- 2/3 cup low-fat milk
- 1 cup low-fat vanilla yogurt, for garnish

IN A BOWL, combine the berries, lemon juice and maple syrup or honey. Cover the mixture with plastic wrap. Let marinate for 3 hours.

PREHEAT the oven to 350°F. Lightly oil a large baking sheet. In a large bowl, sift together the flour, baking powder, cinnamon and salt. In another bowl, cream the honey, butter or oil and milk until smooth. Gradually add the milk mixture to the dry ingredients, mixing to form a soft dough. Roll out the dough on a floured board to a 1/2-inch thickness and cut with a large cookie cutter into eight circles. Place the circles on the baking sheet and bake 15 minutes.

LET THE SHORTCAKES cool slightly, then cut each one in half like an English muffin. Spoon the berry mixture between each half and on top. Garnish with a dollop of vanilla yogurt.

Helpful hint:

Unfilled shortcakes may be baked, cooled, then wrapped tightly in plastic wrap and frozen.

PER SERVING:
283 Cal.; 6g Prot.; 7g Fat; 51g Carb.;
17mg Chol.; 231mg Sod.; 6g Fiber.

Strawberry Angel Food Cake with Red and Green Holiday Sauces

serves 12

Angel food cake is known for its incredible lightness. This one is dressed with festive holiday sauces.

CAKE

> 1 cup sifted unbleached white flour
>
> 1 cup finely ground date sugar or superfine sugar
>
> 10 egg whites
>
> 1 1/4 teaspoons cream of tartar
>
> 1 1/2 teaspoons vanilla extract
>
> 1/2 cup thinly sliced fresh or frozen strawberries

SAUCES

> 1 cup fresh or frozen sliced strawberries
>
> 1 cup honey
>
> 2 tablespoons arrowroot powder or cornstarch
>
> 2 cups peeled and sliced kiwifruit
>
> Chunks of fresh kiwifruit as garnish (optional)

CAKE: Preheat the oven to 350°F. Sift together the flour and 1/2 cup sugar into a large bowl. In another bowl, beat the egg whites until foamy. Add the cream of tartar, and continue beating until soft peaks form. Add the remaining 1/2 cup sugar, 2 tablespoons at a time, beating until stiff peaks form. Fold in the flour-sugar mixture, 1/2 cup at a time. Fold in the vanilla and strawberries.

POUR the batter into an ungreased 10-inch tube pan, spreading evenly and deflating any large air pockets with a knife. Bake until the cake is lightly browned and springy, about 40 minutes. Invert the pan and let the cake cool for 40 minutes. Remove the cake from the pan and set it on a serving plate.

SAUCES: In a blender, combine the strawberries, 1/2 cup honey and 1 tablespoon arrowroot or cornstarch. Purée until smooth. Pour the mixture into a saucepan and heat, whisking, until slightly thickened. Pour it into a bowl to let cool.

PRESS the kiwifruit through a fine sieve to remove the seeds. In a blender, combine the strained kiwifruit with remaining 1 tablespoon arrowroot or cornstarch, and 1/2 cup honey. Purée until smooth. Pour the sauce into a clean saucepan and heat, whisking, until slightly thickened. Pour into a bowl to let cool.

TO SERVE, ladle a small amount of red sauce on half of a dessert plate, and an equal amount of green sauce on the other half. Place a slice of cake in the center and drizzle with stripes of the two sauces and chunks of kiwifruit. Serve at once.

Helpful hint:

> The trick to a successful angel food cake is the lightness of the beaten egg whites, so fold them quickly into the batter before they have a chance to separate.

PER SERVING:
222 Cal.; 4g Prot.; 0.2g Fat; 14g Carb.;
0mg Chol.; 177mg Sod.; 1g Fiber.

Grilled Angel Food Cake with Nectarines and Blueberries

serves 6

> 6 ripe nectarines
>
> 3 tablespoons confectioners' sugar
>
> Grated zest of 1 lemon
>
> Juice of 1/2 lemon
>
> 6 slices angel food cake
>
> 1 pint fresh blueberries

PREPARE the grill and cover it to build an intense heat. Remove the nectarine pits and slice each nectarine into 6 slices. (Don't peel nectarines.) Combine the confectioners' sugar, lemon zest and lemon juice in a small bowl. Spear 6 nectarine slices on each skewer and place the skewers on the grill. Cook 5 minutes, turn and baste with the lemon glaze. Continue cooking and basting until the fruit is hot and tender, about 7 minutes more.

WHEN THE FRUIT is just about done, toast the cake slices on a cooler part of the grill, turning once. Serve the toasted cake with skewered fruit and a generous handful of fresh blueberries.

Variation:

Purée 1 cup strawberries, sweeten to taste with honey or sugar and drizzle over the cake slices.

> **PER SERVING:**
> 284 Cal.; 6g Prot.; 0.7g Fat; 63g Carb.;
> 0mg Chol.; 175mg Sod.; 5g Fiber.

Easy Holiday Fruitcake

serves 15

If you're tired of commercially produced candied fruit-cakes, you'll enjoy this easy, flavorful, moist version.

- 1 cup unbleached white flour
- 1 cup sugar
- 1 teaspoon salt
- 1/2 teaspoon baking powder
- 1/2 cup plus 2 teaspoons thawed orange juice concentrate
- 2 eggs, slightly beaten, plus 2 egg whites (or equivalent egg substitute)
- 1 cup chopped pecans
- 1 cup chopped walnuts
- One 10-ounce jar maraschino cherries, drained and patted dry
- 1 cup chopped pitted dates
- 1 cup chopped dried figs or raisins
- 1/2 cup confectioners' sugar
- 1 teaspoon water

PREHEAT the oven to 300°F. Grease a 9 × 5-inch loaf pan. In a large bowl, stir together the flour, sugar, salt, baking powder, 1/2 cup orange juice concentrate, and eggs or egg substitute. Blend in the nuts, cherries, dates, and figs or raisins. Mix well. Spoon the batter into the pan. Bake 2 hours. Then cover the cake with foil and bake until a toothpick inserted in the center comes out clean, about 15 minutes more. Let sit 15 minutes before removing the cake from the pan.

MEANWHILE, in a small bowl, stir together the confectioners' sugar, water and remaining 2 teaspoons orange juice concentrate. Drizzle over the cake while it's still hot. Cool the cake completely. To store, wrap it in plastic wrap, then in foil, and refrigerate.

> **PER SERVING:**
> 364 Cal.; 5g Prot.; 14g Fat; 64g Carb.;
> 22mg Chol.; 185mg Sod.; 4g Fiber.

Shamrock Torte

serves 10

Kiwifruit tops this tasty carob cake.

CAROB CAKE

| 1/2 cup plus 2 tablespoons whole-wheat pastry flour
1/2 cup unbleached white flour
1/4 cup carob powder or unsweetened cocoa powder
1/4 cup granulated sugarcane juice
1/2 teaspoon baking soda
1/8 teaspoon salt
1/4 cup corn oil
6 tablespoons water
1/2 cup plus 2 tablespoons honey or maple syrup
1/2 tablespoon cider vinegar
1 teaspoon vanilla extract

TOPPING

2 pounds firm tofu
3/4 cup brown rice syrup
1/2 cup honey
3/4 cup fresh lime juice (preferably key lime juice)
1 tablespoon arrowroot
2 tablespoons corn oil

GLAZE AND GARNISH

3/4 teaspoons agar-agar flakes
6 tablespoons water
6 tablespoons brown rice syrup (see Note)
1 to 2 drops peppermint extract
2 to 3 kiwifruit, peeled and sliced (or 1 cup sliced strawberries)

CAROB CAKE: Preheat the oven to 350°F. Sift together the dry ingredients into a medium bowl. Whisk in the remaining cake ingredients until no lumps remain.

LIGHTLY OIL AND FLOUR an 8- or 10-inch round springform pan. Pour the batter into the pan. Bake until a toothpick inserted into the center comes out clean, about 25 to 35 minutes.

TOPPING: In a food processor, blend the topping ingredients. Pour the mixture into a double boiler. Heat until the mixture thickens to the consistency of heavy cream. Let cool.

WHEN THE TOPPING IS COOL, pour it onto the cake and spread it evenly with a spatula. Refrigerate until the topping sets completely, about 2 hours.

GLAZE AND GARNISH: In a small saucepan, dissolve the agar-agar in water. Add the syrup and peppermint extract. Bring to a simmer then remove from heat. Let cool slightly.

REMOVE the chilled torte from your refrigerator. Arrange the fruit on top. While the glaze is still warm, drizzle it over the fruit. Refrigerate the torte for 10 to 15 minutes before cutting.

Note:

Brown rice syrup, available in natural foods stores and through mail order, has the consistency and golden color of honey but is less pronounced in flavor. It works well in sweetening baked goods and other desserts.

PER SERVING:
511 Cal.; 9g Prot.; 13g Fat; 95g Carb.; 0mg Chol.; 88mg Sod.; 0g Fiber.

Cherry Heart Tartlets

serves 2

These delicious—and romantic—tartlets can be made in round or heart-shaped tart pans, found at gourmet kitchenware shops.

CRUST

3/4 cup rolled oats

1 teaspoon walnuts, lightly toasted (page 106)

1/2 cup whole-wheat pastry flour

Pinch salt

1/4 teaspoon ground cinnamon

2 teaspoons safflower oil

2 teaspoons apple juice

1 to 2 tablespoons maple syrup

FILLING

1 cup apple-cherry juice

1 tablespoon agar-agar flakes

1 cup frozen pitted cherries

1/2 teaspoon vanilla extract

1 teaspoon lemon juice

2 teaspoons arrowroot powder or cornstarch, dissolved in 2 tablespoons cold water

CRUST: Preheat the oven to 350°F. In a food processor or blender, grind the oats and walnuts to a coarse meal. Combine with the flour, salt and cinnamon in a medium bowl. Stir in the oil, apple juice and maple syrup to form a soft dough. Press the dough evenly into the bottoms and sides of two 4-inch circular or heart-shaped tart pans. Prick the dough several times with a fork and bake until golden, about 15 to 20 minutes. Let cool before filling.

FILLING: In a small saucepan, stir together the juice and agar. Simmer over low heat for 10 minutes, stirring frequently, until the agar dissolves. Stir in the cherries, vanilla and lemon juice, cooking until warmed through. In a small bowl, mix together the arrowroot or cornstarch and water until dissolved, then add to the saucepan. Simmer 3 minutes, stirring constantly. Remove from the heat and transfer the filling to a medium bowl. Cover the bowl with plastic wrap and let stand at room temperature for 20 minutes to thicken slightly. Pour the filling into the baked crusts, smoothing the tops with a spatula. Let the tarts set until the filling is firm, about 30 minutes.

Variations:

- If desired, top each tart with a dollop of low-fat vanilla yogurt.
- Substitute almonds or other nuts for walnuts.
- Substitute other juices and fruits. Raspberries and strawberries are good possibilities.

> **PER SERVING:**
> 490 Cal.; 11g Prot.; 7g Fat; 67g Carb.;
> 0mg Chol.; 142mg Sod.; 8g Fiber.

Pear Tart with Almond Crust

serves 8

French bakery windows tempt passersby with colorful jewel-like tarts, filled with seasonal fruits, custards or jams. Here's a lower-fat version—employing a rather unusual ingredient (jarred baby food) with great success. This recipe has all the appeal of the original buttery tart.

CRUST

- 1 1/4 cups rolled oats
- 1 1/4 cups whole-wheat pastry flour or unbleached white flour
- Pinch salt
- 1/4 teaspoon baking soda
- 1/4 teaspoon baking powder
- 1/4 to 1/2 teaspoon ground allspice (optional)
- 1 teaspoon freshly grated lemon zest
- 2 tablespoons fresh lemon juice
- 1 teaspoon almond extract
- 1/4 cup canola oil
- 1/3 cup maple syrup

FILLING

- One 4-ounce jar pear baby food
- 4 to 5 tablespoons apricot jam
- 1 teaspoon vanilla extract
- Pinch salt
- 3 pears (cornice, bartlett or anjou), ripe but not mushy
- 1 tablespoon fresh lemon juice

CRUST: In a food processor or blender, grind the rolled oats into a coarse meal. Combine the ground oats, flour, salt, baking soda, baking powder and allspice in a bowl. In a separate bowl, combine the lemon rind and juice, almond extract, oil and maple syrup. Add the wet ingredients to the dry ingredients and mix well. The dough will be sticky. Chill at least 20 minutes.

PREHEAT the oven to 350°F. Dust two sheets of waxed paper with flour. Roll out the dough between the waxed paper into an 11-inch circle. Fit the crust into a greased 10-inch tart pan and trim edges. Prick the crust with a fork several times and bake 10 minutes.

FILLING: Mix the pear baby food with 2 tablespoons jam, vanilla and salt. Spread evenly over the baked crust. Slice the pears in half lengthwise (peeling is optional), scoop out the seeds and trim tops and bottoms. Slice each half into thin pieces lengthwise (see Helpful hint) and fan out. Lift the sliced pear halves with a knife or spatula and place them on the tart. Arrange them in a circle over the top of the filling. Use an extra pear half if needed to fill in the spaces. Bake 20 to 25 minutes.

LOWER the oven temperature to 325°F. Stir together the remaining 2 to 3 tablespoons jam and lemon juice in a small pan. Heat until warm. When the tart is baked, remove it from your oven and gently brush the warm jam over the sliced pears. Bake 5 to 7 minutes more. Cool before slicing.

Helpful hint:

To slice pears, place a pear half on a cutting board; hold the pear with wide end toward you. With a sharp knife, slice toward you. Try to make the pear slices as thin as possible.

PER SERVING:
250 Cal.; 5g Prot.; 8g Fat; 30g Carb.;
0mg Chol.; 109mg Sod.; 5g Fiber.

Apple Tart

serves 8

CRUST
- 1 cup unbleached white flour
- Pinch salt
- 1 tablespoon brown sugar
- 4 tablespoons margarine, chilled
- 2 tablespoons cold water

FILLING
- 3 Granny Smith apples, peeled and sliced thinly
- 1/4 cup sugar
- 1/2 cup raspberry, apricot or strawberry preserves

CRUST: Combine the flour, salt and brown sugar in a food processor. Process, using a standard cutting blade, for 30 seconds. With the machine running, add the margarine in bits through the feed tube. Then add the cold water and process until the dough forms a ball, about 20 seconds. Wrap the dough in plastic and chill at least 30 minutes. Or, by hand, stir together the flour, salt and brown sugar in a bowl. Cut in the margarine, and distribute evenly using a fork or your fingers. Add the water, a bit at a time, stirring to form a ball.

FILLING: Preheat the oven to 375°F. With your fingers, press the dough into a 10-inch tart pan, evenly distributing the dough up the sides. Arrange the apple slices in a concentric circle, overlapping slightly. Sprinkle with the sugar. Bake until the crust is slightly golden, about 45 minutes. Meanwhile, in a small saucepan, melt the preserves over medium heat, stirring well. Remove the tart from your oven. Transfer the melted preserves to a small sieve and pour evenly over the tart. Let cool at least 30 minutes. Serve warm or at room temperature.

> **PER SERVING:**
> 214 Cal.; 2g Prot.; 6g Fat; 41g Carb.;
> 0mg Chol.; 112mg Sod.; 1g Fiber.

Apricot Creme Tart

serves 6

Phyllo, a paper-thin flaky pastry, replaces the usual butter-and-flour pie crust in this light sweet-tart dessert.

- 8 sheets frozen phyllo
- 1 cup dried apricots
- 1/2 cup honey
- 2 cups water
- 1/2 teaspoon agar-agar powder (or 1 tablespoon agar-agar flakes), dissolved in 2 tablespoons water
- 8 ounces soft tofu
- 1/2 teaspoon vanilla extract
- 2 to 3 teaspoons fresh lemon juice
- One 16-ounce can apricot halves
- 1/4 to 1/3 cup fruit-sweetened apricot jam
- 1 ounce melted chocolate for decorating (optional)

PREHEAT the oven to 350°F. Spray a 9-inch pie pan with nonstick cooking spray. Place a sheet of phyllo in the pan and spray it with nonstick cooking spray. Fold the edges inward so they do not extend beyond the rim of the pan. Put down another phyllo layer; spray and fold. Repeat this procedure with the remaining phyllo until the pan is covered. Bake until crispy and golden brown, about 15 to 20 minutes.

PLACE the dried apricots, honey and water in a saucepan, and simmer gently until the apricots are very soft and the liquid has reduced to a heavy syrup. Add the dissolved agar-agar to the apricot mixture; simmer for a couple of minutes. Transfer the mixture to a blender or food processor. Add the tofu, vanilla and lemon juice, and purée until smooth. Pour into the crust. Drain the apricot halves and arrange them on the tart. Melt the apricot jam in a small saucepan over low heat and brush it on top. Drizzle the chocolate on top in a zigzag fashion. Chill at least 1 hour before serving.

PER SERVING:
330 Cal.; 8g Prot.; 3g Fat; 67g Carb.;
0mg Chol.; 119mg Sod.; 5g Fiber.

Banana-Raspberry Ice Cream Pie

serves 10

Here's a no-bake pie that's quick to whip up for company. (And there's no need to wash your food processor between steps!)

CRUST

- **2 cups crumbled chocolate cookies**
- **2 to 3 tablespoons vanilla ice cream, soy ice cream or frozen yogurt**

FILLING

- **2 ripe bananas, peeled and frozen**
- **1 pint vanilla ice cream, soy ice cream or frozen yogurt, slightly softened**
- **2 cups frozen raspberries**
- **3 to 4 tablespoons raspberry jam, extra cookies and raspberries, for garnish (optional)**

CRUST: Place the cookies and 2 tablespoons ice cream in a food processor. Pulse until the mixture looks like crumbly sand. (You may have to add additional ice cream to make the crumbs hold together.) Spoon the mixture into a 9-inch pie pan and press to form a crust.

FILLING: Let the bananas soften for a few minutes. Chop them into 1-inch pieces. Place in the food processor and pulse until coarse. Add 1 cup ice cream. Pulse until evenly blended, about 30 to 60 seconds. Spoon the mixture into the pie shell and spread it evenly.

PLACE the frozen raspberries in the food processor and pulse until they look like ruby-red seeds. Add the remaining 1 cup ice cream and blend until smooth. Stop the machine occasionally to scrape down the mixture if necessary. Spoon the raspberry mixture over the banana layer and spread evenly. Freeze until firm. At serving time, garnish the pie with raspberry jam, cookies and raspberries.

Helpful hint:

To prevent the cookie crumb mixture from sticking to your fingers as you form the pie crust, cover the crumbs in the pie pan with a piece of plastic wrap. Or place a plastic sandwich bag over your hand like a mitten before pressing the crumbs.

Variations:

- For a topping, heat the raspberry jam and thin with 1 to 3 teaspoons fruit liqueur. Strain the topping to remove the seeds.

- Experiment with your favorite cookies for the crust or with other ice cream flavors and fruit combinations. However, use frozen fruit; fresh fruit will make the ice cream soupy and will crystallize when frozen.

PER SERVING:
231 Cal.; 3g Prot.; 6g Fat; 42g Carb.;
6mg Chol.; 76mg Sod.; 3g Fiber.

Tofu-Pumpkin Pie

serves 10

This tasty version of a classic Thanksgiving dessert is egg- and dairy free. Candied ginger adds a festive touch.

CRUST

2 cups all-purpose flour

1/2 cup (1 stick) margarine or butter

1 teaspoon salt

3 to 4 tablespoons cold water

FILLING

1 pound firm tofu

One 16-ounce can puréed pumpkin

1 teaspoon ground cinnamon

1/4 teaspoon ground nutmeg

1/2 teaspoon salt

1 teaspoon vanilla extract

3/4 cup light brown sugar

1/4 teaspoon ground cloves

1/3 cup safflower oil

5 tablespoons candied ginger, chopped (or 1 teaspoon ground ginger)

CRUST: Combine the flour, margarine or butter, and salt in a food processor using the standard cutting blade. Process for 30 seconds using a standard cutting blade. Add the water through the feed tube and process the dough to form a ball. (Or, by hand, stir together the flour and salt in a bowl. Cut in the margarine or butter, and distribute evenly using a fork or your fingers. Add the water, stirring to form a ball.) Wrap the dough in plastic wrap or wax paper and chill at least 30 minutes. Then roll out the dough with a rolling pin and place it in a 10-inch tart pan or a deep-dish pie pan. Set aside.

FILLING: Preheat the oven to 350°F. Combine all the filling ingredients except the candied ginger in a food processor or blender. (If using ground ginger, add it at this time.) Process until smooth, about 3 minutes. Add 3 tablespoons candied ginger, and process 30 seconds more. Pour the filling into the crust and bake 1 hour. Let cool. Place the remaining 2 tablespoons candied ginger in the food processor or blender and process until coarsely ground. Sprinkle over the pie. Serve warm or chilled.

> **PER SERVING:**
> 293 Cal.; 6g Prot.; 13g Fat; 38g Carb.;
> 0mg Chol.; 440mg Sod.; 1g Fiber.

Louisiana Sweet Potato Pie

serves 8

1/2 cup evaporated skim milk

1 teaspoon apple cider vinegar

1 teaspoon baking soda

2 cups freshly cooked and mashed sweet potatoes

1 tablespoon butter or margarine, melted

1/3 cup honey, or to taste

1 teaspoon baking powder

1/2 teaspoon ground cinnamon

1/2 teaspoon ground nutmeg

1/4 teaspoon salt

3/4 cup egg substitute (or 3 eggs), beaten

One 9-inch pie crust, chilled (see No-Roll Pie Crust on page 436)

Ground cinnamon, for garnish (optional)

PREHEAT the oven to 400°F. In a small bowl, stir together the evaporated milk, vinegar and baking soda; set aside. In a large bowl, mix together the remaining ingredients except the pie crust and cinnamon; add the milk mixture. Process the sweet potato mixture in a blender or food processor until smooth.

POUR the filling into a chilled pie crust and bake 10 minutes. Lower the heat to 300°F and bake 45 to 50 minutes more. Let cool. Serve the pie chilled or at room temperature, with a sprinkle of cinnamon.

> **PER SERVING:**
> 234 Cal.; 4g Prot.; 6g Fat; 29g Carb.;
> 15mg Chol.; 323mg Sod.; 3g Fiber.

Upside-Down Peach Pie

serves 8

Who needs a fat-laden crust when this pie has a delicious crunchy-sweet oat topping? A slice has only 52 calories and next to no fat.

FILLING

- 4 cups sliced, fresh peaches
- 3 tablespoons whole-wheat flour
- 1/3 cup unsweetened apricot preserves
- 2 teaspoons fresh lemon juice
- 1/8 teaspoon nutmeg

TOPPING

- 1 tablespoon maple syrup
- 1/2 teaspoon vanilla extract
- 1/4 cup quick-cooking rolled oats
- 1 tablespoon cornmeal

FILLING: Preheat the oven to 375°F. Gently mix the peaches with the flour and place in a 9-inch pie pan. Mix together the preserves, lemon juice and nutmeg. Spoon over the peaches. Bake 30 minutes. Remove the pan and lower the oven temperature to 350°F.

TOPPING: While the peach mixture is baking, make the topping. Combine the maple syrup and vanilla in a bowl. Stir in the oats and cornmeal, mixing well. Crumble the topping mixture over the cooked peach filling and return the pie to your oven for 15 minutes more. Serve warm or cold.

> **PER SERVING:**
> 52 Cal.; 1g Prot.; 0.2g Fat; 13g Carb.;
> 0mg Chol.; 1mg Sod.; 3g Fiber.

Mixed Fruit Turnovers

makes 16

- 1 cup coarsely chopped mixed dried fruit
- 1/2 cup apple juice
- 1/4 cup water
- 1/4 cup chopped walnuts
- 1 1/4 teaspoons ground cinnamon
- 1/8 teaspoon black walnut extract (optional)
- 1/4 cup sugar
- 3 tablespoons vegetable oil
- 8 sheets frozen phyllo, thawed

COMBINE the dried fruit, apple juice and water in a small saucepan; let soak 1 hour. Bring to a boil, cover (keeping the lid ajar) and simmer until the liquid is absorbed and the fruit is soft, about 10 minutes. Add the walnuts, 1/4 teaspoon cinnamon and walnut extract. Set aside.

COMBINE the sugar and remaining 1 teaspoon cinnamon in a dish. Pour the oil into another dish. Cut a sheet of phyllo lengthwise into 4 strips. (Keep the remaining sheets covered with a damp dishcloth to prevent them from drying out.) Brush the strips lightly with oil and sprinkle with the cinnamon-sugar mixture. Lay another strip on top of the first and brush with the oil again and sprinkle with the cinnamon-sugar mixture. Spoon 1 tablespoon of the fruit-nut mixture at one end of strip. Fold the short edge at a diagonal over the filling so that it meets the long edge and forms a triangle. Brush the triangle lightly with the oil and sprinkle with the cinnamon-sugar mixture. Continue folding the strip back and forth like a flag, brushing with the oil and sprinkling with the cinnamon-sugar, until you reach the end. Place the turnover on a cookie sheet. Repeat the process with the remaining phyllo, oil, cinnamon-sugar mixture and filling.

PREHEAT the oven to 400°F. Bake turnovers, turning once, until lightly browned, about 10 minutes.

PER TURNOVER:
101 Cal.; 2g Prot.; 4g Fat; 17g Carb.;
0mg Chol.; 41mg Sod.; 1g Fiber.

Pear Cobbler

serves 4

Serve this dessert with scoops of ice cream, or try it for breakfast the next morning with a dollop of yogurt.

> 4 peeled, sliced pears
> 1/4 cup raisins or currants
> 4 teaspoons brown sugar
> 1/4 teaspoon ground cinnamon
> 1/4 teaspoon vanilla extract
> 1 cup rolled oats
> 3 tablespoons whole-wheat pastry flour
> 4 teaspoons margarine

PREHEAT the oven to 325°F. Combine the pears, raisins or currants, 3 teaspoons brown sugar, cinnamon and vanilla in a medium bowl. Transfer this mixture to an 8-inch square baking pan.

IN A SMALL BOWL, mix the oats, remaining 1 teaspoon brown sugar, flour and margarine with a fork until the margarine is evenly distributed and the mixture is crumbly. Spoon it on top of the pear mixture. Bake until browned, about 45 minutes. Let cool slightly before serving. Serve warm or chilled.

Variation:

Substitute apples, plums, nectarines, peaches, cherries or blueberries for the pears.

PER SERVING:
245 Cal.; 5g Prot.; 4g Fat; 41g Carb.;
0mg Chol.; 27mg Sod.; 7g Fiber.

Cran-Raspberry Crisp

serves 6

This old-time dessert was a simple affair in the Old World, made with the kind of sour cherries that grew wild. Here we've substituted cranberries and given them even more sparkle with raspberries.

- 4 cups fresh or frozen cranberries
- One 10-ounce package frozen sweetened raspberries, thawed
- 3/4 cup quick-cooking rolled oats
- 1/2 cup brown sugar
- 1/2 cup unsifted unbleached all-purpose flour
- 1 teaspoon ground cinnamon
- 1/4 cup cold butter or margarine
- Frozen vanilla yogurt (optional)

PREHEAT the oven to 375°F. If you're using fresh cranberries, wash them in cold water. If you're using frozen berries, place them in a colander and run warm water over them to thaw slightly. Drain. Place the cranberries in a 9-inch round or square baking pan, and spoon the raspberries over them.

IN A SMALL MIXING BOWL, combine the oats, brown sugar, flour and cinnamon. With your fingertips, rub the cold butter or margarine into the mixture until it resembles cornmeal. Sprinkle the mixture evenly over the berries.

BAKE until the crumb topping is crisp and brown, about 30 minutes. Serve warm with scoops of frozen yogurt.

> **PER SERVING:**
> 290 Cal.; 3g Prot.; 8g Fat; 26g Carb.;
> 20mg Chol.; 86mg Sod.; 6g Fiber.

Banana-Blueberry Crisp

serves 4

This dish makes a great dessert, breakfast or snack. Serve it with yogurt or ice cream.

- 2 cups cooked rice or cooked bulgur
- 2/3 cup skim milk
- 1/4 cup brown sugar
- 1 tablespoon margarine, melted (optional)
- 1 teaspoon ground cinnamon
- 2 bananas, peeled and sliced
- 2 cups fresh or frozen blueberries

PREHEAT the oven to 350°F. In a bowl, combine the rice or bulgur, milk, brown sugar, margarine and cinnamon. Add the fruit and mix gently. Transfer the mixture to an 8-inch square baking pan, and cover with foil. Bake 30 minutes. Let cool slightly before serving.

> **PER SERVING:**
> 277 Cal.; 5g Prot.; 0.9g Fat; 49g Carb.;
> 1mg Chol.; 35mg Sod.; 4g Fiber.

Pear-Almond Clafouti with Red Wine Glaze

serves 8

This is an adaptation of a classic French clafouti, a baked custardy puff somewhat similar to a popover but with the tasty addition of fresh fruit. This version takes only minutes to assemble.

CLAFOUTI

- 2 cups whole-wheat pastry flour or unbleached white flour
- 1 1/2 cups almond meal (see Note)
- 2 1/2 teaspoons baking powder
- 1/3 cup soymilk or low-fat milk
- 2/3 cup honey or fruit juice concentrate
- 1 teaspoon vanilla extract
- 1/3 cup honey or apple juice concentrate
- 2 teaspoons fresh lemon juice
- 2 firm pears, cored and sliced lengthwise

GLAZE

- 2/3 cup red wine
- 1/3 cup honey or fruit juice concentrate
- 3 to 4 tablespoons arrowroot or cornstarch
- 3 to 4 tablespoons water

CLAFOUTI: Preheat the oven to 375°F. Combine the flour with 1 cup almond meal and baking powder in a bowl. Mix together the soymilk or milk, 2/3 cup honey or fruit juice concentrate, and vanilla; pour into the flour mixture, mixing well. Pat the dough into a greased 9-inch cake pan or quiche pan. Combine the remaining 1/2 cup almond meal with 1/3 cup honey or apple juice concen-trate, and lemon juice; spread over the dough. Arrange the pear slices on top in a spiral pattern. Bake 30 to 35 minutes.

GLAZE: Combine the wine and honey or fruit juice concentrate in a small saucepan and heat to a simmer. Dissolve the arrowroot or cornstarch in an equal amount of water and whisk into the wine mixture, cooking until thickened. Brush the hot glaze over the pears. Serve hot or warm.

Note:

To make almond meal, chop the nuts in a blender or food processor and transfer to a bowl. Place 1/2 cup in your blender or food processor, blend briefly, stir and repeat until you have a fine grind. Do not over-grind—you may end up with almond butter.

Helpful hint:

Cornstarch will thicken the glaze as well as arrow-root, but arrowroot will give pears a glossier appear-ance.

> **PER SERVING:**
> 502 Cal.; 19g Prot.; 8g Fat; 84g Carb.;
> 0mg Chol.; 144mg Sod.; 6g Fiber.

Apple-Cinnamon Strudel

serves 14

Less than a gram of fat per serving? You better believe it—and the strudel is absolutely delicious.

STRUDEL

- 8 medium Granny Smith apples, peeled, cored and sliced
- 1/2 cup raisins
- 2 tablespoons honey or brown sugar
- Ground cinnamon to taste
- Ground nutmeg to taste
- 6 sheets frozen phyllo, partially thawed and covered with a damp dishcloth

CINNAMON SAUCE

- 2 cups apple cider
- 4 teaspoons cornstarch or arrowroot
- Ground cinnamon to taste
- Ground nutmeg to taste

STRUDEL: Preheat the oven to 400°F. Mix the apples and raisins with the sweetener; sprinkle with the cinnamon and nutmeg. Lay 1 sheet of phyllo on a greased cookie sheet. Spray the phyllo with nonstick cooking spray or a mist of water. Lay another sheet of phyllo on top of the first one, spray with cooking spray or water and place a third sheet on top.

SPOON half of the apple mixture on the phyllo and roll up lengthwise, turning in the ends to enclose the filling. Cut 3/4 of the way through the roll to make 7 servings. Repeat the procedure with the other 3 sheets of phyllo and the remaining apple mixture. Bake until lightly browned, about 15 to 20 minutes.

CINNAMON SAUCE: Combine the cider, cornstarch or arrowroot, and spices in a small saucepan. Whisk thoroughly. Heat to a boil, stirring constantly.

TO SERVE, use a sharp knife to separate slices of strudel. Top with the warm sauce.

> **PER SERVING WITH 2 TABLESPOONS SAUCE:**
> 105 Cal.; 1g Prot.; 0.2g Fat; 24g Carb.;
> 0mg Chol.; 38mg Sod.; 3g Fiber.

Cream Cheese Frosting

makes 2/3 cup

This guilt-free frosting is made with fat-free cream cheese. For flavor sensations, check out the variations.

- 3 ounces fat-free cream cheese, at room temperature
- 1 tablespoon nonfat plain or vanilla yogurt
- 1/2 teaspoon vanilla extract
- 1 to 3 tablespoons confectioners sugar

IN A BLENDER, blend the cream cheese, yogurt and vanilla extract until smooth. Add the confectioners sugar and continue blending until creamy.

Variations:

- Berry Frosting: Substitute 1 tablespoon frozen cranberry or raspberry juice concentrate for vanilla extract and add an additional tablespoon of confectioners sugar.
- Lemon Frosting: Substitute an equal quantity of lemon extract for vanilla extract and add 1 teaspoon grated lemon zest.
- Coconut Frosting: Substitute an equal quantity of coconut extract for vanilla extract. Frost the cake and sprinkle it with sweetened coconut shreds.

> **PER 2/3 CUP:**
> 120 Cal.; 18g Prot.; 0g Fat; 10g Carb.;
> 2mg Chol.; 450mg Sod.; 0g Fiber.

Chocolate Glaze

makes 1/4 cup

| 1 square unsweetened baking chocolate
| 2 tablespoons honey, or more to taste
| 1/2 teaspoon vanilla extract

IN A HEAVY SAUCEPAN or double boiler, melt the chocolate over very low heat. Stir in the honey and vanilla.

> **PER 1/4 CUP:**
> 275 Cal.; 3g Prot.; 15g Fat; 42g Carb.;
> 0mg Chol.; 3mg Sod.; 2g Fiber.

Mock Whipped Cream

makes 1 cup

After you've tasted this low-fat whipped cream, you won't want to serve the regular version. Be sure to buy very fresh tofu to avoid bitterness.

| 8 ounces soft tofu, drained
| 2 tablespoons maple syrup, or to taste
| 1 teaspoon vanilla extract
| 1 teaspoon grated orange rind
| Dash ground nutmeg

PURÉE all the ingredients in a blender or food processor until very smooth and creamy. Add more maple syrup to taste. Cover and chill 20 minutes before serving.

> **PER TABLESPOON:**
> 19 Cal.; 1g Prot.; 0.5g Fat; 1g Carb.;
> 0mg Chol.; 1mg Sod.; 0g Fiber.

No-Roll Pie Crust

makes one 9-inch pie crust

This crust becomes its flaky best if allowed to chill at least 20 minutes before filling.

| 3/4 cup unbleached white flour
| 1 tablespoon sesame seeds
| 3 tablespoons butter or margarine
| 1 tablespoon white vinegar
| 1/2 to 1 tablespoon ice water, as needed

SPRAY a 9-inch pie pan with nonstick cooking spray; set aside. Place the flour, sesame seeds, and butter or margarine in a food processor fitted with a steel blade. Process the mixture to a coarse meal.

WHILE THE MACHINE is running, slowly add the vinegar through the feed tube, then add tiny dribbles of the ice water, stopping the machine as soon as the dough leaves the sides of bowl. Transfer the dough to the pie pan and press it with your fingertips to cover the bottom and sides evenly. Chill 20 to 30 minutes. Fill and bake the crust as your recipe directs.

Helpful hint:

For pies with an uncooked filling, poke the chilled pie crust with the tines of a fork, then bake at 400°F for 10 minutes. Cool before filling.

> **PER 1/8 CRUST:**
> 81 Cal.; 1g Prot.; 5g Fat; 8g Carb.;
> 11mg Chol.; 44mg Sod.; 0g Fiber.

23

baked goods

NO WORDS CAN ADEQUATELY DESCRIBE THE TASTE AND AROMA of fresh-baked bread. Your senses delight in homemade breads, rolls, muffins, ethnic specialties and other baked goods; their store-bought counterparts pale in comparison. True, homemade baked goods may take some time and effort to make, but the payoff . . . well, taste it for yourself. By the way, the secret to baking yeasted breads successfully is experience. So if your first loaves don't turn out as well as you'd like, try again. For baked goods without yeast, simply measure the ingredients and follow the directions exactly.

Whole-Wheat Bread

makes 2 loaves • serves 16

2 teaspoons active dry yeast

1/2 cup warm water (about 110°F)

6 cups whole-wheat flour

1/2 teaspoon salt

2 tablespoons honey

2 1/4 cups lukewarm water

2 tablespoons vegetable oil (optional)

DISSOLVE yeast in warm water. Set aside. In a large bowl, mix together flour and salt, and make a well in the center. Dissolve honey in lukewarm water and add oil if desired. Pour the yeast and honey mixtures into the well. Stir from the center outward, incorporating the liquid ingredients into the flour. Fold in the remaining flour from the sides of the bowl and stir until the mixture forms a soft dough. Add a small amount of water if the dough is too dry, or a bit of flour if the dough is too sticky.

TURN OUT the dough onto a breadboard. For best results, knead the dough about 20 minutes, or 600 strokes, without adding any more flour. The dough should be elastic and smooth.

FORM the dough into a smooth ball and place in a large clean bowl. Cover the bowl with a platter or plastic sheet and place in a warm, draft-free spot so the dough can rise. At about 80°F, the rising will take 1 1/2 to 2 hours; at 70°F, 2 1/2 hours.

AFTER THE ALLOTTED TIME, wet your finger with water and poke it about 1/2 inch into the dough. The dough is ready if the hole doesn't fill in. Gently press out the air, making the dough into a smooth ball. Return it to the bowl for a second rise, which will take about half as long as the first. Use the finger-poke test again.

AFTER THE SECOND RISING, turn the dough onto a lightly floured tabletop or breadboard. Wet or flour your hands and deflate the dough by pressing it gently from one side to the other. Cut it in half and form each part into a round ball. Let the rounded balls rest, covered, about 10 minutes.

SHAPE each ball into a loaf, and place the loaves in 2 greased 8×4-inch loaf pans. Let rise again, about 30 to 45 minutes. Preheat the oven to 425°F. Bake 10 minutes, then lower the temperature to 325°F. Bake until done, about 45 to 60 minutes. When done, the loaves should slide easily out of the pans and be a golden brown color. Tap their bottoms with your fingertips; they should sound hollow. Let cool before slicing.

> **PER SERVING:**
> 127 Cal.; 5g Prot.; 0.7g Fat; 27g Carb.;
> 0 Chol.; 268mg Sod.; 8g Fiber.

Challah

serves 24

Challah is a braided, slightly sweet egg bread served every Friday night for the Jewish Sabbath meal. On Rosh Hashanah it is made into a circle to symbolize the cycle of the year, and it contains raisins for added sweetness in the year ahead.

1 teaspoon salt

1 tablespoon sugar

2 tablespoons canola oil

2 cups hot water

1 tablespoon instant potato flakes

2 packages rapid-rise yeast

1/4 cup lukewarm water

3 large eggs, beaten (or 3/4 cup egg substitute)

1 cup golden raisins (optional)

8 cups unbleached white flour, plus extra for kneading

1 egg yolk mixed with 1 to 2 tablespons water
(or 2 tablespoons egg substitute)

COMBINE salt, sugar, oil, hot water and potato flakes in a large mixing bowl. Stir to dissolve, then set aside and let cool. In a small cup, dissolve yeast in lukewarm water and set aside. When the yeast begins to foam, it's ready to use.

WHEN the potato mixture has cooled to lukewarm, stir in the yeast mixture and eggs or egg substitute. Add raisins if desired. Gradually stir in flour until the mixture holds together as a ball and is no longer sticky. Transfer the dough to a well-floured work surface.

KNEAD the dough for 10 minutes. Add flour as needed to keep the dough from sticking to the work surface and your hands. When done, the dough should be smooth, warm and springy.

WASH, dry and oil the mixing bowl. Place the dough in the bowl and turn it over so the oiled surface is on top. Cover the bowl with a dishcloth and set it in a warm, draft-free spot for 1 1/2 hours. It should triple in bulk. Deflate the dough, cover the bowl, and let the dough rise again until tripled in bulk, about 30 minutes to 1 hour. (Omit this second rising if you're short on time.)

DEFLATE the dough and place it on a clean, floured surface. Cut off 1/3 of the dough, cover it with a dishcloth, and set aside. Cut the remaining dough into 3 equal parts. With floured hands, roll each piece back and forth into a thick rope about 16 inches long. Place the 3 ropes on an oiled baking sheet, pinch together firmly at one end and braid loosely. Pinch together the other end. Join the ends to make a circle, cover the dough with a dishcloth, and set aside.

CUT the remaining dough into 3 equal parts. Roll each into a thin rope 16 inches long and make a thin braid, pinching the top and bottom together as before. Center this braid on top of the large one and tuck the ends of the smaller braid into the last fold of the large braid. Cover with a dishcloth and let rise until doubled in bulk, about 30 minutes.

PREHEAT the oven to 400°F. Lightly brush the challah with the egg-water mixture or egg substitute. Bake for 20 minutes. Lower the temperature to 375°F and continue baking until golden brown, about 40 to 45 minutes. Cool on a rack before serving.

> **PER SERVING:**
> 162 Cal.; 5g Prot.; 2g Fat; 30g Carb.;
> 36mg Chol.; 99mg Sod.; 1g Fiber.

Three Kings Bread

serves 16

Here's the perfect bread to serve at the Epiphany, celebrating the time when the wise men find Jesus in the manger.

Basic Sweetened Bread Dough (recipe follows)

3/4 cup raisins

3/4 cup chopped nuts

1/3 cup chopped or dried cherries

1 1/2 tablespoons grated orange peel

Golden Glaze (page 441) or glaze of your choice

Whole nuts and candied or dried fruit for decoration
(optional)

MAKE the Basic Sweetened Bread Dough, adding raisins, nuts, cherries and orange peel with the final 3 cups flour.

DIVIDE the risen dough into thirds. Roll each third into a 20-inch-long roll. Join the ends of each roll to form 3 separate rings. Place the rings on greased cookie sheets. Cover with a dishcloth and let rise until doubled in bulk, about 1 to 2 hours.

PREHEAT the oven to 350°F. Bake until the crusts are golden brown, about 30 minutes. Cool on racks, then glaze with Golden Glaze. Decorate with nuts and fruit to resemble the "crowns" of the Three Kings.

> **PER SERVING
> (WITHOUT GLAZE):**
> 281 Cal.; 6g Prot.; 7g Fat; 50g Carb.;
> 0 Chol.; 269mg Sod.; 3g Fiber.

Basic Sweetened Bread Dough

serves 16

This dough may be used to make other sweetened breads, including some wonderful holiday breads.

2 cups soymilk

1/2 cup plus 1 teaspoon honey

2 tablespoons fresh lemon juice

2 teaspoons salt

1/2 cup vegetable oil

3/4 cup warm water

2 tablespoons active dry yeast

2 tablespoons potato flour or starch

7 cups unbleached white flour or whole-wheat bread
flour (or use half of each)

IN A SMALL SAUCEPAN. heat the soymilk just until bubbles form around the edges. Remove from the heat. Stir in 1/2 cup honey, lemon juice, salt and oil. Let cool.

PLACE the warm water in a large mixing bowl and stir in the 1 teaspoon honey. Sprinkle in the yeast and potato flour or starch and let dissolve. Pour in the soymilk mixture. Stir in 3 cups flour of choice. Beat 2 minutes with a wooden spoon or an electric mixer. Add 1 more cup flour and beat 2 minutes more. Then work in the remaining 3 cups flour and knead on a lightly floured surface for 10 minutes, adding a little more flour if necessary. The dough should feel velvety smooth, not sticky.

PLACE the dough in a lightly oiled bowl, cover with a dishcloth and let rise in a warm place until doubled, about 1 1/2 hours. Deflate the dough. To finish making the bread, see the specific recipe you are using for instructions.

> **PER SERVING:**
> 281 Cal.; 6g Prot.; 8g Fat; 48g Carb.;
> 0 Chol.; 269mg Sod.; 2g Fiber.

Golden Glaze

makes 1 cup

| 1/4 cup soya-lecithin spread or margarine
| 1/4 cup light honey or maple syrup
| 1/2 cup instant soymilk powder
| Pinch salt
| 1 teaspoon vanilla extract or grated citrus fruit rind
| Soymilk for thinning (optional)

In a food processor or blender, process all ingredients until smooth. Thin the mixture with a little soymilk if it is too thick to spread.

> **PER CUP:**
> 860 Cal.; 12g Prot.; 55g Fat; 87g Carb.;
> 0 Chol.; 216mg Sod.; 0 Fiber.

Basic Dinner Crepes

makes 12 to 16

| 4 eggs
| 1 1/4 cups water
| 1 cup low-fat milk or soymilk
| 1/2 teaspoon salt
| 2 tablespoons vegetable oil
| 2 cups whole-wheat pastry flour or unbleached white
| flour

PROCESS all the ingredients in a blender or food processor at high speed for 1 minute. Pour the mixture into a bowl. Cover and refrigerate for 2 hours before cooking. The batter should be the consistency of heavy cream. If necessary, thin with more liquid.

TO COOK CREPES, use either a well-seasoned omelet or crepe pan, or a nonstick 8-inch skillet. Brush the pan lightly with oil, and place over low heat for a few minutes. Remove from the heat, pour in 3 or 4 tablespoons of batter, and tilt the pan so the batter coats the bottom of the pan lightly. Return the pan to medium-low heat and cook for a few minutes until the crepe is lightly browned or begins to bubble. Using a spatula, flip the crepe and cook 30 seconds more. Gently remove the crepe from the pan and place on a plate. Repeat process with the remaining batter, stacking the crepes as they're cooked. The crepes may be used at once or wrapped well in plastic and refrigerated for up to one week. They also freeze well.

> **PER CREPE:**
> 124 Cal.; 5g Prot.; 5g Fat; 16g Carb.;
> 73mg Chol.; 123mg Sod.; 0.5g Fiber.

No-Cholesterol Dinner Crepes

makes 12 to 16

| 2 tablespoons egg substitute
| 1 1/2 cups water
| 1 cup soymilk
| 1/2 teaspoon salt
| 2 tablespoons oil
| 2 cups whole-wheat pastry flour or unbleached white
| flour
| 1/2 cup chickpea flour

COMBINE the egg substitute with 1/2 cup water in a blender or food processor and blend until smoth. Add remaining ingredients and blend 1 minute at high speed. Cook the crepes according to directions for Basic Dinner Crepes.

PER CREPE:
115 Cal.; 4g Prot.; 3g Fat; 19g Carb.;
0 Chol.; 90mg Sod.; 0.8g Fiber.

Feather-Bed Biscuits

makes 12

- 2 cups unbleached white flour
- 1 tablespoon sugar
- 1 tablespoon baking powder
- 1/2 to 1 teaspoon salt (optional)
- 1/4 cup vegetable shortening
- 1 package active dry yeast
- 1/3 cup lukewarm water
- 3/4 cup lukewarm skim milk
- Melted butter (optional)

IN A LARGE BOWL, sift together the flour, sugar, baking powder and salt. Cut in the shortening until the mixture resembles coarse meal. Set aside.

IN A SMALL BOWL, sprinkle the yeast over the warm water. Stir until the yeast dissolves. Add the milk and mix well. Add the yeast mixture to the dry ingredients and stir with a fork until moistened. The dough will be sticky.

TURN OUT the dough onto a heavily floured breadboard and knead gently until smooth, about 30 seconds. Cover the dough with a dishcloth and let rise for 20 minutes.

GENTLY ROLL out the dough to a 1/2-inch thickness. Cut it with a floured heart-shaped cutter and arrange the hearts 2 inches apart on an ungreased baking sheet. Preheat the oven to 400°F while the biscuits rise on the baking sheet for 15 minutes. After they have risen, place the biscuits in your oven and bake for 12 to 15 minutes. If desired, brush the tops of the hot biscuits with melted butter. Cool on a rack.

PER BISCUIT:
116 Cal.; 3g Prot.; 4g Fat; 16g Carb.;
1mg Chol.; 204mg Sod.; 1g Fiber.

One-Rise Breadsticks

makes 12

- 1 package active dry yeast
- 1/2 cup lukewarm water
- 1 teaspoon plus 1 1/2 tablespoons honey
- 1/3 cup canola oil
- 1/2 cup boiling water
- 1/2 cup egg substitute, divided
- 3 1/2 to 4 cups whole-wheat pastry flour
- Sesame seeds

IN A SMALL BOWL, combine the yeast, water and 1 teaspoon honey; set aside for 5 minutes. In a large bowl, mix the oil, remaining honey and boiling water. Let cool to lukewarm. Add 1/4 cup egg substitute and the yeast mixture; mix well.

GRADUALLY STIR in 3 1/2 cups flour; mix well, but do not knead. If the dough is too soft and sticky to handle, add a small amount of additional flour. Cover with a dishcloth and place in your refrigerator to chill until firm.

SPRAY a baking sheet with nonstick cooking spray. Divide the dough into 12 equal parts. With floured hands, roll each part into a stick about 12 inches long. Place the sticks 1 1/2 inches apart on the prepared baking sheet. Brush with the remaining 1/4 cup egg substitute, then sprinkle with sesame seeds. Let rise in a warm place for 30 minutes. Preheat the oven to 425°F. Bake 15 minutes. Serve warm.

> **PER BREADSTICK:**
> 199 Cal.; 6g Prot.; 8g Fat; 24g Carb.;
> 0 Chol.; 22mg Sod.; 5g Fiber.

Hot Corn Sticks

makes 14

| 1 cup unbleached white flour
| 3/4 cup cornmeal
| 1/4 cup sugar
| 2 teaspoons baking powder
| 1/4 teaspoon salt
| 3/4 cup skim milk or soymilk
| 1/4 cup canola oil
| 1 egg, lightly beaten

PREHEAT the oven to 450°F. Generously spray 2 cast iron "ear of corn" pans with nonstick cooking spray. In a medium bowl, sift the flour with the cornmeal, sugar, baking powder and salt. Add the milk or soymilk, oil and egg. Stir with a fork until just blended. Do not overmix. Fill the pans 3/4 full.

BAKE until golden brown, about 20 minutes. Serve at once. Or remove the cornbread from the pans, let cool, and wrap them tightly in foil. Reheat before serving.

> **PER STICK:**
> 111 Cal.; 3g Prot.; 4g Fat; 15g Carb.;
> 20mg Chol.; 114mg Sod.; 1g Fiber.

Orange Almond Scones

makes 6

SCONES
| 2 cups flour (unbleached white flour or whole-wheat pastry flour, or a combination)
| 1/4 teaspoon salt
| 2 teaspoons baking powder
| 1/2 teaspoon baking soda
| 1/4 cup vegetable oil or margarine
| 1/3 cup honey or maple syrup
| 1/3 cup thawed frozen orange juice concentrate
| Grated zest of 1 orange
| 1/2 to 3/4 ripe banana, mashed
| 1/2 teaspoon almond extract (optional)
| 1/3 to 1/2 cup soymilk or low-fat milk

TOPPING
| 2 tablespoons thawed frozen orange juice concentrate
| 2 tablespoons honey
| 1/3 cup sliced almonds (optional)

TO MAKE the scones, in a large bowl, combine the flour with the salt, baking powder and baking soda. With a fork, stir in the oil or margarine. Add the honey or maple syrup, orange juice concentrate, orange zest, banana and almond extract if desired. Mix lightly. Stir in the soymilk or milk. Let stand 10 minutes.

PREHEAT the oven to 350°F. Form the dough into 6 circles or triangles about 1/2 inch thick. Place on a lightly greased baking sheet.

FOR THE TOPPING, mix together the orange juice concentrate and honey and brush the topping onto the dough. Sprinkle with almonds if desired. Bake 15 minutes.

PER SCONE:
318 Cal.; 5g Prot.; 8g Fat; 37g Carb.;
0 Chol.; 302mg Sod.; 1g Fiber.

PREHEAT the oven to 350°F. Oil a 9×5-inch loaf pan. In a large bowl, blend the tofu, soymilk or milk, juice, maple syrup and vanilla with a fork. Stir in the cornmeal, flour, starch, baking powder, baking soda and salt; mix well. Set aside for 10 minutes.

FOLD IN the remaining ingredients. Pour the batter into the prepared pan and bake until a toothpick inserted in the center comes out clean, about 45 minutes.

PER SERVING:
393 Cal.; 9g Prot.; 9g Fat; 68g Carb.;
0 Chol.; 469mg Sod.; 6g Fiber.

Berry-Pecan Cornbread

serves 6

1/3 cup silken tofu
1 3/4 cups soymilk or milk
1/2 cup cranberry-apple juice
1/4 cup maple syrup
2 teaspoons vanilla extract
1 3/4 cups cornmeal
1/2 cup unbleached white flour
1/4 cup tapioca starch, potato starch or cornstarch
2 teaspoons baking powder
1 teaspoon baking soda
1/2 teaspoon salt
1/4 cup sesame seeds
1 1/2 cups dried tart cherries or chopped cranberries
1/3 cup toasted whole pecans (page 106)

Focaccia with Coarse Salt and Fennel

serves 6

1 teaspoon active dry yeast
1 teaspoon sugar
1 1/2 cups warm water
5 to 6 cups all-purpose flour
1 1/2 teaspoons salt
1/4 cup olive oil
Olive oil for brushing dough
2 to 4 teaspoons coarse salt
1 to 2 teaspoons fennel seeds

DISSOLVE the yeast and sugar in 1/2 cup warm water. Let sit until bubbly, about 10 minutes. Combine 5 cups flour and salt in a mixing bowl. Make a well in the center and pour in the yeast mixture and olive oil. Stir until combined, adding enough of the remaining water to make a dough.

TURN OUT the dough onto a floured surface and knead until smooth, about 10 minutes. Knead in just enough of the remaining 1 cup flour to make the dough easy to handle. Place the dough in an oiled bowl and cover with a damp dishcloth. Let rise in a warm spot until doubled in bulk, about 1 hour.

DIVIDE the dough into 2 or 3 pieces and knead each piece briefly. Shape each piece into a ball and let rest for about 10 minutes. Then roll out each ball into a 5- to 6-inch circle or oval about 1/2 inch thick. Place the dough on a heavy baking sheet. Make small slits all the way through the dough in a pattern; then stretch the dough to form openings.

PREHEAT the oven to 425°F. Brush the dough with olive oil and sprinkle coarse salt and fennel seeds over. (At this point, you may cover the dough and refrigerate it up to 1 day. Then let the chilled dough sit at room temperature for about 30 minutes before baking.) Bake on the middle shelf of your oven for about 10 minutes. Then lower the heat to 400°F and continue baking until bread is browned, about 10 to 20 minutes more.

> **PER SERVING:**
> 444 Cal.; 10g Prot.; 12g Fat; 63g Carb.;
> 0 Chol.; 1,246mg Sod.; 3g Fiber.

Whole-Wheat Apple Bread

makes 1 loaf, 12 slices

- 1 1/4 cups whole-wheat pastry flour
- 1/2 cup bran cereal
- 2 teaspoons ground cinnamon
- 1 teaspoon ground nutmeg
- 1 teaspoon ground allspice
- 1 teaspoon baking powder
- 1/2 teaspoon baking soda
- 1/2 teaspoon salt
- 1 1/2 cups peeled and diced tart apples, such as Granny Smith
- 1/2 cup chopped pitted dates
- 1/2 cup unsweetened applesauce
- 1/3 cup buttermilk or soymilk
- 3 tablespoons safflower oil
- 1 egg, lightly beaten (or equivalent egg substitute)
- 1/3 cup thawed apple juice concentrate

PREHEAT the oven to 400°F. Lightly oil a 9×5-inch loaf pan or spray it with nonstick cooking spray. Dust with flour. Shake out excess flour.

IN A LARGE BOWL, combine the flour, cereal, cinnamon, nutmeg, allspice, baking powder, baking soda and salt. Add the apples and dates, then toss to coat. In another bowl, lightly whisk together the remaining ingredients.

COMBINE the contents of both bowls, folding until the wet and dry ingredients are just blended. Spoon the batter into the prepared pan. Bake 25 minutes, then lower the heat to 300°F and bake until a toothpick inserted in the center comes out clean, about 15 minutes more.

Pizza Crust

makes one 13-to-14-inch crust

More nutritious than takeout. When you top it, go heavy on the vegetables and light on the cheese.

- 1 1/4 cups whole-wheat flour
- 1/4 cup gluten flour
- 1/2 teaspoon reduced-sodium salt
- 1 tablespoon fast-rising yeast
- 2/3 to 3/4 cup very hot tap water (about 130°F)

IN A FOOD PROCESSOR fitted with a metal "S" blade, combine the flours, salt and yeast. Pulse on and off to mix. With the machine running, pour hot water slowly through the feed tube. Stop adding water as soon as the dough forms a ball.

TURN OFF the machine and feel the dough. It should be sticky, stretchy and quite moist. If the dough is dry, add an additional tablespoon water; if the dough is water-logged, add flour as needed. Process the dough for about 40 seconds to knead. Transfer the dough to a well-floured board and let sit for 2 minutes. Then roll out to a diameter of 13 to 14 inches. Top the dough as desired and bake at 450°F until the crust begins to brown, about 10 minutes.

Basic Biscuit Crust

makes 1 crust to cover a
9×12-inch baking pan

This biscuit crust makes a delicious base for pot pies. You may use soymilk in place of buttermilk but the result will be heavier.

- 1 3/4 cups unbleached white flour or whole-wheat pastry flour
- 2 teaspoons baking powder
- 1/2 teaspoon baking soda
- 1/2 teaspoon salt (optional)
- 2 tablespoons butter or safflower margarine
- 3/4 cup buttermilk or soymilk
- 2 teaspoons honey

IN A LARGE BOWL, sift together the flour, baking powder, baking soda and salt if desired. Using a pastry blender or fork, cut the butter or margarine into the flour mixture until it resembles coarse meal. In a measuring cup, combine the buttermilk or soymilk and honey. Add the liquid measure to the flour mixture, stirring with a fork to form a stiff dough. Add more buttermilk or soymilk if the dough is too dry. Knead lightly in the bowl until the dough is no longer sticky, about 3 to 5 minutes. Then turn out the dough onto a lightly floured surface. Roll out into the desired shape.

Blueberry Buttermilk Coffeecake

serves 12

- 1 cup whole-wheat flour
- 1 cup unbleached white flour
- 2 teaspoons baking powder
- 2 teaspoons baking soda
- 1/4 teaspoon salt
- 2 cups fresh or frozen blueberries
- 3/4 cup honey or maple syrup
- 1 egg plus 3 egg whites (or equivalent egg substitute)
- 1/4 cup canola oil
- 1/3 cup pureed pitted prunes
- 3/4 cup buttermilk or soymilk
- 1/2 cup mashed banana
- 1 tablespoon chopped walnuts
- 1/3 cup brown sugar

PREHEAT the oven to 350°F. Lightly oil a 13×9-inch baking dish or spray with nonstick cooking spray. In a large bowl, sift together the flours, baking powder, baking soda and salt. Fold in the blueberries. In another bowl, whisk together the honey or maple syrup, egg and egg whites, oil, prunes, buttermilk or soymilk, and banana.

COMBINE the contents of both bowls, mixing briefly, then pour the batter into the baking dish. Smooth the top of the batter with a spatula. Sprinkle with walnuts and brown sugar. Bake until a toothpick inserted in the center comes out clean, about 40 to 50 minutes. Let cool, then cut into serving pieces.

> **PER SERVING:**
> 245 Cal.; 5g Prot.; 5g Fat; 22g Carb.;
> 14mg Chol.; 292mg Sod.; 3g Fiber.

Fruity Bran Muffins

makes 12

Most muffins are high in fat, but not these nutritious treats.

- 1 1/4 cups whole-wheat flour
- 1/2 cup oat bran
- 1/4 cup wheat bran
- 2 teaspoons baking powder
- 1 tablespoon vegetable oil
- 1/4 cup honey
- 1 whole egg (or 2 egg whites), beaten
- 2/3 cup skim milk or soymilk
- 1/2 cup unsweetened applesauce
- 1/2 teaspoon vanilla extract
- 2 medium ripe bananas, mashed

PREHEAT the oven to 350°F. Grease muffin tins. Stir together the dry ingredients and set aside. In a bowl, combine the oil and honey. Whisk in the egg or egg whites, milk, applesauce and vanilla. Combine the dry and wet ingredients until just blended. Gently fold the bananas into the batter. Spoon the batter into the muffin tins. Bake until the muffins just begin to brown, about 20 to 30 minutes. Serve warm.

Variation:

Substitute 1 cup blueberries, or 1 cup chopped cranberries and 3 tablespoons granulated sugarcane juice, for the bananas.

> **PER MUFFIN:**
> 120 Cal.; 3g Prot.; 2g Fat; 23g Carb.;
> 18mg Chol.; 71mg Sod.; 3g Fiber.

Sweet-Tart Cranberry Muffins

makes 12

  1 1/4 cups unbleached white flour
  1/2 teaspoon ground cinnamon
  1/2 teaspoon ground cardamom
  1/2 teaspoon ground nutmeg
  1 teaspoon baking powder
  1/2 teaspoon baking soda
  1/2 teaspoon salt
  1/2 cup finely chopped pitted prunes
  1/2 cup rolled oats
  3/4 cup buttermilk or soymilk
  3 tablespoons canola oil
  6 tablespoons maple syrup
  1/2 cup fresh or frozen cranberries
  3 egg whites (or egg substitute), lightly beaten

PREHEAT the oven to 400°F. Line a 12-cup muffin tin with muffin papers (or spray it with nonstick cooking spray).

IN A LARGE BOWL, sift together the flour, cinnamon, cardamom, nutmeg, baking powder, baking soda and salt. Add the prunes and oats and toss to coat. In another bowl, whisk together the buttermilk or soymilk, oil, maple syrup and cranberries. In a third bowl, beat the egg whites or substitute to soft peaks. Set aside.

GENTLY combine the dry and wet ingredients, then fold in the eggs, until just incorporated. Spoon the batter into the muffin tins, filling 3/4 full. Bake until the muffins are light and springy to the touch, about 12 to 15 minutes.

> **PER MUFFIN:**
> 140 Cal.; 4g Prot.; 4g Fat; 17g Carb.;
> 1mg Chol.; 212mg Sod.; 2g Fiber.

Cheese Muffins

makes 12

  2 tablespoons chopped onion
  2 tablespoons butter or oil
  1 egg, beaten
  1 1/4 cups buttermilk
  1/2 cup grated Swiss or cheddar cheese
  3/4 teaspoon dill weed or parsley flakes
    (or 1/2 teaspoon dry mustard)
  1/2 cup whole-wheat pastry flour
  1/2 teaspoon salt
  1/2 teaspoon baking soda
  2 teaspoons baking powder
  2 1/4 cups rolled oats, coarsely ground into
    1 3/4 cups flour

PREHEAT the oven to 375°F. Oil a 12-cup muffin tin and set aside. Cook the onion in butter or oil, stirring, over medium heat until soft. Let cool. Transfer the onion to a large bowl and stir in the egg, buttermilk, cheese and seasonings. (Choose dill weed or parsley with Swiss and mustard with cheddar.)

SIFT together the whole-wheat flour, salt, baking soda and baking powder. Combine with the oat flour. Stir the dry ingredients into the cheese mixture until just blended. Spoon the batter into the muffin tins and bake about 15 minutes. When done, the muffins will be a creamy color on top and golden brown on the bottom and sides.

> **PER MUFFIN:**
> 111 Cal.; 6g Prot.; 6g Fat; 10g Carb.;
> 33mg Chol.; 230mg Sod.; 0.5g Fiber.

Simple Tortillas

makes 12

M any cooks use a tortilla press to make these Hispanic breads, but a rolling pin works just as well.

- **2 cups *masa harina* (available in the Mexican foods section of supermarkets)**
- **1 cup warm water**

MIX the *masa harina* with the water in a bowl to form a ball. If the dough is too dry to hold together, add a few more tablespoons of water. Knead the dough lightly for a few minutes, cover with a dishcloth, and let sit for 1 hour.

DIVIDE the dough into 2-inch balls. Preheat a heavy skillet or griddle over medium-high heat, and place a cloth napkin in a shallow basket. Place a ball of dough between two plastic bags and roll it into a 6-inch circle; place the circle on the hot griddle and cook until bubbles begin to form on the surface. Turn the tortilla and cook the other side for a few seconds only. As each tortilla is cooked, place it in the napkin and cover it completely. Repeat the procedure with the remaining dough. If desired, dip the tortillas briefly in hot oil to soften them for rolling or shaping into shells.

> **PER TORTILLA:**
> 72 Cal.; 2g Prot.; 0.5g Fat; 15g Carb.;
> 0 Chol.; 0 Sod.; 3g Fiber.

Flame Toasted Whole-Wheat Tortilla

makes 6

- **6 whole-wheat tortillas**
- **Flavored oil or melted butter (optional)**

PLACE one tortilla directly over a medium-high gas flame or on a cookie rack set over an electric burner. Toast until the surface becomes lightly flecked with char, about 10 to 20 seconds, and the tortilla begins to fill with steam. Turn over and toast the other side. The perfect tortilla will fill with steam and puff up if it has no tears or holes.

IF DESIRED, brush the tortilla with oil or butter. Place it in a towel-lined basket while toasting the remaining tortillas. Serve hot.

> **PER TORTILLA:**
> 130 Cal.; 4g Prot.; 1g Fat.; 26g Carb.;
> 0 Chol.; 250mg Sod.; 3g Fiber.

Simple Chapatis

Makes 12

I ndia's daily flatbread is called chapati. Made with wheat flour and water, it is very thin, soft and pliable.

- **1/2 cup unbleached white flour**
- **1 cup whole-wheat flour**
- **1 cup whole-wheat pastry flour**
- **1/2 teaspoon salt**
- **1 scant cup water**

MIX together the flours and salt in a bowl. Add the water a little at a time, tossing the flour with a fork as you pour. When the dough comes together in a ball, turn it out onto a floured board. Knead until firm, smooth and elastic, about 5 to 8 minutes. Let sit at room temperature for 30 minutes.

WITH YOUR HANDS, form the dough into 12 balls the size of large walnuts. On a lightly floured surface, roll each ball into a very thin, flat circle about 7 inches in diameter.

HEAT a cast-iron skillet until a drop of water bounces off the surface. Cook the chapatis on one side until a big bubble of steam forms in the center, then cook the other side. There should be toasty brown spots on each side. Keep the chapatis warm by stacking them in a towel-lined basket and placing the basket in a 200°F oven.

> **PER CHAPATI:**
> 83 Cal.; 3g Prot.; 0.4g Fat; 18g Carb.;
> 0 Chol.; 90mg Sod.; 1g Fiber.

Cumin Nan

serves 6

DOUGH

- 2 cups unbleached white flour
- 1 teaspoon active dry yeast
- 1 tablespoon sugar
- 1 teaspoon salt (optional)
- 3 cloves garlic, minced
- 1 tablespoon corn oil
- 1/3 cup packaged mashed potato flakes
- 1 teaspoon cumin seeds, toasted
- 1 cup warm water

GLAZE

- 1 to 2 tablespoons corn oil
- 2 cloves garlic, minced

TO MAKE THE DOUGH, combine all the dough ingredients except the water in a food processor and process for 30 seconds. With the machine running, gradually add the water in a thin stream through the feeder tube. Pulse on and off until the dough forms a soft ball. Transfer the dough to a floured board. Knead for 5 minutes by hand, sprinkling with flour as needed to prevent sticking. The dough should be very soft and pliable. Lightly flour a plastic bag. Place the dough in the bag, seal it, and let it sit 15 to 20 minutes in a warm, dark place.

PREPARE your grill. Keep it covered to build an intense heat. Combine the glaze ingredients and reserve. Remove the dough from the bag and cut it into 6 equal pieces. On a floured board, roll each piece into a circle as thin as a flour tortilla and about 8 inches in diameter. (The circle need not be perfect, and a few holes are fine.) As each piece is rolled, brush it lightly with the glaze and place it glazed-side down onto the grill. When all of the dough has been placed on the grill, cover the grill and bake for 5 minutes, then brush the tops with the glaze, flip, and brown the other side. There should be bubbles and brown patches on both sides when the bread is done.

> **PER SERVING:**
> 227 Cal.; 5g Prot.; 5g Fat; 41g Carb.;
> 0 Chol.; 17mg Sod.; 3g Fiber.

24

breakfast

AFTER YOU CRAWL OUT OF BED AND HEAD TO THE KITCHEN, you may have only enough energy to pour cereal into a bowl and top it with milk or soymilk and maybe a sliced banana. But breakfast can be more exciting than packaged cereal. You may not have the time to make some of these recipes during the hectic workweek, whether you work in an office, at home or in school. But don't pass them by; just save the time-consuming recipes for the weekends and cook up the quick ones during the week.

Good Grains Pancake Mix

makes 3 batches

For a high-fiber meal in minutes, keep a supply of this pancake mix in your freezer. You also can use it to make waffles.

| 1 cup rye flour
| 1/2 cup wheat germ
| 1 cup whole-wheat flour
| 1 1/2 cups unbleached white flour
| 1/2 cup cornmeal
| 1/3 cup sugar
| 2 tablespoons baking powder
| 1 teaspoon baking soda
| 1 tablespoon salt

STIR together all the ingredients. Divide into thirds (just under 2 cups each) and seal each batch in a plastic bag. Store in your freezer.

Good Grains Pancakes

makes 10 · serves 5

| 1 1/4 cups skim milk or soymilk
| 1/4 cup egg substitute (or 2 eggs)
| 2 tablespoons canola oil
| 1 batch Good Grains Pancake Mix (previous recipe)

IN A BOWL, whisk together the milk or soymilk, egg substitute or eggs, and oil. Whisk in the pancake mix until the dry ingredients are just moist. (The batter will be somewhat lumpy.)

TO COOK the pancakes, pour 1/4 cup batter per pancake onto a hot nonstick griddle. Cook until bubbles form and the underside is lightly browned, turn and cook the other side until browned. Repeat with the remaining batter.

Variation:

To make waffles, cook according to the manufacturer's directions for your waffle iron.

> **PER PANCAKE:**
> 230 Cal.; 8g Prot.; 8g Fat; 30g Carb.;
> ?mg Chol · 708mg Sod · 4g Fiber

Butternut Squash Pancakes

makes 12 · serves 5

| 1 small butternut squash
| 1 egg
| 1 egg white
| 1/2 cup skim milk or water
| 2 cups whole-wheat pastry flour
| 2 teaspoons baking powder
| 1 teaspoon salt
| 1/2 teaspoon ground cinnamon
| 1/4 teaspoon ground cloves
| 1 tablespoon vegetable oil

PREHEAT the oven to 350°F. Bake the squash until tender when pierced with a fork, about 40 minutes. Peel, seed and mash the squash. Let cool. In a bowl, combine the squash with the egg, egg white and milk or water. In a separate bowl, stir together the flour, baking powder, salt, ground cinnamon and cloves. Add the dry ingredients to the squash mixture, mixing well.

HEAT the oil over medium-high heat in a nonstick skillet. Pour 1/4 cup batter per pancake, and cook about 3 minutes. Flip the pancakes and press down to flatten. Cook until lightly browned, about 3 minutes more. Repeat with the remaining batter.

> **PER PANCAKE:**
> 101 Cal.; 4g Prot.; 2g Fat; 18g Carb.;
> 17mg Chol.; 227mg Sod.; 3g Fiber.

Blue Plate Pancakes

makes 12 • serves 5

- 1 cup buckwheat flour
- 1/2 cup amaranth flour
- 1/2 cup finely ground cornmeal (yellow or blue)
- 1/2 teaspoon salt
- 1 tablespoon baking powder
- 2 cups soymilk or skim milk
- 1 egg
- 2 tablespoons vegetable oil
- 3 tablespoons maple syrup
- Oil for frying
- Blueberry Sauce (page 489)

IN A LARGE BOWL, combine the flours, cornmeal, salt and baking powder. In a small bowl, whisk together the soymilk or milk, egg, oil and maple syrup. Add to the dry ingredients, stirring to dissolve any lumps. Let sit 10 minutes.

HEAT a well-seasoned skillet. Lightly oil the skillet and pour 1/3 cup batter per pancake. Cook until bubbles begin to form on the surface of the pancakes. Flip the pancakes and cook the other side until lightly browned, about 3 to 5 minutes. Repeat with the remaining batter. Serve with blueberry sauce.

> **PER SERVING (WITHOUT SAUCE):**
> 302 Cal.; 11g Prot.; 11g Fat; 40g Carb.;
> 33mg Chol.; 493mg Sod.; 6g Fiber.

Pumpkin-and-Brown Rice Pancakes

makes 12 • serves 5

Try these golden pancakes when you're in the mood for an out-of-the-ordinary breakfast.

- 1/2 cup cooked brown rice
- 1 cup buttermilk
- 1 egg
- 2 egg whites
- 1 teaspoon canola oil
- 2 tablespoons honey
- 1/2 cup fresh, cooked pumpkin or canned pumpkin
- 1/3 cup apple juice
- 3/4 cup whole-wheat pastry flour or unbleached white flour
- 1 teaspoon baking powder
- 1/2 teaspoon ground cinnamon
- 1/4 teaspoon ground nutmeg

IN A SMALL BOWL, combine the rice, buttermilk, egg and egg whites, oil, honey, pumpkin and apple juice. Sift the remaining ingredients into a second bowl. Combine the contents of the 2 bowls, mixing until just blended.

PREHEAT a nonstick griddle over medium heat. Drop the batter by the spoonful onto the griddle. Cook until bubbles appear; then flip the pancakes and cook other side until lightly browned.

PER PANCAKE:
74 Cal.; 3g Prot.; 1g Fat; 13g Carb.;
19mg Chol.; 72mg Sod.; 1g Fiber.

Almost-Classic Quiche with Broccoli

serves 6

Here's a trimmed-down and tasty version of quiche. It's lower in fat, cholesterol and calories than the original but still is rich in flavor.

CRUST

1/2 cup rolled oats

1/2 cup whole-wheat flour

1/2 cup unbleached white flour

1/4 teaspoon salt

1/8 teaspoon baking powder

1/4 to 1/3 cup canola oil

2 tablespoons fresh lemon juice

1 1/2 teaspoon honey

2 to 3 tablespoons cold water

1 to 2 teaspoons sesame seeds

FILLING

1 teaspoon water

1 cup diced onion

1 teaspoon minced garlic

3 cups small broccoli florets

1 to 2 tablespoons water

1 egg

2 egg whites

One 10-ounce package soft tofu

1 tablespoon prepared mustard

1 teaspoon dried basil or rosemary

1/4 teaspoon ground nutmeg

1/4 teaspoon salt

1/4 teaspoon white pepper

1 to 2 tablespoons grated Parmesan cheese

Red pepper strips or sliced black olives, for garnish (optional)

CRUST: Preheat the oven to 375°F. Grind the oats to a coarse flour in a blender or food processor. Place the ground oats in a large bowl. Stir in the flours, salt and baking powder. Drizzle 1/4 cup canola oil over the flour mixture and mix lightly; add more oil if necessary, until the mixture looks like wet sand. Drizzle the lemon juice, honey and 2 tablespoons water over the dough. Mix lightly with a fork until the dough forms a ball. (Add more water if necessary.)

ROLL OUT the dough between sheets of waxed paper. Sprinkle the sesame seeds evenly over bottom of a quiche or pie pan, then place the dough in the pan. (If using a pie pan, fold excess dough over to form an edge about 1/4 inch thick.) Prick the sides and bottom of the crust with a fork. Bake for 10 minutes, remove from the oven and lower the temperature to 350°F.

FILLING: Heat 1 teaspoon water or oil in a skillet over medium heat. Add the onion and cook, stirring, 3 to 5 minutes. Add the garlic and cook 30 seconds more. Add the broccoli florets and 1 to 2 tablespoons water. Cover. Steam until the broccoli is bright green and slightly tender but not soft, about 2 minutes. Drain the vegetables if necessary; then spread them evenly over the bottom of the prebaked pie crust.

IN A BLENDER or food processor, whip the egg and egg whites until frothy. Add the tofu, mustard, basil or rosemary, nutmeg, salt, white pepper and Parmesan. Blend until very smooth, about 1 to 2 minutes. Pour the egg-tofu mixture over the vegetables in the pie crust. Place the red pepper or black olives on top. Bake until slightly puffy, about 40 minutes. Let cool 5 to 10 minutes before slicing.

Helpful hint:

Quiche keeps for several days in the refrigerator; reheat slices in a 325°F oven for 15 to 20 minutes.

Variations:

- Substitute 3 cups of any vegetable for the broccoli. Try lightly steamed asparagus, sautéed mushrooms and leeks, or red pepper and zucchini.
- Eliminate egg and egg whites and substitute 8 ounces soft tofu. Add with the remaining tofu for a total of 18 ounces of tofu.

> **PER SERVING:**
> 267 Cal.; 11g Prot.; 13g Fat; 25g Carb.;
> 28mg Chol.; 408mg Sod.; 4g Fiber.

Raisin-Cheese Blintzes

serves 6

Blintzes are rolled crepes traditionally filled with cheese, fruit or potatoes. To keep the cholesterol content low in this version, a combination of bananas and cornstarch is used in making the crepes.

CREPE BATTER

 3/4 cup whole-wheat pastry flour

 1 cup skim milk or soymilk

 4 tablespoons cornstarch

 1 small banana, peeled and mashed

FILLING

 1 cup low-fat cottage cheese

 1/4 cup raisins

 1/4 teaspoon ground cinnamon

BATTER: Mix the batter ingredients in a bowl. Heat a nonstick pan lightly coated with nonstick cooking spray over medium heat. Pour in about 6 or 7 tablespoons of batter into the pan to make a crepe. Lift and tilt pan gently to spread the batter evenly and thinly. Cook until top is slightly dry. Remove with a spatula and place on a napkin. Repeat with the remaining batter. Preheat the oven to 350°F.

FILLING: Combine the filling ingredients in a bowl. Place a few tablespoons of the filling in the center of each crepe. Roll up and fold the ends under to make rectangular "packages." Place the blintzes in a lightly oiled baking pan. Bake until golden, about 30 minutes.

Helpful hint:

Go easy on the oil or the blintzes will be greasy. If the crepes fall apart, they may not have been cooked long enough; if the crepes are too crisp, they are overcooked.

Variation:

Fill the blintzes with a combination of 3 medium potatoes, cooked and mashed, and 1 small onion, finely chopped and sautéed.

> **PER SERVING:**
> 147 Cal.; 9g Prot.; 2g Fat; 26g Carb.;
> 2mg Chol.; 176mg Sod.; 3g Fiber.

Yogurt-Cheese Blintzes with Raspberries

makes 12 to 16

These blintzes have a wonderfully sweet-creamy filling.

FILLING

1/4 cup egg substitute

1 tablespoon sugar

1/8 teaspoon ground cinnamon, or to taste

Pinch salt

1 teaspoon grated lemon rind

1 teaspoon farina

1 1/2 cups yogurt cheese, made from 4 to 5 cups plain low-fat or whole milk yogurt (page 486)

CREPE

2 eggs (or 1/2 cup egg substitute)

1/2 teaspoon salt

1/2 teaspoon sugar

1 cup water

1 cup unbleached white flour mixed with 1/4 teaspoon baking powder

1 tablespoon margarine, melted

CONCASSEE AND TOPPING

Two 10-ounce packages frozen raspberries in light syrup (or 2 pints fresh raspberries, crushed and simmered with 1/2 cup sugar)

2 cups plain or vanilla yogurt

FILLING: In a large bowl, combine all the filling ingredients except the yogurt cheese. Stir well, then gently blend in the cheese with a fork.

CREPES: Combine all the crepe ingredients except the margarine in a bowl. With a whisk (or in a blender or food processor), blend until smooth. Heat a nonstick 6- or 7-inch skillet over medium-high heat. Brush the inside surface with margarine. Pour enough batter into the pan to cover the surface, then immediately pour the batter back into the bowl. (You'll have the right amount of batter in the pan to make a thin crepe.) Return the pan to your stovetop, lower the heat to low, and cook on one side only, until the top is dry. Turn out the crepe, bottom side up, onto a dishcloth. Repeat, brushing the pan with margarine each time, until all of the batter is used up. Cover the crepes and set aside.

CONCASSEE: Process the raspberries in a blender or food processor fitted with a steel blade; then force the fruit with its juices through a fine strainer to remove the seeds. Chill.

PREHEAT the oven to 350°F. To make the blintzes, place each crepe, brown side up, on a flat surface. Spoon

1 tablespoon of the filling in the center, bring the bottom edge up to cover it, then fold in the two sides and roll the package to the edge to enclose the filling. Repeat with the remaining crepes. Warm the blintzes in your oven until heated through. Place 1 to 2 tablespoons of cold raspberry concassee on a flat dessert plate, center a hot blintz on it, and top with a dollop of yogurt.

> **PER BLINTZ:**
> 269 Cal.; 15g Prot.; 6g Fat; 27g Carb.;
> 74mg Chol.; 368mg Sod.; 3g Fiber.

Nutty Blintzes

serves 4

These unusual blintzes are dairy-free and delicious.

- 12 ounces firm tofu
- 3 tablespoons honey or maple syrup
- 1/3 cup raisins or currants
- 1/3 cup lightly toasted walnuts, chopped (page 106)
- 1/4 cup lightly toasted slivered almonds (page 106) (optional)
- 1/4 teaspoon ground nutmeg
- Dash ground cinnamon
- 4 to 6 No-Cholesterol Crepes (page 441)

MASH the tofu with a fork until almost smooth. Mix in the honey or maple syrup, raisins or currants, nuts and spices. Fill the crepes with the tofu mixture and fold by rolling up the crepes or folding them into packages.

PREHEAT the oven to 350°F. Place the blintzes on a lightly greased baking sheet. Cover with aluminum foil. Bake the blintzes for 10 to 15 minutes. (Or, place the blintzes in a serving dish, cover the dish with plastic wrap, and heat the blintzes in your microwave oven on high power for 2 to 4 minutes.) Serve at once.

> **PER SERVING:**
> 352 Cal.; 11g Prot.; 10g Fat; 58g Carb.;
> 0mg Chol.; 222mg Sod.; 4g Fiber.

Cherry Clafouti

serves 6

A clafouti is a cross between a pudding and a pancake. It's a delicious start to your day.

- 1/4 cup unbleached white flour
- 1/3 cup sugar
- 2 eggs, lightly beaten
- 2 egg yolks
- 2 cups low-fat milk
- 1/2 teaspoon vanilla extract
- 2 cups pitted fresh sweet cherries

SIFT together the flour and sugar into a mixing bowl. Make a well in the center and add eggs and egg yolks. Then, in a steady stream, pour in half of the milk. Whisk the mixture to make a smooth paste. Whisk in the remaining milk and vanilla.

SPREAD the cherries evenly on the bottom of a lightly oiled 8-inch deep-dish pie pan. Hold a strainer over the fruit and pour in the batter. With a spoon, stir the batter and press it against the strainer to push the batter through. Remove the strainer and let the mixture sit for 30 minutes.

PREHEAT the oven to 375°F. Bake until the clafouti is puffy and golden brown, about 40 to 45 minutes. Let cool 5 minutes before serving.

> **PER SERVING:**
> 162 Cal.; 7g Prot.; 4g Fat; 23g Carb.;
> 129mg Chol.; 63mg Sod.; 1g Fiber.

Pineapple Breakfast Cheesecake

serves 8

2 cups bread cubes

One 9-ounce can crushed pineapple, packed in juice

1 tablespoon cornstarch

15 ounces part-skim ricotta cheese

1 tablespoon egg substitute

2 tablespoons wheat germ

2 tablespoons dry bread crumbs

1 tablespoon brown sugar

PREHEAT the oven to 350°F. Layer the bread cubes in a nonstick 1 1/2-quart casserole dish. Set aside. Drain the pineapple, reserving the juice. In a small saucepan, combine the pineapple juice with the cornstarch. Heat, stirring, until the mixture becomes clear. Set aside. In a medium bowl, stir together the ricotta, egg substitute and the crushed pineapple. Add the cornstarch mixture. Mix gently and spoon it on top of the bread cubes in the casserole. Combine the wheat germ, bread crumbs and brown sugar. Sprinkle on the cheesecake. Bake 35 to 40 minutes.

> **PER SERVING:**
> 190 Cal.; 11g Prot.; 6g Fat; 24g Carb.;
> 19mg Chol.; 224mg Sod.; 1g Fiber.

Maple-Walnut Granola

makes 8 cups

6 cups rolled oats

2 cups walnuts, chopped coarsely

1/2 to 1 cup sesame seeds

1 cup barley flour or whole-wheat pastry flour

1 teaspoon ground cinnamon

1/2 teaspoon ground allspice

1/2 teaspoon ground nutmeg or cardamom

1/2 teaspoon salt

3/4 cup maple syrup

3/4 cup honey

1/2 cup vegetable oil

2 tablespoons frozen orange juice concentrate (or 2 teaspoons vanilla extract), optional

PREHEAT the oven to 300°F. Combine the dry ingredients in a large mixing bowl. In a separate bowl, whisk the wet ingredients to a creamy consistency or blend in a blender for 1 minute. Pour the wet ingredients into the dry ingredients, and blend well. Place half of the mixture on each of two cookie sheets or two large baking pans. The granola shouldn't be more than an inch deep.

BAKE 1 hour gently turning over the granola with a spatula every 15 minutes. Switch the position of the trays, placing the top tray on bottom shelf, after 20 minutes of baking. Let cool. (The granola will become crunchy as it cools.) Store in an airtight container in your refrigerator.

> **PER 1/4-CUP SERVING:**
> 201 Cal.; 5g Prot.; 10g Fat; 26g Carb.;
> 0mg Chol.; 37mg Sod.; 0.5g Fiber.

Hot Cereal with Raisins

serves 2

This quick hot cereal is an energy-boosting sendoff. It includes triticale, a man-made hybrid of wheat and rye, with higher protein content than either grain.

> 3 cups water
>
> 1/2 cup raisins or other dried fruits
>
> 2 cups oat, rye and triticale flakes (often available already mixed together) or instant rolled oats
>
> Sweetener of choice (optional)
>
> Skim milk, soymilk or nonfat powdered milk, reconstituted (optional)

IN A MEDIUM POT, bring the water and dried fruit to a boil. Add the grains, stir and return to a boil. Then remove from the heat, cover and let sit until the grains are soft, about 5 to 10 minutes. Add the sweetener and milk.

Variation:

Stir in one or more of the following: chopped nuts, banana chips, wheat germ, ground cinnamon or ground nutmeg.

> **PER SERVING:**
> 254 Cal.; 7g Prot.; 2g Fat; 54g Carb.;
> 0mg Chol.; 6mg Sod.; 7g Fiber.

Oat Muesli with Dried Peaches

serves 4

This sweet muesli, an uncooked cereal of soaked grains and raw nuts, is a favorite breakfast dish with children. Prepare it the night before serving.

> 1 cup uncooked rolled oats
>
> 1/2 cup uncooked rolled barley (see Note)
>
> 1 cup skim milk or plain soymilk
>
> 1 tablespoon low-sugar peach preserves or apricot preserves
>
> 1/2 teaspoon vanilla extract
>
> 1 1/2 tablespoons honey
>
> 2 tablespoons raisins
>
> 2 tablespoons chopped dried peaches or dried apricots
>
> 1 tablespoon chopped raw cashews or other nuts (optional)
>
> Additional milk, soymilk or yogurt (optional)

IN A BOWL, combine the oats, barley, milk or soymilk, preserves, vanilla and honey. Cover the bowl and refrigerate overnight. Before serving, stir in the raisins, peaches or apricots, and nuts. Top with additional milk, soymilk or yogurt.

Note:

If you are unable to find rolled barley, substitute rolled oats.

> **PER SERVING:**
> 221 Cal.; 8g Prot.; 2g Fat; 44g Carb.;
> 1mg Chol.; 35mg Sod.; 3g Fiber.

Overnight Whole-Grain Cereal

serves 2

This breakfast cereal requires just a few minutes of advance preparation the night before serving. You can find the grains in the bulk-food section of a well-stocked supermarket, at a natural food store or through a mail-order supplier.

 1 tablespoon uncooked wheat berries

 1 tablespoon uncooked rye berries

 1 tablespoon uncooked barley

 1 tablespoon uncooked millet

 1 tablespoon uncooked rolled oats

 1 1/2 cups water or apple juice

 2 tablespoons uncooked oat bran

 2 tablespoons raisins

IN A GRAIN MILL or blender on high speed, coarsely grind the wheat berries, rye berries, barley, millet and oats for 30 seconds. Place the mixture in a pot with the water or apple juice, bran and raisins. Bring to a boil over medium-high heat. Simmer the cereal for 10 minutes, then remove from the heat. Cover the pot and let sit overnight on the stove. The next morning, reheat over medium heat.

Helpful hint:

You may double or triple the amount of grains to be ground for use on other days. Keep the ground grains in an airtight container in your refrigerator to ensure freshness.

> **PER SERVING:**
> 103 Cal.; 3g Prot.; 1g Fat; 21g Carb.;
> 0mg Chol.; 4mg Sod.; 2g Fiber.

Cream of Rice Cereal

serves 2

Topped with sliced bananas, this homemade creamed cereal is a favorite kids' breakfast.

 2/3 cup uncooked short-grain brown rice

 2 cups water

 2/3 cup nonfat dry milk or powdered soymilk (optional)

 1/4 teaspoon salt

 1/4 cup raisins

IN A LARGE DRY SKILLET toast the brown rice over medium heat for 1 minute, stirring constantly. Place the rice in a grain mill, food processor or blender, and grind to a fine powder. Combine with the remaining ingredients and let sit overnight in a covered bowl in your refrigerator. In the morning, transfer the cereal to a pot. Bring to a boil and cook 5 minutes, stirring frequently. Serve hot.

> **PER SERVING:**
> 276 Cal.; 5g Prot.; 1g Fat; 62g Carb.;
> 0mg Chol.; 274mg Sod.; 3g Fiber.

Berry Pancake Topping

serves 8

| 1 1/2 tablespoons cornstarch
| 2 tablespoons honey
| 2 tablespoons water
| 2 cups unsweetened berries of your choice

IN A SMALL SAUCEPAN, blend the cornstarch, honey and water. Add 1/2 cup berries. Heat until the mixture thickens slightly. Stir in the remaining 1 1/2 cups fruit.

PER SERVING:
33 Cal.; 0g Prot.; 0g Fat; 8g Carb.;
0mg Chol.; 1mg Sod.; 1g Fiber.

Tropical Yogurt Smoothie

serves 2

For potassium and vitamins A and C, it's hard to beat this smoothie.

| 1 papaya, peeled, seeded and cubed
| 1 kiwifruit, unpeeled and sliced into rounds (optional)
| 1 fresh or frozen banana, sliced
| 1 cup frozen strawberries
| 8 ounces nonfat plain yogurt
| 2 cups fresh orange juice

IN A BLENDER or food processor, purée all the ingredients until smooth.

Helpful hint:

Using frozen fruit gives a pleasing chill to smoothies. Buy fruit in season, then freeze in freezer bags. When bananas become overripe, peel and freeze in freezer bags.

PER SERVING:
381 Cal.; 9g Prot.; 2g Fat; 83g Carb.;
3mg Chol.; 95mg Sod.; 5g Fiber.

Raspberry-Peach Super Smoothie

serves 2

This morning brightener is rich in vitamin C and potassium.

| 1/2 cup fresh or frozen unsweetened raspberries
| 1 fresh or frozen peach, sliced
| 1 fresh or frozen banana, sliced
| 8 ounces soft tofu
| 2 cups fresh orange juice

IN A BLENDER or food processor, purée all the ingredients until smooth.

PER SERVING:
283 Cal.; 10g Prot.; 5g Fat; 47g Carb.;
0mg Chol.; 11mg Sod.; 4g Fiber.

Hawaiian Smoothie

serves 2

This wake-up drink supplies a generous dose of vitamins and fiber.

> 1 cup unsweetened pineapple juice
> 1 banana
> 1/4 cup oat bran
> 4 ice cubes

PROCESS all the ingredients in a blender at high speed for 1 minute.

PER SERVING:
186 Cal.; 4g Prot.; 2g Fat; 38g Carb.;
0mg Chol.; 7mg Sod.; 5g Fiber.

25

sandwiches

NOTHING COULD BE MORE UNIVERSAL THAN THE SANDWICH. It seems that every cuisine has its own version of a portable feast. This selection emphasizes the American idea of a sandwich (two slices of bread with something delicious in between), but some of the recipes have a definite ethnic flair. We've included kid-pleasing sandwiches as well, including a lower-fat version of PB and J.

Submarine Sandwich

serves 8

Crusty French bread and generous amounts of lettuce, onions, tomatoes, mushrooms and condiments combine to make a satisfying lunch or light dinner.

  4 cups white button mushroom caps

  1/2 cup milk or plain soymilk

  1 cup dry seasoned bread crumbs

  2 tablespoons virgin olive oil

  2 loaves French bread

  4 cups lettuce or sprouts

  2 ripe medium tomatoes, sliced thinly

  1 large sweet onion, sliced thinly

  Sliced dill pickles

  Condiments of choice: Mustard, ketchup, and
    mayonnaise or soy mayonnaise (optional)

DIP the mushrooms in the milk or soymilk, and roll in the bread crumbs. Heat the oil in a skillet. Stir-fry the coated mushrooms until the bread crumbs are golden brown and the mushrooms are hot. Set aside.

SLICE the loaves lengthwise and remove the top halves. Generously cover the bottom halves with the mushrooms. Top with the lettuce or sprouts, tomatoes, onions, pickles and condiments. Replace the top halves of the bread. Cut each loaf into quarters.

Helpful hint:

Your bread should be crusty on the outside and soft on the inside. If the crust is soft, place the bread in a 250°F oven for 5 to 10 minutes.

PER SERVING:
430 Cal.; 15g Prot.; 9g Fat; 71g Carb.;
1mg Chol.; 1,219mg Sod.; 4g Fiber.

"Egg" Salad Sandwich

serves 4

Tofu takes the place of egg in this delicious taste-alike.

  8 ounces firm tofu, drained and diced

  1 red bell pepper, chopped finely

  2 scallions (green and white parts), chopped finely

  1 small carrot, shredded finely

  1 tablespoon chopped fresh parsley

  1 tablespoon chopped dill pickle

  1 teaspoon Dijon mustard

  2 tablespoons mayonnaise or soy mayonnaise

  1/4 teaspoon salt

  1/8 teaspoon freshly ground black pepper

  8 slices whole-wheat bread

  Shredded lettuce

MIX together all the ingredients except the bread and lettuce in a mixing bowl. Divide the mixture evenly among 4 slices of bread. Top with the lettuce and remaining bread slices.

PER SERVING:
241 Cal.; 9g Prot.; 10g Fat; 30g Carb.;
4mg Chol.; 650mg Sod.; 5g Fiber.

Tempeh Mock Chicken Salad

serves 6

Tempeh remains moist and tender when microwaved. Serve this tasty salad in pita bread or on lettuce leaves.

> 8 ounces tempeh, cubed
>
> 2 tablespoons soy sauce
>
> 2 tablespoons water
>
> 1 teaspoon rice vinegar or other mild vinegar
>
> 1 cup chopped celery
>
> 1/2 cup chopped carrot
>
> 4 scallions (green and white parts), minced
>
> 1/2 cup minced fresh parsley
>
> 1/2 cup reduced-fat mayonnaise

COMBINE the tempeh, soy sauce, water and vinegar in a 1-quart casserole dish. Cover. Cook on high power for 5 minutes, stirring once. Uncover and let cool to room temperature. Add the remaining ingredients to the tempeh mixture. Stir well and chill.

> **PER SERVING:**
> 158 Cal.; 8g Prot.; 10g Fat; 7g Carb.;
> 0mg Chol.; 513mg Sod.; 0.9g Fiber.

Herbed White Bean and Cucumber Sandwich

serves 4

The creamy bean spread complements the crunchy vegetables in this sandwich.

> 1 cup cooked white beans
>
> 2 tablespoons chopped fresh parsley
>
> 1 tablespoon chopped fresh chives
>
> 1 tablespoon chopped fresh dillweed (or 1 teaspoon dried)
>
> 1/4 teaspoon salt
>
> 1/8 teaspoon freshly ground black pepper
>
> 2 ounces creamy goat cheese or light cream cheese
>
> 1 tablespoon fresh lemon juice
>
> 8 slices black bread or whole-grain bread
>
> 1 cucumber, peeled and sliced thinly
>
> Boston lettuce
>
> Sprouts

COMBINE the beans, parsley, chives, dillweed, salt, pepper, cheese and lemon juice in a food processor and process until smooth. Add more herbs or lemon juice as desired. Spread the mixture on 4 slices of bread. Top with a layer of cucumber, lettuce and sprouts. Top with the remaining bread slices.

> **PER SERVING:**
> 250 Cal.; 12g Prot.; 7g Fat; 36g Carb.;
> 4mg Chol.; 404mg Sod.; 7g Fiber.

Cream Cheese Sandwich

serves 4

Combining ricotta cheese with cream cheese keeps the fat content in check in this kid-pleasing sandwich.

- 1/2 cup low-fat ricotta cheese
- One 3-ounce package light cream cheese
- 1/4 cup plain nonfat yogurt
- 1 clove garlic, crushed
- 1 tablespoon chopped fresh chives
- 1 tablespoon chopped fresh basil leaves (or 1 teaspoon dried)
- 1 tablespoon chopped fresh parsley
- 1/8 teaspoon salt
- 1/8 teaspoon freshly ground black pepper
- 8 slices whole-grain bread
- Shredded lettuce
- Sprouts
- 1 tomato, sliced

IN A MEDIUM BOWL, mix together the cheeses, yogurt, garlic, herbs, salt and pepper until smooth. Spread the mixture on 4 slices of bread. Top with the lettuce, sprouts, tomato and remaining bread slices.

> **PER SERVING:**
> 256 Cal.; 14g Prot.; 8g Fat; 33g Carb.;
> 22mg Chol.; 605mg Sod.; 4g Fiber.

Sloppy Joes

serves 4

Here's a variation on a favorite mess of a meal.

- 3/4 cup uncooked couscous
- 1 1/2 cups boiling water
- 2 tablespoons vegetable oil
- 2/3 cup finely chopped onions
- 1/2 cup minced green bell pepper
- 1/4 cup ketchup
- 1 cup cooked pinto or kidney beans, lightly mashed
- 1 cup low-fat or regular sour cream, or soy substitute
- 4 whole-wheat burger buns

PLACE the couscous and boiling water in a heat-proof bowl. Cover and let sit 15 minutes. Then fluff with a fork. Set aside.

HEAT the oil in a medium skillet and cook the onions and bell pepper, stirring, until soft, about 10 minutes. Stir in the couscous and pinto or kidney beans. Lower the heat to a simmer.

COMBINE the ketchup and sour cream or soy substitute, and stir the mixture into the skillet a little at a time. Continue to stir over low heat until heated through, about 8 minutes. Spoon the sloppy joes over the burger buns. Serve at once.

> **PER SERVING:**
> 401 Cal.; 13g Prot.; 13g Fat; 53g Carb.;
> 0mg Chol.; 581mg Sod.; 9g Fiber.

Sloppy Falafel Sandwiches

serves 4

One 6-ounce package falafel mix

1 teaspoon vegetable oil

One 28-ounce can tomatoes (with juice), chopped

1/2 teaspoon salt

Chili powder to taste

4 whole-wheat burger buns

PREPARE the falafel according to the package directions. Heat the oil in a large skillet and fry the falafel, breaking it up as it cooks. When the falafel begins to dry out and become crumbly, add the tomatoes with juice, salt and chili powder. Stir, lower the heat and simmer until thickened. Serve the sauce over the buns.

Helpful hint:

Add canned red or pinto beans to the recipe to make an excellent quick chili.

> **PER SERVING:**
> 236 Cal.; 11g Prot.; 4g Fat; 30g Carb.;
> 0mg Chol.; 1,129mg Sod.; 12g Fiber.

Pita Pockets Stuffed with Vegetables and Chickpeas

serves 4

2 cloves garlic, minced

1/2 cup finely chopped scallions (green and white parts)

2 teaspoons vegetable oil

1/3 cup chopped green bell pepper

3 tablespoons chopped fresh parsley

1 tablespoon sesame seeds

1/2 teaspoon dried oregano

1/2 teaspoon dried mint

One 15-ounce can chickpeas, rinsed

Dash salt (optional)

Dash hot pepper sauce (optional)

2 whole-wheat pita rounds, cut in half

2 small tomatoes, cut into 4 slices each

1 small onion, sliced

4 leaves romaine or other lettuce

1 cup alfalfa or other sprouts

1 cup shredded low-fat Monterey Jack or soy cheese (optional)

IN A SKILLET, cook the garlic and scallions, stirring, in the oil over medium heat until the scallions are soft. Add the bell pepper, parsley and sesame seeds. Cook until the pepper is soft. Add the oregano and mint and cook, stirring, 1 minute more. Place the vegetable mixture and chickpeas in a food processor and process until smooth. Add the salt and hot pepper sauce. Stuff the mixture into pita pockets. Garnish with the tomatoes, onion, lettuce, sprouts and cheese.

> **PER SERVING:**
> 276 Cal.; 13g Prot.; 7g Fat; 42g Carb.;
> 0mg Chol.; 220mg Sod.; 8g Fiber.

Eggplant Pita Sandwiches

serves 4

| 1 cup uncooked quick-cooking brown rice
| 1 tablespoon virgin olive oil
| 1 eggplant, peeled and chopped
| 1 onion, chopped
| 2 cloves garlic, minced
| One 16-ounce can whole tomatoes, chopped (reserve liquid)
| Salt and freshly ground black pepper to taste
| 1/4 teaspoon cayenne pepper
| 4 large pita rounds, cut in half

PREPARE the rice according to the package directions. Set aside. In a wok or large skillet, heat the oil and stir-fry the eggplant for 5 to 10 minutes. Add the onion and garlic, and stir-fry a few minutes more. Stir in the tomatoes, tomato liquid and seasonings. Cover and simmer until the eggplant reaches desired tenderness. Place the mixture in a medium bowl. Stir in the cooked rice.

FILL the pita pockets with the rice-eggplant mixture. Heat the filled pockets in your microwave.

Variation:

Omit the rice and serve the eggplant mixture over thin spaghetti, vermicelli or linguine.

PER SERVING:
430 Cal.; 12g Prot.; 6g Fat; 83g Carb.;
0mg Chol.; 805mg Sod.; 8g Fiber.

Falafel Updated

serves 4

This Middle Eastern classic gets the skinny treatment in this remake.

YOGURT SAUCE

| 1 cup nonfat plain yogurt
| 1/4 teaspoon salt
| Pinch sugar
| Freshly ground black pepper to taste
| 1 tablespoon chopped fresh mint leaves (or 1 teaspoon dried)
| 2 cloves garlic

HOT SAUCE

| 1 cup vegetable stock (page 178)
| 6 tablespoons tomato paste
| 2 teaspoons red chili paste
| 1 tablespoon fresh lemon juice
| 1/2 teaspoon ground cumin
| 1 tablespoon minced fresh parsley (or 1 1/2 teaspoons dried)
| 1 tablespoon minced fresh cilantro leaves (or 1 1/2 teaspoons dried coriander leaves)

FALAFEL

- 3 cloves garlic
- 1/2 medium onion, chopped
- 1/2 cup minced fresh parsley
- 1 1/2 cups cooked chickpeas
- 1 tablespoon fresh lemon juice
- 1 teaspoon ground cumin
- 1/2 teaspoon dried basil
- 1/2 teaspoon ground coriander
- 1/2 teaspoon dried thyme
- 1/2 teaspoon salt
- 1/2 teaspoon hot pepper sauce
- Freshly ground black pepper to taste
- 2 slices French bread, torn into large pieces and soaked in cold water to cover
- 1/2 cup whole-wheat flour
- 1 tablespoon virgin olive oil
- 4 whole-wheat pita rounds
- Lettuce, sliced tomatoes, sliced cucumbers and chopped onions, for garnish

YOGURT SAUCE: Blend all the ingredients in a blender or food processor until smooth. Set aside.

HOT SAUCE: Combine all the ingredients in a small saucepan. Simmer over medium heat until the mixture has thickened slightly, about 5 minutes. Set aside.

FALAFEL: Preheat the oven to 375°F. Process the garlic, onion and parsley in a food processor or blender until finely minced. Add the chickpeas and blend until finely chopped and somewhat pasty. Add the lemon juice, cumin, basil, coriander, thyme, salt, hot pepper sauce and black pepper. Squeeze the water out of bread and add the bread. Process until well mixed.

FORM the falafel mixture into 16 balls. Flatten each ball to form 1/2-inch-thick patties. Dredge the patties in the flour and place them on a lightly greased baking sheet. Bake for 10 minutes. Turn the patties and bake 10 minutes more.

IN A LARGE SKILLET, heat half of the olive oil over medium-high heat. Add the patties and fry until golden brown and crispy on the bottom. Turn the patties and add the remaining oil, swirling the oil so that it comes into contact with all the patties. Fry until golden brown and crispy, then drain on paper towels.

TO SERVE, cut off about 1/3 of each pita round and open the larger section to form a pocket. Fill each pocket with the hot falafel patties. Garnish with lettuce, tomatoes, cucumbers, onions, yogurt sauce and hot sauce.

Variation:

For a dairy-free sauce, omit the yogurt from the yogurt sauce and substitute half of a 10 1/2-ounce package of firm tofu plus 1/4 cup fresh lemon juice.

> **PER SERVING
> WITH 1 TABLESPOON
> OF EACH SAUCE:**
> 386 Cal.; 15g Prot.; 7g Fat; 68g Carb.;
> 0.1mg Chol.; 774mg Sod.; 10g Fiber.

Beet-Apple Pita Sandwiches

serves 4

Add prepared horseradish to this sandwich for a zesty lunch or light supper.

| 1 beet, peeled and grated
| 1 large Granny Smith apple, peeled, cored and grated
| 1/2 cup plain nonfat yogurt
| 2 teaspoons fresh lemon juice
| Dash salt
| 1 teaspoon prepared horseradish (optional)
| 2 whole-wheat pita rounds
| Alfalfa sprouts or shredded greens

IN A BOWL, mix the beet, apple, yogurt, lemon juice, salt and horseradish. Cut the pita rounds in half. Fill each half with 1/4 of the beet mixture. Stuff with sprouts or greens.

> **PER SERVING:**
> 115 Cal.; 5g Prot.; 0.9g Fat; 22g Carb.;
> 1mg Chol.; 257mg Sod.; 4g Fiber.

Pita Pizzas

makes 12

| 12 small pita rounds (4 inches in diameter)
| 1 cup mild Italian-style tomato sauce
| 1 cup grated mozzarella cheese or mozzarella-style soy cheese

PREHEAT the oven to 450°F. Place the pitas on a cookie sheet. Spread with the tomato sauce, then sprinkle with the cheese. (You may add other toppings.) Bake until the cheese melts, about 5 minutes. Cool slightly before serving.

> **PER PIZZA:**
> 111 Cal.; 5g Prot.; 2g Fat; 18g Carb.;
> 5mg Chol.; 318mg Sod.; 1g Fiber.

English Muffin Pizza

serves 1

| 1 English muffin, split in half
| 3 tomato slices
| Chopped green bell peppers, white button mushrooms and/or other vegetable toppings
| 1/2 teaspoon dried oregano
| 1/2 teaspoon dried basil
| 1 slice cheese of choice

TOP the English muffin halves with the tomato slices and remaining ingredients. Place under your broiler until the cheese melts.

> **PER SERVING:**
> 263 Cal.; 12g Prot.; 10g Fat; 28g Carb.;
> 27mg Chol.; 788mg Sod.; 2g Fiber.

Cottage Cheese and Vegetable Spread

makes 3 cups

This spread is a great warm-weather filling for pita pockets or whole-grain bread.

> 2 cups low-fat cottage cheese
>
> 2 scallions (green and white parts), sliced thinly
>
> 2/3 cup finely chopped green bell pepper
>
> 2/3 cup finely chopped red bell pepper
>
> 1 tablespoon minced fresh basil leaves
>
> 1 tablespoon minced jalapeño peppers
>
> 1 teaspoon dried dillweed
>
> 1 teaspoon curry powder
>
> 1 tablespoon salt, or to taste
>
> Freshly ground black pepper to taste
>
> 2 teaspoons rice vinegar
>
> 1 teaspoon minced garlic

COMBINE all the ingredients in a bowl and mix well.

> **PER 1/2-CUP SERVING
> WITH HALF OF A PITA ROUND:**
> 152 Cal.; 14g Prot.; 2g Fat; 18g Carb.;
> 6mg Chol.; 511mg Sod.; 2g Fiber.

Peanut-Ricotta Spread

makes 2 cups

Combining peanut butter and ricotta cheese produces a spread that's far lower in fat than straight peanut butter and just as delicious. Try it with jelly on bread as a sandwich or with low-fat crackers as a spread.

> One 15-ounce carton low-fat or nonfat ricotta cheese
>
> 1/4 cup peanut butter
>
> 1 tablespoon honey
>
> 1/4 teaspoon almond extract
>
> 1/4 teaspoon vanilla extract
>
> 1/4 teaspoon ground cinnamon

BLEND all the ingredients in a food processor or blender until smooth. Store the spread in your refrigerator.

Variation:

Replace ricotta cheese with cottage cheese.

> **PER 2-TABLESPOON SERVING:**
> 70 Cal.; 5g Prot.; 4g Fat; 4g Carb.;
> 10mg Chol.; 56mg Sod.; 0g Fiber.

Any Bean Sandwich Spread

serves 6

Serve this spread on slices of whole-grain bread and top it with your favorite vegetables and condiments.

- 1 1/2 cups cooked beans of choice
- 2 tablespoons grated onion
- 1 teaspoon fresh lemon juice
- 1/2 teaspoon dried thyme or sage
- 1/2 cup plain nonfat yogurt
- 1/2 teaspoon salt (optional)
- 1 tablespoon honey

MASH the beans thoroughly. Mix in the remaining ingredients and chill.

PER SERVING:
80 Cal.; 5g Prot.; 0g Fat; 15g Carb.;
0mg Chol.; 434mg Sod.; 5g Fiber.

26

sauces and such

SAUCES HAVE A SPECIAL WAY of enlivening an otherwise ordinary dish—whether the dish is the main part of the meal or on the side. Many classic sauces rely on fat for flavor. But for the sake of nutrition and good taste, our selection includes delicious low-fat remakes, exotic ethnic specialties and fruit toppings. You'll also find eggless mayonnaise, several marinades, yogurt cheese and other recipes to round out your culinary repertoire. (They are the "such" in this selection.)

Low-Fat Pesto

serves 6

Adelicious topping for pasta, pesto typically is high in fat due to generous amounts of cheese and nuts. This low-fat version highlights fresh herbs instead.

- 2 cups chopped fresh basil leaves
- 1 cup chopped fresh Italian flat-leaf parsley
- 1/4 cup toasted bread crumbs (page 106)
- 2 tablespoons grated Parmesan cheese
- 2 cloves garlic, minced
- 3 tablespoons light miso
- 1/4 to 1/3 cup water

IN A FOOD PROCESSOR, combine the basil, parsley, bread crumbs, Parmesan, garlic and miso; pulse until the mixture is finely minced. With the machine running, add water until the pesto is smooth and creamy.

> **PER SERVING:**
> 53 Cal.; 3g Prot.; 1g Fat; 8g Carb.;
> 2mg Chol.; 74mg Sod.; 2g Fiber.

Low-Fat Cheese Sauce

serves 6

Surprisingly, making low-fat sauces doesn't necessarily mean giving up cheese. A trio of low-fat cheeses gives this sauce a rich flavor. Try it over linguine or other pasta.

- 1/3 cup white wine
- 2 large cloves garlic, minced
- 1/2 cup sliced scallions (green and white parts)
- 1 large red bell pepper, seeded and chopped finely
- 2 tablespoons grated Parmesan cheese
- 1/4 cup grated part-skim mozzarella cheese
- 1/4 cup low-fat or nonfat cottage cheese
- 2 tablespoons chopped fresh basil leaves

IN A LARGE SKILLET over medium-high heat, heat the wine to bubbling; add the garlic and cook 1 minute. Add the scallions and bell pepper. Cook until the pepper is soft, stirring frequently, about 5 to 6 minutes. In a food processor or blender, purée the Parmesan cheese, mozzarella cheese and cottage cheese until smooth. Stir into the sautéed vegetables. Remove from the heat. Sprinkle with basil.

> **PER SERVING:**
> 76 Cal.; 8g Prot.; 2g Fat; 3g Carb.;
> 9mg Chol.; 218mg Sod.; 0.1 Fiber.

Béchamel Sauce

makes 2 cups

This traditional white sauce usually contains dairy products, but not this version. Spoon it over vegetables, croquettes, pasta or grains.

> 3 tablespoons margarine or corn oil
>
> 4 tablespoons unbleached white flour
>
> 2 cups soymilk, heated
>
> 1/4 onion, separated into sections
>
> 4 whole cloves
>
> Several dashes ground nutmeg
>
> 6 or 7 peppercorns (or white pepper to taste)
>
> Salt to taste

HEAT the margarine or oil in a saucepan over low heat. Whisk in the flour, stirring constantly for 2 or 3 minutes. Slowly add the hot milk, stirring until thickened. Add the remaining ingredients.

CONTINUE to cook, covered, for 10 to 15 minutes, stirring frequently. Strain through a sieve. Serve at once.

Variation:

For a quick white sauce, omit onion, cloves and peppercorns. Cook only until thickened.

> **PER 2-TABLESPOON SERVING**
> 35 Cal.; 1g Prot.; 3g Fat; 2g Carb.;
> 0mg Chol.; 58mg Sod.; 0g Fiber.

Almond Sauce

makes 2 1/2 cups

Based on a béchamel sauce, this version goes a step further, turning something basic into an especially flavorful sauce with a very fine almond crunch. Spoon this sauce over any dish where you'd like a nutty touch: vegetables, pilafs, croquettes and so on.

> 1/2 cup whole almonds with skins
>
> 3 tablespoons margarine or corn oil
>
> 4 tablespoons unbleached white flour
>
> 2 1/2 cups soymilk, heated
>
> 1 teaspoon soy sauce (optional)

PREHEAT the oven to 350°F. Place the almonds on a baking sheet and roast them to a golden brown, about 10 minutes. Transfer to a food processor or nut grinder, and grind finely. Set aside.

HEAT the margarine or oil in a saucepan, letting it brown slightly. Add the flour and cook 2 or 3 minutes over low heat, stirring so that the flour doesn't burn. Slowly add the hot milk, whisking until thickened. Add the ground almonds, and cook for 4 or 5 minutes. Stir in the soy sauce.

> **PER 2-TABLESPOON SERVING:**
> 46 Cal.; 2g Prot.; 4g Fat; 2g Carb.;
> 0mg Chol.; 20mg Sod.; 0g Fiber.

Sauce Bourguignonne

serves 8

This red wine, tomato and rosemary sauce is unusual and wonderful. Instead of the traditional butter-and-flour roux, arrowroot or cornstarch thickens this sauce, and the fat content drops to virtually nil. Try it on pasta of various shapes.

| 1 cup minced onion
| 1 cup diced carrots
| 1/2 cup diced celery
| 3 cloves garlic, minced
| 3 cups water
| 1 tablespoon tomato paste
| 1 cup red wine
| 2 tablespoons dry red wine vinegar
| Salt to taste
| 1 tablespoon chopped fresh rosemary leaves (or 1 teaspoon dried)
| 1/2 teaspoon dried thyme
| 1 teaspoon dried basil
| 1/2 teaspoon white pepper
| 1/3 cup cold water
| 2 tablespoons arrowroot powder or cornstarch

IN A SKILLET over medium heat, cook the onion, carrots, celery and garlic, stirring, in a little water for 5 minutes. Transfer the sautéed vegetables to a large pot. Stir in the remaining ingredients except 1/3 cup water and arrowroot or cornstarch. Bring to a boil, cover with the lid ajar, and simmer until the vegetables are tender, about 15 to 20 minutes.

WHISK together the cold water and arrowroot or cornstarch until smooth. Pour slowly into the simmering sauce, stirring constantly. Lower the heat and continue stirring as the sauce thickens and becomes shiny, about 5 minutes. If necessary, add more dissolved arrowroot or cornstarch, a teaspoon at a time, until the sauce reaches desired consistency.

Variations:

- Substitute another cup of wine for 1 cup of water.
- Add 1 cup of sliced, sautéed white button mushrooms to the sauce just before stirring in the dissolved arrowroot or cornstarch.

> **PER SERVING:**
> 50 Cal · 0.5g Prot · 0.1g Fat· 7g Carb ·
> 0mg Chol.; 172mg Sod.; 1g Fiber.

Tofu-Cilantro Sauce

makes 2 1/2 cups

Try this on vegetables.

| 1 pound firm tofu, drained and cut into 8 pieces
| 4 tablespoons plain nonfat yogurt
| 1 teaspoon stone-ground mustard
| 3 to 4 tablespoons fresh lemon juice
| 1 tablespoon coarsely chopped fresh cilantro leaves
| 1 scallion (green part only), chopped
| 1/4 teaspoon salt

STEAM the tofu for 3 to 5 minutes. Set aside. In a blender, purée the remaining ingredients. Add the tofu a piece at a time and blend until smooth. Serve warm.

> **PER 2-TABLESPOON SERVING:**
> 19 Cal.; 2g Prot.; 1g Fat; 1g Carb.;
> 0mg Chol.; 35mg Sod.; 0g Fiber.

Mushroom Sauce

makes 3 cups

Once the shiitake mushrooms are reconstituted in water, this sauce takes only minutes to make. It tastes great over noodles and burgers.

- 8 to 10 dried shiitake mushrooms, soaked in 2 cups warm water for 1 hour
- 4 tablespoons oil or margarine
- 2 1/3 cups sliced white button mushrooms
- 1/4 cup sherry or sake
- 2 cloves garlic, minced
- 1 cup tomato juice
- 1 tablespoon soy sauce
- 2 tablespoons mirin (or 4 teaspoons sherry and 2 teaspoons honey)
- 2 teaspoons to 2 tablespoons nutritional yeast
- 1 tablespoon white or barley miso
- 3 tablespoons arrowroot (or 4 teaspoons kudzu), dissolved in a small amount of water

DRAIN the shiitake mushrooms, reserving the soaking water. Heat the oil or margarine in a saucepan over medium heat; cook the shiitake and other mushrooms, stirring, for a few minutes. Cover and simmer until the mushrooms have reduced in size and have begun to let out their juices, about 4 to 5 minutes.

ADD the sherry or sake, raise heat to high, and add the garlic, reserved soaking water and tomato juice. Boil rapidly for a minute. Add the soy sauce and mirin, and boil 2 to 3 minutes more. Lower the heat, and add the nutritional yeast and miso. While stirring, add the dissolved arrowroot or kudzu, and cook until the sauce has thickened and become transparent. Serve at once.

> **PER 2-TABLESPOON SERVING:**
> 35 Cal.; 1g Prot.; 2g Fat; 2g Carb.;
> 0mg Chol.; 67mg Sod.; 0.7g Fiber.

Spicy Sesame Sauce

serves 6

Asian noodles, such as udon or soba, pair deliciously with this spicy sesame sauce.

- 2 tablespoons cornstarch
- 1/4 cup low-sodium soy sauce
- 1/4 cup water
- 1 tablespoon dark sesame oil
- 1 tablespoon honey
- 1/4 cup mirin or dry sherry
- 1/2 pound extra-firm tofu, cut into thin strips
- 2 red bell peppers, seeded and julienned
- 2 large cloves garlic, minced
- 2 tablespoons minced fresh ginger root
- 6 scallions (green and white parts), sliced diagonally
- 1 teaspoon cayenne pepper
- 1/4 cup chopped fresh cilantro leaves

IN A SMALL BOWL, combine the cornstarch, soy sauce, water, oil and honey. Set aside. In a wok or skillet, heat the mirin or sherry to bubbling over medium-high heat. Add the tofu, bell peppers, garlic, ginger root and scallions, and stir-fry until the peppers are soft, about 5 minutes. Add the cornstarch mixture and simmer until thick, about 5 minutes. Remove from the heat. Stir in the cayenne and cilantro.

> **PER SERVING:**
> 125 Cal.; 7g Prot.; 5g Fat; 10g Carb.;
> 0mg Chol.; 408mg Sod.; 1g Fiber.

Eggplant Sauce

serves 6

If cooked slowly, eggplant adds delicious richness to low-fat pasta sauces. Here eggplant is simmered in wine and Italian spices. Try it over angel-hair pasta.

- 1 teaspoon virgin olive oil
- 1/4 cup water or dry sherry
- 1 small onion, chopped
- 2 large cloves garlic, minced
- 1/2 green bell pepper, diced
- 1 pound eggplant, peeled and diced
- 2 pounds fresh tomatoes, diced
- 1/2 cup dry red wine or vegetable stock (page 178)
- 2 tablespoons chopped fresh basil leaves
- 2 tablespoons chopped fresh oregano leaves
- Salt to taste
- Freshly ground black pepper to taste

IN A LARGE SKILLET or saucepan, heat the oil and water or sherry to bubbling over medium-high heat. Add the onion and garlic; cook, stirring frequently, until the onion is soft but not browned. Add the bell pepper, eggplant, tomatoes, wine or stock, basil and oregano. Lower the heat, cover and simmer until the sauce is thick, about 30 to 45 minutes. Season with salt and pepper.

> **PER SERVING:**
> 82 Cal.; 2g Prot.; 1g Fat; 13g Carb.;
> 0mg Chol.; 195mg Sod.; 4g Fiber.

Peanutty Sauce

makes 2 cups

Serve this sauce with pasta, vegetables and other dishes. It also makes a wonderful dip for vegetables.

- 1 cup peanut butter
- 1 cup water
- 2 tablespoons low-sodium soy sauce
- 1 1/2 tablespoons sugar
- 1/4 teaspoon salt
- Dash cayenne pepper
- 1/4 cup chopped scallions (green and white parts)

PLACE the peanut butter in a bowl. Gradually add the water, whisking to blend. Stir in the remaining ingredients. Just before serving, place the sauce in a lightly oiled saucepan. Cook over low heat, uncovered, stirring constantly, until heated through. The sauce will thicken as it warms.

> **PER 2-TABLESPOON SERVING:**
> 100 Cal.; 5g Prot.; 8g Fat; 4g Carb.;
> 0mg Chol.; 140mg Sod.; 0.3g Fiber.

Romesco Sauce

makes 1 to 1 1/2 cups

Romesco takes its name from a variety of small, hot red chilies grown in Spain. Though these chilies are hard to find in the United States, you'll get good results with any kind of small, dried hot pepper. Full in intriguing and unexpected flavors, this sauce is excellent served with steamed new potatoes or other steamed vegetables speared with wooden toothpicks for dipping.

> 1 small dried hot pepper
> 1/2 cup hot water
> 3 medium ripe tomatoes
> 1/2 cup blanched almonds
> 2 cloves garlic, pressed or minced
> 1 teaspoon paprika
> 1/2 teaspoon salt
> 1/4 to 1/2 cup virgin olive oil
> 2 to 3 tablespoons red wine vinegar

SOAK the dried pepper in the hot water until soft, about 10 minutes. Meanwhile, broil the tomatoes until soft, about 6 minutes. Peel, seed and mash the tomatoes. Set aside. Toast the almonds in a dry skillet over low heat until golden brown, about 5 minutes. Finely grind the almonds in a blender or food processor. Set aside. Drain the hot pepper, then seed and coarsely chop.

IN A BLENDER or food processor, process the pepper, tomatoes, garlic, paprika and salt until smooth. Drizzle in the oil a little at a time, blending until the sauce is creamy. Add the vinegar 1 tablespoon at a time to taste. Stir in the ground almonds and serve.

Helpful hint:

You may use 2/3 cup canned, stewed tomatoes, seeded and mashed, in place of fresh tomatoes.

> **PER 3-TABLESPOON SERVING:**
> 116 Cal.; 3g Prot.; 10g Fat; 6g Carb.;
> 0mg Chol.; 185mg Sod.; 2g Fiber.

Miso Sauce

makes 1 1/2 cups

Here's a simple-to-make sauce with the complex flavor of miso, an Asian condiment that may be mellow or intensely flavored. Serve the sauce over hot pasta, rice or steamed vegetables.

> 2 tablespoons safflower oil
> 8 scallions (green and white parts), chopped finely
> 2 cloves garlic, minced
> 1/4 cup yellow miso
> 1 to 1 1/2 cups water or vegetable stock (page 178), warmed
> 4 tablespoons chopped fresh parsley

IN A MEDIUM SKILLET, heat the oil over medium-high heat. Add the scallions and garlic, and cook, stirring, 3 minutes. Transfer the mixture to a medium bowl. Add the miso. Slowly add 1 cup water or stock while stirring. Add the parsley. (Adjust the thickness of the sauce by adding more liquid.)

> **PER 1/3-CUP SERVING:**
> 99 Cal.; 2g Prot.; 8g Fat; 5g Carb.;
> 0mg Chol.; 510mg Sod.; 0g Fiber.

Red Pepper Sauce

makes 2 1/2 cups

Here's a marvelous sauce where you need an intense flavor. Try it on potatoes and other vegetables, pasta, grains and other dishes.

> 3 large red bell peppers
>
> Oil for brushing peppers
>
> 2 tablespoons virgin olive oil
>
> 1 onion, minced
>
> 1 1/2 teaspoons dried basil
>
> 1/2 teaspoon dried marjoram
>
> 1/2 teaspoon salt
>
> 1/2 cup white wine
>
> 1/2 cup tomato purée
>
> 2 cups water
>
> 1 tablespoon tomato paste
>
> 2 to 3 teaspoons white wine vinegar
>
> 1 tablespoon butter
>
> 2 tablespoons chopped fresh basil leaves

PREHEAT the broiler. Cut the bell peppers in half lengthwise, remove the seeds and press open to flatten. Brush the skins with oil. Place the peppers skin side up in the broiler and cook until lightly charred, about 10 minutes. Remove the pepper halves, stacking one on top of another to create steam. Let sit 10 minutes, then remove as much charred skin as possible. (Don't rinse the peppers or you'll lose much of the flavor.) Slice into strips.

HEAT 2 tablespoons virgin olive oil in a skillet. Cook the pepper strips, onion, basil, marjoram and salt, stirring, for 5 minutes over medium-high heat. Add the wine and cook until the mixture is reduced to a sauce, about

15 minutes. Add the tomato purée, water and tomato paste. Lower the heat and simmer 25 minutes. Transfer to a food processor and purée, then pass through a food mill (if you own one). Return the sauce to the skillet and barely simmer. Season with the vinegar. Stir in the butter and basil. Serve warm.

> **PER 3-TABLESPOON SERVING:**
> 47 Cal.; 0.6g Prot.; 3g Fat; 2mg Chol.;
> 140mg Sod.; 0.4g Fiber.

Yellow Curry Paste

makes 3 tablespoons

Indian and Thai cuisine meld in this curry paste. Serve with dishes when you want added spice.

> 1 teaspoon coriander seed
>
> 1 teaspoon caraway seed
>
> 4 dried red chilies
>
> Pinch ground cinnamon
>
> Pinch ground cloves
>
> 1/4 cup minced red onion
>
> 2 to 4 cloves garlic, minced
>
> 1 tablespoon minced lemongrass bulb (or 1/2 tablespoon lemon zest)
>
> 1 teaspoon salt
>
> 1 teaspoon dry mustard
>
> 2 teaspoons mild curry powder

ROAST the coriander and caraway seeds in a dry skillet pan over low heat until lightly browned. Crush the seeds in a mortar and pestle, blender or food processor. Set aside.

REMOVE and discard the seeds from the dried chilies. Soak the chilies in warm water for 15 minutes. Drain and chop finely. In a mortar and pestle, blender or food processor, blend the chilies, ground seeds and remaining ingredients to a paste.

Helpful hint:

This paste stays fresh for about a month in a covered container in your refrigerator.

> **PER TABLESPOON:**
> 36 Cal.; 0.1g Prot.; 0.4g Fat; 7g Carb.;
> 0mg Chol.; 538mg Sod.; 1g Fiber.

Green Curry Paste

makes 1/4 cup

This paste heats up Thai and Indian dishes. Stir in as much or as little as you desire.

- 8 fresh small green chilies, such as serranos
- 2 tablespoons minced lemongrass bulb (or 1 tablespoon lemon zest)
- 2 tablespoons chopped fresh cilantro leaves
- 1 large shallot, minced
- 2 medium cloves garlic, minced
- 1 teaspoon fresh shredded ginger root
- A few slivers lime zest
- 1 teaspoon coriander seed
- 1/2 teaspoon caraway seed
- 10 peppercorns
- 1 teaspoon salt

IN A SMALL SKILLET, roast all the ingredients over medium-high heat until smoking, about 3 minutes. Transfer to a blender or food processor, and process to a thick paste, adding some water if necessary.

Helpful hint:

This paste stays fresh for about a month in a covered container in your refrigerator.

> **PER TABLESPOON:**
> 56 Cal.; 0.3g Prot.; 0g Fat; 14g Carb.;
> 0mg Chol.; 630mg Sod.; 8g Fiber.

Pineapple-Cucumber Chutney

serves 4

Place a platter of chutney on your table along with your favorite Indian foods.

- 1/2 small pineapple, cored, peeled and chopped finely
- 2 medium cucumbers, peeled, seeded and chopped finely
- 1 bunch fresh mint leaves, chopped
- 1/4 to 1/2 serrano pepper, seeded and chopped finely
- 1 tablespoon brown sugar
- 1 tablespoon finely minced ginger root
- Juice and zest of 1 lime
- Pinch salt (optional)
- Mint leaves, for garnish

COMBINE all the ingredients except the garnish in a non-metallic bowl and toss well. Refrigerate for at least 40 minutes. Place on a serving platter and garnish with mint.

PER SERVING:
123 Cal.; 1g Prot.; 0.6g Fat; 28g Carb.;
0mg Chol.; 6mg Sod.; 4g Fiber.

Pineapple-Mango Chutney

makes 4 cups · 16 servings

2 cups diced fresh pineapple

1 large mango, peeled, pitted and chopped

1 cup diced onion

1 apple or pear, cored and diced

1/2 cup brown sugar (or 1/3 cup maple syrup)

1 cup red wine vinegar

1/2 cup dry white wine or apple juice

1 jalapeño pepper, seeded and minced

1 tablespoon minced fresh ginger root

3 to 4 cloves garlic, minced

1 teaspoon ground cumin

1/2 teaspoon ground cloves

1/4 teaspoon salt

SIMMER all the ingredients in a large saucepan over low heat, stirring occasionally, until the mixture has a jam-like consistency, about 15 to 20 minutes.

Helpful hints:

- The chutney will keep for several weeks in the refrigerator.
- Use plastic gloves when removing seeds from the jalapeño pepper. It may irritate bare skin.

PER SERVING:
51 Cal.; 0g Prot.; 0g Fat; 12g Carb.;
0mg Chol.; 38mg Sod.; 1g Fiber.

Avocado Salsa

makes 2 1/2 cups

Depending on how hot you like your salsa, remove the seeds (the hottest part) of the pepper or leave them in.

1 1/2 cups canned tomatoes, drained and diced

1 small avocado, diced

2 tablespoons fresh lime juice

2 tablespoons fresh lemon juice

1 tablespoon honey or other liquid sweetener

2 tablespoons chopped fresh mint leaves

2 tablespoons chopped fresh cilantro leaves

1 jalapeño pepper, minced

Salt and freshly ground black pepper to taste

IN A FOOD PROCESSOR or blender, process 1/4 cup tomatoes and 1/4 cup avocado. Transfer to a medium bowl. Mix in the remaining ingredients.

PER SERVING:
17 Cal.; 0.3g Prot.; 0.7g Fat; 1g Carb.;
0mg Chol.; 27mg Sod.; 0.1g Fiber.

No-Oil Spaghetti Sauce

serves 12

There's only 1 gram of fat in a serving of this aromatic tomato sauce. Spoon it over your favorite pasta.

- 1 1/3 cups diced onions
- 1 1/3 cups diced celery
- 1/2 cup diced green bell pepper
- 1/2 pound white button mushrooms, sliced
- 2 cloves garlic, minced
- 4 cups diced tomatoes
- 4 cups tomato sauce
- 2 cups tomato purée
- 1 teaspoon dried basil
- 1 teaspoon dried oregano
- 1 bay leaf

SAUTÉ the onions in a small amount of water until soft, about 5 minutes. Add the celery, green pepper, mushrooms and garlic; cook 5 minutes more. Mix in the remaining ingredients and simmer, uncovered, for 30 minutes. Remove the bay leaf. Serve hot.

> **PER SERVING:**
> 91 Cal.; 4g Prot.; 1g Fat; 20g Carb.;
> 0mg Chol.; 534mg Sod.; 6g Fiber.

Quick Tomato Sauce

makes 4 cups

This barely cooked sauce has a light, fresh taste.

- 2 tablespoons virgin olive oil
- 2 cloves garlic, minced
- 1 large onion, chopped finely
- 2/3 cup sliced white button mushrooms (optional)
- 5 cups chopped fresh, ripe tomatoes
- 1/4 cup red wine
- 2 teaspoons chopped fresh basil leaves (or 1 teaspoon dried)
- 1/2 teaspoon dried rosemary
- Salt and freshly ground black pepper to taste

IN A LARGE SKILLET, heat the oil and cook the garlic, onion and mushrooms, stirring, until soft. Add the tomatoes and wine, cover and simmer 5 minutes. Add the basil and rosemary, cover and simmer 20 minutes, stirring occasionally. Season with salt and pepper.

> **PER 1/2-CUP SERVING:**
> 57 Cal.; 0.8g Prot.; 4g Fat; 5g Carb.;
> 0mg Chol.; 73mg Sod.; 4g Fiber.

Chunky Tomato Gravy

serves 4

This pretty gravy goes well with any stuffing. It may not be traditional, but who's to quibble?

2 tablespoons margarine or butter

1 onion, minced

1 garlic clove, minced

1/2 pound plum tomatoes, peeled, seeded and chopped

2 teaspoons arrowroot powder or cornstarch

1/4 teaspoon salt

1/8 teaspoon freshly ground black pepper

1 cup water

1/4 cup chopped fresh parsley

MELT the margarine or butter in a medium saucepan. Add the onion and garlic and cook, stirring, over medium-high heat about 1 minute. Add the tomatoes and cook 2 minutes more. Stir in the arrowroot or cornstarch, salt, pepper and water. Cook, stirring, until thickened, about 4 to 5 minutes. Stir in the parsley. Serve hot.

> **PER SERVING:**
> 51 Cal.; 1g Prot.; 3g Fat; 5g Carb.;
> 0mg Chol.; 208mg Sod.; 2g Fiber.

Mustard Marinade

makes 1/2 cup

These marinades—pungent mixtures typically including oil and vinegar—add flavor to roasted vegetables; skewered vegetables, tofu and/or fruit; and bean burgers. Marinate your dish before cooking. You also may use the marinade to baste during cooking. Here are several to try.

2 tablespoons Dijon mustard

3 cloves garlic, crushed

3 tablespoons tamari or soy sauce

3 tablespoons fresh lemon or lime juice

1 tablespoon vegetable oil

WHISK together all the ingredients except the oil. Add the oil 1/2 teaspoon at a time, whisking vigorously after each addition.

> **PER TABLESPOON:**
> 28 Cal.; 1g Prot.; 2g Fat; 1g Carb.;
> 0mg Chol.; 482mg Sod.; 0g Fiber.

Tart White Wine Marinade

makes 1 cup

1/2 cup white wine

2 small lemons, sliced thinly

1 teaspoon chopped fresh thyme leaves

3 small bay leaves

10 peppercorns, crushed

1/4 teaspoon salt

MIX together all the ingredients.

> **PER TABLESPOON:**
> 8 Cal.; 0g Prot.; 0g Fat; 1g Carb.;
> 0mg Chol.; 1mg Sod.; 0g Fiber.

Apple-Ginger Marinade

makes 1 1/2 cups

1/4 cup apple juice or cider

1 tablespoon minced fresh ginger root

1/4 cup cider vinegar

1/3 cup vegetable oil

1/3 cup tamari

1/3 cup honey

2 cloves garlic, crushed

MIX together all the ingredients.

> **PER TABLESPOON:**
> 45 Cal.; 0g Prot.; 3g Fat; 5g Carb.;
> 0mg Chol.; 221mg Sod.; 0g Fiber.

Sweet and Tangy Marinade

makes 2 cups

3 tablespoons vegetable oil

1/2 cup cider vinegar

3/4 cup ketchup

1/4 cup vegetarian Worcestershire sauce

1 tablespoon molasses

3 tablespoons honey

1 teaspoon salt (optional)

Pinch allspice

COMBINE all the ingredients in a saucepan. Bring to a boil, cover, lower the heat and simmer 5 minutes. Let cool.

> **PER TABLESPOON:**
> 27 Cal.; 0g Prot.; 1g Fat; 4g Carb.;
> 0mg Chol.; 79mg Sod.; 0g Fiber.

Citrus Marinade

makes 2 cups

This marinade is especially tasty with tempeh.

1 cup fresh lime juice

1/2 cup fresh orange juice

1/4 cup fresh lemon juice

1 onion, sliced

3 tablespoons virgin olive oil

Pinch ground coriander

Salt and freshly ground black pepper to taste

MIX together all the ingredients.

> **PER TABLESPOON:**
> 17 Cal.; 0g Prot.; 1g Fat; 1g Carb.;
> 0mg Chol.; 33mg Sod.; 0g Fiber.

Mock Sour Cream

makes 1 1/2 cups

With a flavor surprisingly similar to genuine sour cream, this mixture is tasty on blintzes, potatoes, Mexican dishes—whenever you desire a creamy, piquant sensation.

1 cup low-fat cottage cheese

2 tablespoons fresh lemon juice

2 tablespoons mayonnaise

1/4 cup buttermilk

Zest of 1/2 lemon

Pinch salt

IN A BLENDER or food processor, blend all the ingredients until smooth. Chill.

> **PER TABLESPOON:**
> 16 Cal.; 1g Prot.; 1g Fat; 0.5g Carb.;
> 1mg Chol.; 59mg Sod.; 0g Fiber.

Yogurt Cheese

makes 1/2 cup

One 8-ounce container plain yogurt (see Note)

PLACE the yogurt in a fine mesh strainer on top of a bowl and cover with plastic wrap. Refrigerate for 24 hours. The whey will drop through the cheesecloth, leaving a mild, sweet cheese in the strainer.

Variation:

To make a sandwich spread, heat 1/4 cup sherry or vegetable broth over medium-high heat. Stir in some chopped onion, chives and minced carrot and cook about 5 minutes. Combine with the yogurt cheese.

Notes:

- Use a brand without stabilizers (starch, gelatin or gums).
- Store in a tightly covered container in your refrigerator; it keeps for about 10 days.

> **PER 1/2 CUP:**
> 144 Cal.; 12g Prot.; 4g Fat; 16g Carb.;
> 14mg Chol.; 159mg Sod.; 0g Fiber.

Homemade Mayonnaise

makes 1 1/2 cups

Use this mayonnaise as a condiment or to garnish soups and entrées.

1 cup fresh bread crumbs

1/4 cup fresh lemon juice

2 to 4 cloves garlic, minced

Pinch salt

1/3 cup virgin olive oil

2 teaspoons prepared mustard (optional)

PLACE the bread crumbs in a small bowl. Sprinkle with the lemon juice and let sit. Place the garlic and salt in a food processor or mortar and pestle. If you're using a food processor, add the lemon-soaked crumbs and purée, adding the oil a few teaspoons at a time through the feed tube while the machine is running. Blend to a thick paste. Stir in the mustard. If using a mortar and pestle, pound the garlic and salt. Add the lemon-soaked bread crumbs, oil and mustard a few tablespoons at a time. Pound to a thick paste.

STORE, covered, in your refrigerator for up to 3 days. If the mayonnaise separates simply stir it with a fork.

> **PER TABLESPOON:**
> 44 Cal.; 0.6g Prot.; 3g Fat; 3g Carb.;
> 0mg Chol.; 42mg Sod.; 0g Fiber.

Tofu Relish

serves 6

This relish keeps for three days in your refrigerator.

> 1/2 pound extra-firm tofu
>
> 1/2 pound white turnip, shredded
>
> 1/2 cup thinly sliced scallions (green and white parts)
>
> 1 plum tomato, diced finely
>
> 1/4 cup low-sodium soy sauce
>
> 2 tablespoons grated fresh ginger root
>
> 3 tablespoons sesame seeds, toasted (page 106) (optional)

CUT the tofu into 1/4-inch cubes or pulse in a food processor until crumbly. Combine with the turnip, scallions and tomato in a bowl. Mix together the soy sauce and ginger, and pour over the tofu mixture. Stir well and chill for at least 1 hour. Just before serving, stir in the sesame seeds.

PER SERVING:
77 Cal.; 7g Prot.; 3g Fat; 7g Carb.;
0mg Chol.; 427mg Sod.; 2g Fiber.

Sun-Dried Tomatoes Marinated in Red Wine

makes 1 pint

Marinated dried tomatoes may be stirred into sauces, pasta, grains and casseroles to heighten the richness of your dish.

> 1 1/2 cups sun-dried tomatoes (see Note)
>
> 1/4 cup canola oil
>
> 1/4 cup virgin olive oil
>
> 1/2 cup dry red wine
>
> 2 cloves garlic, minced
>
> 1 teaspoon salt
>
> 1 bay leaf
>
> 1/2 teaspoon dried thyme (or a sprig of fresh thyme)
>
> 1/4 teaspoon dried basil
>
> 1/4 teaspoon dried oregano or marjoram
>
> Freshly ground black pepper to taste

COMBINE all the ingredients in a nonaluminum bowl or jar. Cover and let sit in refrigerator 12 hours, stirring occasionally. Transfer the marinated tomatoes to a sterilized pint jar and close tightly. Refrigerate up to 3 months.

Note:

If your sun-dried tomatoes are hard, steam them until they are soft enough to chew. Then proceed with the recipe.

**PER TABLESPOON
(WITH DRAINED TOMATOES):**
18 Cal.; 0.2g Prot.; 1g Fat; 1g Carb.;
0mg Chol.; 69mg Sod.; 0.1g Fiber.

Banana Condiment

makes 1 cup

Here's a sweet complement to savory dishes. Stored in a jar in the refrigerator, it will last two to three weeks.

- **5 very ripe bananas**
- **Juice of 1 lemon**
- **1/4 cup raisins or fresh berries in season**

AT LEAST ONE DAY BEFORE PREPARATION, place the bananas in your refrigerator to blacken. Peel the bananas and mash them in a bowl until almost smooth. Add the lemon juice and raisins or berries. Transfer to a saucepan and bring to a boil, stirring constantly, until the mixture thickens, about 10 minutes. (The longer it cooks, the thicker it will become.) Cool slightly before serving.

> **PER SERVING:**
> 40 Cal.; 0.5g Prot.; 0.1g Fat; 9g Carb.;
> 0mg Chol.; 1mg Sod.; 1g Fiber.

Herb-Flavored Vinegars

makes 3 quarts

Vinegars flavored with herbs add zest to meals. Use fresh herbs if possible; otherwise use high-quality dried herbs.

- **3 cups fresh herbs (or 1 1/2 cups dried herbs)**
- **3 quarts vinegar of choice (see Note)**

IF YOU'RE USING FRESH HERBS, rinse them well and dry them with a dishcloth. Rub the fresh or dried herbs between your fingers to release their oils. If you're using herb seeds, crush them a bit. Place the herbs in a glass gallon jar or crock, and pour the vinegar over them. Cover with a nonmetallic lid.

LET SIT for 2 weeks at room temperature. Or heat the vinegar to just below the boiling point, remove from the heat and let sit 1 to 3 days. Strain the vinegar through a colander lined with cheesecloth and set over a bowl. Pour the liquid into sterilized jars or bottles. For identification and decoration, add a sprig or two of the herbs to the bottle. Cap with a nonmetal cap or cork stopper.

Flavor ideas:

Try these herbs alone or in combination: dill, chives, thyme, oregano, marjoram, tarragon, basil or rosemary. Or opt for some more exotic herbs, such as opal basil (which turns white wine vinegar a dark burgundy), lemon verbena or lovage.

Note:

Apple cider vinegar is the best all-purpose vinegar to use, but you can also use red wine vinegar, white wine vinegar, malt vinegar or rice vinegar. Do not use distilled white vinegar; its flavor is too strong.

> **PER TABLESPOON:**
> 2 Cal.; 0g Prot.; 0g Fat; 0.9g Carb.;
> 0mg Chol.; 0mg Sod.; 0g Fiber.

Flavored Oils

makes 3 cups

Oils flavored with herbs and spices enhance many foods. Use oils sparingly because they're all fat.

| Fresh or dried herbs and spices (except garlic)
| 3 cups vegetable oil, preferably virgin olive oil

GENTLY rinse the fresh herbs; dry on towels. (Moisture clouds and spoils oil.) Place several sprigs of the fresh herbs or several tablespoons of the dried herbs into a large clean, dry jar. Pour in the oil. Cover tightly and let sit in a cool, dark place for no less than 1 week and up to several months, depending on the strength you desire.

CHECK the oils weekly to see if the herbs seem to be decomposing. If they appear to be decomposing, strain the oil through a fine-mesh strainer or several layers of cheesecloth. Discard the herbs and rebottle the oil. (The oil is safe to use.)

WHEN THE OIL TASTES JUST RIGHT to you, strain it and decant into dry, sterilized bottles. Add a sprig of fresh herb to each bottle and cap tightly. Store the bottles in your refrigerator.

Helpful hints:

- To be on the safe side, do not use garlic to flavor oil. Garlic is very low in acid and it can cause botulism if it isn't acidified.

- Using fresh herbs makes a more intensely flavored oil. Dried herbs have the plus of not containing moisture. In the winter, it's often best to use good-quality dried herbs (choose those with bright color and aroma), and use a sprig of fresh herb from your window or grocer in each bottle for identification and decoration.

- Any herb or combination of herbs can be used except basil, which turns black in oil. Try oregano, dill, rosemary, thyme, lemon thyme, fennel (both the feathery stems and the seeds, slightly crushed), sage, tarragon and marjoram.

> **PER TABLESPOON:**
> 120 Cal.; 0g Prot.; 14g Fat; 0mg Carb.;
> 0mg Chol.; 0mg Sod.; 0g Fiber.

Blueberry Sauce

serves 8

| 2 cups apple or mixed berry juice
| One 10-ounce jar blueberry preserves
| 2 to 3 teaspoons arrowroot or kudzu dissolved in 1/2 cup cold water
| Pinch salt
| Pinch ground cinnamon or nutmeg
| 1 teaspoon vanilla extract
| 1 pint blueberries (fresh or frozen)
| 1 to 2 teaspoons fresh lemon juice (optional)

BRING the apple or berry juice to a boil in a saucepan, add the preserves, lower the heat and simmer. Add the dissolved arrowroot or kudzu and stir until the sauce thickens and becomes shiny. Stir in the salt, cinnamon or nutmeg, vanilla, blueberries and lemon juice. Lower the heat and keep warm until ready to serve.

> **PER SERVING:**
> 140 Cal.; 0g Prot.; 0g Fat; 34g Carb.;
> 0mg Chol.; 37mg Sod.; 1g Fiber.

Raspberry Sauce

makes 1 1/4 cups

1 cup frozen raspberries
2 tablespoons fresh lemon juice
1/4 to 1/3 cup honey

PURÉE the frozen raspberries and lemon juice in a blender. Sweeten with the honey and purée until smooth.

PER 2-TABLESPOON SERVING:
65 Cal.; 0.3g Prot.; 0g Fat; 17g Carb.;
0mg Chol.; 1mg Sod.; 1g Fiber.

Chocolate Sauce

makes 1 1/2 cups

1 1/2 cups skim milk or low-fat vanilla soymilk
4 tablespoons unsweetened cocoa powder
1 egg (or equivalent egg substitute)
5 tablespoons honey or brown sugar
1 teaspoon vanilla extract

IN A BLENDER, combine all the ingredients and blend until smooth. Transfer to a small saucepan. Heat, stirring constantly, until thickened and beginning to boil. Remove from the heat. Chill before serving.

PER 2-TABLESPOON SERVING:
43 Cal.; 2g Prot.; 1g Fat; 7g Carb.;
18mg Chol.; 6mg Sod.; 0g Fiber.

yields, weights and measures

YIELDS

BREADS
1 pound = 12 to 16 slices

1 slice fresh = 1/2 cup soft crumbs

1 slice dried = 1/3 cup dry crumbs

28 saltine crackers = 1 cup fine crumbs

CHEESES
Grating cheeses (i.e., Parmesan)

3 ounces = 1 cup grated

Hard cheeses (i.e., cheddar, mozzarella)

4 ounces = 1 cup shredded

DRY BEANS
Large beans (i.e., kidney)

1 cup = 2 to 3 cups cooked

1 pound = 2 cups uncooked = 5 1/2 cups cooked

Small beans (i.e., navy)

1 cup = 2 to 3 cups cooked

1 pound = 2 1/3 cups uncooked = 5 1/2 cups cooked

Lentils

1 cup = 3 cups cooked

Split peas

1 cup = 2 1/2 cups cooked

EGGS
White

1 large = 2 tablespoons

Yolk

1 large = 1 tablespoon

FATS

Butter or margarine
1 stick = 1/2 cup = 4 ounces

1 pound = 2 cups

1 pound whipped = 3 cups

Vegetable oil
8 ounces = 1 cup

FRUITS, VEGETABLES, HERBS

Apple
1 medium chopped = 1 cup

Garlic
1 medium clove = 3/4 teaspoon minced

Herbs
1 tablespoon fresh = 1/2 to 1 teaspoon dried

Lemon
Juice of 1 lemon = 3 tablespoons

Grated zest of 1 lemon = 1 teaspoon

Onion
1 medium chopped = 1/2 cup

Orange
Juice of 1 orange = 1/3 cup

Grated zest of 1 orange = 2 teaspoons

Potatoes
1 pound = 3 medium

GRAINS

Barley
1 cup = 3 1/2 cups cooked

Bulgur
1 cup = 2 1/2 to 3 cups cooked

Cornmeal
1 cup = 4 cups cooked

Kasha (buckwheat groats)
1 cup = 2 1/2 to 3 cups cooked

Millet
1 cup = 3 1/2 cups cooked

Pasta
1 pound macaroni = 5 cups uncooked = 8 to 10 cups cooked

4 ounces spaghetti = 2 cups cooked

Rice (white or brown)
1 pound = 2 1/2 cups uncooked

1 cup = 3 cups cooked

Rolled oats
1 pound = 5 cups uncooked

1 cup = 1 3/4 cups cooked

Wild rice
1 cup = 4 cups cooked

Nuts
1 cup whole = 1/4 pound = 1 cup chopped (approx.)

WEIGHTS AND MEASURES

Pinch = about 1/16 teaspoon

Dash = about 1/8 teaspoon

3 teaspoons = 1 tablespoon

4 tablespoons = 1/4 cup

5 1/3 tablespoons = 1/3 cup

8 tablespoons = 1/2 cup

10 2/3 tablespoons = 2/3 cup

12 tablespoons = 3/4 cup

16 tablespoons = 1 cup

1 ounce = 28.35 grams

1 gram = 0.035 ounces

1 cup = 8 fluid ounces

1 cup = 1/2 pint

2 cups = 1 pint

4 cups = 1 quart

4 quarts = 1 gallon

1 quart = 946.4 milliliters

1 liter = 1.06 quarts

mail-order sources

ARROWHEAD MILLS, INC.: You can find the company's products in natural food stores and well-stocked supermarkets, but if you live in a more remote area, their catalog will come in handy. Arrowhead Mills has a wide range of products: grains, legumes, peanut butter, seeds and waffle and pancake mixes. Free catalog. Arrowhead Mills, Inc., P.O. Box 2059, Hereford, TX 79045; (800) 749-0730.

THE BEAN BAG: Specializes in legumes, with more than a hundred varieties available. Also carries various rices, corn flour, nuts, Western African foods (such as yam flour and ground melon seeds) and dried herbs and spices. Catalog costs $1, refundable with a purchase. The Bean Bag, 8118 Jefferson Street, Oakland, CA 94607; (800) 845-2326.

GARDEN SPOT DISTRIBUTORS: A wide variety of bulk staples: cereals, grains (both common and ancient varieties, including teff and quinoa), legumes, dried fruits, breads, organic produce, organic milk, tofu, tempeh, convenience foods, juices and desserts (such as fat-free cheesecake). Free catalog. Garden Spot Distributors, 438 White Oak Road, New Holland, PA 17557; (800) 829-5100.

GOLD MINE NATURAL FOOD CO.: Vegetarian staples include grains and legumes, plus dried shiitake mushrooms, umeboshi plums, chestnut flour and Asian foods such as miso, shoyu and tamari. Free catalog. Gold Mine Natural Food Co., 3419 Hancock Street, San Diego, CA 92110; (800) 475-3663.

THE MAIL ORDER CATALOG: Textured vegetable protein, gluten flour and nutritional yeast available. The Mail Order Catalog, P.O. Box 180-TC, Summertown, TN 38483; (800) 695-2241.

MOUNTAIN ARK TRADING CO.: Carries a variety of foods, including some unusual selections: sea vegetables, nonwheat pasta, kudzu, Asian noodles and other Asian products such as umeboshi plums, tofu, grains, flours, dried fruits, nuts and legumes. Free catalog. Mountain Ark Trading Co., P.O. Box 3170, Fayetteville, AR 72702; (800) 643-8909.

THE ORIENTAL PANTRY: Has a gamut of Asian foods. Free catalog. The Oriental Pantry, 423 Great Road, Acton, MA 01720; (800) 828-0368.

WALNUT ACRES: You want it, they've got it—whole food staples, pasta, organic canned goods and soups, organic cheeses, convenience foods, preserves, cookies, and even baking supplies and kitchen gadgets. Free catalog. Walnut Acres, Penns Creek, PA 17862; (800) 433-3998.

A

index

SAMPLE CALCULATION OF RENAL DIET PLAN FOR HEMODIALYSIS

Food Choices	Choices no.	Energy kcal	PRO g	Na mg	K mg	P mg
Milk	1	120	4	80	185	110
Nondairy milk substitute	1	140	0.5	40	80	30
Meat	9	585	63	225	900	585
Starch	10	900	20	800	350	350
Vegetable	2	50	2	30	...	40
Low potassium		...	...	...	...	...
Medium potassium	(1)	...	...	...	150	...
High potassium	(1)	...	...	...	270	...
Fruit	3	210	1.5	...	...	45
Low potassium	...	...	...	...	...	
Medium potassium	(1)	...	...	...	150	...
High potassium	(2)	...	...	...	540	...
Fat	10	450	...	550	100	50
High-calorie	5	500	...	75	100	25
Salt	1	...	...	250	...	...
Totals		2955	91	2050	2825	1235

*Because control of fat and carbohydrate intake is not a priority for all patients, practitioners may include their calculation in the meal plan on a case-by-case basis. Table abbreviations: PRO = protein, CHO = carbohydrate, Na = sodium, K = potassium, P = phosphorus, tr = trace, HBW = healthy body weight.

Source: Monsen, ER: Meeting the challenge of the renal diet. Copyright The American Dietetic Association. Reprinted by permission from Journal of the American Dietetic Association 93:638, 1993.

and sample meal plan are shown. Box 20–3 is a condensed food list for the client with chronic renal failure who is receiving hemodialysis treatments. A sample menu derived from the condensed renal food list and the sample daily meal plan is shown in Table 20–4.

Nutrient Guidelines for Adults with Renal Disease

As you can see, the nutritional care of renal clients is complex. Table 20–5 is a summary that lists clinical situations, dietary interventions, and the rationale for nutrient control.

Renal Disease in Children

Growth failure is commonly seen in children with chronic renal failure treated with dialysis, but it is not an inevitable complication. Inadequate kilocaloric consumption and/or metabolic acidosis are reasons for the poor growth. These children often need to have their sodium, potassium, and protein intake rigidly controlled, and this may contribute to poor food intake. Anorexia and emotional disturbances are also contributing factors. Suggestions for improving children's intake might include involving the children in selecting and preparing foods (insofar as possible); serving meals in an appealing, attractive manner (e.g., serving contrasting colors and textures of foods, using decorative tableware and dishes; serving small, frequent meals; ensuring that the child has someone with him or her at mealtime; and planning special mealtime events such as picnics (even if they have to be held in the hospital playroom).

Kidney Stones

Kidney stones may be found in the bladder, kidney, ureter, or urethra. During urine formation, the urine moves from the collecting tubules and into the **renal pelvis.** From the renal pelvis, the urine moves

---

BOX 20–3   CONDENSED RENAL FOOD LISTS FOR CHRONIC RENAL FAILURE, HEMODIALYSIS

MILK LIST

Approximate Nutrient Content: 4 g protein, 120 kcal, 80 mg sodium (Na), 185 mg potassium (K), 110 mg phosphorus (P)

Item	*Amount*
Milk	1/2 cup
Alterna (low-sodium milk substitute)	1 cup
Cream cheese	3 tbsp

NONDAIRY MILK SUBSTITUTES

Approximate Nutrient Content: 0.5 g protein, 140 kcal, 40 mg Na, 80 mg K, 30 mg P

Liquid nondairy creamer, polyunsaturated	1/2 cup
Dessert topping, nondairy, frozen	1/2 cup

MEAT LIST

Approximate Nutrient Content: 7 g protein, 65 kcal, 25 mg Na, 100 mg K, 65 mg P

Low-cholesterol egg substitute	1/4 cup
Lean beef, pork, poultry	1 oz
Unsalted canned tuna	1/4 cup

STARCH LIST

Approximate Nutrient Content: 2 g protein, 90 kcal, 80 mg Na, 35 mg K, 35 mg P

Bread (white, light rye, sourdough)	1 slice
Saltines, unsalted	4
Puffed wheat	1 cup
Rice, cooked	1/2 cup
Angel Food Cake	1 oz

VEGETABLE LIST

Approximate Nutrient Content: 1 g protein, 25 kcal, 15 mg Na, 20 mg P; serving size is ½ cup unless otherwise noted; prepared or canned without salt

Low Potassium (0–100 mg K)	
Lettuce, all varieties	1 cup
Cucumber, peeled	
Medium Potassium (101 to 200 mg K)	
Carrots	1 small, raw
Corn	1/2 ear
Broccoli	1/2 cup
High Potassium (201–350 mg K)	
Tomato	1 medium
Potato, baked	1/2 medium
Spinach, ckd.	

Item	Amount
FRUIT LIST	
Approximate Nutrient Content: 0.5 g protein, 70 kcal, 15 mg P; serving size is 1/2 cup, unless otherwise noted	
Low Potassium (0–100 mg K)	
Applesauce	
Pears, canned	
Medium Potassium (101–200 mg K)	
Apple, fresh	1 small
Watermelon	1 cup
High Potassium (201–350 mg K)	
Orange juice	
Pear, fresh	1 medium
FAT LIST	
Approximate Nutrient Content: trace protein, 45 kcal, 55 mg Na, 10 mg K, 5 mg P	
Unsaturated Fats	
Margarine	1 tsp
Mayo	1 tsp
Saturated Fats	
Coconut	2 tbsp
Powdered coffee whitener	1 tbsp
HIGH-KILOCALORIE CHOICES	
Approximate Nutrient Content: 100 kcal, 15 mg ligrams Na, 20 mg K, 5 mg P	
Carbonated beverages, fruit flavors, root beer	1 cup
Kool-Aid	1 cup
Lemonade	1 cup
Tang	1 cup
Gum drops	15

down the **ureter** and into the urinary bladder. Finally, urine passes from the bladder, down the urethra, and exits the body. A stone, also called a **urinary calculus,** is a deposit of mineral salts held together by a thick, syrupy substance. A urinary calculus can block the movement of urine out of the body. Symptoms of a blockage include sudden severe pain with chills, fever, hematuria (blood in the urine), and an increased desire to urinate. A kidney stone can also pass out of the body via the urine.

Causes

The cause of most kidney stones is unknown. Some possible causes include an abnormal function of the parathyroid gland, disordered uric acid metabolism (as in gout), an excessive intake of animal protein, and immobility. At higher risk for kidney stones are men, people with a sedentary lifestyle, and Asians and Caucasians. Typically, kidney stones occur in clients who are between ages 30 and 50. A determination of the stones's composition may lead to a restriction of dietary substrates (the substance acted on). Frequent dietary substrates of kidney stones are oxalic acid and purines.

> **Urinary calculus**—Calculus (stone) in any part of the renal system, which can block the movement of urine out of the body.

TABLE 20–4 Chronic Renal Failure, Hemodialysis Meal Plan and Sample Menu

Meal Plan	Sample Menu	Meal Plan	Sample Menu
Breakfast		*Afternoon Snack*	
1 nondairy milk substitute	1/2 cup liquid nondairy creamer, polyunsaturated	1 high-kilocalorie	1 cup Kool-Aid
1 high-potassium fruit	1/2 cup orange juice	*Supper*	
2 starches	1 cup puffed wheat and 1 slice light rye toast	1 high-potassium vegetable	1/2 cup ckd. drained spinach
1 meat	1/4 cup low-cholesterol egg substitute	1 high-potassium fruit	1 fresh pear
2 fats	2 tsp margarine	2 starches	1/2 cup rice and 1 oz angel food cake
Morning Snack		4 meat	4 oz broiled chicken breast
1 high-kilocalorie	1 cup Tang	2 fats	2 tsp margarine (used on chicken)
Lunch		1 high-kilocalorie	1 cup root beer
1 medium-potassium vegetable	1 small raw carrot	*Bedtime Snack*	
1 medium-potassium fruit	1 small apple	1 milk	1/2 cup low-fat milk
2 starches	2 slices of sourdough white bread	2 starches	8 unsalted saltine crackers
4 meats	4 oz unsalted lean beef	1 meat	1/4 cup unsalted canned tuna
2 fats	2 tsp mayo	2 fats	2 tsp mayo (for tuna salad)
1 high-kilocalorie	1 cup lemonade	1 high-kilocalorie	1 cup limeade

TABLE 20–5 Clinical Situation, Dietary Intervention, and Rationale for Nutrient Control

Clinical Situation	Rationale	Intervention
Proteinuria	Protein lost in urine	Increase dietary protein
CAPD	Protein lost in dialysate	Increase dietary protein
Elevated BUN and creatinine (Uremia)	Body unable to excrete waste generated from protein metabolism in the amounts eaten and/or catabolized	Decrease dietary protein Increase nonprotein kilocalories Emphasis on proteins with high biologic value
Edema (Anuria)	Body unable to reabsorb and excrete sodium and fluid in the amounts consumed	Fluid restrictions Sodium restriction
Hyperkalemia	Body unable to excrete potassium	Potassium restriction
Hyperphosphatemia	May be related to an inability to activate vitamin D Body unable to excrete the amounts of phosphorus consumed and absorbed	Phosphorus restriction Phosphate binders
Low ferritin levels	Iron deficiency; may be caused by blood loss and/or poor food intake	Increase kilocalories Increase nutrient density Iron supplements Vitamin C enhances iron absorption and should be consumed with meals
Poor growth, especially in children	Insufficient energy	Increase kilocalories to spare protein
Low number of red blood cells with normal ferritin level	Inability to manufacture erythropoietin	Epoetin alfa supplement
Elevated triglyceride levels	Common in renal patients	Type 4 hyperlipoproteinemia diet with modifications in fat and carbohydrate intake

Treatment

All clients with kidney stones should be advised to drink sufficient water to keep the urine volume above 2 liters per day. About 3000 milliliters or 13 cups of water per day are necessary to produce this amount of urine. The primary reason for increasing fluid intake is to prevent formation of concentrated urine, in which crystals arc morc likcly to combine and precipitate.

Oxalates

A diet that excludes foods high in oxalates (see Clinical Application 20–2) is frequently prescribed for clients with kidney stones if laboratory analysis of a surgically removed or passed stone is found to be high in oxalates.

Calcium

Historically, if laboratory analysis of a surgically removed or passed stone was found to be high in calcium, a low-calcium diet was prescribed (600 milligrams per day). Recent research has shown, however, that there is no benefit to the time-honored advice to eat a diet low in calcium (LeMann, 1993). In fact, calcium restriction increases the absorption of oxalate in the gastrointestinal tract and leads to an increase in urinary oxalate excretion. Urinary oxalate may be more important than urinary calcium for stone formation, because calcium oxalate saturation of urine increases rapidly with small increases in the oxalate concentration (Curhan, et al, 1993).

Uric Acid Stones

Stones composed of uric acid are sometimes a complication of gout. **Gout** is a hereditary metabolic disease that is a form of arthritis. One symptom of gout is inflammation of the joints. The metabolism of uric acid is related to dietary purines. **Purines** are an end product of protein digestion. Thus, a purine-restricted diet is often prescribed for gout. Table 20–6 shows foods that are high, moderate, and low in purines. Many physicians do not prescribe a low-purine diet for the treatment of gout because the condition can be more effectively controlled by medications.

CLINICAL APPLICATION 20–2
Foods High in Oxalic Acid

Beverages	mg/100 g
coffee, instant dry	143.0
tea, brewed	12.5

Fruits	
blackberries, raw	12.4
gooseberries, raw	19.3
plums, raw	11.9

Grains	
bread, whole-wheat	20.9

Vegetables	
beets, raw	72.2
beets, boiled	109.0
carrots, boiled	14.5
green beans, raw	43.7
green beans, boiled	29.7
rhubarb, raw	537.0
rhubarb, stewed	447.0
spinach, boiled	571.0

Miscellaneous	
cocoa, dry	623.0
Ovaltine, powder	45.9

Values taken from Pennington, JAT, and Church, HN: *Food Values of Portions Commonly Used*, 14th ed. Harper & Row Publishers, NY, 1985, p 232.

Surgery

Surgery is sometimes necessary to remove large kidney stones. Surgical removal of the stones prevents infection, reduces pain, and prevents a loss of kidney function.

Gout—Hereditary metabolic disease that is a form of acute arthritis. Marked by inflammation in the joints.

Purines—End product of nucleoprotein digestion. Purines may be synthesized in the body. A purine-restricted diet is occasionally prescribed for gout.

TABLE 20–6 Purines in Food

GROUP A: HIGH CONCENTRATION (150–1000 mg/100 g)	
Liver	Sardines (in oil)
Kidney	Meat extracts
Sweetbreads	Consomme
Brain	Gravies
Heart	Fish roes
Anchovies	Herring

GROUP B: MODERATE AMOUNTS (50–150 mg/100 g)	
Meat, game, and fish other than those mentioned in Group A	
Fowl	Asparagus
Lentils	Cauliflower
Whole-grain cereals	Mushrooms
Beans	Spinach
Peas	

GROUP C: VERY SMALL AMOUNTS NEED NOT BE RESTRICTED IN DIET OF PERSONS WITH GOUT	
Vegetables other than those mentioned above	
Fruits of all kinds	Coffee
Milk	Tea
Cheese	Chocolate
Eggs	Carbonated beverages
Refined cereals, spaghetti, macaroni	Tapioca
Butter, fats, nuts, peanut butter*	Yeast
Sugars and sweets	
Vegetable soups	

* Fats interfere with the urinary excretion of urates and thus should be limited when attempting to promote excretion of uric acid.

Source: From Thomas, CL (ed): Taber's Cyclopedic Medical Dictionary, ed 17. FA Davis, Philadelphia, 1993, p 1643, with permission.

Urinary Tract Infections

One form of **urinary tract infection** (UTI) is **cystitis** or an inflammation of the bladder. This condition is prevalent in young women. Recurrent UTI means that the individual has three or more bouts of infection per year. A general nutrition measure includes acidifying the urine by taking large doses of vitamin C. One study found the regular intake of a cranberry juice beverage reduced the frequency of bacteriuria with pyuria in older women (Avorn, et al, 1994) and another small study confirmed this (Haverkorn, and Mandigers, 1994). Cranberry juice contains a substance with biologic activity that inhibits the growth of *E coli* in the urinary tract. Although clinical interventions are seldom based on one or two studies, ingestion of moderate amounts of cranberry juice would be harmless and acceptable to most clients. In any event, clients with UTIs should be encouraged to drink ample fluids.

Summary

The basic functional unit of the kidney is the nephron. Millions of nephrons work together to form urine and remove unnecessary substances from the blood. Glomerular filtration rate (GFR) is a measure of kidney function. The kidneys also are the site where vitamin D_3 (calcitriol) and erythropoietin are activated. No other body organ can replace the kidneys. Kidney disease is a feared complication of many disease states such as atherosclerosis, diabetes, hypertension, and septic shock. Kidney failure can be acute or chronic. Chronic renal disease is progressive. Much research is aimed at finding a way to stop the downward spiral in GFR in clients diagnosed with chronic renal failure. Current research is focused on the relationship of dietary protein and phosphorus on the progression of kidney failure. Treatment for kidney failure is dialysis or a kidney transplant.

Nutritional management of clients with renal disease is a fundamental part of treatment. Clients with kidney disease require constant assessment, monitoring, and counseling. The dietary components that may need modification are kilocalories, protein, sodium, potassium, phosphorus, fluid, cholesterol, and saturated fat. Vitamin and mineral supplements are often prescribed. Frequently, the diet these clients follow must be further modified as their medical condition and treatment approach changes. Recently, a National Renal Diet was developed for use by these clients.

Some nutritional intervention is necessary for clients with kidney stones and UTIs. The fluid intake of these clients should be high. Usually, clients with kidney stones need to avoid foods that contain substances likely to form stones.

Case Study 20–1

Mr. U a 25-year-old man, was admitted to the hospital from his doctor's office for a shunt implantation with subsequent hemodialysis planned. A college graduate, he is employed as an engineer. His medical record indicates that he had an episode of acute glomerulonephritis about 10 years ago. He contracted the disease after a streptococcal throat infection. At that time his symptoms were hematuria, oliguria, proteinuria, hypertension, and edema. He was discharged on a 4-g sodium diet.

Mr U now complains of swollen ankles, headaches, and fatigue. He reports to have had a 10-lb weight gain over the past 6 weeks. His usual body weight is 170 lb; he is 5 ft, 10 in tall and has a large frame. He now weighs 181 lb. His blood pressure is 155/99. Laboratory test results follow:

Test	Results	Normal Range
BUN	75 mg/dL	9–25 mg/dL
Creatinine	2 mg/dL	0.6–1.5 mg/dL
Serum phosphorus	4.4 mg/dL	3.0–4.5 mg/dL
Serum calcium	3.5 mg/dL	3.5–5.0 mg/dL
Hemoglobin	6 mg/dL	14–18 g/dL
Hematocrit	19 percent	42–52 percent
Potassium	4.0 mEq/L	3.5–5.0 mEq/L
Albumin	3.5 g/dL	3.5–5.5 g/dL
Urine volume	900 mL/day	1000–1500 mL
Proteinuria	1 +	None
GFR	10 mL/min	125 mL/min
Cholesterol	280 mg/dL	<200 mg/dL
Triglycerides	140 mg/dL	40–150 mg/dL

The doctor has prescribed a 60-g protein, 2000-kcal, 2-g sodium, low-saturated-fat, low-cholesterol diet and a fluid restriction of output plus 500 mL. Hemodialysis is ordered for three times a week. His medications include docusate sodium, furosemide, a multivitamin, vitamin B_6, and folic acid. Mr U stated that the protein, fluid, saturated fat, and cholesterol restrictions are new to him.

NURSING CARE PLAN FOR MR. U

Assessment

Subjective Data Client complains of headaches, swollen ankles, and fatigue.

Objective Data Client has an elevated BUN, phosphorus, blood pressure, and creatinine. The client also has edema; a decreased GFR, hemoglobin, and hematocrit; and a decreased urinary output.

Continued on following page

Urinary tract infection—Infection of the urinary tract with microorganisms.

Nursing Diagnosis	Fluid volume excess: related to renal insufficiency as evidenced by client complaints of headaches, swollen ankles, fatigue and decreased urinary output, edema formation, and hypertension.

Desired Outcome/ Evaluation Criteria	Nursing Actions	Rationale
The client will demonstrate a stabilized fluid volume, with balanced intake and output, and a decrease in BUN/ creatinine. Vital signs will decrease from admission values within 24 hours.	Assist client in the restoration of homeostasis. Measure urinary output q shift (q = every).	Client's urinary output may vary, and fluid intake must be adjusted accordingly.
	Plan fluid intake with client; monitor fluid intake and body weight.	Fluid intake must be controlled to prevent excessive edema and control blood pressure. Daily weight is best measure of fluid balance.
	Monitor BUN/creatinine results, as needed.	The client is currently unable to excrete waste generated from protein metabolism in amounts eaten and/or catabolized. As the client begins dialysis treatments, the BUN/creatinine levels should decrease, and the protein content of the diet will need to be adjusted accordingly.
	Assess mentation using standard tool q shift. Provide for dietary restrictions as prescribed, while providing adequate kilocalories to meet the body's needs.	The client's mental status may be altered by increased BUN/ creatinine levels which in turn are increased by a kilocalorie deficit.
	Monitor blood pressure, pulses, lung sounds q 4 hours.	The client's fluid volume excess and decreased GFR may increase secretion of renin and raise blood pressure.
	Encourage adequate kilocaloric intake.	The diet will not be effective in controlling BUN/creatinine levels unless adequate kilocalories are consumed.
The client will verbalize knowledge of condition and therapy regimen.	Discuss necessary changes in lifestyle and assist client to incorporate disease management into activities of daily living.	Because the client has a chronic disease, long-term compliance with the treatment approach will be necessary.
	Teach client to measure urinary output.	The client will need to learn to measure his own urinary output.
	Teach client to measure fluid intake daily; fluid intake should be 500 mL plus urinary output in milliliters.	The client will need to learn how to calculate his daily fluid intake based on his urinary output and insensible losses of fluid.
	Discuss with client the relationships of his symptoms (headaches, swollen ankles, fatigue) and signs (edema; decreased GFR, hemoglobin, hematocrit, urinary output; and elevated BUN/ creatinine to treatment approaches (hemodialysis and dietary restrictions).	Relating signs and symptoms to the client's treatment approach will assist him in understanding his treatment regimen.

Desired Outcome/ Evaluation Criteria	Nursing Actions	Rationale
	Refer to the dietitian for dietary teaching.	The client's needs will best be met if referral to the dietitian is made as soon as possible. A diet as complicated as this client's will require several hours of instruction. Information is usually better retained if small amounts of information are given at frequent intervals.
	Discuss with the client the importance of regular hemodialysis treatments.	Failure to receive regular hemodialysis treatments will result in an excessive fluid gain and abnormal laboratory values between treatments. Subsequent efforts to remove this excess fluid may result in a dangerous drop in blood pressure during the dialysis treatment.
The client will demonstrate behaviors consistent with dietary program.	Monitor client's food intake.	The best method to evaluate whether the client has learned his dietary restrictions is to monitor food intake.

Study Aids

Chapter Review

1. Which of the following is not always a nutritional goal for a child with renal disease?
   a. Promote normal growth and development
   b. Maintain current hydration status
   c. Minimize uremic toxicity
   d. Stimulate client well-being

2. Kidney disease cannot be caused by:
   a. Consumption of toxic metals
   b. Habitual consumption of water
   c. Consumption of a diet habitually high in protein
   d. Trauma

3. Kilocalories usually need to be increased in protein-restricted diets because an adequate kilocalorie intake _____.
   a. Assists in the control of serum potassium
   b. Is necessary to prevent the renal anemia
   c. Controls and prevents osteodystrophy
   d. Spares protein

4. The _____ intake from food is not monitored in renal clients.

   a. Vitamin D
   b. Fluid
   c. Protein
   d. Sodium

5. The most important nutritional consideration in treating clients with kidney stones is to:
   a. Limit calcium intake.
   b. Restrict all end products of protein metabolism.
   c. Restrict all food sources of calcium, oxalic acid, and purines.
   d. Increase fluid intake.

Clinical Analysis

1. Bill, age 10, has acute glomerulonephritis. His mother explains that Bill had a streptococcal infection 1 week prior to the illness. When planning Bill's care, the nurse recognizes that he needs help in understanding his diet. Bill's restrictions will include:
   a. A low-fat diet
   b. A potassium restriction
   c. Measuring urine output (if any) daily and planning his fluid intake
   d. A high-protein diet

2. Mr. Jones, a 49-year-old mechanic, has been admitted to the hospital with diagnosis of renal failure. Mr. Jones has been following a 40-gram protein, 2-gram sodium, 2-gram potassium, 1000-milliliter fluid restriction for the past 5 years. Mr. Jones is scheduled for surgery tomorrow to have a permanent shunt implanted for hemodialysis. Mr. Jones's nutritional needs will most likely change after he is maintained on hemodialysis so as to:
   a. Include more oranges, bananas, and baked potatoes.
   b. Include more lean meat, eggs, low-fat milk, and low-fat cheeses.
   c. Include less starches, breads, and cereals.
   d. Include less margarine, oil, and salad dressings.

3. Mr. Jones is found to have an elevated serum phosphorus level after 6 months on hemodialysis. He should:
   a. Restrict his intake of dairy products.
   b. Restrict his intake of red meats.
   c. Increase his intake of sugar, honey, jam, jelly, and other simple sugars.
   d. Discontinue his phosphate binders.

Bibliography

Ahmed, FE: Effect of diet on progression of chronic renal disease. J Am Diet Assoc 10:1266, 1991.

American Dietetic Association: Manual of Clinical Dietetics, ed 4. American Dietetic Association, Chicago, 1992.

Avorn, J, et al: In reply [letter]. JAMA 272:589, 1994.

Avorn, J, et al: Reduction of bacteriuria and pyuria after ingestion of cranberry juice, JAMA 271:751, 1994.

Burton, BT, and Hirschman, GH: Current concepts of nutritional therapy in chronic renal disease: An update. J Am Diet Assoc 82:4, 1983.

Curhan, GC, et al: A prospective study of dietary calcium and other nutrients and the risk of symptomatic kidney stones. N Engl J Med 328:12, 1993.

Doenges, M, and Moorhouse, M: Nursing Diagnoses with Interventions, ed 2. FA Davis, Philadelphia, 1985.

Feldman, EB: Essentials of Clinical Nutrition. FA Davis, Philadelphia, 1988.

Guyton, AC: Textbook of Medical Physiology, ed 7. WB Saunders, Philadelphia, 1986.

Gylys, BA, and Wedding, ME: Medical Terminology: A Systems Approach, ed 3. FA Davis, Philadelphia, 1995.

Haverkorn, MJ, and Mandigers, J: Reduction of bacteriuria and pyuria using cranberry juice [letter]. JAMA 272:590, 1994.

Klahr, S, et al: The effects of dietary protein restriction and blood-pressure control on the progression of chronic renal disease. N Engl J Med 330:877–884, 1994.

LeMann, J: Composition of diet and calcium kidney stones. N Engl J Med 328:12, 1993.

Monsen, ER: Meeting the challenge of the renal diet. J Am Diet Assoc 93:6, 1993.

Moore, MC: Pocket Guide to Nutrition and Diet Therapy, ed 2. Mosby Year Book, St Louis, 1993.

National Live Stock and Meat Board: Iron in Human Nutrition. National Live Stock and Meat Board, Chicago, 1990.

Oksa, H, et al: Malnutrition in hemodialysis patients. Scand J Urol Nephrol 25:157, 1990.

Paragis, J: Nutrition and end-stage Renal Disease. Patient Care News. Sherwood Medical, St. Louis, 1995.

Pennington, JAT, and Church, HN: Food Values of Portions Commonly Used. Harper and Row, New York, 1985.

Robinson, CH, and Weigley, ES: Basic Nutrition and Diet Therapy, ed 6. Macmillan, New York, 1989.

Ross Laboratories: Specialized Nutrition for Patients with Renal Disease. Ross Laboratories, Columbus, OH, 1990.

Wesley, JR, et al: Parenteral and Enteral Nutrition Manual, ed 4. University of Michigan Medical Center, 1986.

Williams, SR: Essentials of Nutrition and Diet Therapy, ed 5. Times Mirror/Mosby St Louis, 1990.

Wolfson, M: Use of water-soluble vitamins in patients with chronic renal failure. Semin Dialysis 1:28, 1988.

Young, GA, et al: Nutritional assessment of continuous ambulatory peritoneal dialysis patients: An international study. Am J Kidney Dis. 17:462, 1991.

Zeller, K, et al: Effect of restricting dietary protein on the progression of renal failure in patients with insulin-dependent diabetes mellitus. N Engl J Med 324:78, 1991.

CHAPTER 21

Diet in Gastrointestinal Disease

After completing this chapter, the student should be able to:

1   Distinguish the dietary preparation for gastrointestinal surgery from dietary preparation for surgery on other body systems.

2   Identify nutritional deficiencies that may accompany diseases of or resection of regions of the gastrointestinal tract.

3   Describe nutritional deficiencies associated with steatorrhea.

4   List several nutritional consequences of cirrhosis of the liver.

5   Discuss dietary modifications for common gastrointestinal diseases treated medically and surgically.

Many disorders affecting the gastrointestinal tract and its accessory organs (liver, gallbladder, and pancreas) influence the nutritional status of clients. Most surgical procedures impact gastrointestinal tract function and require special dietary measures, both preoperatively and postoperatively. This chapter discusses diet modifications for surgical clients and for clients with common gastrointestinal diseases.

Dietary Considerations with Surgical Clients

Postoperatively, the healing process requires increased protein, vitamins C and K, and zinc, along with adequate amounts of other nutrients. Vitamin C is necessary for collagen formation; vitamin K for blood clotting; and zinc for tissue growth, bone formation, skin integrity, cell-mediated immunity and generalized host defense.

Protein depletion causes increased risk of infection and shock. Protein is essential for the manufacture of antibodies and white blood cells, which help the body fight infection. Hypoalbuminemia (low serum albumin) prevents the return of interstitial fluid to the venous system, decreasing intravascular fluid. This results in an increased risk of shock due to low intravascular volume. Local edema, which accompanies any trauma, including surgery, hampers circulation and healing. A low serum albumin level will increase the time needed to reduce edema. The serum albumin level, then, becomes a useful and readily available measure of protein status. Clinical Application 21–1 elaborates the possible consequence of malnutrition in surgical clients.

Persons with gastrointestinal disease are at special risk when facing surgery because their diseases interfere with nutrition. In cases involving gastrointestinal surgery the gastrointestinal tract is incised and sutured, so postoperative feeding is postponed to allow healing. Clients with postoperative complications following gastrointestinal surgery were four times as likely to have been severely malnourished preoperatively as those without complications. Signs of severe malnutrition in this study were subcutaneous tissue loss and muscle wasting, often with edema, and ongoing weight loss of 10 percent or

---

CLINICAL APPLICATION 21–1

Surgical Clients with Rampant Dental Caries

Within a period of weeks, three clients on a gynecological surgical unit suffered postoperative wound disruptions. Each disruption was a dehiscence, a separation of the wound edges. Dehiscence occurs most frequently between the fifth and twelfth postoperative days. Risk factors for dehiscence include obesity, malnutrition, dehydration, abdominal distention, increased abdominal pressure from improper deep breathing and coughing, and infection.

All three clients had at least one of the risk factors. One client ran a postoperative fever, which could have been caused by infection or dehydration. The other two clients had such severely carious teeth it would have been difficult for them to chew in the months before surgery. They probably were malnourished.

It is suggested that nurses refer preoperative clients with marked dental caries to the dietitian for nutritional assessment. Carious teeth can cause and be caused by poor eating habits.

more of body weight (Detsky, Smalley, and Chang, 1994). A more complicated prognostic nutritional index (PNI) uses serum albumin, serum tranferrin, triceps skinfold and cutaneous delayed hypersensitivity in a formula to predict the risk of operative complications. In clients identified as high risk, seven days of preoperative TPN produced a sixfold reduction in major sepsis (Mullen, 1981).

Special notice should be given to the surgical client with liver disease. The liver has many functions, some of which are reviewed in Table 21–1. Because of the liver's role in metabolizing and detoxifying drugs, the client with liver disease must be carefully managed when surgery is necessary. Drugs may accumulate in the bloodstream because the liver cannot metabolize them. Some anesthetics, analgesics, and anti-infectives are toxic to the liver.

Preoperative Nutrition

Before elective surgery is undertaken, nutritional deficiencies should be identified and corrected. Many obese clients are instructed to lose weight to reduce the risk of surgery. If the client is anemic, an iron preparation can be prescribed. Other nutrients can be provided as needed. At least 2 to 3 weeks are required for objective evidence of the effectiveness of nutritional therapy. All surgical clients should receive instruction in the weeks before surgery.

If general anesthesia is employed, the stomach should be empty to prevent aspiration of gastric contents into the lungs. The usual procedure is to have the client take nothing by mouth (NPO) during the 8 hours prior to surgery. Surgery of the gastrointestinal tract demands additional bowel preparation.

TABLE 21–1   Liver Functions

Related to	Produces	Stores	Breaks Down
Carbohydrate	Glucose from galactose and fructose Glucose from glycogen Glucose from glycerol and protein	Glycogen	
Fat	Fat from glucose Cholesterol Fatty acids and glycerol from cholesterol, phospholipids, and lipoproteins Lipoproteins Water-soluble bilirubin (from fat-soluble) Bile	Fat	
Protein	Albumin Some globulins Prothrombin Fibrinogen Transferrin Enzymes to convert ammonia to urea		
Vitamins	Retinol-binding protein Other transport proteins Activate thiamine Activate pyridoxine	A, D, E, K Thiamin Riboflavin Pyridoxine Folic acid B_{12} Biotin	
Minerals		Iron	
Other			Worn-out red blood cells Acetaminophen Alcohol Aldosterone Bacteria Barbiturates Estrogen Glucocorticoids Morphine Progesterone Some anesthetics

Anti-infectives such as neomycin sulfate, which remain predominantly in the bowel, may be given to kill intestinal bacteria. A low-residue diet for 2 to 3 days will minimize the feces left in the bowel.

A low-residue diet reduces the fecal bulk by reducing food residue. Residue is the total solid material in the large intestine after digestion. A low-residue diet usually consists of foods that are easily digested and absorbed. Table 21–2 details the low-residue diet.

TABLE 21–2   Low-Residue Diet

Description	Indications	Adequacy
The low-residue diet limits milk and milk products and excludes any food made with seeds, nuts, and raw or dried fruits and vegetables. The purpose of the diet is to decrease colonic contents.	The diet can be used for severe diarrhea, partial bowel obstruction, and acute phases of inflammatory bowel diseases. Preoperatively the diet is used to minimize fecal volume and residue. Postoperatively the diet is used in the progression to a general diet. Long-term use of the diet is not recommended since it may aggravate symptoms during nonacute phases of disease.	Strict reduction in milk and milk products, vegetables, and fruits may necessitate supplementation of calcium, vitamin C, folate, and other nutrients.

Food Group	Allowed	Avoided
Milk	2 cups/day Mild cheese	Strong cheese
Breads and cereals	White bread Refined cereals: cream of wheat, cream of rice, puffed rice, Rice Krispies, corn flakes Crackers without whole grains or seeds Rice, noodles, macaroni, spaghetti	Whole-grain breads Bread made with seeds, nuts, or bran Cracked wheat bread Whole-grain rice or pasta
Fruits	Juice without pulp Ripe banana Cooked or canned apples, apricots, Royal Anne cherries, peaches, pears Strained fruit	Prunes and prune juice Fruits not on "allowed" list Dried fruit
Vegetables	Juice without pulp Lettuce Cooked or canned asparagus, green and wax beans, beets, carrots, eggplant, pumpkin, spinach, acorn squash, seedless tomatoes, tomato sauce or puree, white or sweet potatoes without skin Strained vegetables	Vegetables not on "allowed" list Dried peas and beans Potato skins or chips Fried potatoes
Meat, poultry, fish, shellfish, eggs	Lean tender meat without grease: ground or well-cooked (roasted, baked, or broiled) beef, lamb, ham, veal, pork, poultry, organ meats, fish Eggs except fried	Tough, fried, or spiced meats Fried eggs

TABLE 21-2   Low-Residue Diet (Continued)

Food Group	Allowed	Avoided
Fats and oils	Smooth peanut butter Butter, oils Cream (deduct from milk allowance) Margarine	All other nuts Coconut Olives
Desserts and miscellaneous	Plain dessert made with allowed foods: fruit, ices, sherbet, ice cream, gelatin Candy: gum drops, hard candy, jelly beans, plain chocolate, marshmallows, butterscotch Honey, sugar, molasses Salt, pepper, ground seasonings Plain gravy Milk sauces (deduct milk allowance) Mayo Coffee, decaffeinated coffee Jelly Tea Soda	Popcorn Seeds of any kind Whole spices Chili sauce Rich gravy Vinegar Alcohol Jam, marmalade

Sample Menu

Breakfast	Lunch/Dinner
Strained grapefruit juice	Baked halibut with clear lemon juice
Cream of wheat	Twice baked potato (no onions)
Poached egg	Candied sweet potato (no nuts or whole spices)
White bagel with butter and honey	Canned pear and banana on lettuce
1/2 cup milk	French bread and margarine
Coffee	Rice pudding (no raisins; deduct milk from allowance)

Postoperative Nutrition

Intravenous fluids are continued after surgery. The usual minimum replacement is 2 liters of 5 percent glucose in water in 24 hours. This amount contains 100 grams of glucose and delivers 340 kilocalories. Although this will not meet a person's resting energy expenditure, it will prevent ketosis. A previously well-nourished adult would most likely have nutrient reserves for 3 to 4 days of semistarvation. To prevent excessive muscle protein from being used for energy, adequate nourishment must be delivered to the client within 3 days.

To avoid abdominal distention, oral feedings are delayed until peristalsis returns and is detected with a stethoscope. Another sign of peristalsis is the passage via the rectum of **flatus** (gas). Ambulation as permitted will help the client pass the flatus and avoid uncomfortable distention.

Clients are usually progressed from clear liquids to full liquids, soft diet, and then a regular diet as soon as possible. The progression time varies with the client and surgical procedure from hours to days. If "diet as tolerated" is ordered, the client should be asked what foods sound appealing. Sometimes, a full dinner tray when the client does not feel well "turns off" the appetite. After gastrointestinal surgery, oral food and fluids are deferred longer than with other surgeries to allow healing. It is not advisable to give red liquids after surgery on the mouth and throat no red liquids are given to prevent vomitus being mistaken for blood or vice versa.

Surgical removal of a specific part of the gastrointestinal tract, such as the stomach, duodenum, jejunum, or ileum, may result in malabsorption of specific nutrients, as illustrated in Figure 21-1. For example, intrinsic factor, which is secreted by the stomach, carries vitamin B_{12} to the ileum for absorption. Iron absorbed from the duodenum and

Flatus—Gas in the digestive tract, averaging 400 to 1200 mL/day.

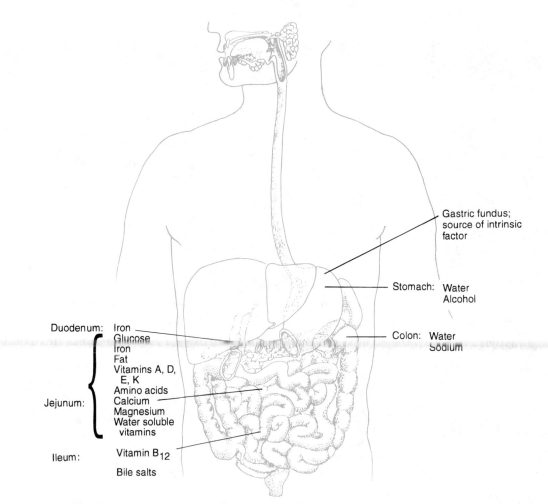

FIGURE 21–1 The chief sites of absorption for various nutrients. Disease or resection of an area will increase the risk of deficiency of specific nutrients. (Adapted from Scanlon, VC, and Sanders, T: Student Workbook for Essentials of Anatomy and Physiology, ed 2. FA Davis, Philadelphia, 1995, p 252, with permission.)

the jejunum is necessary for hemoglobin synthesis. Glucose, amino acids, fat- and water-soluble vitamins, calcium, and magnesium, all absorbed in the jejunum, are necessary for metabolism. Bile salts are absorbed in the ileum. Although the loss of bile salts in the feces may seem harmless, the body ordinarily recycles these salts over and over in the management of fats. Prolonged impaired absorption of bile salts can result in failure to absorb fat and fat-soluble vitamins.

Disorders of the Mouth and Throat

Varied conditions such as dental caries, oral surgery, surgery of the head and neck, fractured jaw, and cancer chemotherapy or radiation therapy can cause difficulty with chewing and swallowing. Often the client will require a feeding tube as discussed in the Chapter 15, "Nutrient Delivery." Suggestions to manage dysphagia were given in Chapter 10, "Digestion, Absorption, Metabolism, and Execution."

Disorders of the Esophagus

The **esophagus** just conducts food to the stomach, but sometimes malfunctions. Achalasia, esophageal reflux, and hiatal hernia are examples of esophageal disorders.

Achalasia

Failure of the gastrointestinal muscle fibers to relax where one part joins another is called **achalasia.** Often the term is applied to the **cardiac sphincter,** which separates the stomach from the esophagus. Sometimes the condition is termed *cardiospasm.* The cause of achalasia is unknown. Very hot or cold foods may trigger esophageal spasm, and anxiety seems to aggravate the condition. Symptoms are described as "something sticking in my throat" and a feeling of fullness behind the breastbone (sternum). Vomiting is associated with achalasia, and aspiration of vomitus can cause pneumonia.

In mild cases, avoiding spicy foods and dietary bulk may be effective. Diets for these clients require much individual attention. Rarely does one achalasia client display an intolerance for the same foods as another client. Plenty of liquids with small, frequent meals may help. Treatment of more severe cases involves stretching the cardiac sphincter or surgically slitting it.

Esophageal Reflux

Esophageal reflux refers to the regurgitation of the stomach contents into the esophagus. Esophageal reflux can usually be managed without surgery. This regurgitation is common in infancy and disappears with age often to reappear in old age due to poor muscle tone of the sphincter. In infants, usually no treatment is undertaken unless there is evidence of aspiration of food into the respiratory tract or of failure to thrive. In adults, the most common underlying cause of esophageal reflux is hiatal hernia, which is discussed in the next section. Some experts believe that esophageal reflux may be caused by failure of the cardiac sphincter to operate properly. The stomach is normally protected from hydrochloric acid by a thick layer of mucus. Because the esophagus is not so protected, esophageal reflux can lead to ulcer formation. The prominent symptom is heartburn with pain occurring behind the sternum or breastbone. Sometimes the pain radiates to the neck and the back of the throat. Lying down or bending over may increase reflux and aggravate the pain.

Treatment involves a number of conservative measures. Small, frequent meals often help. Protein is associated with tightening of the cardiac sphincter. Foods often avoided because they relax the sphincter are fat, alcohol, caffeine, peppermint, spearmint, and chocolate. Smoking also relaxes the sphincter. Decaffeinated coffee and pepper are frequently avoided because they stimulate gastric secretion. Acidic juices, such as citrus juices and tomato juice, may be irritating.

A change in eating behaviors may assist in the control of esophageal reflux. Chewing the food thoroughly, not eating within 3 hours of bedtime, and sitting upright for 2 hours after meals may increase food tolerance. Liquids may accompany meals unless the client reports early satiety or distention. Raising the head of the bed 6 to 8 inches enables gravity to help keep stomach contents contained. Symptoms of overweight clients may improve with weight loss. Table 21–3 details the diet for esophageal reflux.

Hiatal Hernia

The *esophageal hiatus* is the opening in the diaphragm through which the esophagus is attached to the stomach. A **hiatal hernia** is a protrusion of the stomach through the esophageal hiatus into the chest cavity (Fig. 21–2). The symptoms of hiatal hernia are similar to those of esophageal reflux and its medical treatment is the same. Persistent symptoms despite conservative treatment might lead the client to elect surgical repair of the hernia.

Disorders of the Stomach

Disorders of the stomach often require diet modification and in some cases, surgery. In this section we will discuss gastritis and peptic ulcers.

Gastritis

Inflammation of the stomach is **gastritis.** Common causes of gastritis are the chronic use of aspirin and alcohol abuse. Other conditions that result in gastritis are food allergies, food poisoning, infections, ra-

---

Achalasia—Failure of the gastrointestinal muscle fibers to relax where one part joins another.

Cardiac sphincter—The circular muscle between the esophagus and the stomach.

Esophageal reflux—Regurgitation of the stomach contents into the esophagus.

Hiatal hernia—Protrusion of part of stomach into chest cavity.

Gastritis—Inflammation of the stomach.

TABLE 21–3   Diet for Esophageal Reflux and Hiatal Hernia

Description	Indications	Adequacy
The diet is designed to minimize reflux through timing of intake, texture control, limiting fat, and exclusive of sphincter relaxants and gas-forming foods. Adjunctive treatment involves positioning.	Esophageal reflux, hiatal hernia, esophageal uclers, esophagitis, esophageal strictures, heartburn.	The diet may not meet the RDAs for vitamin C and iron in the premenopausal woman.

	Allowed	Avoided
Meal pattern	6 small meals 1/2 cup liquid with meals Other liquids >1 1/2 hours after meals >1/2 hour before meals	Eating within 3 hours of bedtime
Adjunction therapy	Elevate head of bed 6 in Relax at mealtime Consider weight loss if needed	Lying down in the hour after eating
Food Group Milk	Skim milk, buttermilk, evaporated skim milk Skim milk cheese Cottage cheese Low-fat yogurt	Other milk Hot chocolate
Breads and cereals	White and whole-grain breads Plain rolls, biscuits, and muffins Plain crackers Any cereals except those on "Avoided" list Rice Pasta	Pancakes, waffles, French toast Doughnuts, sweet rolls, nut breads Granola-type cereals with nuts and/or coconut
Fruits	Mild juices Any cereals except those on "Avoided" list	Avocado Raw apples and melons Orange, grapefruit, and tomato juices
Vegetables	Any cereals except those on "Avoided" list	Creamed or fried vegetables Hashed brown potatoes Broccoli, brussels sprouts, cabbage, cauliflower, cucumber, dried peas or beans, onions, green pepper, rutabagas, sauerkraut, turnips
Meat, poultry, fish, shellfish eggs	6 oz lean beef, pork, ham, lamb, liver, veal, fish, skinless poultry/day Eggs	Sausage, bacon, frankfurters, luncheon meats, canned meats and fish, duck, goose
Fats and oils	3 tsp/day: oil, butter, margarine, mild salad dressing 2 tbsp of the following may substitute for 1 tsp of fat: light cream, sour cream, nondairy cream Vegetable pan sprays as desired Low-fat salad dressings	Fried foods Gravies and sauces Cream Salad dressing Shortening, lard, or oils in excess of allowance Nuts, peanut butter

TABLE 21–3   Diet for Esophageal Reflux and Hiatal Hernia (Continued)

	Allowed	*Avoided*
Desserts and miscellaneous	Plain cakes and cookies Gelatin, popsicles Sherbet and pudding made with skim milk Caffeine-free carbonated beverages Decaffeinated tea Fat-free broth, boullion, consomme Soup made from allowed foods Cream soup made with skim milk Sugar, honey, syrup, molasses Jam, jelly, preserves Plain candy Salt Condiments and spices in small amounts Vanilla Vinegar	Ice cream, ice milk Pie, pastry Butter cake and icings Chocolate, coconut, cream, cream cheese, whipped cream, nuts, peppermint, spearmint Caffeinated beverages Decaffeinated coffee Tea Alcohol Potato chips Candy containing chocolate, nuts, coconut, or peppermint Popcorn Snack chips Pickles, relish Catsup, chili sauce Mustard Steak sauce

Sample Menus

35 Minutes Before Breakfast
2 glasses of water

Breakfast
1/2 banana
1/2 cup oatmeal
1/2 cup skim milk
1 slice toast with jam

Midmorning Snack
1/2 cup pineapple juice
3 graham crackers

35 Minutes Before Meal
2 glasses of water

Lunch/Dinner
3 oz skinless chicken breast baked in lemon juice
1/2 baked potato with 1 tbsp sour cream
1/2 cup whole kernel corn
3 small celery sticks
Hard roll with 1 tsp margarine
1/2 cup decaffeinated tea

35 Minutes Before Snack
2 glasses of water

Midafternoon/Evening snack
1 cup low-fat yogurt

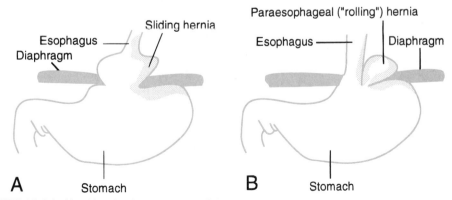

FIGURE 21–2 In hiatal hernia, the upper part of the stomach squeezes into the chest cavity through the esophageal opening in the diaphragm. (*A*) Sliding hernia; (*B*) paraesophageal hernia. (From Long and Phipps, p 937, with permission.)

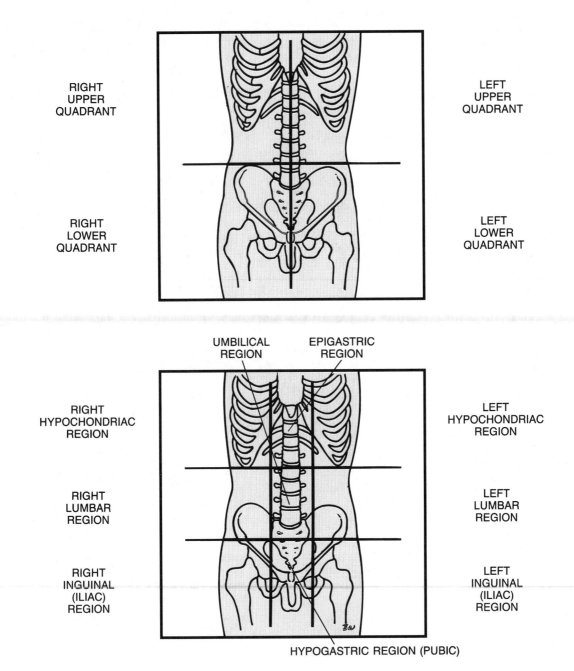

ABDOMINAL QUADRANTS AND REGIONS

FIGURE 21–3   Quadrants and regions of the abdomen that are used to describe locations of signs and symptoms. (From Thomas, CL [ed]: Taber's Cyclopedic Medical Dictionary, ed 18. FA Davis, Philadelphia, 1997, pp 3, 4, by Beth Anne Willert, MS, Dictionary Illustrator, with permission.)

diation exposure, and stress. Symptoms of gastritis are anorexia, nausea, a feeling of fullness, and epigastric pain. Figure 21–3 illustrates the abdominal quadrants and regions used to describe signs and symptoms. Signs of gastritis are vomiting and eructating (belching).

The dietary treatment plan for gastritis includes having the client:

1. Eat at regular intervals.
2. Chew food, especially fibrous food, slowly and thoroughly.
3. Avoid foods that cause pain.
4. Avoid foods that cause gas, especially vegetables in the cabbage family, including broccoli, cauliflower, and brussels sprouts.
5. Avoid gastric irritants such as caffeine and alcohol; nonsteroidal anti-inflammatory drugs (NSAIDs) such as aspirin; and strong spices, including nutmeg, pepper, garlic, and chili powder.
6. Eat in a relaxed manner.

More often than not, discovering which foods are responsible for the pain and discomfort of gastritis is a trial-and-error process. Individual tolerances will vary from person to person. Prolonged or recurrent gastritis deserves medical attention.

Peptic Ulcers

Both gastric (stomach) and duodenal ulcers are called *peptic ulcers.* Peptic ulcers affect 10 percent of the world's population, men and women equally. Duodenal ulcer incidence peaks in clients in their 50s and 60s; gastric ulcers in those between 60 and 80.

Pathophysiology

An ulcer client's mucosa is not sufficiently resistant to the acids secreted by the stomach. If just the superficial cells are involved, the lesion is called an **erosion.** Once the muscular layer of the stomach or duodenum is involved, the person has an **ulcer.**

Gastric ulcers are most common on the lesser curvature or right side of the stomach, rather than on the greater curvature. Duodenal ulcers account for 60 percent of all ulcers and are associated with increased acidity of the stomach. The majority of gastric and duodenal ulcers are related to infection with *Helicobacter pylori* (Soll, 1996). The organism occurs worldwide and is found in about 20 to 50 percent of adults in developed countries but only a small fraction develop peptic ulcers.

The second most common form of peptic ulcer is related to the use of nonsteroidal anti-inflammatory drugs (Soll, 1996). Long-term use of other medications such as potassium chloride and corticosteroids is also associated with ulcer formation.

Factors predisposing a person to ulcer formation and complicating treatment are smoking, caffeine, and alcohol. Stress and lack of rest contribute to ulcer development. Thus, ICU clients are often treated prohylactically.

Although the stereotypical ulcer client is a hard-driving executive, ulcers are actually more common in the lower socioeconomic class. Low socioeconomic status is a risk factor and may be linked with two other risk factors, poor nutrition and stress. The latter two factors may be related to irregular consumption of meals, which may contribute to ulcer formation in susceptible clients. Ulcer formation is associated with long-term use of medications, including aspirin, potassium chloride, and corticosteroids.

Signs and Symptoms

A gnawing, burning epigastric pain when the stomach is empty is characteristic of peptic ulcer. This occurs 1 to 3 hours after eating or at night. One quarter of ulcer clients experience bleeding, more often with duodenal than with gastric ulcers. If the blood is vomited immediately, it is bright red. If it stays in contact with digestive juices for a while, the vomitus will resemble coffee grounds. The medical term for this is *coffee-ground emesis.* Other symptoms of peptic ulcer are nausea, anorexia, and sometimes, weight loss.

Complications of Peptic Ulcers

Hemorrhage is a common complication of peptic ulcers. Scar tissue from a healed ulcer can restrict the gastric outlet, causing pyloric obstruction. If the ulcer continues to erode through the entire stomach or intestinal wall, the result is a **perforated ulcer.** Spilling gastrointestinal contents into the ster-

---

Erosion—Destruction of the surface of a tissue either on the surface of or inside the body.

Ulcer—Open sore or lesion of skin or mucous membrane.

Perforated ulcer—Condition in which an ulcer penetrates completely through the stomach or intestinal wall, spilling the organ's contents into the peritoneal cavity.

ile abdominal cavity causes **peritonitis,** an inflammation of the peritoneum, the lining of the abdominal cavity.

Treatment of Peptic Ulcers

Usually a course of medical treatment is prescribed at first. If *Helicobacter pylori* infection is the cause, combinations of antibiotics and other drugs are recommended (Soll, 1996). Only if such treatment should prove ineffective is surgery recommended.

MEDICAL TREATMENT   Before the advent of antiulcer medications, clients with peptic ulcers were usually advised to take antacids every 2 hours, alternating with milk and cream. One adverse effect of treatment was milk alkali syndrome as discussed in Chapter 8, "Minerals." New medications have revolutionized the treatment. They are almost always effective without a drastic change in diet. Commonly prescribed medications are cimetidine, ranitidine, and famotidine, which block histamine-stimulated gastric acid secretion, and omeprazole, which suppresses gastric acid production.

Diet does require some modification, however. Some experts recommend only three regular meals with no snacking because food, including milk, stimulates gastric secretion. Other authorities recommend midmorning and midafternoon snacks. In both regimens, substances that cause gastric irritation are avoided. These include the same gastric irritants discussed in the section on gastritis. Clients should be encouraged to avoid or limit spices or foods that are not well tolerated.

Definite changes in the ulcer client's lifestyle will improve the chances of successful treatment. Clients need counseling for stress reduction. They should obtain enough sleep. Since smoking stimulates secretion of gastric acid, ulcer clients should be advised not to smoke.

SURGICAL TREATMENT   When surgery is necessary, the ulcer is removed and the remaining gastrointestinal tract is sutured together. Surgical procedures designed to eliminate the diseased area include the gastroduodenostomy (stomach and duodenum anastomosed), the gastrojejunostomy (stomach and jejunum anastomosed) and the total gastrectomy (esophagus and duodenum anastomosed). **Anastomosis** is the surgical connection between tubular structures. Figure 21–4 illustrates these three procedures.

Following gastric surgery, parenteral and tube feeding are used singly or in combination. If a tube feeding is used, the tube must be inserted beyond the area resected. Once a client is advanced to an oral diet, he or she may experience the **dumping syndrome.** Dumping syndrome may develop as a complication of any surgical procedure that removes, disrupts, or bypasses the pyloric sphincter. Clinical Application 21–2 describes the dumping syndrome in more detail. Table 21–4 contains instructions for a diet to prevent or treat the dumping syndrome.

Disorders of the Intestines

Successful diagnostic studies of the bowel depend upon proper preparation. It is imperative to empty the bowel for clear radiographic visualization. This is accomplished by laxatives and enemas. Often the client is advised to follow a low-residue diet for several days prior to diagnostic studies. Explaining the procedures and the necessity for them is helpful in gaining the client's cooperation. The radiography department or the institution's diet manual will list the procedures. The nurse should ensure that the client receives maximum nourishment when tests

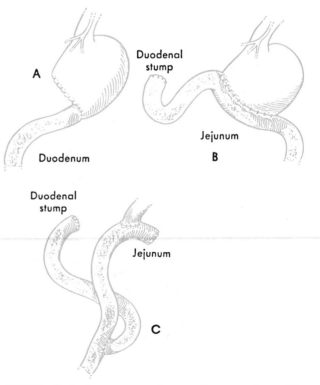

FIGURE 21–4   Common gastric resection procedures. (A) Gastroduodenostomy, Billroth I; (B) Gastrojejunostomy Billroth II: (C) total gastrectomy. (From Long and Phipps, p 948, with permission.)

When a concentrated liquid suddenly enters the intestine, water is pulled from the bowel wall just as in osmotic diarrhea. Local effects are hyperperistalsis, diarrhea, abdominal pain, and vomiting 30 to 60 min after a meal. Systemic effects relate to fluid volume deficit: weakness, dizziness, sweating, decreased blood pressure, tachycardia, and palpitations. The dumping syndrome is most often associated with total gastrectomy or resection of two-thirds of the stomach. The same signs and symptoms can occur in a client receiving a tube feeding if the nasogastric tube is accidentally carried down into the duodenum.

Dietary treatment of the dumping syndrome attempts to delay gastric emptying and to distribute the increased osmolality in the bowel over time. This can be achieved by limiting the intake of simple sugars, consuming frequent meals, and limiting fluids with meals. Simple sugars increase the osmolality of the gastric contents and enhance the movement of food out of the stomach. Small, frequent meals will reduce the load on the intestine. Liquids should be taken between, rather than with, meals. Beverages should be low in simple carbohydrate. Very hot or cold foods will stimulate peristalsis and should be avoided. A nondietary intervention also helps to control the symptoms of the dumping syndrome. Lying down for 30 to 60 min after eating retains the meal in the stomach longer.

are completed for the day. Frequently, another series of tests is scheduled for the next day.

Problems with Elimination

Several problems with frequency and consistency of bowel movements are common. These include irritable bowel syndrome, diarrhea, and constipation.

Irritable Bowel Syndrome

Signs and symptoms of **irritable bowel syndrome** are diarrhea, constipation, or alternating diarrhea and constipation; abdominal pain; and flatulence. Investigation often reveals no organic cause for the symptoms. Irritable bowel syndrome is often related to stress and emotional tension triggering overactivity of the nervous system.

Treatment is symptomatic. Offending foods should be identified and avoided. Stress management techniques and bowel hygiene principles should be part of the teaching plan. A high-fiber diet helps to avoid both constipation and an increase in pressure on the walls of the intestine. This often provides symptomatic relief.

Diarrhea

Diarrhea was discussed in Chapter 12, "Life Cycle Nutrition: Infancy Childhood, Adolescence." Of special note here are the foods that are hazardous for travelers. Especially in primitive areas, raw vegetables, raw meat, raw seafood, tap water, ice, and unpasteurized dairy products are best avoided. If an adult is in little jeopardy from electrolyte imbalance, self-treatment for diarrhea by following the regimen listed in Table 21–5 is appropriate. If the diarrhea is protracted or if a client has medical conditions for which dehydration is a hazard, a physician should be consulted.

Constipation

A person is constipated when bowel movements are infrequent. Each person develops a usual bowel pattern so that a bowel movement every second or third day may be perfectly normal for a given individual. Objective evidence of colonic constipation is stool that is hard and dry, with small round pieces like marbles. Rectal constipation is characterized by delayed passage of soft stool. It is essential that changes in bowel habits be investigated thoroughly to discover possible bowel cancers. Aside from disease conditions, the causes of constipation are lack of water and fiber in the diet, lack of exercise, and voluntary retention.

Treatment for constipation involves dietary and lifestyle changes, not laxatives. Unfortunately, the message has not yet been widely heard, especially by the elderly. Up to 50 percent of adults over age 70 regularly use laxatives. Overall, Americans spend $250 million on laxatives each year. Increasing the

Peritonitis—Inflammation of the peritoneal cavity.

Anastomosis—A surgical connection between tubular structures.

Dumping syndrome—Condition in which the stomach contents move into the duodenum too rapidly; often associated with gastric resections.

Irritable bowel syndrome—Diarrhea, or alternating constipation and diarrhea with no discernible organic cause.

TABLE 21–4 Diet for Dumping Syndrome

Description	*Indications*	*Adequacy*
This diet consists of 6 small feedings, high in protein and low in simple sugars.	This diet and adjunct therapy, used after surgical removal of the pyloric sphincter or other treatments that speed gastric emptying is designed to prevent rapid emptying of hypertonic gastric contents into the small intestine. Examples of such operative procedures include vagotomy, pyloroplasty, hemigastrectomy, total gastrectomy, esophagogastrectomy, Whipple's procedure, gastroenterostomy, and gastrojejunostomy. It is as the body adapts to its new condition, specific foods may be tolerated later in convalescence.	Deficiencies secondary to surgery or malabsorption may require supplementation. Among the nutrients likely to be needed are the vitamins B_{12}, D, and folic acid, and the minerals calcium and iron.

	Allowed	*Avoided*
Meal pattern	Six small servings Eat slowly and chew thoroughly	Fluids with meals
Adjunct therapy	Lie down for 1/2 hour after meals	
Food Group		
Milk	LactAid Aged cheese (>90 days)	Milk if lactose intolerant*
Breads and cereals	White, whole wheat, rye, Jewish, Italian, and Vienna breads* Rolls, crackers, biscuits, and muffins (milk-free)* Any cooked or dry cereal, milk-free* Rice, noodles, spaghetti, macaroni	Frosted breads Sweet rolls, doughnuts, coffeecake Bread made with milk (unless tolerated)* Sugar sweetened cereal Cereal containing milk*
Fruits	Fresh, frozen or unsweetened canned fruits, banana Juices, fresh, frozen, canned, unsweetened between meals only	Sweetened canned or frozen juices and fruits, dried fruit Raw fruits unless tolerated Juices with meals
Vegetables	Any as tolerated Juices between meals only	Those causing discomfort Juices with meals
Meat group	Any as tolerated	None
Fats and oils	Milk-free margarine if lactose intolerant* Oils Vegetable shortening	Any containing milk unless tolerated*

TABLE 21–4 Diet for Dumping Syndrome (Continued)

	Allowed	Avoided
Desserts and miscellaneous	Artificially sweetened gelatin Angel food and sponge cakes Salt, pepper, spices as tolerated Mustard, catsup, pickles, relishes as tolerated Artificially sweetened beverages Decaffeinated tea and coffee, herbal tea Dietetic jam and jelly	Sugar containing cakes, pies, cookies, ice cream,* sherbert* Seasonings that cause discomfort Caffeine-containing beverages Sugar, honey, syrup, molasses Jam, jelly Candy

Sample Menu	
30 Minutes Before Breakfast Decaffeinated beverage Artificial sweetener *Breakfast* 1/2 banana 1 egg, poached 1 tsp milk-free margarine Dietetic jelly *1 1/2 Hours After Breakfast* Orange juice *Midmorning Snack* 1 slice whole-wheat toast Dietetic jam	*30 Minutes Before Lunch* 1 cup LactAid *Lunch/Dinner* 3 oz roast pork Barley with butter 1/2 cup squash 1/2 cup fruit cocktail, drained *1 1/2 Hours After Meal* Decaffeinated beverage Artificial sweetener

* If lactose-free restriction is necessary.

fiber in the diet with adequate amounts of water, and exercising regularly are the keys to overcoming constipation. Even laxative habits established for years can be overcome this way.

In cases of fecal impaction, the client may exhibit diarrhea. Clinical Application 21–3 explains this paradox.

Problems with Absorption

Fat malabsorption may follow many diseases that damage the intestine. Celiac disease, or nontropical sprue, is a specific response to gluten-containing foods.

Fat Malabsorption

Several conditions hinder fat absorption. Many of the resulting symptoms are similar despite the differences in the underlying pathology.

When fat is not well absorbed, the fat-soluble vitamins also are poorly absorbed and the fat content of the feces is increased. These extra fatty acids bind with calcium and magnesium to form soaps in the bowel. (A chemical soap results from the union of fatty acid and alkali.) The calcium bound in the soap is thus unavailable to bind with oxalate. An increased amount of oxalate is excreted through the kidney. This is not a harmless rerouting, however, because oxalate kidney stones can form as a result.

CLINICAL APPLICATION 21–3

Distinguishing Diarrhea from Fecal Impaction

If a client usually is constipated and then has diarrhea, the nurse should check the rectum for impacted stool. The stool will be dry and hard and the client will not be able to pass it unassisted. The diarrheal stool is passed around the impaction. This type of constipation is not treated with diet. As in many cases, prevention is preferable to diagnosis and treatment. Institutionalized clients should be monitored for elimination problems. Frequency and consistency of bowel movements should be charted.

TABLE 21–5   Self-Treatment for Diarrhea*

Time	Oral Intake	Comments
1st 12 h	Nothing by mouth	Anything additional in the GI tract will stimulate peristalsis.
2nd 12 h	Clear liquids	If up to 5 percent body weight lost; if more than 5 percent lost, seek medical attention.
3rd 12 h	Full liquids	Experiment with milk in case lactose intolerance has developed.
4th 12 h	Soft diet	Include applesauce or banana for pectin; rice, pasta, and bread without fat (digested by enzymes usually unaffected by gastroenteritis).
By 48th h	Regular diet	If diarrhea has not resolved and regular diet is not tolerated, seek medical treatment.

* Appropriate for healthy adults.

Treatment centers upon careful selection of fats in the diet and appropriate supplementation of unavailable nutrients. Table 21–8 compares some food choices that are low in fat to similar items that are high in fat. Low-fat diets will be discussed later in the chapter. Because pancreatic lipase or bile are unnecessary for their absorption, medium-chain triglycerides (MCTs) are often given to increase kilocalories. MCTs are absorbed into the portal vein, as are amino acids and monosaccharides, rather than into the lymphatic system as are other lipids. Usually, MCTs are added to salad dressings, skim milk, or desserts. Because linoleic acid, an essential fatty acid, is missing from MCT, some regular fat is still needed in the diet. Supplements of the fat-soluble vitamins should be given in water-soluble form. To overcome malabsorption, the commonly used dose of supplements is twice the RDA.

Celiac Disease

Celiac disease is also called gluten enteropathy or nontropical **sprue.** Usually diagnosed in childhood, it occasionally is not discovered until late adulthood (Scully, et al, 1994). The cause is unknown but there is a genetic predisposition. Researchers are attempting to identify the components of gluten causing the disease, but a single trigger seems unlikely (Saltzman and Clifford, 1994). The affected person is sensitive to gluten, a protein in wheat, oats, rye, and barley. As little as 3 grams per day may cause symptoms. Ingestion of gluten by these sensitive people causes atrophy of the intestinal villi in the jejunum. Malabsorption of all the classes of nutrients except water follows.

The outstanding sign of celiac disease is **steatorrhea,** or excessive fat in the stools, which are foul-smelling, frothy, and bulky. Clients complain of bloating, diarrhea, and cramping abdominal pain. Some of this may be temporary, the result of lactase insufficiency. Untreated, the client's anorexia leads to weight loss and malnutrition marked by anemia, muscle wasting, edema from hypoalbuminemia, bleeding due to vitamin-K deficiency, and bone pain and tetary from hypocalcemia.

The treatment is to remove gluten permanently from the diet. The disease is not outgrown, and damage to the villi continues even without symptoms. Removing gluten from the diet is easier said than done. It involves analyzing the label of every food the client takes. See Chapter 10, "Digestion, Absorption, Metabolism, and Excretion," which outlines a gluten-restricted diet. Fortunately, this treatment reverses the pathology almost completely, but it might take 3 to 6 months. Sometimes, a secondary lactose intolerance results from mucosal damage and requires long-term management.

Inflammatory Bowel Diseases

Inflammatory bowel diseases are a group of syndromes that share similar characteristics but have some major differences. The two most common inflammatory bowel diseases are **Crohn's disease,** also known as ileitis or regional enteritis, and **ulcerative colitis.** Although the cause of both of these conditions is unknown, autoimmunity and genetic susceptibility may be partially responsible. The most common signs and symptoms of both Crohn's disease and ulcerative colitis are diarrhea, abdominal pain, and fever. Differences between the two diseases include their location in the gastrointestinal tract, the type of lesions involved, and complications (Table 21–6). The nutritional care of clients with inflammatory bowel disease is variable and dependent on the nutritional status of the individual, the location and extent of the disease, and the nature of the surgical and medical management. Elemental diets have

TABLE 21-6 Differences between Crohn's Disease and Ulcerative Colitis

	Crohn's Disease	Ulcerative Colitis
Location	Anywhere in bowel	Large intestine
	Diseased areas alternate with healthy tissue	Usually starts in rectum and spreads upward in continuous pattern
Lesions	Involves all layers of intestinal wall	Confined to mucosal and submucosal layers
Complications	Fistula, obstruction, stricture	Toxic megacolon, fistula
		Increased risk of colon cancer

promoted remission in Crohn's disease of the small bowel, but not of the large bowel, and not in ulcerative colitis (Sullivan, and Heyman, 1995).

Nutritional Therapy in Crohn's Disease

Crohn's disease may involve either the small or large intestine or both, as well as the stomach and esophagus, in some cases. The emphasis of treatment is (1) to support the healing of tissue, (2) to avoid and/or prevent nutritional deficiencies, and (3) to prevent local trauma to inflamed areas. Parenteral and tube feedings may be used together or separately to meet nutritional goals. The diet modifications are usually based on high-kilocaloric, high-protein, low-fat, and sometimes low-fiber or low-residue intake. Small, frequent feedings may assist in promoting comfort and adequate nutrition. Seasonings and chilled foods often aggravate symptoms. Restricting lactose is only appropriate in documented intolerance (Sullivan, and Heyman, 1995).

Nutritional Therapy in Ulcerative Colitis

During an acute exacerbation of ulcerative colitis, tube feedings or TPN are often given. A 4- to 6-week course of TPN achieves complete bowel rest. This choice is necessary when the client has a fistula, obstruction, or abscess. As many as 60 to 80 percent of clients undergo remission with these therapies. Con-valescent clients with ulcerative colitis must avoid irritating foods. Dietary modification is usually based on client tolerance. To maintain nutritional status, foods should not be eliminated from the diet without a fair trial. Restrictions should be limited to foods that produce gas or loose stools. Suspected foods should be tried in small amounts to determine tolerance levels. Parenteral supplements of iron and vitamin B_{12} may also be prescribed for these clients.

Surgical Treatment in Inflammatory Bowel Disease

Surgery may be recommended when inflammatory bowel disease becomes medically unmanageable. It may be curative in ulcerative colitis but is palliative in Crohn's disease (Sullivan and Heyman, 1995). The portion of the bowel that is inflamed can be surgically removed (resected). This results in a shorter gut. Resection of the small intestine may create additional nutritional hazards for the client (Clinical Application 21–4). A **colectomy** is the surgical removal of part or all of the colon. Other surgical procedures include ileostomy and colostomy, which may be either permanent or temporary.

In an **ileostomy,** the end of the remaining portion of the small intestine (the **ileum**) is attached to a surgically established opening in the abdominal wall called a **stoma,** from which the intestinal contents are discharged. In a **colostomy,** a part of the large intes-

---

Celiac disease (Gluten enteropathy)—Intolerance to dietary gluten, which damages the intestine and produces diarrhea and malabsorption.

Crohn's Disease—Inflammatory disease appearing in any area of the bowel, with diseased areas alternating with healthy tissue.

Ulcerative colitis—Inflammatory disease of the large intestine that usually begins in the rectum and spreads upward in a continuous pattern.

Colectomy—Surgical removal of all or part of the colon.

Ileostomy—Surgical procedure in which an opening to the small intestine (ileum) is constructed on the abdomen.

Stoma—A surgically created opening in the abdominal wall.

Colostomy—Surgical procedure in which an opening to the large intestine is constructed on the abdomen.

tine is resected and a stoma is created on the abdomen. Clients who have surgery to divert intestinal contents onto the abdominal wall often suffer psychological trauma in addition to the physical change.

ILEOSTOMY   An ileostomy produces liquid drainage containing active enzymes, which irritate the skin. In addition, nutrient losses are great. A loss of as much as 2 liters of fluid per day immediately following surgery is possible. Clinical Application 21–5 discusses innovations for controlling ileostomy drainage. Over time the bowel adapts to some extent, and drainage decreases to 300 to 500 milliliters. This amount, however, is more than the 100 to 200 milliliters of water lost in the normal stool. Additional nutrient losses in ileostomy clients are those of sodium, potassium, and vitamin B_{12}.

COLOSTOMY   In contrast to an ileostomy, a colostomy, after the convalescent period, may be so continent that a dry dressing is all that is necessary to cover the stoma. The client may do daily irrigations or not, as the surgeon suggests. Sometimes the client knows best, after the initial learning process.

DIETARY GUIDELINES FOR OSTOMY CLIENTS   A soft or general diet is usually served to ostomy clients after recovery from surgery. Stringy, high-fiber foods are initially avoided until a definite tolerance has been demonstrated. Stringy, high-fiber foods include celery, coconut, corn, cabbage, coleslaw, membranes on citrus fruits, peas, popcorn, spinach, dried fruit, nuts, sauerkraut, pineapple, seeds, and fruit and vegetable skins. Some clients avoid fish, eggs, beer, and carbonated beverages because they produce excessive odor.

Clients with ostomies should be encouraged to (1) eat at regular intervals; (2) chew food well to avoid blockage at the stoma site; (3) drink adequate amounts of fluid; (4) avoid foods that produce excessive gas, loose stools, offensive odors and/or undesirable bulk; and (5) avoid excessive weight gain. Dietary restrictions are usually based on individual tolerance.

Diverticular Disease

A **diverticulum** (plural—diverticula) is an outpouching of intestinal membrane through a weakness in the intestine's muscular layer. Diverticula are present in 10 percent of the US population. About one-third to one-half of the elderly have diverticula, 60 percent among people older than 80. A low-fiber diet is believed to increase the risk for diverticula. A low-fiber diet contains less than 15 grams of fiber per day.

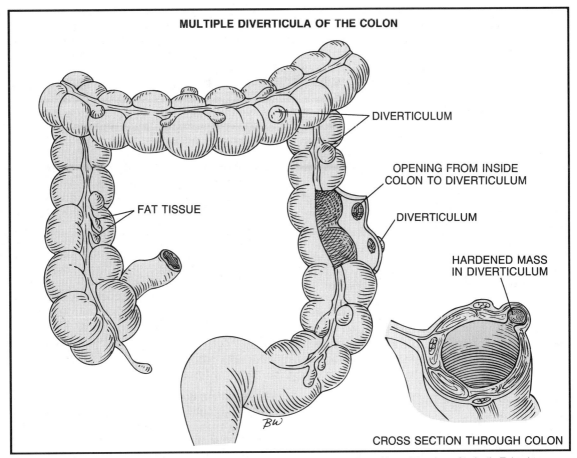

FIGURE 21–5 Diverticula of the transverse and descending colon. (From Thomas, CL [ed]: Taber's Cyclopedic Medical Dictionary, ed 18. FA Davis, Philadelphia, 1997, p 565, by Beth Anne Willert, MS, Dictionary Illustrator, with permission.)

Diverticulosis

The presence of diverticula is called **diverticulosis.** The usual site is the sigmoid colon (Fig. 21–5). Diverticula often occur at the points at which blood vessels enter the intestinal muscle. A proposed cause for diverticulosis is the increased force needed to propel insufficient intestinal contents through the lumen. Often the person with diverticulosis has no signs or symptoms. Once an individual knows the diverticula are present, a high-fiber diet of 30 grams per day is advised. This should be accompanied by an adequate fluid intake.

Diverticulitis

When diverticula become inflamed, the condition is termed **diverticulitis.** Inflammation occurs in the elderly at about the same rate as in younger people

with diverticulosis, 25 percent. Following the prescribed diet improves the condition of 85 percent of the clients.

Signs and symptoms of diverticulitis, with the exception of fever, are focused in the abdomen. The client complains of cramps, pain in the lower left quadrant, dyspepsia, nausea and vomiting, distention and flatus, and alternating constipation and diarrhea. Some serious complications can follow di-

Diverticulum—A sac or pouch in the walls of an organ of the alimentary canal.

Diverticulosis—Presence of one or more diverticula (outpouching of the inner mucosa through a weakness in the gastrointestinal muscle).

Diverticulitis—Inflammation of a diverticulum.

verticulitis. The inflammatory process can lead to adhesions or fistulas. A thickened intestinal wall from the scar tissue can cause an obstruction. Rupture of a diverticulum can initiate peritonitis.

Dietary treatment of diverticulitis has changed radically over the years. Whereas once a low-fiber diet was the rule, now it is only a temporary measure. While the inflammation is severe, elemental or predigested formulas or a low-fiber diet is given. After that, a high-fiber diet as for diverticulosis is prescribed. Although not proven to be helpful, avoiding foods with small seeds that could get caught in the diverticulum may be recommended.

Diseases and Conditions of the Liver

The infiltration of liver cells by fat is called **fatty liver.** Many situations can cause fatty liver, including a low-protein or a starvation diet, (because of the breakdown of adipose tissue for energy), and alcoholism. Usually no harm is done by fatty liver unless it progresses. Treatment is to correct the cause. If it is alcohol consumption, abstinence reverses the pathology. More serious liver diseases are hepatitis and cirrhosis.

Hepatitis

Inflammation of the liver, or **hepatitis,** can result from viral infections, alcohol, drugs, or toxins. Two well-known viral infections are hepatitis A and hepatitis B. Hepatitis A is spread by the fecal-oral route and, rarely, by blood transfusion. It was discussed in Chapter 14, "Food Management." Hepatitis B is spread by body fluids such as blood, saliva, semen, and vaginal secretions. Hepatitis C (formerly called non-A, non-B) is parenterally transmitted with the highest incidence being in drug users and hemophilia clients.

SIGNS AND SYMPTOMS OF HEPATITIS Regardless of type or cause, symptoms are anorexia, nausea, epigastric discomfort, and weakness. Signs of hepatitis are vomiting, diarrhea, and jaundice due to the inability of the liver to convert fat-soluble bilirubin to a water-soluble (conjugated) form. The degree of jaundice gives a rough estimate of the severity of the disease. Physical examination shows an enlarged and tender liver and an enlarged spleen.

TREATMENT OF HEPATITIS Currently, no specific medications can be given to cure hepatitis. Bed rest, abstinence from alcohol, and optimum nutrition are the treatment. Convalescence may take

from 3 weeks to 3 months. Clients on bed rest, especially debilitated clients, are more susceptible to pressure ulcers than the average client because of decreased synthesis of albumin and the globulins. If the client abstains from alcohol, the hepatitis is often reversible.

A high-kilocalorie, high-protein, and moderate-fat diet is frequently prescribed for the hepatitis client. Energy intake should come from as much as 400 grams of carbohydrate daily. Protein in amounts up to 100 grams will help heal the liver. Emulsified fats in dairy products and eggs may be accepted better by the client than other fats. Up to 35 percent of kilocalories in fat will provide high energy in a lower volume of food. Fluid intake should be 3 to 3.5 liters per day.

Coaxing a person with hepatitis to accept such a substantial meal pattern is an enormous task, in view of the anorexia and nausea that accompany the disease. Since the nausea is often less in the morning than later in the day, the hepatitis client should be encouraged to eat a big breakfast. Polymeric oral feedings that are high in kilocalories and protein are widely used for between meal feedings.

Cirrhosis of the Liver

The word cirrhosis comes from a French word for orange. In **cirrhosis** the liver becomes fibrous and contains orange-colored nodules resembling the skin of an orange.

In the United States, chronic alcohol abuse is the most common but not the only cause of cirrhosis. About half of the 13 million alcoholics in this country will develop cirrhosis.

A diagnosis of cirrhosis cannot always be linked to alcoholism. Cirrhosis has occurred in nondrinkers. Insults to the liver such as infection, biliary obstruction, and toxic chemicals, including medications, may precede cirrhosis.

Alcohol is toxic to all body tissues, including the liver. A summary of the nutritional effects of alcoholism appears in Clinical Application 21–6 and of

---

Fatty liver—Accumulation of triglycerides in the liver cells; usually reversible if the cause, of which there are many, is removed.

Hepatitis—Inflammation of the liver, caused by viruses, drugs, alcohol, or toxic substances.

Cirrhosis—Chronic disease of the liver in which functioning cells degenerate and are replaced by fibrosed connective tissue.

CLINICAL APPLICATION 21–6

Nutritional Effects of Alcohol

Alcoholism is a disease of alcohol consumption that produces tolerance, physical dependence, and characteristic organ pathology in the body. Ingestion of prodigious amounts of alcohol is not necessary for someone to become an alcoholic. The disease may be produced in some persons by 3–5 oz/day of whiskey. The first notion to dispel is the cliché of the skid row alcoholic. There still are alcoholics on skid row, of course, but the disease is far more pervasive than that. In an affluent society alcoholics may be obese, usually early in the disease, rather than later.

In the United States, alcoholism is the single most important factor in nutrient deficiencies. Associating the numerous functions of the liver with the fact that alcohol is toxic to all body cells, the nutritional havoc accompanying alcoholism becomes obvious. Even without liver damage, alcohol injures the intestine, thereby reducing absorption of vitamins A, D, K, thiamin, pyridoxine, folic acid, and B_{12}. Folic acid deficiency occurs in 50–80 percent of alcoholics.

The vitamin deficiency that is almost synonymous with alcoholism is that of thiamin because it is necessary to convert alcohol to energy. In the United States, thiamin deficiency is seen almost exclusively in alcoholics, affecting from 30–80 percent of them. The neurological symptoms of thiamin deficiency present a disheartening picture. Clients have atrophy of many nerves, weakness in the ankles and toes, and numbness and tingling in the feet.

The behavior of an intoxicated person readily shows that alcohol penetrates the blood-brain barrier. In fact, brain damage may occur before severe liver damage. The **Wernicke-Korsakoff syndrome** is a disorder of the CNS caused by thiamin deficiency in alcoholics. The clients display disorientation, memory dysfunction, and ataxia. Weakness of the muscles controlling the eyes produces double vision (diplopia) and abnormal movements of the eyeball (nystagmus).

Thiamin helps to oxidize glucose and to metabolize alcohol to energy. This is a critical piece of information for health care workers taking care of alcoholics. Administering a simple solution of glucose intravenously can precipitate symptoms of Wernicke-Korsakoff syndrome if the client is thiamin deficient. For this reason thiamin is routinely administered parenterally to alcoholics.

Other vitamin deficiencies in alcoholics in order of frequency after folic acid and thiamin, are pyridoxine, niacin, vitamin C, and vitamin A. Niacin deficiency occurs in one-third of alcoholics. Scurvy in the United States is almost exclusively found in alcoholics. Vitamin C, besides being necessary for tissue repair, plays a role in folic acid metabolism and in iron absorption. Storage of vitamin A in the liver is impaired. A prominent result of hypovitaminosis A is night blindness.

Other nutritional effects possible in alcoholics are bone loss and bleeding tendencies. One-half of alcoholics show bone loss. Albumin carries calcium in the bloodstream. Hypoalbuminemia, reduced stores and faulty metabolism of vitamin D, low calcium intake, and steatorrhea causing binding of calcium in the intestine may all combine to produce bone loss.

Prothrombin, normally manufactured by the liver using vitamin K, is necessary for blood clotting. Vitamin-E deficiency produces neurological changes, cerebellar degeneration, and peripheral neuropathy.

Potassium, phosphorus, and magnesium are the most common major mineral deficiencies in alcoholics. Because some of the symptoms of delirium tremens are the same as symptoms of magnesium deficiency, it was postulated that magnesium deficiency causes delirium tremens. At present, there is no consensus on this issue.

Iron and zinc are the trace minerals most often deficient in alcoholics. Low iron stores are related to gastrointestinal bleeding, rather than poor absorption. Alcohol damages the intestinal mucosa and thereby permits increased absorption of iron. With low folic acid levels, however, red blood cell production cannot proceed normally. Anemia or bone marrow abnormalities have been found in 75 percent of clients hospitalized with alcoholism.

Up to 50 percent of alcoholic clients are deficient in zinc. Zinc is needed for many enzymes that function in DNA and RNA metabolism. It plays a vital role in the growth and repair of essential organs, such as the liver. Zinc is also necessary to convert vitamin A to a functional form in the retina.

Lastly, alcoholics suffer from protein-energy malnutrition. Even in early alcoholism, albumin levels are low-normal. The typical alcoholic consumes only 75 percent of required energy. The result of low-protein, low-energy intake is muscle wasting. Fat is not an adequate source of energy for alcoholics, owing to malabsorption. Steatorrhea is seen in half the clients.

its connection to mortality in Clinical Application 21–7.

A number of barriers interfere with alcoholism case-finding: (1) alcoholism's multiple and varied manifestations; (2) the health care provider's personal definition and meaning of alcoholism; and (3) denial by the client and family. The CAGE questionnaire shown in Clinical Application 21–8 is a brief, effective screening tool to identify possible alcohol abusers. In addition, the presence of recent morning drinking in women appears to indicate a current or impending alcohol problem (York, 1995).

PATHOPHYSIOLOGY Alcohol needs no digestion. It is absorbed rapidly, 20 percent from the stomach and 80 percent from the small intestine. Immediately after absorption, the alcohol is carried to the liver. The rate of breakdown by the liver is 0.5 ounce of alcohol per hour. This refers to the alcohol content, not the whole beverage. This step cannot be rushed. So giving coffee or other stimulants to an intoxicated person will not induce sobriety, merely a "wide-awake drunk."

If the liver is not able to repair the damage, dying liver cells are replaced by scar tissue. Figure 21–6 traces the path from cell death to several cardinal signs of cirrhosis. Because of the multiple functions of the liver, one pathological change reinforces another. The **ascites** is worsened by hypoalbuminemia and is partly caused by and also worsened by sodium retention. Depressed plasma protein production, as evidenced by decreasing albumin levels, indicates a poor client outcome.

SIGNS AND SYMPTOMS OF CIRRHOSIS Cirrhosis causes anorexia, epigastric pain, and nausea that worsens as the day goes on. Signs of the disease are abdominal distention, vomiting, steatorrhea, jaundice, ascites, edema, and gastrointestinal bleeding. Of clients with advanced cirrhosis, 70 percent develop esophageal varices, varicose veins of the esophagus. Muscle tremors are attributed to hypomagnesemia. Laboratory tests will show hypoglycemia and elevated serum triglyceride levels. The lack of enzymes for converting noncarbohydrate sources to energy causes hypoglycemia. Insufficient lipoprotein synthesis causes the elevated triglycerides and fatty liver. The end result of cirrhosis is liver failure, which leads to hepatic coma (Clinical Application 21–9).

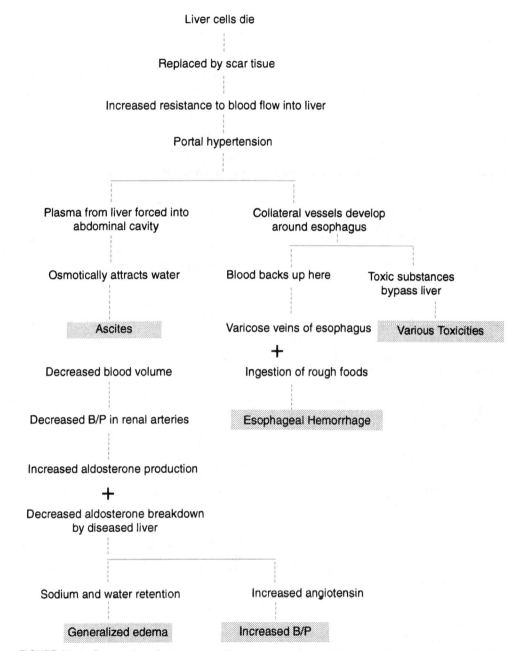

FIGURE 21–6 Progression of pathology leading to the classic symptoms of cirrhosis of the liver. The signs and symptoms are shaded.

DIETARY TREATMENT OF CIRRHOSIS Treatment is ineffective if the client continues to drink. Even so, once portal hypertension has set in, abstinence does not halt progression of cirrhosis.

A protein-restricted diet, between 20 and 40 grams per day, may be prescribed when the liver cannot process the end products of protein metabolism. Esophageal varices necessitate a soft diet.

As the client improves, protein can sometimes be increased to aid liver regeneration. It is necessary to monitor the client carefully for signs of excessive protein intake. Frequent blood ammonia levels are drawn to assess the client's ability to metabolize dietary protein effectively.

Sufficient kilocalories must be provided to prevent catabolism of tissue protein for energy. Simple

---

Hepatic Encephalopathy

Hepatic encephalopathy is the result of liver failure. The precise mechanism involved in the pathology is uncertain. Because hepatic encephalopathy is associated with increased serum levels of ammonia and aromatic amino acids, treatments to control one or both of these factors have been suggested. Since elevated serum ammonia levels interfere with normal mentation, caution is recommended when interpreting interview data.

Because of its clinical similarity to hepatic encephalopathy, manganese toxicity is proposed as a mechanism contributing to the manifestations of both. Manganese is a component of an enzyme, glutamine synthetase, which detoxifies ammonia. If this theory holds, metal-chelating agents may be added to the treatment of hepatic encephalopathy (Krieger, et al, 1995).

Ammonia is produced by intestinal bacteria, and by digestive enzymes breaking down protein. Even if the person consumes no protein foods, the bacteria work on the cast-off cells of the gastrointestinal tract and on the blood from gastrointestinal bleeding, which is so common in alcoholic cirrhosis. Ordinarily, the liver degrades ammonia to urea, which is then excreted by the kidneys in urine. In liver failure, blood ammonia levels rise. Ammonia is toxic to all cells, including those of the liver and the brain. The laboratory values are not clearly correlated with the degree of encephalopathy, so a series of tests is necessary to monitor each client. Hypokalemia with resulting alklosis for instance, causes ammonia retention in the brain.

The liver normally breaks down amino acids. The client with liver failure exhibits a change in the ratio of aromatic amino acids (phenylalanine, tryptophan, and tyrosine) to branched-chain amino acids (leucine, isoleucine, and valine). In the healthy client this ratio is approximately 1:1; in hepatic coma it is 3:1 or higher. The elevated levels of aromatic amino acids interfere with the formation of the neurotransmitters dopamine and norepinephrine, and may contribute to hepatic coma.

Some signs of hepatic encephalopathy can be observed prior to the onset of coma. These are personality changes, irritability, weakness, apathy, confusion, and sleepiness. More specific signs are asterixis and fetor hepaticus. Asterixis, or liver flap, refers to involuntary jerking movements or a flapping of the hand when the arm is outstretched. Fetor hepaticus is a fecal odor to the breath. Lastly, there is coma.

Treatment consists of medications and dietary modifications, along with symptomatic care. Oral neomycin kills the bacteria in the intestine, thereby decreasing ammonia production. Lactulose acidifies the large intestine, causing ammonia to be converted to ammonium ions, which are not absorbed but eliminated in the feces. Diet must be carefully planned. Some foods produce higher ammonia levels than most others. These include chicken, salami, ground beef, ham, gelatin, peanut butter, potatoes, onions, buttermilk, and blue, American, and cheddar cheese (Rudman, 1973).

When coma is approaching, protein is limited to 40–60 g of high-quality protein per day. Because they contain fewer aromatic amino acids, vegetable proteins may be tolerated better than animal protein. If enteral feeding is necessary, special preparations low in aromatic amino acids are available. Two of them are Hepatic-Aid II and Travasorb-Hepatic. According to theory, these should be beneficial, but more data are being collected. Aspartame (NutraSweet) contains phenylalanine, an aromatic amino acid. If the theory holds, it too should be avoided.

If the client's condition continues to deteriorate, even greater restrictions are placed on diet. Adequate kilocaloric intake, 1500–2000 kcal, must be maintained to prevent tissue protein from being used for energy. Dietary protein is decreased to 10–20 g/day. As the client recovers, dietary protein is added in increments of 10 g every 2 days. If signs of encephalopathy occur, protein is reduced to the previous restriction.

---

carbohydrates are encouraged. Enough fat is offered for palatability. Dietary fats that are already emulsified, such as those in homogenized milk and eggs, need less bile for digestion.

Fluid and electrolyte balance demands careful attention. If the client has ascites, sodium will likely be restricted. An amount of 250 milligrams to 1 gram per day is common. Fluid is restricted also, often to 1.5 to 2 liters in 24 hours. If the serum sodium level is low, fluid may be limited to 1 to 1.5 liters. Monitoring signs of ascites reduction include measuring abdominal girth and weighing daily. If the client has ascites without peripheral edema, a reasonable goal for weight loss is 0.5 kilogram (1.1 pounds) per day. If both ascites and peripheral edema are displayed, the goal for weight loss is 1 kilogram per day.

Table 21–7 displays various protein-controlled diets which assume the client tolerates fats. Exten-

TABLE 21-7   Protein-Controlled Diets for Liver Disease

Description	Indications	Adequacy
These diets are prescribed to attain and maintain normal amino acid balance, reduce blood ammonia levels, and improve clinical status. In addition to protein, fluid and sodium are often restricted.	These diets are used in severe liver disease such as acute hepatitis or advanced cirrhosis.	The diets may not meet the RDA for B complex vitamins, especially folic acid, calcium, and iron.

Meal Plan	Sample Menu

20-GRAM PROTEIN DIET

Meal Plan	Sample Menu
Breakfast	
1/2 cup milk	1/2 cup whole milk
1 fruit	1/2 cup orange juice with 2 tbsp modular carbohydrate supplement*
2 starches	1/2 cup Cream of Wheat with 1 tbsp modular carbohydrate supplement and 1 slice of toast with 1 tbsp margarine and jelly
Fat (as tolerated)	2 tbsp cream
Beverage	As tolerated and per fluid restriction
Lunch	
2 starches	1 cup rice with 1/4 cup unsalted tomato sauce and 1 tbsp olive oil
Vegetable	1/2 cup green beans with 1 tsp margarine
Fruit	1/2 cup canned peaches with 1 tbsp modular carbohydrate supplement
Beverage	As tolerated and per fluid restriction
Dinner	
2 starches	1 baked potato with 2 tbsp sour cream and 1 slice of bread with 1 tsp margarine and jelly
Vegetable	1/2 cup mushrooms (for potato topping)
Fruit	1/2 cup strawberries with 1 tbsp modular carbohydrate supplement
Beverage	As tolerated and per fluid restriction

40-GRAM PROTEIN DIET

Add to the Above:

1/2 cup milk	1 starch exchange
2 meat exchanges	

60-GRAM PROTEIN DIET

Add to the 20-Gram Protein Diet Meal Plan:

2 cups milk

1 starch exchange	1 vegetable exchange
	3 meat exchanges

80-GRAM PROTEIN DIET

Add to the 20-Gram Diet Meal Plan:

2 cups milk	1 vegetable exchange
5 meat exchanges	4 starch exchanges

* Polycose, Sumacal, and Moducal are all modular carbohydrate supplements.

sive low-protein exchange lists have been developed to treat liver failure. The dietary management of these clients is complex and constantly changing, requiring the services of a dietitian. Because of the high risk of vitamin deficiencies cirrhosis clients are given pharmaceutical supplements. Up to 5 times the RDA of water-soluble vitamins may be necessary.

Gallbladder Disease

On the underside of the liver is a small pouch-like organ called the **gallbladder.** Its function is to concentrate and store bile until it is needed for digestion. The liver secretes 600 to 800 milliliters of bile per day. The gallbladder reduces this to 60 to 160 milliliters.

Gallbladder disease is usually related to gallstones. The presence of gallstones is called **cholelithiasis.** One–fifth of adults over 40 years of age and one-third over 70 have gallstones. Most gallstones form when the bile is too scant, too concentrated or contains excessive cholesterol. When the gallbladder becomes inflamed from the stones' irritation, the condition is labeled **cholecystitis.**

Causative Factors

Women are three times more likely than men to have gallbladder disease. Heredity and hypercholesterolemia are associated with gallstones. Obesity is the only nutritional factor definitely linked to gallbladder disease in humans. Other conditions associated with gallbladder disease include cardiovascular disease, diabetes mellitus, ileal disease or resection, long-term total parenteral nutrition, multiple pregnancies, and oral contraceptive use. Some of these, once present, are unchangeable risk factors. Gallstone disease is also associated with a habitual long overnight fast, with dieting, and with a low fiber intake. A long fast between the evening meal and the first meal of the next day could be modified by a light bedtime snack and/or drinking 2 glasses of water on arising if breakfast will be delayed. Either practice will stimulate the gallbladder to empty, thus decreasing the likelihood of very concentrated bile.

Symptoms of Gallbladder Disease

The cardinal symptom of gallbladder disease is pain after ingestion of fat. The pain is located in the right upper quadrant and often radiates to the right shoulder.

Treatment of Gallbladder Disease

Dietary modification and medical and surgical interventions are used to treat gallbladder disease. Usually, conservative medical management is tried for a time before surgery.

Dietary Modifications

During an acute attack, a full liquid diet with minimal fat is recommended. For chronic gallbladder disease, the client should limit fat and correct obesity. Some clients obtain relief with the restriction of dietary fat; others do not. A reasonable approach to fat restriction is to (1) select skim milk dairy products, (2) limit fats or oils to 3 teaspoons per day, and (3) consume no more than 6 ounces of very lean meat per day. Gas-forming foods also are often poorly tolerated.

Another approach is to eliminate foods that cause symptoms. Clients usually can identify foods that cause pain. Fried foods are the worst offenders. Table 21–8 identifies some foods that are low in fat and some that are high in fat. The high-fat list contains 4 times as much fat as the possible substitutions on the low-fat list.

Medical Interventions

New procedures have been devised to treat gallstones without surgery. One technique involves injecting solvents into the gallbladder. Another method is to break up the stones using shock waves, a procedure called *lithotripsy.* Clients and physicians still may opt for removal of the gallbladder, cholecystectomy, through a laparoscope or the traditional abdominal incision.

Postoperative diet routines are similar to those for other gastrointestinal surgery. When the client begins to take oral nourishment, clear liquids are given for 24 hours. The diet is progressed as tolerated. Because bile enters the duodenum continuously, balanced meals should be well tolerated. Many clients can eat a regular diet without difficulty 1 month after surgery. Clients who became nauseated after eating certain foods preoperatively, however, may avoid them postoperatively because of the association.

Diseases and Disorders of the Pancreas

In addition to the endocrine secretions insulin, glucagon, and somatostatin, the **pancreas** secretes

TABLE 21–8 Comparison of Fat Content of Selected Foods

Low-Fat Foods	Fat(g)	High-Fat Foods	Fat(g)
STARCH/BREADS			
Angel food cake, 1/12	<1	Pecan pie, 1/6 of pie	24
Italian bread, 1 slice	<1	Bread stuffing, 1/2 cup	13
English muffin, 1	1	Danish pastry	12
Raisin toast, 1 slice	1	Croissant, 1	12
Pancake, 4-in, 1	2	Glazed raised doughnut, 1	13
MEATS, FISH, AND POULTRY			
Beef round, 3 oz lean roasted	9	Beef prime rib, 3 oz, lean only	24
Chicken breast, 3 oz rst., without skin	9	Chicken, deep-fried thigh, 1	14
Boiled ham, 3 oz	9	Spare ribs, 3 oz	24
Tuna, 1/2 cup water-packed	6	Tuna, 1/2 cup oil-packed, drained	24
FRUITS AND VEGETABLES			
Banana, 8 3/4 in long, 1	1	Avocado, 1	30
Raisins, 1 cup	1	Coconut, dried, 1 cup	50
Potato, baked, 1	<1	French fried potato, 2 × 3 1/2 in, 15 pieces	12
Onion, raw, sliced, 1 cup	<1	French fried onion rings, 4	10
MILK PRODUCTS			
Cottage cheese, 1 percent, 1/2 cup	1	Cottage cheese, 4 percent, 1/2 cup	5
Mozzarella, part skim, 1 oz	5	Cheddar, 1 oz	9
Skim milk, with added milk solids, 1 cup	1	Whole milk, 1 cup	8
Frozen yogurt, low-fat, 1 cup	4	Ice cream, regular, hard, vanilla, 1 cup	14
FAST FOODS			
Arby's Regular roast beef sandwich	15	Chicken breast sandwich	26
Burger King Whopper Junior	17	Whopper with cheese	48
McDonald's Chicken McNuggets, 6	16	Quarter pounder with cheese	29
Wendy's Chili, 1 cup	9	Bacon cheeseburger	28

amylase, lipase, trypsin, and chymotrypsin. Disorders of the pancreas include pancreatitis and cystic fibrosis.

Pancreatitis

When the blood vessels of the pancreas become abnormally permeable, plasma and plasma protein leak into the interstitial spaces. The resulting edema damages the pancreatic cells. Normally, the pancreatic enzymes necessary for digestion are inactive in the pancreas and become activated only upon entering the duodenum. Otherwise, the active enzymes would digest the pancreas itself. In **pancreatitis,** the retained pancreatic enzymes, especially trypsin, become activated and digest the pancreatic tissue.

Cholelithiasis—The presence of gallstones.

Cholecystitis—Inflammation of the gallbladder.

Pancreatitis—Inflammation of the pancreas.

Alcoholism is the most common cause of pancreatitis, generating up to 75 percent of the cases. Other conditions that can lead to pancreatitis are biliary tract disease or surgery; stomach surgery; and the administration of cancer chemotherapy, steroids, thiazides, or estrogens. In some cases, viral infection, pregnancy, or trauma have preceded pancreatitis. The characteristic symptom of pancreatitis is excruciating pain in the left upper quadrant. Nausea and vomiting accompany an attack. Laboratory tests reveal elevated levels of serum amylase and lipase.

In the treatment of pancreatitis, the client is advised to avoid alcohol. The acutely ill client is usually allowed nothing by mouth for 24 to 48 hours to reduce secretions. A nasogastric tube is used to suction stomach contents. Ice chips may be prescribed to lessen dryness of the mouth. Because plain water stimulates gastric secretions, the ice chips may be made by freezing electrolyte solutions instead. Increased secretions when administering gastric suction would only escalate electrolyte losses. If necessary, the client is maintained on intravenous or TPN feedings until the acute phase subsides.

When the pain subsides and bowel sounds return, oral intake is started. Clear liquids, progressing to a low-fat, high-carbohydrate diet, are given. The use of elemental formulas may be necessary. Medium-chain triglycerides may be a better tolerated source of fats than normal dietary fats. Six small meals per day is the usual pattern. The client's comfort level is monitored, and serum amylase concentrations are periodically checked. If the client's condition worsens, the acute care regimen is reinstituted.

Acute pancreatitis may or may not progress to chronic pancreatitis. For chronic pancreatitis clients, alcohol is not recommended. Fat restriction similar to that for gallbladder disease may be helpful. Pancreatic enzymes can be given orally before or with meals to aid digestion. Because vitamin B_{12} is not absorbed adequately by pancreatitis clients, it is given parenterally.

Cystic Fibrosis

The most common cause of pancreatic insufficiency in children and young adults is **cystic fibrosis.** It occurs once in 2500 live births. One in 20 caucasians carries the recessive gene for this disorder.

Pathophysiology

The underlying pathology of cystic fibrosis is thick glandular mucus production. This dense mucus affects the pancreas, lungs, liver, heart, gallbladder, and small intestine. The mucus plugs the ducts through which it and other secretions are supposed to flow. The stagnant secretions then become a hospitable environment for bacteria. Fifty percent of children with cystic fibrosis show lung symptoms. Lung infection is the most common cause of death.

The pancreas is affected in 80 percent of the cases. Here the thick mucus interferes with digestive secretions, leading to malabsorption of many nutrients and stunted growth. The sign of cystic fibrosis related to the gastrointestinal tract is the passage of bulky, fatty, foul-smelling feces. This is caused by the impairment of fat digestion. With increased life expectancy, more cystic fibrosis clients display hyperglycemia or diabetes mellitus.

The sweat of a cystic fibrosis client has more sodium chloride than normal. A sweat chloride level greater than 60 milliequivalents per liter is diagnostic of cystic fibrosis. The high electrolyte content of the sweat also puts the client at increased risk of imbalance during hot weather, fever, or bouts of diarrhea.

Treatment of Cystic Fibrosis

Supportive care is the foundation of cystic fibrosis treatment. Pulmonary congestion and infections are treated as required. The client's energy needs may be double those of others the same age. When the lungs are involved, much of the client's energy is expended in respiratory effort. Because starches require amylase for digestion, carbohydrates in the form of simple sugars are a better source of energy. If the client also has diabetes mellitus, the diet will include more simple sugars than the usual diet for diabetes mellitus. Intensive therapy of the diabetes mellitus can be maintained with self-monitoring of blood glucose and multiple doses of insulin (Hayes, et al, 1994).

For the cystic fibrosis client, protein needs are double the RDA. Fat content should be as high as possible because it is a concentrated energy source. If necessary, medium-chain triglycerides can be used to increase fat intake without overtaxing the weak digestive system.

Pancreatic enzymes are administered orally. These help, but they do not completely substitute for a normally functioning pancreas. Fat-soluble vitamins are supplemented in water-miscible form. Riboflavin needs are increased because of the client's high energy expenditure. Vitamin A should be readily available, to help maintain the integrity of the respiratory and gastrointestinal mucosa. Vitamin K is required because frequent courses of antibiotics kill the intestinal flora. Mineral intake is watched carefully if the weather is hot or the client is feverish. Extra salt is given if sweat losses are increased. Zinc levels often are low as a result of loss in the feces. Deficiency of zinc contributes to failure of bone growth and to increased susceptibility to infection.

Summary

Diseases of other body systems may be more immediately life threatening, but over the long term, gastrointestinal diseases can profoundly affect quality of life and life expectancy. Health care workers should make nutrition a priority for clients undergoing diagnostic tests or surgery.

Almost everyone with a gastrointestinal disorder benefits from small, frequent meals. Hiatal hernia clients should remain upright after meals. In contrast, postgastrectomy clients with dumping syndrome are treated with frequent dry meals, low in simple sugar, and should maintain a horizontal position following meals.

Celiac disease and cystic fibrosis are gastrointestinal diseases found in children as well as in adults. In celiac disease, gluten destroys the intestinal villi, causing major malabsorption problems. In cystic fibrosis, thick glandular secretions plug the pancreatic ducts, causing malabsorption. The excessive mucus produced in the lungs by cystic fibrosis is life threatening, however.

Nourishing clients with Crohn's disease and ulcerative colitis poses significant challenges. Use of elemental formulas or total parenteral nutrition is often necessary to permit healing. In intractable cases, colon resection and ileostomy may be performed. This drastic surgery presents a new set of management problems, including fluid balance, odor control, and skin integrity.

In cirrhosis, the liver becomes scarred and hard. The result is portal hypertension, absorption of toxins through collateral channels, esophageal varices, ascites, bleeding problems, and possible hepatic coma. Alcohol abuse underlies most cases of cirrhosis and pancreatitis. Treatment is abstinence and supportive therapy. Diet is modified according to the client's current clinical status.

Cystic fibrosis—Hereditary disease often affecting the lungs and pancreas in which glandular secretions are abnormally thick.

Case Study 21–1

An outpatient, Ms. C, a 40-year-old white woman, has just been evaluated for right upper quadrant pain. The pain occurs after meals and radiates to the right shoulder. Ms. C has noticed her stools have become pale gray in the past 2 months. Ms. C is 5 ft, 4 in tall, has a medium frame, and weights 151 lb.

Ultrasound examination of the gallbladder showed the presence of numerous stones. None is obstructing the duct system yet.

Ms. C is a single parent of four children, aged 4 to 17, and is employed as a secretary. If surgery does become necessary, she would like to delay it until the youngest child is in school. For that reason, she is electing conservative treatment.

The nurse taking a dietary history discovers that Ms. C seldom eats breakfast, substituting a doughnut and coffee during her morning coffee break. Lunch is generally a bologna sandwich with chips. Dinner at home often consists of hamburgers, pizza, or macaroni and cheese. Ms. C told the nurse she does not know much about nutrition, that she shops as her mother did, and cooks food her children will eat.

NURSING CARE PLAN FOR MS. C

Assessment

Subjective Data	Pain in right upper quadrant immediately after eating
	Pale stools for 2 months by history
	High-fat, low-fiber diet by history
	Admitted lack of knowledge about nutrition
Objective Data	Gallstones per ultrasound
	115 percent of healthy body weight

Nursing Diagnosis Knowledge deficit, related to prescribed low-fat diet for cholecystitis as evidenced by admitted lack of knowledge about nutrition

Desired Outcome/ Evaluation Criteria	Nursing Actions	Rationale
Client will verbalize foods to avoid to maintain low-fat diet by end of teaching session.	Explain low-fat diet, working in client's lifestyle. Provide written instructions for client to take home.	Having written instructions available as a teaching tool structures the session and may stimulate questions the client would not think of otherwise. Her taking the material home will reinforce the instruction.
Client will state means of modifying meals to accommodate prescribed diet by end of teaching session.	Explore Ms. C's preferences for adding fiber to her diet.	Soluble fiber will combine with cholesterol, which comprises most gallstones, and carry it out of the body. Building on the client's choices increases chances of compliance.
	Obtain client's reaction to diet and offer alternatives to her present meal pattern.	Considering the client's wishes affirms her status as an individual. Personalizing the diet for her circumstances will increase the chances of success.
	Suggest Ms. C either eat breakfast or drink 2 glasses of water first thing in the morning.	Either of these actions will stimulate the gallbladder to empty and rid itself of the concentrated bile that has accumulated overnight.
Client will return to follow-up session in 1 week with report of the week's meals and any questions she may have.	Try to obtain a commitment to return for follow-up in 1 week.	This is quite a radical change from Ms. C's usual eating habits. Follow-up in 1 week will give the nurse an opportunity to reinforce the teaching, answer questions, and counsel the client to remain committed to the therapeutic regimen.

Study Aids

Chapter Review

1. Which of the following foods would be allowed for a preoperative client on a low-residue diet?
   a. 8 ounces of milk with each of the three main meals
   b. Minestrone soup containing peas and lentils
   c. Ground beef on a white bun
   d. A fresh fruit salad

2. Increased fat in the bowel due to absorption problems may lead to kidney stones because:
   a. Fatty acids form the core of kidney stones.
   b. Less calcium is available to bind with oxalate to promote its excretion.
   c. The bile supply cannot meet demand, so fats are absorbed without emulsification.
   d. Waste material moves through the intestine so fast that insufficient water is absorbed to keep the urine dilute.

3. Clients who have had resection of the ileum must be protected from:
   a. Iron-deficiency anemia
   b. Fat-soluble vitamin deficiency
   c. Calcium and phosphorus deficiency
   d. Vitamin B_{12} deficiency

4. A client with cirrhosis of the liver should be asked if _____ has been experienced before ordering a diet.
   a. Headache
   b. Vomiting of blood
   c. Vomiting followed by pneumonia
   d. Hives

5. Which of the following meal components is likely to improve symptoms of the dumping syndrome?
   a. Mashed fresh strawberries
   b. Orange sherbet
   c. Salt-free tomato juice
   d. Whole-wheat toast with dietetic jelly

Clinical Analysis

Mr. W is a 55-year-old white man admitted to the acute care unit with jaundice and ascites secondary to cirrhosis of the liver. He has gained 15 pounds in the last 3 weeks. He is a known alcoholic who went through detoxification several times in the past 5 years. The dietitian has instructed Mr. W on a 1000-milligram sodium diet with a fluid restriction of 1000 milliliters per day.

1. When the nurse does the beginning of shift assessment, Mr. W says he has tried "cutting down on salt" when he started gaining weight, but it didn't work. Which of the following statements best reflects the nurse's understanding of Mr. W's pathology and treatment?
   a. Just cutting out added salt is not enough, because many foods are naturally high in sodium.
   b. Fluids are always restricted with a low-sodium diet.
   c. The ascites is caused by the inability of the liver to produce water-soluble bilirubin.
   d. Besides retaining sodium, Mr. W has ascites due to decreased blood pressure in the liver.

2. Mr. W vomits immediately after his next meal. The physician then orders a hydrating solution of 5 percent dextrose in water intravenously. If thiamin is not included in that order, the nurse should inquire about it because:
   a. Thiamin is necessary to predigest the dextrose for immediate absorption.
   b. Intravenous glucose without thiamin in the cirrhosis client can precipitate the Wernicke-Korsakoff syndrome.
   c. Thiamin prevents folic acid stores from being diluted by the hydrating solution.
   d. Deficiency of thiamin causes delirium tremens.

3. Mr. W's condition worsens. He is placed on a 30-gram protein diet. Ms. W has been told the purpose of the protein restriction. The next day, Ms. W asks the nurse, "If protein breakdown is causing the problem, why is he getting any at all?" Which of the following responses by the nurse would be most accurate.
   a. Some protein is necessary to spare glucose for basic energy needs.
   b. If the body receives no protein, it will destroy its own tissue to obtain it.
   c. The proteins in this diet are predigested and more easily absorbed than most.
   d. Laboratory tests will show the doctor how much and what kinds of protein can be tolerated.

Bibliography

Adams, WL, et al: Alcohol-related hospitalization of elderly people. JAMA 270:1222–1225, 1993.

Archer, L, Grant, BF, and Dawson, DA: What if Americans drank less? The potential effect on the prevalence of alcohol abuse and dependence. Am J Public Health 85:61–66, 1995.

Benenson, AS (ed): Control of Communicable Diseases Manual, ed 16. American Public Health Association, Washington, DC, 1995.

Beresford, TP, et al: Comparison of CAGE questionnaire and computer-assisted laboratory profiles in screening for covert alcoholism. Lancet 336:482–485, 1990.

Blackburn, GL, et al: Surgical nutrition. In Halpern, SL (ed): Quick Reference to Clinical Nutrition. JB Lippincott, Philadelphia, 1987.

Brensilver, JM, and Goldberger, E: A Primer of Water, Electrolyte, and Acid-Base Syndromes, ed 8. FA Davis, Philadelphia, 1996.

Bush, B, et al: Screening for alcohol abuse using the CAGE questionnaire. Am J Med 82:231–235, 1987.

Chan, AWK, Pristach, EA, and Welte, JW: Detection by the CAGE of alcoholism or heavy drinking in primary care outpatients and the general population. J Substance Abuse 6:123, 1994.

Committee on Diet and Health. Food and Nutrition Board. Commission on Life Sciences. National Research Council: Diet and Health: Implications for Reducing Chronic Disease Risk. National Academy Press, Washington, DC, 1989.

Deglin, JH, and Vallerand, AH: Davis's Drug Guide for Nurses, ed 4. FA Davis, Philadelphia, 1995.

Detsky, AS, Smalley, PS, and Chang, J: Is this patient malnourished? JAMA 271:54, 1994.

Ewing, JA: Detecting alcoholism: The CAGE questionnaire. JAMA 252:1905–1907, 1984.

Feldman, EB: Essentials of Clinical Nutrition. FA Davis, Philadelphia, 1988.

Ferry, GD, and Price-Jones, BA: Nutrition and disorders of the colon. In Halpern, SL (ed): Quick Reference to Clinical Nutrition. JB Lippincott, Philadelphia, 1987.

Girela, E, et al: Comparison of the CAGE questionnaire versus some biochemical markers in the diagnosis of alcoholism. Alcohol-Alcohol 29:337–343, 1994.

Hayes, DR, et al: Management dilemmas in the individual with cystic fibrosis and diabetes. J Am Diet Assoc 94:78, 1994.

Kerr, EC: Celiac disease in childhood. Gastroenterol Nurs 18:67–70, 1995.

Klish, WJ, and Montandon, CM: Nutrition and upper gastrointestinal disorders. In Feldman, EB (ed): Essentials of Clinical Nutrition. FA Davis, Philadelphia, 1988.

Krieger, D, et al: Manganese and chronic hepatic encephalopathy. Lancet 346:270–274, 1995.

Liskow, B, et al: Validity of the Cage questionnaire in screening for alcohol dependence in a walk-in (triage) clinic. J Stud Alcohol 56:277–281, 1995.

Long, BC, and Phipps, WJ: Medical-Surgical Nursing, A Nursing Process Approach, 3 ed. CV Mosby Company, St. Louis, 1993.

Monahan, FD, Drake, T, and Neighbors, M: Nursing Care of Adults. Saunders, Philadelphia, 1994.

Mullen, JL: Consequences of malnutrition in the surgical patient. Surg Clin North Am 61:465, 1981.

Noone, J: Acute pancreatitis: An Orem approach to nursing assessment and care. Crit Care Nurse 15:27–37, 1995.

Nour, B, Van Thiel, DH, and Kocoshis, S: Intestinal failure and intestinal transplantation: New therapy for individuals sustaining large losses of bowel: A review. J Okla State Med Assoc 88:191–197, 1995.

Reisner, EH: Nutrition and the anemias. In Halpern, SL (ed): Quick Reference to Clinical Nutrition. JB Lippincott, Philadelphia, 1987.

Rudman, D, et al: Ammonia content of food. Am J Clin Nutr 26:487, 1973.

Saltzman, JR, and Clifford, BD: Identification of the triggers of celiac sprue. Nutr Rev 52:317–319, 1994.

Scanlon, VT and Sanders, T: Essentials of Anatomy and Physiology ed 2. FA Davis, Philadelphia, 1995.

Scanlon, VT, and Sanders, T: Student Workbook for Essentials of Anatomy and Physiology. FA Davis, Philadelphia, 1991.

Scully, RE, et al: Case records of the Massachusetts General Hospital. N Engl J Med 331:383–389, 1994.

Shaw, EW, and Maddrey, WC: Nutritional therapy in patients with liver disease. In Halpern, SL (ed): Quick Reference to Clinical Nutrition. JB Lippincott, Philadelphia, 1987.

Sichiere, R, Everhart, JE, and Rothe, H: A prospective study of hospitalization with gallstone disease among women: Role of dietary factors, fasting period, and dieting. Am J Public Health 81:880, 1991.

Soll, AH: Medical treatment of peptic ulcer disease: Practice guidelines. JAMA 275:622, 1996.

Sullivan, M, and Heyman, MB: Increasing use of nutritional therapy in pediatric inflammatory bowel disease. RD (Health Communications, Darien, CT) 15:1, 4–6, 8–9, 1995.

Tamburro, CH: Nutritional management of alcoholism, drug addiction, and acute toxicity syndromes. In Halpern, SL (ed): Quick Reference to Clinical Nutrition. JB Lippincott, Philadelphia, 1987.

Thomas, CL, ed: Taber's Cyclopedic Medical Dictionary, 17 ed. FA Davis, Philadelphia, 1993.

York, JL: Progression of alcohol consumption across the drinking career in alcoholics and social drinkers. J Stud Alcohol 56:328, 1995.

CHAPTER 22

Diet in Cancer

LEARNING OBJECTIVES

After completing this chapter, the student should be able to:

1 Describe the ways in which foods are implicated in the development of cancer.

2 List several correlations between dietary intake and cancers of specific sites.

3 Interpret dietary guidelines on the prevention of cancer.

4 Name several factors thought to contribute loss of appetite in cancer clients.

5 Discuss measures to increase oral intake for clients with cancer.

Cancer has been known since 3400 B.C. Amazingly one substance now linked to prevention was used as a treatment. Crushed cabbage leaves were applied to cancerous ulcers in ancient Rome (Albert-Puleo, 1983). Cancer means crab, for the creeping way in which it spreads.

Cancer encompasses more than 100 types of malignant neoplastic disease. Cancer is a **neoplasm,** a new and abnormal formation of tissue (tumor) that grows at the expense of the healthy organism. Two of the main types of cancer are sarcomas and carcinomas. **Sarcomas** arise from connective tissue, such as muscle or bone and are more common in young people. **Carcinomas** occur in epithelial tissue, such as skin and mucous membranes and are more common in older people. The characteristics common to all types of cancer are uncontrolled growth and the ability to spread to distant sites (to **metastasize**). Clinical Application 22–1 discusses the transformation of normal cells into cancer cells.

Cancer is the second most common cause of death in the United States. Clients who are alive and without recurrence of cancer 5 years after diagnosis are considered cured. This is termed the *5-year survival rate*. It is now 52 percent for whites and 38 percent for blacks (Alberts, and Garcia, 1995). Regardless of ethnicity, the 5-year survival rate for poor Americans is estimated to be 10 to 15 percent lower than that of middle-class and affluent Americans (Kagawa-Singer, 1995). Depending on the site in which the cancer occurs, the survival rates vary greatly.

CLINICAL APPLICATION 22–1

Transformation of Normal Cells into Cancer Cells

Within all cells are genes that make up the DNA molecule. Genes carry the traits that the individual inherited from his or her parents. Within tumor cells, **oncogenes** have been located that transform normal cells into cancer cells. Forty different oncogenes have been identified. Just having an oncogene is not enough to produce a cancer. The transformation of normal cells to cancer cells is a two-step process. The first step is **initiation.** The second step is promotion.

Initiation

Physical forces, chemicals, or biologic agents can cause a mutation, an alteration in the cell's DNA. If the mutation affects both strands of the DNA helix it is not repairable, resulting in a permanently altered gene. This altered gene is not significant until the second step of **promotion** takes place. In fact, 10 to 30 years may elapse between initiation and the diagnosis of cancer.

Promotion

For promoters to enhance the expression of the altered gene, they must be present in high levels for a prolonged period. Repeated exposure to promoting agents causes expression of the altered gene. Promoters are tissue-specific; for instance, bile acids for colon cancer and saccharin for cancer of the urinary bladder. In contrast to initiation, which results in permanent change, the process of promotion is reversible. Reducing exposure to high levels of promoters allows the body to repair the damaged cells.

Evidence Linking Cancer to Diet

The causes of cancer are complex and often poorly understood. Certain cancers appear in great numbers in particular countries. Clinical Application 22–2 summarizes some of these findings.

Dietary Components Associated with Cancer

It is difficult to assess the role of dietary components without also considering the other factors that might contribute to the development of cancer. An estimated 50 percent of cancers may be related to diet, including 40 percent of those in men and 60 percent of those in women, despite the fact that women consume a more varied diet and less alcohol than men (Patterson, RE, et al, 1995). Much data has been compiled on breast cancer and diet. Clinical Application 22–3 gives a synopsis.

Excesses of Certain Substances

Some substances are associated with cancer when they are consumed in large quantities. This is the case with fat, alcohol, and pickled and smoked foods. The cooking method also may influence the development of cancer.

FAT   Some of the end products of fat metabolism are thought to be *carcinogenic.* That, plus the slow intestinal transit time, which increases the duration of exposure to the **carcinogen,** may contribute to the development of bowel cancer. Saturated fatty acids and animal fat from red meat were associated with a greater risk of aggressive or advanced prostate cancer (Giovannucci, et al, 1993; Greco, and Kulawiak, rectal cancer. Risk of esophageal cancer increases two to four times if 41 to 80 grams of alcohol is ingested per day, and 18 times if more than 80 grams per day is drunk (Feldman, 1988). When combined with cigarettes or chewing tobacco, alcohol increases the risk of mouth, larynx, and throat cancers.

Alcohol has been related to increased risk of breast cancer. An estimated increase in risk of 40 percent was associated with each 24 grams (about 2 drinks) of alcohol consumed per day (Hunter, and Willett, 1993). A possible pathophysiological reason for the correlation is discussed in Clinical Application 22–3.

PICKLED AND SMOKED FOODS   Cancers of the esophagus and stomach are correlated with large intakes of pickled and smoked foods. It is postulated that the process of smoking foods may result in their absorbing tar similar to that in tobacco smoke. Charcoal broiling presents the same type of danger, in that carcinogens may be deposited on the surface of the food.

CARCINOGENS RELATED TO COOKING   Recent data have shown that high-temperature cooking of meat—frying, broiling, and grilling—produces substances known to produce cancer in animals. Low-temperature, high-moisture cooking, such as stewing and pot roasting, does not produce the same level of carcinogens.

Protective Nutrients

Excessive amounts of a cancer-promoting food seems to be neutralized by other foods. Of particular note are fiber, vitamin A and carotene, and vitamin C.

FIBER   Approximately one-third of all cancers are attributed to the typical high-fat, low-fiber American

1994). In the breast and prostatic cancers, body fat is thought to affect hormonal activity.

Linoleic acid, an essential fatty acid, is classified as a promoter of cancer rather than an initiator. Although some polyunsaturated fats are recommended for protection against heart disease, excessive intakes of polyunsaturated fats have been connected to cancer. In animal studies, the omega-3 fatty acids have been protective against cancer development, and monounsaturated fatty acids have been neutral, neither promoting nor protecting.

ALCOHOL   Alcohol-induced cirrhosis, with resulting increased liver cell turnover, is associated with liver cancer. Heavy beer drinking is identified with colo-

Neoplasm—A new and abnormal formation of tissue (tumor) that grows at the expense of the healthy organism.

Carcinoma—A malignant neoplasm that occurs in epithelial tissue.

Metastasis—The "seeding" of cancer cells to distant sites of the body by blood or lymph vessels or by spilling into a body cavity.

Oncogene—A gene found in tumor cells making the host cells susceptible to initiation and promotion by carcinogens.

Breast Cancer and Diet

Early epidemiological research related high-dietary fat intake to breast cancer in many countries, but later case-control and prospective studies did not support a cause-and-effect relationship except in post-menopausal women (Howe, et al, 1990; van't Veer, 1994). Some experts suggest that fat intake must be less than 25 percent of kilocalories to affect breast cancer rates (Position of the ADA and CDA, 1995). A large primary prevention trial, including an intervention to reduce fat intake to 20 percent of kilocalories, is underway among postmenopausal women in the United States and Canada (Hulka, and Stark, 1995). Given a possible 30-year promotion phase in cancer development, any dietary intervention late in life may not be helpful. Furthermore, the international data likely reflect lifetime food consumption habits. Indeed, a pooled analysis of 4980 cases of breast cancer occurring among 337,819 women aged 28 to 93 at baseline found little association between the percent of kilocalories from fat and the risk of breast cancer. This was true even among women who derived less than 20 percent of energy from fat. The conclusion drawn is that fat reduction in midlife or later would be unlikely to substantially diminish the risk of breast cancer, however the data on adult women cannot exclude the effect of fat intake in childhood or adolescence on later breast cancer (Hunter, et al, 1996). Further evidence of youthful diet affecting breast cancer is the positive correlation between height and breast cancer, particularly linked to energy intake during peripubertal growth (Hunter, and Willett, 1993; Vatten, and Kvinnsland, 1990).

One key aspect of breast cancer involves the metabolism of estrogen. Risk of breast cancer increases 40 to 50 percent with estrogen replacement therapy and decreases with bilateral oophorectomy early in life (Hulka, and Stark, 1995). Breast cancers with a high ability to take up estrogen, labelled estrogen receptor positive, are often treated by counteracting the hormone.

Estrogen is produced not only by the ovaries but by body fat cells. Thus the fact that obesity increases the risk of breast cancer in postmenopausal women may be related to this source of estrogen. Of women with estrogen receptor positive breast tumors, 66 percent of the obese women had lymph node involvement compared to 32 percent of the lean women (Niwa, Swaneck, and Bradlow, 1994).

Manipulating the fat in the diet has been shown to affect the amounts of estrogen in the blood even in the short-term. A 10 to 22 week trial to lower dietary fat intake from 37 to 20 percent of kilocalories reduced blood estradiol 17 percent (Prentice, et al, 1990). The women also lost an average of 3.4 kg (7.5 lb) and showed an average drop in plasma cholesterol of 12 mg/dL.

Estrogen is degraded by the liver, so impairment of liver function would increase the estrogen level in the blood. An increased risk among women who consume alcohol is probably the best established dietary risk factor for breast cancer (Hunter and Willett, 1993). As with the association between peripubertal energy intake and breast cancer, some evidence suggests youthful alcohol consumption influences development of breast cancer, even if the women later stopped drinking.

Enhanced excretion of estrogen would also decrease blood levels. A high-fiber diet seemed to protect women against breast cancer in two Chinese cities (Yuan, et al, 1995). Lack of fiber in the bowel is thought to promote the reabsorption of estrogen that otherwise would be excreted via bile.

In another report, even a slightly lower fat intake seemingly protected breast cancer clients from treatment failure (recurrence, a tumor in the opposite breast, or metastasis). Women with estrogen receptor positive tumors without treatment failure recounted an average fat intake of 36 percent of kilocalories in the year before diagnosis compared to 38.5 percent reported by women with treatment failure (Holm, et al, 1993).

Besides estrogen receptors, vitamin D receptors have been found on breast tumor cells. Their presence seems to be protective because clients whose tumors showed these receptors had a longer-disease free survival than those without them. These vitamin D receptors may help to explain the 55 percent higher breast cancer mortality in the Northeastern United States than that in the Southeast and Southwest. Breast cancer rates are low in Japan which is relatively far north, but the native Japanese diet contains large amounts of fish high in vitamin D. Immigration, and presumed adoption of a Western diet, affects cancer development: age-adjusted breast cancer incidence rates per 100,000 Japanese women were 14 in Japan, 44 in Hawaii, and 57 in Los Angeles (Tomlinson, 1994). These differences were originally attributed to excess dietary fat, but lack of vitamin D may be a greater factor.

Attempts to correlate specific vitamins with lower risk of breast cancer have been unsuccessful, but intake of fruits and vegetables have been shown to be protective (Hulka, and Stark, 1995). Large intakes of vitamins C or E did not protect women from breast cancer, but low vitamin A intake was associated with increased tumors, suggesting any benefit from increased vitamin A may be limited to women consuming diets low in the vitamin (Hunter, et al, 1993).

Awareness that knowledge about disease etiology accrues in small increments will help to interpret the conflicting reports in the scientific and general press. Eating a balanced, varied diet in moderation, rather than supplementing with individual nutrients, still is the recommended course.

diet (Foerster, 1995). Increased intake of cereals and vegetables were related to decreased risk of prostate cancer (Greco, and Kulawick, 1994). Low-fiber diets are associated with colon cancer. It has been suggested, however, that all fiber is not of equal value, and that perhaps a particular subset of fiber, as yet unspecified, confers all the protection.

VITAMIN A AND CAROTENOIDS High intakes of vitamin A and carotene may reduce the risk of lung, larynx, esophagus, bladder, upper gastrointestinal tract, and breast cancers. Vitamin A may control cell differentiation or influence host immune defenses; carotene may protect against oxidation. Studies have shown that individuals with the overall highest cancer rates have lower serum retinol levels than other people.

Carotenoids, other than beta-carotene, provitamin A, seem to be protective against cancer. Intake of tomatoes, tomato sauce, and pizza was inversely associated with risk of prostatic cancer (Giovannucci, et al, 1995). **Lycopene,** found in tomatoes, is the most efficient antioxidant of the carotenoids but has no vitamin A potential, and is retained after heating (Franceschi, et al, 1994). This carotenoid may explain the low rates of prostatic cancer seen in Italy and Greece where the Mediterranean diet includes many tomato-based dishes.

A high intake of raw tomatoes, more than 7 servings per week, was significantly related to decreased risk for gastrointestinal cancers compared to an intake of less than 2 servings per week (Franceschi, et al, 1994). Tomatoes have other components besides vitamin C and lycopene that may contribute to these findings, suggesting that at this stage of understanding, eating a variety of whole foods, not individual micronutrients, is the appropriate formula to decrease the risk of cancer.

VITAMIN C Diets high in fruits and vegetables are associated with a decreased incidence of cancers of the stomach and esophagus. Vitamin C intake was inversely related to breast cancer (Howe, et al, 1990) and to stomach cancer mortality (Ocke, et al, 1995).

VITAMIN E AND SELENIUM Vitamin E and selenium are both antioxidants that protect cells against breakdown. These two nutrients have a reciprocal sparing relationship, so relating one alone to cancer is a complicated process.

A very large Finnish trial found no reduction in the incidence of lung cancer after 5 to 8 years of supplementation with alpha-tocopherol (vitamin E) or beta carotene (Alpha-Tocopherol, Beta Carotene Cancer Prevention Study Group, 1994). Consider-

ing that a malignancy may develop over decades, the trial was relatively short. At the beginning of the study, the men had smoked an average 20.4 cigarettes a day for an average of 35.9 years. Although a high dose of beta carotene with high bioavailability was used, the dose of vitamin E was quite small and not highly bioavailable (Hennekens, Buring, and Peto, 1994). For these reasons, and the fact that cigarette smoke is both an initiator and promoter of cancer, the conclusion cannot be made that vitamins are useless. Clinical Application 22–4 discusses vegetable intake, as opposed to pharmaceutical vitamin supplementation, in relation to cancer.

People with the highest intakes of selenium had half the cancer risk of people with the lowest intakes (Feldman, 1988). Conversely, selenium in drinking water was positively correlated with colorectal cancer. Because of the small database and selenium's narrow margin of safety, selenium supplementation is not recommended.

CALCIUM In both animals and humans, calcium seems to protect against colon cancer. Experts theorize that calcium reduces cell turnover rates.

Questionable Relationships to Cancer

Studies have produced inconclusive data or conflicting reports on the relationship of certain substances to cancer. Two of these are caffeine and coffee. Total epidemiological evidence shows no substantial increase in breast cancer risk due to coffee-drinking (Hunter, and Willett, 1993).

Aflatoxins are inconclusively linked to cancer. **Aflatoxins** from molds are contaminants of improperly stored food. Aflatoxin contamination of peanuts and corn is related to primary liver cancer, especially in Africa and Asia. Interpreting this information is complicated, since hepatitis B is endemic to both continents. The cancer may be caused by the aflatoxins or by hepatitis B virus, or both. There is no evidence relating aflatoxins to cancer risk in the United States.

Reducing the Risk of Cancer

Cancer encompasses a constellation of pathologies and evolves from genetic and environmental factors, of which diet is only one. Diet is likely to influence the premalignant phase of cancer development, not frank tumor growth (Alberts, and Garcia, 1995). Mental attitude, too, influences the body's immune system.

Nevertheless, certain dietary practices are widely recommended to decrease one's risk of cancer.

Some of them also are advised to decrease risk of heart disease. Following the rules, however, does not guarantee a disease-free life.

Food Practices to Avoid

Persons attempting to minimize the risk of cancer should avoid excessive intakes of meat, fat, and alcohol.

Excessive Meat Consumption

Vegetarians have lower cancer rates, even when the effects of smoking and alcohol are eliminated. Population studies link low cancer rates with low meat intake and high intake of vegetables and grains. Seventh Day Adventists and Mormons have a lower incidence of bowel cancer than other Americans, even when caffeine and alcohol differences between the study groups are equalized. A diet high in meat and fat from animal sources is associated with increased risk of non-Hodgkin lymphoma in older women (Chiu, et al, 1996).

Of particular concern is the consumption of smoked, salted, or nitrate-cured meat. These foods should be consumed infrequently. Matching these preserved foods with a good source of vitamin C to counter the effects of nitrosamines would be wise planning. Likewise, limiting the consumption of meats cooked at high temperature may be desirable.

Excessive Fat Consumption

Cancers of the uterus, colon, and prostate are linked to excessive fat consumption. Limiting fat intake to 30 percent of kilocalories is recommended. Substituting skim-milk dairy products for whole-milk products would be a significant change. Selecting lean meats and trimming fat is another step. Limiting fat intake without adding other foods in place of it would also limit kilocalories, which seems to be beneficial.

Alcohol Consumption

Along with tobacco, alcohol is linked to head and neck cancers. Liver cancer risk is increased by alcoholic cirrhosis. Excessive beer consumption is associated with rectal cancer. Evidence links alcohol consumption with breast cancer, however whether abstinence later in life reduces the risk is uncertain (Hunter, and Willett, 1993). The recommendation is to drink alcohol moderately, if at all.

Food Practices to Cultivate

Along with food practices to avoid, there are some food practices to cultivate to minimize cancer risk. These concern fiber, carotene, and cruciferous vegetables. All of these were addressed in a California program to promote fruit and vegetable consumption. Its logo is shown in Figure 22–1. The campaign used broadcast and print media and point of sale reminders, posters, and recipes to educate consumers.

FIGURE 22–1 The national 5 a Day program logo. The program logo and slogan are registered servicemarks. To use them, food industry and state health authority partners sign a license agreement to follow guidelines that maintain the scientific integrity of all messages and other communications to the public. (From American Journal of Preventive Medicine 11:126, 1995, with permission.)

(Foerster, et al, 1995). Unfortunately, a survey of cancer risk behavior indicated pressure from others (extrinsic motivation) may be less effective than beliefs (intrinsic motivation) in promoting healthful behaviors (Patterson, RE, et al, 1995).

Increase Fiber Intake

To reduce the risk of colon cancer, a high-fiber diet is recommended. Fiber promotes bile excretion and speeds up intestinal transit time so that carcinogens are eliminated quicker. The Finnish people have a low cancer rate despite high-fat diets, but their diets are also high in fiber.

Increase Carotene Intake

These precursors of vitamin A have been associated with lower cancer rates. Because of the function of vitamin A in maintaining the integrity of epithelial tissue, carotene intake may help prevent cancers of these tissues. Preformed vitamin A as a supplement is not recommended because of possible toxicity.

Increase Consumption of Cruciferous Vegetables

Cancer clients have been found to eat less cabbage, broccoli, and brussels sprouts than cancer-free persons. The other members of this vegetable family are cauliflower, collards, kale, and kohlrabi.

Consuming these vegetables regularly may reduce risk of cancer of the gastrointestinal and respiratory tracts.

Nutrition for Cancer Clients

Once a person has cancer, nutrition becomes part of the treatment. With the possible exception of clients with acquired immune deficiency syndrome (AIDS), clients with cancer have the highest incidence of malnutrition of hospitalized clients (Ottery, 1995).

Cachexia

A state of malnutrition and wasting is called **cachexia.** Often associated with cancer, it is also seen in AIDS, alcoholism, malaria, tuberculosis, and pituitary disease. Cachexia affects one-third to two-thirds of cancer clients. It occurs despite efforts to nourish the client, because of the tumor's effects on the client's metabolism. Figure 22–2 shows a woman with cachexia.

Cancer changes the client's carbohydrate metabolism. Insulin resistance is common. The client can no longer produce glucose efficiently from carbohydrate but instead uses tissue protein for energy. In traumatized noncancer clients, catabolism of fat for fuel gradually replaces protein breakdown. The cancer client's body does not make this adaptive change.

Special Needs

Food is therapy for cancer clients. Energy needs are one and a half to two times the resting energy expenditure. Protein needs are 1.5 to 2 grams per kilogram of body weight. Often, increased folate is needed (Theologides, 1987). Within the cancer client, the tumor cells are multiplying rapidly and consuming folic acid, which is necessary for DNA formation. Good nutrition enhances medical treat-

Indoles—Compounds found in vegetables of the cruciferous family which activate enzymes to destroy carcinogens.

Cachexia—State of malnutrition and wasting seen in chronic conditions such as cancer, AIDS, malaria, tuberculosis, and pituitary disease.

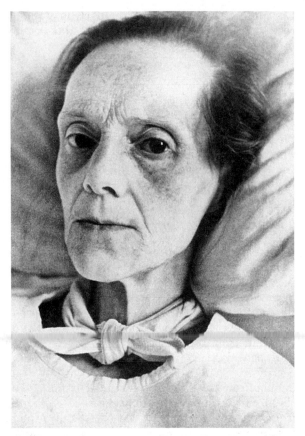

FIGURE 22–2   This woman is cachectic. (From Nutrition Today 16:(3), cover, © by Williams & Wilkins, 1981, with permission.)

ments. During radiation therapy good nutrition and elemented diets seem to lower the incidence of significant bowel injury (Nussbaum, Campana, and Weese, 1993).

Assessment

Unexplained weight loss is one of the seven danger signals of cancer. Anorexia and changes in the sense of taste often precede the diagnosis of cancer. Because the tumor alters the person's metabolism, it is possible for weight loss to occur without a reduction in food intake. Pretreatment weight loss has been related to poor response to therapy (Ottery, 1994).

Cancer clients develop ascites, as well as accumulation of fluids in other body cavities. Interpreting the weight gain or loss may be difficult because of third-space sequestering of fluids. Nevertheless, weight is an important measure of progress.

Serum proteins, particularly albumin, reflect skeletal muscle and visceral protein status. Serum protein levels were lower in clients with pressure ulcers (pressure sores) if they also had cancer than if they did not. Increased breakdown of the body's tissues and catabolism of the albumin will produce low serum albumin levels. Values below 3.4 grams per deciliter are associated with increased morbidity and mortality after therapy (Daly, and Shinkwin, 1991). Hypoalbuminemia also may be due to nephrotic syndrome or loss of proteins from removal of third-space fluids.

Serum transferrin is also used as a marker for protein status. Because its half-life is 8 days compared to 20 days for albumin, serum transferrin levels will reflect responses to stress or to nutritional support faster than will serum albumin levels.

A relatively simple summary measure of malnutrition uses three parameters: weight loss of 10 percent or more of body weight, serum albumin less than 3.4 grams per deciliter, and serum transferrin less than 190 milligrams per deciliter. The presence of any two of those findings indicates a need for nutritional support (Daly, and Shinkwin, 1991).

Common Nutritional Problems in Cancer Clients

Some nutritional problems in cancer clients are due to the disease. Some are due to treatment modalities. Common problems affecting meals and nourishments are early satiety and anorexia, taste alterations, local effects in the mouth, nausea, vomiting and diarrhea, and altered immune response.

Early Satiety and Anorexia

Although they may look starved, cancer clients may take a few bites of food and declare that they are full. They may say that they have no appetite at all. The main source of these symptoms is the cancer itself, by a mechanism that is poorly understood (Tchekmedyian, 1993). Control of the disease improves the appetite.

Sometimes, though, the physical pressure from the tumor or third-space fluid accumulation may give a feeling of fullness. Relieving those problems may improve food intake.

Some additional factors may interfere with appetite. The psychological stress of dealing with cancer may produce anxiety or depression. The person may be grappling with a body image change and may be going through the grieving process for the loss of a body function or the potential loss of life itself.

Taste Alterations

Cancer clients often have changes in taste perceptions, particularly a decreased threshold for bitterness. Accordingly, they will often say that beef and pork taste bitter or metallic. Some clients report a decreased sensation of sweet, salty, and sour tastes and desire increased seasonings. These taste changes are due to the cancer and the various modes of therapy.

Local Effects in the Mouth

Clients who are being treated for head and neck cancers often experience mouth ulcers, decreased and thick saliva, and swallowing difficulty. Any of these may interfere with nutritional intake.

Nausea, Vomiting, and Diarrhea

This triad of symptoms often accompany cancer treatment, either radiation or chemotherapy, as well as certain types of tumors. Since the gastrointestinal tract cells are replaced every few days, these rapidly dividing cells are more vulnerable to the cancer treatments than are more slowly reproducing cells. Not all clients suffer these side effects to the same extent. Health care workers must be careful not to program clients to be sick.

Altered Immune Response

Sometimes, antineoplastic agents also suppress the client's **immune system.** Clients receiving them are at risk of overwhelming infections from organisms that would not affect other persons. Clinical Application 22–5 discusses the role of the immune system in preventing cancer.

Nutritional Interventions

After the disease is controlled, vitamin and mineral deficiencies can be corrected rapidly. Tissue loss responds more slowly to treatment. Severely restricting carbohydrate to minimize glucose available to brain tumors has been tried (Nebling, and Lerner, 1995). Unorthodox diets have not proven effective in extending life or improving its quality (Dwyer, 1992). In a quality of life study, however, appetite and ability to eat were the most important aspects of physical well-being for cancer clients (Padilla, et al, 1983).

CLINICAL APPLICATION 22–5

Role of the Immune System in Preventing Cancer

Some experts believe that many cancers begin in a person's lifetime, only to be stopped by the body's defense system. The increased incidence of cancer in AIDS clients and organ transplant clients on immunosuppressive drugs offers credence to this theory.

One of the body's defenses is provided by certain white blood cells called **T-lymphocytes.** These cells have the task of recognizing foreign materials, including cancer cells, as "non-self" and acting to destroy the invaders. Some of the T-lymphocytes develop into killer cells, which bind to the foreign cell membrane and release lysosomal enzymes into the cancer cell which destroys it. The T-lymphocytes mature in the **thymus** gland in the chest, hence the name, thymic lymphocytes.

Contributing to the development of cancer in the elderly is the deterioration of the immune system. The thymus gland begins to shrink at sexual maturity. By age 50 only 10 percent of the original gland remains.

For Early Satiety and Anorexia

Many nutrient-dense feedings are offered to the cancer client. To maximize the nutrition, creative concoctions are in order. For instance, adding 1 1/3 cups of instant dry skim milk powder to 1 quart of liquid milk increases the nutrient density, with little or no change in palatability.

Cancer clients should be encouraged to eat whether they are hungry or not. Food is therapy, too. Appropriate exercise before meals may help to stimulate appetite. Attractively prepared food served in a pleasant environment is enticing. Very small servings, offered frequently, may increase the client's intake. For clients in the hospital, receiving favorite foods from home or sharing a meal with the family may help overcome the client's aversion to food. Children sometimes can be coaxed to eat by decorating their food with faces or serving it in the

---

T-lymphocytes (T-cells)—White blood cells which recognize and fight foreign cells such as cancer.

Thymus—Gland in the chest, above and in front of the heart, which contributes to the immune response, including the maturation of T-lymphocytes.

form of designs such as cars or dolls or the child's name. Involving the child in food preparation or in choosing the menu can help to pique the appetite. As a last attempt to encourage nourishment in the severely anorexic client, suggest offering 1 ounce of a complete nutritional supplement every hour.

Clients with severe, chronic anorexia who can tolerate oral intake may benefit from drug therapy with megestrol acetate. This progesterone-like hormone with antineoplastic action has improved appetite and food intake in cancer clients but increased survival time has not been documented (Tchekmedyian, 1993).

To Combat Bitter or Metallic Tastes

Oral hygiene before meals will freshen the mouth. Cooking in the microwave oven or in glass utensils may minimize the metallic taste. As protein sources, eggs, fish, poultry, and dairy products may be better received than beef or pork. Serving meat cold or at room temperature lessens the bitter taste. Sometimes sauces and seasonings added to the meat will improve its palatability.

For Local Effects about the Mouth

A single canker sore can be remarkably painful. A cancer client with multiple oral ulcerations may complain of severe pain upon food ingestion. In addition, some clients also have dry mouths and difficulty swallowing. For all of these problems, good oral hygiene, before and after meals, is essential.

MOUTH ULCERATIONS   Foods should be soft and mild. Sauces, gravies, and dressings may make foods easier to eat. Cream soups and milk provide much nutrition for the volume ingested. Cold foods have a somewhat numbing effect and may be better tolerated than hot food. Taking liquids with meals will help to wash down the food. Soda straws may help get the liquids past mouth ulcerations. Substances likely to irritate the mouth ulcerations should be avoided. These may include hot items, salty or spicy foods, and acidic juices.

To maintain oral intake, it may be necessary to resort to an anesthetic mouthwash. If the mouth is anesthetized, clients should be instructed to chew slowly and carefully to avoid biting their lips or tongue or cheeks. A small study demonstrated the effectiveness of topical vitamin E oil in healing chemotherapy-induced mouth lesions (Wadleigh, et al, 1992).

DRY MOUTH   Adequate hydration will help keep the mouth moist. Food lubricants can be of value: gravy, butter, margarine, milk, beer, or bouillon may aid in consuming a near-adequate diet when the mouth is dry (Theologides, 1987). Synthetic salivas are available also, but sips of water are often preferred. Sugarless hard candy, chewing gum, or popsicles may stimulate saliva production (Ganley, 1995).

SWALLOWING DIFFICULTY   This problem may linger throughout a 6-week course of treatment. To combat it, clients should make swallowing a conscious act. They should inhale, swallow, and exhale. Experiment with head position. Tilting the head backward or forward may help. Foods for these clients should be nonsticky and of even consistency. "Dunking" bread products in beverages helps lubricate the passage. Lumpy gravy and mixed vegetables are hard to manage.

For Nausea, Vomiting, and Diarrhea

Antiemetic medications should be given 6 hours before chemotherapy begins, and continued on a regular schedule. These drugs are most effective if given prophylactically, before the client becomes nauseated.

Similarly, medications for pain and insomnia must be given liberally. Nausea and vomiting frequently accompany pain in clients without cancer, also. Controlling the pain may alleviate nausea to a great extent.

As with morning sickness, eating dry crackers before arising may alleviate the nausea. Liquids taken between, rather than with, meals will reduce the volume in the stomach. Similarly, a low-fat diet is digested faster, leaving less content in the stomach to cause nausea or be vomited. Adding nutmeg to food to decrease gastric motility is suggested (Lowdermilk, 1995).

Clients should eat slowly and chew thoroughly. Resting after eating helps. Foods the client especially likes should be saved for times the client feels good, lest these favorite foods become associated with vomiting, and afterwards avoided.

As with the client who has gastrointestinal upset, clear liquids should be tried first, after vomiting ceases, and the diet progressed as tolerated. Unconventional mealtimes may be instituted to ensure that the client receives nourishment when nausea is minimal. If this means that breakfast is eaten at 2 A.M. and lunch at 6 A.M., so be it. That is truly individualized care.

Diarrhea may be countered by adding pectin-containing foods to the client's intake. A low-residue diet helps reduce intestinal stimulation. The possibility of lactose intolerance should be considered because of the destruction of the gastrointestinal mucosa. Active cultures of yogurt have been used to repopulate the intestine with bacteria, when the flora normally present have been killed by the therapy or washed out by the diarrheal stools.

For Altered Immune Response

Clients may be placed in protective isolation to minimize their exposure to microorganisms. As for dietary interventions, fresh fruits and vegetables may be restricted since they cannot be disinfected adequately. Yogurt also may have to be avoided because of the possibility of translocation of bacteria from the intestine to the bloodstream. Other measures are similar to those taken to protect AIDS clients and are discussed in Chapter 24, "Diet in HIV and Aids."

Total Parenteral Nutrition or Tube Feedings

The principles of tube feeding and TPN apply to cancer clients as well as clients generally. Clients should be started on appropriate feeding methods before they become severely malnourished. Clients whose weight is 5 kilograms below their healthy body weights and whose serum albumin is less than 3 grams per 100 milliliters should be considered candidates for intensive nutritional support. Charting Tips 22–1 discusses documenting cancer clients' at-home treatment and diet plans.

Other Nursing Interventions

Oral hygiene before and after meals may help clients to eat better. Oral hygiene with isotonic saline alone or combined with soda bicarbonate is recommended. Alcohol and glycerine products dry the mucosa and hydrogen peroxide damages new tissue.

Massage and relaxation techniques may assist clients to cope. They can either stimulate or relax a person, depending on the techniques used. Besides the local effects, the client receives the benefit of touch from another person. This can be very valuable, since cancer clients sometimes feel, rightly or wrongly, shunned. In one type of relaxation exercise, clients are coached to relax areas of the body in sequence. Others focus the client's mind on controlled breathing or mental images. These procedures have the added advantage of as-

CHARTING TIPS 20 1

When admitting a client who provides much of his or her own care at home, try to learn all about treatments and dietary preferences and document them. If the client becomes less self-sufficient after surgery or after beginning cancer therapy, the staff will not have to ask multiple questions before providing care. Recording this information ensures that others besides the nurse who obtained it will be able meet the client's needs.

---

sisting the client to achieve some control over an oppressive situation.

Physical therapy to prevent further loss of muscle tissue due to weight loss is proposed (Ottery, 1994). Clients respond differently to nursing interventions. No single technique will work in every situation.

Nursing the cancer client requires creativity and patience. It also exemplifies one of the magical features of nursing. We often enter clients' lives at critical times. For the most part, they share their hopes and fears with us. As often as not, we can learn as much from them as they can from us. Cancer clients, by confronting a potentially fatal disease, can teach themselves, their families, and their caregivers the truth of the adage that life is a journey, not a destination.

Summary

Cancer is the second leading cause of death in the United States. Many different kinds of cancer exist, but all occur when normal cells reproduce uncontrollably both at the site of origin and in metastatic sites of the body. Substances called initiators and promoters are necessary for cancer to begin.

Dietary guidelines to prevent cancer are similar to those discussed throughout this book. People should avoid excessive consumption of meat, fat, kilocalories, and alcohol. Positive dietary steps are to increase intake of fiber, carotene, and cruciferous vegetables, and to consume adequate amounts of vitamin C.

Cancer clients often present difficult nutritional problems. Both the disease and its treatment cause early satiety and anorexia, taste alterations, local effects in the mouth, nausea, vomiting, diarrhea, and altered immune responses. Creative interventions for these problems will make the client's life significantly more comfortable and can give a sense of accomplishment to the nurse.

Case Study 22–1   Ms. X is admitted to the hospital for a third course of chemotherapy. She is divorced, with no children, and lives with her mother, who is very supportive. Hopeful that this therapy will stem the cancer, Ms. X is determined to complete the prescribed treatments. Nausea and vomiting in the past two courses of chemotherapy caused her to suspend treatment before it was completed.

Ms. X is 42 years old, 5 ft, 5 in tall, and weighs 123 lb. Her wrist measurement is 5 1/2 in. The mucous membranes of her oral cavity are intact. Her favorite foods are ice cream and steak, although for the past 2 months beef has tasted bitter to her.

NURSING CARE PLAN FOR MS. X

Assessment

Subjective Data	History of intolerance to chemotherapy due to excessive nausea and vomiting
	Taste alteration for beef
	Stated determination to complete treatment
Objective Data	94 percent healthy body weight (131 lb)
	No breaks in mucous membranes of mouth

Nursing Diagnosis   Nutrition, altered: less than body requirements, related to cancer cachexia as evidenced by 6 percent under healthy body weight for height

Desired Outcome/ Evaluation Criteria	Nursing Actions	Rationale
Client will maintain current weight during chemotherapy treatments.	Give antiemetics on scheduled basis beginning 6 hours before first treatment.	Antiemetics work better as preventive medicine than as curative.
	Assess daily the times nausea occurs. Schedule three main meals at other times. Offer dry crackers whenever nausea occurs.	Individualizing meal schedules for clients at high risk of malnutrition takes priority over maintaining hospital routines.
	Give gentle oral hygiene every 4 hours.	Keeping the oral cavity clean and in good condition will help maintain intake.
	Encourage client to eat slowly and chew thoroughly.	Eating slowly and chewing thoroughly reduce the incidence and severity of nausea.
	Provide a back rub and quiet time after meals.	Rest after eating will lesson pressure on stomach and intestines. Massage induces relaxation.

Desired Outcome/ Evaluation Criteria	Nursing Actions	Rationale
	Teach relaxation exercises and controlled breathing to be used when nausea occurs.	These exercises give the client some control over her environment. Teaching the exercises before treatments begin will be more effective rather than trying to interrupt the cycle of nausea and vomiting once begun.
	Consult with clinical dietitian and physician regarding high-protein, low-fat diet; enteral feeding; or TPN.	Although this client is not 10 percent below minimum body weight, the loss of an additional 5 lb will put her there. Aggressive nutritional support should begin before the client becomes severely malnourished.

Study Aids

Chapter Review

1. A high-fiber diet is thought to reduce the risk of colon cancer because it:
   a. Absorbs water from the intestinal wall
   b. Promotes the excretion of bile
   c. Stops diarrhea
   d. Is low in kilocalories

2. Cruciferous vegetables that are specifically thought to protect against cancer are:
   a. Corn, lima beans, and peas
   b. Carrots, green beans, and tomatoes
   c. Brussels sprouts, bean sprouts, and water chestnuts
   d. Broccoli, cauliflower, and cabbage

3. Which of the following foods is likely to be well received by a cancer client with mouth ulcerations?
   a. Hot chicken noodle soup
   b. Orange juice with orange sherbet
   c. Vanilla milkshake
   d. Soda crackers with cream cheese

4. Which of the following is the best advice to increase oral intake for the chemotherapy client who suffers from nausea and vomiting?
   a. Drink plenty of fluids with the meal
   b. Eat high-fat, high-protein meals
   c. Take only foods that are well liked
   d. Eat slowly and chew thoroughly

5. If visitors brought all of the following to a client in protective isolation, which should the nurse question?
   a. Fruit basket
   b. Homemade vegetable soup
   c. Apple pie
   d. Malted milk and french fries

Clinical Analysis

Ms. P is a 38-year-old single mother of three who has returned to the clinic for follow up after a breast biopsy. The tissue removed from her left breast was diagnosed as benign.

Ms. P is 5 feet, 6 inches tall and weighs 180 pounds. Meals at the P house are often hamburger dishes or ethnic combinations. Italian and Mexican foods are favorites of her children.

Ms. P's mother was treated for breast cancer at age 60, but is living and well. When interviewed by the nurse, Ms. P expressed interest in learning what she could do to lessen her chances of developing a malignancy of the breast.

1. Knowing that too radical a change is likely to be rejected by the client, the nurse concentrates on

one improvement to be made in Ms. P's diet. Which of the following is likely to make the biggest difference in Ms. P's health?
   a. Substituting vegetable oil margarine for butter
   b. Increasing fluid intake
   c. Limiting fats to 30 percent of kilocalories
   d. Increasing protein to 20 percent of kilocalories

2. Which of the following suggestions should help Ms. P meet her new dietary goal?
   a. Avoiding gas-forming vegetables of the cabbage family
   b. Draining and rinsing cooked ground beef for one-dish meals
   c. Minimizing the use of tomato-based sauces
   d. Selecting aged cheddar rather than processed American cheese

3. Ms. P confides that her mother is a recovering alcoholic. She wonders if heavy alcohol consumption contributed to her mother's breast cancer. Which of the following answers would be best for the nurse to give?
   a. "Much evidence has shown alcohol is related to cancers of the gastrointestinal system and some evidence links it to breast cancer."
   b. "Probably not. Alcohol intake is related to liver cancer only."
   c. "Only if she also smoked. Alcohol must be potentiated by cigarettes to produce breast cancer."
   d. "Not at all. Alcohol has a sterilizing effect on the internal organs, so that any bacteria likely to translocate to the bloodstream would be eliminated."

Bibliography

Albert-Puleo, M: Physiological effects of cabbage with reference to its potential as a dietary cancer-inhibitor and its use in ancient medicine. J Ethnopharmacol 9:261, 1983.

Alberts, DS, and Garcia, DJ: An overview of clinical cancer chemoprevention studies with emphasis on positive Phase III studies. J Nutr 125:692S–697S, 1995.

Alpha-Tocopherol, Beta Carotene Cancer Prevention Study Group: The effect of vitamin E and beta carotene on the incidence of lung cancer and other cancers in male smokers. N Engl J Med 330:1029, 1994.

Chiu, BC-H, et al: Diet and risk of non-Hodgkin lymphoma in older women. JAMA 275:1315, 1996.

Daly, HM, and Shinkwin, M: Nutrition and the cancer patient. In Holleb, AI, Fink, DJ, and Murphy, GP (eds): American Cancer Society Textbook of Clinical Oncology. American Cancer Society, Atlanta, GA, 1991.

Dwyer, JT: Unproven nutritional remedies and cancer. Nutr Rev 50:106, 1992.

Feldman, EB: Essentials of Clinical Nutrition. FA Davis, Philadelphia, 1988.

Foerster, SB, et al: California's "5 a Day—for Better Health" campaign: An innovative population-based effort to effect large-scale dietary change. Am J Prev Med 11:124–31, 1995.

Franceschi, S, et al: Tomatoes and risk of digestive-tract cancers. Int J Cancer 59:181, 1994.

Freedman, LS, et al: Dietary fat and breast cancer: Where we are. J Natl Cancer Inst 85:764, 1993.

Ganley, BJ: Effective mouth care for head and neck radiation therapy patients. Medsurg Nurs 4:133, 1995.

Giovannucci, E, et al: Intake of carotenoids and retinol in relation to risk of prostatic cancer. J Natl Cancer Inst 87:1767, 1995.

Giovannucci, E, et al: A prospective study of dietary fat and risk of prostate cancer. J Natl Cancer Inst 85:1571, 1993.

Greco, KE, and Kulawiak, L: Prostate cancer prevention: Risk reduction through lifestyle, diet and chemoprevention. Oncol Nurs Forum 21:1504, 1994.

Greenwald, P: Antioxidant vitamins and cancer risk. Nutrition 10:433, 1994.

Hennekens, CH, Buring, JE, and Peto, R: Antioxidant vitamins—benefits not yet proved. N Engl J Med 330:1080, 1994.

Ho, C-T, et al: Phytochemicals in teas and rosemary and their cancer-preventive properties. In Huang, M-T, et al (eds): Food Phytochemicals II: Teas, Spices, and Herbs. American Chemical Society, Washington, DC, 1994.

Holm, LE, et al: Treatment failure and dietary habits in women with breast cancer. J Natl Cancer Inst 85:32, 1993.

Howe, GR: High-fat diets and breast cancer risk. JAMA 268:2080, 1992.

Howe, GR, et al: Dietary factors and risk of breast cancer: Combined analysis of 12 case-control studies. J Natl Cancer Inst 82:561, 1990.

Huang, M-T, Ferraro, T, and Ho, C-T: Cancer chemoprevention by phytochemicals in fruits and vegetables. In Huang, M-T, et al (eds): Food Phytochemicals I: Fruits and Vegetables. American Chemical Society, Washington, DC, 1994.

Hulka, BS, and Stark, A: Breast cancer: Cause and prevention. Lancet 346:883, 1995.

Hunter, DJ, et al: Cohort studies of fat intake and the risk of breast cancer—a pooled analysis. N Engl J Med 334:356, 1996.

Hunter, DJ, et al: A prospective study of the intake of vitamins C, E, and A and the risk of breast cancer. N Engl J Med 329:234, 1993.

Hunter, DJ, and Willett, WC: Diet, body size, and breast cancer. Epidemiologic Reviews 15:110, 1993.

Hunter, M: Dietary therapies for cancer: Challenging the alternatives. Eur J Cancer Care 1:27, 1991.

Kagawa-Singer, J: Socioeconomic and cultural influences on cancer care of women. Semin Oncol Nurs 11:109, 1995.

Kelly, R: Nursing patients with oral cancer. Nurs Stand 8:25, 1994.

Kendler, BS: Free radicals in health and disease: Implications for primary health care providers. Nurse Pract 20:29, 1995.

Kim, M, et al: Preventive effect of green tea polyphenols on colon carcinogenesis. In Huang, M-T, et al (eds): Food Phytochemicals II: Teas, Spices, and Herbs. American Chemical Society, Washington, DC, 1994.

Lachance, PA: Micronutrients in cancer prevention. In Huang, M-T, et al (eds): Food Phytochemicals I: Fruits and Vegetables. American Chemical Society, Washington, DC, 1994.

Lowdermilk, DL: Home care of the patient with gynecologic cancer. J Obstetr Gynecol Neonatal Nurs 24:157, 1995.

Nebling, LC, and Lerner, E: Implementing a ketogenic diet based on medium-chain triglyceride oil in pediatric patients with cancer. J Am Diet Assoc 95:693, 1995.

Niwa, T, Swaneck, G, and Bradlow, HL: Alterations in estradiol metabolism in MCF-7 cells induced by treatment with indole-3-carbinol and related compounds. Steroids 59:523, 1994.

Nowak, R: Beta-carotene: Helpful or harmful? Science 264:500–1, 1994.

Nussbaum, ML, Campana, TJ, and Weese, JL: Radiation-induced intestinal injury. Clin Plastic Surg 20:573, 1993.

Ocke, MC, et al: Average intake of anti-oxidant (pro)vitamins and subsequent cancer mortality in the 16 cohorts of the seven countries study. Int J Cancer 61:480, 1995.

Ottery, FD: Rethinking nutritional support of the cancer patient: The new field of nutritional oncology. Sem Oncol 21:770, 1994.

Padilla, GV, et al: Quality of life index for patients with cancer. Res Nurs Health 6:117–126, 1983.

Patterson, BH, et al: Food choices of whites, blacks, and Hispanics: Data from the 1987 National Health Interview Survey. Nutr Cancer 23:105, 1995.

Patterson, RE, et al: Diet-cancer related beliefs, knowledge, norms, and their relationship to healthful diets. J Nutr Educ 27:86, 1995.

Position of the American Dietetic Association and the Canadian Dietetic Association: Women's health and nutrition. J Am Diet Assoc 95:362, 1995.

Prentice, R, et al: Dietary fat reduction and plasma estradiol concentration in healthy postmenopausal women. J Natl Cancer Inst 82:129, 1990.

Siegel, BS: Love, Medicine, and Miracles. Harper and Row, New York, 1986.

Stewart, GS: Trends in radiation therapy for the treatment of lung cancer. Nurs Clin North Am 27:643, 1992.

Stoewsand, GS: Bioactive organosulfur phytochemicals in Brassica oleracea vegetables—A review. Fd Chem Toxic 33:537, 1995.

Taubes, G: Pesticides and breast cancer: No link? Science 264:499–500, 1994.

Tchekmedyian, NS: Treatment of anorexia with megestrol acetate. Nutr Clin Prac 8:115–118, 1993.

Theologides, A: Nutrition in cancer. In Halpern, SL: Quick Reference to Clinical Nutrition. JB Lippincott, Philadelphia, 1987.

Tomlinson, SS: Dietary and lifestyle factors associated with breast cancer rates. J Am Acad Phys Assist 7:622–34, 1994.

van't Veer, P: Diet and breast cancer: Trial and error? Ann Med 26:453–460, 1994.

Vatten, LJ, and Kvinnsland, S: Body height and risk of breast cancer. A prospective study of 23,831 Norwegian women. Br J Cancer 61:881, 1990.

Wadleigh, RD, et al: Vitamin E in the treatment of chemotherapy-induced mucositis. Am J Med 92:481, 1992.

Waltman, NL, et al: Nutritional status, pressure sores, and mortality in elderly patients with cancer. Oncol Nurs Forum 18:867, 1991.

Weisburger, JH, and Horn, CL: The causes of cancer. In Holleb, AI, Fink, DJ, and Murphy, GP (eds): American Cancer Society Textbook of Clinical Oncology, American Cancer Society, Atlanta, GA, 1991.

Willett, WC, et al: Dietary fat and fiber in relation to the risk of breast cancer. JAMA 268:2037, 1992.

Wilson, BA, Shannon, MT, and Stang, CL: Nurses Drug Guide 1996. Appleton Lange, Stamford, CT, 1996.

Work Study Group on Diet, Nutrition, and Cancer: American Cancer Society guidelines on diet nutrition and cancer. CA 41:334, 1991.

Yuan, JM, et al: Diet and breast cancer in Shanghai and Tianjin, China. Br J Cancer 71:1353, 1995.

CHAPTER 23

Nutrition During Stress

LEARNING OBJECTIVES

After completing this chapter, the student should be able to:

1 Explain how people can protect themselves nutritionally from the effects of excessive mental stress.

2 List four hypermetabolic conditions that increase resting energy expenditure and hence, kilocaloric requirements.

3 Discuss the relationship between uncomplicated starvation and resting energy expenditure.

4 Discuss the effects of impaired respiratory function on nutritional status and appropriate nutritional therapy.

5 List six recommendations for the safe refeeding of malnourished clients.

We have all experienced stress. Within the content of this chapter, **stress** is defined as any stimulus or condition that threatens the body's homeostasis. Starvation is one form of stress. The effect of a food deprivation in the absence of disease is discussed in this chapter. Also discussed are the relationships of mental health to nutrition and that of nutrition to metabolic stress from illness, trauma, and infections. The safe principles of refeeding a nutritionally deprived client conclude the chapter.

Nutrition and Mental Health

The effects of mental stress cannot be isolated easily from the effects of physical stress. The physical self is structurally related to the emotional self. For example, in the presence of danger, a series of chemical reactions occurs and is associated with our feeling of fear. The fight-or-flight response discussed in Chapter 1, "Evolution and the Science of Nutrition" is mediated by hormones. In other words, the fear (emotional factor) triggers the hormones (physical factors).

Genetics and Mental Health

Genetics may play a role in our response to stress. For example, one person may perceive a given situation to be more stressful than another person. We all know people who anger easily at events others regard as insignificant. Some individuals may also be more genetically susceptible to the negative effects of stress than others. For example, highly stressful situations have been known to precipitate heart attacks in some people, whereas in others the heart is not affected. In this regard the effect of genetics, although known to have an impact on our response to stress, is poorly understood.

Not All Stress Is Negative

A balanced amount of stress maximizes health. Human beings need some stress for emotional well-being. For example, boredom is stressful to many people. Emotional stress such as ambition, drive, and desire may in fact be perceived as positive. Stress such as strain, tension, and/or anxiety is commonly perceived as negative. The death of a spouse, divorce, unemployment, financial problems, and personal injury are all perceived by most people as negative. Clearly, we cannot control all of the events that affect us. However, we do have some control over how we respond to such events. The relationship between nutritional status and people's response to emotional stress has not been completely researched.

Chronic Disease

Emotional stress does appear to be related to the prevalence of cancer, cardiovascular disease, hypertension, and some forms of gastrointestinal diseases. All of these chronic diseases are related to nutrition. Emotional health is known to be important in reducing the risk of heart disease. People who are ordinarily tense, impatient, and ambitious tend to have a high serum cholesterol level.

Gastrointestinal Complication

Ulcers and some intestinal diseases are aggravated by perceived excessive mental stress. A client may report that he or she has specific food intolerances when under emotional stress, but that the same food is easily tolerated in the absence of stress. This is partially due to impairment of gastrointestinal function during episodes of stress. Decreased motility often causes development of anorexia, abdominal distention, gas pains, and constipation. These symptoms may contribute to reduced food intake and/or food intolerances. Thus, the effects of emotional stress, including food intolerances, can vary not only from person to person, but also in the same person from time to time.

Food Intake

The volume of food a client consumes and the desire to prepare food are sometimes related to emotional stress. Some people respond to stress by eating more; others respond by eating less. Mental stress can cause a person to lose interest in food preparation. Thus, mental stress can be related to both overnutrition and undernutrition. An individual's perceived stress should always be taken into consideration when formulating the nutritional component of a care plan.

The time food is eaten also may be important. Undernutrition is related to cognition. Extensive evidence indicates that relatively modest increases in circulating glucose concentrations enhance learning

> **Stress**—The total biological reaction to a stimulus; physical, mental, or emotional, which threatens to disturb the human body's equilibrium.

and memory processes in rats and humans (Gold, 1995). For example, a student who eats breakfast will score higher on an examination.

Requirements for Nutrients

Nutrition experts believe the need for most nutrients is not increased solely as a result of excessive mental activity. The needs for kilocalories, protein, calcium, and vitamins have all received some attention from scientists.

Kilocalories

Mental stress alone does not increase our need for kilocalories. For example, mental effort used in studying demands few if any additional kilocalories. Likewise, a single parent coping with financial problems, a job, and child rearing does not require extra kilocalories solely as a result of excessive mental activity. Because mental stress does not require additional kilocalories, our requirement for certain vitamins is not increased solely as a result of mental activity. Thiamin, riboflavin, and niacin requirements are based on kilocalorie requirements; if the need for kilocalories is not increased, neither is the requirement for these vitamins.

A person who responds to mental stress by increased physical movement or muscle activity will require additional kilocalories to maintain his or her body weight. Mental stress may cause a person to sleep less, walk more, tremble, fidget, or otherwise increase the work of the muscles. In this situation, additional kilocalories are needed in underweight clients. Underweight clients who complain of a recent weight loss or an inability to gain weight are likely to need additional kilocalories.

Protein and Calcium Balance

Some research has been done on the effects of emotional stress on both protein and calcium balance. Emotional stress such as fear, anxiety, or anger increases the secretion of epinephrine, which in turn causes a series of changes that result in a loss of nitrogen. Most Americans consume protein in excess of their recommended dietary allowances. However, large amounts of dietary protein provide no insurance against the effects of a stressful lifestyle, since excessive protein intake is thought to stress kidney function.

Calcium is another nutrient that has been studied in people under stress. In a classical study, individuals in calcium balance have gone suddenly into negative balance under the stress of student examinations (National Center for Health Statistics, 1967). In another study, a group of emotionally distressed young women was found to require a higher intake of calcium to maintain calcium balance than a comparable group of happy, relaxed women. Calcium intake varies widely among individuals in the United States (National Research Council, 1989). Because many Americans do not routinely consume the RDA for calcium, the authors advocate that individuals experiencing excessive mental stress pay close attention to their calcium intake.

Vitamins and Minerals

The majority of evidence gathered thus far indicates that vitamins in excess of the RDA do not counterbalance the negative effects of mental stress. An example illustrates this principle. In one study, persons on low thiamin intakes showed pronounced mood changes, vague feelings of uneasiness, fear, disorderly thinking, and other signs of mental depression (Guthrie, 1986). When their diets were supplemented with thiamin, they responded readily. The subjects in this study were not habitually consuming their RDA for thiamin. The results of this study have been erroneously interpreted by some lay consumers to mean that thiamin supplements cure mental ailments. This is not true. The purchase of over-the-counter vitamins and/or minerals for stress has limited scientific basis. A healthy, well-balanced diet with adequate protein, calcium and other minerals, and vitamins is the best insurance against excessive stress. Maintenance of a healthy body weight is an indication that kilocaloric intake is appropriate.

The Stress of Starvation

Starvation is a form of stress to the human body. Biologically, our bodies developed to cope with periods of feast or famine. Our response to the stress of starvation evolved slowly over the course of millions of years. The human body's response to a food deprivation differs from the body's response to other forms of stress.

Uncomplicated starvation means that the client has a food deprivation without an underlying stress state. A stress state may be an underlying disease. During uncomplicated starvation, clients will expend about 70 percent of the kilocalories they normally need to maintain their body weight. Because of the biochemical adaptation to starvation, these clients require fewer kilocalories than is normal for their height and weight.

The human body has a well-defined response to starvation. The breakdown or catabolism of nutrient stores to meet energy needs characterizes our response. Every cell within the human body needs a constant supply of energy to function. During starvation, a series of chemical reactions occurs to meet each cell's energy needs. A summary of these chemical reactions follows:

1. **Glycogenolysis** is the breakdown of glycogen (the liver's carbohydrate stores). This releases glucose into the bloodstream. However, the body's limited glycogen stores will last only a few hours.
2. **Gluconeogenesis** is the production of glucose from noncarbohydrate stores. The primary source of glucose in early starvation is the increased rate of gluconeogenesis.

3. **Lipolysis** is the breakdown of adipose tissue for energy. This releases free fatty acids into the bloodstream. In prolonged starvation, adaptive mechanisms conserve body protein stores by enabling a greater proportion of energy needs to be met by increased fatty acids, with a decreased requirement for glucose. (See the following.)
4. **Ketosis** is the accumulation in the body of the ketone bodies: acetone, beta-hydroxybutyric acid, and acetoacetic acid. Ketosis results from the incomplete metabolism of fatty acids, generally from carbohydrate deficiency, and is commonly seen in starvation. The body will utilize some ketone bodies for energy during prolonged starvation. This reduces but does not eliminate the need for glucose.

These chemical reactions are summarized in Figure 23–1.

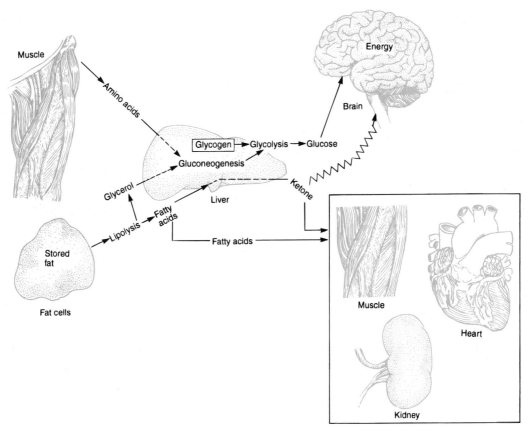

FIGURE 23–1 Origin of fuel and fuel consumption during starvation. The primary source of glucose in early starvation (after the depletion of glycogen stores) is the increased rate of gluconeogenesis. In prolonged starvation, adaptive mechanisms conserve protein by enabling a greater proportion of energy needs to be met by ketone bodies, with a decreased requirement for glucose (after adaptation to starvation).

Each body cell ultimately needs glucose, fatty acids, or the end products of fatty acids and amino acids for energy. Body cells need fuel constantly. Amino acids can be utilized for energy, but only after the liver converts them into glucose and/or fat. Specific organs have a preference for glucose as a fuel source. The brain prefers glucose for energy. Ketone bodies can also be utilized by some cells for energy. The brain will use ketone bodies but prefers glucose. For the most part, the human body can utilize only a very small part of the fat molecule, the glycerol portion, to manufacture glucose. This means that body protein stores must be continually broken down to supply the brain with glucose during starvation after the liver's glycogen stores are depleted.

The heart, kidney, and skeletal muscle tissues prefer fatty acids and/or ketone bodies for their fuel sources. This means that even if a starving person is fed glucose (as in TPN), some fat is still needed to prevent the breakdown of adipose tissue. A balance of the end products of fat and carbohydrate metabolism is necessary for survival.

In prolonged starvation, most body organs will switch to a less preferred fuel source. Even the brain will increasingly begin to utilize more ketone bodies for energy after adaptation to starvation than before. The breakdown of muscle tissue continues in prolonged starvation, but at a much lower rate than previously. The human body also becomes more efficient in reusing amino acids for protein synthesis. Thus, urea nitrogen excretion decreases during prolonged starvation. The rate of tissue breakdown in prolonged starvation also decreases because the metabolic rate and total energy expenditure decrease to conserve energy and prolong life. The catabolic or starved individual will spontaneously decrease physical activity, increase sleep, and run a decreased body temperature. All of these adaptations during prolonged starvation serve one purpose—to prolong life. The human body gets "more miles per gallon" as a result of individual body organs switching to a less preferred fuel source.

The Stress Response

The term *stress response* refers to major changes in metabolism that occur after severe injury, illness, and/or infection. Kilocaloric needs decrease during uncomplicated starvation and increase (sometimes markedly) as a result of bodily response to stress. The stress response is a dynamic process that has an ebb phase, a flow phase, and an anabolic phase. A client can progress or regress from one phase to another during his or her clinical course. The need for protein varies according to the client's stress level.

Ebb Phase

The **ebb phase** begins with an initial stress stimulus and typically lasts for approximately 24 hours. Blood pressure, cardiac output, body temperature, and oxygen consumption are all reduced during the ebb phase. The body does this so that it has the capacity to meet the increased demands of the environment. These clients require about 1.5 grams of protein per kilogram of body weight per day.

Flow Phase

Increased cardiac output, increased urinary nitrogen losses, altered glucose metabolism, and accelerated catabolism characterize the **flow phase.** In addition, the flow phase is marked by pronounced hormonal changes. Table 23–1 lists hormones secreted during this stage of the stress response and describes the impact these hormones have on metabolism. These hormonal conditions favor the breakdown of body protein stores to provide glucose. This leads to a rapid loss of nitrogen in the urine as lean body mass is broken down to furnish

TABLE 23–1 Hormonal Secretion during Phase Two of the Stress Response and the Metabolic Effect of These Hormones*

Hormonal Secretion	Effect of Metabolism
Increased epinephrine	Rate of lipolysis increased Rate of glycolysis increased Rate of gluconeogenesis increased
Decreased insulin	Storage of glucose, fatty acids, and amino acids ceases. Glucose delivery to the cells thus decreases. For this reason, hyperglycemia is commonly seen in stressed clients.
Increased glucagon	Rate of gluconeogenesis increases
Increased antidiuretic hormone	Increase in water retention
Increased aldosterone	Increase in sodium retention

* Net effect: decrease in body protein and fat stores.

the cells with glucose. The need for protein is about 2 grams per kilogram of body weight during the flow phase (Cerra, 1993).

Blood flow to the GI tract is often diminished during this phase of the stress response. This decreases the supply of both oxygen and nutrients to the GI tract. The secretion of mucus is diminished and the secretion of gastric acid is increased. Cells that line the GI tract waste away and die as a result of these changes. The client may complain of diarrhea and bloating.

Recovery or Anabolic Phase

The third stage of the stress response, the **anabolic phase,** is also marked by changes in hormonal secretions. Insulin and growth hormone increase in the bloodstream during the anabolic phases. Secretion of most of the other hormones decreases. The building up of body tissue and nutrient stores (anabolism) characterizes this phase. Protein need during the anabolic phase is between 2 to 3 grams per kilogram of body weight.

Obviously it is desirable for a client to progress to the third phase of the stress stage as rapidly as possible. Tissue building, or anabolism, is beneficial. The ability of a client to rebuild tissue after a physical stress depends on several factors. Age is one factor. The client's prior nutritional status, the severity of the stress, and the duration of the stress particularly influence tissue growth. Clients who have ample nutrient stores to draw on during stress are better able to tolerate the negative effects of the stress. Good nutrition is a form of insurance. The nutrient stores are available to be used if an unexpected stress occurs. Recent research has shown that early supplementation with the amino acid glutamine may enhance the progression to the anabolic phase of the stress response (see Clinical Application 23–1).

Nutrition and Metabolic Stress from Illness, Trauma, and Infection

Cancer, major surgery, burns, infections, and trauma are the physical stressors that have the greatest impact on metabolism. The needs of clients with cancer were described previously. This section of the text focuses on the nutritional needs of clients subjected to surgery, burns, infections and fevers, and trauma. Nutritional support during extreme stress is needed to decrease the length of the stress, prevent complications, and minimize human suffering.

CLINICAL APPLICATION 23–1

Glutamine and Stress

Glutamine is a nonessential amino acid. During stress the body's requirement for glutamine appears to exceed the individual's ability to produce it in sufficient amounts. Current research is exploring the provision of supplemental glutamine to enhance the recovery of the seriously ill client. Alitraq, manufactured by Ross Laboratories, is a specialized elemental formula for medical use that is high in glutamine.

Hypermetabolism

Hypermetabolism is an abnormal increase in the rate at which fuel or kilocalories are burned. Hypermetabolism can be identified by an increased metabolic rate, negative nitrogen balance, hyperglycemia, and increased oxygen consumption. Clients are hypermetabolic during the flow phase of the stress response.

Protein Needs

Protein needs are elevated during hypermetabolism. Injury or illness requires active protein formation. Surgical wounds, tissue repair, replacement of red blood cells and plasma protein lost in hemorrhage, and the immune response to infection all require a constant supply of protein. For these reasons, a client who is hypermetabolic has an increased need for protein. A hypermetabolic client may lose as much as 250 grams (about 1/2 pound) of muscle tissue per day.

URINE ASSESSMENT OF PROTEIN STATUS Total urinary excretion of nitrogen increases with the client's

---

Ebb phase—The first phase in the stress response; the body reduces blood pressure, cardiac output, body temperature, and oxygen consumption to meet increased demands.

Flow phase—The second stage in the stress response; usually lasts from 2 to 10 days and is marked by pronounced hormonal changes.

Anabolic phase—The third stage in the stress response in which the body begins to rebuild tissue.

Hypermetabolism—An abnormal increase in the rate at which fuel or kilocalories is burned.

stress level. Urinary creatinine measurements may be used to estimate muscle protein reserves. One problem common to the use of all urinary measurements is the completion of an accurate 24-hour urine collection. The nurse is typically responsible for collecting a 24-hour urine specimen from the client. If even one voiding is discarded measurements will be inaccurate.

Kilocalories and Hypermetabolic Stress

Clients who are hypermetabolic have an increased need for kilocalories. The negative nitrogen balance observed in hypermetabolic clients may be the result of an inadequate kilocaloric intake rather than an insufficient protein intake.

EARLY FEEDING   The use of early nutritional support during the ebb phase of the stress response has been studied. The use of enteral nutrition shortly after the event that precipitated the stress may be advantageous because it supplies essential nutrients, keeps the GI tract active, and halts the elevation of the catabolic stress hormones.

KILOCALORIC NEEDS   Energy expenditure means the number of kilocalories that an individual uses to meet the body's demand for fuel. The kilocalorie need of a person is calculated by the following formula:

Resting Energy Expenditure × Activity Factor
= Daily Energy Allowance

The hypermetabolic client's kilocaloric need has been well researched. Major body stressors increase kilocaloric needs. The kilocaloric need of a hypermetabolic client is often calculated with the following formula:

Resting Energy Expenditure × Activity Factor
× Stress Factor = Estimated Energy Need

Each part of this formula is discussed in detail below.

RESTING ENERGY EXPENDITURE   The **Harris-Benedict equation** is widely used to estimate REE for critically ill clients. The Harris-Benedict equation is presented in Clinical Calculation 23–1 along with an example of these calculations. Please note that different equations are used for male and female clients. The Harris-Benedict equation allows the health care provider to calculate kilocalories based on an individual client's height, age, and weight.

ACTIVITY FACTOR   The Harris-Benedict equation calculates the patient's REE. Physical activity is not

---

CLINICAL CALCULATION 23–1

Calculation of Kilocaloric Need for Both a Male and a Female

Male Client

Energy Need = REE
× Activity Factor × Stress Factor

Step 1: Use the following Harris-Benedict equation to calculate the male client's resting energy expenditure:

REE = 66 + (13.7 × weight in kg)
+ (5 × height in cm) − (6.8 × age)

Step 2: Multiply an activity factor by the client's REE (from Table 23–2).

Step 3: Multiply the answer obtained in step 2 by the appropriate stress factor (Table 23–3).

Female Client

Energy Need = REE
× Activity Factor × Stress Factor

Step 1: Use the following Harris-Benedict equation to calculate the female client's resting energy expenditure:

REE = 655 + (9.6 × weight in kg)
+ (1.7 × height in cm) − (4.7 × age)

Step 2: Multiply an activity factor by the client's REE (Table 23–2):

REE × Activity Factor

Step 3: Multiply the answer obtained in step 2 by the appropriate stress factor (from Table 23–3):

REE × Activity Factor × Stress Factor

Example Calculation

Assume you need to estimate the kilocaloric need of a 154-lb (70-kg) male who is 5 ft, 5 in (165 cm) tall and 25 years old. Assume he is confined to bed and has a fractured long bone.

Sample calculation for step 1:

70-kg male who is 165 cm tall and 25 years old

REE = 66 + (13.7 × 70) + (5 × 165) − (6.8 × 25)
REE = 66 + 959 + 825 − 170
REE = 1680

Sample calculation for step 2:

REE × Activity Factor
1680 × 1.2
2016

Sample calculation for step 3:

Answer from step 2 × Stress Factor
2016 × 1.35
2721.6 = client's estimated energy need

TABLE 23–2 Activity Factors Commonly Used to Calculate a Client's Activity Kilocalories

For a client confined to bed	0.2, or 20 percent
For a client out of bed	0.3, or 30 percent

TABLE 23–3 Stress Factors Commonly Used to Determine a Client's Need for Kilocalories

Stressor	Factor
Uncomplicated minor surgery	1.05
Starvation	0.70
For each degree F above 98.6	1.07
Cancer	1.1–1.45
Soft tissue trauma	1.14–1.37
Skeletal trauma (fracture)	1.35
Burns (10–30 percent of body surface area)	1.5
Burns (30–50 percent of body surface area)	1.75
Burns (>50 percent of body surface area)	2.0
Peritonitis	1.2–1.5
Major sepsis	1.4–1.8

SOURCE: Adapted from Bronson-Adatto, 1984.

included in REE and must be calculated. Table 23–2 shows activity factors for clients confined to bed as 0.20 or 20 percent and for those not confined to bed as 0.30 or 30 percent.

STRESS FACTOR   Research has shown that different types of stress increase kilocaloric needs differently. A **stress factor** is a number assigned to a given pathological state to predict how much a client's kilocaloric need has increased as a result of the type of stress the client is experiencing from that state. Table 23–3 lists various types of physical stress and the stress factor used for each disease state.

As you can see in the table, a client with burns over 50 percent of his or her body has a stress factor of 2.0. This means kilocaloric need is twice (200 percent) his or her resting energy expenditure. By contrast, the stress factor for minor surgery is 1.05. This means a client who has had minor surgery needs only 5 percent more kilocalories than his or her REE multiplied by the previously determined physical activity factor. Stress factors are convenient to use in estimating kilocaloric needs.

Kilocalorie:Nitrogen Ratios in the Hypermetabolic Client

Protein requirements cannot be totally separated from energy requirements because protein is used as an energy source in the absence of adequate kilocalories. The current practice is to calculate **kilocalorie:nitrogen ratios** for hypermetabolic clients. As a rule, the average healthy person needs 1 gram of nitrogen per 300 kilocalories (Branson-Adatto, 1984). One gram of nitrogen is derived from 6.25 grams of protein. The hypermetabolic client needs approximately 1 gram of nitrogen per 100 to 150 kilocalories (Branson-Adatto, 1984). The hypermetabolic client needs about twice as much protein as the client not in a state of hypermetabolism. Clinical Calculation 23–2 demonstrates the calculation of kilocalorie:nitrogen ratios in a TPN solution.

Most nutritional supplements have the kilocalorie:nitrogen ratio of the product listed either on the label or in a package insert.

Vitamin Needs

The hypermetabolic client usually requires an increase in the B vitamins and vitamin C. The B vitamins help release the chemical energy stored in foods. Any time a client requires increased kilocalories, the need for the B-vitamin complex automatically increases. When anabolism or the building of body tissue is indicated, vitamin C requirements are increased. Hypermetabolic clients usually need to build up depleted tissue stores.

Examples of Hypermetabolic Conditions

The hypermetabolic conditions that influence nutritional needs most profoundly are major surgery, burns, infections and fevers, and trauma. All of these conditions increase resting energy expenditure and hence, kilocaloric requirements. This section of the chapter discusses these conditions.

Kilocalorie:Nitrogen Ratios—A mathematical relationship expressed as the number of kilocalories to grams of nitrogen provided in a feeding.

CLINICAL CALCULATION 23–2

Calculation of a Sample TPN Solution

Please calculate the total kilocalories, nonprotein calories, grams of nitrogen, calorie/nitrogen ratio, and percent calories from fat in the following TPN solution: 500 cc D_{50}, 500 cc amino acids 10 percent, 250 cc lipid 20 percent.

Dextrose:

$$D_{50} = 0.50 \times 500 \text{ cc} = 250 \text{ g dextrose}$$
$$250 \text{ g} \times 3.4 \text{ kcal/g} = 850 \text{ kcal}$$

Amino Acids:

$$500 \text{ cc} \times 0.10 = 50 \text{ g protein}$$
$$50 \text{ g protein} \times 4 \text{ kcal/g} = 200 \text{ kcal}$$

Lipids:

$$250 \text{ cc} \times 1.1 \text{ kcal/cc} = 275 \text{ kcal}$$

Total Calories:

$$850 \text{ from dextrose} + 200 \text{ from protein} + 275 \text{ from lipid} = 1325 \text{ kcal}$$

Nonprotein Calories:

$$\text{Kcal from dextrose } 850 + \text{ kcal from lipid } 275 = 1125 \text{ nonprotein kcal}$$

Grams of Nitrogen:

$$50 \div 6.25 = 8.0 \text{ g nitrogen}$$

Calorie:Nitrogen Ratio:

$$850 \text{ (from dextrose)} + 275 \text{ (from lipid)} = 1125 \text{ nonprotein kcal}$$
$$1125 \div 8.0 \text{ g nitrogen} = 141$$
$$\text{Calorie:nitrogen ratio} = 141 \text{ to } 1$$

Percent Kilocalories from Fat:

$$\text{Total kcal} \div \text{kcal from fat}$$
$$275 \text{ total kcal} \div 1325 \text{ kcal from fat} = 21 \text{ percent}$$

Surgery

Uncomplicated minor surgery increases the surgical client's kilocaloric requirement by only 5 percent. Surgery needed to repair a soft tissue trauma requires between a 14 and 37 percent increase in kilo-calories. A surgical client with complications may require a large increase in kilocalories. Please refer again to Table 23–3 for more specific numbers.

Burns

Major burns represent the most extreme state of stress a client can sustain. They produce a hypermetabolic state that raises kilocaloric needs higher than those of most other stress states. Kilocaloric requirements may be as large as 8000 kilocalories per day. Even a client who was well nourished before becoming burned may rapidly develop protein-calorie malnutrition. As indicated in Table 23–3, the degree to which the metabolic rate increases is directly related to the body surface area burned. Although it is not reflected in the stress factors listed in the table, the deeper the burn, the higher the client's kilocaloric need. Burn clients may remain in a hypermetabolic state for many weeks.

Figure 23–2 classifies burns according to the depth of the burn. Determination of the surface area burned is also provided in this figure. Note that a first-degree burn includes minimal depth. Superficial burns, where the damage is limited to the outer layer of the skin, are considered first-degree burns. Second-degree burns include some damage to both layers of the skin; blisters are present. Second-degree burns that become infected, however, may be equivalent to a third-degree burn. Third-degree burns include damage to the tissue beneath the skin. The percentage of body surface area burned is determined by totaling the individual percentages given in the figure.

The increased load of waste products produced in clients with burns is one reason for an increase in fluid requirements. Extra fluids will assist the kidneys in eliminating these waste products. Capillary permeability is increased in the burn client; hence, plasma proteins, fluids, and electrolytes escape into the burn area and interstitial space. This shift reduces the volume of the plasma, so fluid volume needs to be replaced.

Physicians disagree on the best time to begin feeding the burn client. Some physicians initiate tube feedings within 4 hours following burn injury. Here, an important consideration is that **peristalsis,** the wavelike motion that propels food through the gastrointestinal tract, ceases in some burn clients. Until peristalsis returns, the client's stomach should not be the site of choice for a tube feeding. Instead, the tube should be inserted into the client's intestines and a very slow continuous drip feeding used.

BURNS

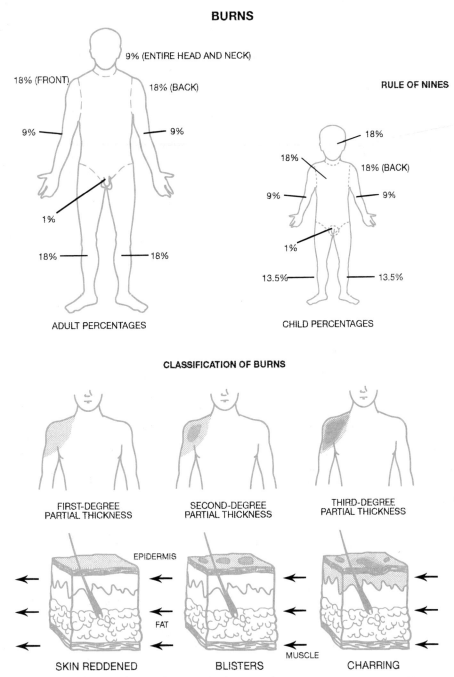

RULE OF NINES

9% (ENTIRE HEAD AND NECK)

18% (FRONT)   18% (BACK)

9%   9%

1%

18%   18%

ADULT PERCENTAGES

18%

18%   18% (BACK)

9%   9%

1%

13.5%   13.5%

CHILD PERCENTAGES

CLASSIFICATION OF BURNS

FIRST-DEGREE
PARTIAL THICKNESS

SECOND-DEGREE
PARTIAL THICKNESS

THIRD-DEGREE
PARTIAL THICKNESS

EPIDERMIS

FAT

MUSCLE

SKIN REDDENED   BLISTERS   CHARRING

FIGURE 23–2   Classification of burns. Percentage of body surface area burned is determined by comparing the body surface area of the client's burns to percentages given in this chart. For example, if a client has extensive burns over both legs, the total body surface area burned would be 36 percent (18 percent for the first leg plus 18 percent for the second leg). The depth of the burn determines whether the burn is classified as first, second, or third degree. (From Thomas, CL[ed]: Taber's Cyclopedic Medical Dictionary, ed 18. FA Davis, Philadelphia, 1997, p 278, by Beth Anne Willert, MS, Dictionary Illustrator, with permission.)

Rather than beginning the feedings on the day of injury, other physicians resume oral feeding of the client with the return of normal bowel activity. For most clients this is 2 to 4 days after the initial burn. The burn client is usually allowed a clear or full liquid diet at this time. Dietary progression begins 4 to 10 days after the injury, as tolerated.

Burn clients are particularly susceptible to **sepsis,** the state in which disease-producing organisms are present in the blood. Major sepsis further increases a clients metabolic rate. See Table 23–3 for the stress factor to use in determining kilocaloric needs during sepsis.

Stress factors can be multiplied by each other. For example, the formula to use for a client with greater than 50 percent burns over the body surface area and major sepsis is:

Kilocalorie Need = REE × Activity Factor
× Stress Factor No. 1 (2.0 for 50 percent burn)
× Stress Factor No. 2 (1.5 for major sepsis)

Sepsis is of course not limited to burn clients; surgical and trauma clients may also suffer from sepsis.

For all burn clients, a nutritional assessment is essential to minimize complications and allow the nutritional therapy to be effectively evaluated. These clients should have their food intake monitored and documented. The kilocalories consumed or taken intravenously should be charted daily.

Most burn clients have a high-protein, high-kilocalorie diet ordered; often the diet is initially offered in six small meals. Complete nutritional oral supplements are commonly used to increase the client's kilocaloric and protein intake. The protein content of the diet can be increased by providing a between-meal feeding high in protein, a serving of two eggs at breakfast, and a large serving of meat at both lunch and supper. If the client drinks a full 8 ounces of milk with each meal, this will further increase the protein content of the diet.

Infections and Fever

Malnutrition decreases resistance to infection, and infection aggravates malnutrition by depleting body nutrient stores. Fever characteristically accompanies infection but can also result from a variety of causes. Fever is an adaptive response by the body that modern therapy supports rather than suppresses (Vanden Bosch, et al, 1993). Infection often results in decreased food intake and absorption of nutrients, altered metabolism, and increased excretion of nutrients. Extra kilocalories are needed by the body during fever because it takes more energy to support the higher metabolic rate. Also, as in any hypermetabolic state, extra kilocalories are needed because the client's REE increases. Table 23–3 shows a stress factor of 1 + 0.07 for each degree Fahrenheit the temperature exceeds normal. For example, to determine the kilocaloric need of a client with a prolonged fever of 104.6°F, the stress factor is 1.49 (1 + 7 degrees × 0.07).

Protein requirements for the client with an infection are increased. Extra protein is also needed to enable the human body to produce antibodies and white blood cells to fight the infection. For every degree of fever elevation there is a proportional degree of immune system enhancement up to 104°F (Vanden Bosch, et al, 1993).

The fluid requirements of a client with a fever are increased. Perspiration entails a loss of fluids from the body, and clients with fever have increased perspiration. Fluid will also be lost in vomiting and diarrhea. This fluid needs to be replaced.

Trauma

Trauma may be defined as a physical injury or wound caused by an external source of violence. Stab and gunshot wounds, multiple fractures, and motor vehicle accidents that include crushing are some examples of trauma. Victims of these traumas may become hypermetabolic, depending on the severity of the injury. Vitamin supplements may be necessary. These clients are at a nutritional risk and may need extra kilocalories and protein.

Nutrition and Respiration

The scientific literature addresses the relationship between good nutrition and **respiration.** Respiration refers to the exchange of gases (oxygen and carbon dioxide) between a living organism and its environment. The air or oxygen inhaled and the carbon dioxide exhaled is the act of **ventilation.** Ventilation means breathing. **Pulmonary** means concerning or involving the lungs. **Chronic obstructive pulmonary disease** (COPD) refers to a group of lung diseases with a common characteristic of chronic airflow obstruction. COPD has become the fourth leading cause of death in the United States. Malnutrition is commonly seen in clients with respiratory diseases.

Effects of Impaired Nutritional Status on Respiratory Function

Poor nutrition is related to inadequate pulmonary function in five important ways. First, these clients frequently have an inadequate food intake, which is related to anorexia, shortness of breath, and/or gastrointestinal distress. Shortness of breath during food preparation and consumption of meals may limit kilocaloric intake. Inadequate oxygen delivery to the cells causes fatigue. Impaired gastrointestinal tract motility is common in clients with respiratory diseases (see the following section).

Second, kilocaloric requirements are often increased in clients with pulmonary disease. Recent research has estimated that while the kilocaloric cost of breathing ranges from 36 to 72 kilocalories per day in normal individuals, the kilocaloric cost of breathing increases to 430 to 720 kilocalories per day in clients with COPD (Brown, and Light, 1983). Owing to the combined effects of decreased food intake and increased energy requirements, weight loss is commonly seen in these clients.

The third important relationship between nutrition and pulmonary function is the effect of catabolism. When kilocaloric intake is decreased, the body begins to break down muscle stores, including those of the respiratory muscles. A loss of the lean mass of any muscle will have an impact on the muscle's function. The lung's structure itself is thus affected as a result of catabolism. Malnutrition may also result in decreased lung-tissue cell replacement or growth.

The gastrointestinal distress common in clients with pulmonary disease may be related to malnutrition. A loss of the structure within the GI tract may lead to hemorrhage and paralytic ileus. **Paralytic ileus** is defined as the temporary reduction of peristalsis. This contributes to the feeling of anorexia and decreased food intake. In addition, paralytic ileus may lead to a translocation of bacteria. Decreased peristalsis in the GI tract fosters the movement (translocation) of bacteria from the GI tract into the bloodstream. This, in turn, leads to sepsis, or blood-borne infection, a sometimes fatal complication.

The fourth important relationship between nutrition and pulmonary function is that malnutrition decreases resistance to infection. Lung infection is frequently the cause of death in pulmonary clients.

In a state of malnutrition, the body decreases the production of antibodies, which are necessary to fight infection. Also, as a result of starvation, the lungs will decrease production of pulmonary phospholipid (a fat-like structure). Phospholipids assist in keeping the lung tissue lubricated and help to protect both lungs from any disease-producing organisms that are inhaled.

The fifth important relationship between nutrition and pulmonary function is that improved nutritional status has been associated with an increased ability to wean clients from respirators or ventilators. A **respirator** (also called a ventilator) is a machine for prolonged artificial or mechanical respiration. Clients on artificial respirators do not have to use their respiratory muscles to breathe. Active muscle movement stimulates muscle growth via protein stimulus. This is the same principle as physical exercise increasing muscle size. To some extent, all the respiratory muscles **atrophy** or waste away, due to inactivity while a client is artificially breathing.

Clients on ventilators are usually weaned slowly from these machines as their condition improves. Some experts have attributed clients' ability to be successfully weaned from respirators to an increase in protein synthesis. Good nutrition stimulates respiratory muscle growth.

Nutritional Therapy

Respiratory disease can affect both food intake and nutrient utilization. Many clients with respiratory diseases also have problems with water balance.

Energy Nutrient Utilization

Many clients with COPD suffer from carbon dioxide retention and oxygen depletion. Such clients are said to be carbon dioxide retainers. The medical goal with these clients is to decrease their blood level

---

Sepsis—A condition in which disease-producing organisms are present in the blood.

Trauma—A physical injury or wound caused by an external force.

Chronic obstructive pulmonary disease (COPD)—A group of chronic diseases with a common characteristic of chronic airflow obstruction.

Paralytic ileus—A temporary cessation in peristalsis that causes symptoms of intestinal obstruction.

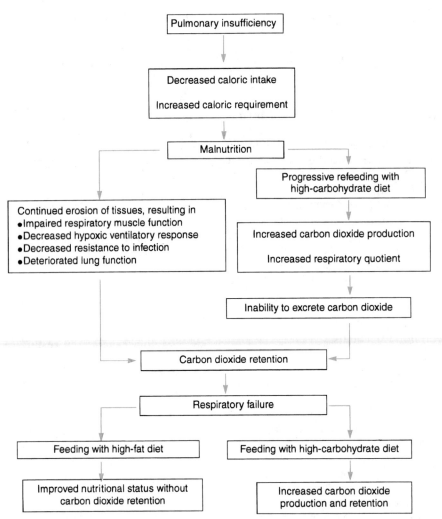

FIGURE 23–3 Interrelationship between nutrition and respiratory status in clients with pulmonary insufficiency. Influence of high-carbohydrate and high-fat diets is shown. (From Specialized Nutrition for Pulmonary Patients, December 1984, p 14, Ross Laboratories, with permission.)

of carbon dioxide. The following formula may assist the understanding of this concept:

Protein (or Carbohydrate or Fat) + Oxygen
= Heat Energy + Water + Carbon Dioxide

Fat kilocalories produce less carbon dioxide than carbohydrate kilocalories. For this reason, a diet high in fat is often used for carbon dioxide retainers. A high-fat diet may also assist the client with respiratory failure who must be weaned from mechanical ventilation. A high-fat diet may provide as much as 50 percent of the kilocalories in the form of fat. Figure 23–3 illustrates the relationship between nutrition and respiratory status in clients with pulmonary insufficiency. The influence of high-carbohydrate and high-fat diets is shown.

Some physicians may oppose the use of a high-fat diet for carbon dioxide retainers. This opposition is based on research that has shown that a high-fat intake may be immunosuppressive in some clients. (Juskelis, 1991). For this reason, fat in excess of 50 percent of total kilocalories is rarely prescribed.

Care must be taken not to overfeed these clients. Excess intake can raise the demand for oxygen and production of carbon dioxide beyond the capacity of the client with reduced respiratory function. The total number of kilocalories fed to the pulmonary client should be closely monitored. A nutritional assessment will help predict the client's kilocaloric need and assist in therapy. Several companies have complete nutritional supplements on the market that are targeted to clients who need a greater percentage of kilocalories provided from fat.

Vitamins A and C

An adequate intake of vitamins A and C is essential in helping to prevent pulmonary infections and to help decrease the extent of lung tissue damage. Foods high in vitamin A, such as fortified milk, dark green or yellow fruits and vegetables, some breakfast cereals (check the label), cheese, and eggs should be included in the diet. Foods high in vitamin C, such as citrus fruits and juices, strawberries, and fortified breakfast cereals (check the label) should also be included. Sources of vitamins A and C that are used should not increase flatus.

Water and Phosphorus

Water balance and serum phosphorus levels need to be closely monitored in these clients. Clients with COPD and acute respiratory failure often need a fluid restriction. A fluid restriction will assist in the control of pulmonary edema or a movement of fluid into interstitial lung tissue. Low serum phosphorus levels or hypophosphatemia are often seen in clients who are respirator-dependent. Phosphorus leaves the intracellular space and moves into the extracellular space during starvation. Serum phosphorus levels are in the normal or near-normal range at this point. With refeeding, phosphate moves back into the intracellular space. At this point, the serum phosphorus level may drop below normal. In the event that this occurs, it is crucial that the client receive phosphate therapy. Because acute hypophosphatemia has been reported to cause respiratory failure, serum phosphorus levels should be monitored in all clients receiving aggressive nutritional support.

Feeding Techniques

Many of these clients lack the energy to eat. Complaints of fatigue are common. The gastrointestinal distress experienced by these clients contributes to the anorexia. Foods from the cabbage family such as broccoli, cabbage, and brussels sprouts may produce gas and contribute to gastrointestinal distress. Small, frequent feeding of foods with a high-nutrient density should be encouraged. Serving food items that require little or no chewing may help with difficulties chewing, breathlessness, and swallowing.

Refeeding Syndrome

Many of the types of clients discussed in this chapter will require aggressive nutritional support. Several metabolic and physiological changes occur when refeeding the chronically protein-calorie malnourished client. These complications can occur regardless of the route nutrients are delivered—oral, enteral, and/or parenteral.

Refeeding syndrome has been used to describe a series of metabolic and physiological reactions that occur in some malnourished clients when nutritional rehabilitation is begun. Improper refeeding of a chronically malnourished client can result in CHF and respiratory failure. Clients at risk include those with alcoholism, chronic weight loss, hyperglycemia, insulin-dependent diabetes mellitus, or those on chronic antacid or diuretic therapy (Solomon, and Kirby, 1990).

Starvation leads to both a loss of the lean body mass in the heart and respiratory muscles and decreased insulin secretion. When carbohydrate intake is low, the pancreas adapts by decreasing insulin secretion. With the reintroduction of carbohydrates into the diet, insulin secretion will increase. The increased insulin secretion is associated with increased sodium and water retention. Other hormones are also activated with carbohydrate feeding. As a result of hormone action, increases in metabolic rate, oxygen consumption, and carbon dioxide production occur (Alfin-Slater, 1991). The net effect of these metabolic changes is an increased workload for the cardiopulmonary system. Refeeding may increase the work of the cardiopulmonary system beyond its diminished capacity (due to the loss of lean body mass) and cause CHF and respiratory failure.

Starvation also leads to an increase in extracellular fluid and an increased loss of intracellular phosphorus, potassium, and magnesium. The degree of intracellular loss of these minerals reflects the degree of loss of lean body mass. Before refeeding, serum phosphorus and magnesium levels may remain in the lower range of normal, while the intracellular and total body stores of these minerals are depleted. After refeeding, these minerals are redistributed from the extracellular to the intracellular compartments. Repeated laboratory measurements

Refeeding Syndrome—A series of metabolic reactions that occur in some malnourished clients when they are refed; characterized by CHF and respiratory failure.

taken after refeeding is started may show low serum levels of phosphorus, magnesium, and potassium. Failure to correct for these mineral deficiencies may be fatal for the client.

Principles of Safe Refeeding of the Malnourished Client

Health care workers need to be aware of the dangers of refeeding a malnourished client. Starved clients can be found in outpatient settings as well as in hospital intensive care units. A high prevalence of malnutrition is common in the outpatient setting. The following recommendations may help the health care worker to avoid the refeeding syndrome in malnourished clients.

1. Recognize the "client at risk." Refeeding syndrome occurs in clients with frank starvation, including war victims undergoing repletion, chronically ill clients who are malnourished, those clients on prolonged intravenous dextrose solutions without other modes of nutritional support, hypermetabolic clients who have not received nutritional support for 1 to 2 weeks, clients who report prolonged fasting, obese clients who report a recent loss of a considerable amount of weight, chronic alcoholics, and clients with anorexia nervosa.

2. Health care workers practicing in an outpatient setting and not directly under the supervision of a physician need to develop a referral plan in the event they suspect a client is a likely candidate for the refeeding syndrome. These clients require the expertise of a physician. Many physicians will accept referrals from any health care worker.

3. A physician needs to test for and correct all electrolyte abnormalities before initiating nutritional support, whether by oral, enteral, or parenteral routes. Many physicians depend on other health care workers to assist in the monitoring of serum phosphorus, magnesium, and potassium values. For the nurse practicing within the hospital, this means notifying the physician upon receipt of laboratory test results showing low serum levels of these minerals. It is especially important to notify the physician before implementing changes in tube feedings, oral diets, or the rate of hyperalimentation. In larger hospitals, the nutrition support service will perform this service.

4. The physician needs to restore circulatory volume and to monitor pulse rate and intake and output before initiating nutritional support. Again, many physicians depend on nurses and other health care workers to assist in monitoring these signs.

5. The kilocaloric delivery of previously starved clients should be slow. Tube-fed and parenterally fed clients need to be closely monitored. The rate, the total volume, and the concentration of kilocalories delivered should be carefully monitored and documented. The concentration, volume, or rate of kilocaloric intake should be increased one at a time. Stepwise advancement to a higher kilocalorie intake should not occur unless the client is metabolically and physiologically stable.

6. Electrolytes should be monitored before nutritional support is started and at designed intervals thereafter.

Refeeding the malnourished client requires a team effort. A careful diet history performed by the dietitian can assist in the identification of clients likely to become victims of the refeeding syndrome. Changes in taste, appetite, intake, weight, or consumption of a special diet may indicate significantly altered status. Correction of electrolyte abnormalities by the physician before implementing nutritional support can prevent death. Careful observation and monitoring by the nutritional support service can identify early signs of this syndrome. Open and prompt communication between all health care team members may be crucial to the client's survival.

Summary

Stress is defined as any condition that threatens the body's equilibrium. Because the physical and emotional aspects of the self are closely related, it is difficult to separate the effects of mental from physical stress. Mental stress has been shown to have an impact on nitrogen and calcium balance. The best insurance against unexpected stress is good nutrient stores developed from the previous consumption of a well-balanced diet.

The stress response has three well-defined phases, which are mediated by hormones: the ebb phase, the flow phase, and the recovery (or anabolic) phase. Hypermetabolism differs from starvation in that resting energy expenditure (REE) increases during hypermetabolism and decreases during a prolonged state of starvation. Major surgery, severe infections, fever, major burns, and severe trauma are all examples of hypermetabolic states. All of these conditions require a high-kilocaloric, high-protein diet.

Respiratory status profoundly affects nutrient need and utilization as well as food intake. Nutritional support can decrease catabolism of the respiratory muscles, improve immune function, minimize carbon dioxide production, and improve the likelihood of successfully weaning clients who are on mechanical respirators.

Refeeding a previously starved client has some risks. Refeeding may increase the work of the cardiorespiratory system beyond its diminished capacity and cause congestive heart failure and respiratory failure. Refeeding syndrome is a series of metabolic reactions seen in some malnourished clients when they are re-fed. All health care workers have a responsibility to understand this syndrome. A team approach to refeeding the malnourished client is necessary to prevent tragic complications.

Case Study 23–1

Mr. X is a 42-year-old man who was admitted to the intensive care unit (ICU) with a diagnosis of acute bronchitis. He has a known history of carbon dioxide retention and chronic obstructive pulmonary disease. Mr. X is 5 ft, 11 in (180 cm), 140 lbs (63.6 kg), and has a medium body frame (HBW = 87.5 percent). He reports a recent 9 lb weight loss over a 3-week period. The client is on a mechanical respirator. The physician's goal is to wean the client from the ventilator as soon as possible. Mr. X complains of fatigue, gas pains, anorexia, dyspnea (difficulty breathing), and early satiety. The client consumed a cup of coffee and one slice of toast for breakfast before falling asleep. The physician has ordered a 50 percent fat high-kilocalorie, high-protein diet.

NURSING CARE PLAN FOR MR. X

Assessment

Subjective Data	Reports a 3-lb/week loss over the last 3 weeks.
	Complains of fatigue, gas pains, anorexia, dyspnea, and early satiety.
Objective Data	87.5 percent HBW
	Observed low-food intake
	Known history of COPD with carbon dioxide retention

Nursing Diagnosis Nutrition, altered: less than body requirements, related to poor food intake, recent weight loss, fatigue, gas pains, anorexia, dyspnea, and early satiety as evidenced by 87.5 percent HBW and known history of COPD and carbon dioxide retention.

Desired Outcome/ Evaluation Criteria	Nursing Actions	Rationale
States that good nutrition is important to independent respiration in one day.	Stress the importance of the prescribed diet to independent respiration.	Successful weaning to independent respiration is enhanced by good nutrition. Current thought is that good nutrition decreases respiratory muscle catabolism, fosters protein synthesis, and facilitates production of pulmonary phospholipids.

Table continued on following page

Desired Outcome/ Evaluation Criteria	Nursing Actions	Rationale
Consumes an appropriate food intake in 3 days.	Consult with the dietitian to set a nutritional goal for the client based on the client's estimated energy expenditure using the Harris-Benedict formula, total energy requirements, and protein requirements.	The pulmonary client should not be over- or underfed. Determination of the client's energy and protein requirements will provide baseline information to determine nutritional needs. Kilocalories and carbohydrates in excess will increase carbon dioxide retention. A deficiency of kilocalories and protein will increase catabolism of the respiratory muscles.
	Promote a pleasant, relaxed environment, including socialization if possible at mealtime.	Eating is both a social and biological experience. Kilocaloric intake will be greater if an attempt is made to provide a pleasant eating environment.
	Consult with the dietitian to provide a diet with modifications that meet the needs such as: • Texture and modification as necessary. • Avoidance of foods not tolerated due to questionable limited GI tract motility such as gassy vegetables, spicy foods, milk products (secondary to lactase deficiency), etc. • Between meal supplements that are acceptable to the client. • Limitation of empty kilocalories. • Meal size and volume limits. Monitor the client's food intakes (i.e., kilocalorie count).	Clients with pulmonary disease are often too tired to eat and may have gastrointestinal complaints. Small frequent meals, easily chewed foods, and reduction of empty kilocalories may assist in helping the client to meet estimated kilocalorie and protein needs. Documentation of food intake with subsequent analysis of protein and kilocaloric content will provide an objective measure of nursing care plan effectiveness. The results of the analysis can be used to provide feedback to the client.
	Provide oral care before/after meals.	A fresh mouth increases appetite.

Desired Outcome/ Evaluation Criteria	Nursing Actions	Rationale
Maintains his weight during hospitalization.	Weigh client daily.	The best way to evaluate the effectiveness of nutritional therapy is to weigh the nonedematous client. For this client, weight gain will require a considerable effort, hence, an intermediate goal of weight maintenance is realistic.
Demonstrates progressive weight gain toward his HBW over the next 3 months.	Instruct client to weigh himself weekly.	The ultimate goal for this client is anabolism with a weight gain. A slow progressive weight gain means the approach taken is succeeding.

Study Aids

Chapter Review

1. Clients who complain about excessive mental stress would benefit the most by counseling to:
   a. Supplement their diet with thiamin
   b. Drink extra fluids
   c. Eat a balanced diet
   d. Increase their protein intake

2. Which condition does not increase a client's resting energy expenditure. Identify the exception.
   a. Infection
   b. Chronic obstructive pulmonary disease
   c. Starvation
   d. Burn

3. The burn client's need for kilocalories relates directly to:
   a. The amount of protein eaten
   b. The total body surface area burned
   c. The volume of food tolerated
   d. Existing nutrient stores

4. Malnutrition is commonly seen in clients with pulmonary disease, for all except one of the following reasons. Identify the *exception*.
   a. Many of these clients have a decreased food intake.
   b. Many of these clients expend more kilocalories to breathe.
   c. Many of these clients have impaired gastrointestinal tract function.
   d. Many of these clients have an extraordinary ability to fight infection.

5. Experts advocate the following when refeeding a malnourished client:
   a. Immediately pushing kilocalories and protein to replenish lost stores
   b. Progressing the rate, volume, and concentration of a tube feeding as rapidly as possible
   c. Full participation of all members of the health care team to manage commonly seen metabolic abnormalities
   d. Correction of the hyperphosphatemia seen during the refeeding of a malnourished client

Clinical Analysis

1. Mr. X is suffering from second- and third-degree burns over 40 percent of his body. His physician has decided to use topical agents and leave the wound open to air. In the first 30 to 40 days postburn, the nurse is planning nutritional support. The best supplemental feedings for the client would use:
   a. A modular feeding with a kilocalorie:nitrogen ratio of 150:1
   b. A modular feeding with a kilocalorie:nitrogen ratio of 300:1

c. A polymeric (complete nutritional) supplement that is acceptable to the client

d. High-kilocalorie desserts such as apple pie, cake, and ice cream

2. Mrs. J is an alcoholic who has previously reported that she has not eaten "food" for at least the last 3 months. She stated that her sole source of kilocalories had been in the form of alcohol. She was just recently transferred to the unit in which you work after treatment for alcohol withdrawal on another unit. The physician has ordered a high-kilocalorie, high-protein diet. So far, she has eaten 100 percent of the three high-kilocalorie, high-protein trays she has received while on your unit. While reviewing the client's laboratory values, you notice her serum phosphorus, magnesium, and calcium levels are decreased. Mrs. J's depressed phosphorus values may be related to:

a. A movement of phosphorus into the extracellular space

b. A total compartmental depletion of phosphorus

c. A lack of phosphorus in the client's present dietary intake

d. A movement of phosphorus into the intracellular space

3. Mr. C is a heavy smoker. He was recently admitted to your unit with carbon dioxide retention and a diagnosis of chronic obstructive pulmonary disease. He complains of gas pains. His diet should include all except the following:

a. A high-fat complete nutritional supplement

b. Broccoli, onions, peas, melons, and cabbage

c. Six small meals

d. Custard, hot cooked cereals, bananas, ground meats, and mashed potatoes

Bibliography

Bronson-Adatto, C (ed): Suggested Guidelines for Nutrition Management of the Critically Ill Patient. American Dietetic Association, Chicago, 1984.

Brown, SE, and Light, RW: What is now known about protein-energy depletion: When COPD patients are malnourished. J Respir Dis, May 1983.

Bullock, BL, and Rosendahl, PP: Pathophysiology: Adaptations and Alterations in Function, ed 3. JB Lippincott, Philadelphia, 1992.

Cerra, FB: Branched-chain amino acids and stress staging. Current concepts in nutritional support. Biomedical Information Corp, New York, 1993.

Cohen, S, et al: Psychological stress and susceptibility to the common cold. N Engl J Med. 325:606–612, 1991.

Gold, PE: Role of glucose in regulating brain and cognition. Am J Clin Nutr. (suppl) 61:9875–955, 1995.

Henningfield, MF: Specialized Elemental Nutrition with Glutamine. Ross Laboratories Division of Abbott Laboratories. Columbus, OH, 1991.

Juskelis, D: Starvation in patients: Guidelines for refeeding. Registered Dietitian Clinical Interactions. Norwich Eaton Pharmaceuticals, Inc. 11:2, 1991.

Lacey, JM, and Wilmore, DW: Is Glutamine a conditional essential amino acid? Nutrition Reviews 48:297, 1990.

National Research Council: Recommended Dietary Allowances, ed 10. National Academy Press, Washington DC, 1989.

Olson, AK: Refeeding in the setting of chronic protein-calorie malnutrition. Nutrition and the MD 17:1, 1991.

Solomon, SM, and Kirby, DF: The Refeeding Syndrome: A Review. JPEN 14:90–97, 1991.

Thomas, CL (ed): Taber's Cyclopedic Medical Dictionary, ed 17. FA Davis, Philadelphia, 1993.

Vanden Bosch, TM, et al: Redesigning fever management through research utilization. Michigan Nurse 66:9, 1993.

CHAPTER 24

Diet in HIV and AIDS

LEARNING OBJECTIVES

After completing this chapter, the student should be able to:

1   Define AIDS and HIV and list transmittal routes for the virus.
2   List nutrition-related complications seen in clients infected with HIV and for each complication describe interventions to improve nutritional status.
3   Discuss why malnutrition is commonly seen in these clients.
4   Describe why each client with AIDS needs an individualized nutritional assessment.

Acquired immune deficiency syndrome (AIDS) is a life-threatening disease and a major public health issue. The **human immunodeficiency virus (HIV)** causes AIDS. The impact of this virus on our society is and will continue to be a challenge. This chapter discusses the prevention, diagnosis, and treatment of HIV infection. The course of acquired immune deficiency syndrome is often complicated by malnutrition. For this reason, a major portion of this chapter is devoted to the nutritional care of the client infected with the human immunodeficiency virus.

Human Immunodeficiency Virus

The human immunodeficiency virus attacks both the immune system and the nervous system. **Immunity** refers to resistance to or protection against a specified disease. When the AIDS virus enters the bloodstream, it begins to attack one type of white blood cell called the T-lymphocyte, or T cell. As is the case with viruses generally, the HIV lives within the cell and conscripts its DNA—reprograms it, in effect—to reproduce the virus. Figure 24–1 diagrams this process. Loss of T-lymphocyte function leaves an individual susceptible to infections and certain cancers. Evidence shows that the AIDS virus may also attack the nervous system, causing damage to the brain.

Acquired Immune Deficiency Syndrome

AIDS is a disease complex characterized by a collapse of the body's natural immunity against disease. Every part of the human body may be affected. The disease is progressive but runs an unpredictable course with periods of remission. AIDS is diagnosed by finding certain indicator opportunistic diseases such as infection, tumor, wasting, or dementia. The Centers for Disease Control have published a specific list of infections and cancers that are used to diagnose AIDS. This list is constantly being reviewed and revised as more information is gathered on the course of this disease. The World Health Organization defines AIDS more simply (Table 24–1).

No Known Cure

Presently, most researchers believe the invariable outcome of AIDS is death. At this time, there is no cure and no vaccine to prevent this disease, although researchers continue to search for both.

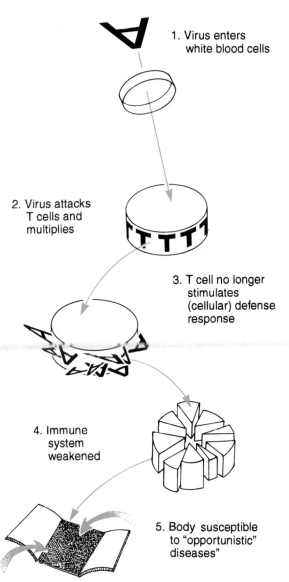

1. Virus enters white blood cells

2. Virus attacks T cells and multiplies

3. T cell no longer stimulates (cellular) defense response

4. Immune system weakened

5. Body susceptible to "opportunistic" diseases

FIGURE 24–1 Diagram of AIDS virus entering the bloodstream. (From Koop, CE: Surgeon General's Report on Acquired Immune Deficiency Syndrome. US Public Health Service Pub. No. HE20.9002:AC, Washington, DC, 1987.)

Signs and Symptoms

Once the HIV enters the body, the affected person may be without any signs or symptoms of disease or may develop AIDS.

The HIV-infected individual may develop an acute flu-like illness, with symptoms appearing in about 2 to 6 weeks after exposure to the virus. After this phase, the individual may be **asymptomatic** (without symptoms) for years. Most HIV-infected

TABLE 24–1   World Health Organization's Case Definition of Adult AIDS*

Major Signs
Weight loss of greater than 10 percent of body weight
Chronic diarrhea of longer than 1 month's duration
Fever of longer than 1 month's duration, either intermittent or constant

Minor Signs
Persistent cough for greater than 1 month
General pruritic dermatitis (severe itching due to inflammation of the skin)
Recurrent herpes zoster (recurrent infectious disease caused by the varicella-zoster virus)
Oropharyngeal candidiasis (infection of the throat with any species of *Candida*)
Chronic progressive and disseminated herpes simplex infections (an acute infectious disease caused by the herpes simplex virus Type I)
Generalized lymphadenopathy (disease of the lymph nodes)

* AIDS in an adult is diagnosed if at least two major and one minor signs are present in the absence of a known cause of immunosuppression, such as cancer or severe malnutrition.

persons have no symptoms and are not even aware that they are infected. The danger lies in their ability to infect other people unknowingly. Some people remain well for years after infection with the HIV virus.

The Epidemic

AIDS Worldwide

The World Health Organization (WHO) has endeavored to collect information on the number of reported cases of AIDS. This has been difficult because reporting in many countries is unreliable and the definitions used to identify AIDS vary. WHO estimates that about 4.5 million AIDS cases (with more than one-half in Sub-Saharan Africa) had occurred by 1995 (Beneson, 1995). It is estimated that 50 million to 100 million persons worldwide could develop AIDS in the next 2 decades (Cross, 1992).

AIDS in the United States

The Centers for Disease Control and Prevention estimates that approximately 1 million people, or one in every 250 people in the United States, are infected with HIV. As of December 31, 1995, 513,486 cases of AIDS have been reported to the Centers for Disease Control.

Transmittal Routes

The human immunodeficiency virus is not easily transmissible. Evidence indicates that the AIDS virus is spread through blood and body fluids. Direct contact of blood to blood or of virus to mucous membrane must occur for disease transmittal. In practical terms, there are three transmittal routes: bloodborne, perinatal, and sexual.

Bloodborne Route

HIV may be transmitted by exposure to contaminated blood or blood products through transfusion, sharing of drug apparatus, and injuries to health care workers from needles and other sharp objects. Box 24–1 outlines precautions to prevent needlestick injuries. Intravenous drug abusers often share needles and other equipment for drug injection. This practice can result in a minute amount of blood from an infected person being injected into the bloodstream of the next user. In addition, cases of AIDS have been linked with receipt of blood products from HIV-infected donors, acupuncture treatments performed with improperly sterilized needles, and receipt of transplanted organs from a person later discovered to have been HIV infected.

Perinatal Transmission

Most children with AIDS contract the virus from their infected mothers through blood-to-blood transmission prior to or at birth. Breast-feeding has been implicated in transmission, since HIV has been isolated from breast milk. In the United States, the Centers for Disease Control advise HIV-positive women against breast-feeding. On the other hand, in developing countries, breast-feeding is still cur-

Acquired immune deficiency syndrome(AIDS)—A disease complex caused by a virus that attacks the immune system and permits opportunistic infections, malignancies, and neurological disease.

Human Immunodeficiency virus(HIV)—The virus that causes AIDS.

Immunity—Resistance or protection against a specified disease.

BOX 24–1   NEEDLE-STICK INJURIES

To prevent needle-stick injuries, needles should not be:
- Recapped
- Purposely bent or broken by hand
- Removed from disposable syringes
- Otherwise manipulated by hand

Guidelines for disposal of syringes, needles, scalpel blades, and other sharp objects include:
- Placing them in a puncture-resistant container located as close to the area of use as is practical
- Placing large-bore reusable needles in a puncture-resistant container for transport to the processing area

---

rently being advocated by the WHO because of the concern about infant morbidity and mortality due to poor sanitation.

Sexual Transmission

The most likely way to become infected with the HIV is to have intimate sexual contact with an infected individual's blood, semen, and possibly vaginal secretions. The virus enters a person's bloodstream through the rectum, vagina, or penis. Small tears in the surface lining of the vagina or rectum may occur during insertion of the penis, fingers, or other objects, thus opening an avenue for entrance of the virus directly into the bloodstream. Both homosexual and heterosexual persons are at risk for AIDS. The only people not at risk of infection by this route are couples who have maintained mutually faithful monogamous relationships (only one continuing sexual partner) for at least 7 years. Celibate individuals are also not at risk.

AIDS: You Can Protect Yourself

The best advice to avoid infection is to avoid direct contact with anyone's blood or body fluids. This involves practicing safer sexual behaviors and following universal precautions or body substance isolation procedures. People need to be advised to adopt safer sexual practices. As precautions to prevent sexual transmission have been described elsewhere (Durham and Cohen, 1991), we will not discuss this important subject here.

Universal Precautions or Body Substance Isolation

Health care workers need to consider all clients as potentially infected with HIV and/or other blood-borne pathogens. **Universal precautions** means that every client and every client's blood and certain body fluids should be considered contaminated and treated as such. **Body substance isolation** is used when all body fluids should be considered contaminated and treated as such. Body substance isolation is thus more comprehensive than universal precautions. Whether universal precautions or body substance isolation procedures are followed in a given facility varies.

Clinical Application 24–1 discusses the myth of risk via casual contact.

Diagnosis and Treatment

Test Screening

A blood test can detect antibodies to the human immunodeficiency virus. The presence of HIV antibodies in the bloodstream means that a person has been exposed to the virus and can be assumed to be infected. The newly infected individual develops antibodies about 3 weeks to 6 months after exposure to the virus. Consequently, antibodies to HIV take a minimum of 3 weeks following exposure to the virus before they can be found in the blood. However, this time frame is not absolute; a negative test does not always mean that the person is free of infection. False-positive results also occur. In rare situations, there is viral infection without the formation of antiviral antibodies.

Complications of HIV Infection

AIDS is characterized by weakness, anorexia, diarrhea, weight loss, fever, and a decreased white blood cell count, or **leukopenia.** Commonly occurring problems associated with AIDS include opportunistic infections, gastrointestinal dysfunction, tumors, AIDS dementia complex (ADC), and organ dysfunction.

Opportunistic Infections

Parasitic, bacterial, viral, and fungal organisms are everywhere in our environment. The healthy person's immune system keeps these organisms in check and under control. AIDS places the client at high risk for certain infections, called **opportunistic infections.** Some of the infections these clients develop were rarely seen in the United States before the onset of the AIDS epidemic. We will discuss three opportunistic infections commonly seen in AIDS clients: thrush, tuberculosis, and pneumocystis pneumonia.

THRUSH   A physical assessment may show signs of **thrush,** which include a thick whitish coating on the tongue or in the throat, which may be accompanied by sore throat. Thrush is a fungal infection that can cause oral ulcers, frequent fevers, and gastrointestinal inflammation.

TUBERCULOSIS   Tuberculosis (TB) is spread from person to person through tiny airborne particles. By sharing surroundings with a person who has active pulmonary TB, a susceptible person may inhale the disease-producing particles. Fortunately, most people who have inhaled these particles never become contagious or develop active TB. Even a healthy immune system cannot kill all the particles. HIV infection weakens the body's immune system and makes it more likely that the individual who has inhaled TB-related particles will develop active TB.

PNEUMOCYSTIS PNEUMONIA   Pneumonia, characterized by shortness of breath, fatigue, and anorexia, is also seen in these clients. About 60 percent of AIDS clients are infected with one type of pneumonia-causing organism called *Pneumocystis carinii,* hence the name **pneumocystis pneumonia.** The organisms take up residence in the person's lungs, causing progressively worsening breathing problems, eventually leading to death.

Gastrointestinal Dysfunction

The gastrointestinal tract is a common site for expression of HIV-related symptoms. The client may feel pain in the mouth or esophagus due to the growth of opportunistic infections. The client may have difficulty swallowing because of open lesions or sores. Both the small and large intestine are commonly affected by AIDS. The enzymes necessary for digestion and absorption in the wall of the small intestine may be lacking or present in insufficient amounts. Malabsorption may occur with diarrhea. Gut failure may follow. The medications these clients receive to control their infections also contribute to the gastrointestinal dysfunction.

AIDS Dementia Complex

AIDS dementia complex (ADC) is the most common HIV-caused central nervous system illness as-

Universal precautions—A list of procedures developed by the Centers for Disease Control for when blood and other certain body fluids should be considered contaminated and treated as such.

Body substance isolation—A situation in which all body fluids are considered contaminated and treated as such by all health care workers.

Leukopenia—Abnormal decrease in the number of white blood corpuscles, usually below 5000 per cubic millimeter.

Opportunistic infection—An infection caused by normally nonpathogenic organisms in a person whose resistance is impaired.

Thrush—An infection caused by the organism Candida albicans that is characterized by the formation of white patches and ulcers in the mouth and throat.

Pneumocystis pneumonia—A type of lung infection frequently seen in AIDS clients; caused by the organism Pneumocystis carinii

AIDS dementia complex(ADC)—A central nervous system disorder caused by the HIV virus.

sociated with AIDS. It is estimated that at least 40 to 50 percent of adults with AIDS have some neurological dysfunction. Experts believe ADC frequently is misdiagnosed as Alzheimer's disease in persons over 50 (Scharnhorst, 1992). This dysfunction is usually chronic and progressive. Early symptoms of ADC are difficulty in concentration, slowness in thinking and response, and memory impairment. Behavioral symptoms include social withdrawal, apathy, and personality changes. Such symptoms may be interpreted solely as a psychiatric disorder. Motor symptoms include clumsiness of gait, difficulty with fine motor movements, and poor balance and coordination.

Tumors

Kaposi's sarcoma is the most frequently seen malignancy among AIDS clients. The most common manifestation of Kaposi's sarcoma is single or multiple lesions appearing on the lower extremities, especially of the feet and ankles. These open areas appear reddish, purple, or brown. Treatment consist of radiation, surgery, and/or chemotherapy.

Organ Dysfunction

AIDS affects many organs in the body, leading to organ dysfunction. Diseases of the gallbladder, liver, and kidneys are seen in some AIDS clients. **Cholecystitis,** inflammation of the gallbladder, can occur in conjunction with certain opportunistic infections seen in AIDS victims. *Hepatomegaly,* or an enlarged liver, is frequently seen with pain, fever, and abnormal liver function tests, especially alkaline phosphatase (Kotler, 1989). **Pancreatitis,** inflammation of the pancreas, has also been noted in some infected clients. AIDS can lead to **end-stage renal failure** within weeks.

Clearly, AIDS is a disease with many complications. Ongoing research has yet to discover a cure for this terrible disease.

Treatment

Treatment for AIDS is still in its infancy. A variety of new medications show some promise of killing or inhibiting the activity of the HIV virus. No drug is available to cure AIDS. Most treatment is directed at the specific infections or cancers that attack HIV-infected people. Clinical Application 24–2 discusses drug treatment for AIDS. Realistically, health care intervention can only suppress most infections for these clients, not cure them.

CLINICAL APPLICATION 24–2

Medications Used for HIV and AIDS

Drug therapy for clients with HIV has increased in complexity. Clients must often take 10 or more different medications each day to treat HIV infections, suppress opportunistic infections, and control symptoms (Volberding, 1996). Three antiretroviral medications currently used for these clients include Zidovuine (AZT), didanosine (ddI), and zalcitabine or (ddc). Zidovuine has been shown to decrease disease progression of HIV in asymptomatic persons with CD4 counts below 200 and 500 cells/mm^3. Some authorities initiate combination AZT and ddI or AZT and ddc when the CD4 count decreases with AZT alone. *CD4* is a protein on the surface of human T-lymphocytes. HIV attacks the lymphocytes at the CD4 marker site. As the number of lymphocytes decrease in infected clients, the number and severity of complicating symptoms increases (Universal Standard Medical Laboratories, 1994). One study has shown that clients who took ddI alone or ddI plus AZT fared better than those taking AZT alone (American Health Consultants, 1995).

A new class of drugs known as protease inhibitors when used in combination with antiretroviral therapy shows great promise. Norvir (ritonavir) manufactured by Abbott Laboratories and Crixivan (indinavir sulfate) manufactured by Merck are two examples of protease inhibitors. These drugs prevent the intracellular maturation of newly produced HIV. The hope is these drugs will suppress the HIV's ability to reproduce and keep to a minimum the development of resistant strains of HIV. No long-term studies have been completed to evaluate clinical progression of HIV infection.

New information suggests that certain medications may be useful in reversing the nutritional decline and sequelae associated with AIDS. Marinal, dronabinal, and megace have all been shown to have significant efficacy in appetite stimulation, increasing caloric intake, reversing weight loss, and improving patient's sense of well-being.

Prevention and Counseling

Notification of a positive HIV test finding creates a crisis for the individual. The person who has had pretest counseling is more prepared and likely to cope better. Counseling the individual on how best to fight the virus is important; for example, the HIV-positive individual needs to receive all current immunizations to boost his or her immunity. Behaviors that interfere with wellness and reduce immunity like alcohol, smoking, and illegal drug use should be discouraged. Adequate rest, good nutrition, and exercise all can improve general good health and should be encouraged.

Prognosis

Most clients want to know their **prognosis** and what is likely to happen to them. Currently, only general guidelines are available. The only estimates are from the date of the infection, and most clients do not know when they became infected. The median time between HIV infection and full blown AIDS is 8.5 years. One-half of all people diagnosed with AIDS will die within two years. Five percent of HIV positive clients are still in good health after ten or more years. This later group is the subject of intense research.

Nutrition and HIV Infection

Nutritional management is both a preventive and a therapeutic treatment in HIV infection. A malnourished client has a limited ability to fight infection. Well-nourished individuals infected with the HIV virus are better able to offer some resistance to opportunistic infections and tolerate the side effects of treatment. Good nutritional status may influence response to medications by decreasing the incidence of adverse drug reactions, providing available raw materials for reactions evoked by medications, and supporting organ functions. Some experts believe that the most effective medical intervention involves the prevention, early identification, and early treatment of enteric infections and malabsorption. Keeping AIDS clients well nourished is often a challenge because of their numerous medical complications. Dietary modifications are frequently indicated for many of these clients.

Nutrition and Immunity

The function of the immune system is to protect the body against foreign invasion. Foreign invaders include viruses, bacteria, tumor cells, fungi, and transplant material. Studies have shown that a deficiency of almost any nutrient affects a cell's ability to fight infection and handle foreign invaders. Therefore, malnutrition by itself can produce an immune deficiency. Many experts believe that malnutrition aggravates AIDS and may suppress any residual immune function. Deficiencies of iron, zinc, pyridoxine, folic acid, and vitamins B_{12}, C, and A are associated with immunologic changes. The mal-

nourished client with AIDS has minimal internal resources to fight opportunistic infections.

Malnutrition among AIDS Clients

Malnutrition causes a number of physiological alterations that may lead to decreased resistance to infection. For example, malnutrition can cause increased gut permeability, which allows more alien material to be absorbed into the body. Malnutrition may also result in decreased intestinal secretions. Some of these secretions are necessary for the proper digestion and absorption of food. Malnutrition may also cause a change in intestinal flora. This may affect the utilization of nutrients. Malnutrition may lead to hormonal imbalances and decreased tissue repair. The body ceases to replace and repair tissue because it lacks the raw materials to do so. A well-balanced diet is essential to optimal immune function.

Recent research has shown that some HIV positive clients need an additional 400 kilocalories per day to maintain their weights due to metabolic abnormalities. Some experts believe these clients lose lean body mass preferentially over body fat. Thus, some HIV positive clients lose lean body mass although they have not lost body weight and seem to eat a balanced diet. Early intervention is important. Clients who are HIV positive should receive nutrition education (Box 24–2).

Malabsorption

Diarrhea and malabsorption are probably the major nutrition-related problems occurring in AIDS clients. Mucosal atrophy and decreased digestive enzyme activity contribute to the malabsorption seen among persons with AIDS. Carbohydrate malabsorption and steatorrhea are frequently seen in AIDS clients with diarrhea. Gastrointestinal problems such as diarrhea may occur in children with HIV infection due to disaccharide intolerance, rather than to enteric infection with known pathogens. Malabsorption of fat, simple sugars, and

---

Kaposi's sarcoma—A type of cancer related to the immunocompromised state that accompanies AIDS; multiple areas of cell proliferation occur initially in the skin and eventually in other body sites.

Prognosis—Probable outcome of disease based on individual's condition and usual course of the disease.

BOX 24–2   COUNSELING THE CLIENT WITH HIV AND AIDS

1. Offer nutrition education soon after the initial diagnosis. Even if the client has not lost weight or seems to be eating a balanced diet, teach the client the basics of good nutrition.
2. Decreased fat and cholesterol levels have been linked to adverse clinical outcomes (Chlebowski, 1995). Closely monitor blood lipids and cholesterol levels.
3. Evaluate the client's diet which should contain at least 100 percent of the RDA for all vitamins and minerals. A multivitamin/mineral supplement may or may not be indicated.
4. Recommend the HIV-infected person consume a few hundred more kilocalories per day than usual. Discourage weight loss as many HIV clients lose lean body mass first and fat second.
5. Encourage more and frequent meals to increase energy intake. Snacks, complete nutritional supplements, and intravenous feedings may be necessary.

vitamin B_{12} is known to occur in clients with intestinal infections.

Other factors may contribute to the diarrhea seen in these clients. Malnutrition can cause a decrease in pancreatic secretions, decreased levels of the enzymes found in the walls of the small intestine (lactase, sucrase, maltase), villous atrophy, and decreased absorptive surfaces. A low serum albumin level may cause diarrhea. Side effects of medication therapy may be related to malabsorption. For example, bacterial overgrowth of organisms not susceptible to the chosen antibiotic may occur with long-term anti-infective therapy.

Initially, dietary treatment involves identification of the cause of the diarrhea and a determination of which nutrients the client cannot absorb. The concentration of hydrogen in the breath can be measured after oral lactose or sucrose administration to determine if the client is intolerant to either of these sugars. An elevated breath hydrogen implies intolerance, since the hydrogen is primarily a product of metabolism of these sugars by colon bacteria. Fecal microbiologic evaluations and intestinal biopsies are used to determine absorptive capability. In some clients infected with HIV, malabsorption of sucrose, maltose, lactose, and fat has been documented, even in the absence of diarrhea.

Clients with a form of carbohydrate intolerance may benefit from either a lactose-restricted diet or a disaccharide-free diet. A disaccharide-free diet is indicated for severe intolerance to sugar. Sucrose needs to be broken down into glucose and fructose (lactose into glucose and galactose; maltose into glucose and glucose) before absorption is possible. A disaccharide-free diet excludes most fruits and veg-

etables and many starches and is nutritionally inadequate. Vitamin C will be deficient and daily supplementation is recommended. Some of these clients may tolerate a small amount of sugar, but they usually need assistance in understanding their tolerance level. A lactose-free diet may be sufficient for clients who are deficient only in lactase.

A low-fat diet may be necessary to control steatorrhea. In cases of a severe fat intolerance, medium-chain triglycerides are more readily absorbed. Clinical Application 24–3 discusses several ways medium-chain triglycerides can be incorporated into table foods.

Several additional meal-planning tips are suggested to promote the client's well-being and control the malabsorption. (1) Fluids should be encouraged to maintain hydration when large fluid volume is lost in stools. (2) Yogurt and other foods that contain the *Lactobacillus acidophilus* culture may be helpful if bacteria overgrowth is a problem secondary to long-term anti-infective use. (3) Small frequent meals make best use of a limited absorptive capacity of the gut. (4) A multivitamin supplement is indicated to increase the amount of vitamin available for absorption. (5) An elemental formula for medical use or parenteral nutrition may be necessary during severe bouts of malabsorption. (6) Avoidance of sorbital, which is used as a sweetening agent in both sugar-free candies and some medications. An elemental formula for medical use contains partially digested nutrients. Promising studies have shown that clients experienced increased weight gain and good tolerance when this type of formula was given at home (Trujillo, et al, 1992).

In some situations, the malabsorption is highly re-

CLINICAL APPLICATION 24-3

Incorporating Medium-Chain Triglyceride Oil Into Table Foods

Medium-chain triglyceride (MCT) oil can replace vegetable oil in most recipes with satisfactory results. The easiest ways to introduce MCT oil in food preparation are in salad dressings, blended with milk (pretreated with lactase enzyme if necessary) or fruit juices, and in sauteed foods. MCT oil can be used to make cookies, bread, pancakes, French toast, muffins, and pie crusts. MCT oil is made by Mead-Johnson and can usually be purchased from a pharmacy.

sistant to any treatment. Nutritional therapy goals should be those that maximize client comfort. Fiber-containing supplements or foods high in fiber may be beneficial for decreasing diarrhea; eliminating caffeine intake also may help control it. The benefits of overly restricting the client's diet may not suffice to offset the resulting loss in client comfort in an incurable situation.

Increased Nutritional Requirements

Clients with AIDS have moderate-to-severe metabolic stress similar to that found in other critically ill clients (Trujillo et al, 1992). Fever and infection increase kilocaloric, protein, and certain mineral and vitamin requirements. Dietitians frequently use the **Harris-Benedict equation** and multiply by appropriate stress and activity factors to determine kilocaloric requirements. Protein requirements should reflect a 150 : 1 kilocalorie-to-nitrogen ratio (McCorkindale, 1990) if the client shows signs of hypermetabolism.

Decreased Food Intake

Anorexia can be a major problem for many clients with AIDS. A poor food intake may be the result of fever, respiratory infections, drug side effects, gastrointestinal complications, oral and esophageal pain, and emotional stress. Clients with ADC may experience mechanical problems with eating. Some drugs used in these clients, such as bactrim and pentamine, may cause nausea, vomiting, and taste changes that decrease the desire to eat (Resler, 1988). Interaction with the client to encourage food intake is particularly important when the person is feeling relatively well.

Nutritional Care in AIDS

Manifestations of the HIV virus vary greatly from one client to another. Therefore, the nutritional care must be tailored to each client's unique set of symptoms. Quality nutritional care starts with screening.

Screening

Screening HIV-infected clients for nutritional problems is a crucial component of quality client care. Early indicators of decreased nutritional status include decreases in body weight, percent body fat, and BMI (McCorkindale, 1990). All clients infected with the HIV virus should have an assessment made of their recent food intake. An effort should be made to correct all nutritional deficiencies as soon as possible. This intervention will help support response to treatment of opportunistic infections and improve client strength and comfort.

Planning Nutrient Delivery

In keeping with the general principle, "if the gut works, use it," every effort should be made to feed the client orally. The anorexia commonly seen in AIDS clients can sometimes be resolved by changing the meal plan. Try offering smaller, frequent feedings. Serving food cold or at room temperature may help some clients consume more kilocalories. Modification of seasonings and kilocaloric density may also improve intake. Modification of texture may assist the client with poor chewing ability or oral lesions.

The Centers for Disease Control recommend the use of regular dishware for clients with bloodborne diseases. Because AIDS is not transmitted through food, food handling, or dishes, regular dishes and utensils may be used without risk. This means an isolation setup is not necessary. Historically, an isolation setup included only disposable dishware, a cardboard tray, and plastic utensils. Disposable dishware compounds the client's feelings of social isolation. Regular dishware provides better quality food at appropriate temperatures and allows the food to appear more appetizing. Many health care institutions require all workers to wear protective gloves when handling soiled dishes.

If the client is unable to consume sufficient nutrients in the form of table foods, supplemental feedings and/or other enteral feedings should be considered. The type of malnutrition should influence the food and supplements offered. The dietitian usually determines the kind of supplement the client should be offered. For example, if the client's protein status is adequate but the client has an energy deficit, a carbohydrate and/or fat supplement may be the best choice. In such a situation the client's serum albumin level would be normal but the client still may be losing weight. On the other hand, if the client's albumin is low but his or her body weight is stable, a protein supplement would be preferable. (Of course, water balance also influences body weight, so this example is necessarily an oversimplification.) The point is that not all supplemental feedings are equally desirable at any given stage of illness. Clients are encouraged to consume particular nutrients based on individual assessment data.

If the client is unable to consume sufficient nutrients orally and the gut is working, a tube feeding may be considered. If the gut is not functioning properly, PPN or TPN may be considered. The goal with these clients should always be to prolong living, not to prolong dying. A client has the right to refuse any alternate feeding route offered.

Monitoring

Periodic evaluation of the client is necessary to ensure that adequate nutrients are being consumed. Body weight and nutritional intake should be monitored frequently. Body mass index and percent body fat should be monitored every few weeks. Throughout this process, health care workers should maintain a supportive, nonjudgmental approach, which is the key to establishing a trusting relationship.

Client Teaching

Nutritional education is an important part of total client care. All AIDS clients need instruction on food safety since low immune-system functioning makes them much more susceptible to foodborne illnesses. This will minimize the likelihood of opportunistic infection. Instructions on dietary modifications and the use of supplemental feedings are also indicated. Many of these clients need instruction on the importance of good nutrition and how to prepare nutrient-dense meals. An assessment of the client's knowledge level and understanding of the individualized meal plan is appropriate. (See Table 24–2.)

Follow-up Care

The nutritional status of a client often depends on appropriate follow-up care. A referral to a community agency, home health care program, outpatient clinic, or a dietitian should be made to provide continuity of care.

TABLE 24–2   Food Tips for Travelers with HIV Infection

Travel, particularly to third world countries, may carry a significant risk for the exposure of HIV-infected persons to opportunistic pathogens. For this reason, HIV-infected travelers should be counseled on the following prior to departure from home:

- Raw or undercooked seafood, eggs (Caesar dressings), and poultry should be avoided.
- Unpasteurized milk and dairy products should be avoided.
- Items purchased from street vendors should be avoided.
- Tap water and ice made from tap water should be avoided. Hot coffee or tea, beer, wine, or water brought to a rolling boil for 1 min is preferable. Treatment of water with iodine or chlorine may not be as effective as boiling but can be used, perhaps in conjunction with filtration, when boiling is not practical.
- Items generally considered safe include: steaming hot foods served, fruits peeled by the traveler, and bottled (especially carbonated) beverages.
- Accidental ingestion of lake or river water while swimming or engaging in other recreational activities may carry a risk. In the severely immunocompromised client, an additional restriction may be necessary. Some soft cheese and ready-to-eat foods (e.g., hot dogs and cold cuts from delicatessen counters) have been known to cause listeriosis. These foods should be reheated until they are steaming hot before ingestion.

Summary

The AIDS epidemic is worldwide. Known transmittal routes include blood-to-blood, perinatal, and sexual contact. As health care professionals we can all protect ourselves from AIDS by using extreme care when handling blood and equipment that has been in contact with blood, and as private individuals by practicing safer sexual behaviors. The human immunodeficiency virus attacks the immune system and leaves its victims defenseless against opportunistic infections. AIDS is a disease with many clinical complications. Nutritional management is both a preventive and a therapeutic treatment in clients infected with the human immunodeficiency virus. Increased nutrient needs, decreased food intake, and impaired nutrient absorption contribute to the malnutrition seen in AIDS clients.

Case Study 24–1 Ms. S is a 30-year-old white woman who acquired HIV from her drug-abusing husband and subsequently infected their son in utero. She could not believe the test results when she was first told. Now she is seeking nutritional information to allow her to increase her chance for a quality life and her son's chance to survive infancy. Her knowledge of basic nutrition is good.

NURSING CARE PLAN FOR MS. S AND HER SON

Assessment

Subjective Data Lack of information on relationship of nutrition to AIDS

Concrete goals established

Objective Data HIV-positive tests, both mother and infant

Nursing Diagnosis Knowledge deficit, related to AIDS progression and/or inhibition, as evidenced by verbal statements.

Desired Outcome/ Evaluation Criteria	Nursing Actions	Rationale
Client will verbalize areas in which nutrition could affect AIDS development.	Reinforce need for regular, balanced meals. Emphasize adequate kilocalories.	The stress of receiving this diagnosis may impede use of previously learned information.
	Instruct Ms. S to keep home environment clean, especially kitchen, bathrooms, and basements where molds and fungi could thrive.	Organisms that are harmless to persons with normal immune systems can cause opportunistic infections in HIV-infected persons.
	Teach client to monitor herself and her son for changes in health related to food intake or digestion.	Discovering beginning malabsorption problems would permit treatment before malnutrition becomes apparent.

Study Aids

Chapter Review

1. AIDS is transmitted through:
   a. Casual contact with dishes and utensils handled by an AIDS client
   b. Casual contact with an infected person's saliva or sputum
   c. Intimate contact with an infected person's blood or semen
   d. Close household contact through airborne organisms

2. The major nutrition-related problems in AIDS clients are:
   a. Diarrhea and malabsorption
   b. Financial and housing related
   c. Swallowing difficulties and general weakness
   d. Social ostracism and unclean surroundings

3. Which of the following diet modifications is designed to compensate for the limited absorptive capacity of the gut in AIDS clients?

a. Giving yogurt or buttermilk regularly
b. Forcing fluids
c. Offering small, frequent meals
d. Cooking foods thoroughly

4. Put the following types of feedings in the recommended order to be used.
   1. Oral
   2. Total parenteral nutrition
   3. Tube feeding
      a. 1, 2, 3
      b. 1, 3, 2
      c. 2, 3, 1
      d. 3, 2, 1

5. A person who is HIV positive should use good hygiene to decrease the risk of:
   a. Rare tumors
   b. Malabsorption problems
   c. Renal failure
   d. Opportunistic infections

Clinical Analysis

Mr. M is 5 feet, 8 inches tall, with advanced AIDS. His male companion died of AIDS 1 year ago. Mr. M lives alone in an urban apartment. He has been losing weight steadily; he now weighs 118 pounds. Mr. M has found it difficult to shop for groceries due to progressive weakness and chronic diarrhea.

1. Which of the following interventions would be most appropriate at this stage?
   a. Referral to a social service agency for a friendly visitor
   b. Arranging for Meals on Wheels service
   c. Obtaining a dietitian's recommendation for a complete nutritional supplement to replace meals
   d. Suggesting to the physician that tube feeding be started

2. Mr. M develops pneumocystis pneumonia. In addition to monitoring nutrient intake, the nurse now would suggest which of the following interventions?
   a. Lying down after meals
   b. Encouraging fluids
   c. Strict isolation
   d. Use of an antiseptic mouthwash

3. If Mr. M becomes anemic before the pneumonia is resolved, which of the following signs should alert the nurse to the need for closer supervision of the client?

a. Complaints of nausea and loss of appetite
b. Increased bitter taste to foods
c. Forgetfulness and sleepiness
d. Appearance of white patches in his mouth

Bibliography

Bartletti, JG (ed): New Trials Reach Same Conclusion: Two Drugs are Better than AZT alone. AIDS ALERT. 10:133, 1995.

Berenson, AS (ed): Control of Communicable Diseases Manual. 16 ed. American Public Health Assoc., Washington DC, 1995.

Casey, K: Nursing Issues in Weight Loss Associated With Acquired Immunodeficiency Syndrome (AIDS). Bristol-Myers Squibb Oncology and Immunology Medical Services, Princeton, NJ, 1995.

Centers for Disease Control. AIDS Information Hotline (404/332-4565). Document No. 320210, 1994.

Centers for Disease Control. AIDS due to HIV-2 Infection: New Jersey. MMWR 37:33, 1988.

Chlebowski, RT, et al: Diet intake and counseling, weight maintenance, and the course of HIV infection. J Am Diete Assoc 95:428, 1995.

Collier, AC, et al: Treatment of human immunodeficiency virus infection with saquinavir, zidovudine, and zalcitabine. New Engl J Med 334:1011, 1996.

Cross, EW: AIDS: Legal implications for managers. J Am Diet Assoc 92:74, 1992.

Durham, JD, and Cohen, FL (eds): The Person with AIDS: Nursing Perspectives. Springer, New York, 1991.

Eron, JJ, et al: Treatment with lamivudine, zidovudine, or both in HIV-positive patients with 200 to 500 CD4+ cells per cubic millimeter. New Engl J Med 333:1662, 1995.

Greene, WC: Denying HIV safe haven. New Engl J Med 334:1264, 1996.

Koo, MB: Disaccharide intolerance in children with HIV. Nutrition and the MD 17:5, 1991.

Koop, CE: Surgeon General's Report on Acquired Immune Deficiency Syndrome. US Public Health Service, Pub. No. HE 20, 9002: AC, Washington, DC 1987.

Kotler, DP: Intestinal and hepatic manifestations of AIDS. Adv Inter Med 34:43, 1989.

Mandell, GL, Bennett, JE, and Dolin, R: Principles and Practice of Infectious Diseases, ed 4. Churchill Livingstone, New York, 1995.

Mann, JM, et al: The international epidemiology of AIDS. Scientific American 259:82, 1988.

McCorkindale, C: Nutrition status of HIV infected patients during early disease stages. J Am Diet Assoc 90:1236, 1990.

Position Paper of the American and Canadian Dietetic Association: Nutrition intervention in the care of persons with human immunodeficiency virus infection. Am Diet Assoc, 94:1042, 1994.

Resler, SS: Nutrition care of AIDS patients. J Am Diet Assoc 88:828, 1988.

Scharnhorst, S: AIDS dementia complex in the elderly. Nurse Pract 17(8):41, 1992.

Trujillo, EB, et al: Assessment of nutritional status, nutrient intake, and nutrition support in AIDS patients. J Am Diet Assoc 92:477, 1992.

Universal Standard Medical Laboratories, Inc.: Specimen Requirement Manual. Lexi-Comp, Inc., Hudson, OH, 1994.

US Department of Health and Human Services Public Health Service. Centers for Disease Control: TB: The HIV Connection, Atlanta, p. 1. Pub. No. HE 20.7302:T79, 1991.

US Public Health Service: Guidelines for the prevention of opportunistic infections in persons infected with human immunodeficiency virus: A Summary. Ann Intern Med 124:349, 1996.

Volberding, PA: Improving the outcomes of care for patients with human immunodeficiency virus infection. New Engl J Med 334:729, 1996.

Woods, SE: Nutrition beliefs of men with human immunodeficiency virus disease in a self-selected population. The American Dietetic Association 78th Annual Meeting and Exhibition (abstracts). J Am Diet Assoc 95:A-88, 1995.

CHAPTER 25

Nutritional Care of the Terminally Ill

LEARNING OBJECTIVES

After completing this chapter, the student should be able to:

1   Differentiate between palliative and curative nutritional care.
2   State appropriate nutritional screening questions for the terminally ill client.
3   List at least two appropriate dietary management techniques for symptom control for: anemia, anorexia, bowel obstruction, cachexia, constipation, cough, dehydration, diarrhea, dysgeusia, esophageal reflux, fever, fluid accumulation, hiccups, incontinence, jaundice and hepatic encephalopathy, migraine headache, nausea and vomiting, pruritus, stomatitis, weakness, wounds and pressure sores, and xerostomia.
4   State appropriate assessment questions for the terminally ill client.
5   Discuss the ethical and legal considerations of feeding a terminally ill client.

Dealing with Death

Our culture emphasizes the enjoyment of life. Many of us have chosen to ignore and shield ourselves from death. At the beginning of this century, most people died at home. Many died young. Death was a part of everyday life. During the last fifty years, most people typically died in hospitals or long-term care facilities. Often an ambulance is called if a person is dying. Health care workers have received much training on how to reverse the effects of disease. We have received much less training on how to assist our clients with dying. With changes in the health care system bringing decreased lengths of hospital stays an increasing number of clients will again be cared for in their homes. The need to train health care workers to provide home care for terminally ill clients is becoming essential.

To help the dying, health care workers must first contemplate and then accept their own mortality. Nurses deny death as much as lay people. Evidence of this is often seen in behavior such as avoiding conversation with a terminally ill client. We may also become attached to a particular client and become overwhelmed by our feelings, thereby becoming ineffective as helping care givers. Nutritional and dietary issues are at the crux of some ethical questions concerning the care of these clients. Becoming an advocate for clients' best interests is paramount to providing quality care.

The Dying Process

Death is an unavoidable part of the life cycle. There are both physiological and psychological changes that occur as part of the dying process. The client's age, diagnosis, and physical condition influence the physiological changes. Regardless of the underlying disease, it is cardiopulmonary failure that is the final cause of death. Pulmonary and circulatory failure may be gradual or sudden. The major signs and symptoms in the final days and hours of life include: cessation of eating and drinking; oliguria and incontinence; muscle weakness; difficulty in breathing; cyanosis; decreased mental alertness; and changes in vital signs.

Cessation of Eating and Drinking

Life will soon cease when a client's eating and drinking diminishes critically. One study reported that 8 percent of clients with cancer will completely cease to eat and/or drink (Feuz, and Rapin, 1994). Oral intake dwindles because a client has no desire to eat or disease may prevent digestion. This greatly decreased oral intake is often worrisome to family members. Health care workers need to counsel family members that dehydration at this time is believed to have an euphoric effect and is not painful. Oral dryness can be alleviated by good oral care, the use of ice chips, giving sips of fluids, and applying oil to the lips. It is unkind to force food or fluids on a client who is actively dying.

Oliguria and Incontinence

Because oral intake is usually decreased for several days before death, urine output is often diminished. The color of the urine may become very dark. A period of incontinence often precedes the oliguria. General fatigue, muscle weakness, decreased mental acuity are among the reasons for the incontinence. Bedding should be changed as quickly as possible to avoid skin irritation. Death usually occurs within 48 to 72 hours after urine output stops.

Difficulty in Breathing

Most clients have some difficulty breathing before death. The *death rattle*, which is a loud, hoarse, and bubbling sound alarms many caregivers. This sound is caused by the passage of breath through pharyngeal and pulmonary secretions that lodge at the back of the client's throat. Atropine is often administered to decrease the secretions. Elevating the head of the bed, gentle suctioning, and positioning the client onto his or her side help maintain a clear airway.

Cyanosis

Slightly bluish, grayish, or dark purple discoloration of the skin is called *cyanosis*. The client's feet, legs, hands, and groin feel cold. Many health care workers feel this is one of the most useful indicators that the end of life is approaching. These signs are caused by slowed circulation and decreased tissue perfusion.

Decreased Mental Alertness

The amount of blood reaching the brain, lungs, liver, and kidneys decreases as general circulation slows. Sleepiness, apathy, disorientation, confusion, restlessness, and finally a decreased level of consciousness that frequently progresses to a coma are among the signs that death is imminent.

Changes in the Vital Signs

A decrease in body temperature, an increase in pulse rate, a rise and then a decrease in respirations, and a fall in blood pressure are signs that it is time to summon family members for their final goodbyes. Death occurs when respiration ceases.

Family members and caregivers of terminally ill clients often express fear at the thought of being alone with an actively dying client. For this reason, health care workers often remain with the client and their loved ones during this time. Some nurses resist working with the terminally ill because they think that they cannot cope with this experience. However, death is not always a painful experience. Death can provide an opportunity for personal growth, meaningful attachments, and joyous affirmation in life.

Palliative Versus Curative Care

Clients are considered terminally ill when they have an irreversible disease with a prognosis of 6 months or less. The goal of curative care is arresting the disease. The goal of palliative care is the relief of symptoms to alleviate or ease pain and discomfort. Emphasis in palliative care is placed on addressing the problems of pain, loneliness, and loss of control that are common in dying clients. Palliative care programs address and/or include the client and family members in the plan of care.

The major palliative care program in the United States for terminally ill clients is hospice. *Hospice* is a concept that dates back to medieval times. During the crusades, travelers needed a place to stop for comfort. The Knights of Hospitallers of the Order of St. John of Jerusalem in the twelfth century sheltered the sick and religious pilgrims. They established hospices in England, Germany, Italy, Cyprus, and Rhodes. The soul, the mind, and the spirit were considered as much in need of help as the body. Around the fifteenth century, anatomic and surgical practices developed. Physicians moved into hospitals that emphasized curative treatments. Monks and nuns remained in cloisters and cared for the people the physicians could not heal (the disabled, the chronically ill, and the terminally ill). During the eighteenth and nineteenth centuries great advances in curative treatments occurred and hospitals became highly specialized in acute life-threatening situations. Hospitals were less able to offer shelter to people nearing their life's end. At the same time, dying became less a private or religious function and more a public and governmental function.

The modern day hospice draws its roots from the late nineteenth century when a place of shelter for the incurable ill was founded in Dublin. The hospice movement in the United States was inspired by the British physician, Dr. Cicely Saunders. Dr. Saunders is noted for her work in pain control and founding of St. Christopher's Hospice in London in 1967. The first operational hospice program in the United States was established in New Haven, Connecticut in the early 1970s (Hospice of Jackson, 1992).

Hospice philosophy includes the belief that death is a natural part of life. Hospice is committed to the philosophy that persons have the right to die in the setting of their choice and to be as comfortable as possible. The idea that palliative care is appropriate when treatment of the client's disease becomes ineffective and irrelevant is central to the hospice philosophy.

Nutrition Screening

The goal of palliative nutritional care is to assist the client and/or caregiver(s) with any food-related concerns. These difficulties may be related to uncomfortable symptoms and/or attitudes and beliefs held about food. Screening the client with a terminal illness for food-related concerns is the first step. This task can be performed by a dietitian or as part of the nurse's initial assessment of the client. There are major differences between screening a client who is undergoing curative and/or preventative treatment and the terminally ill client who is receiving palliative care. First, the health care worker needs to ascertain if the client has any symptoms that may be diminished by nutritional intervention. Second, a determination of the client's and/or caregiver(s) attitudes and beliefs about food needs to be examined. Some clients and their caregivers have a difficult time accepting that the terminally ill client frequently eats much less than is needed to sustain life. Table 25–1 is an example of a nutrition screening form for the client with a terminal condition.

Assessment

During the nutritional assessment, it is important that every question posed to the client and/or caregiver has a purpose. Health care workers need to know the results of laboratory tests, diagnostic procedures, physical examinations, anthropometric measures, level of immune function, and food intake information to determine the client's nutritional sta-

TABLE 25–1   A Sample Nutrition Screening Form for the Client with a Terminal Condition

Name _____ Caregiver's Name _____

Date _____ Diagnosis _____

1. Have you had any concerns about weight changes or food intake?
   _____ No _____ Yes   Describe _____
2. (For clients on tube feedings or parenteral feedings only): Have your feedings created or increased discomfort, diarrhea, distension, etc.?
   Type: _____ Amt. _____ Infusion rate _____
   _____ No _____ Yes   Describe _____
3. Do you feel your symptoms could be decreased/controlled through dietary change?
   _____ No _____ Yes Describe _____
4. Do you feel diet or nutritional supplement would benefit you or your disease process?
   _____ No _____ Yes Type _____
5. Do you believe that your diet caused your disease or will slow the progression of your disease?
   _____ No _____ Yes Describe _____
6. Do you find eating enhances comfort? _____ No _____ Yes
7. What concerns do you have regarding your diet intake?
   _____
8. Would you (client or caregiver) like to discuss food-related concerns with the dietition? _____ No _____ Yes

tus. The importance of these nutritional parameters in the provision of nutritional care for the terminally ill client is dubious. For example, why ask if the client drinks milk? Is it to estimate if the client is meeting the calcium, riboflavin, and vitamin D allowances? If it is determined that the milk intake is suboptimal, would anything be done about the inadequacy? If however, the client has diarrhea with severe abdominal cramping after the ingestion of milk, a recommendation to drink lactose-free milk would be appropriate. Unless the client would experience symptomatic relief from bothersome symptoms it is best not to recommend behavioral changes that may be difficult for the client to make.

Intervention and Symptom Control

Table 25–2 discusses appropriate dietary management for symptom control for a client with a terminal illness. If a nurse feels comfortable with the interventions, he or she may elect to counsel the client. If a nurse feels uncomfortable or lacks the time to counsel the client, a referral to the dietitian is indicated.

Ethical and Legal Considerations

Before the advancement of nutritional support technology, whether to feed a client was not an ethical or legal consideration. Now the situation has changed. Feeding, once an ordinary treatment, has become what many people consider an extraordinary treatment. *Ordinary care* means a procedure or treatment that is simple, natural, and common. Oral feeding is an example of ordinary care. *Extraordinary care* means complicated, unnatural, infrequent, mechanical, and artificial. Hyperalimentation is thought by many to be extraordinary care. For this reason, most hospice services have a policy of discharging a client from their service if he or she desires aggressive nutritional support. The client is not abandoned but rather referred to another program that provides extraordinary care.

Ethics uses rational processes for determining the most morally desirable course of action in the face of conflicting value choices. The process of deciding on an ethical course of action involves medical goals and proportionally, client preferences, quality of life, and contextual features. *Contextual features* means in a given situation.

Medical Care Goals and Proportionality

The medical care goals that apply to the client with a terminal illness include:

Relieving symptoms, pain, and suffering
Preventing untimely death ("I want to live long enough to _____.")
Improving of functional status or maintaining of compromised status

TABLE 25–2   Dietary Management for Symptom Control

Anemia

1. Recommend vitamin C source with red meats and iron fortified foods.
2. Discourage use of coffee, tea, and chocolate if the client has gastrointestinal bleeding.
3. Recommend multivitamin supplement if client desires, but avoid megadose vitamins.

Anorexia

1. Discuss practical issues with client and/or caregiver such as food attitudes, social aspects of eating, and unpredictable food preferences (Dietitians Assoc of Australia Position Paper, 1992).
2. Evaluate client's desire for a sense of well-being.
3. Suggest use of small frequent feedings.
4. Educate caregiver to recognize early signs of malnutrition and provide protein supplements, make food accessible, and encourage eating as desired by the client and/or caregiver, if the client's prognosis is more than a few weeks.
5. Evaluate client acceptance of a liquid diet and recommend complete oral nutritional supplements.
6. Teach caregiver that the client has the right to self-determination and may refuse to eat and/or drink when actively dying. The caregiver should continue to offer nourishment as a sign of love and caring but not harass the client to eat or drink.

Bowel Obstruction

1. Recommend limiting intake to sips of fluids if the client has a complete obstruction.
2. Encourage small meals low in fiber and residue if oral intake is not contraindicated.
3. Encourage the client to eat slowly, chew food well, and rest after each meal.
4. Recommend dry feedings.
5. Recommend avoidance of sugary fatty foods, alcohol, and foods with a strong odor.

Cachexia

1. Teach relaxation techniques and encourage use before mealtime.
2. Encourage client and/or caregiver to concentrate on the sensual pleasures of eating such as setting an attractive table and plate, the use of food garnishes, and the importance of an appetizing eating environment (remove bedpans and emesis basin, etc. before serving the food).
3. Evaluate client for dysgeusia and dysphagia, and xerostomia. Refer to symptoms and definitions of terms on this table.

Constipation

1. Encourage high-fiber foods (bran, whole grains, fruits, vegetables, nuts, and legumes) if an adequate fluid intake can be maintained.
2. Instruct the client to avoid high-fiber foods if dehydration or an obstruction is suspected or anticipated.
3. Assess the client's fluid intake and recommend an increased intake if needed.
4. Recommend taking 1–2 oz with the evening meal of a special recipe: 2 cups applesauce, 2 cups unprocessed bran (All bran), and 1 cup of 100 percent prune juice. (Gallagher-Allred, 1989). Refrigerate this mixture between uses and discard after 5 days if not used.
5. Suggest limiting cheese and high-fat, sugary foods (doughnuts, cakes, pies, cookies) that may be constipating.
6. Discontinue calcium and iron supplements if contributing to constipation.
7. Review the client's medications. If the client is taking bulking agents (milk of magnesia, magnesium citrate, metamucil, or Golytely), a large fluid intake is essential. Suggest the client and/or caregiver mask the taste of these medications in applesauce, mashed potatoes, gravy, orange juice, and nectars.

Cough

1. Encourage fluids and ice chips.
2. Recommend hard candy including sour balls.
3. Have the client try tea and coffee to dilate pulmonary vessels.

TABLE 25–2   Dietary Management for Symptom Control (Continued)

Dehydration

1. Encourage fluids such as juices, ice cream, gelatin, custards, puddings, soups, and juices, if the client's life expectancy is more than a few days.
2. Encourage the client to try creative beverages such as orange sherbet and milk shake.
3. Consider a nasogastric tube feeding for fluid delivery only after a discussion with other team members, client, and caregivers. Plain water and foods high in electrolytes can be delivered via a tube feeding.
4. Consider a parenteral line only after a tube feeding is considered and rejected and after an in depth discussion with the team members, client, and family. Client goals, expectations, and quality of life issues should all be very carefully considered. Parenteral lines for the delivery of nutrients and water are rarely indicated in terminally ill clients.
5. Be prepared to accept that dehydration is still considered by some health professionals to be painful or uncomfortable. The impression that starvation and dehydration are terrible ways to die is especially prominent among nonhospice physicians. Generally, the impression of hospice clinicians is that starvation and dehydration do not contribute to suffering among the dying and might contribute to a comfortable passage from life (Byock, 1995). Evidence for the potential benefits of not rehydrating and for the withdrawal of intravenous fluids for terminally ill clients is increasing but is still not conclusive (Malone, 1994). This is an area of active research.

Diarrhea

1. Consider modification of diet to omit lactose, gluten, or fat if related to diarrhea.
2. Suggest a decrease in dietary fiber content.
3. Consider the omission of gas-forming vegetables if an association between the consumption of these foods and diarrhea can be ascertained.
4. Consider the use of a low-residue diet.
5. Encourage high-potassium foods (bananas, tomato juice, orange juice, potatoes, etc.) if the client is dehydrated.
6. Recommend dry feedings (drink fluids 1 hour before or 30–60 min after meals).
7. Encourage intake of medium-chain triglycerides and a diet high in protein and carbohydrates for steatorrhea due to pancreatic insufficiency.
8. Consider the use of a complete oral nutritional supplement to provide adequate nutrient composition while helping the client overcome mild-to-moderate malabsorption.
9. For copious diarrhea and/or diarrhea combined with a decubitus on the coccyx, consider use of a clear liquid complete nutritional supplement or a predigested oral nutritional supplement.

Dysgeusia (Abnormal taste)

1. Encourage oral care before mealtime.
2. Evaluate whether client experiences a bitter, sweet, or no taste after food consumption.
   If foods taste bitter encourage consumption of poultry, fish, milk and milk products, and legumes. Recommend the use of marinated meats and poultry in juices or wine. Sour and salty foods are generally not liked when a client experiences a bitter taste. Cook food in a glass or porcelain container to improve taste. Recommend a decreased use of red meats, sour juices, coffee, tea, tomatoes, and chocolate. The use of a modular protein supplement may be helpful if the client's protein intake is suboptimal.
   If food has no taste, recommend foods served at room temperature, highly seasoned foods, and sugary foods.
   If foods have a sweet taste, recommend sour juices, tart foods, lemon juice, vinegar, pickles, spices, herbs, and the use of a modular carbohydrate supplement.

Table continued on following page

TABLE 25–2   Dietary Management for Symptom Control (Continued)

Dyspnea (Difficulty Breathing)

1. Encourage coffee, tea, carbonated beverages, and chocolate. These foods are bronchodilators that increase blood pressure, dilate pulmonary vessels, increase glomerular filtration rate, and thereby break up and expel pulmonary secretions and fluids (Gallagher-Allred, 1989).
2. Encourage use of a soft diet. Liquids are usually better tolerated than solids. Cold foods are often better accepted than hot foods.
3. Recommend small frequent feedings.
4. Encourage ice chips, frozen fruit juices, and popsicles; these are often well accepted.
5. Consider the use of a complete high-fat, low-carbohydrate nutritional supplement. This decreases carbon dioxide retention and assists in breathing.

Esophageal Reflux

1. Recommend small feedings.
2. Discourage foods that lower esophageal sphincter pressure such as high-fat foods, chocolate, peppermint, spearmint, and alcohol.
3. Encourage client to sit up while eating and for 1 hour afterward.
4. Recommend avoidance of food within 3 hours before bedtime.
5. Teach relaxation techniques.

Fever

1. Recommend a high-fluid intake.
2. Consider a tube feeding for severe dehydration to maintain hydration after a discussion with team members. This is not recommended if death is imminent (hours/days).
3. Recommend high-protein, high-caloric foods.

Fluid Accumulation

1. Recommend a mild sodium restriction (3–4 g/day).
   Recommend a lower sodium restriction only if this is the wish of the client.
2. Discourage a fluid restriction unless the client has significant hyponatremia.
3. Provide a list of foods high in protein and potassium.

Hiccups

1. Recommend smaller meals and slow eating.
2. Discourage the use of a straw.
3. Add peppermint to food to decrease gastric distention (Gallagher-Allred, 1989).
4. Recommend client swallow a large teaspoon of granulated sugar.

Hypoglycemia

1. Assess the client's and/or caregiver's knowledge about diabetes and hypoglycemia.
2. Determine if the client is truly insulin dependent as part of the admission assessment process. The following suggest true insulin-dependence (Tatling, Houston, and Hill, 1985):
   a. The introduction of insulin soon after the diagnosis
   b. A history of previous ketoacidosis
   c. Use of more than one daily dose of insulin for years
3. Evaluate the client's expressed desire for extent of medical care. The primary guide for determining the level of nutritional intervention is the wish of the client.
4. Determine the last time the client experienced the signs of a hypoglycemic episode. Many of these clients have deficiencies in the counterregulatory hormones, especially epinephrine, and may lapse into a coma without any warning signs. Caregivers need to be informed of this potential complication. Educate the client and/or caregiver on the treatment of hypoglycemia (15–15 rule, see Chapter 18, "Diet in Diabetes Mellitus and Hypoglycemia").

TABLE 25–2 Dietary Management for Symptom Control (Continued)

5. Monitor client's blood glucose level. A suitable range for blood sugars would be 127–309 mg/dL in the hospice population (Boyd, 1993).
6. Encourage 30–50 g of carbohydrate every 3 hours to prevent starvation ketosis. Each of the following is equal to 30–50 g of carbohydrate:
     3/4 cup Carnation Instant Breakfast
     1 cup regular gelatin
     1 cup vanilla ice cream
     1 1/2 cups gingerale
     1 cup orange juice
     1 cup apple juice

Incontinence

1. Discourage intake of coffee, tea, carbonated beverages containing caffeine, especially before bedtime.
2. Continue to encourage adequate fluid intake.

Jaundice and Hepatic Encephalopathy

1. Encourage a high-carbohydrate diet.
2. Encourage a protein-restricted diet only if the client desires.
3. Specialized oral nutritional supplements for clients with liver disease are often ineffective for the terminally ill but may be beneficial when the client desires to "live long enough to _____."

Nausea and Vomiting

1. Discuss practical issues with client and/or caregiver such as food attitudes, social aspects of eating, and unpredictable food preferences (Dietitians Association of Australia, 1992).
2. Recommend client restrict fluids to 1 hour before or after meals to prevent early satiety.
3. Assess if sweet, fried, or fatty foods are poorly tolerated, recommend avoidance if necessary.
4. Evaluate if starchy foods such as crackers, breads, potatoes, rice, and pasta are better tolerated. Encourage increased consumption if helpful.
5. Encourage the client to eat slowly, chew feed well, and rest after each meal as these behaviors may increase food intake.
6. Recommend the client avoid offensive odors during food preparation.
7. Recommend that the person who has recently experienced severe nausea and vomiting try 1–2 bites of food per hour.
8. Emphasize the sensual aspects of food including: appearance (serve garnished food on attractive tableware); odor of environment (remove bedpans and emesis basins from room); taste (cater to the client's likes and dislikes); and the importance of companionship during mealtime.
9. Recommend the avoidance of food if nausea and vomiting becomes severe and food makes the client feel worse. Feeding may not be desirable if death is expected within hours or a few days and the effects of partial dehydration or the withdrawal of nutrition support will not adversely alter client comfort (American Dietetic Association, 1987).

Migraine Headaches

1. Recommend that the client eat at regular intervals. Hunger or missed meals can trigger a migraine headache.
2. Recommend that the highly motivated client keep a food diary and record the onset of any headaches. Migraine headaches can be triggered by one or many foods. Common food offenders include: many common food additives, processed meats, peanuts and peanut products, soybeans, yeast, chocolate, aged cheeses, seasonings, caffeine, some types of alcohol, and flavorings.

Table continued on following page

TABLE 25–2 Dietary Management for Symptom Control (Continued)

Pruritus (Severe itching)

1. Recommend avoidance of known allergy foods.
2. Encourage fluid intake for clients receiving antihistamines.
3. Recommend avoidance of coffee, tea, carbonated beverages containing caffeine, alcohol, and cocoa that can cause vasodilation and itching.

Stomatitis (Inflammation of the mouth)

1. Consider multivitamin supplement with folic acid and vitamin B_{12}.
2. Recommend avoidance of spicy, acidic, rough, hot, and salty foods.
3. Recommend a consistency modification such as pureed, soft, or liquid.
4. Consider the use of a complete nutritional supplement.
5. Recommend creamy foods, whites sauces, and gravies.
6. Consider between meal supplements such as milkshakes, eggnogs, and puddings.
7. Recommend caregiver add sugar to acid or salty foods to alter the food's taste.
8. Recommend meals be served when the client's pain is under control.
9. Recommend good oral care before and after meals.

Weakness

1. Recommend multivitamin-mineral supplement with folic acid, vitamin B_{12}, and iron.
2. Encourage high-potassium foods (bananas, cantaloupe, milk, baked winter squash, etc.) if client vomits easily.
3. Recommend a modification in the food's consistency (mechanical soft or full liquid) to decrease the energy cost of eating.

Wounds and Pressure Sores

1. Recommend caregiver cater to the client's food preferences.
2. Use of aggressive nutritional support is rarely effective, but may be appropriate if the client and family desire quantity. For example, "I want to live and see my _____."
3. Correct elevated glucose levels to decrease risk of infection.
4. Evaluate the use of a multiple vitamin and mineral supplement which contains zinc and vitamin C. As excess dietary zinc impedes healing, do not routinely recommend a zinc supplement without assessment information.
5. Encourage protein and caloric intake equal to estimated needs only if the client desires and is able.

Xerostomia (Dry Mouth)

1. Encourage frequent sips of water, fruit juices, ice chips, popsicles, ice cream, and sherbet.
2. Recommend the use of hard candy.
3. Consider a modification of food consistency such as soft, mechanical soft, or full liquids.
4. Recommend avoidance of extremely hot or cold foods. Foods served at room temperature are generally better tolerated.
5. Recommend creamy foods, white sauces, and gravies.
6. Encourage the client to dip foods in gravy, margarine, butter, olive oil, coffee, and broth.
7. Consider the need for a complete liquid nutritional supplement between meals.

Educating and counseling the client and his or her significant others regarding condition and prognosis

Avoiding harming the client in the course of care

Promoting of health and preventing of disease not related to the terminal disease

The physician is responsible for the initial education and counseling of clients regarding his or her condition and prognosis.

The principle of proportionality is an important ethical consideration in treatment for the terminally ill client. *Proportionality* means a medical treatment is ethically mandatory to the extent that it is likely to confer greater benefits than burdens to the client. For example, many experts feel a client who is actively dying and slightly dehydrated has a more comfortable death. Dehydration has been reported to reduce a client's secretions and excretions, thus decreasing breathing problems, emesis, and incontinence. Dehydration can sedate the brain just before death. Greatly diminished or cessation of oral intake is one of the signs that death is imminent. In another context, a client who is terminally ill but whose condition is stable and enjoys many activities of daily living may appreciate or request education on how to maintain hydration. A nutritional intervention is appropriate if the client would receive greater benefits than burdens.

Client Preference

The most important ethical principle to consider is the client's right to self-determination. Some individuals may perceive suffering as an important means of personal growth or a religious experience. Other individuals may hope a miracle cure will be discovered for his or her disease. Health care workers have a responsibility to provide a combination of emotional support and technical nutritional advice on how best to achieve each client's goals.

Quality of Life

The most fundamental goal of medical care is the improvement of the quality of life of those who seek care. If improvement is not possible, a goal of medical care is maintenance, or slowing the decline, or raising the quality of life. Oral feeding is part of being human and synonymous with human dignity. One study found that 92 percent of all cancer clients could eat and/or drink until the day they died (Feuz, and Rapin, 1994). These clients derived some pleasure from the sensual aspect of food and the socialization which accompanies meals. Food conveys emotional, spiritual, sociological, and biologic meanings. If food remains enjoyable for a client with a terminal illness, the health care worker should encourage mealtimes to be shared with loved ones. If eating is not a pleasant experience, however, it should not be overemphasized.

Contextual

Every terminally ill client has his or her own story, with both a history and a future. A client's decision to eat or not to eat is part of his or her narrative. The fear of abandonment is among the most frequently cited apprehensions of dying (American Dietetic Association, 1987). Even if the client refuses to eat, health care workers should remain supportive. The client may change his or her mind. The rejection of food should not be considered by the

health care worker as a sign of personal or professional failure.

A consideration of a client's medical goals, preferences, quality of life, and contextual features may provide a framework for resolution of ethical dietary issues. The interdisciplinary team conference is the best arena to discuss ethical feeding conflicts. Hospice programs often have interdisciplinary care teams.

Legal Issues

The issue of whether to discontinue food and fluid to the client with a terminal illness first emerged in the 1960s. Clients have the legal right to refuse treatment, including artificial feedings. This right is based on the 14th Amendment to the Constitution, which refers to the right to liberty, and includes the right to be left alone and not invaded or treated against his or her will. Courts have recognized that competent adults have the right to refuse treatment, including artificial feeding. The state may exert its authority to expand the individuals's right to liberty on the basis of several concepts. The preservation of life, the prevention of suicide, the protection of innocent third parties (such as minor children), and the protection of the ethical integrity and professional discretion of the medical profession are among these concepts. Health care workers need to be familiar with the laws in their individual states and the policies and procedures of the organization for which they work. They should also be familiar with their professional organizations standards of practice. In some states, a charge of battery can be made if a client is fed artificially against his or her wishes. In some states, a charge of negligence can be made if a client is allowed to intentionally starve themselves to death. Situations such as these should be discussed at the interdisciplinary team meeting or brought to the risk manager's attention. A *risk manager* is an individual hired by a health care organization to identify, evaluate, and correct potential risks of injuring clients, staff, visitors, or property.

With incompetent adult clients, caretakers and family should try to ascertain the client's wishes from past written and oral statements and actions. State laws differ as to whether nutrition and hydration are medically obligatory or medically optional. Some clients may wish for the withdrawal of antibiotics and ventilators but continue nutritional support. This situation may occur when an individual has a permanent tube feeding in place because of an inability to swallow, such as may occur with cancer of the esophagus. What legally should the nurse do if the client is incompetent and the family wants the feeding tube removed? What legally should the nurse do if family members disagree about whether to have the feeding tube removed? The best advice is "when in doubt" continue to feed the client until the health care team, the institution's ethics committee, or the facility's risk manager reviews the case. The artificial feeding can be stopped at a future time. A deceased person cannot be resuscitated or brought back to life.

Individuals may make their wishes known in writing through advanced directives, living wills, and durable power of attorneys. Although each of these legal documents technically differ from one another, the common element is that trust is given to another party to make decisions for an individual if he or she becomes incompetent. In the event that a client does not have a written directive, the next of kin or guardian should be consulted about probable preference for the level of nutrition intervention (American Dietetic Association, 1987).

General Considerations

Oral feedings should be advocated over tube and intravenous feedings in the terminally ill client. Food and control of food intake remain one of life's last pleasures. The client's decision to eat or not to eat is his or her right. An effort should be made to enhance the individual's enjoyment of food. A pleasant dining environment that includes a cheerful attitude on the part of caregivers may encourage food intake. The use of complete oral nutrition supplements may provide some relief from the symptoms associated with hunger, thirst, and malnutrition. Many previously prescribed dietary restrictions should be re-evaluated and liberalized. The client's right to self-determination should guide the health care worker in determining whether to allow foods that are not permitted within the diet prescription.

Palliative care does not automatically preclude aggressive nutritional support. The client's informed preference for the level of nutrition intervention is important. If the client wants maximal nutrition support and the policy of the organization is not to provide hyperalimentation and/or tube feedings for terminally ill clients, the client has the right to be informed of the name of a facility that will provide this service. Artificial feeding is generally not desirable if death is expected within hours or a few days. The effects of partial dehydration and the withdrawal of nutritional support will not adversely alter client comfort. Enteral or parenteral feeding will probably worsen the condition, symptoms, or discomfort when shock, pulmonary edema, diarrhea, or aspiration is a potential or actual complication. The client or surrogate needs to be informed of these facts when he or she requests maximal support.

Summary

Death is a part of life. If we want to help the dying, we must examine our own attitudes toward death. Treatment for the terminally ill client is palliative. The goal of care is symptomatic relief to reduce or alleviate pain. Nutritional intervention can frequently alleviate or reduce the pain and suffering of the terminally ill client. The use of oral feedings should always be given preferential consideration over tube and parenteral feedings. Oral feeding is ordinary care while tube feedings and hyperalimentation are considered by some to be extraordinary care.

In the United States, the client's expressed desire is the primary guide for determining the extent of nutritional and hydration therapy. Our constitution guarantees clients the right to self-determination. Ethical and legal dilemmas should promptly be brought to the attention of the interdisciplinary team, the risk manager, or the facility's ethics committee. An artificial feeding should never be stopped unless one of these parties has investigated the situation and made a legal and ethical determination that the feeding should cease.

| Case Study 25–1 | Ms. Z is a 60-year-old woman who has a diagnosis of amyotrophic lateral sclerosis (ALS), also called Lou Gehrig's Disease, with a prognosis of less than 6 months. The client has at least two swallowing impediments. She is unable to dislodge food that collects under her tongue, in cheeks, and on her hard palate. She does not have adequate swallow control (the bolus goes down before she wants it to). Because of these impediments, Ms. Z is unable to tolerate thin liquids and the maintenance of hydration and aspiration are of concern to the caregiver. Ms. Z is alert, oriented, and highly educated. She saw a television program that led her to believe that a high-protein diet would delay the progression of ALS. She would like instruction on a high-protein diet. |

Assessment

Subjective Data Client believes a high-protein diet will delay the progression of her ALS

The caregiver is concerned about the danger of aspiration and the maintenance of hydration.

Objective Data Diagnosis ALS with a prognosis of less than 6 months

Lack of swallowing control

Nursing Diagnosis Knowledge deficit related to lack of desired information about foods high in protein as evidenced by verbal statements. Knowledge deficit related to a lack of understanding of how to increase and/or maintain hydration with the client's swallowing impediments as evidenced by the caregiver's verbal statements.

Desired Outcome/ Evaluation Criteria	Nursing Actions	Rationale
The client will indicate how she can incorporate foods high in protein and of semisolid or pureed consistency into her diet.	Plan a 70–80 g protein semiliquid/pureed diet (2 cups thickened milk, 6 oz meat or equivalent, 2 vegetables, and 6 starches) for the client or refer the client to the dietitian to plan and instruct the client and/or caregiver on the diet.	Because a 70–80 g protein diet would most likely not harm the client and would make her feel in control, instruction on the diet is appropriate.
The caregiver will verbalize how to reduce the likelihood of aspiration by following safety precautions for clients with dysphagia.	Discuss feeding issues with the caregiver such as the correct body positioning and eating conditions (American Dietetic Association, 1992). Eliminate distractions Position individual in an upright position (90-degrees at the hip) with feet flat on floor. Give semiliquids in very small amounts (syringe) and only after food has been cleared from the mouth. Feed the client very small bites. Encourage several dry swallows between bites of food. If the Adam's apple rises, it is likely the food is being swallowed and not deposited in the cheeks. A wet sounding voice with a gurgle may mean food is resting on the vocal cords.	The risk of aspiration is high in clients with dysphagia.

Table continued on following page

Sample Menu for a 70–80 Gram Protein Diet, Semiliquid Pureed Consistency

Breakfast	Lunch	Dinner
1/2 cup orange juice thickened with gelatin 2 scrambled eggs Oatmeal mixed with milk and applesauce Coffee, if desired, in very small amounts as tolerated	Soup with coarsely chpd. meat and vegetable (use of a food processor will aid in achieving the desired consistency) Warm peach cobbler, made with angel food cake, thickened peach sauce, and canned chpd. peaches Vegetable juice thickened with a commercial thickener	Chpd. meat with gravy over mashed potatoes Vegetable aspic salad (puree vegetables and serve in tomato flavored gelatin) Fruit juice thickened with commercial thickener or applesauce
Snack Milk thickened with commercial thickener and vanilla Plain toast softened with flavored gelatin	*Snack* Mashed banana	*Snack* Thickened milk made with ice cream or sherbet and commercial thickener

---

Study Aids

Chapter Review

1. A diet prescription consistent with palliative care goals is:
   a. One-gram sodium for congestive heart failure
   b. Forty-gram protein for liver failure
   c. Low-cholesterol, low-saturated fat diet for hyperlipoproteinemia
   d. Gluten-free diet for diarrhea and celiac disease
   e. High-calorie, high-protein diet for anorexia in the actively dying client

2. An appropriate nutritional screening question for the client with a terminal illness is:
   a. "How many servings of meats do you eat each day?"
   b. "How much weight have you lost in the past month?"
   c. "Do you look forward to meals?"
   d. "Do you include a green or yellow vegetable in your diet each day?"
   e. "How many times a day do you eat?"

3. The most important ethical principle to consider when a decision must be made whether or not to feed a client is:
   a. The client's right to self-determination
   b. Proportionality
   c. Medical goals
   d. The client's quality of life
   e. Contextual features

4. Which recommendation would be appropriate for a client with congestive heart failure who requests dietary advice:
   a. Recommend a low potassium diet
   b. Recommend a 1000 cc fluid restriction
   c. Monitor the client's fluid intake and output
   d. Recommend a low-protein diet
   e. Recommend a 3 or 4 gram sodium diet

5. The intervention appropriate for a terminally ill client with dyspnea who requests dietary treatment is:
   a. Encourage a high-fiber diet
   b. Encourage a low-fat diet
   c. Recommend fresh fruits, whole grains, and vegetables
   d. Consider a high-fat and low-carbohydrate diet
   e. Encourage avoidance of caffeine

Clinical Analysis

1. Mr. O is actively dying. Mr. O's wife is concerned because her husband adamantly refuses all food and fluids. The nurse should:
   a. Call the doctor and request an order for a tube feeding
   b. Call the doctor and request an order for an intravenous feeding
   c. Instruct the caregiver to be more creative in the type of food and fluids she gives the client
   d. Counsel the caregiver that oral intake often ceases near the end of life
   e. Counsel the client to drink more fluids to prevent dehydration

2. Mrs. P has diagnoses of brain cancer and insulin-dependent diabetes mellitus and a prognosis of a few days. She and her caregiver have been taught to self-monitor the blood glucose levels. The caregiver is quite concerned because Mrs. P's blood glucose levels are running between 400 to 500 milligrams per deciliter. Historically, the client claims to have followed her 1200 calorie diet faithfully. Recently, her appetite is markedly reduced and her blood glucose levels are elevated (hypermetabolism). The physician has been contacted and refuses to increase the client's insulin further and recommended to Mrs. P's caregiver to stop monitoring the client's blood glucose levels. The nurse should:
   a. Encourage the caregiver to offer Mrs. P frequent sips of clear liquid fruit juices (about 30 grams of carbohydrate every 3 hours)
   b. Encourage the caregiver to continue to offer the client the 1200 calorie diet to avoid a hypoglycemic episode
   c. Recommend the caregiver look for a new doctor because obviously the doctor does not know how to treat clients with insulin-dependent diabetes
   d. Contact the Hospice medical director and ask for an order to increase the client's insulin
   e. Tell the caregiver not to offer food and fluids to the client

3. Mr. J has a partial bowel obstruction and shows signs of dehydration. He has an order for metamucil prn. The nurse should immediately recommend:
   a. High-fiber foods such as bran, whole grains, fruits, vegetables, etc.
   b. Discontinuation of the metamucil
   c. Increasing the dose of metamucil
   d. Encourage the use of cheese, cakes, pies, cookies, and doughnuts
   e. An intravenous feeding

Bibliography

Albert, SM: Do family caregivers recognize malnutrition in frail elderly? J Am Geriatr Soc 93:617, 1993.
American Dietetic Association: Manual of Clinical Dietetics. American Dietetic Association, Chicago, 1992, p 144.
American Dietetic Association: Migraine headaches and food. The "trigger" factor. J Am Diet Assoc 95:1240, 1995.
American Dietetic Association: Position of the American Dietetic Association: Issues in feeding the terminally ill adult. J Am Diete Assoc 87:76, 1987.
American Dietetic Association: Position of the American Dietetic Association: Legal and ethical issues in feeding permanently unconscious patients. J Am Diete Assoc 95:231, 1995.
Boyd, K: Diabetes mellitus in hospice patients: Some guidelines. Palliative Med 7:163, 1993.
Byock, I: Patient refusal of nutrition and hydration: Walking the ever-fine line. Am J Hospice Palliative Care 12:8, 1995.
Dietitians Association of Australia: Position Paper: Nutrition priorities in palliative care of oncology patients. Dietitians Association of Australia. 92–93, 1992.
Feuz, A, and Rapin C: An observational study of the role of pain management and food adaptation of elderly patients with terminal cancer. J Am Diet Assoc 94:767, 1994.
Gallagher-Allred, CR: Nutritional Care of the Terminally Ill. Aspen Publishers, Gaithersburg, MD, 1989.
Hospice of Jackson: Unpublished manual, 1992.
Malone, N: Hydration in the terminally ill patient. Clin Palliative Care 8:20, 1994.
McKinley, MJ, et al: Improved body weight as a result of nutrition intervention in adult, HIV-positive outpatients. J Am Diet Assoc 94:1014, 1994.
Morley, JE, and Kraenzle, D: Causes of weight loss in a community nursing home. J Am Geriatr Soc 94:583, 1994.
Tatling, W, Houston, DC, and Hill, Rd: The prevalence of diabetes mellitus in a typical English community. Jr Coll Phys Lond 19:248, 1985.
Towers, AL, et al: Constipation in the elderly: Influence of dietary, psychological, and physiological factors. J Am Geriatr Soc 94:701, 1994.

Exchange Lists of the American Dietetic and American Diabetes Associations

STARCH LIST

One starch exchange equals 15 g carbohydrate, 3 g protein, 0–1 g fat, and 80 cal.

Bread		*Oats* (cont.)	
Bagel	1/2 (1 oz)	Oats	1/2 cup
Bread, reduced-calorie	2 slices (1 1/2 oz)	Pasta	1/2 cup
Bread, white, whole-wheat, pumpernickel, rye	1 slice (1 oz)	Puffed cereal	1 1/2 cups
		Rice milk	1/2 cup
Bread sticks, crisp, 4 in long × 1/2 in	2 (2/3 oz)	Rice, white or brown	1/3 cup
		Shredded Wheat	1/2 cup
English muffin	1/2	Sugar-frosted cereal	1/2 cup
Hot dog or hamburger bun	1/2 (1 oz)	Wheat germ	3 tbsp
Pita, 6 in across	1/2	*Starchy Vegetables*	
Roll, plain, small	1 (1 oz)	Baked beans	1/3 cup
Raisin bread, unfrosted	1 slice (1 oz)	Corn	1/2 cup
Tortilla, corn, 6 in across	1	Corn on cob, medium	1 (5 oz)
Tortilla, flour, 7–8 in across	1	Mixed vegetables with corn, peas, or pasta	1 cup
Waffle, 4 1/2 in square, reduced-fat	1	Peas, green	1/2 cup
Cereals and Grains		Plantain	1/2 cup
Bran cereals	1/2 cup	Potato, baked or boiled	1 small (3 oz)
Bulgur	1/2 cup	Potato, mashed	1/2 cup
Cereals	1/2 cup	Squash, winter (acorn, butternut)	1 cup
Cereals, unsweetened, ready-to-eat	3/4 cup	Yam, sweet potato, plain	1/2 cup
Cornmeal (dry)	3 tbsp	*Crackers and Snacks*	
Couscous	1/3 cup	Animal crackers	8
Flour (dry)	3 tbsp	Graham crackers, 2 1/2 in square	3
Granola, low-fat	1/4 cup		
Grape-Nuts	1/4 cup	Matzoh	3/4 oz
Grits	1/2 cup	Melba toast	4 slices
Kasha	1/2 cup	Oyster crackers	24
Millet	1/4 cup	Popcorn (popped, no fat added or low-fat microwave)	3 cups
Muesli	1/4 cup	Pretzels	3/4 oz
		Rice cakes, 4 in across	2

Saltine-type crackers	6	Chow mein noodles	1/2 cup
Snack chips, fat-free (tortilla, potato)	15–20 (3/4 oz)	Corn bread, 2 in cube	1 (2 oz)
		Crackers, round butter type	6
Whole-wheat crackers, no fat added	2–5 (3/4 oz)	Croutons	1 cup
		French-fried potatoes	16–25 (3 oz)

Dried Beans, Peas, and Lentils
(Count as 1 starch exchange, plus 1 very lean meat exchange.)

		Granola	1/4 cup
Beans and peas (garbanzo, pinto, kidney, white, split, black-eyed)	1/2 cup	Muffin, small	1 (1 1/2 oz)
		Pancake, 4 in across	2
		Popcorn, microwave	3 cups
Lima beans	2/3 cup	Sandwich crackers, cheese or peanut butter filling	3
Lentils	1/2 cup		
Misc*	3 tbsp	Stuffing, bread (prepared)	1/3 cup
		Taco shell, 6 in across	2

Starchy Foods Prepared with Fat
(Count as 1 starch exchange, plus 1 fat exchange.)

		Waffle, 4 1/2 in square	1
Biscuit, 2 1/2 in across	1	Whole-wheat crackers, fat added	4–6 (1 oz)

* = 400 mg or more of sodium per serving.

FRUIT LIST

One fruit exchange equals 15 g carbohydrate and 60 cal. The weight includes skin, core, seeds, and rind.

Fruit

Apple, unpeeled, small	1 (4 oz)	Papaya	1/2 fruit (8 oz) or 1 cup cubes
Applesauce, unsweetened	1/2 cup		
Apples, dried	4 rings	Peach, medium, fresh	1 (6 oz)
Apricots, fresh	4 whole (5 1/2 oz)	Peaches, canned	1/2 cup
Apricots, dried	8 halves	Pear, lg, fresh	1/2 (4 oz)
Apricots, canned	1/2 cup	Pears, canned	1/2 cup
Banana, small	1 (4 oz)	Pineapple, fresh	3/4 cup
Blackberries	3/4 cup	Pineapple, canned	1/2 cup
Blueberries	3/4 cup	Plums, small	2 (5 oz)
Cantaloupe, small	1/3 melon (11 oz) or 1 cup cubes	Plums, canned	1/2 cup
		Prunes, dried	3
Cherries, sweet, fresh	12 (3 oz)	Raisins	2 tbsp
Cherries, sweet, canned	1/2 cup	Raspberries	1 cup
Dates	3	Strawberries	1 1/4 cup whole berries
Figs, fresh	1 1/2 large or 2 medium (3 1/2 oz)		
		Tangerines, small	2 (8 oz)
Figs, dried	1 1/2	Watermelon	1 slice (13 1/2 oz) or 1 1/4 cup cubes
Fruit cocktail	1/2 cup		
Grapefruit, lg	1/2 (11 oz)	*Fruit Juice*	
Grapefruit sections, canned	3/4 cup	Apple juice/cider	1/2 cup
Grapes, small	17 (3 oz)	Cranberry juice cocktail	1/3 cup
Honeydew melon	1 slice (10 oz) or 1 cup cubes	Cranberry juice cocktail reduced-calorie	1 cup
		Fruit juice blends, 100 percent juice	1/3 cup
Kiwi	1 (3 1/2 oz)		
Mandarin oranges, canned	3/4 cup	Grape juice	1/3 cup
Mango, small	1/2 fruit (5 1/2 oz) or 1/2 cup	Grapefruit juice	1/2 cup
		Orange juice	1/2 cup
Nectarine, small	1 (5 oz)	Pineapple juice	1/2 cup
Orange, small	1 (6 1/2 oz)	Prune juice	1/3 cup

MILK LIST

One milk exchange equals 12 g carbohydrate and 8 g protein.

Skim and Very Low-Fat Milk
(0–3 g fat per serving)

Skim milk	1 cup
1/2 percent milk	1 cup
1 percent milk	1 cup
Nonfat or low-fat buttermilk	1 cup
Evaporated skim milk	1/2 cup
Nonfat dry milk	1/3 cup dry
Plain nonfat yogurt	3/4 cup
Nonfat or low-fat fruit-flavored yogurt sweetened with aspartame or with a nonnutritive sweetener	1 cup

Low-Fat
(5 g fat per serving)

2 percent milk	1 cup
Plain low-fat yogurt	3/4 cup
Sweet acidophilus milk	1 cup

Whole Milk
(8 g fat per serving)

Whole milk	1 cup
Evaporated whole milk	1/2 cup
Goat's milk	1 cup
Kefir	1 cup

OTHER CARBOHYDRATES LIST

One exchange equals 15 g carbohydrate, or 1 starch, or 1 fruit, or 1 milk.

Food	Serving Size	Exchanges Per Serving
Angel food cake, unfrosted	1/12th cake	2 carbohydrates
Brownie, small, unfrosted	2 in square	1 carbohydrate, 1 fat
Cake, unfrosted	2 in square	1 carbohydrate, 1 fat
Cake, frosted	2 in square	2 carbohydrates, 1 fat
Cookie, fat-free	2 small	1 carbohydrate
Cookie or sandwich cookie with creme filling	2 small	1 carbohydrate, 1 fat
Cupcake, frosted	1 small	2 carbohydrates, 1 fat
Cranberry sauce, jellied	1/4 cup	2 carbohydrates
Doughnut, plain cake	1 medium (1 1/2 oz)	1 1/2 carbohydrates, 2 fats
Doughnut, glazed	3 3/4 in across (2 oz)	2 carbohydrates, 2 fats
Fruit juice bars, frozen, 100 percent juice	1 bar (3 oz)	1 carbohydrate
Fruit snacks, chewy (pureed fruit concentrate)	1 roll (3/4 oz)	1 carbohydrate
Fruit spreads, 100 percent fruit	1 tbsp	1 carbohydrate
Gelatin, regular	1/2 cup	1 carbohydrate
Gingersnaps	3	1 carbohydrate
Granola bar	1 bar	1 carbohydrate, 1 fat
Granola bar, fat-free	1 bar	2 carbohydrates
Hummus	1/3 cup	1 carbohydrate, 1 fat
Ice cream	1/2 cup	1 carbohydrate, 2 fats
Ice cream, light	1/2 cup	1 carbohydrate, 1 fat
Ice cream, fat-free, no sugar added	1/2 cup	1 carbohydrate
Jam or jelly, regular	1 tbsp	1 carbohydrate
Milk, chocolate, whole	1 cup	2 carbohydrates, 1 fat
Pie, fruit, 2 crusts	1/6 pie	3 carbohydrates, 2 fats
Pie, pumpkin or custard	1/8 pie	1 carbohydrate, 2 fats
Potato chips	12–18 (1 oz)	1 carbohydrate, 2 fats
Pudding, regular (made with low-fat milk)	1/2 cup	2 carbohydrates
Pudding, sugar-free (made with low-fat milk)	1/2 cup	1 carbohydrate
Salad dressing, fat-free*	1/4 cup	1 carbohydrate
Sherbet, sorbet	1/2 cup	2 carbohydrates
Spaghetti or pasta sauce, canned*	1/2 cup	1 carbohydrate, 1 fat
Sweet roll or Danish	1 (2 1/2 oz)	2 1/2 carbohydrates, 2 fats
Syrup, light	2 tbsp	1 carbohydrate

Food	Serving Size	Exchanges Per Serving
Syrup, regular	1 tbsp	1 carbohydrate
Syrup, regular	1/4 cup	4 carbohydrates
Tortilla chips	6–12 (1 oz)	1 carbohydrate, 2 fats
Yogurt, frozen, low-fat, fat-free	1/3 cup	1 carbohydrate, 0–1 fat
Yogurt, frozen, fat-free, no sugar added	1/2 cup	1 carbohydrate
Yogurt, low-fat with fruit	1 cup	3 carbohydrates, 0–1 fat
Vanilla wafers	5	1 carbohydrate, 1 fat

* = 400 mg or more sodium per exchange.

VEGETABLE LIST

In general, one vegetable exchange is 1/2 cup cooked vegetable or juice or 1 cup raw vegetable.
One vegetable exchange equals 5 g carbohydrate, 2 g protein, 0 g fat, and 25 cal.

Artichoke
Artichoke hearts
Asparagus
Beans (green, wax, Italian)
Bean sprouts
Beets
Broccoli
Brussels sprouts
Cabbage
Carrots
Cauliflower
Celery
Cucumber
Eggplant
Green onions or scallions
Greens (collard, kale, mustard, turnip)
Kohlrabi
Leeks
Mixed vegetables (without corn, peas, or pasta)

Mushrooms
Okra
Onions
Pea pods
Peppers (all varieties)
Radishes
Salad greens (endive, escarole, lettuce, romaine, spinach)
Sauerkraut*
Spinach
Summer squash
Tomato
Tomatoes, canned
Tomato sauce*
Tomato/vegetable juice*
Turnips
Water chestnuts
Watercress
Zucchini

* = 400 mg or more sodium per exchange.

MEAT AND MEAT SUBSTITUTES LIST

Very Lean Meat and Substitutes List
One exchange equals 0 g carbohydrate, 7 g protein, 0–1 g fat, and 35 cal. One very lean meat exchange is equal to any one of the following items.

Poultry: Chicken or turkey (white meat, no skin), Cornish hen (no skin) — 1 oz

Fish: Fresh or frozen cod, flounder, haddock, halibut, trout; tuna fresh or canned in water — 1 oz

Shellfish: Clams, crab, lobster, scallops, shrimp, imitation shellfish — 1 oz

Game: Duck or pheasant (no skin), venison, buffalo, ostrich — 1 oz

Cheese with 1 g or less fat per ounce:
Nonfat or low-fat cottage cheese — 3/4 cup
Fat-free cheese — 1 oz

Other: Processed sandwich meats with 1 g or less fat per ounce, such as deli thin, shaved meats, chipped beef,* turkey ham — 1 oz

Egg whites — 2
Egg substitutes, plain — 1/4 cup
Hot dogs with 1 g or less fat per ounce* — 1 oz
Kidney (high in cholesterol) — 1 oz
Sausage with 1 g or less fat per ounce — 1 oz

Count as one very lean meat and one starch exchange.
Dried beans, peas, lentils (cooked) — 1/2 cup

Lean Meat and Substitutes List
One exchange equals 0 g carbohydrate, 7 g protein, 3 g fat, and 55 cal. One lean meat exchange is equal to any one of the following items.

Beef: USDA Select or Choice grades of lean beef trimmed of fat, such as round, sirloin, and flank steak; tenderloin; roast (rib, chuck, rump); steak (T-bone, porterhouse, cubed), ground round — 1 oz

Pork: Lean pork, such as fresh ham; canned, cured, or boiled ham; Canadian bacon*; tenderloin, center loin chop — 1 oz

Lamb: Roast, chop, leg — 1 oz

Veal: Lean chop, roast — 1 oz

Poultry: Chicken, turkey (dark meat, no skin), chicken white meat (with skin), domestic duck or goose (well drained of fat, no skin) — 1 oz

Fish:

Herring (uncreamed or smoked)	1 oz
Oysters	6 medium
Salmon (fresh or canned), catfish	1 oz
Sardines (canned)	2 medium
Tuna (canned in oil, drained)	1 oz

Game: Goose (no skin), rabbit — 1 oz

Cheese:

4.5 percent fat cottage cheese	1/2 cup
Grated Parmesan	2 tbsp
Cheeses with 3 g or less fat per ounce	1 oz

Other:

Hot dogs with 3 g or less fat per ounce*	1 1/2 oz
Processed sandwich meat with 3 g or less fat per ounce, such as turkey pastrami or kielbasa	1 oz
Liver, heart (high in cholesterol)	1 oz

Medium-Fat Meat and Substitutes List

One exchange equals 0 g carbohydrate, 7 g protein, 5 g fat, and 75 cal. One medium-fat meat exchange is equal to any one of the following items.

Beef: Most beef products fall into this category (ground beef, meatloaf, corned beef, short ribs, Prime grades of meat trimmed of fat, such as prime rib) — 1 oz

Pork: Top loin, chop, Boston butt, cutlet — 1 oz

Lamb: Rib roast, ground — 1 oz

Veal: Cutlet (ground or cubed, unbreaded) — 1 oz

* = 400 mg or more sodium per exchange.

Poultry: Chicken dark meat (with skin), ground turkey or ground chicken, fried chicken (with skin) — 1 oz

Fish: Any fried fish product — 1 oz

Cheese: With 5 g or less fat per ounce

Feta	1 oz
Mozzarella	1 oz
Ricotta	1/4 cup (2 oz)

Other:

Egg (high in cholesterol, limit to 3 per week)	1
Sausage with 5 g or less fat per ounce	1 oz
Soy milk	1 cup
Tempeh	1/4 cup
Tofu	4 oz or 1/2 cup

High-Fat Meat and Substitutes List

One exchange equals 0 g carbohydrate, 7 g protein, 8 g fat, and 100 cal.

Remember these items are high in saturated fat, cholesterol, and calories and may raise blood cholesterol levels if eaten on a regular basis. One high-fat meat exchange is equal to any one of the following items.

Pork: Spareribs, ground pork, pork sausage — 1 oz

Cheese: All regular cheeses, such as American*, cheddar, Monterey Jack, Swiss — 1 oz

Other: Processed sandwich meats with 8 g or less fat per ounce, such as bologna, pimento loaf, salami — 1 oz

Sausage, such as bratwurst, Italian, knockwurst, Polish, smoked	1 oz
Hot dog (turkey or chicken)*	1 (10/lb)
Bacon	3 slices (20 slices/lb)

Count as one high-fat meat plus one fat exchange.

Hot dog (beef, pork, or combination)*	1 (10/lb)
Peanut butter (contains unsaturated fat)	2 tbsp

FAT LIST

Monounsaturated Fats List

One fat exchange equals 5 g fat and 45 cal.

Avocado, medium	1/8 (1 oz)
Oil (canola, olive, peanut)	1 tsp
Olives: ripe (black)	8 large
green, stuffed*	10 large
Nuts	
almonds, cashews	6 nuts
mixed (50% peanuts)	6 nuts
peanuts	10 nuts
pecans	4 halves
Peanut butter, smooth or crunchy	2 tsp
Sesame seeds	1 tbsp
Tahini paste	2 tsp

Polyunsaturated Fats List

One fat exchange equals 5 g fat and 45 cal.

Margarine: stick, tub, or squeeze	1 tsp
lower-fat (30 percent to 50 percent vegetable oil)	1 tbsp
Mayo: regular	1 tsp
reduced-fat	1 tbsp
Nuts, walnuts, English	4 halves
Oil (corn, safflower, soybean)	1 tsp
Salad dressing: regular*	1 tbsp
reduced-fat	2 tbsp
Miracle Whip Salad Dressing®:	
regular	2 tsp
reduced-fat	1 tbsp
Seeds: pumpkin, sunflower	1 tbsp

Saturated Fats List†
One fat exchange equals 5 g of fat and 45 cal.

Bacon, cooked	1 slice (20 slices/lb)		Coconut, sweetened, shredded	2 tbsp
			Cream, half and half	2 tbsp
			Cream cheese: regular	1 tbsp (1/2 oz)
Bacon, grease	1 tsp		reduced-fat	2 tbsp (1 oz)
Butter: stick	1 tsp			
whipped	2 tsp		Fatback or salt pork, see below‡	
reduced-fat	1 tbsp		Shortening or lard	1 tsp
Chitterlings, boiled	2 tbsp (1/2 oz)		Sour cream: regular	2 tbsp
			reduced-fat	3 tbsp

* = 400 mg or more sodium per exchange.
† Saturated fats can raise blood cholesterol levels.
‡ Use a piece 1 in × 1 in × 1/4 in if you plan to eat the fatback cooked with vegetables. Use a piece 2 in × 1 in × 1/2 in when eating only the vegetables with the fatback removed.

FREE FOODS LIST

A *free food* is any food or drink that contains less than 20 cal or less than 5 g of carbohydrate per serving. Foods with a serving size listed should be limited to three servings per day. Be sure to spread them out throughout the day. If you eat all three servings at one time, it could affect your blood glucose level. Foods listed without a serving size can be eaten as often as you like.

Fat-Free Or Reduced-Fat Foods

Cream cheese, fat-free	1 tbsp
Creamers, nondairy, liquid	1 tbsp
Creamers, nondairy, powdered	2 tsp
Mayo, fat-free	1 tbsp
Mayo, reduced-fat	1 tsp
Margarine, fat-free	4 tbsp
Margarine, reduced-fat	1 tsp
Miracle Whip®, nonfat	1 tbsp
Miracle Whip®, reduced-fat	1 tsp
Nonstick cooking spray	
Salad dressing, fat-free	1 tbsp
Salad dressing, fat-free, Italian	2 tbsp
Salsa	1/4 cup
Sour cream, fat-free, reduced-fat	1 tbsp
Whipped topping, regular or light	2 tbsp

Sugar-Free or Low-Sugar Foods

Candy, hard, sugar-free	1 candy
Gelatin dessert, sugar-free	2 tsp
Gelatin, unflavored	
Gum, sugar-free	
Jam or jelly, low-sugar or light	
Sugar substitutes*	
Syrup, sugar-free	2 tbsp

Drinks

Bouillon, broth, consommé†	1 tbsp
Bouillon or broth, low-sodium	
Carbonated or mineral water	
Cocoa powder, unsweetened	
Coffee	
Club soda	
Diet soft drinks, sugar-free	
Drink mixes, sugar-free	
Tea	
Tonic water, sugar-free	

Condiments

Catsup	1 tbsp
Horseradish	
Lemon juice	
Lime juice	
Mustard	
Pickles, dill†	1 1/2 large
Soy sauce, regular or light†	
Taco sauce	1 tbsp
Vinegar	

Seasonings

Be careful with seasonings that contain sodium or are salts, such as garlic or celery salt, and lemon pepper.

Flavoring extracts
Garlic
Herbs, fresh or dried
Pimento
Spices
Tabasco® or hot pepper sauce
Wine, used in cooking
Worcestershire sauce

* Sugar substitutes, alternatives, or replacements that are approved by the Food and Drug Administration (FDA) are safe to use. Common brand names include: Equal® (aspartame), Sprinkle Sweet® (saccharin), Sweet One® (acesulfame K), Sweet-10® (saccharin), Sugar Twin® (saccharin), Sweet 'n Low® (saccharin).

† = 400 mg or more of sodium per choice.

COMBINATION FOODS LIST

Many of the foods we eat are mixed together in various combinations. These combination foods do not fit into any one exchange list. Often it is hard to tell what is in a casserole dish or prepared food item. This is a list of exchanges for some typical combination foods. This list will help you fit these foods into your meal plan. Ask your dietitian for information about any other combination foods you would like to eat.

Food	Serving Size	Exchanges Per Serving
Entrees		
Tuna noodle casserole, lasagna, spaghetti with meatballs, chili with beans, macaroni and cheese*	1 cup (8 oz)	2 carbohydrates, 2 medium-fat meats
Chow mein (without noodles or rice)	2 cups (16 oz)	1 carbohydrate, 2 lean meats
Pizza, cheese, thin crust*	1/4 of 10 in (5 oz)	2 carbohydrates, 2 medium-fat meats, 1 fat
Pizza, meat topping, thin crust*	1/4 of 10 in (5 oz)	2 carbohydrates, 2 medium-fat meats, 2 fats
Pot pie*	1 (7 oz)	2 carbohydrates, 1 medium-fat meat, 4 fats
Frozen entrees		
Salisbury steak with gravy, mashed potato*	1 (11 oz)	2 carbohydrates, 3 medium-fat meats, 3–4 fats
Turkey with gravy, mashed potato, dressing*	1 (11 oz)	2 carbohydrates, 2 medium-fat meats, 2 fats
Entree with less than 300 cal*	1 (8 oz)	2 carbohydrates, 3 lean meats
Soups		
Bean*	1 cup	1 carbohydrate, 1 very lean meat
Cream (made with water)*	1 cup (8 oz)	1 carbohydrate, 1 fat
Split pea (made with water)*	1/2 cup (4 oz)	1 carbohydrate
Tomato (made with water)*	1 cup (8 oz)	1 carbohydrate
Vegetable beef, chicken noodle, or other broth-type*	1 cup (8 oz)	1 carbohydrate

* = 400 mg or more of sodium per choice.

FAST FOODS*

Food	Serving Size	Exchanges Per Serving
Burritos with beef†	2	4 carbohydrates, 2 medium-fat meats, 2 fats
Chicken nuggets†	6	1 carbohydrate, 2 medium-fat meats, 1 fat
Chicken breast and wing, breaded and fried†	1 ea.	1 carbohydrate, 4 medium-fat meats, 2 fats
Fish sandwich/tartar sauce†	1	3 carbohydrates, 1 medium-fat meat, 3 fats
French fries, thin	20–25	2 carbohydrates, 2 fats
Hamburger, regular	1	2 carbohydrates, 2 medium-fat meats
Hamburger, large†	1	2 carbohydrates, 3 medium-fat meats, 1 fat
Hot dog with bun†	1	1 carbohydrate, 1 high-fat meat, 1 fat
Individual pan pizza†	1	5 carbohydrates, 3 medium-fat meats, 3 fats
Soft-serve cone	1 medium	2 carbohydrates, 1 fat
Submarine sandwich†	1 sub (6 in)	3 carbohydrates, 1 vegetable, 2 medium-fat meats, 1 fat
Taco, hard shell†	1 (6 oz)	2 carbohydrates, 2 medium-fat meats, 2 fats
Taco, soft shell†	1 (3 oz)	1 carbohydrate, 1 medium-fat meat, 1 fat

* = 400 mg or more sodium per exchange.

† Ask at your fast-food restaurant for nutrition information about your favorite fast foods.

USING FOOD LABELS

Nutrition Facts on food labels can help you with food choices. These labels are required by law for most foods and are based on standard serving sizes. However, these serving sizes may not always be the same as the serving sizes in this booklet.

- Check the serving size on the label. Is it nearly the same size as the food exchange? You may need to adjust the size of the serving to fit your meal plan.
- Look at the grams of carbohydrate in the serving size. (One starch, fruit, milk, or other carbohydrate has about 15 grams of carbohydrate.) So, if 1 cup of cereal has 30 grams of carbohydrate, it will count as 2 starch choices in your meal plan. You may need to adjust the size of the serving so it contains the number of carbohydrate choices you have for a meal or a snack.
- Look at the grams of protein in the serving size. (One meat choice has 7 grams of protein.) If the food has more than 7 grams of protein in a serving, you can figure out the number of meat choices by dividing the grams of protein by 7. Meats generally contain fat, too.
- Look at the grams of fat in the serving size. (One fat choice has 5 grams of fat.) If one waffle has 15 grams of carbohydrate and 5 grams of fat, it counts as 1 starch choice and 1 fat choice.
- Look at the number of calories in the serving size. If there are less than 20 calories per serving, it is a free food. However, if it has more than 20 calories, follow the steps listed above to count the food choices.

Ask your dietitian for help using information on food labels. Some food labels may also give exchanges. These are based on information in this appendix.

Chili With Beans Nutrition Facts	
Serving Size 1 cup (253 g) Servings Per Container 2	
Amount Per Serving	
Calories 260 Calories from Fat 72	
	% Daily Value
Total Fat 8 g	13%
Saturated Fat 3 g	17%
Cholesterol 130 mg	44%
Sodium 1010 mg	42%
Total Carbohydrate 22 g	7%
Dietary Fiber 9 g	36%
Sugars 4 g	
Protein 25 g	

The Exchange Lists are the basis of a meal-planning system designed by a committee of the American Diabetes Association and the American Dietetic Association. While designed primarily for people with diabetes and others who must follow special diets, the Exchange Lists are based on principles of good nutrition that apply to everyone. Copied with permission.

Source: Adapted from Exchange Lists for Meal Planning ©1995, American Diabetes Association, The American Dietetic Association.

Nutritive Values of Foods

Foods, approximate measures, units, and weight (weight of edible portion only)		Water	Food energy	Pro- tein	Fat	Fatty Acids		
						Satu- rated	Mono- unsatu- rated	Poly- unsatu- rated
		Grams	Per- cent	Cal- ories	Grams	Grams	Grams	Grams
BEVERAGES		Grams						
Alcoholic:								
Beer:								
Regular-----------	12 fl oz--------	360	92	150	1	0	0.0	0.0	0
Light------------	12 fl oz--------	355	95	95	1	0	0.0	0.0	0.0
Gin, rum, vodka, whiskey:								
86-proof------------	1½ fl oz	42	64	105	0	0	0.0	0.0	0.0
Wines:								
Dessert-----------	3½ fl oz--------	103	77	140	Tr	0	0.0	0.0	0.0
Table:								
Red------------	3½ fl oz--------	102	88	75	Tr	0	0.0	0.0	0.0
White----------	3½ fl oz--------	102	87	80	Tr	0	0.0	0.0	0.0
Carbonated:[2]								
Club soda--------	12 fl oz--------	355	100	0	0	0	0.0	0.0	0.0
Cola type:								
Regular-----------	12 fl oz--------	369	89	160	0	0	0.0	0.0	0.0
Diet, artificially sweet-								
ened------------	12 fl oz--------	355	100	Tr	0	0	0.0	0.0	0.0
Ginger ale----------	12 fl oz--------	366	91	125	0	0	0.0	0.0	0.0
Root beer-----------	12 fl oz--------	370	89	165	0	0	0.0	0.0	0.0
Coffee:								
Brewed-------------	6 fl oz--------	180	100	Tr	Tr	Tr	Tr	Tr	Tr
Instant, prepared (2 tsp powder plus 6 fl oz water)-----------	6 fl oz--------	182	99	Tr	Tr	Tr	Tr	Tr	Tr
Fruit drinks, noncarbonated:								
Canned:								
Fruit punch drink-----	6 fl oz--------	190	88	85	Tr	0	0.0	0.0	0.0
Grape drink--------	6 fl oz--------	187	86	100	Tr	0	0.0	0.0	0.0
Pineapple-grapefruit juice drink--------	6 fl oz--------	187	87	90	Tr	Tr	Tr	Tr	Tr
Fruit juices. See type under Fruits and Fruit Juices.								
Milk beverages. See Dairy Products								
Tea:								
Brewed-------------	8 fl oz--------	240	100	Tr	Tr	Tr	Tr	Tr	Tr
Instant, powder, prepared:								
Unsweetened (1 tsp powder plus 8 fl oz water)-----------	8 fl oz--------	241	100	Tr	Tr	Tr	Tr	Tr	Tr
Sweetened (3 tsp powder plus 8 fl oz water)---	8 fl oz--------	262	91	85	Tr	Tr	Tr	Tr	Tr
DAIRY PRODUCTS								
Cheese:								
Natural:								
Blue-------------	1 oz----------	28	42	100	6	8	5.3	2.2	0.2

(Tr indicates nutrient present in trace amounts.)

Nutrients in Indicated Quantity

| Cho-les-terol | Carbo-hydrate | Calcium | Phos-phorus | Iron | Potas-sium | Sodium | Vitamin A value | | Thiamin | Ribo-flavin | Niacin | Ascorbic acid |
| | | | | | | | (IU) | (RE) | | | | |
Milli-grams	Grams	Milli-grams	Milli-grams	Milli-grams	Milli-grams	Milli-grams	Inter-national units	Retinol equiva-lents	Milli-grams	Milli-grams	Milli-grams	Milli-grams
0	13	14	50	0.1	115	18	0	0	0.02	0.09	1.8	0
0	5	14	43	0.1	64	11	0	0	0.03	0.11	1.4	0
0	Tr	Tr	Tr	Tr	1	Tr	0	0	Tr	Tr	Tr	0
0	8	8	9	0.2	95	9	(¹)	(¹)	0.01	0.02	0.2	0
0	3	8	18	0.4	113	5	(¹)	(¹)	0.00	0.03	0.1	0
0	3	9	14	0.3	83	5	(¹)	(¹)	0.00	0.01	0.1	0
0	0	18	0	Tr	0	78	0	0	0.00	0.00	0.0	0
0	41	11	52	0.2	7	18	0	0	0.00	0.00	0.0	0
0	Tr	14	39	0.2	7	³32	0	0	0.00	0.00	0.0	0
0	32	11	0	0.1	4	29	0	0	0.00	0.00	0.0	0
0	42	15	0	0.2	4	48	0	0	0.00	0.00	0.0	0
0	Tr	4	2	Tr	124	2	0	0	0.00	0.02	0.4	0
0	1	2	6	0.1	71	Tr	0	0	0.00	0.03	0.6	0
0	22	15	2	0.4	48	15	20	2	0.03	0.04	Tr	⁴61
0	26	2	2	0.3	9	11	Tr	Tr	0.01	0.01	Tr	⁴64
0	23	13	7	0.9	97	24	60	6	0.06	0.04	0.5	⁴110
0	Tr	0	2	Tr	36	1	0	0	0.00	0.03	Tr	0
0	1	1	4	Tr	61	1	0	0	0.00	0.02	0.1	0
0	22	1	3	Tr	49	Tr	0	0	0.00	0.04	0.1	0
21	1	150	110	0.1	73	396	200	65	0.01	0.11	0.3	0

Nutritive Value of Foods *(Continued)*

Foods, approximate measures, units, and weight (weight of edible portion only)		Water	Food energy	Pro-tein	Fat	Fatty Acids Satu-rated	Mono-unsatu-rated	Poly-unsatu-rated
		Grams	Per-cent	Cal-ories	Grams	Grams	Grams	Grams	Grams
DAIRY PRODUCTS—Con.								
Camembert (3 wedges per 4-oz container)- - - - -	1 wedge- - - - - - - -	38	52	115	8	9	5.8	2.7	0.3
Cheddar:								
Cut pieces- - - - - - - -	1 oz- - - - - - - - - -	28	37	115	7	9	6.0	2.7	0.3
	1 in³- - - - - - - - -	17	37	70	4	6	3.6	1.6	0.2
Shredded- - - - - - - -	1 cup- - - - - - - -	113	37	455	28	37	23.8	10.6	1.1
Cottage (curd not pressed down):								
Lowfat (2%)- - - - - -	1 cup- - - - - - - - -	226	79	205	31	4	2.8	1.2	0.1
Uncreamed (cottage cheese dry curd, less than ½% fat)- - - - -	1 cup- - - - - - - - -	145	80	125	25	1	0.4	0.2	Tr
Cream- - - - - - - - - - - - -	1 oz- - - - - - - - - -	28	54	100	2	10	6.2	2.8	0.4
Feta- - - - - - - - - - - - -	1 oz- - - - - - - - - -	28	55	75	4	6	4.2	1.3	0.2
Mozzarella, made with:								
Whole milk- - - - - - - -	1 oz- - - - - - - - - -	28	54	80	6	6	3.7	1.9	0.2
Parmesan, grated:								
Tablespoon- - - - - - - - -	1 tbsp- - - - - - - - -	5	18	25	2	2	1.0	0.4	Tr
Ounce- - - - - - - - - - -	1 oz- - - - - - - - - -	28	18	130	12	9	5.4	2.5	0.2
Provolone- - - - - - - - - -	1 oz- - - - - - - - - -	28	41	100	7	8	4.8	2.1	0.2
Ricotta, made with:								
Whole milk- - - - - - - -	1 cup- - - - - - - -	246	72	430	28	32	20.4	8.9	0.9
Part skim milk- - - - -	1 cup- - - - - - - -	246	74	340	28	19	12.1	5.7	0.6
Swiss- - - - - - - - - - - -	1 oz- - - - - - - - - -	28	37	105	8	8	5.0	2.1	0.3
Pasteurized process cheese:								
American- - - - - - - - - -	1 oz- - - - - - - - - -	28	39	105	6	9	5.6	2.5	0.3
Swiss- - - - - - - - - - - -	1 oz- - - - - - - - - -	28	42	95	7	7	4.5	2.0	0.2
Pasteurized process cheese food, American- - - - -	1 oz- - - - - - - - - -	28	43	95	6	7	4.4	2.0	0.2
Cream, sweet:								
Half-and-half (cream and milk)- - - - - - - - - - - -	1 cup- - - - - - - -	242	81	315	7	28	17.3	8.0	1.0
	1 tbsp- - - - - - - -	15	81	20	Tr	2	1.1	0.5	0.1
Light, coffee, or table- - - -	1 cup- - - - - - - -	240	74	470	6	46	28.8	13.4	1.7
	1 tbsp- - - - - - - -	15	74	30	Tr	3	1.8	0.8	0.1
Whipping, unwhipped (volume about double when whipped):								
Light- - - - - - - - - - - - -	1 tbsp- - - - - - - -	15	64	45	Tr	5	2.9	1.4	0.1
Heavy- - - - - - - - - - - -	1 tbsp- - - - - - - -	15	58	50	Tr	6	3.5	1.6	0.2
Whipped topping, (pressurized)- - - - - - - - - - - -	1 tbsp- - - - - - - -	3	61	10	Tr	1	0.4	0.2	Tr
Cream, sour- - - - - - - - - - -	1 tbsp- - - - - - - -	12	71	25	Tr	3	1.6	0.7	0.1
Cream products, imitation (made with vegetable fat):								

(Tr indicates nutrient present in trace amounts.)

Nutrients in Indicated Quantity

Cholesterol	Carbohydrate	Calcium	Phosphorus	Iron	Potassium	Sodium	Vitamin A value (IU)	(RE)	Thiamin	Riboflavin	Niacin	Ascorbic acid
Milligrams	Grams	Milligrams	Milligrams	Milligrams	Milligrams	Milligrams	International units	Retinol equivalents	Milligrams	Milligrams	Milligrams	Milligrams
27	Tr	147	132	0.1	71	320	350	96	0.01	0.19	0.2	0
30	Tr	204	145	0.2	28	176	300	86	0.01	0.11	Tr	0
18	Tr	123	87	0.1	17	105	180	52	Tr	0.06	Tr	0
119	1	815	579	0.8	111	701	1,200	342	0.03	0.42	0.1	0
19	8	155	340	0.4	217	918	160	45	0.05	0.42	0.3	Tr
10	3	46	151	0.3	47	19	40	12	0.04	0.21	0.2	0
31	1	23	30	0.3	34	84	400	124	Tr	0.06	Tr	0
25	1	140	96	0.2	18	316	130	36	0.04	0.24	0.3	0
22	1	147	105	0.1	19	106	220	68	Tr	0.07	Tr	0
4	Tr	69	40	Tr	5	93	40	9	Tr	0.02	Tr	0
22	1	390	229	0.3	30	528	200	49	0.01	0.11	0.1	0
20	1	214	141	0.1	39	248	230	75	0.01	0.09	Tr	0
124	7	509	389	0.9	257	207	1,210	330	0.03	0.48	0.3	0
76	13	669	449	1.1	307	307	1,060	278	0.05	0.46	0.2	0
26	1	272	171	Tr	31	74	240	72	0.01	0.10	Tr	0
27	Tr	174	211	0.1	46	406	340	82	0.01	0.10	Tr	0
24	1	219	216	0.2	61	388	230	65	Tr	0.08	Tr	0
18	2	163	130	0.2	79	337	260	62	0.01	0.13	Tr	0
89	10	254	230	0.2	314	98	1,050	259	0.08	0.36	0.2	2
6	1	16	14	Tr	19	6	70	16	0.01	0.02	Tr	Tr
159	9	231	192	0.1	292	95	1,730	437	0.08	0.36	0.1	2
10	1	14	12	Tr	18	6	110	27	Tr	0.02	Tr	Tr
17	Tr	10	9	Tr	15	5	170	44	Tr	0.02	Tr	Tr
21	Tr	10	9	Tr	11	6	220	63	Tr	0.02	Tr	Tr
2	Tr	3	3	Tr	4	4	30	6	Tr	Tr	Tr	0
5	1	14	10	Tr	17	6	90	23	Tr	0.02	Tr	Tr

Nutritive Value of Foods *(Continued)*

Foods, approximate measures, units, and weight (weight of edible portion only)		Water	Food energy	Pro-tein	Fat	Fatty Acids		
						Satu-rated	Mono-unsatu-rated	Poly-unsatu-rated
	Grams	Per-cent	Cal-ories	Grams	Grams	Grams	Grams	Grams
DAIRY PRODUCTS—Con.								
Sweet:								
Creamers:								
Powdered- - - - - - - - - 1 tsp- - - - - - - - - -	2	2	10	Tr	1	0.7	Tr	Tr
Whipped topping:								
Frozen- - - - - - - - - - - 1 cup- - - - - - - -	75	50	240	1	19	16.3	1.2	0.4
1 tbsp- - - - - - - -	4	50	15	Tr	1	0.9	0.1	Tr
1 tbsp- - - - - - - -	12	75	20	Tr	2	1.6	0.2	0.1
Ice cream. See Milk desserts, frozen.								
Ice milk. See Milk desserts, frozen.								
Milk:								
Fluid:								
Whole (3.3% fat)- - - - - 1 cup- - - - - - - -	244	88	150	8	8	5.1	2.4	0.3
Lowfat (2%):								
No milk solids added- 1 cup- - - - - - - -	244	89	120	8	5	2.9	1.4	0.2
Lowfat (1%):								
No milk solids added- 1 cup- - - - - - - -	244	90	100	8	3	1.6	0.7	0.1
Nonfat (skim):								
No milk solids added- 1 cup- - - - - - - -	245	91	85	8	Tr	0.3	0.1	Tr
Buttermilk- - - - - - - - - 1 cup- - - - - - - -	245	90	100	8	2	1.3	0.6	0.1
Canned:								
Evaporated:								
Whole milk- - - - - - - 1 cup- - - - - - - -	252	74	340	17	19	11.6	5.9	0.6
Skim milk- - - - - - - 1 cup- - - - - - - -	255	79	200	19	1	0.3	0.2	Tr
Dried:								
Nonfat, instantized:								
Envelope, 3.2 oz, net wt.[6]- - - - - - - - - - 1 envelope- - - - - -	91	4	325	32	1	0.4	0.2	Tr
Milk beverages:								
Chocolate milk (commer-cial):								
Regular- - - - - - - - - - - 1 cup- - - - - - - -	250	82	210	8	8	5.3	2.5	0.3
Lowfat (2%)- - - - - - - 1 cup- - - - - - - -	250	84	180	8	5	3.1	1.5	0.2
Cocoa and chocolate-flavored beverages:								
Eggnog (commercial)- - - - 1 cup- - - - - - - -	254	74	340	10	19	11.3	5.7	0.9
Malted milk:								
Chocolate:								
Powder								
Prepared (8 oz whole milk plus ¾ powder)- - - - - - - 1 serving- - - - - -	265	81	235	9	9	5.5	2.7	0.4
Shakes, thick:								
Chocolate- - - - - - - - - - 10-oz container- -	283	72	335	9	8	4.8	2.2	0.3
Vanilla- - - - - - - - - - - - 10-oz container- -	283	74	315	11	9	5.3	2.5	0.3

(Tr indicates nutrient present in trace amounts.)

Nutrients in Indicated Quantity

Cholesterol	Carbohydrate	Calcium	Phosphorus	Iron	Potassium	Sodium	Vitamin A value (IU)	Vitamin A value (RE)	Thiamin	Riboflavin	Niacin	Ascorbic acid
Milligrams	Grams	Milligrams	Milligrams	Milligrams	Milligrams	Milligrams	International units	Retinol equivalents	Milligrams	Milligrams	Milligrams	Milligrams
0	1	Tr	8	Tr	16	4	Tr	Tr	0.00	Tr	0.0	0
0	17	5	6	0.1	14	19	[5]650	[5]65	0.00	0.00	0.0	0
0	1	Tr	Tr	Tr	1	1	[5]30	[5]3	0.00	0.00	0.0	0
1	1	14	10	Tr	19	6	Tr	Tr	Tr	0.02	Tr	Tr
33	11	291	228	0.1	370	120	310	76	0.09	0.40	0.2	2
18	12	297	232	0.1	377	122	500	139	0.10	0.40	0.2	2
10	12	300	235	0.1	381	123	500	144	0.10	0.41	0.2	2
4	12	302	247	0.1	406	126	500	149	0.09	0.34	0.2	2
9	12	285	219	0.1	371	257	80	20	0.08	0.38	0.1	2
74	25	657	510	0.5	764	267	610	136	0.12	0.80	0.5	5
9	29	738	497	0.7	845	293	1,000	298	0.11	0.79	0.4	3
17	47	1,120	896	0.3	1,552	499	[7]2,160	[7]646	0.38	1.59	0.8	5
31	26	280	251	0.6	417	149	300	73	0.09	0.41	0.3	2
17	26	284	254	0.6	422	151	500	143	0.09	0.41	0.3	2
149	34	330	278	0.5	420	138	890	203	0.09	0.48	0.3	4
34	29	304	265	0.5	500	168	330	80	0.14	0.43	0.7	2
30	60	374	357	0.9	634	314	240	59	0.13	0.63	0.4	0
33	50	413	326	0.3	517	270	320	79	0.08	0.55	0.4	0

Nutritive Value of Foods *(Continued)*

Foods, approximate measures, units, and weight (weight of edible portion only)		Water	Food energy	Pro- tein	Fat	Fatty Acids		
						Satu- rated	Mono- unsatu- rated	Poly- unsatu- rated
DAIRY PRODUCTS—Con.		Grams	Per- cent	Cal- ories	Grams	Grams	Grams	Grams
Milk desserts, frozen:								
Ice cream, vanilla:								
Regular (about 11% fat):								
Hardened	1 cup	133	61	270	5	14	8.9	4.1	0.5
	3 fl oz	50	61	100	2	5	3.4	1.6	0.2
Soft serve (frozen cus-								
tard)	1 cup	173	60	375	7	23	13.5	6.7	1.0
Rich (about 16% fat),								
hardened	1 cup	148	59	350	4	24	14.7	6.8	0.9
Ice milk, vanilla:								
Hardened (about								
4% fat)	1 cup	131	69	185	5	6	3.5	1.6	0.2
Soft serve (about								
3% fat)	1 cup	175	70	225	8	5	2.9	1.3	0.2
Sherbert (about 2% fat)	1 cup	193	66	270	2	4	2.4	1.1	0.1
Yogurt:								
With added milk solids:								
Made with lowfat milk:								
Fruit-flavored[8]	8-oz container	227	74	230	10	2	1.6	0.7	0.1
Plain	8-oz container	227	85	145	12	4	2.3	1.0	0.1
Made with nonfat milk	8-oz container	227	85	125	13	Tr	0.3	0.1	Tr
EGGS								
Eggs, large (24 oz per dozen):								
Raw:								
Whole, without shell	1 egg	50	75	80	6	6	1.7	2.2	0.7
White	1 white	33	88	15	3	Tr	0.0	0.0	0.0
Yolk	1 yolk	17	49	65	3	6	1.7	2.2	0.7
Cooked:								
Fried in butter	1 egg	46	68	95	6	7	2.7	2.7	0.8
Hard-cooked, shell								
removed	1 egg	50	75	80	6	6	1.7	2.2	0.7
Poached	1 egg	50	74	80	6	6	1.7	2.2	0.7
Scrambled (milk added)								
in butter. Also omelet	1 egg	64	73	110	7	8	3.2	2.9	0.8
FATS AND OILS								
Butter (4 sticks per lb):								
Tablespoon (⅛ stick)	1 tbsp	14	16	100	Tr	11	7.1	3.3	0.4
Pat (1 in square, ⅓ in high;								
90 per lb)	1 pat	5	16	35	Tr	4	2.5	1.2	0.2
Fats, cooking (vegetable								
shortenings)	1 tbsp	13	0	115	0	13	3.3	5.8	3.4
Lard	1 tbsp	13	0	115	0	13	5.1	5.9	1.5
Margarine:								
Imitation (about 40% fat),								
soft	1 tbsp	14	58	50	Tr	5	1.1	2.2	1.9

(Tr indicates nutrient present in trace amounts.)

Nutrients in Indicated Quantity

Cholesterol	Carbohydrate	Calcium	Phosphorus	Iron	Potassium	Sodium	Vitamin A value (IU)	Vitamin A value (RE)	Thiamin	Riboflavin	Niacin	Ascorbic acid
Milligrams	Grams	Milligrams	Milligrams	Milligrams	Milligrams	Milligrams	International units	Retinol equivalents	Milligrams	Milligrams	Milligrams	Milligrams
59	32	176	134	0.1	257	116	540	133	0.05	0.33	0.1	1
22	12	66	51	Tr	96	44	200	50	0.02	0.12	0.1	Tr
153	38	236	199	0.4	338	153	790	199	0.08	0.45	0.2	1
88	32	151	115	0.1	221	108	900	219	0.04	0.28	0.1	1
18	29	176	129	0.2	265	105	210	52	0.08	0.35	0.1	1
13	38	274	202	0.3	412	163	175	44	0.12	0.54	0.2	1
14	59	103	74	0.3	198	88	190	39	0.03	0.09	0.1	4
10	43	345	271	0.2	442	133	100	25	0.08	0.40	0.2	1
14	16	415	326	0.2	531	159	150	36	0.10	0.49	0.3	2
4	17	452	355	0.2	579	174	20	5	0.11	0.53	0.3	2
274	1	28	90	1.0	65	69	260	78	0.04	0.15	Tr	0
0	Tr	4	4	Tr	45	50	0	0	Tr	0.09	Tr	0
272	Tr	26	86	0.9	15	8	310	94	0.04	0.07	Tr	0
278	1	29	91	1.1	66	162	320	94	0.04	0.14	Tr	0
274	1	28	90	1.0	65	69	260	78	0.04	0.14	Tr	0
273	1	28	90	1.0	65	146	260	78	0.03	0.13	Tr	0
282	2	54	109	1.0	97	176	350	102	0.04	0.18	Tr	Tr
31	Tr	3	3	Tr	4	[9]116	[10]430	[10]106	Tr	Tr	Tr	0
11	Tr	1	1	Tr	1	[9]41	[10]150	[10]38	Tr	Tr	Tr	0
0	0	0	0	0.0	0	0	0	0	0.00	0.00	0.0	0
12	0	0	0	0.0	0	0	0	0	0.00	0.00	0.0	0
0	Tr	2	2	0.0	4	[11]134	[12]460	[12]139	Tr	Tr	Tr	Tr

Nutritive Value of Foods *(Continued)*

Foods, approximate measures, units, and weight (weight of edible portion only)		Water	Food energy	Pro-tein	Fat	Fatty Acids		
						Satu-rated	Mono-unsatu-rated	Poly-unsatu-rated
		Percent	*Cal-ories*	*Grams*	*Grams*	*Grams*	*Grams*	*Grams*
		Grams						

Foods, approximate measures, units, and weight (weight of edible portion only)		Water *Percent*	Food energy *Cal-ories*	Pro-tein *Grams*	Fat *Grams*	Satu-rated *Grams*	Mono-unsatu-rated *Grams*	Poly-unsatu-rated *Grams*
FATS AND OILS—Con. *(Grams)*								
Regular (about 80% fat):								
Hard (4 sticks per lb):								
Tablespoon (⅛ stick)-	1 tbsp- - - - - - - -	14	16	100	Tr	11	2.2	5.0	3.6
Pat (1 in square, ⅓ in high; 90 per lb)- - - -	1 pat- - - - - - - -	5	16	35	Tr	4	0.8	1.8	1.3
Soft- - - - - - - - - - - - -	1 tbsp- - - - - - - -	14	16	100	Tr	11	1.9	4.0	4.8
Spread (about 60% fat):								
Hard (4 sticks per lb):								
Tablespoon (⅛ stick)-	1 tbsp- - - - - - - -	14	37	75	Tr	9	2.0	3.6	2.5
Pat (1 in square, ⅓ in high; 90 per lb)- - - -	1 pat- - - - - - - -	5	37	25	Tr	3	0.7	1.3	0.9
Soft- - - - - - - - - - - - -	8-oz container- - -	227	37	1,225	1	138	29.1	71.5	31.3
	1 tbsp- - - - - - - -	14	37	75	Tr	9	1.8	4.4	1.9
Oils, salad or cooking:								
Corn- - - - - - - - - - - - -	1 tbsp- - - - - - - -	14	0	125	0	14	1.8	3.4	8.2
Olive- - - - - - - - - - - - -	1 tbsp- - - - - - - -	14	0	125	0	14	1.9	10.3	1.2
Peanut- - - - - - - - - - - -	1 tbsp- - - - - - - -	14	0	125	0	14	2.4	6.5	4.3
Safflower	1 tbsp- - - - - - - -	14	0	125	0	14	1.3	1.7	10.4
Soybean oil, hydrogenated (partially hardened)- - -	1 tbsp- - - - - - - -	14	0	125	0	14	2.1	6.0	5.3
Soybean-cottonseed oil blend, hydrogenated- - -	1 tbsp- - - - - - - -	14	0	125	0	14	2.5	4.1	6.7
Sunflower- - - - - - - - - - -	1 tbsp- - - - - - - -	14	0	125	0	14	1.4	2.7	9.2
Salad dressings:								
Commercial:								
Blue cheese- - - - - - - -	1 tbsp- - - - - - - -	15	32	75	1	8	1.5	1.8	4.2
French:								
Regular- - - - - - - - - -	1 tbsp- - - - - - - -	16	35	85	Tr	9	1.4	4.0	3.5
Low calorie- - - - - - -	1 tbsp- - - - - - - -	16	75	25	Tr	2	0.2	0.3	1.0
Italian:								
Regular- - - - - - - - - -	1 tbsp- - - - - - - -	15	34	80	Tr	9	1.3	3.7	3.2
Low calorie- - - - - - -	1 tbsp- - - - - - - -	15	86	5	Tr	Tr	Tr	Tr	Tr
Mayonnaise:								
Regular- - - - - - - - - -	1 tbsp- - - - - - - -	14	15	100	Tr	11	1.7	3.2	5.8
Imitation- - - - - - - - -	1 tbsp- - - - - - - -	15	63	35	Tr	3	0.5	0.7	1.6
Mayonnaise type- - - - -	1 tbsp- - - - - - - -	15	40	60	Tr	5	0.7	1.4	2.7
Tartar sauce- - - - - - -	1 tbsp- - - - - - - -	14	34	75	Tr	8	1.2	2.6	3.9
Thousand island:								
Regular- - - - - - - - - -	1 tbsp- - - - - - - -	16	46	60	Tr	6	1.0	1.3	3.2
Low calorie- - - - - - -	1 tbsp- - - - - - - -	15	69	25	Tr	2	0.2	0.4	0.9
Prepared from home recipe:								
Cooked type[13]-	1 tbsp- - - - - - - -	16	69	25	1	2	0.5	0.6	0.3
FISH AND SHELLFISH								
Clams:								
Raw, meat only- - - - - - -	3 oz- - - - - - - - - -	85	82	65	11	1	0.3	0.3	0.3
Canned, drained solids- - -	3 oz- - - - - - - - - -	85	77	85	13	2	0.5	0.5	0.4
Crabmeat, canned- - - - - - -	1 cup- - - - - - - -	135	77	135	23	3	0.5	0.8	1.4

(Tr indicates nutrient present in trace amounts.)

Nutrients in Indicated Quantity

Cholesterol	Carbohydrate	Calcium	Phosphorus	Iron	Potassium	Sodium	Vitamin A value (IU)	Vitamin A value (RE)	Thiamin	Riboflavin	Niacin	Ascorbic acid
Milligrams	Grams	Milligrams	Milligrams	Milligrams	Milligrams	Milligrams	International units	Retinol equivalents	Milligrams	Milligrams	Milligrams	Milligrams
0	Tr	4	3	Tr	6	[11]132	[12]460	[12]139	Tr	0.01	Tr	Tr
0	Tr	1	1	Tr	2	[11]47	[12]170	[12]50	Tr	Tr	Tr	Tr
0	Tr	4	3	0.0	5	[11]151	[12]460	[12]139	Tr	Tr	Tr	Tr
0	0	3	2	0.0	4	[11]139	[12]460	[12]139	Tr	Tr	Tr	Tr
0	0	1	1	0.0	1	[11]50	[12]170	[12]50	Tr	Tr	Tr	Tr
0	0	47	37	0.0	68	[11]2,256	[12]7,510	[12]2,254	0.02	0.06	Tr	Tr
0	0	3	2	0.0	4	[11]139	[12]460	[12]139	Tr	Tr	Tr	Tr
0	0	0	0	0.0	0	0	0	0	0.00	0.00	0.0	0
0	0	0	0	0.0	0	0	0	0	0.00	0.00	0.0	0
0	0	0	0	0.0	0	0	0	0	0.00	0.00	0.0	0
0	0	0	0	0.0	0	0	0	0	0.00	0.00	0.0	0
0	0	0	0	0.0	0	0	0	0	0.00	0.00	0.0	0
0	0	0	0	0.0	0	0	0	0	0.00	0.00	0.0	0
0	0	0	0	0.0	0	0	0	0	0.00	0.00	0.0	0
3	1	12	11	Tr	6	164	30	10	Tr	0.02	Tr	Tr
0	1	2	1	Tr	2	188	Tr	Tr	Tr	Tr	Tr	Tr
0	2	6	5	Tr	3	306	Tr	Tr	Tr	Tr	Tr	Tr
0	1	1	1	Tr	5	162	30	3	Tr	Tr	Tr	Tr
0	2	1	1	Tr	4	136	Tr	Tr	Tr	Tr	Tr	Tr
8	Tr	3	4	0.1	5	80	40	12	0.00	0.00	Tr	0
4	2	Tr	Tr	0.0	2	75	0	0	0.00	0.00	0.0	0
4	4	2	4	Tr	1	107	30	13	Tr	Tr	Tr	0
4	1	3	4	0.1	11	182	30	9	Tr	Tr	0.0	Tr
4	2	2	3	0.1	18	112	50	15	Tr	Tr	Tr	0
2	2	2	3	0.1	17	150	50	14	Tr	Tr	Tr	0
9	2	13	14	0.1	19	117	70	20	0.01	0.02	Tr	Tr
43	2	59	138	2.6	154	102	90	26	0.09	0.15	1.1	9
54	2	47	116	3.5	119	102	90	26	0.01	0.09	0.9	3
135	1	61	246	1.1	149	1,350	50	14	0.11	0.11	2.6	0

Nutritive Value of Foods *(Continued)*

Foods, approximate measures, units, and weight (weight of edible portion only)		Water	Food energy	Pro-tein	Fat	*Fatty Acids* Satu-rated	Mono-unsatu-rated	Poly-unsatu-rated
		Grams	Per-cent	Cal-ories	Grams	Grams	Grams	Grams	Grams

Foods, approximate measures, units, and weight		Grams	Per-cent	Cal-ories	Grams	Grams	Grams	Grams	Grams
FISH AND SHELLFISH—Con.									
Fish sticks, frozen, reheated, (stick, 4 by 1 by ½ in)--	1 fish stick-----	28	52	70	6	3	0.8	1.4	0.8
Flounder or Sole, baked, with lemon juice:									
With butter----------	3 oz----------	85	73	120	16	6	3.2	1.5	0.5
With margarine--------	3 oz----------	85	73	120	16	6	1.2	2.3	1.9
Without added fat------	3 oz----------	85	78	80	17	1	0.3	0.2	0.4
Haddock, breaded, fried[14]---	3 oz----------	85	61	175	17	9	2.4	3.9	2.4
Halibut, broiled, with butter and lemon juice------	3 oz----------	85	67	140	20	6	3.3	1.6	0.7
Herring, pickled--------	3 oz----------	85	59	190	17	13	4.3	4.6	3.1
Ocean perch, breaded, fried[14]	1 fillet--------	85	59	185	16	11	2.6	4.6	2.8
Oysters:									
Raw, meat only (13–19 medium Selects)--------	1 cup--------	240	85	160	20	4	1.4	0.5	1.4
Breaded, fried[14]--------	1 oyster-------	45	65	90	5	5	1.4	2.1	1.4
Salmon:									
Canned (pink), solids and liquid------------	3 oz----------	85	71	120	17	5	0.9	1.5	2.1
Baked (red)-----------	3 oz----------	85	67	140	21	5	1.2	2.4	1.4
Smoked-------------	3 oz----------	85	59	150	18	8	2.6	3.9	0.7
Sardines, Atlantic, canned in oil, drained solids-----	3 oz----------	85	62	175	20	9	2.1	3.7	2.9
Scallops, breaded, frozen, reheated-------------	6 scallops------	90	59	195	15	10	2.5	4.1	2.5
Shrimp:									
Canned, drained solids---	3 oz----------	85	70	100	21	1	0.2	0.2	0.4
French fried (7 medium)[16]-	3 oz----------	85	55	200	16	10	2.5	4.1	2.6
Trout, broiled, with butter and lemon juice---------	3 oz----------	85	63	175	21	9	4.1	2.9	1.6
Tuna, canned, drained solids:									
Oil pack, chunk light----	3 oz----------	85	61	165	24	7	1.4	1.9	3.1
Water pack, solid white--	3 oz----------	85	63	135	30	1	0.3	0.2	0.3
Tuna salad[17]-----------	1 cup--------	205	63	375	33	19	3.3	4.9	9.2
FRUITS AND FRUIT JUICES									
Apples:									
Raw:									
Unpeeled, without cores:									
2¾-in diam. (about 3 per lb with cores)--	1 apple-------	138	84	80	Tr	Tr	0.1	Tr	0.1
3¼-in diam. (about 2 per lb with cores)--	1 apple-------	212	84	125	Tr	1	0.1	Tr	0.2
Dried, sulfured--------	10 rings------	64	32	155	1	Tr	Tr	Tr	0.1
Apple juice, bottled or canned[19]-----------	1 cup--------	248	88	115	Tr	Tr	Tr	Tr	0.1
Applesauce, canned:									
Sweetened-----------	1 cup--------	255	80	195	Tr	Tr	0.1	Tr	0.1

(Tr indicates nutrient present in trace amounts.)

Nutrients in Indicated Quantity

Cholesterol	Carbohydrate	Calcium	Phosphorus	Iron	Potassium	Sodium	Vitamin A value		Thiamin	Riboflavin	Niacin	Ascorbic acid
							(IU)	(RE)				
Milligrams	Grams	Milligrams	Milligrams	Milligrams	Milligrams	Milligrams	International units	Retinol equivalents	Milligrams	Milligrams	Milligrams	Milligrams
26	4	11	58	0.3	94	53	20	5	0.03	0.05	0.6	0
68	Tr	13	187	0.3	272	145	210	54	0.05	0.08	1.6	1
55	Tr	14	187	0.3	273	151	230	69	0.05	0.08	1.6	1
59	Tr	13	197	0.3	286	101	30	10	0.05	0.08	1.7	1
75	7	34	183	1.0	270	123	70	20	0.06	0.10	2.9	0
62	Tr	14	206	0.7	441	103	610	174	0.06	0.07	7.7	1
85	0	29	128	0.9	85	850	110	33	0.04	0.18	2.8	0
66	7	31	191	1.2	241	138	70	20	0.10	0.11	2.0	0
120	8	226	343	15.6	290	175	740	223	0.34	0.43	6.0	24
35	5	49	73	3.0	64	70	150	44	0.07	0.10	1.3	4
34	0	[15]167	243	0.7	307	443	60	18	0.03	0.15	6.8	0
60	0	26	269	0.5	305	55	290	87	0.18	0.14	5.5	0
51	0	12	208	0.8	327	1,700	260	77	0.17	0.17	6.8	0
85	0	[15]371	424	2.6	349	425	190	56	0.03	0.17	4.6	0
70	10	39	203	2.0	369	298	70	21	0.11	0.11	1.6	0
128	1	98	224	1.4	104	1,955	50	15	0.01	0.03	1.5	0
168	11	61	154	2.0	189	384	90	26	0.06	0.09	2.8	0
71	Tr	26	259	1.0	297	122	230	60	0.07	0.07	2.3	1
55	0	7	199	1.6	298	303	70	20	0.04	0.09	10.1	0
48	0	17	202	0.6	255	468	110	32	0.03	0.10	13.4	0
80	19	31	281	2.5	531	877	230	53	0.06	0.14	13.3	6
0	21	10	10	0.2	159	Tr	70	7	0.02	0.02	0.1	8
0	32	15	15	0.4	244	Tr	110	11	0.04	0.03	0.2	12
0	42	9	24	0.9	288	[18]56	0	0	0.00	0.10	0.6	2
0	29	17	17	0.9	295	7	Tr	Tr	0.05	0.04	0.2	[20]2
0	51	10	18	0.9	156	8	30	3	0.03	0.07	0.5	[20]4

Nutritive Value of Foods *(Continued)*

Foods, approximate measures, units, and weight (weight of edible portion only)			Water	Food energy	Pro-tein	Fat	Fatty Acids		
							Satu-rated	Mono-unsatu-rated	Poly-unsatu-rated
		Grams	*Per-cent*	*Cal-ories*	*Grams*	*Grams*	*Grams*	*Grams*	*Grams*
FRUITS AND FRUIT JUICES—Con.									
Unsweetened	1 cup	244	88	105	Tr	Tr	Tr	Tr	Tr
Apricots:									
Raw, without pits (about 12 per lb with pits)	3 apricots	106	86	50	1	Tr	Tr	0.2	0.1
Canned (fruit and liquid):									
Heavy syrup pack	3 halves	85	78	70	Tr	Tr	Tr	Tr	Tr
Juice pack	3 halves	84	87	40	1	Tr	Tr	Tr	Tr
Dried:									
Uncooked (28 large or 37 medium halves per cup)	1 cup	130	31	310	5	1	Tr	0.3	0.1
Cooked, unsweetened, fruit and liquid	1 cup	250	76	210	3	Tr	Tr	0.2	0.1
Apricot nectar, canned	1 cup	251	85	140	1	Tr	Tr	0.1	Tr
Avocados, raw, whole, without skin and seed:									
California (about 2 per lb with skin and seed)	1 avocado	173	73	305	4	30	4.5	19.4	3.5
Florida (about 1 per lb with skin and seed)	1 avocado	304	80	340	5	27	5.3	14.8	4.5
Bananas, raw, without peel:									
Whole (about 2½ per lb with peel)	1 banana	114	74	105	1	1	0.2	Tr	0.1
Sliced	1 cup	150	74	140	2	1	0.3	0.1	0.1
Blackberries, raw	1 cup	144	86	75	1	1	0.2	0.1	0.1
Blueberries:									
Raw	1 cup	145	85	80	1	1	Tr	0.1	0.3
Frozen, sweetened	10-oz container	284	77	230	1	Tr	Tr	0.1	0.2
	1 cup	230	77	185	1	Tr	Tr	Tr	0.1
Cantaloup. See Melons.									
Cherries:									
Sour, red, pitted, canned, water pack	1 cup	244	90	90	2	Tr	0.1	0.1	0.1
Sweet, raw, without pits and stems	10 cherries	68	81	50	1	1	0.1	0.2	0.2
Cranberry juice cocktail, bottled, sweetened	1 cup	253	85	145	Tr	Tr	Tr	Tr	0.1
Cranberry sauce, sweetened, canned, strained	1 cup	277	61	420	1	Tr	Tr	0.1	0.2
Dates:									
Whole, without pits	10 dates	83	23	230	2	Tr	0.1	0.1	Tr
Figs, dried	10 figs	187	28	475	6	2	0.4	0.5	1.0
Fruit cocktail, canned, fruit and liquid:									
Heavy syrup pack	1 cup	255	80	185	1	Tr	Tr	Tr	0.1
Juice pack	1 cup	248	87	115	1	Tr	Tr	Tr	Tr

(Tr indicates nutrient present in trace amounts.)

Nutrients in Indicated Quantity

Cholesterol	Carbohydrate	Calcium	Phosphorus	Iron	Potassium	Sodium	Vitamin A value (IU)	Vitamin A value (RE)	Thiamin	Riboflavin	Niacin	Ascorbic acid
Milligrams	Grams	Milligrams	Milligrams	Milligrams	Milligrams	Milligrams	International units	Retinol equivalents	Milligrams	Milligrams	Milligrams	Milligrams
0	28	7	17	0.3	183	5	70	7	0.03	0.06	0.5	[20]3
0	12	15	20	0.6	314	1	2,770	277	0.03	0.04	0.6	11
0	18	8	10	0.3	119	3	1,050	105	0.02	0.02	0.3	3
0	10	10	17	0.3	139	3	1,420	142	0.02	0.02	0.3	4
0	80	59	152	6.1	1,791	13	9,410	941	0.01	0.20	3.9	3
0	55	40	103	4.2	1,222	8	5,910	591	0.02	0.08	2.4	4
0	36	18	23	1.0	286	8	3,300	330	0.02	0.04	0.7	[20]2
0	12	19	73	2.0	1,097	21	1,060	106	0.19	0.21	3.3	14
0	27	33	119	1.6	1,484	15	1,860	186	0.33	0.37	5.8	24
0	27	7	23	0.4	451	1	90	9	0.05	0.11	0.6	10
0	35	9	30	0.5	594	2	120	12	0.07	0.15	0.8	14
0	18	46	30	0.8	282	Tr	240	24	0.04	0.06	0.6	30
0	20	9	15	0.2	129	9	150	15	0.07	0.07	0.5	19
0	62	17	20	1.1	170	3	120	12	0.06	0.15	0.7	3
0	50	14	16	0.9	138	2	100	10	0.05	0.12	0.6	2
0	22	27	24	3.3	239	17	1,840	184	0.04	0.10	0.4	5
0	11	10	13	0.3	152	Tr	150	15	0.03	0.04	0.3	5
0	38	8	3	0.4	61	10	10	1	0.01	0.04	0.1	[21]108
0	108	11	17	0.6	72	80	60	6	0.04	0.06	0.3	6
0	61	27	33	1.0	541	2	40	4	0.07	0.08	1.8	0
0	122	269	127	4.2	1,331	21	250	25	0.13	0.16	1.3	1
0	48	15	28	0.7	224	15	520	52	0.05	0.05	1.0	5
0	29	20	35	0.5	236	10	760	76	0.03	0.04	1.0	7

Nutritive Value of Foods *(Continued)*

Foods, approximate measures, units, and weight (weight of edible portion only)	Water	Food energy	Pro-tein	Fat	Fatty Acids Satu-rated	Mono-unsatu-rated	Poly-unsatu-rated
	Grams	Per-cent	Cal-ories	Grams	Grams	Grams	Grams	Grams

FRUITS AND FRUIT JUICES—Con.

Grapefruit:								
Raw, without peel, mem-brane and seeds (3¾-in diam., 1 lb 1 oz, whole, with refuse)- - - - - - - - ½ grapefruit- - - -	120	91	40	1	Tr	Tr	Tr	Tr
Canned, sections with syrup)- - - - - - - - - - - - 1 cup- - - - - - - - -	254	84	150	1	Tr	Tr	Tr	0.1
Grapefruit juice:								
Raw- - - - - - - - - - - - - - - 1 cup- - - - - - - - -	247	90	95	1	Tr	Tr	Tr	0.1
Canned:								
Unsweetened- - - - - - - - 1 cup- - - - - - - - -	247	90	95	1	Tr	Tr	Tr	0.1
Frozen concentrate, unsweetened								
Diluted with 3 parts water by volume- - - - - - - - 1 cup- - - - - - - - -	247	89	100	1	Tr	Tr	Tr	0.1
Grapes, European type (ad-herent skin), raw;								
Thompson Seedless- - - - - 10 grapes- - - - - -	50	81	35	Tr	Tr	0.1	Tr	0.1
Tokay and Emperor, seeded types- - - - - - - - - - - - - 10 grapes- - - - - -	57	81	40	Tr	Tr	0.1	Tr	0.1
Grape juice:								
Canned or bottled- - - - - - 1 cup- - - - - - - - -	253	84	155	1	Tr	0.1	Tr	0.1
Kiwifruit, raw, without skin (about 5 per lb with skin)- 1 kiwifruit- - - - - -	76	83	45	1	Tr	Tr	0.1	0.1
Lemons, raw, without peel and seeds (about 4 per lb with peel and seeds)- - - - - - - - 1 lemon- - - - - - -	58	89	15	1	Tr	Tr	Tr	0.1
Lemon juice:								
Raw- - - - - - - - - - - - - - - 1 cup- - - - - - - - -	244	91	60	1	Tr	Tr	Tr	Tr
Canned or bottled, unsweet-ened- - - - - - - - - - - - - 1 cup- - - - - - - - -	244	92	50	1	1	0.1	Tr	0.2
1 tbsp- - - - - - - - -	15	92	5	Tr	Tr	Tr	Tr	Tr
Lime juice:								
Raw- - - - - - - - - - - - - - - 1 cup- - - - - - - - -	246	90	65	1	Tr	Tr	Tr	0.1
Canned, unsweetened- - - - 1 cup- - - - - - - - -	246	93	50	1	1	0.1	0.1	0.2
Mangos, raw, without skin and seed (about 1½ per lb with skin and seed)- - - - 1 mango- - - - - -	207	82	135	1	1	0.1	0.2	0.1
Melons, raw, without rind and cavity contents:								
Cantaloup, orange-fleshed (5-in diam., 2⅓ lb, whole, with rind and cavity con-tents)- - - - - - - - - - - - - ½ melon- - - - - - -	267	90	95	2	1	0.1	0.1	0.3
Honeydew (6½-in diam., 5¼ lb, whole, with rind and cavity contents)- - - - - - ¹⁄₁₀ melon- - - - - - -	129	90	45	1	Tr	Tr	Tr	0.1

(Tr indicates nutrient present in trace amounts.)

Nutrients in Indicated Quantity

Cholesterol	Carbohydrate	Calcium	Phosphorus	Iron	Potassium	Sodium	Vitamin A value (IU)	Vitamin A value (RE)	Thiamin	Riboflavin	Niacin	Ascorbic acid
Milligrams	Grams	Milligrams	Milligrams	Milligrams	Milligrams	Milligrams	International units	Retinol equivalents	Milligrams	Milligrams	Milligrams	Milligrams
0	10	14	10	0.1	167	Tr	[22]10	[22]1	0.04	0.02	0.3	41
0	39	36	25	1.0	328	5	Tr	Tr	0.10	0.05	0.6	54
0	23	22	37	0.5	400	2	20	2	0.10	0.05	0.5	94
0	22	17	27	0.5	378	2	20	2	0.10	0.05	0.6	72
0	24	20	35	0.3	336	2	20	2	0.10	0.05	0.5	83
0	9	6	7	0.1	93	1	40	4	0.05	0.03	0.2	5
0	10	6	7	0.1	105	1	40	4	0.05	0.03	0.2	6
0	38	23	28	0.6	334	8	20	2	0.07	0.09	0.7	[20]Tr
0	11	20	30	0.3	252	4	130	13	0.02	0.04	1.4	74
0	5	15	9	0.3	80	1	20	2	0.02	0.01	0.1	31
0	21	17	15	0.1	303	2	50	5	0.07	0.02	0.2	112
0	16	27	22	0.3	249	[23]51	40	4	0.10	0.02	0.5	61
0	1	2	1	Tr	15	[23]3	Tr	Tr	0.01	Tr	Tr	4
0	22	22	17	0.1	268	2	20	2	0.05	0.02	0.2	72
0	16	30	25	0.6	185	[23]39	40	4	0.08	0.01	0.4	16
0	35	21	23	0.3	323	4	8,060	806	0.12	0.12	1.2	57
0	22	29	45	0.6	825	24	8,610	861	0.10	0.06	1.5	113
0	12	8	13	0.1	350	13	50	5	0.10	0.02	0.8	32

Nutritive Value of Foods *(Continued)*

Foods, approximate measures, units, and weight (weight of edible portion only)		Water	Food energy	Pro-tein	Fat	Fatty Acids		
						Satu-rated	Mono-unsatu-rated	Poly-unsatu-rated
		Per-cent	*Cal-ories*	*Grams*	*Grams*	*Grams*	*Grams*	*Grams*
FRUITS AND FRUIT JUICES—Con.	*Grams*							
Nectarines, raw, without pits (about 3 per lb with pits) 1 nectarine- - - - -	136	86	65	1	1	0.1	0.2	0.3
Oranges, raw:								
Whole, without peel and seeds (2⅞-in diam., about 2½ per lb, with peel and seeds)- - - - - - - - - - - 1 orange- - - - - - -	131	87	60	1	Tr	Tr	Tr	Tr
Orange juice:								
Raw, all varieties- - - - - - - 1 cup- - - - - - - - -	248	88	110	2	Tr	0.1	0.1	0.1
Canned, unsweetened- - - - 1 cup- - - - - - - - -	249	89	105	1	Tr	Tr	0.1	0.1
Chilled- - - - - - - - - - - - - 1 cup- - - - - - - - -	249	88	110	2	1	0.1	0.1	0.2
Frozen concentrate:								
Diluted with 3 parts water by volume- - - - - - - - - 1 cup- - - - - - - - -	249	88	110	2	Tr	Tr	Tr	Tr
Orange and grapefruit juice, canned- - - - - - - - - - - - - 1 cup- - - - - - - - -	247	89	105	1	Tr	Tr	Tr	Tr
Papayas, raw, ½-in cubes 1 cup- - - - - - - - -	140	86	65	1	Tr	0.1	0.1	Tr
Peaches:								
Raw: Whole, 2½-in diam., peeled, pitted (about 4 per lb with peels and pits)- - - - - - - - - - - 1 peach- - - - - - - -	87	88	35	1	Tr	Tr	Tr	Tr
Canned, fruit and liquid:								
Heavy syrup pack- - - - - 1 half- - - - - - - - -	81	79	60	Tr	Tr	Tr	Tr	Tr
Juice pack- - - - - - - - - - 1 half- - - - - - - - -	77	87	35	Tr	Tr	Tr	Tr	Tr
Dried:								
Uncooked- - - - - - - - - - 1 cup- - - - - - - - -	160	32	380	6	1	0.1	0.4	0.6
Cooked, unsweetened, fruit and liquid- - - - - 1 cup- - - - - - - - -	258	78	200	3	1	0.1	0.2	0.3
Frozen, sliced, sweetened- 10-oz container- -	284	75	265	2	Tr	Tr	0.1	0.2
1 cup- - - - - - - - -	250	75	235	2	Tr	Tr	0.1	0.2
Pears:								
Raw, with skin, cored:								
Bartlett, 2½-in diam. (about 2½ per lb with cores and stems)- - - - 1 pear- - - - - - - - -	166	84	100	1	1	Tr	0.1	0.2
Bosc, 2½-in diam. (about 3 per lb with cores and stems)- - - - - - - - - - - 1 pear- - - - - - - - -	141	84	85	1	1	Tr	0.1	0.1
D'Anjou, 3-in diam. (about 2 per lb with cores and stems)- - - - 1 pear- - - - - - - - -	200	84	120	1	1	Tr	0.2	0.2
Canned, fruit and liquid:								
Heavy syrup pack- - - - - 1 half- - - - - - - -	79	80	60	Tr	Tr	Tr	Tr	Tr
Juice pack- - - - - - - - - - 1 half- - - - - - - -	77	86	40	Tr	Tr	Tr	Tr	Tr
Pineapple:								
Raw, diced- - - - - - - - - - - 1 cup- - - - - - - - -	155	87	75	1	1	Tr	0.1	0.2

(Tr indicates nutrient present in trace amounts.)

Nutrients in Indicated Quantity

Cho-les-terol	Carbo-hydrate	Calcium	Phos-phorus	Iron	Potas-sium	Sodium	Vitamin A value		Thiamin	Ribo-flavin	Niacin	Ascorbic acid
							(IU)	(RE)				
Milli-grams	Grams	Milli-grams	Milli-grams	Milli-grams	Milli-grams	Milli-grams	Inter-national units	Retinol equiva-lents	Milli-grams	Milli-grams	Milli-grams	Milli-grams
0	16	7	22	0.2	288	Tr	1,000	100	0.02	0.06	1.3	7
0	15	52	18	0.1	237	Tr	270	27	0.11	0.05	0.4	70
0	26	27	42	0.5	496	2	500	50	0.22	0.07	1.0	124
0	25	20	35	1.1	436	5	440	44	0.15	0.07	0.8	86
0	25	25	27	0.4	473	2	190	19	0.28	0.05	0.7	82
0	27	22	40	0.2	473	2	190	19	0.20	0.04	0.5	97
0	25	20	35	1.1	390	7	290	29	0.14	0.07	0.8	72
0	17	35	12	0.3	247	9	400	40	0.04	0.04	0.5	92
0	10	4	10	0.1	171	Tr	470	47	0.01	0.04	0.9	6
0	16	2	9	0.2	75	5	270	27	0.01	0.02	0.5	2
0	9	5	13	0.2	99	3	290	29	0.01	0.01	0.4	3
0	98	45	190	6.5	1,594	11	3,460	346	Tr	0.34	7.0	8
0	51	23	98	3.4	826	5	510	51	0.01	0.05	3.9	10
0	68	9	31	1.1	369	17	810	81	0.04	0.10	1.9	[21]268
0	60	8	28	0.9	325	15	710	71	0.03	0.09	1.6	[21]236
0	25	18	18	0.4	208	Tr	30	3	0.03	0.07	0.2	7
0	21	16	16	0.4	176	Tr	30	3	0.03	0.06	0.1	6
0	30	22	22	0.5	250	Tr	40	4	0.04	0.08	0.2	8
0	15	4	6	0.2	51	4	Tr	Tr	0.01	0.02	0.2	1
0	10	7	9	0.2	74	3	Tr	Tr	0.01	0.01	0.2	1
0	19	11	11	0.6	175	2	40	4	0.14	0.06	0.7	24

Nutritive Value of Foods *(Continued)*

Foods, approximate measures, units, and weight (weight of edible portion only)		Water	Food energy	Pro- tein	Fat	Fatty Acids		
						Satu- rated	Mono- unsatu- rated	Poly- unsatu- rated
		Grams	Per- cent	Cal- ories	Grams	Grams	Grams	Grams	Grams

		Grams	Per- cent	Cal- ories	Grams	Grams	Grams	Grams	Grams
FRUITS AND FRUIT JUICES—Con.									
Canned, fruit and liquid:									
Heavy syrup pack:									
Slices- - - - - - - - - - -	1 slice- - - - - - - - -	58	79	45	Tr	Tr	Tr	Tr	Tr
Juice pack:									
Slices- - - - - - - - - - -	1 slice- - - - - - - -	58	84	35	Tr	Tr	Tr	Tr	Tr
Pineapple juice, unsweetened, canned- - - - - - - - - - - - - -	1 cup- - - - - - - - -	250	86	140	1	Tr	Tr	Tr	0.1
Plantains, without peel:									
Cooked, boiled, sliced- - - -	1 cup- - - - - - - - -	154	67	180	1	Tr	0.1	Tr	0.1
Plums, without pits:									
Raw:									
2⅛-in diam. (about 6½ per lb with pits)- - - - - - -	1 plum- - - - - - - -	66	85	35	1	Tr	Tr	0.3	0.1
1½-in diam. (about 15 per lb with pits)- - - - - - -	1 plum- - - - - - - -	28	85	15	Tr	Tr	Tr	0.1	Tr
Canned, purple, fruit and liquid:									
Heavy syrup pack- - - - -	3 plums- - - - - - - -	133	76	120	Tr	Tr	Tr	0.1	Tr
Juice pack- - - - - - - - - -	3 plums- - - - - - - -	95	84	55	Tr	Tr	Tr	Tr	Tr
Prunes, dried:									
Uncooked- - - - - - - - - - -	4 extra large or 5 large prunes- - -	49	32	115	1	Tr	Tr	0.2	0.1
Cooked, unsweetened, fruit and liquid- - - - - - - - - -	1 cup- - - - - - - - -	212	70	225	2	Tr	Tr	0.3	0.1
Prune juice, canned or bottled- - - - - - - - - - -	1 cup- - - - - - - - -	256	81	180	2	Tr	Tr	0.1	Tr
Raisins, seedless:									
Cup, not pressed down- - -	1 cup- - - - - - - - -	145	15	435	5	1	0.2	Tr	0.2
Packet, ½ oz (1½ tbsp)- - -	1 packet- - - - - - -	14	15	40	Tr	Tr	Tr	Tr	Tr
Raspberries:									
Raw- - - - - - - - - - - - - - -	1 cup- - - - - - - - -	123	87	60	1	1	Tr	0.1	0.4
Frozen, sweetened- - - - - -	10-oz container- -	284	73	295	2	Tr	Tr	Tr	0.3
Rhubarb, cooked, added sugar- - - - - - - - -	1 cup- - - - - - - - -	240	68	280	1	Tr	Tr	Tr	0.1
Strawberries:									
Raw, capped, whole- - - - -	1 cup- - - - - - - - -	149	92	45	1	1	Tr	0.1	0.3
Frozen, sweetened, sliced-	10-oz container- -	284	73	275	2	Tr	Tr	0.1	0.2
	1 cup- - - - - - - - -	255	73	245	1	Tr	Tr	Tr	0.2
Tangerines:									
Raw, without peel and seeds (2⅜-in diam., (about 4 per lb, with peel and seeds)-	1 tangerine- - - - -	84	88	35	1	Tr	Tr	Tr	Tr
Watermelon, raw, without rind and seeds:									
Piece (4 by 8 in wedge with rind and seeds; ¹⁄₁₆ of 32⅝- lb melon, 10 by 16 in)- -	1 piece- - - - - - - -	482	92	155	3	2	0.3	0.2	1.0

(Tr indicates nutrient present in trace amounts.)

Nutrients in Indicated Quantity

Cho-les-terol	Carbo-hydrate	Calcium	Phos-phorus	Iron	Potas-sium	Sodium	Vitamin A value (IU)	Vitamin A value (RE)	Thiamin	Ribo-flavin	Niacin	Ascorbic acid
Milli-grams	Grams	Milli-grams	Milli-grams	Milli-grams	Milli-grams	Milli-grams	Inter-national units	Retinol equiva-lents	Milli-grams	Milli-grams	Milli-grams	Milli-grams
0	12	8	4	0.2	60	1	10	1	0.05	0.01	0.2	4
0	9	8	3	0.2	71	1	20	2	0.06	0.01	0.2	6
0	34	43	20	0.7	335	3	10	1	0.14	0.06	0.6	27
0	48	3	43	0.9	716	8	1,400	140	0.07	0.08	1.2	17
0	9	3	7	0.1	114	Tr	210	21	0.03	0.06	0.3	6
0	4	1	3	Tr	48	Tr	90	9	0.01	0.03	0.1	3
0	31	12	17	1.1	121	25	340	34	0.02	0.05	0.4	1
0	14	10	14	0.3	146	1	960	96	0.02	0.06	0.4	3
0	31	25	39	1.2	365	2	970	97	0.04	0.08	1.0	2
0	60	49	74	2.4	708	4	650	65	0.05	0.21	1.5	6
0	45	31	64	3.0	707	10	10	1	0.04	0.18	2.0	10
0	115	71	141	3.0	1,089	17	10	1	0.23	0.13	1.2	5
0	11	7	14	0.3	105	2	Tr	Tr	0.02	0.01	0.1	Tr
0	14	27	15	0.7	187	Tr	160	16	0.04	0.11	1.1	31
0	74	43	48	1.8	324	3	170	17	0.05	0.13	0.7	47
0	75	348	19	0.5	230	2	170	17	0.04	0.06	0.5	8
0	10	21	28	0.6	247	1	40	4	0.03	0.10	0.3	84
0	74	31	37	1.7	278	9	70	7	0.05	0.14	1.1	118
0	66	28	33	1.5	250	8	60	6	0.04	0.13	1.0	106
0	9	12	8	0.1	132	1	770	77	0.09	0.02	0.1	26
0	35	39	43	0.8	559	10	1,760	176	0.39	0.10	1.0	46

Nutritive Value of Foods *(Continued)*

Foods, approximate measures, units, and weight (weight of edible portion only)		Water	Food energy	Pro-tein	Fat	Fatty Acids		
						Satu-rated	Mono-unsatu-rated	Poly-unsatu-rated
		Grams	Per-cent	Cal-ories	Grams	Grams	Grams	Grams	Grams

GRAIN PRODUCTS

Foods, approximate measures, units, and weight (weight of edible portion only)		Grams	Per-cent	Cal-ories	Grams	Grams	Grams	Grams	Grams
Bagels, plain or water, enriched, 3½-in diam.[24]	1 bagel	68	29	200	7	2	0.3	0.5	0.7
Barley, pearled, light, uncooked	1 cup	200	11	700	16	2	0.3	0.2	0.9
Biscuits, baking powder, 2-in diam. (enriched flour, vegetable shortening):									
From home recipe	1 biscuit	28	28	100	2	5	1.2	2.0	1.3
Breadcrumbs, enriched: Soft. See White bread.									
Breads:									
Boston brown bread, canned, slice, 3¼ in by ½ in[25]	1 slice	45	45	95	2	1	0.3	0.1	0.1
Cracked-wheat bread (¾ enriched wheat flour, ⅓ enriched wheat flour):[26]									
Slice (18 per loaf)	1 slice	25	35	65	2	1	0.2	0.2	0.3
French or vienna bread, enriched:[25]									
Slice:									
French, 5 by 2½ by 1 in	1 slice	35	34	100	3	1	0.3	0.4	0.5
Vienna, 4¾ by 4 by ½ in	1 slice	25	34	70	2	1	0.2	0.3	0.3
Italian bread, enriched:									
Slice, 4½ by 3¼ by ¾ in	1 slice	30	32	85	3	Tr	Tr	Tr	0.1
Mixed grain bread, enriched:[25]									
Slice (18 per loaf)	1 slice	25	37	65	2	1	0.2	0.2	0.4
Oatmeal bread, enriched:[25]									
Slice (18 per loaf)	1 slice	25	37	65	2	1	0.2	0.4	0.5
Pita bread, enriched, white, 6½-in diam.	1 pita	60	31	165	6	1	0.1	0.1	0.4
Pumpernickel (⅔ rye flour, ⅓ enriched wheat flour):[25]									
Slice, 5 by 4 by ⅜ in	1 slice	32	37	80	3	1	0.2	0.3	0.5
Raisin bread, enriched:[25]									
Slice (18 per loaf)	1 slice	25	33	65	2	1	0.2	0.3	0.4
Rye bread, light (⅔ enriched wheat flour, ⅓ rye flour):[25]									
Slice, 4¾ by 3¾ by ⁷⁄₁₆ in	1 slice	25	37	65	2	1	0.2	0.3	0.3
Wheat bread, enriched:[25]									
Slice (18 per loaf)	1 slice	25	37	65	2	1	0.2	0.4	0.3

(Tr indicates nutrient present in trace amounts.)

Nutrients in Indicated Quantity

Cholesterol	Carbohydrate	Calcium	Phosphorus	Iron	Potassium	Sodium	Vitamin A value		Thiamin	Riboflavin	Niacin	Ascorbic acid
							(IU)	(RE)				
Milligrams	Grams	Milligrams	Milligrams	Milligrams	Milligrams	Milligrams	International units	Retinol equivalents	Milligrams	Milligrams	Milligrams	Milligrams
0	38	29	46	1.8	50	245	0	0	0.26	0.20	2.4	0
0	158	32	378	4.2	320	6	0	0	0.24	0.10	6.2	0
Tr	13	47	36	0.7	32	195	10	3	0.08	0.08	0.8	Tr
3	21	41	72	0.9	131	113	[26]0	[26]0	0.06	0.04	0.7	0
0	12	16	32	0.7	34	106	Tr	Tr	0.10	0.09	0.8	Tr
0	18	39	30	1.1	32	203	Tr	Tr	0.16	0.12	1.4	Tr
0	13	28	21	0.8	23	145	Tr	Tr	0.12	0.09	1.0	Tr
0	17	5	23	0.8	22	176	0	0	0.12	0.07	1.0	0
0	12	27	55	0.8	56	106	Tr	Tr	0.10	0.10	1.1	Tr
0	12	15	31	0.7	39	124	0	0	0.12	0.07	0.9	0
0	33	49	60	1.4	71	339	0	0	0.27	0.12	2.2	0
0	16	23	71	0.9	141	177	0	0	0.11	0.17	1.1	0
0	13	25	22	0.8	59	92	Tr	Tr	0.08	0.15	1.0	Tr
0	12	20	36	0.7	51	175	0	0	0.10	0.08	0.8	0
0	12	32	47	0.9	35	138	Tr	Tr	0.12	0.08	1.2	Tr

Nutritive Value of Foods *(Continued)*

Foods, approximate measures, units, and weight (weight of edible portion only)			*Water*	*Food energy*	*Protein*	*Fat*	Fatty Acids: *Saturated*	Fatty Acids: *Monounsaturated*	Fatty Acids: *Polyunsaturated*
GRAIN PRODUCTS—Con.		*Grams*	*Percent*	*Calories*	*Grams*	*Grams*	*Grams*	*Grams*	*Grams*
Wheat bread, enriched:[25]									
Slice (18 per loaf)	1 slice	25	37	65	2	1	0.3	0.4	0.2
Whole-wheat bread:[25]									
Slice (16 per loaf)	1 slice	28	38	70	3	1	0.4	0.4	0.3
Breakfast cereals:									
Hot type, cooked:									
Corn, (hominy) grits:									
Regular and quick, enriched	1 cup	242	85	145	3	Tr	Tr	0.1	0.2
Instant, plain	1 pkt	137	85	80	2	Tr	Tr	Tr	0.1
Cream of Wheat®:									
Regular, quick, instant	1 cup	244	86	140	4	Tr	0.1	Tr	0.2
Mix'n Eat, plain	1 pkt	142	82	100	3	Tr	Tr	Tr	0.1
Malt-O-Meal®	1 cup	240	88	120	4	Tr	Tr	Tr	0.1
Oatmeal or rolled oats:									
Regular, quick, instant, nonfortified	1 cup	234	85	145	6	2	0.4	0.8	1.0
Ready to eat:									
All-Bran® (about ⅓ cup)	1 oz	28	3	70	4	1	0.1	0.1	0.3
Cap'n Crunch® (about ¾ cup)	1 oz	28	3	120	1	3	1.7	0.3	0.4
Cheerios® (about 1¼ cup)	1 oz	28	5	110	4	2	0.3	0.6	0.7
Corn Flakes (about 1¼ cup):									
Kellogg's®	1 oz	28	3	110	2	Tr	Tr	Tr	Tr
40% Bran Flakes:									
Kellogg's® (about ¾ cup)	1 oz	28	3	90	4	1	0.1	0.1	0.3
Post® (about ⅔ cup)	1 oz	28	3	90	3	Tr	0.1	0.1	0.2
Froot Loops® (about 1 cup)	1 oz	28	3	110	2	1	0.2	0.1	0.1
Golden Grahams® (about ¾ cup)	1 oz	28	2	110	2	1	0.7	0.1	0.2
Grape-Nuts® (about ¼ cup)	1 oz	28	3	100	3	Tr	Tr	Tr	0.1
Honey Nut Cheerios® (about ¾ cup)	1 oz	28	3	105	3	1	0.1	0.3	0.3
Lucky Charms® (about 1 cup)	1 oz	28	3	110	3	1	0.2	0.4	0.4
Nature Valley® Granola (about ⅓ cup)	1 oz	28	4	125	3	5	3.3	0.7	0.7
100% Natural Cereal (about ¼ cup)	1 oz	28	2	135	3	6	4.1	1.2	0.5

(Tr indicates nutrient present in trace amounts.)

Nutrients in Indicated Quantity

Cholesterol	Carbohydrate	Calcium	Phosphorus	Iron	Potassium	Sodium	Vitamin A value		Thiamin	Riboflavin	Niacin	Ascorbic acid
							(IU)	(RE)				
Milligrams	Grams	Milligrams	Milligrams	Milligrams	Milligrams	Milligrams	International units	Retinol equivalents	Milligrams	Milligrams	Milligrams	Milligrams
0	12	32	27	0.7	28	129	Tr	Tr	0.12	0.08	0.9	Tr
0	13	20	74	1.0	50	180	Tr	Tr	0.10	0.06	1.1	Tr
0	31	0	29	[27]1.5	53	[28]0	[29]0	[29]0	[27]0.24	[27]0.15	[27]2.0	0
0	18	7	16	[27]1.0	29	343	0	0	[27]0.18	[27]0.08	[27]1.3	0
0	29	[30]54	[31]43	[30]10.9	46	[31,32]5	0	0	[30]0.24	[30]0.07	[30]1.5	0
0	21	[30]20	[30]20	[30]8.1	38	241	[30]1,250	[30]376	[30]0.43	[30]0.28	[30]5.0	0
0	26	5	[30]24	[30]9.6	31	[33]2	0	0	[30]0.48	[30]0.24	[30]5.8	0
0	19	178		1.6	131	[34]2	40	4	0.26	0.05	0.3	0
0	21	23	264	[30]4.5	350	320	[30]1,250	[30]375	[30]0.37	[30]0.43	[30]5.0	[30]15
0	23	5	36	[27]7.5	37	213	40	4	[27]0.50	[27]0.55	[27]6.6	0
0	20	48	134	[30]4.5	101	307	[30]1,250	[30]375	[30]0.37	[30]0.43	[30]5.0	[30]15
0	24	1	18	[30]1.8	26	351	[30]1,250	[30]375	[30]0.37	[30]0.43	[30]5.0	[30]15
0	22	14	139	[30]8.1	180	264	[30]1,250	[30]375	[30]0.37	[30]0.43	[30]5.0	0
0	22	12	179	[30]4.5	151	260	[30]1,250	[30]375	[30]0.37	[30]0.43	[30]5.0	0
0	25	3	24	[30]4.5	26	145	[30]1,250	[30]375	[30]0.37	[30]0.43	[30]5.0	[30]15
Tr	24	17	41	[30]4.5	63	346	[30]1,250	[30]375	[30]0.37	[30]0.43	[30]5.0	[30]15
0	23	11	71	1.2	95	197	[30]1,250	[30]375	[30]0.37	[30]0.43	[30]5.0	0
0	23	20	105	[30]4.5	99	257	[30]1,250	[30]375	[30]0.37	[30]0.43	[30]5.0	[30]15
0	23	32	79	[30]4.5	59	201	[30]1,250	[30]375	[30]0.37	[30]0.43	[30]5.0	[30]15
0	19	18	89	0.9	98	58	20	2	0.10	0.05	0.2	0
Tr	18	49	104	0.8	140	12	20	2	0.09	0.15	0.6	0

Nutritive Value of Foods *(Continued)*

Foods, approximate measures, units, and weight (weight of edible portion only)		Water	Food energy	Pro-tein	Fat	Fatty Acids		
						Satu-rated	Mono-unsatu-rated	Poly-unsatu-rated
		Grams	Per-cent	Cal-ories	Grams	Grams	Grams	Grams	Grams

		Grams	Per-cent	Cal-ories	Grams	Grams	Grams	Grams	Grams
GRAIN PRODUCTS—Con.									
Product 19® (about ¾ cup)	1 oz	28	3	110	3	Tr	Tr	Tr	0.1
Raisin Bran:									
Kellogg's® (about ¾ cup)	1 oz	28	8	90	3	1	0.1	0.1	0.3
Post® (about ½ cup)	1 oz	28	9	85	3	1	0.1	0.1	0.3
Rice Krispies® (about 1 cup)	1 oz	28	2	110	2	Tr	Tr	Tr	0.1
Shredded Wheat (about ⅔ cup)	1 oz	28	5	100	3	1	0.1	0.1	0.3
Special K® (about 1⅓ cup)	1 oz	28	2	110	6	Tr	Tr	Tr	Tr
Super Sugar Crisp® (about ⅞ cup)	1 oz	28	2	105	2	Tr	Tr	Tr	0.1
Sugar Frosted Flakes, Kellogg's® (about ¾ cup)	1 oz	28	3	110	1	Tr	Tr	Tr	Tr
Sugar Smacks® (about ¾ cup)	1 oz	28	3	105	2	1	0.1	0.1	0.2
Total® (about 1 cup)	1 oz	28	4	100	3	1	0.1	0.1	0.3
Trix® (about 1 cup)	1 oz	28	3	110	2	Tr	0.2	0.1	0.1
Wheaties® (about 1 cup)	1 oz	28	5	100	3	Tr	0.1	Tr	0.2
Buckwheat flour, light, sifted	1 cup	98	12	340	6	1	0.2	0.4	0.4
Bulgur, uncooked	1 cup	170	10	600	19	3	1.2	0.3	1.2
Cakes prepared from cake mixes with enriched flour:[35]									
Angelfood:									
Piece, 1/12 of cake	1 piece	53	38	125	3	Tr	Tr	Tr	0.1
Coffeecake, crumb:									
Piece, ⅙ of cake	1 piece	72	30	230	5	7	2.0	2.8	1.6
Devil's food with chocolate frosting:									
Piece, 1/16 of cake	1 piece	69	24	235	3	8	3.5	3.2	1.2
Cupcake, 2½-in diam.	1 cupcake	35	24	120	2	4	1.8	1.6	0.6
Gingerbread:									
Piece, ⅑ of cake	1 piece	63	37	175	2	4	1.1	1.8	1.2
Yellow with chocolate frosting:									
Piece, 1/16 of cake	1 piece	69	26	235	3	8	3.0	3.0	1.4
Cakes prepared from home recipes using enriched flour:									
Carrot, with cream cheese frosting:[36]									
Piece, 1/16 of cake	1 piece	96	23	385	4	21	4.1	8.4	6.7

(Tr indicates nutrient present in trace amounts.)

Nutrients in Indicated Quantity

Cholesterol	Carbohydrate	Calcium	Phosphorus	Iron	Potassium	Sodium	Vitamin A value (IU)	Vitamin A value (RE)	Thiamin	Riboflavin	Niacin	Ascorbic acid
Milligrams	Grams	Milligrams	Milligrams	Milligrams	Milligrams	Milligrams	International units	Retinol equivalents	Milligrams	Milligrams	Milligrams	Milligrams
0	24	3	40	[30]18.0	44	325	[30]5,000	[30]1,501	[30]1.50	[30]1.70	[30]20.0	[30]60
0	21	10	105	[30]3.5	147	207	[30]960	[30]288	[30]0.28	[30]0.34	[30]3.9	0
0	21	13	119	[30]4.5	175	185	[30]1,250	[30]375	[30]0.37	[30]0.43	[30]5.0	0
0	25	4	34	[30]1.8	29	340	[30]1,250	[30]375	[30]0.37	[30]0.43	[30]5.0	[30]15
0	23	11	100	1.2	102	3	0	0	0.07	0.08	1.5	0
Tr	21	8	55	[30]4.5	49	265	[30]1,250	[30]375	[30]0.37	[30]0.43	[30]5.0	[30]15
0	26	6	52	[30]1.8	105	25	[30]1,250	[30]375	[30]0.37	[30]0.43	[30]5.0	0
0	26	1	21	[30]1.8	18	230	[30]1,250	[30]375	[30]0.37	[30]0.43	[30]5.0	[30]15
0	25	3	31	[30]1.8	42	75	[30]1,250	[30]375	[30]0.37	[30]0.43	[30]5.0	[30]15
0	22	48	118	[30]18.0	106	352	[30]5,000	[30]1,501	[30]1.50	[30]1.70	[30]20.0	[30]60
0	25	6	19	[30]4.5	27	181	[30]1,250	[30]375	[30]0.37	[30]0.43	[30]5.0	[30]15
0	23	43	98	[30]4.5	106	354	[30]1,250	[30]375	[30]0.37	[30]0.43	[30]5.0	[30]15
0	78	11	86	1.0	314	2	0	0	0.08	0.04	0.4	0
0	129	49	575	9.5	389	7	0	0	0.48	0.24	7.7	0
0	29	44	91	0.2	71	269	0	0	0.03	0.11	0.1	0
47	38	44	125	1.2	78	310	120	32	0.14	0.15	1.3	Tr
37	40	41	72	1.4	90	181	100	31	0.07	0.10	0.6	Tr
19	20	21	37	0.7	46	92	50	16	0.04	0.05	0.3	Tr
1	32	57	63	1.2	173	192	0	0	0.09	0.11	0.8	Tr
36	40	63	126	1.0	75	157	100	29	0.08	0.10	0.7	Tr
74	48	44	62	1.3	108	279	140	15	0.11	0.12	0.9	1

Nutritive Value of Foods *(Continued)*

Foods, approximate measures, units, and weight (weight of edible portion only)			Water	Food energy	Protein	Fat	Fatty Acids: Saturated	Fatty Acids: Monounsaturated	Fatty Acids: Polyunsaturated
		Grams	*Percent*	*Calories*	*Grams*	*Grams*	*Grams*	*Grams*	*Grams*
GRAIN PRODUCTS—Con.									
Fruitcake, dark:[36]									
Piece, 1/32 of cake, 2/3-in arc	1 piece	43	18	165	2	7	1.5	3.6	1.6
Plain sheet cake:[37]									
Without frosting:									
Piece, 1/9 of cake	1 piece	86	25	315	4	12	3.3	5.0	2.8
With uncooked white frosting:									
Piece, 1/9 of cake	1 piece	121	21	445	4	14	4.6	5.6	2.9
Pound:[38]									
Slice, 1/17 of loaf	1 slice	30	22	120	2	5	1.2	2.4	1.6
Cakes, commercial, made with enriched flour:									
Pound:									
Slice, 1/17 of loaf	1 slice	29	24	110	2	5	3.0	1.7	0.2
Snack cakes:									
Devil's food with creme filling (2 small cakes per pkg)	1 small cake	28	20	105	1	4	1.7	1.5	0.6
Sponge with creme filling (2 small cakes per pkg)	1 small cake	42	19	155	1	5	2.3	2.1	0.5
White with white frosting:									
Piece, 1/16 of cake	1 piece	71	24	260	3	9	2.1	3.8	2.6
Yellow with chocolate frosting:									
Piece, 1/16 of cake	1 piece	69	23	245	2	11	5.7	3.7	0.6
Cheesecake:									
Piece, 1/12 of cake	1 piece	92	46	280	5	18	9.9	5.4	1.2
Cookies made with enriched flour:									
Brownies with nuts:									
Commercial, with frosting, 1 1/2 by 1 3/4 by 7/8 in	1 brownie	25	13	100	1	4	1.6	2.0	0.6
From home recipe, 1 3/4 by 1 3/4 by 7/8 in[36]	1 brownie	20	10	95	1	6	1.4	2.8	1.2
Chocolate chip:									
Commercial, 2 1/4-in diam., 3/8 in thick	4 cookies	42	4	180	2	9	2.9	3.1	2.6
From home recipe, 2 1/3-in diam.[25]	4 cookies	40	3	185	2	11	3.9	4.3	2.0
From refrigerated dough, 2 1/4-in diam., 3/8 in thick	4 cookies	48	5	225	2	11	4.0	4.4	2.0
Oatmeal with raisins, 2 5/8-in diam., 1/4 in thick	4 cookies	52	4	245	3	10	2.5	4.5	2.8
Peanut butter cookie, from home recipe, 2 5/8-in diam.[25]	4 cookies	48	3	245	4	14	4.0	5.8	2.8

(Tr indicates nutrient present in trace amounts.)

Nutrients in Indicated Quantity

Cho-les-terol	Carbo-hydrate	Calcium	Phos-phorus	Iron	Potas-sium	Sodium	Vitamin A value		Thiamin	Ribo-flavin	Niacin	Ascorbic acid
							(IU)	(RE)				
Milli-grams	Grams	Milli-grams	Milli-grams	Milli-grams	Milli-grams	Milli-grams	Inter-national units	Retinol equiva-lents	Milli-grams	Milli-grams	Milli-grams	Milli-grams
20	25	41	50	1.2	194	67	50	13	0.08	0.08	0.5	16
61	48	55	88	1.3	68	258	150	41	0.14	0.15	1.1	Tr
70	77	61	91	1.2	74	275	240	71	0.13	0.16	1.1	Tr
32	15	20	28	0.5	28	96	200	60	0.05	0.06	0.5	Tr
64	15	8	30	0.5	26	108	160	41	0.06	0.06	0.5	0
15	17	21	26	1.0	34	105	20	4	0.06	0.09	0.7	0
7	27	14	44	0.6	37	155	30	9	0.07	0.06	0.6	0
3	42	33	99	1.0	52	176	40	12	0.20	0.13	1.7	0
38	39	23	117	1.2	123	192	120	30	0.05	0.14	0.6	0
170	26	52	81	0.4	90	204	230	69	0.03	0.12	0.4	5
14	16	13	26	0.6	50	59	70	18	0.08	0.07	0.3	Tr
18	11	9	26	0.4	35	51	20	6	0.05	0.05	0.3	Tr
5	28	13	41	0.8	68	140	50	15	0.10	0.23	1.0	Tr
18	26	13	34	1.0	82	82	20	5	0.06	0.06	0.6	0
22	32	13	34	1.0	62	173	30	8	0.06	0.10	0.9	0
2	36	18	58	1.1	90	148	40	12	0.09	0.08	1.0	0
22	28	21	60	1.1	110	142	20	5	0.07	0.07	1.9	0

Nutritive Value of Foods *(Continued)*

Foods, approximate measures, units, and weight (weight of edible portion only)			Water	Food energy	Pro-tein	Fat	Satu-rated	Mono-unsatu-rated	Poly-unsatu-rated
								Fatty Acids	
		Grams	Per-cent	Cal-ories	Grams	Grams	Grams	Grams	Grams
GRAIN PRODUCTS—Con.									
Sandwich type (chocolate or vanilla), 1¾-in diam., ⅜ in thick - - - -	4 cookies - - - - - - -	40	2	195	2	8	2.0	3.6	2.2
Shortbread:									
Commercial - - - - - - - - -	4 small cookies - - -	32	6	155	2	8	2.9	3.0	1.1
Sugar cookie, from refrigerated dough, 2½-in diam., ¼ in thick - - - -	4 cookies - - - - - - -	48	4	235	2	12	2.3	5.0	3.6
Vanilla wafers, 1¾-in diam., ¼ in thick - - - - - - - - -	10 cookies - - - - - -	40	4	185	2	7	1.8	3.0	1.8
Corn chips - - - - - - - - - - - - -	1-oz package - - - -	28	1	155	2	9	1.4	2.4	3.7
Cornmeal:									
Whole-ground, unbolted, dry form - - - - - - - - - -	1 cup - - - - - - - - -	122	12	435	11	5	0.5	1.1	2.5
Bolted (nearly whole-grain), dry form - - - - -	1 cup - - - - - - - - -	122	12	440	11	4	0.5	0.9	2.2
Degermed, enriched:									
Dry form	1 cup	138	12	500	11	2	0.2	0.4	0.9
Crackers:[39]									
Cheese:									
Plain, 1 in square - - - - -	10 crackers - - - - -	10	4	50	1	3	0.9	1.2	0.3
Sandwich type (peanut butter) - - - - - - - - - - -	1 sandwich - - - - -	8	3	40	1	2	0.4	0.8	0.3
Graham, plain, 2½ in square - - - - - - -	2 crackers - - - - - -	14	5	60	1	1	0.4	0.6	0.4
Melba toast, plain - - - - -	1 piece - - - - - - - -	5	4	20	1	Tr	0.1	0.1	0.1
Rye wafers, whole-grain, 1⅞ by 3½ in - - - - - - - - - - -	2 wafers - - - - - - -	14	5	55	1	1	0.3	0.4	0.3
Saltines[40] - - - - - - - - - - - -	4 crackers - - - - - -	12	4	50	1	1	0.5	0.4	0.2
Snack-type, standard - - - -	1 round cracker - -	3	3	15	Tr	1	0.2	0.4	0.1
Wheat, thin - - - - - - - - -	4 crackers - - - - - -	8	3	35	1	1	0.5	0.5	0.4
Whole-wheat wafers - - - - -	2 crackers - - - - - -	8	4	35	1	2	0.5	0.6	0.4
Croissants, made with enriched flour, 4½ by 4 by 1¾ in - - - - - - - - - - - - - - -	1 croissant - - - - -	57	22	235	5	12	3.5	6.7	1.4
Danish pastry, made with enriched flour:									
Plain without fruit or nuts:									
Round piece, about 4¼-in diam., 1 in high - - - - -	1 pastry - - - - - - -	57	27	220	4	12	3.6	4.8	2.6
Fruit, round piece - - - - - -	1 pastry - - - - - - -	65	30	235	4	13	3.9	5.2	2.9
Doughnuts, made with enriched flour:									
Cake type, plain, 3¼-in diam., 1 in high - - - - - -	1 doughnut - - - - -	50	21	210	3	12	2.8	5.0	3.0
Yeast-leavened, glazed, 3¾-in diam., 1¼ in high - - -	1 doughnut - - - - -	60	27	235	4	13	5.2	5.5	0.9

(Tr indicates nutrient present in trace amounts.)

Nutrients in Indicated Quantity

Cho-les-terol	Carbo-hydrate	Calcium	Phos-phorus	Iron	Potas-sium	Sodium	Vitamin A value		Thiamin	Ribo-flavin	Niacin	Ascorbic acid
							(IU)	(RE)				
Milli-grams	Grams	Milli-grams	Milli-grams	Milli-grams	Milli-grams	Milli-grams	Inter-national units	Retinol equiva-lents	Milli-grams	Milli-grams	Milli-grams	Milli-grams
0	29	12	40	1.4	66	189	0	0	0.09	0.07	0.8	0
27	20	13	39	0.8	38	123	30	8	0.10	0.09	0.9	0
29	31	50	91	0.9	33	261	40	11	0.09	0.06	1.1	0
25	29	16	36	0.8	50	150	50	14	0.07	0.10	1.0	0
0	16	35	52	0.5	52	233	110	11	0.04	0.05	0.4	1
0	90	24	312	2.2	346	1	620	62	0.46	0.13	2.4	0
0	91	21	272	2.2	303	1	590	59	0.37	0.10	2.3	0
0	108	8	137	5.9	166	1	610	61	0.61	0.36	4.8	0
6	6	11	17	0.3	17	112	20	5	0.05	0.04	0.4	0
1	5	7	25	0.3	17	90	Tr	Tr	0.04	0.03	0.6	0
0	11	6	20	0.4	36	86	0	0	0.02	0.03	0.6	0
0	4	6	10	0.1	11	44	0	0	0.01	0.01	0.1	0
0	10	7	44	0.5	65	115	0	0	0.06	0.03	0.5	0
4	9	3	12	0.5	17	165	0	0	0.06	0.05	0.6	0
0	2	3	6	0.1	4	30	Tr	Tr	0.01	0.01	0.1	0
0	5	3	15	0.3	17	69	Tr	Tr	0.04	0.03	0.4	0
0	5	3	22	0.2	31	59	0	0	0.02	0.03	0.4	0
13	27	20	64	2.1	68	452	50	13	0.17	0.13	1.3	0
49	26	60	58	1.1	53	218	60	17	0.16	0.17	1.4	Tr
56	28	17	80	1.3	57	233	40	11	0.16	0.14	1.4	Tr
20	24	22	111	1.0	58	192	20	5	0.12	0.12	1.1	Tr
21	26	17	55	1.4	64	222	Tr	Tr	0.28	0.12	1.8	0

Nutritive Value of Foods *(Continued)*

Foods, approximate measures, units, and weight (weight of edible portion only)		Water	Food energy	Pro-tein	Fat	*Fatty Acids*		
						Satu-rated	Mono-unsatu-rated	Poly-unsatu-rated
	Grams	Per-cent	Cal-ories	Grams	Grams	Grams	Grams	Grams
GRAIN PRODUCTS—Con.								
English muffins, plain,								
enriched- - - - - - - - - - 1 muffin- - - - - - -	57	42	140	5	1	0.3	0.2	0.3
Toasted- - - - - - - - - - - - 1 muffin- - - - - - -	50	29	140	5	1	0.3	0.2	0.3
French toast, from home								
recipe- - - - - - - - - - - - - - 1 slice- - - - - - - - -	65	53	155	6	7	1.6	2.0	1.6
Macaroni, enriched, cooked (cut lengths, elbows, shells):								
Firm stage (hot)- - - - - - 1 cup- - - - - - - - -	130	64	190	7	1	0.1	0.1	0.3
Tender stage:								
Cold- - - - - - - - - - - - - - 1 cup- - - - - - - - -	105	72	115	4	Tr	0.1	0.1	0.2
Hot- - - - - - - - - - - - - - 1 cup- - - - - - - - -	140	72	155	5	1	0.1	0.1	0.2
Muffins made with enriched flour, 2½-in diam., 1½ in high:								
From home recipe:								
Blueberry[25]- - - - - - - - - 1 muffin- - - - - - -	45	37	135	3	5	1.5	2.1	1.2
Bran[36]- - - - - - - - - - - - - 1 muffin- - - - - - -	45	35	125	3	6	1.4	1.0	2.0
Corn (enriched, de-germed cornmeal and flour)[36]- - - - - - - - - - - 1 muffin- - - - - - -	45	33	145	3	5	1.5	2.2	1.4
From commercial mix (egg and water added):								
Blueberry- - - - - - - - - - 1 muffin- - - - - - -	45	33	140	3	5	1.4	2.0	1.2
Bran- - - - - - - - - - - - - - 1 muffin- - - - - - -	45	28	140	3	4	1.3	1.6	1.0
Corn- - - - - - - - - - - - - - 1 muffin- - - - - - -	45	30	145	3	6	1.7	2.3	1.4
Noodles (egg noodles), enriched, cooked- - - - - - 1 cup- - - - - - - - -	160	70	200	7	2	0.5	0.6	0.6
Noodles, chow mein, canned 1 cup- - - - - - - - -	45	11	220	6	11	2.1	7.3	0.4
Pancakes, 4-in diam.:								
Buckwheat, from mix (with buckwheat and enriched flours), egg and milk added- - - - - 1 pancake- - - - - -	27	58	55	2	2	0.9	0.9	0.5
Plain:								
From home recipe using enriched flour- - - - - - 1 pancake- - - - - -	27	50	60	2	2	0.5	0.8	0.5
From mix (with enriched flour), egg, milk, and oil added- - - - - - - - - - - 1 pancake- - - - - -	27	54	60	2	2	0.5	0.9	0.5
Piecrust, made with enriched flour and vegetable short-ening, baked:								
From home recipe, 9-in diam.- - - - - - - - - - - - 1 pie shell- - - - - -	180	15	900	11	60	14.8	25.9	15.7
From mix, 9-in diam.- - - - Piecrust for 2-crust pie- - - - - - - -	320	19	1,485	20	93	22.7	41.0	25.0

(Tr indicates nutrient present in trace amounts.)

Nutrients in Indicated Quantity

Cholesterol	Carbohydrate	Calcium	Phosphorus	Iron	Potassium	Sodium	Vitamin A value		Thiamin	Riboflavin	Niacin	Ascorbic acid
							(IU)	(RE)				
Milligrams	Grams	Milligrams	Milligrams	Milligrams	Milligrams	Milligrams	International units	Retinol equivalents	Milligrams	Milligrams	Milligrams	Milligrams
0	27	96	67	1.7	331	378	0	0	0.26	0.19	2.2	0
0	27	96	67	1.7	331	378	0	0	0.23	0.19	2.2	0
112	17	72	85	1.3	86	257	110	32	0.12	0.16	1.0	Tr
0	39	14	85	2.1	103	1	0	0	0.23	0.13	1.8	0
0	24	8	53	1.3	64	1	0	0	0.15	0.08	1.2	0
0	32	11	70	1.7	85	1	0	0	0.20	0.11	1.5	0
19	20	54	46	0.9	47	198	40	9	0.10	0.11	0.9	1
24	19	60	125	1.4	99	189	230	30	0.11	0.13	1.3	3
23	21	66	59	0.9	57	169	80	15	0.11	0.11	0.9	Tr
45	22	15	90	0.9	54	225	50	11	0.10	0.17	1.1	Tr
28	24	27	182	1.7	50	385	100	14	0.08	0.12	1.9	0
42	22	30	128	1.3	31	291	90	16	0.09	0.09	0.8	Tr
50	37	16	94	2.6	70	3	110	34	0.22	0.13	1.9	0
5	26	14	41	0.4	33	450	0	0	0.05	0.03	0.6	0
20	6	59	91	0.4	66	125	60	17	0.04	0.05	0.2	Tr
16	9	27	38	0.5	33	115	30	10	0.06	0.07	0.5	Tr
16	8	36	71	0.7	43	160	30	7	0.09	0.12	0.8	Tr
0	79	25	90	4.5	90	1,100	0	0	0.54	0.40	5.0	0
0	141	131	272	9.3	179	2,602	0	0	1.06	0.80	9.9	0

Nutritive Value of Foods *(Continued)*

Foods, approximate measures, units, and weight (weight of edible portion only)		Water	Food energy	Pro-tein	Fat	Fatty Acids		
						Satu-rated	Mono-unsatu-rated	Poly-unsatu-rated
		Grams	*Per-cent*	*Cal-ories*	*Grams*	*Grams*	*Grams*	*Grams*
GRAIN PRODUCTS—Con.								
Pies, piecrust made with enriched flour, vegetable shortening, 9-in diam.:								
Apple:								
Piece, ⅙ of pie	1 piece	158	48	405	3	18	4.6	7.4	4.4
Blueberry:								
Piece, ⅙ of pie	1 piece	158	51	380	4	17	4.3	7.4	4.6
Cherry:								
Piece, ⅙ of pie	1 piece	158	47	410	4	18	4.7	7.7	4.6
Creme:								
Piece, ⅙ of pie	1 piece	152	43	455	3	23	15.0	4.0	1.1
Custard:								
Piece, ⅙ of pie	1 piece	152	58	330	9	17	5.6	6.7	3.2
Lemon meringue:								
Piece, ⅙ of pie	1 piece	140	47	355	5	14	4.3	5.7	2.9
Peach:								
Piece, ⅙ of pie	1 piece	158	48	405	4	17	4.1	7.3	4.4
Pecan:								
Piece, ⅙ of pie	1 piece	138	20	575	7	32	4.7	17.0	7.9
Pumpkin:								
Piece, ⅙ of pie	1 piece	152	59	320	6	17	6.4	6.7	3.0
Pies, fried:								
Apple	1 pie	85	43	255	2	14	5.8	6.6	0.6
Cherry	1 pie	85	42	250	2	14	5.8	6.7	0.6
Popcorn, popped:								
Air-popped, unsalted	1 cup	8	4	30	1	Tr	Tr	0.1	0.2
Popped in vegetable oil, salted	1 cup	11	3	55	1	3	0.5	1.4	1.2
Sugar syrup coated	1 cup	35	4	135	2	1	0.1	0.3	0.6
Pretzels, made with enriched flour:								
Stick 2¼ in long	10 pretzels	3	3	10	Tr	Tr	Tr	Tr	Tr
Twisted, dutch 2¾ by 2⅝ in	1 pretzel	16	3	65	2	1	0.1	0.2	0.2
Twisted, thin, 3¼ by 2¼ by ¼ in	10 pretzels	60	3	240	6	2	0.4	0.8	0.6
Rice:								
Brown, cooked, served hot	1 cup	195	70	230	5	1	0.3	0.3	0.4
White enriched:								
Commercial varieties, all types:								
Cooked, served hot	1 cup	205	73	225	4	Tr	0.1	0.1	0.1
Instant, ready-to-serve, hot	1 cup	165	73	180	4	0	0.1	0.1	0.1
Parboiled:								
Cooked, served hot	1 cup	175	73	185	4	Tr	Tr	Tr	0.1

(Tr indicates nutrient present in trace amounts.)

Nutrients in Indicated Quantity

Cholesterol	Carbohydrate	Calcium	Phosphorus	Iron	Potassium	Sodium	Vitamin A value		Thiamin	Riboflavin	Niacin	Ascorbic acid
							(IU)	(RE)				
Milligrams	Grams	Milligrams	Milligrams	Milligrams	Milligrams	Milligrams	International units	Retinol equivalents	Milligrams	Milligrams	Milligrams	Milligrams
0	60	13	35	1.6	126	476	50	5	0.17	0.13	1.6	2
0	55	17	36	2.1	158	423	140	14	0.17	0.14	1.7	6
0	61	22	40	1.6	166	480	700	70	0.19	0.14	1.6	0
8	59	46	154	1.1	133	369	210	65	0.06	0.15	1.1	0
169	36	146	172	1.5	208	436	350	96	0.14	0.32	Œ0.9	0
143	53	20	69	1.4	70	395	240	66	0.10	0.14	0.8	4
0	60	16	46	1.9	235	423	1,150	115	0.17	0.16	2.4	5
95	71	65	142	4.6	170	305	220	54	0.30	0.17	1.1	0
109	37	78	105	1.4	243	325	3,750	416	0.14	0.21	1.2	0
14	31	12	34	0.9	42	326	30	3	0.09	0.06	1.0	1
13	32	11	41	0.7	61	371	190	19	0.06	0.06	0.6	1
0	6	1	22	0.2	20	Tr	10	1	0.03	0.01	0.2	0
0	6	3	31	0.3	19	86	20	2	0.01	0.02	0.1	0
0	30	2	47	0.5	90	Tr	30	3	0.13	0.02	0.4	0
0	2	1	3	0.1	3	48	0	0	0.01	0.01	0.1	0
0	13	4	15	0.3	16	258	0	0	0.05	0.04	0.7	0
0	48	16	55	1.2	61	966	0	0	0.19	0.15	2.6	0
0	50	23	142	1.0	137	0	0	0	0.18	0.04	2.7	0
0	50	21	57	1.8	57	0	0	0	0.23	0.02	2.1	0
0	40	5	31	1.3	0	0	0	0	0.21	0.02	1.7	0
0	41	33	100	1.4	75	0	0	0	0.19	0.02	2.1	0

Nutritive Value of Foods *(Continued)*

Foods, approximate measures, units, and weight (weight of edible portion only)		Water	Food energy	Pro- tein	Fat	Fatty Acids		
						Satu- rated	Mono- unsatu- rated	Poly- unsatu- rated
		Grams	Per- cent	Cal- ories	Grams	Grams	Grams	Grams	Grams

		Grams	Per- cent	Cal- ories	Grams	Grams	Grams	Grams	Grams
GRAIN PRODUCTS—Con.									
Rolls, enriched:									
Commercial:									
Dinner, 2½-in diam., 2 in high	1 roll	28	32	85	2	2	0.5	0.8	0.6
Frankfurter and ham- burger (8 per 11½-oz pkg.)	1 roll	40	34	115	3	2	0.5	0.8	0.6
Hard, 3¾-in diam., 2 in high	1 roll	50	25	155	5	2	0.4	0.5	0.6
Hoagie or submarine, 11½ by 3 by 2½ in	1 roll	135	31	400	11	8	1.8	3.0	2.2
From home recipe:									
Dinner, 2½-in diam., 2 in high	1 roll	35	26	120	3	3	0.8	1.2	0.9
Spaghetti, enriched, cooked:									
Firm stage, "al dente," served hot	1 cup	130	64	190	7	1	0.1	0.1	0.3
Tortillas, corn	1 tortilla	30	45	65	2	1	0.1	0.3	0.6
Waffles, made with enriched flour, 7-in diam.:									
From home recipe	1 waffle	75	37	245	7	13	4.0	4.9	2.6
From mix, egg and milk added	1 waffle	75	42	205	7	8	2.7	2.9	1.5
Wheat flours:									
All-purpose or family flour, enriched:									
Sifted, spooned	1 cup	115	12	420	12	1	0.2	0.1	0.5
Cake or pastry flour, enriched, sifted, spooned	1 cup	96	12	350	7	1	0.1	0.1	0.3
Self-rising, enriched, unsifted, spooned	1 cup	125	12	440	12	1	0.2	0.1	0.5
Whole-wheat, from hard wheats, stirred	1 cup	120	12	400	16	2	0.3	0.3	1.1
LEGUMES, NUTS, AND SEEDS									
Almonds, shelled:									
Slivered, packed	1 cup	135	4	795	27	70	6.7	45.8	14.8
Whole	1 oz	28	4	165	6	15	1.4	9.6	3.1
Beans, dry:									
Cooked, drained:									
Black	1 cup	171	66	225	15	1	0.1	0.1	0.5
Great Northern	1 cup	180	69	210	14	1	0.1	0.1	0.6
Lima	1 cup	190	64	260	16	1	0.2	0.1	0.5
Pea (navy)	1 cup	190	69	225	15	1	0.1	0.1	0.7
Pinto	1 cup	180	65	265	15	1	0.1	0.1	0.5

(Tr indicates nutrient present in trace amounts.)

Nutrients in Indicated Quantity

Cholesterol	Carbohydrate	Calcium	Phosphorus	Iron	Potassium	Sodium	Vitamin A value (IU)	Vitamin A value (RE)	Thiamin	Riboflavin	Niacin	Ascorbic acid
Milligrams	Grams	Milligrams	Milligrams	Milligrams	Milligrams	Milligrams	International units	Retinol equivalents	Milligrams	Milligrams	Milligrams	Milligrams
Tr	14	33	44	0.8	36	155	Tr	Tr	0.14	0.09	1.1	Tr
Tr	20	54	44	1.2	56	241	Tr	Tr	0.20	0.13	1.6	Tr
Tr	30	24	46	1.4	49	313	0	0	0.20	0.12	1.7	0
Tr	72	100	115	3.8	128	683	0	0	0.54	0.33	4.5	0
12	20	16	36	1.1	41	98	30	8	0.12	0.12	1.2	0
0	39	14	85	2.0	103	1	0	0	0.23	0.13	1.8	0
0	13	42	55	0.6	43	1	80	8	0.05	0.03	0.4	0
102	26	154	135	1.5	129	445	140	39	0.18	0.24	1.5	Tr
59	27	179	257	1.2	146	515	170	49	0.14	0.23	0.9	Tr
0	88	18	100	5.1	109	2	0	0	0.73	0.46	6.1	0
0	76	16	70	4.2	91	2	0	0	0.58	0.38	5.1	0
0	93	331	583	5.5	113	1,349	0	0	0.80	0.50	6.6	0
0	85	49	446	5.2	444	4	0	0	0.66	0.14	5.2	0
0	28	359	702	4.9	988	15	0	0	0.28	1.05	4.5	1
0	6	75	147	1.0	208	3	0	0	0.06	0.22	1.0	Tr
0	41	47	239	2.9	608	1	Tr	Tr	0.43	0.05	0.9	0
0	38	90	266	4.9	749	13	0	0	0.25	0.13	1.3	0
0	49	55	293	5.9	1,163	4	0	0	0.25	0.11	1.3	0
0	40	95	281	5.1	790	13	0	0	0.27	0.13	1.3	0
0	49	86	296	5.4	882	3	Tr	Tr	0.33	0.16	0.7	0

Nutritive Value of Foods *(Continued)*

Foods, approximate measures, units, and weight (weight of edible portion only)		Water	Food energy	Pro-tein	Fat	Fatty Acids		
						Satu-rated	Mono-unsatu-rated	Poly-unsatu-rated
		Grams	Per-cent	Cal-ories	Grams	Grams	Grams	Grams	Grams

		Grams	Per-cent	Cal-ories	Grams	Grams	Grams	Grams
LEGUMES, NUTS, AND SEEDS—Con.								
Canned, solids and liquid:								
White with:								
Frankfurters (sliced)-	1 cup- - - - - - - - -	255	71	365	19	18	7.4	8.8	0.7
Pork and tomato								
sauce- - - - - - - - - -	1 cup- - - - - - - - -	255	71	310	16	7	2.4	2.7	0.7
Pork and sweet sauce-	1 cup- - - - - - - - -	255	66	385	16	12	4.3	4.9	1.2
Red kidney- - - - - - - - -	1 cup- - - - - - - - -	255	76	230	15	1	0.1	0.1	0.6
Black-eyed peas, dry, cooked (with residual cooking liquid)- - - - - - - - - - - - -	1 cup- - - - - - - - -	250	80	190	13	1	0.2	Tr	0.3
Brazil nuts, shelled- - - - - -	1 oz- - - - - - - - -	28	3	185	4	19	4.6	6.5	6.8
Carob flour- - - - - - - - - - -	1 cup- - - - - - - - -	140	3	255	6	Tr	Tr	0.1	0.1
Cashew nuts, salted:								
Dry roasted- - - - - - - - - -	1 oz- - - - - - - - -	28	2	165	4	13	2.6	7.7	2.2
Roasted in oil- - - - - - - -	1 oz- - - - - - - - -	28	4	165	5	14	2.7	8.1	2.3
Chestnuts, European (Italian), roasted, shelled- - - - - - - - - - - - -	1 cup - - - - - - -	143	40	350	5	3	0.6	1.1	1.2
Chickpeas, cooked, drained-	1 cup- - - - - - - - -	163	60	270	15	4	0.4	0.9	1.9
Coconut:								
Raw:								
Piece, about 2 by 2 by ½ in- - - - - - - - -	1 piece- - - - - - -	45	47	160	1	15	13.4	0.6	0.2
Dried, sweetened, shredded- - - - - - - -	1 cup- - - - - - - - -	93	13	470	3	33	29.3	1.4	0.4
Filberts (hazelnuts), chopped- - - - - - - - - - - - -	1 oz- - - - - - - - -	28	5	180	4	18	1.3	13.9	1.7
Lentils, dry, cooked- - - - - - -	1 cup- - - - - - - - -	200	72	215	16	1	0.1	0.2	0.5
Macadamia nuts, roasted in oil, salted- - - - - - - - - - -	1 oz- - - - - - - - -	28	2	205	2	22	3.2	17.1	0.4
Mixed nuts, with peanuts, salted:								
Dry roasted- - - - - - - - - -	1 oz- - - - - - - - -	28	2	170	5	15	2.0	8.9	3.1
Roasted in oil- - - - - - - -	1 oz- - - - - - - - -	28	2	175	5	16	2.5	9.0	3.8
Peanuts, roasted in oil, salted- - - - - - - - - - - - -	1 oz- - - - - - - - -	28	2	165	8	14	1.9	6.9	4.4
Peanut butter- - - - - - - - - - -	1 tbsp- - - - - - -	16	1	95	5	8	1.4	4.0	2.5
Peas, split, dry, cooked- - - -	1 cup- - - - - - - - -	200	70	230	16	1	0.1	0.1	0.3
Pecans, halves- - - - - - - - -	1 oz- - - - - - - - -	28	5	190	2	19	1.5	12.0	4.7
Pine nuts (pinyons), shelled-	1 oz- - - - - - - - -	28	6	160	3	17	2.7	6.5	7.3
Pistachio nuts, dried, shelled	1 oz- - - - - - - - -	28	4	165	6	14	1.7	9.3	2.1
Pumpkin and squash kernels, dry, hulled- - - - - - - - - - -	1 oz- - - - - - - - -	28	7	155	7	13	2.5	4.0	5.9
Refried beans, canned- - - - -	1 cup- - - - - - - - -	290	72	295	18	3	0.4	0.6	1.4
Sesame seeds, dry, hulled- - -	1 tbsp- - - - - - - -	8	5	45	2	4	0.6	1.7	1.9
Soybeans, dry, cooked, drained- - - - - - - - - - - - -	1 cup- - - - - - - - -	180	71	235	20	10	1.3	1.9	5.3

(Tr indicates nutrient present in trace amounts.)

Nutrients in Indicated Quantity

Cho-les-terol	Carbo-hydrate	Calcium	Phos-phorus	Iron	Potas-sium	Sodium	Vitamin A value		Thiamin	Ribo-flavin	Niacin	Ascorbic acid
							(IU)	(RE)				
Milli-grams	Grams	Milli-grams	Milli-grams	Milli-grams	Milli-grams	Milli-grams	Inter-national units	Retinol equiva-lents	Milli-grams	Milli-grams	Milli-grams	Milli-grams
30	32	94	303	4.8	668	1,374	330	33	0.18	0.15	3.3	Tr
10	48	138	235	4.6	536	1,181	330	33	0.20	0.08	1.5	5
10	54	161	291	5.9	536	969	330	33	0.15	0.10	1.3	5
0	42	74	278	4.6	673	968	10	1	0.13	0.10	1.5	0
0	35	43	238	3.3	573	20	30	3	0.40	0.10	1.0	0
0	4	50	170	1.0	170	1	Tr	Tr	0.28	0.03	0.5	Tr
0	126	390	102	5.7	1,275	24	Tr	Tr	0.07	0.07	2.2	Tr
0	9	13	139	1.7	160	[41]181	0	0	0.06	0.06	0.4	0
0	8	12	121	1.2	150	[42]177	0	0	0.12	0.05	0.5	0
0	76	41	153	1.3	847	3	30	3	0.35	0.25	1.9	37
0	45	80	273	4.9	475	11	Tr	Tr	0.18	0.09	0.9	0
0	7	6	51	1.1	160	9	0	0	0.03	0.01	0.2	1
0	44	14	99	1.8	313	244	0	0	0.03	0.02	0.4	1
0	4	53	88	0.9	126	1	20	2	0.14	0.03	0.3	Tr
0	38	50	238	4.2	498	26	40	4	0.14	0.12	1.2	0
0	4	13	57	0.5	93	[43]74	Tr	Tr	0.06	0.03	0.6	0
0	7	20	123	1.0	169	[44]190	Tr	Tr	0.06	0.06	1.3	0
0	6	31	131	0.9	165	[44]185	10	1	0.14	0.06	1.4	Tr
0	5	24	143	0.5	199	[45]122	0	0	0.08	0.03	4.2	0
0	3	5	60	0.3	110	75	0	0	0.02	0.02	2.2	0
0	42	22	178	3.4	592	26	80	8	0.30	0.18	1.8	0
0	5	10	83	0.6	111	Tr	40	4	0.24	0.04	0.3	1
0	5	2	10	0.9	178	20	10	1	0.35	0.06	1.2	1
0	7	38	143	1.9	310	2	70	7	0.23	0.05	0.3	Tr
0	5	12	333	4.2	229	5	110	11	0.06	0.09	0.5	Tr
0	51	141	245	5.1	1,141	1,228	0	0	0.14	0.16	1.4	17
0	1	11	62	0.6	33	3	10	1	0.06	0.01	0.4	0
0	19	131	322	4.9	972	4	50	5	0.38	0.16	1.1	0

Nutritive Value of Foods *(Continued)*

Foods, approximate measures, units, and weight (weight of edible portion only)		Grams	Water Per-cent	Food energy Cal-ories	Pro-tein Grams	Fat Grams	Fatty Acids		
							Satu-rated Grams	Mono-unsatu-rated Grams	Poly-unsatu-rated Grams
LEGUMES, NUTS, AND SEEDS—Con.									
Soy products:									
Miso	1 cup	276	53	470	29	13	1.8	2.6	7.3
Tofu, piece 2½ by 2¾ by 1 in	1 piece	120	85	85	9	5	0.7	1.0	2.9
Sunflower seeds, dry, hulled	1 oz	28	5	160	6	14	1.5	2.7	9.3
Tahini	1 tbsp	15	3	90	3	8	1.1	3.0	3.5
Walnuts:									
Black, chopped	1 oz	28	4	170	7	16	1.0	3.6	10.6
English or Persian, pieces or chips	1 oz	28	4	180	4	18	1.6	4.0	11.1
MEAT AND MEAT PRODUCTS									
Beef, cooked:[46]									
Cuts braised, simmered, or pot roasted:									
Relatively fat such as chuck blade:									
Lean and fat, piece, 2½ by 2½ by ¾ in	3 oz	85	43	325	22	26	10.8	11.7	0.9
Lean only	2.2 oz	62	53	170	19	9	3.9	4.2	0.3
Relatively lean, such as bottom round:									
Lean and fat, piece, 4⅛ by 2¼ by ½ in	3 oz	85	54	220	25	13	4.8	5.7	0.5
Lean only	2.8 oz	78	57	175	25	8	2.7	3.4	0.3
Ground beef, broiled, patty, 3 by ⅝ in:									
Lean	3 oz	85	56	230	21	16	6.2	6.9	0.6
Regular	3 oz	85	54	245	20	18	6.9	7.7	0.7
Liver, fried, slice, 6½ by 2⅜ by ⅜ in[47]	3 oz	85	56	185	23	7	2.5	3.6	1.3
Roast, oven cooked, no liquid added:									
Relatively fat, such as rib:									
Lean and fat, 2 pieces, 4⅛ by 2¼ by ¼ in	3 oz	85	46	315	19	26	10.8	11.4	0.9
Lean only	2.2 oz	61	57	150	17	9	3.6	3.7	0.3
Relatively lean, such as eye of round:									
Lean and fat, 2 pieces, 2½ by 2½ by ⅜ in	3 oz	85	57	205	23	12	4.9	5.4	0.5
Lean only	2.6 oz	75	63	135	22	5	1.9	2.1	0.2
Steak:									
Sirloin, broiled:									
Lean and fat, piece, 2½ by 2½ by ¾ in	3 oz	85	53	240	23	15	6.4	6.9	0.6
Lean only	2.5 oz	72	59	150	22	6	2.6	2.8	0.3
Beef, canned, corned	3 oz	85	59	185	22	10	4.2	4.9	0.4

(Tr indicates nutrient present in trace amounts.)

Nutrients in Indicated Quantity

Cho-les-terol	Carbo-hydrate	Calcium	Phos-phorus	Iron	Potas-sium	Sodium	Vitamin A value (IU)	Vitamin A value (RE)	Thiamin	Ribo-flavin	Niacin	Ascorbic acid
Milli-grams	Grams	Milli-grams	Milli-grams	Milli-grams	Milli-grams	Milli-grams	Inter-national units	Retinol equiva-lents	Milli-grams	Milli-grams	Milli-grams	Milli-grams
0	65	188	853	4.7	922	8,142	110	11	0.17	0.28	0.8	0
0	3	108	151	2.3	50	8	0	0	0.07	0.04	0.1	0
0	5	33	200	1.9	195	1	10	1	0.65	0.07	1.3	Tr
0	3	21	119	0.7	69	5	10	1	0.24	0.02	0.8	1
0	3	16	132	0.9	149	Tr	80	8	0.06	0.03	0.2	Tr
0	5	27	90	0.7	142	3	40	4	0.11	0.04	0.3	1
87	0	11	163	2.5	163	53	Tr	Tr	0.06	0.19	2.0	0
66	0	8	146	2.3	163	44	Tr	Tr	0.05	0.17	1.7	0
81	0	5	217	2.8	248	43	Tr	Tr	0.06	0.21	3.3	0
75	0	4	212	2.7	240	40	Tr	Tr	0.06	0.20	3.0	0
74	0	9	134	1.8	256	65	Tr	Tr	0.04	0.18	4.4	0
76	0	9	144	2.1	248	70	Tr	Tr	0.03	0.16	4.9	0
410	7	9	392	5.3	309	90	[48]30,690	[48]9,120	0.18	3.52	12.3	23
72	0	8	145	2.0	246	54	Tr	Tr	0.06	0.16	3.1	0
49	0	5	127	1.7	218	45	Tr	Tr	0.05	0.13	2.7	0
62	0	5	177	1.6	308	50	Tr	Tr	0.07	0.14	3.0	0
52	0	3	170	1.5	297	46	Tr	Tr	0.07	0.13	2.8	0
77	0	9	186	2.6	306	53	Tr	Tr	0.10	0.23	3.3	0
64	0	8	176	2.4	290	48	Tr	Tr	0.09	0.22	3.1	0
80	0	17	90	3.7	51	802	Tr	Tr	0.02	0.20	2.9	0

Nutritive Value of Foods *(Continued)*

Foods, approximate measures, units, and weight (weight of edible portion only)		Water	Food energy	Pro- tein	Fat	Fatty Acids		
						Satu- rated	Mono- unsatu- rated	Poly- unsatu- rated
	Grams	Per- cent	Cal- ories	Grams	Grams	Grams	Grams	Grams
MEAT AND MEAT PRODUCTS—Con.								
Beef, dried, chipped - - - - - - 2.5 oz - - - - - - - -	72	48	145	24	4	1.8	2.0	0.2
Lamb, cooked:								
Chops, (3 per lb with bone):								
Arm, braised:								
Lean and fat - - - - - - 2.2 oz - - - - - - - -	63	44	220	20	15	6.9	6.0	0.9
Lean only - - - - - - - - 1.7 oz - - - - - - - -	48	49	135	17	7	2.9	2.6	0.4
Loin, broiled:								
Lean and fat - - - - - - 2.8 oz - - - - - - - -	80	54	235	22	16	7.3	6.4	1.0
Lean only - - - - - - - - 2.3 oz - - - - - - - -	64	61	140	19	6	2.6	2.4	0.4
Leg, roasted:								
Lean and fat, 2 pieces, 4⅛ by 2¼ by ¼ in - - - - - 3 oz - - - - - - - - -	85	59	205	22	13	5.6	4.9	0.8
Lean only - - - - - - - - 2.6 oz - - - - - - - -	73	64	140	20	6	2.4	2.2	0.4
Rib, roasted:								
Lean and fat, 3 pieces, 2½ by 2½ by ¼ in - - - - 3 oz - - - - - - - - -	85	47	315	18	26	12.1	10.6	1.5
Lean only - - - - - - - - 2 oz - - - - - - - - -	57	60	150	18	7	3.2	2.8	0.5
Pork, cured, cooked:								
Bacon:								
Regular - - - - - - - - - - 3 medium slices - -	19	13	110	6	9	3.3	4.5	1.1
Canadian-style - - - - - - 2 slices - - - - - - - -	46	62	85	11	4	1.3	1.9	0.4
Ham, light cure, roasted:								
Lean and fat, 2 pieces, 4⅛ by 2¼ by ¼ in - - - - - 3 oz - - - - - - - - -	85	58	205	18	14	5.1	6.7	1.5
Lean only - - - - - - - - 2.4 oz - - - - - - - -	68	66	105	17	4	1.3	1.7	0.4
Luncheon meat:								
Canned, spiced or un- spiced, slice, 3 by 2 by ½ in - - - - - - - - - - - - - 2 slices - - - - - - - -	42	52	140	5	13	4.5	6.0	1.5
Cooked ham (8 slices per 8-oz pkg):								
Regular - - - - - - - - - 2 slices - - - - - - - -	57	65	105	10	6	1.9	2.8	0.7
Extra lean - - - - - - - - 2 slices - - - - - - - -	57	71	75	11	3	0.9	1.3	0.3
Pork, fresh, cooked:								
Chop, loin (cut 3 per lb with bone):								
Broiled:								
Lean and fat - - - - - - 3.1 oz - - - - - - - -	87	50	275	24	19	7.0	8.8	2.2
Lean only - - - - - - - - 2.5 oz - - - - - - - -	72	57	165	23	8	2.6	3.4	0.9
Pan fried:								
Lean and fat - - - - - - 3.1 oz - - - - - - - -	89	45	335	21	27	9.8	12.5	3.1
Lean only - - - - - - - - 2.4 oz - - - - - - - -	67	54	180	19	11	3.7	4.8	1.3
Ham (leg), roasted:								
Lean and fat, piece, 2½ by 2½ by ¾ in - - - - - - 3 oz - - - - - - - - -	85	53	250	21	18	6.4	8.1	2.0
Lean only - - - - - - - - 2.5 oz - - - - - - - -	72	60	160	20	8	2.7	3.6	1.0

(Tr indicates nutrient present in trace amounts.)

Nutrients in Indicated Quantity

Cholesterol	Carbohydrate	Calcium	Phosphorus	Iron	Potassium	Sodium	Vitamin A Value (IU)	Vitamin A Value (RE)	Thiamin	Riboflavin	Niacin	Ascorbic acid
Milligrams	Grams	Milligrams	Milligrams	Milligrams	Milligrams	Milligrams	International units	Retinol equivalents	Milligrams	Milligrams	Milligrams	Milligrams
46	0	14	287	2.3	142	3,053	Tr	Tr	0.05	0.23	2.7	0
77	0	16	132	1.5	195	46	Tr	Tr	0.04	0.16	4.4	0
59	0	12	111	1.3	162	36	Tr	Tr	0.03	0.13	3.0	0
78	0	16	162	1.4	272	62	Tr	Tr	0.09	0.21	5.5	0
60	0	12	145	1.3	241	54	Tr	Tr	0.08	0.18	4.4	0
78	0	8	162	1.7	273	57	Tr	Tr	0.09	0.24	5.5	0
65	0	6	150	1.5	247	50	Tr	Tr	0.08	0.20	4.6	0
77	0	19	139	1.4	224	60	Tr	Tr	0.08	0.18	5.5	0
50	0	12	111	1.0	179	46	Tr	Tr	0.05	0.13	3.5	0
16	Tr	2	64	0.3	92	303	0	0	0.13	0.05	1.4	6
27	1	5	136	0.4	179	711	0	0	0.38	0.09	3.2	10
53	0	6	182	0.7	243	1,009	0	0	0.51	0.19	3.8	0
37	0	5	154	0.6	215	902	0	0	0.46	0.17	3.4	0
26	1	3	34	0.3	90	541	0	0	0.15	0.08	1.3	Tr
32	2	4	141	0.6	189	751	0	0	0.49	0.14	3.0	[49]16
27	1	4	124	0.4	200	815	0	0	0.53	0.13	2.8	[49]15
84	0	3	184	0.7	312	61	10	3	0.87	0.24	4.3	Tr
71	0	4	176	0.7	302	56	10	1	0.83	0.22	4.0	Tr
92	0	4	190	0.7	323	64	10	3	0.91	0.24	4.6	Tr
72	0	3	178	0.7	305	57	10	1	0.84	0.22	4.0	Tr
79	0	5	210	0.9	280	50	10	2	0.54	0.27	3.9	Tr
68	0	5	202	0.8	269	46	10	1	0.50	0.25	3.6	Tr

Nutritive Value of Foods *(Continued)*

Foods, approximate measures, units, and weight (weight of edible portion only)		Water	Food energy	Pro-tein	Fat	Fatty Acids		
						Satu-rated	Mono-unsatu-rated	Poly-unsatu-rated
		Grams	Per-cent	Cal-ories	Grams	Grams	Grams	Grams
MEAT AND MEAT PRODUCTS—Con.								
Rib, roasted:								
Lean and fat, piece, 2½ by								
¾ in	3 oz	85	51	270	21	20	7.2	9.2	2.3
Lean only	2.5 oz	71	57	175	20	10	3.4	4.4	1.2
Shoulder cut, braised:								
Lean and fat, 3 pieces, 2½								
by 2½ by ¼ in	3 oz	85	47	295	23	22	7.9	10.0	2.4
Lean only	2.4 oz	67	54	165	22	8	2.8	3.7	1.0
Sausages (See also Luncheon meats):								
Bologna, slice (8 per 8-oz pkg)	2 slices	57	54	180	7	16	6.1	7.6	1.4
Braunschweiger, slice (6 per 6-oz pkg)	2 slices	57	48	205	8	18	6.2	8.5	2.1
Brown and serve (10–11 per 8-oz pkg), browned	1 link	13	45	50	2	5	1.7	2.2	0.5
Frankfurter (10 per 1-lb pkg), cooked (reheated)	1 frankfurter	45	54	145	5	13	4.8	6.2	1.2
Pork link (16 per 1-lb pkg), cooked[50]	1 link	13	45	50	3	4	1.4	1.8	0.5
Salami:								
Cooked type, slice (8 per 8-oz pkg)	2 slices	57	60	145	8	11	4.6	5.2	1.2
Dry type, slice (12 per 4-oz pkg)	2 slices	20	35	85	5	7	2.4	3.4	0.6
Sandwich spread (pork, beef)	1 tbsp	15	60	35	1	3	0.9	1.1	0.4
Vienna sausage (7 per 4-oz can)	1 sausage	16	60	45	2	4	1.5	2.0	0.3
Veal, medium fat, cooked, bone removed:								
Cutlet, 4⅛ by 2¼ by ½ in, braised or broiled	3 oz	85	60	185	23	9	4.1	4.1	0.6
Rib, 2 pieces, 4⅛ by 2¼ by ¼ in, roasted	3 oz	85	55	230	23	14	6.0	6.0	1.0
MIXED DISHES AND FAST FOODS								
Mixed dishes:								
Chicken potpie, from home recipe, baked, piece, ⅓ of 9-in diam. pie[51]	1 piece	232	57	545	23	31	10.3	15.5	6.6
Chili con carne with beans, canned	1 cup	255	72	340	19	16	5.8	7.2	1.0
Chop suey with beef and pork, from home recipe	1 cup	250	75	300	26	17	4.3	7.4	4.2

(Tr indicates nutrient present in trace amounts.)

Nutrients in Indicated Quantity

Cho-les-terol	Carbo-hydrate	Calcium	Phos-phorus	Iron	Potas-sium	Sodium	Vitamin A value		Thiamin	Ribo-flavin	Niacin	Ascorbic acid
							(IU)	(RE)				
Milli-grams	Grams	Milli-grams	Milli-grams	Milli-grams	Milli-grams	Milli-grams	Inter-national units	Retinol equiva-lents	Milli-grams	Milli-grams	Milli-grams	Milli-grams
69	0	9	190	0.8	313	37	10	3	0.50	0.24	4.2	Tr
56	0	8	182	0.7	300	33	10	2	0.45	0.22	3.8	Tr
93	0	6	162	1.4	286	75	10	3	0.46	0.26	4.4	Tr
76	0	5	151	1.3	271	68	10	1	0.40	0.24	4.0	Tr
31	2	7	52	0.9	103	581	0	0	0.10	0.08	1.5	[49]12
89	2	5	96	5.3	113	652	8,010	2,405	0.14	0.87	4.8	[49]6
9	Tr	1	14	0.1	25	105	0	0	0.05	0.02	0.4	0
23	1	5	39	0.5	75	504	0	0	0.09	0.05	1.2	[49]12
11	Tr	4	24	0.2	47	168	0	0	0.10	0.03	0.6	Tr
37	1	7	66	1.5	113	607	0	0	0.14	0.21	2.0	[49]7
16	1	2	28	0.3	76	372	0	0	0.12	0.06	1.0	[49]5
6	2	2	9	0.1	17	152	10	1	0.03	0.02	0.3	0
8	Tr	2	8	0.1	16	152	0	0	0.01	0.02	0.3	0
109	0	9	196	0.8	258	56	Tr	Tr	0.06	0.21	4.6	0
109	0	10	211	0.7	259	57	Tr	Tr	0.11	0.26	6.6	0
56	42	70	232	3.0	343	594	7,220	735	0.32	0.32	4.9	5
28	31	82	321	4.3	594	1,354	150	15	0.08	0.18	3.3	8
68	13	60	248	4.8	425	1,053	600	60	0.28	0.38	5.0	33

Nutritive Value of Foods *(Continued)*

Foods, approximate measures, units, and weight (weight of edible portion only)		Water	Food energy	Pro-tein	Fat	Satu-rated	Mono-unsatu-rated	Poly-unsatu-rated
							Fatty Acids	
	Grams	Per-cent	Cal-ories	Grams	Grams	Grams	Grams	Grams
MIXED DISHES AND FAST FOODS—Con.								
Macaroni (enriched) and cheese:								
Canned[62]- - - - - - - - - - - 1 cup- - - - - - - - -	240	80	230	9	10	4.7	2.9	1.3
Quiche Lorraine, ⅛ of 8-in diam. quiche[51]- - - - - 1 slice- - - - - - - - -	176	47	600	13	48	23.2	17.8	4.1
Spaghetti (enriched) in to-mato sauce with cheese:								
Canned- - - - - - - - - - - - 1 cup- - - - - - - - -	250	80	190	6	2	0.4	0.4	0.5
From home recipe- - - - - 1 cup- - - - - - - - -	250	77	260	9	9	3.0	3.6	1.2
Spaghetti (enriched) with meatballs and tomato sauce:								
From home recipe- - - - - 1 cup- - - - - - - - -	248	70	330	19	12	3.9	4.4	2.2
Fast food entrees:								
Cheeseburger:								
Regular- - - - - - - - - - - - 1 sandwich- - - - -	112	46	300	15	15	7.3	5.6	1.0
4 oz patty- - - - - - - - - - 1 sandwich- - - - -	194	46	525	30	31	15.1	12.2	1.4
Chicken, fried. See Poultry and Poultry Products.								
Enchilada- - - - - - - - - - - 1 enchilada- - - - -	230	72	235	20	16	7.7	6.7	0.6
English muffin, egg, cheese, and bacon- - - - - - - - - 1 sandwich- - - - -	138	49	360	18	18	8.0	8.0	0.7
Fish sandwich:								
Regular, with cheese- - - 1 sandwich- - - - -	140	43	420	16	23	6.3	6.9	7.7
Large, without cheese- - 1 sandwich- - - - -	170	48	470	18	27	6.3	8.7	9.5
Hamburger:								
Regular- - - - - - - - - - - - 1 sandwich- - - - -	98	46	245	12	11	4.4	5.3	0.5
4 oz patty- - - - - - - - - - 1 sandwich- - - - -	174	50	445	25	21	7.1	11.7	0.6
Pizza, cheese, ⅛ of 15-in diam. pizza[51]- - - - - - 1 slice- - - - - - - - -	120	46	290	15	9	4.1	2.6	1.3
Roast beef sandwich- - - - - 1 sandwich- - - - -	150	52	345	22	13	3.5	6.9	1.8
Taco- - - - - - - - - - - - - - - 1 taco- - - - - - - - -	81	55	195	9	11	4.1	5.5	0.8
POULTRY AND POULTRY PRODUCTS								
Chicken:								
Fried, flesh, with skin:[53]								
Batter dipped:								
Breast, ½ breast (5.6 oz with bones)- - - - - - 4.9 oz- - - - - - - - -	140	52	365	35	18	4.9	7.6	4.3
Drumstick (3.4 oz with bones)- - - - - - - - - - 2.5 oz- - - - - - - - -	72	53	195	16	11	3.0	4.6	2.7
Flour coated:								
Breast, ½ breast (4.2 oz with bones)- - - - - - 3.5 oz- - - - - - - - -	98	57	220	31	9	2.4	3.4	1.9
Drumstick (2.6 oz with bones)- - - - - - - - - 1.7 oz- - - - - - - - -	49	57	120	13	7	1.8	2.7	1.6

(Tr indicates nutrient present in trace amounts.)

							Vitamin A value			Ribo-		Ascorbic
Cho-les-terol	Carbo-hydrate	Calcium	Phos-phorus	Iron	Potas-sium	Sodium	(IU)	(RE)	Thiamin	flavin	Niacin	acid
Milli-grams	Grams	Milli-grams	Milli-grams	Milli-grams	Milli-grams	Milli-grams	Inter-national units	Retinol equiva-lents	Milli-grams	Milli-grams	Milli-grams	Milli-grams
24	26	199	182	1.0	139	730	260	72	0.12	0.24	1.0	Tr
285	29	211	276	1.0	283	653	1,640	454	0.11	0.32	Tr	Tr
3	39	40	88	2.8	303	955	930	120	0.35	0.28	4.5	10
8	37	80	135	2.3	408	955	1,080	140	0.25	0.18	2.3	13
89	39	124	236	3.7	665	1,009	1,590	159	0.25	0.30	4.0	22
44	28	135	174	2.3	219	672	340	65	0.26	0.24	3.7	1
104	40	236	320	4.5	407	1,224	670	128	0.33	0.48	7.4	3
19	24	97	198	3.3	653	1,332	2,720	352	0.18	0.26	Tr	Tr
213	31	197	290	3.1	201	832	650	160	0.46	0.50	3.7	1
56	39	132	223	1.8	274	667	160	25	0.32	0.26	3.3	2
91	41	61	246	2.2	375	621	110	15	0.35	0.23	3.5	1
32	28	56	107	2.2	202	463	80	14	0.23	0.24	3.8	1
71	38	75	225	4.8	404	763	160	28	0.38	0.38	7.8	1
56	39	220	216	1.6	230	699	750	106	0.34	0.29	4.2	2
55	34	60	222	4.0	338	757	240	32	0.40	0.33	6.0	2
21	15	109	134	1.2	263	456	420	57	0.09	0.07	1.4	1
119	13	28	259	1.8	281	385	90	28	0.16	0.20	14.7	0
62	6	12	106	1.0	134	194	60	19	0.08	0.15	3.7	0
87	2	16	228	1.2	254	74	50	15	0.08	0.13	13.5	0
44	1	6	86	0.7	112	44	40	12	0.04	0.11	3.0	0

Nutrients in Indicated Quantity

Nutritive Value of Foods *(Continued)*

Foods, approximate measures, units, and weight (weight of edible portion only)		Water	Food energy	Pro-tein	Fat	Fatty Acids		
						Satu-rated	Mono-unsatu-rated	Poly-unsatu-rated
		Per-cent	*Cal-ories*	*Grams*	*Grams*	*Grams*	*Grams*	*Grams*
POULTRY AND POULTRY PRODUCTS—Con.		*Grams*						
Roasted, flesh only:								
Breast, ½ breast (4.2 oz with bones and skin)- - - - - - -	3.0 oz- - - - - - - -	86	65	140	27	3	0.9	1.1	0.7
Drumstick, (2.9 oz with bones and skin)- - -	1.6 oz- - - - - - - - -	44	67	75	12	2	0.7	0.8	0.6
Stewed, flesh only, light and dark meat, chopped or diced- - - - - - - - -	1 cup- - - - - - - - -	140	67	250	38	9	2.6	3.3	2.2
Chicken liver, cooked- - - - -	1 liver- - - - - - - - -	20	68	30	5	1	0.4	0.3	0.2
Duck, roasted, flesh only- - -	½ duck- - - - - - - -	221	64	445	52	25	9.2	8.2	3.2
Turkey, roasted, flesh only:								
Dark meat, piece, 2½ by 1⅝ by ¼ in- - - - - - - - - - - -	4 pieces- - - - - - - -	85	63	160	24	6	2.1	1.4	1.8
Light meat, piece, 4 by 2 by ¼ in- - - - - - - - - - - - -	2 pieces- - - - - - - -	85	66	135	25	3	0.9	0.5	0.7
Poultry food products:								
Turkey:								
Loaf, breast meat (8 slices per 6-oz pkg)- - - - - -	2 slices- - - - - - - -	42	72	45	10	1	0.2	0.2	0.1
Roast, boneless, frozen, seasoned, light and dark meat, cooked- - -	3 oz- - - - - - - - - -	85	68	130	18	5	1.6	1.0	1.4
SOUPS, SAUCES, AND GRAVIES								
Soups:								
Canned, condensed:								
Prepared with equal volume of milk:								
Clam chowder, New England- - - - - - - -	1 cup- - - - - - - - -	248	85	165	9	7	3.0	2.3	1.1
Cream of chicken- - - -	1 cup- - - - - - - - -	248	85	190	7	11	4.6	4.5	1.6
Cream of mushroom- -	1 cup- - - - - - - - -	248	85	205	6	14	5.1	3.0	4.6
Tomato- - - - - - - - - -	1 cup- - - - - - - - -	248	85	160	6	6	2.9	1.6	1.1
Prepared with equal volume of water:								
Bean with bacon- - - -	1 cup- - - - - - - - -	253	84	170	8	6	1.5	2.2	1.8
Beef broth, bouillon, consomme- - - - - - -	1 cup- - - - - - - - -	240	98	15	3	1	0.3	0.2	Tr
Beef noodle- - - - - - -	1 cup- - - - - - - - -	244	92	85	5	3	1.1	1.2	0.5
Chicken noodle- - - - -	1 cup- - - - - - - - -	241	92	75	4	2	0.7	1.1	0.6
Chicken rice- - - - - - -	1 cup- - - - - - - - -	241	94	60	4	2	0.5	0.9	0.4
Clam chowder, Manhattan- - - - - - - - -	1 cup- - - - - - - - -	244	90	80	4	2	0.4	0.4	1.3
Cream of chicken- - - -	1 cup- - - - - - - - -	244	91	115	3	7	2.1	3.3	1.5
Cream of mushroom- -	1 cup- - - - - - - - -	244	90	130	2	9	2.4	1.7	4.2
Minestrone- - - - - - - -	1 cup- - - - - - - - -	241	91	80	4	3	0.6	0.7	1.1
Pea, green- - - - - - - -	1 cup- - - - - - - - -	250	83	165	9	3	1.4	1.0	0.4

(Tr indicates nutrient present in trace amounts.)

Nutrients in Indicated Quantity

Cholesterol	Carbohydrate	Calcium	Phosphorus	Iron	Potassium	Sodium	Vitamin A value		Thiamin	Riboflavin	Niacin	Ascorbic acid
							(IU)	(RE)				
Milligrams	Grams	Milligrams	Milligrams	Milligrams	Milligrams	Milligrams	International units	Retinol equivalents	Milligrams	Milligrams	Milligrams	Milligrams
73	0	13	196	0.9	220	64	20	5	0.06	0.10	11.8	0
41	0	5	81	0.6	108	42	30	8	0.03	0.10	2.7	0
116	0	20	210	1.6	252	98	70	21	0.07	0.23	8.6	0
126	Tr	3	62	1.7	28	10	3,270	983	0.03	0.35	0.9	3
197	0	27	449	6.0	557	144	170	51	0.57	1.04	11.3	0
72	0	27	173	2.0	246	67	0	0	0.05	0.21	3.1	0
59	0	16	186	1.1	259	54	0	0	0.05	0.11	5.8	0
17	0	3	97	0.2	118	608	0	0	0.02	0.05	3.5	[54]0
45	3	4	207	1.4	253	578	0	0	0.04	0.14	5.3	0
22	17	186	156	1.5	300	992	160	40	0.07	0.24	1.0	3
27	15	181	151	0.7	273	1,047	710	94	0.07	0.26	0.9	1
20	15	179	156	0.6	270	1,076	150	37	0.08	0.28	0.9	2
17	22	159	149	1.8	449	932	850	109	0.13	0.25	1.5	68
3	23	81	132	2.0	402	951	890	89	0.09	0.03	0.6	2
Tr	Tr	14	31	0.4	130	782	0	0	Tr	0.05	1.9	0
5	9	15	46	1.1	100	952	630	63	0.07	0.06	1.1	Tr
7	9	17	36	0.8	55	1,106	710	71	0.05	0.06	1.4	Tr
7	7	17	22	0.7	101	815	660	66	0.02	0.02	1.1	Tr
2	12	34	59	1.9	261	1,808	920	92	0.06	0.05	1.3	3
10	9	34	37	0.6	88	986	560	56	0.03	0.06	0.8	Tr
2	9	46	49	0.5	100	1,032	0	0	0.05	0.09	0.7	1
2	11	34	55	0.9	313	911	2,340	234	0.05	0.04	0.9	1
0	27	28	125	2.0	190	988	200	20	0.11	0.07	1.2	2

Nutritive Value of Foods *(Continued)*

Foods, approximate measures, units, and weight (weight of edible portion only)			Water	Food energy	Pro-tein	Fat	Fatty Acids		
							Satu-rated	Mono-unsatu-rated	Poly-unsatu-rated
SOUPS, SAUCES, AND GRAVIES—Con.		Grams	Per-cent	Cal-ories	Grams	Grams	Grams	Grams	Grams
Tomato	1 cup	244	90	85	2	2	0.4	0.4	1.0
Vegetable beef	1 cup	244	92	80	6	2	0.9	0.8	0.1
Vegetarian	1 cup	241	92	70	2	2	0.3	0.8	0.7
Dehydrated:									
Prepared with water:									
Chicken noodle	1 pkt (6-fl-oz)	188	94	40	2	1	0.2	0.4	0.3
Onion	1 pkt (6-fl-oz)	184	96	20	1	Tr	0.1	0.2	0.1
Tomato vegetable	1 pkt (6-fl-oz)	189	94	40	1	1	0.3	0.2	0.1
Sauces:									
From dry mix:									
Hollandaise, prepared with water	1 cup	259	84	240	5	20	11.6	5.9	0.9
White sauce, prepared with milk	1 cup	264	81	240	10	13	6.4	4.7	1.7
From home recipe:									
White sauce, medium[55]	1 cup	250	73	395	10	30	9.1	11.9	7.2
Ready to serve:									
Barbecue	1 tbsp	16	81	10	Tr	Tr	Tr	0.1	0.1
Soy	1 tbsp	18	68	10	2	0	0.0	0.0	0.0
SUGARS AND SWEETS									
Candy:									
Caramels, plain or chocolate	1 oz	28	8	115	1	3	2.2	0.3	0.1
Chocolate:									
Milk, plain	1 oz	28	1	145	2	9	5.4	3.0	0.3
Milk, with almonds	1 oz	28	2	150	3	10	4.8	4.1	0.7
Milk, with peanuts	1 oz	28	1	155	4	11	4.2	3.5	1.5
Milk, with rice cereal	1 oz	28	2	140	2	7	4.4	2.5	0.2
Semisweet, small pieces (60 per oz)	1 cup or 6 oz	170	1	860	7	61	36.2	19.9	1.9
Sweet (dark)	1 oz	28	1	150	1	10	5.9	3.3	0.3
Fudge, chocolate, plain	1 oz	28	8	115	1	3	2.1	1.0	0.1
Gum drops	1 oz	28	12	100	Tr	Tr	Tr	Tr	0.1
Hard	1 oz	28	1	110	0	0	0.0	0.0	0.0
Jelly beans	1 oz	28	6	105	Tr	Tr	Tr	Tr	0.1
Marshmallows	1 oz	28	17	90	1	0	0.0	0.0	0.0
Custard, baked	1 cup	265	77	305	14	15	6.8	5.4	0.7
Gelatin dessert prepared with gelatin dessert powder and water	½ cup	120	84	70	2	0	0.0	0.0	0.0
Honey, strained or extracted	1 cup	339	17	1,030	1	0	0.0	0.0	0.0
	1 tbsp	21	17	65	Tr	0	0.0	0.0	0.0
Jams and preserves	1 tbsp	20	29	55	Tr	Tr	0.0	Tr	Tr
	1 packet	14	29	40	Tr	Tr	0.0	Tr	Tr
Jellies	1 tbsp	18	28	50	Tr	Tr	Tr	Tr	Tr
	1 packet	14	28	40	Tr	Tr	Tr	Tr	Tr
Popsicle, 3-fl-oz size	1 popsicle	95	80	70	0	0	0.0	0.0	0.0

(Tr indicates nutrient present in trace amounts.)

Nutrients in Indicated Quantity

Cho-les-terol	Carbo-hydrate	Calcium	Phos-phorus	Iron	Potas-sium	Sodium	Vitamin A value		Thiamin	Ribo-flavin	Niacin	Ascorbic acid
							(IU)	(RE)				
Milli-grams	Grams	Milli-grams	Milli-grams	Milli-grams	Milli-grams	Milli-grams	Inter-national units	Retinol equiva-lents	Milli-grams	Milli-grams	Milli-grams	Milli-grams
0	17	12	34	1.8	264	871	690	69	0.09	0.05	1.4	66
5	10	17	41	1.1	173	956	1,890	189	0.04	0.05	1.0	2
0	12	22	34	1.1	210	822	3,010	301	0.05	0.05	0.9	1
2	6	24	24	0.4	23	957	50	5	0.05	0.04	0.7	Tr
0	4	9	22	0.1	48	635	Tr	Tr	0.02	0.04	0.4	Tr
0	8	6	23	0.5	78	856	140	14	0.04	0.03	0.6	5
52	14	124	127	0.9	124	1,564	730	220	0.05	0.18	0.1	Tr
34	21	425	256	0.3	444	797	310	92	0.08	0.45	0.5	3
32	24	292	238	0.9	381	888	1,190	340	0.15	0.43	0.8	2
0	2	3	3	0.1	28	130	140	14	Tr	Tr	0.1	1
0	2	3	38	0.5	64	1,029	0	0	0.01	0.02	0.6	0
1	22	42	35	0.4	54	64	Tr	Tr	0.01	0.05	0.1	Tr
6	16	50	61	0.4	96	23	30	10	0.02	0.10	0.1	Tr
5	15	65	77	0.5	125	23	30	8	0.02	0.12	0.2	Tr
5	13	49	83	0.4	138	19	30	8	0.07	0.07	1.4	Tr
6	18	48	57	0.2	100	46	30	8	0.01	0.08	0.1	Tr
0	97	51	178	5.8	593	24	30	3	0.10	0.14	0.9	Tr
0	16	7	41	0.6	86	5	10	1	0.01	0.04	0.1	Tr
1	21	22	24	0.3	42	54	Tr	Tr	0.01	0.03	0.1	Tr
0	25	2	Tr	0.1	1	10	0	0	0.00	Tr	Tr	0
0	28	Tr	2	0.1	1	7	0	0	0.10	0.00	0.0	0
0	26	1	1	0.3	11	7	0	0	0.00	Tr	Tr	0
0	23	1	2	0.5	2	25	0	0	0.00	Tr	Tr	0
278	29	297	310	1.1	387	209	530	146	0.11	0.50	0.3	1
0	17	2	23	Tr	Tr	55	0	0	0.00	0.00	0.0	0
0	279	17	20	1.7	173	17	0	0	0.02	0.14	1.0	3
0	17	1	1	0.1	11	1	0	0	Tr	0.01	0.1	Tr
0	14	4	2	0.2	18	2	Tr	Tr	Tr	0.01	Tr	Tr
0	10	3	1	0.1	12	2	Tr	Tr	Tr	Tr	Tr	Tr
0	13	2	Tr	0.1	16	5	Tr	Tr	Tr	0.01	Tr	1
0	10	1	Tr	Tr	13	4	Tr	Tr	Tr	Tr	Tr	1
0	18	0	0	Tr	4	11	0	0	0.00	0.00	0.0	0

Nutritive Value of Foods *(Continued)*

Foods, approximate measures, units, and weight (weight of edible portion only)			Water	Food energy	Pro- tein	Fat	Fatty Acids		
							Satu- rated	Mono- unsatu- rated	Poly- unsatu- rated
		Grams	Per- cent	Cal- ories	Grams	Grams	Grams	Grams	Grams
SUGARS AND SWEETS—Con.									
Puddings:									
Canned:									
Vanilla- - - - - - - - - - - -	5-oz can- - - - - - -	142	69	220	2	10	9.5	0.2	0.1
Dry mix, prepared with whole milk:									
Chocolate:									
Instant- - - - - - - - - - -	½ cup- - - - - - - - -	130	71	155	4	4	2.3	1.1	0.2
Regular (cooked)- - - -	½ cup- - - - - - - - -	130	73	150	4	4	2.4	1.1	0.1
Rice- - - - - - - - - - - -	½ cup- - - - - - - - -	132	73	155	4	4	2.3	1.1	0.1
Tapioca- - - - - - - - - - -	½ cup- - - - - - - - -	130	75	145	4	4	2.3	1.1	0.1
Vanilla:									
Instant- - - - - - - - - - -	½ cup- - - - - - - - -	130	73	150	4	4	2.2	1.1	0.2
Sugars:									
Brown, pressed down- - - -	1 cup- - - - - - - - -	220	2	820	0	0	0.0	0.0	0.0
White:									
Granulated- - - - - - - -	1 cup- - - - - - - - -	200	1	770	0	0	0.0	0.0	0.0
	1 tbsp- - - - - - - -	10	1	45	0	0	0.0	0.0	0.0
	1 packet- - - - - - -	6	1	25	0	0	0.0	0.0	0.0
Powdered, sifted, spooned into cup- - - -	1 cup- - - - - - - - -	100	1	385	0	0	0.0	0.0	0.0
Syrups:									
Chocolate-flavored syrup or topping:									
Thin type- - - - - - - - -	2 tbsp- - - - - - - -	38	37	85	1	Tr	0.2	0.1	0.1
Fudge type- - - - - - - - -	2 tbsp- - - - - - - -	38	25	125	2	5	3.1	1.7	0.2
Molasses, cane, blackstrap	2 tbsp- - - - - - - -	40	24	85	0	0	0.0	0.0	0.0
Table syrup (corn and maple)- - - - - - - - - - -	2 tbsp- - - - - - - -	42	25	122	0	0	0.0	0.0	0.0
VEGETABLES AND VEGETABLE PRODUCTS									
Alfalfa seeds, sprouted, raw-	1 cup- - - - - - - - -	33	91	10	1	Tr	Tr	Tr	0.1
Artichokes, globe or French, cooked, drained- - - - - - - -	1 artichoke- - - - -	120	87	55	3	Tr	Tr	Tr	0.1
Asparagus, green:									
Cooked, drained:									
From raw:									
Cuts and tips- - - - - -	1 cup- - - - - - - - -	180	92	45	5	1	0.1	Tr	0.2
Spears, ½-in diam. at base- - - - - - - - - - -	4 spears- - - - - - -	60	92	15	2	Tr	Tr	Tr	0.1
From frozen:									
Cuts and tips- - - - - -	1 cup- - - - - - - - -	180	91	50	5	1	0.2	Tr	0.3
Spears, ½-in diam. at base- - - - - - - - - - -	4 spears- - - - - - -	60	91	15	2	Tr	0.1	Tr	0.1
Canned, spears, ½-in diam. at base- - - - - - - - -	4 spears- - - - - - -	80	95	10	1	Tr	Tr	Tr	0.1
Bamboo shoots, canned, drained- - - - - - - - - - - -	1 cup- - - - - - - - -	131	94	25	2	1	0.1	Tr	0.2

(Tr indicates nutrient present in trace amounts.)

Nutrients in Indicated Quantity

Cho-les-terol	Carbo-hydrate	Calcium	Phos-phorus	Iron	Potas-sium	Sodium	Vitamin A value (IU)	Vitamin A value (RE)	Thiamin	Ribo-flavin	Niacin	Ascorbic acid
Milli-grams	Grams	Milli-grams	Milli-grams	Milli-grams	Milli-grams	Milli-grams	Inter-national units	Retinol equiva-lents	Milli-grams	Milli-grams	Milli-grams	Milli-grams
1	33	79	94	0.2	155	305	Tr	Tr	0.03	0.12	0.6	Tr
14	27	130	329	0.3	176	440	130	33	0.04	0.18	0.1	1
15	25	146	120	0.2	190	167	140	34	0.05	0.20	0.1	1
15	27	133	110	0.5	165	140	140	33	0.10	0.18	0.6	1
15	25	131	103	0.1	167	152	140	34	0.04	0.18	0.1	1
15	27	129	273	0.1	164	375	140	33	0.04	0.17	0.1	1
0	212	187	56	4.8	757	97	0	0	0.02	0.07	0.2	0
0	199	3	Tr	0.1	7	5	0	0	0.00	0.00	0.0	0
0	12	Tr	Tr	Tr	Tr	Tr	0	0	0.00	0.00	0.0	0
0	6	Tr	Tr	Tr	Tr	Tr	0	0	0.00	0.00	0.0	0
0	100	1	Tr	Tr	4	2	0	0	0.00	0.00	0.0	0
0	22	6	49	0.8	85	36	Tr	Tr	Tr	0.02	0.1	0
0	21	38	60	0.5	82	42	40	13	0.02	0.08	0.1	0
0	22	274	34	10.1	1,171	38	0	0	0.04	0.08	0.8	0
0	32	1	4	Tr	7	19	0	0	0.00	0.00	0.0	0
0	1	11	23	0.3	26	2	50	5	0.03	0.04	0.2	3
0	12	47	72	1.6	316	79	170	17	0.07	0.06	0.7	9
0	8	43	110	1.2	558	7	1,490	149	0.18	0.22	1.9	49
0	3	14	37	0.4	186	2	500	50	0.06	0.07	0.6	16
0	9	41	99	1.2	392	7	1,470	147	0.12	0.19	1.9	44
0	3	14	33	0.4	131	2	490	49	0.04	0.06	0.6	15
0	2	11	30	0.5	122	[56]278	380	38	0.04	0.07	0.7	13
0	4	10	33	0.4	105	9	10	1	0.03	0.03	0.2	1

Nutritive Value of Foods *(Continued)*

Foods, approximate measures, units, and weight (weight of edible portion only)			Water	Food energy	Pro-tein	Fat	Fatty Acids		
							Satu-rated	Mono-unsatu-rated	Poly-unsatu-rated
VEGETABLES AND VEGETABLE PRODUCTS—Con.		*Grams*	*Per-cent*	*Cal-ories*	*Grams*	*Grams*	*Grams*	*Grams*	*Grams*
Beans:									
Lima, immature seeds, frozen, cooked, drained:									
Thick-seeded types (Fordhooks)	1 cup	170	74	170	10	1	0.1	Tr	0.3
Thin-seeded types (baby limas)	1 cup	180	72	190	12	1	0.1	Tr	0.3
Snap:									
Cooked, drained:									
From raw (cut and French style)	1 cup	125	89	45	2	Tr	0.1	Tr	0.2
From frozen (cut)	1 cup	135	92	35	2	Tr	Tr	Tr	0.1
Canned, drained solids (cut)	1 cup	135	93	25	2	Tr	Tr	Tr	0.1
Beans, mature. See Beans, dry and Black-eyed peas, dry.									
Bean sprouts (mung):									
Raw	1 cup	104	90	30	3	Tr	Tr	Tr	0.1
Beets:									
Cooked, drained:									
Diced or sliced	1 cup	170	91	55	2	Tr	Tr	Tr	Tr
Canned, drained solids, diced or sliced	1 cup	170	91	55	2	Tr	Tr	Tr	0.1
Beet greens, leaves and stems, cooked, drained	1 cup	144	89	40	4	Tr	Tr	0.1	0.1
Black-eyed peas, immature seeds, cooked and drained:									
From raw	1 cup	165	72	180	13	1	0.3	0.1	0.6
From frozen	1 cup	170	66	225	14	1	0.3	0.1	0.5
Broccoli:									
Raw	1 spear	151	91	40	4	1	0.1	Tr	0.3
Cooked, drained:									
From raw:									
Spear, medium	1 spear	180	90	50	5	1	0.1	Tr	0.2
Spears, cut into ½-in pieces	1 cup	155	90	45	5	Tr	0.1	Tr	0.2
Brussels sprouts, cooked, drained:									
From frozen	1 cup	155	87	65	6	1	0.1	Tr	0.3
Cabbage, common varieties:									
Raw, coarsely shredded or sliced	1 cup	70	93	15	1	Tr	Tr	Tr	0.1
Cooked, drained	1 cup	150	94	30	1	Tr	Tr	Tr	0.2
Cabbage, Chinese:									
Pak-choi, cooked, drained	1 cup	170	96	20	3	Tr	Tr	Tr	0.1
Pe-tsai, raw, 1-in pieces	1 cup	76	94	10	1	Tr	Tr	Tr	0.1

(Tr indicates nutrient present in trace amounts.)

Nutrients in Indicated Quantity

| Cho-les-terol | Carbo-hydrate | Calcium | Phos-phorus | Iron | Potas-sium | Sodium | Vitamin A value | | Thiamin | Ribo-flavin | Niacin | Ascorbic acid |
| | | | | | | | (IU) | (RE) | | | | |
Milli-grams	Grams	Milli-grams	Milli-grams	Milli-grams	Milli-grams	Milli-grams	Inter-national units	Retinol equiva-lents	Milli-grams	Milli-grams	Milli-grams	Milli-grams
0	32	37	107	2.3	694	90	320	32	0.13	0.10	1.8	22
0	35	50	202	3.5	740	52	300	30	0.13	0.10	1.4	10
0	10	58	49	1.6	374	4	[57]830	[58]83	0.09	0.12	0.8	12
0	8	61	32	1.1	151	18	[58]710	[58]71	0.06	0.10	0.6	11
0	6	35	26	1.2	147	[59]339	[60]470	[60]47	0.02	0.08	0.3	6
0	6	14	56	0.9	155	6	20	2	0.09	0.13	0.8	14
0	11	19	53	1.1	530	83	20	2	0.05	0.02	0.5	9
0	12	26	29	3.1	252	[61]466	20	2	0.02	0.07	0.3	7
0	8	164	59	2.7	1,309	347	7,340	734	0.17	0.42	0.7	36
0	30	46	196	2.4	693	7	1,050	105	0.11	0.18	1.8	3
0	40	39	207	3.6	638	9	130	13	0.44	0.11	1.2	4
0	8	72	100	1.3	491	41	2,330	233	0.10	0.18	1.0	141
0	10	205	86	2.1	293	20	2,540	254	0.15	0.37	1.4	113
0	9	177	74	1.8	253	17	2,180	218	0.13	0.32	1.2	97
0	13	37	84	1.1	504	36	910	91	0.16	0.18	0.8	71
0	4	33	16	0.4	172	13	90	9	0.04	0.02	0.2	33
0	7	50	38	0.6	308	29	130	13	0.09	0.08	0.3	36
0	3	158	49	1.8	631	58	4,370	437	0.05	0.11	0.7	44
0	2	59	22	0.2	181	7	910	91	0.03	0.04	0.3	21

Nutritive Value of Foods *(Continued)*

Foods, approximate measures, units, and weight (weight of edible portion only)		Water	Food energy	Pro-tein	Fat	Fatty Acids		
						Satu-rated	Mono-unsatu-rated	Poly-unsatu-rated
		Grams	Per-cent	Cal-ories	Grams	Grams	Grams	Grams
VEGETABLES AND VEGETABLE PRODUCTS—Con.								
Cabbage, red, raw, coarsely shredded or sliced	1 cup	70	92	20	1	Tr	Tr	0.1
Cabbage, savoy, raw, coarsely shredded or sliced	1 cup	70	91	20	1	Tr	Tr	Tr
Carrots:								
Raw, without crowns and tips, scraped:								
Whole, 7½ by 1⅛ in, or strips, 2½ to 3 in long	1 carrot or 18 strips	72	88	30	1	Tr	Tr	0.1
Cooked, sliced, drained:								
From frozen	1 cup	146	90	55	2	Tr	Tr	0.1
Canned, sliced, drained solids	1 cup	146	93	35	1	Tr	0.1	0.1
Cauliflower:								
Cooked, drained:								
From raw (flowerets)	1 cup	125	93	30	2	Tr	Tr	0.1
From frozen (flowerets)	1 cup	180	94	35	3	Tr	0.1	0.2
Celery, pascal type, raw:								
Stalk, large outer, 8 by 1½ in (at root end)	1 stalk	40	95	5	Tr	Tr	Tr	Tr
Collards, cooked, drained:								
From raw (leaves without stems)	1 cup	190	96	25	2	Tr	0.1	0.2
Corn, sweet:								
Cooked, drained:								
From raw, ear 5 by 1¾ in	1 ear	77	70	85	3	1	0.2	0.3	0.5
From frozen:								
Kernels	1 cup	165	76	135	5	Tr	Tr	0.1
Canned:								
Cream style	1 cup	256	79	185	4	1	0.2	0.3	0.5
Whole kernel, vacuum pack	1 cup	210	77	165	5	1	0.2	0.3	0.5
Cowpeas. See Black-eyed peas.								
Cucumber, with peel, slices, ⅛ in thick (large, 2⅛-in diam.; small, 1¾-in diam.)	6 large or 8 small slices	28	96	5	Tr	Tr	Tr	Tr	Tr
Dandelion greens, cooked, drained	1 cup	105	90	35	2	1	0.1	Tr	0.3
Eggplant, cooked, steamed	1 cup	96	92	25	1	Tr	Tr	Tr	0.1
Endive, curly (including escarole), raw, small pieces	1 cup	50	94	10	1	Tr	Tr	Tr	Tr
Jerusalem-artichoke, raw, sliced	1 cup	150	78	115	3	Tr	0.0	Tr	Tr

(Tr indicates nutrient present in trace amounts.)

Nutrients in Indicated Quantity

Cholesterol	Carbohydrate	Calcium	Phosphorus	Iron	Potassium	Sodium	Vitamin A value		Thiamin	Riboflavin	Niacin	Ascorbic acid
							(IU)	(RE)				
Milligrams	Grams	Milligrams	Milligrams	Milligrams	Milligrams	Milligrams	International units	Retinol equivalents	Milligrams	Milligrams	Milligrams	Milligrams
0	4	36	29	0.3	144	8	30	3	0.04	0.02	0.2	40
0	4	25	29	0.3	161	20	700	70	0.05	0.02	0.2	22
0	7	19	32	0.4	233	25	20,250	2,025	0.07	0.04	0.7	7
0	12	41	38	0.7	231	86	25,850	2,585	0.04	0.05	0.6	4
0	8	37	35	0.9	261	[62]352	20,110	2,011	0.03	0.04	0.8	4
0	6	34	44	0.5	404	8	20	2	0.08	0.07	0.7	69
0	7	31	43	0.7	250	32	40	4	0.07	0.10	0.6	56
0	1	14	10	0.2	114	35	50	5	0.01	0.01	0.1	3
0	5	148	19	0.8	177	36	4,220	422	0.03	0.08	0.4	19
0	19	2	79	0.5	192	13	[63]170	[63]17	0.17	0.06	1.2	5
0	34	3	78	0.5	229	8	[63]410	[63]41	0.11	0.12	2.1	4
0	46	8	131	1.0	343	[64]730	[63]250	[63]25	0.06	0.14	2.5	12
0	41	11	134	0.9	391	[65]571	[63]510	[63]51	0.09	0.15	2.5	17
0	1	4	5	0.1	42	1	10	1	0.01	0.01	0.1	1
0	7	147	44	1.9	244	46	12,290	1,229	0.14	0.18	0.5	19
0	6	6	21	0.3	238	3	60	6	0.07	0.02	0.6	1
0	2	26	14	0.4	157	11	1,030	103	0.04	0.04	0.2	3
0	26	21	117	5.1	644	6	30	3	0.30	0.09	2.0	6

Nutritive Value of Foods *(Continued)*

Foods, approximate measures, units, and weight (weight of edible portion only)		Water	Food energy	Pro-tein	Fat	Fatty Acids Satu-rated	Mono-unsatu-rated	Poly-unsatu-rated
VEGETABLES AND VEGETABLE PRODUCTS—Con.	Grams	Per-cent	Cal-ories	Grams	Grams	Grams	Grams	Grams
Kale, cooked, drained:								
From raw, chopped- - - - - 1 cup- - - - - - - - -	130	91	40	2	1	0.1	Tr	0.3
From frozen, chopped- - - - 1 cup- - - - - - - - -	130	91	40	4	1	0.1	Tr	0.3
Kohlrabi, thickened bulb-like stems, cooked, drained, diced- - - - - - - - - - - - - - 1 cup- - - - - - - - -	165	90	50	3	Tr	Tr	Tr	0.1
Lettuce, raw:								
Butterhead, as Boston types:								
Head, 5-in diam- - - - - - 1 head- - - - - - - -	163	96	20	2	Tr	Tr	Tr	0.2
Leaves- - - - - - - - - - - - 1 outer or 2 inner leaves- - - - - - -	15	96	Tr	Tr	Tr	Tr	Tr	Tr
Crisphead, as iceberg:								
Head, 6-in diam- - - - - - 1 head- - - - - - - -	539	96	70	5	1	0.1	Tr	0.5
Looseleaf (bunching varie-ties including romaine or cos), chopped or shredded pieces- - - - - 1 cup- - - - - - - - -	56	94	10	1	Tr	Tr	Tr	0.1
Mushrooms:								
Raw, sliced or chopped- - - 1 cup- - - - - - - - -	70	92	20	1	Tr	Tr	Tr	0.1
Cooked, drained- - - - - - - 1 cup- - - - - - - - -	156	91	40	3	1	0.1	Tr	0.3
Canned, drained solids- - - 1 cup- - - - - - - - -	156	91	35	3	Tr	0.1	Tr	0.2
Mustard greens, without stems and midribs, cooked, drained- - - - - - - - - - - - - 1 cup- - - - - - - - -	140	94	20	3	Tr	Tr	0.2	0.1
Okra pods, 3 by ⅝ in, cooked 8 pods- - - - - - - - -	85	90	25	2	Tr	Tr	Tr	Tr
Onions:								
Raw:								
Sliced- - - - - - - - - - - - - 1 cup- - - - - - - - -	115	91	40	1	Tr	0.1	Tr	0.1
Cooked (whole or sliced), drained- - - - - - - - - 1 cup- - - - - - - - -	210	92	60	2	Tr	0.1	Tr	0.1
Onions, spring, raw, bulb (⅜-in diam.) and white portion of top- - - - - - - - - - - - - - - 6 onions- - - - - - -	30	92	10	1	Tr	Tr	Tr	Tr
Onion rings, breaded, par-fried, frozen, prepared- - - 2 rings- - - - - - - -	20	29	80	1	5	1.7	2.2	1.0
Parsley:								
Raw- - - - - - - - - - - - - - - 10 sprigs- - - - - - -	10	88	5	Tr	Tr	Tr	Tr	Tr
Parsnips, cooked (diced or 2 in lengths), drained- - - - - - - 1 cup- - - - - - - - -	156	78	125	2	Tr	0.1	0.2	0.1
Peas, edible pod, cooked, drained- - - - - - - - - - - - - 1 cup- - - - - - - - -	160	89	65	5	Tr	0.1	Tr	0.2
Peas, green:								
Canned, drained solids- - - 1 cup- - - - - - - - -	170	82	115	8	1	0.1	0.1	0.3
Frozen, cooked, drained- - 1 cup- - - - - - - - -	160	80	125	8	Tr	0.1	Tr	0.2
Peppers:								
Hot chili, raw- - - - - - - - - 1 pepper- - - - - - -	45	88	20	1	Tr	Tr	Tr	Tr

(Tr indicates nutrient present in trace amounts.)

Nutrients in Indicated Quantity

Cho-les-terol	Carbo-hydrate	Calcium	Phos-phorus	Iron	Potas-sium	Sodium	Vitamin A value		Thiamin	Ribo-flavin	Niacin	Ascorbic acid
							(IU)	(RE)				
Milli-grams	Grams	Milli-grams	Milli-grams	Milli-grams	Milli-grams	Milli-grams	Inter-national units	Retinol equiva-lents	Milli-grams	Milli-grams	Milli-grams	Milli-grams
0	7	94	36	1.2	296	30	9,620	962	0.07	0.09	0.7	53
0	7	179	36	1.2	417	20	8,260	826	0.06	0.15	0.9	33
0	11	41	74	0.7	561	35	60	6	0.07	0.03	0.6	89
0	4	52	38	0.5	419	8	1,580	158	0.10	0.10	0.5	13
0	Tr	5	3	Tr	39	1	150	15	0.01	0.01	Tr	1
0	11	102	108	2.7	852	49	1,780	178	0.25	0.16	1.0	21
0	2	38	14	0.8	148	5	1,060	106	0.03	0.04	0.2	10
0	3	4	73	0.9	259	3	0	0	0.07	0.31	2.9	2
0	8	9	136	2.7	555	3	0	0	0.11	0.47	7.0	6
0	8	17	103	1.2	201	663	0	0	0.13	0.03	2.5	0
0	3	104	57	1.0	283	22	4,240	424	0.06	0.09	0.6	35
0	6	54	48	0.4	274	4	490	49	0.11	0.05	0.7	14
0	8	29	33	0.4	178	2	0	0	0.07	0.01	0.1	10
0	13	57	48	0.4	319	17	0	0	0.09	0.02	0.2	12
0	2	18	10	0.6	77	1	1,500	150	0.02	0.04	0.1	14
0	8	6	16	0.3	26	75	50	5	0.06	0.03	0.7	Tr
0	1	13	4	0.6	54	4	520	52	0.01	0.01	0.1	9
0	30	58	108	0.9	573	16	0	0	0.13	0.08	1.1	20
0	11	67	88	3.2	384	6	210	21	0.20	0.12	0.9	77
0	21	34	114	1.6	294	[66]372	1,310	131	0.21	0.13	1.2	16
0	23	38	144	2.5	269	139	1,070	107	0.45	0.16	2.4	16
0	4	8	21	0.5	153	3	[67]4,840	[67]484	0.04	0.04	0.4	109

Nutritive Value of Foods *(Continued)*

Foods, approximate measures, units, and weight (weight of edible portion only)		Water	Food energy	Pro-tein	Fat	Fatty Acids Satu-rated	Mono-unsatu-rated	Poly-unsatu-rated
		Per-cent	*Cal-ories*	*Grams*	*Grams*	*Grams*	*Grams*	*Grams*
VEGETABLES AND VEGETABLE PRODUCTS—Con.		*Grams*						
Sweet (about 5 per lb, whole), stem and seeds removed:								
Raw- - - - - - - - - - - - - -	1 pepper- - - - - - -	74	93	20	1	Tr	Tr	Tr	0.2
Cooked, drained- - - - -	1 pepper- - - - - - -	73	95	15	Tr	Tr	Tr	Tr	0.1
Potatoes, cooked:								
Baked (about 2 per lb, raw):								
With skin- - - - - - - - -	1 potato- - - - - - -	202	71	220	5	Tr	0.1	Tr	0.1
Flesh only- - - - - - - - -	1 potato- - - - - - -	156	75	145	3	Tr	Tr	Tr	0.1
Boiled (about 3 per lb, raw):								
Peeled after boiling- - - -	1 potato- - - - - - -	136	77	120	3	Tr	Tr	Tr	0.1
Peeled before boiling- - -	1 potato- - - - - - -	135	77	115	2	Tr	Tr	Tr	0.1
French fried, strip, 2 to 3½ in long, frozen:								
Oven heated- - - - - - - -	10 strips- - - - - - -	50	53	110	2	4	2.1	1.8	0.3
Fried in vegetable oil- - -	10 strips- - - - - - -	50	38	160	2	8	2.5	1.6	3.8
Potato products, prepared:								
Hashed brown, from frozen	1 cup- - - - - - - - -	100	56	340	5	18	7.0	8.0	2.1
Mashed:								
From home recipe:								
Milk added- - - - - - - -	1 cup- - - - - - - - -	210	78	160	4	1	0.7	0.3	0.1
Milk and margarine added- - - - - - - - - - -	1 cup- - - - - - - - -	210	76	225	4	9	2.2	3.7	2.5
Potato salad, made with mayonnaise- - - - - -	1 cup- - - - - - - - -	250	76	360	7	21	3.6	6.2	9.3
Scalloped:								
From dry mix- - - - - - -	1 cup- - - - - - - - -	245	79	230	5	11	6.5	3.0	0.5
Potato chips- - - - - - - - - - -	10 chips- - - - - - -	20	3	105	1	7	1.8	1.2	3.6
Pumpkin:								
Cooked from raw, mashed-	1 cup- - - - - - - - -	245	94	50	2	Tr	0.1	Tr	Tr
Canned- - - - - - - - - - - -	1 cup- - - - - - - - -	245	90	85	3	1	0.4	0.1	Tr
Radishes, raw, stem ends, rootlets cut off- - - - - - - -	4 radishes- - - - - -	18	95	5	Tr	Tr	Tr	Tr	Tr
Sauerkraut, canned, solids and liquid- - - - - - - - - - -	1 cup- - - - - - - - -	236	93	45	2	Tr	0.1	Tr	0.1
Seaweed:								
Kelp, raw- - - - - - - - - - -	1 oz- - - - - - - - - -	28	82	10	Tr	Tr	0.1	Tr	Tr
Southern peas. See Black-eyed peas.								
Spinach:								
Raw, chopped- - - - - - - -	1 cup- - - - - - - - -	55	92	10	2	Tr	Tr	Tr	0.1
Cooked, drained:								
From raw- - - - - - - - -	1 cup- - - - - - - - -	180	91	40	5	Tr	0.1	Tr	0.2
Canned, drained solids- - -	1 cup- - - - - - - - -	214	92	50	6	1	0.2	Tr	0.4
Squash, cooked:								
Summer (all varieties), sliced, drained- - - - - -	1 cup- - - - - - - - -	180	94	35	2	1	0.1	Tr	0.2

(Tr indicates nutrient present in trace amounts.)

Nutrients in Indicated Quantity

Cholesterol	Carbohydrate	Calcium	Phosphorus	Iron	Potassium	Sodium	Vitamin A value (IU)	Vitamin A value (RE)	Thiamin	Riboflavin	Niacin	Ascorbic acid
Milligrams	Grams	Milligrams	Milligrams	Milligrams	Milligrams	Milligrams	International units	Retinol equivalents	Milligrams	Milligrams	Milligrams	Milligrams
0	4	4	16	0.9	144	2	[68]390	[68]39	0.06	0.04	0.4	[69]95
0	3	3	11	0.6	94	1	[70]280	[70]28	0.04	0.03	0.3	[71]81
0	51	20	115	2.7	844	16	0	0	0.22	0.07	3.3	26
0	34	8	78	0.5	610	8	0	0	0.16	0.03	2.2	20
0	27	7	60	0.4	515	5	0	0	0.14	0.03	2.0	18
0	27	11	54	0.4	443	7	0	0	0.13	0.03	1.8	10
0	17	5	43	0.7	229	16	0	0	0.06	0.02	1.2	5
0	20	10	47	0.4	366	108	0	0	0.09	0.01	1.6	5
0	44	23	112	2.4	680	53	0	0	0.17	0.03	3.8	10
4	37	55	101	0.6	628	636	40	12	0.18	0.08	2.3	14
4	35	55	97	0.5	607	620	360	42	0.18	0.08	2.3	13
170	28	48	130	1.6	635	1,323	520	83	0.19	0.15	2.2	25
27	31	88	137	0.9	497	835	360	51	0.05	0.14	2.5	8
0	10	5	31	0.2	260	94	0	0	0.03	Tr	0.8	8
0	12	37	74	1.4	564	2	2,650	265	0.08	0.19	1.0	12
0	20	64	86	3.4	505	12	54,040	5,404	0.06	0.13	0.9	10
0	1	4	3	0.1	42	4	Tr	Tr	Tr	0.01	0.1	4
0	10	71	47	3.5	401	1,560	40	4	0.05	0.05	0.3	35
0	3	48	12	0.8	25	66	30	3	0.01	0.04	0.1	(1)
0	2	54	27	1.5	307	43	3,690	369	0.04	0.10	0.4	15
0	7	245	101	6.4	839	126	14,740	1,474	0.17	0.42	0.9	18
0	7	272	94	4.9	740	[72]683	18,780	1,878	0.03	0.30	0.8	31
0	8	49	70	0.6	346	2	520	52	0.08	0.07	0.9	10

Nutritive Value of Foods *(Continued)*

Foods, approximate measures, units, and weight (weight of edible portion only)		Water	Food energy	Pro-tein	Fat	Satu-rated	*Fatty Acids* Mono-unsatu-rated	Poly-unsatu-rated
VEGETABLES AND VEGETABLE PRODUCTS—Con.	Grams	Per-cent	Cal-ories	Grams	Grams	Grams	Grams	Grams
Winter (all varieties), baked, cubes- - - - - - -	1 cup- - - - - - - - -	205	89	80	2	1	0.3	0.1	0.5
Sunchoke. See Jerusalem-artichoke.									
Sweet potatoes:									
Cooked (raw, 5 by 2 in; about 2½ per lb):									
Baked in skin, peeled- -	1 potato- - - - - - -	114	73	115	2	Tr	Tr	Tr	0.1
Boiled, without skin- - -	1 potato- - - - - - -	151	73	160	2	Tr	0.1	Tr	0.2
Candied, 2½ by 2-in piece-	1 piece- - - - - - - -	105	67	145	1	3	1.4	0.7	0.2
Canned:									
Solid pack (mashed)- - -	1 cup- - - - - - - - -	255	74	260	5	1	0.1	Tr	0.2
Vacuum pack, piece 2¾ by 1 in- - - - - - - - - - -	1 piece- - - - - - - -	40	76	35	1	Tr	Tr	Tr	Tr
Tomatoes:									
Raw, 2⅗-in diam. (3 per 12 oz pkg.)- - - - - - - - - - -	1 tomato- - - - - - -	123	94	25	1	Tr	Tr	Tr	0.1
Canned, solids and liquid-	1 cup- - - - - - - - -	240	94	50	2	1	0.1	0.1	0.1
Tomato juice, canned- - - - -	1 cup- - - - - - - - -	244	94	40	2	Tr	Tr	Tr	0.1
Tomato products, canned:									
Paste- - - - - - - - - - - - - -	1 cup- - - - - - - - -	262	74	220	10	2	0.3	0.4	0.9
Puree- - - - - - - - - - - - - -	1 cup- - - - - - - - -	250	87	105	4	Tr	Tr	Tr	0.1
Sauce- - - - - - - - - - - - - -	1 cup- - - - - - - - -	245	89	75	3	Tr	0.1	0.1	0.2
Turnips, cooked, diced- - - - -	1 cup- - - - - - - - -	156	94	30	1	Tr	Tr	Tr	0.1
Turnip greens, cooked, drained:									
From raw (leaves and stems)- - - - - - - - - - - -	1 cup- - - - - - - - -	144	93	30	2	Tr	0.1	Tr	0.1
From frozen (chopped)- - -	1 cup- - - - - - - - -	164	90	50	5	1	0.2	Tr	0.3
Vegetable juice cocktail, canned- - - - - - - - - - - - -	1 cup- - - - - - - - -	242	94	45	2	Tr	Tr	Tr	0.1
Vegetables, mixed:									
Frozen, cooked, drained- -	1 cup- - - - - - - - -	182	83	105	5	Tr	0.1	Tr	0.1
Water chestnuts, canned- - -	1 cup- - - - - - - - -	140	86	70	1	Tr	Tr	Tr	Tr
MISCELLANEOUS ITEMS									
Baking powders for home use:									
Sodium aluminum sulfate:									
With monocalcium phos-phate monohydrate- -	1 tsp- - - - - - - - -	3	2	5	Tr	0	0.0	0.0	0.0
Catsup- - - - - - - - - - - - - -	1 cup- - - - - - - - -	273	69	290	5	1	0.2	0.2	0.4
	1 tbsp- - - - - - - -	15	69	15	Tr	Tr	Tr	Tr	Tr
Chili powder- - - - - - - - - - -	1 tsp- - - - - - - - -	2.6	8	10	Tr	Tr	0.1	0.1	0.2
Chocolate:									
Bitter or baking- - - - - - - -	1 oz- - - - - - - - - -	28	2	145	3	15	9.0	4.9	0.5
Semisweet, see Candy									
Cinnamon- - - - - - - - - - - - -	1 tsp- - - - - - - - -	2.3	10	5	Tr	Tr	Tr	Tr	Tr
Curry powder- - - - - - - - - -	1 tsp- - - - - - - - -	2	10	5	Tr	Tr	[1]	[1]	[1]

(Tr indicates nutrient present in trace amounts.)

Nutrients in Indicated Quantity

Cho-les-terol	Carbo-hydrate	Calcium	Phos-phorus	Iron	Potas-sium	Sodium	Vitamin A value		Thiamin	Ribo-flavin	Niacin	Ascorbic acid
							(IU)	(RE)				
Milli-grams	Grams	Milli-grams	Milli-grams	Milli-grams	Milli-grams	Milli-grams	Inter-national units	Retinol equiva-lents	Milli-grams	Milli-grams	Milli-grams	Milli-grams
0	18	29	41	0.7	896	2	7,290	729	0.17	0.05	1.4	20
0	28	32	63	0.5	397	11	24,880	2,488	0.08	0.14	0.7	28
0	37	32	41	0.8	278	20	25,750	2,575	0.08	0.21	1.0	26
8	29	27	27	1.2	198	74	4,400	440	0.02	0.04	0.4	7
0	59	77	133	3.4	536	191	38,570	3,857	0.07	0.23	2.4	13
0	8	9	20	0.4	125	21	3,190	319	0.01	0.02	0.3	11
0	5	9	28	0.6	255	10	1,390	139	0.07	0.06	0.7	22
0	10	62	46	1.5	530	[73]391	1,450	145	0.11	0.07	1.8	36
0	10	22	46	1.4	537	[74]881	1,360	136	0.11	0.08	1.6	45
0	49	92	207	7.8	2,442	[75]170	6,470	647	0.41	0.50	8.4	111
0	25	38	100	2.3	1,050	[76]50	3,400	340	0.18	0.14	4.3	88
0	18	34	78	1.9	909	[77]1,482	2,400	240	0.16	0.14	2.8	32
0	8	34	30	0.3	211	78	0	0	0.04	0.04	0.5	18
0	6	197	42	1.2	292	42	7,920	792	0.06	0.10	0.6	39
0	8	249	56	3.2	367	25	13,080	1,308	0.09	0.12	0.8	36
0	11	27	41	1.0	467	883	2,830	283	0.10	0.07	1.8	67
0	24	46	93	1.5	308	64	7,780	778	0.13	0.22	1.5	6
0	17	6	27	1.2	165	11	10	1	0.02	0.03	0.5	2
0	1	58	87	0.0	5	329	0	0	0.00	0.00	0.0	0
0	69	60	137	2.2	991	2,845	3,820	382	0.25	0.19	4.4	41
0	4	3	8	0.1	54	156	210	21	0.01	0.01	0.2	2
0	1	7	8	0.4	50	26	910	91	0.01	0.02	0.2	2
0	8	22	109	1.9	235	1	10	1	0.01	0.07	0.4	0
0	2	28	1	0.9	12	1	10	1	Tr	Tr	Tr	1
0	1	10	7	0.6	31	1	20	2	0.01	0.01	0.1	Tr

Nutritive Value of Foods *(Continued)*

Foods, approximate measures, units, and weight (weight of edible portion only)		Water	Food energy	Pro-tein	Fat	Fatty Acids Satu-rated	Mono-unsatu-rated	Poly-unsatu-rated
	Grams	Per-cent	Cal-ories	Grams	Grams	Grams	Grams	Grams
MISCELLANEOUS ITEMS—Con.								
Garlic powder	1 tsp	2.8	6	10	Tr	Tr	Tr	Tr	Tr
Gelatin, dry	1 envelope	7	13	25	6	Tr	Tr	Tr	Tr
Mustard, prepared, yellow	1 tsp or individual packet	5	80	5	Tr	Tr	Tr	0.2	Tr
Olives, canned:									
Green	4 medium or 3 extra large	13	78	15	Tr	2	0.2	1.2	0.1
Ripe, Mission, pitted	3 small or 2 large	9	73	15	Tr	2	0.3	1.3	0.2
Oregano	1 tsp	1.5	7	5	Tr	Tr	Tr	Tr	0.1
Paprika	1 tsp	2.1	10	5	Tr	Tr	Tr	Tr	0.2
Pepper, black	1 tsp	2.1	11	5	Tr	Tr	Tr	Tr	Tr
Pickles, cucumber:									
Dill, medium, whole, 3¾ in long, 1¼-in diam.	1 pickle	65	93	5	Tr	Tr	Tr	Tr	0.1
Fresh-pack, slices 1½-in diam., ¼ in thick	2 slices	15	79	10	Tr	Tr	Tr	Tr	Tr
Sweet, gherkin, small, whole, about 2½ in long, ¾-in diam.	1 pickle	15	61	20	Tr	Tr	Tr	Tr	Tr
Popcorn. See Grain Products									
Salt	1 tsp	5.5	0	0	0	0	0.0	0.0	0.0
Vinegar, cider	1 tbsp	15	94	Tr	Tr	0	0.0	0.0	0.0
Yeast:									
Baker's, dry, active	1 pkg	7	5	20	3	Tr	Tr	0.1	Tr

(Tr indicates nutrient present in trace amounts.)

[1] Value not determined.

[2] Mineral content varies depending on water source.

[3] Blend of aspartame and saccharin; if only sodium saccharin is used, sodium is 75 mg; if only aspartame is used, sodium is 23 mg.

[4] With added ascorbic acid.

[5] Vitamin A value is largely from beta-carotene used for coloring.

[6] Yields 1 qt of fluid milk when reconstituted according to package directions.

[7] With added vitamin A.

[8] Carbohydrate content varies widely because of amount of sugar added and amount and solids content of added flavoring. Consult the label if more precise values for carbohydrate and calories are needed.

[9] For salted butter; unsalted butter contains 12 mg sodium per stick, 2 mg per tbsp, or 1 mg per pat.

[10] Values for vitamin are year-round average.

[11] For salted margarine.

[12] Based on average vitamin A content of fortified margarine. Federal specifications for fortified margarine require a minimum of 15,000 IU per pound.

[13] Fatty acid values apply to product made with regular margarine.

[14] Dipped in egg, milk, and breadcrumbs; fried in vegetable shortening.

[15] If bones are discarded, value for calcium will be greatly reduced.

[16] Dipped in egg, breadcrumbs, and flour; fried in vegetable shortening.

[17] Made with drained chunk light tuna, celery, onion, pickle relish, and mayonnaise-type salad dressing.

Nutrients in Indicated Quantity

Cholesterol	Carbohydrate	Calcium	Phosphorus	Iron	Potassium	Sodium	Vitamin A value (IU)	(RE)	Thiamin	Riboflavin	Niacin	Ascorbic acid
Milligrams	Grams	Milligrams	Milligrams	Milligrams	Milligrams	Milligrams	International units	Retinol equivalents	Milligrams	Milligrams	Milligrams	Milligrams
0	2	2	12	0.1	31	1	0	0	0.01	Tr	Tr	Tr
0	0	1	0	0.0	2	6	0	0	0.00	0.00	0.0	0
0	Tr	4	4	0.1	7	63	0	0	Tr	0.01	Tr	Tr
0	Tr	8	2	0.2	7	312	40	4	Tr	Tr	Tr	0
0	Tr	10	2	0.2	2	68	10	1	Tr	Tr	Tr	0
0	1	24	3	0.7	25	Tr	100	10	0.01	Tr	0.1	1
0	1	4	7	0.5	49	1	1,270	127	0.01	0.04	0.3	1
0	1	9	4	0.6	26	1	Tr	Tr	Tr	0.01	Tr	0
0	1	17	14	0.7	130	928	70	7	Tr	0.01	Tr	4
0	3	5	4	0.3	30	101	20	2	Tr	Tr	Tr	1
0	5	2	2	0.2	30	107	10	1	Tr	Tr	Tr	1
0	0	14	3	Tr	Tr	2,132	0	0	0.00	0.00	0.0	0
0	1	1	1	0.1	15	Tr	0	0	0.00	0.00	0.0	0
0	3	3	90	1.1	140	4	Tr	Tr	0.16	0.38	2.6	Tr

[18] Sodium bisulfite used to preserve color; unsulfited product would contain less sodium.

[19] Also applies to pasteurized apple cider.

[20] Without added ascorbic acid. For value with added ascorbic acid, refer to label.

[21] With added ascorbic acid.

[22] For white grapefruit; pink grapefruit have about 310 IU or 31 RE.

[23] Sodium benzoate and sodium bisulfite added as preservatives.

[24] Egg bagels have 44 mg cholesterol and 22 IU or 7 RE vitamin A per bagel.

[25] Made with vegetable shortening.

[26] Made with white cornmeal. If made with yellow cornmeal, value is 32 IU or 3 RE.

[27] Nutrient added.

[28] Cooked without salt. If salt is added according to label recommendations, sodium content is 540 mg.

[29] For white corn grits. Cooked yellow grits contain 145 IU or 14 RE.

[30] Value based on label declaration for added nutrients.

[31] For regular and instant cereal. For quick cereal, phosphorus is 102 mg and sodium is 142 mg.

[32] Cooked without salt. If salt is added according to label recommendations, sodium content is 390 mg.

[33] Cooked without salt. If salt is added according to label recommendations, sodium content is 324 mg.

[34] Cooked without salt. If salt is added according to label recommendations, sodium content is 374 mg.

[35] Excepting angelfood cake, cakes were made from mixes containing vegetable shortening and frostings were made with margarine.

[36] Made with vegetable oil.

(Footnotes continue on next page.)

[37] Cake made with vegetable shortening; frosting with margarine.

[38] Made with margarine.

[39] Crackers made with enriched flour except for rye wafers and whole-wheat wafers.

[40] Made with lard.

[41] Cashews without salt contain 21 mg sodium per cup or 4 mg per oz.

[42] Cashews without salt contain 22 mg sodium per cup or 5 mg per oz.

[43] Macadamia nuts without salt contain 9 mg sodium per cup or 2 mg per oz.

[44] Mixed nuts without salt contain 3 mg sodium per oz.

[45] Peanuts without salt contain 22 mg sodium per cup or 4 mg per oz.

[46] Outer layer of fat was removed to within approximately ½ inch of the lean. Deposits of fat within the cut were not removed.

[47] Fried in vegetable shortening.

[48] Value varies widely.

[49] Contains added sodium ascorbate. If sodium ascorbate is not added, ascorbic acid content is negligible.

[50] One patty (8 per pound) of bulk sausage is equivalent to 2 links.

[51] Crust made with vegetable shortening and enriched flour.

[52] Made with corn oil.

[53] Fried in vegetable shortening.

[54] If sodium ascorbate is added, product contains 11 mg ascorbic acid.

[55] Made with enriched flour, margarine, and whole milk.

[56] For regular pack; special dietary pack contains 3 mg sodium.

[57] For green varieties; yellow varieties contain 101 IU or 10 RE.

[58] For green varieties; yellow varieties contain 151 IU or 15 RE.

[59] For regular pack; special dietary pack contains 3 mg sodium.

[60] For green varieties; yellow varieties contain 142 IU or 14 RE.

[61] For regular pack; special dietary pack contains 78 mg sodium.

[62] For regular pack; special dietary pack contains 61 mg sodium.

[63] For yellow varieties; white varieties contain only a trace of vitamin A.

[64] For regular pack; special dietary pack contains 8 mg sodium.

[65] For regular pack; special dietary pack contains 6 mg sodium.

[66] For regular pack; special dietary pack contains 0 mg sodium.

[67] For red peppers; green peppers contain 350 IU or 35 RE.

[68] For green peppers; red peppers contain 4220 IU or 422 RE.

[69] For green peppers; red peppers contain 141 mg ascorbic acid.

[70] For green peppers; red peppers contain 2740 IU or 274 RE.

[71] For green peppers; red peppers contain 121 mg ascorbic acid.

[72] With added salt; if none is added, sodium content is 58 mg.

[73] For regular pack; special dietary pack contains 31 mg sodium.

[74] With added salt; if none is added, sodium content is 24 mg.

[75] With no added salt; if salt is added, sodium content is 2070 mg.

[76] With no added salt; if salt is added, sodium content is 998 mg.

[77] With salt added.

Adapted from Nutritive Value of Foods, Home and Garden Bulletin, No. 72, U.S. Dept. of Agriculture.

Nutritional Assessment Tools

The Warning Signs of poor nutritional health are often overlooked. Use this checklist to find out if you or someone you know is at nutritional risk.

Read the statements below. Circle the number in the yes column for those that apply to you or someone you know. For each yes answer, score the number in the box. Total your nutritional score.

DETERMINE YOUR NUTRITIONAL HEALTH

		YES
*D	I have an illness or condition that made me change the kind and/or amount of food I eat.	**2**
E	I eat fewer than 2 meals per day.	**3**
	I eat few fruits or vegetables, or milk products.	**2**
	I have 3 or more drinks of beer, liquor or wine almost every day.	**2**
T	I have tooth or mouth problems that make it hard for me to eat.	**2**
E	I don't always have enough money to buy the food I need.	**4**
R	I eat alone most of the time.	**1**
M	I take 3 or more different prescribed or over-the-counter drugs a day.	**1**
I	Without wanting to, I have lost or gained 10 pounds in the last 6 months.	**2**
N	I am not always physically able to shop, cook and/or feed myself.	**2**
E	Age_____ Today's Date_____	**TOTAL**

NAME _____   SEX _____   PHONE # _____

ADDRESS _____   CITY _____   STATE _____   ZIP CODE _____

Total Your Nutritional Score. If It's...

0-2 **Good!** Recheck your nutritional score in 6 months.

3-5 **You are at moderate nutritional risk.** See what can be done to improve your eating habits and lifestyle. Your office of aging, senior nutrition program, senior citizens center or health department can help. Recheck your nutritional score in 3 months.

6 or more **You are at high nutritional risk.** Bring this checklist the next time you see your doctor, dietitian or other qualified health or social service professional. Talk with them about any problems you may have. Ask for help to improve your nutritional health.

These materials developed and distributed by the Nutrition Screening Initiative, a project of:

AMERICAN ACADEMY OF FAMILY PHYSICIANS
THE AMERICAN DIETETIC ASSOCIATION
NATIONAL COUNCIL ON THE AGING, INC.

FOR OFFICE USE ONLY

INTERVENTION RECOMMENDED
- ❑ Social Service
- ❑ Nutrition Education/ Counseling
- ❑ MentalHealth
- ❑ Medication Use
- ❑ Oral Health
- ❑ Nutrition Support

Continued on following page

Remember that warning signs suggest risk, but do not represent diagnosis of any condition.
See below to learn more about the warning signs of poor nutritional health.

DISEASE

Any disease, illness or chronic condition which causes you to change the way you eat, or makes it hard for you to eat, puts your nutritional health at risk. Four out of five adults have chronic diseases that are affected by diet. Confusion or memory loss that keeps getting worse is estimated to affect one out of five or more of older adults. This can make it hard to remember what, when or if you've eaten. Feeling sad or depressed, which happens to about one in eight older adults, can cause big changes in appetite, digestion, energy level, weight and well-being.

EATING POORLY

Eating too little and eating too much both lead to poor health. Eating the same foods day after day or not eating fruit, vegetables, and milk products daily will also cause poor nutritional health. One in five adults skip meals daily. Only 13% of adults eat the minimum amount of fruit and vegetables needed. One in four older adults drink too much alcohol. Many health problems become worse if you drink more than one or two alcoholic beverages per day.

TOOTH LOSS/MOUTH PAIN

A healthy mouth, teeth and gums are needed to eat. Missing, loose or rotten teeth or dentures which don't fit well or cause mouth sores make it hard to eat.

ECONOMIC HARDSHIP

As many as 40% of older Americans have incomes of less than $6,000 per year. Having less–or choosing to spend less–than $25-30 per week for food makes it very hard to get the foods you need to stay healthy.

REDUCED SOCIAL CONTACT

One-third of all older people live alone. Being with people daily has a positive effect on morale, well-being and eating.

MULTIPLE MEDICINES

Many older Americans must take medicines for health problems. Almost half of older Americans take multiple medicines daily. Growing old may change the way we respond to drugs. The more medicines you take, the greater the chance for side effects such as increased or decreased appetite, change in taste, constipation, weakness, drowsiness, diarrhea, nausea, and others. Vitamins or minerals when taken in large doses act like drugs and can cause harm. Alert your doctor to everything you take.

INVOLUNTRY WEIGHT LOSS/GAIN

Losing or gaining a lot of weight when you are not trying to do so is an important warning sign that must not be ignored. Being overweight or underweight also increases your chance of poor health.

NEEDS ASSISTANCE IN SELF CARE

Although most older people are able to eat, one of every five have trouble walking, shopping, buying and cooking food, especially as they get older.

ELDER YEARS ABOVE AGE 80

Most older people lead full and productive lives. But as age increases, risk of frailty and health problems increase. Checking your nutritional health regularly makes good sense.

SOURCE: Reprinted with permission by the Nutrition Screening Initiative, a project of the American Academy of Family Physicians, the American Dietetic Association, and the National Council on the Aging, Inc., and funded in part by a grant from Ross Products Division, Abbott Laboratories.

FEATURES OF SUBJECTIVE GLOBAL ASSESSMENT (SGA)

Select appropriate category with a check mark, or enter numerical value where indicated by "#".

A. History
   1. Weight change
     —Overall loss in past 6 months: amount = # _____ kg; % loss = # _____
     —Change in past 2 weeks: _____ increase
                                     _____ no change
                                     _____ decrease
   2. Dietary intake change (relative to normal)
     _____ No change
     _____ Change _____ duration = # _____ weeks
                   _____ type: _____ suboptimal solid diet _____ full liquid diet
                                 _____ hypocaloric liquids _____ starvation
   3. Gastrointestinal symptoms (that persisted for > 2 weeks)
     _____ none _____ nausea _____ vomiting _____ diarrhea _____ anorexia
   4. Functional capacity
     _____ No dysfunction (eg, full capacity)
     _____ Dysfunction _____ duration = # _____ weeks
                   _____ type: _____ working suboptimally
                                   _____ ambulatory
                                   _____ bedridden
   5. Disease and its relation to nutritional requirements
     Primary diagnosis (specify):
     Metabolic demand (stress): _____ no stress _____ low stress
                                  _____ moderate stress _____ high stress

B. Physical (for each trait specify: 0 = normal, 1+ = mild, 2+ = moderate, 3+ = severe)
   # _____ loss of subcutaneous fat (triceps, chest)
   # _____ muscle wasting (quadriceps, deltoids)
   # _____ ankle edema
   # _____ sacral edema
   # _____ ascites

C. SGA rating (select one):
   _____ A = Well nourished
   _____ B = Moderately (suspected of being) malnourished
   _____ C = Severely malnourished

SOURCE: Detsky, et al: What is subjective global assessment? JPEN 11:8, 1987, with permission.

Growth Charts for Boys and Girls, Ages 0 to 18

Growth charts, such as the eight that follow, are used to evaluate growth in infants and children. They are a valuable tool in nutritional assessment. To plot a measurement on the percentile graph, follow these steps:

- Select the appropriate chart based on age, sex, and type of measurement.
- Locate the child's age on the top or bottom of the chart.
- Locate the child's weight (in pounds or kilograms), length (in inches or centimeters), or head circumference on the left- or-right-hand side of the chart.

- Mark the chart where the age and weight, length, or head circumference lines intersect.

Each chart contains a series of curved lines that represent percentiles. For example, when a mark is on the 95th percentile line of weight for age, it means that only 5 children out of 100 (of the same age and sex) have a greater weight. A series of plot marks on a chart will show the pattern of growth for a particular child. If any marks appear above the 95th percentile or below the 5th percentile, you may want to report this to the physician. Rapid changes above the 75th percentile or below the 25th percentile may also be significant.

BOYS: BIRTH TO 36 MONTHS
PHYSICAL GROWTH
NCHS PERCENTILES*

NAME _____   RECORD # _____

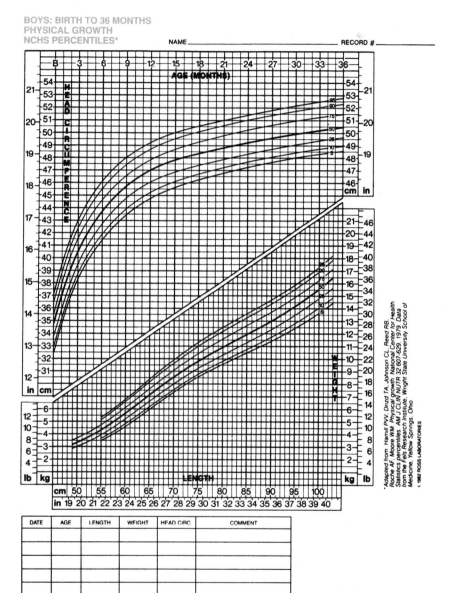

DATE	AGE	LENGTH	WEIGHT	HEAD CIRC.	COMMENT

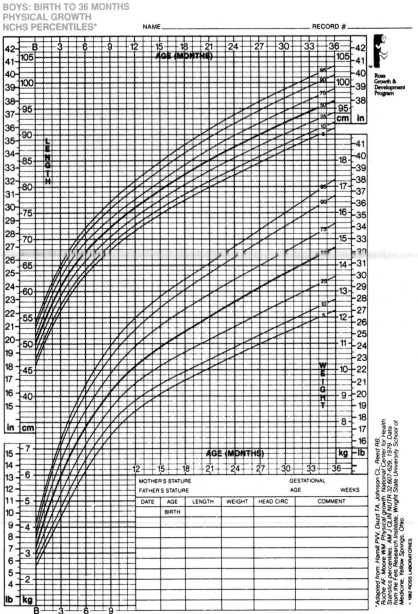

BOYS: BIRTH TO 36 MONTHS
PHYSICAL GROWTH
NCHS PERCENTILES*

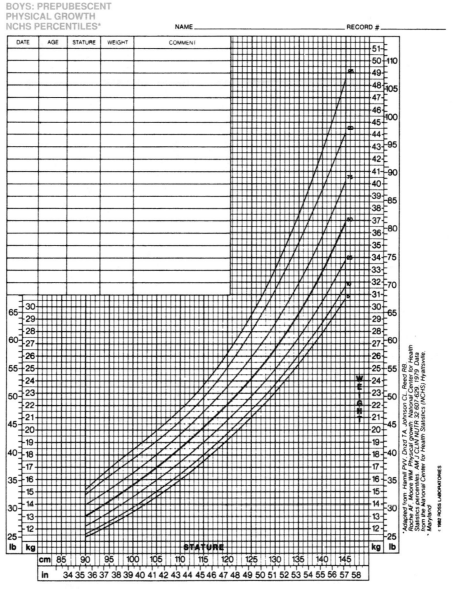

BOYS: PREPUBESCENT
PHYSICAL GROWTH
NCHS PERCENTILES*

BOYS: 2 TO 18 YEARS
PHYSICAL GROWTH
NCHS PERCENTILES*

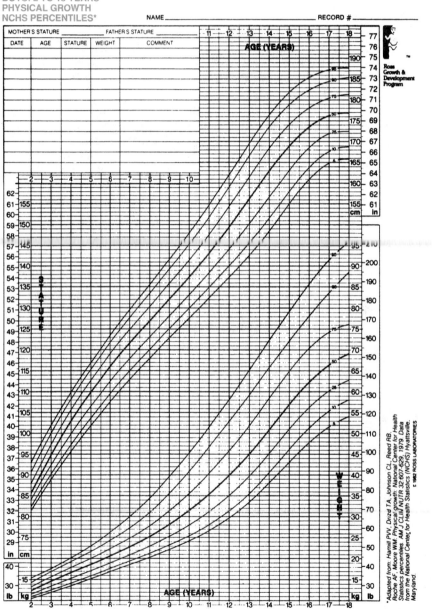

GIRLS: BIRTH TO 36 MONTHS
PHYSICAL GROWTH
NCHS PERCENTILES*

NAME _____ RECORD # _____

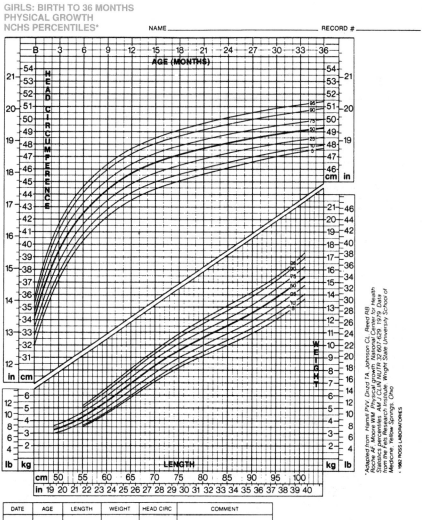

DATE	AGE	LENGTH	WEIGHT	HEAD CIRC	COMMENT

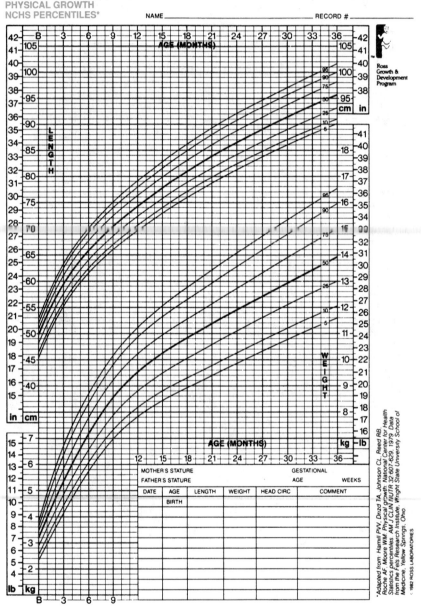

GIRLS: BIRTH TO 36 MONTHS
PHYSICAL GROWTH
NCHS PERCENTILES*

NAME _____ RECORD # _____

GIRLS: PREPUBESCENT
PHYSICAL GROWTH
NCHS PERCENTILES*

NAME _____   RECORD # _____

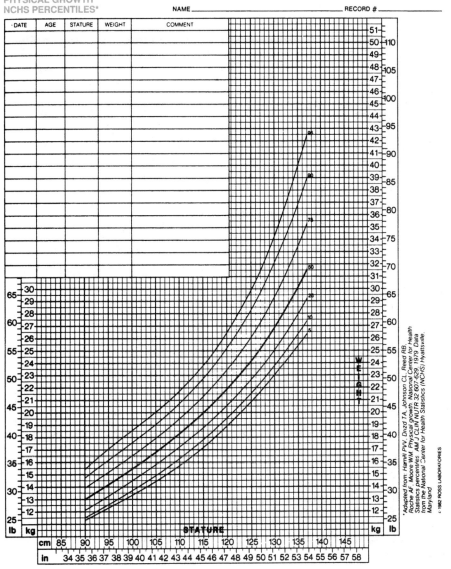

*Adapted from: Hamill PVV, Drizd TA, Johnson CL, Reed RB
Roche AF, Moore WM. Physical growth: National Center for Health
Statistics percentiles. AM J CLIN NUTR 32.607-629,1979 Data
from the National Center for Health Statistics (NCHS) Hyattsville,
Maryland

© 1982 ROSS LABORATORIES

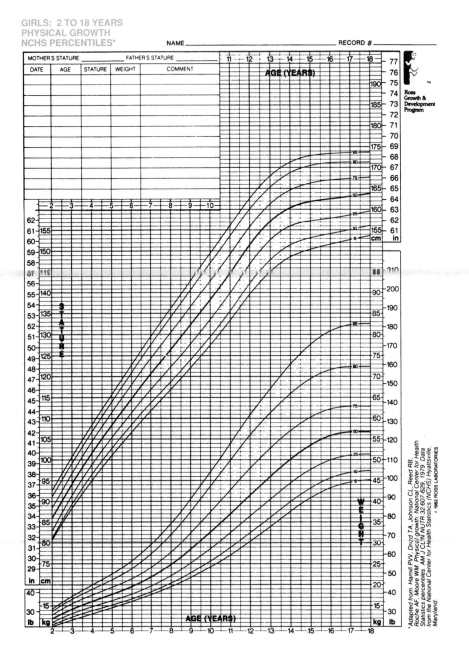

GIRLS: 2 TO 18 YEARS
PHYSICAL GROWTH
NCHS PERCENTILES*

Body Fat and Skinfolds of Adults and Children

TABLE A *Body Fat and Skinfolds of Men*

Skinfolds (mm)	Ages			
	17–29	30–39	40–49	50+
15	4.8	—	—	—
20	8.1	12.2	12.2	12.6
25	10.5	14.2	15.0	15.6
30	12.9	16.2	17.7	18.6
35	14.7	17.7	19.6	20.8
40	16.4	19.2	21.4	22.9
45	17.7	20.4	23.0	24.7
50	19.0	21.5	24.6	26.5
55	20.1	22.5	25.9	27.9
60	21.2	23.5	27.1	29.2
65	22.2	24.3	28.2	30.4
70	23.1	25.1	29.3	31.6
75	24.0	25.9	30.3	32.7
80	24.8	26.6	31.2	33.8
85	25.5	27.2	32.1	34.8
90	26.2	27.8	33.0	35.8
95	26.9	28.4	33.7	36.6
100	27.6	29.0	34.4	37.4
105	28.2	29.6	35.1	38.2
110	28.8	30.1	35.8	39.0
115	29.4	30.6	36.4	39.7
120	30.0	31.1	37.0	40.4
125	30.5	31.5	37.6	41.1
130	31.0	31.9	38.2	41.8
135	31.5	32.3	38.7	42.4
140	32.0	32.7	39.2	43.0
145	32.5	33.1	39.7	43.6
150	32.9	33.5	40.2	44.1

TABLE A   *Body Fat and Skinfolds of Men (Continued)*

| Skinfolds (mm) | Ages | | | |
	17–29	30–39	40–49	50+
155	33.3	33.9	40.7	44.6
160	33.7	34.3	41.2	45.1
165	34.1	34.6	41.6	45.6
170	34.5	34.8	42.0	46.1
175	34.9	—	—	—
180	35.3	—	—	—
185	35.6	—	—	—
190	35.9	—	—	—
195	—	—	—	—
200	—	—	—	—
205	—	—	—	—
210	—	—	—	—

TABLE B   *Body Fat and Skinfolds of Women*

| Skinfolds (mm) | Ages | | | |
	16–29	30–39	40–49	50+
15	10.5	—	—	—
20	14.1	17.0	19.8	21.4
25	16.8	19.4	22.2	24.0
30	19.5	21.8	24.5	26.6
35	21.5	23.7	26.4	28.5
40	23.4	25.5	28.2	30.3
45	25.0	26.9	29.6	31.9
50	26.5	28.2	31.0	33.4
55	27.8	29.4	32.1	34.6
60	29.1	30.6	33.2	35.7
65	30.2	31.6	34.1	36.7
70	31.2	32.5	35.0	37.7
75	32.2	33.4	35.9	38.7
80	33.1	34.3	36.7	39.6
85	34.0	35.1	37.5	40.4
90	34.8	35.8	38.3	41.2
95	35.6	36.5	39.0	41.9
100	36.4	37.2	39.7	42.6
105	37.1	37.9	40.4	43.3
110	37.8	38.6	41.0	43.9
115	38.4	39.1	41.5	44.5
120	39.0	39.6	42.0	45.1
125	39.6	40.1	42.5	45.7
130	40.2	40.6	43.0	46.2
135	40.8	41.1	43.5	46.7
140	41.3	41.6	44.0	47.2
145	41.8	42.1	44.5	47.7
150	42.3	42.6	45.0	48.2

TABLE B   *Body Fat and Skinfolds of Women (Continued)*

Skinfolds (mm)	Ages			
	16–29	30–39	40–49	50+
155	42.8	43.1	45.4	48.7
160	43.3	43.6	45.8	49.2
165	43.7	44.0	46.2	49.6
170	44.1	44.4	46.6	50.0
175	—	44.8	47.0	50.4
180	—	45.2	47.4	50.8
185	—	45.6	47.8	51.2
190	—	45.9	48.2	51.6
195	—	46.2	48.5	52.0
200	—	46.5	48.8	52.4
205	—	—	49.1	52.7
210	—	—	49.4	53.0

In two thirds of the instances, the error was within +3.5% of the body-weight as fat for the women and ±5% for the men.

The relationship of skinfold thickness to body fat in children and individuals under 17 is addressed by The American Alliance for Health, Physical Education, Recreation and Dance in the publication *Lifetime Health Related Physical Fitness Test Manual.* They suggest that national percentile norms provide the best reference. They further suggest that the ideal is at the 50th percentile. Those below the 25th percentile should be encouraged to reduce amount of body fat, while those above the 90th percentile should not be encouraged to lose body fat.

TABLE C *Percentile Norms. Ages 6–18* for Sum of Triceps plus Subscapular Skinfolds (mm) for Boys*

Age	6	7	8	9	10	11	12	13	14	15	16	17
Percentile												
99	7	7	7	7	7	8	8	7	7	8	8	8
95	8	9	9	9	9	9	9	9	9	9	9	9
90	9	9	9	10	10	10	10	10	9	10	10	10
85	10	10	10	10	11	11	10	10	10	11	11	11
80	10	10	10	11	11	12	11	11	11	11	11	12
75	11	11	11	11	12	12	11	12	11	12	12	12
70	11	11	11	12	12	12	12	12	12	12	12	13
65	11	11	12	12	13	13	13	12	12	13	13	13
60	12	12	12	13	13	14	13	13	13	13	13	14
55	12	12	13	13	14	15	14	14	13	14	14	14
50	12	12	13	14	14	16	15	15	14	14	14	15
45	13	13	14	14	15	16	15	16	14	15	15	16
40	13	13	14	15	16	17	16	17	15	16	16	16
35	13	14	15	16	17	19	17	18	16	18	17	17
30	14	14	16	17	18	20	19	19	18	18	18	19

TABLE C *Percentile Norms. Ages 6–18* for Sum of Triceps plus Subscapular Skinfolds (mm) for Boys (Continued)*

Age	6	7	8	9	10	11	12	13	14	15	16	17
Percentile												
25	14	15	17	18	19	22	21	22	20	20	20	21
20	15	16	18	20	21	24	24	25	23	22	22	24
15	16	17	19	23	24	28	27	29	27	25	24	26
10	18	18	21	26	28	33	33	36	31	30	29	30
5	20	24	28	34	33	38	44	46	37	40	37	38

*The norms for age 17 may be used for age 18.

Source: Based on data from Johnston, F.E., Hamill, D.V., and Lemeshow, S.: (1) *Skinfold Thickness of Children 6–11 Years* (Series II, No. 120, 1972), and (2) *Skinfold Thickness of Youths 12–17 Years* (Series II, No. 132, 1974). US National Center for Health Statistics, US Department of HEW, Washington, DC.

TABLE D *Percentile Norms Ages 6–18* for Sum of Triceps plus Subscapular Skinfolds (mm) for Girls*

Age	6	7	8	9	10	11	12	13	14	15	16	17
Percentile												
99	8	8	8	9	9	8	9	10	10	11	11	12
95	9	10	10	10	10	11	11	12	13	14	14	15
90	10	11	11	12	12	12	12	13	15	16	16	16
85	11	12	12	12	13	13	13	14	16	17	18	18
80	12	12	12	13	13	14	14	15	17	18	19	19
75	12	12	13	14	14	15	15	16	18	20	20	20
70	12	13	14	15	15	16	16	17	19	21	21	22
65	13	13	14	15	16	16	17	18	20	22	22	23
60	13	14	15	16	17	17	17	19	21	23	23	24
55	14	15	16	16	18	18	19	20	22	24	24	26
50	14	15	16	17	18	19	19	20	24	25	25	27
45	15	16	17	18	20	20	21	22	25	26	27	28
40	15	16	18	19	20	21	22	23	26	28	29	30
35	16	17	19	20	22	22	24	25	27	29	30	32
30	16	18	20	22	24	23	25	27	30	32	32	34
25	17	19	21	24	25	25	27	30	32	34	34	36
20	18	20	23	26	28	28	31	33	35	37	37	40
15	19	22	25	29	31	31	35	39	39	42	42	42
10	22	25	30	34	35	36	40	43	42	48	46	46
5	26	28	36	40	41	42	48	51	52	56	57	58

*The norms for age 17 may be used for age 18.

Source: Based on data from Johnston, F.E., Hamill, D.V. and Lemeshow, S: (1) *Skinfold Thickness of Children 6–11 Years* (Series II, No. 120, 1972), and (2) *Skinfold Thickness of Youths 12–17 Years* (Series II, No. 132, 1974). US National Center for Health Statistics, US Department of HEW, Washington, DC.

Tables from Lifetime Health Related Physical Fitness Test Manual, ADHPERD, Reston, VA., 1980. With permission of the American Alliance for Health, Physical Education, Recreation and Dance.

APPENDIX F

Recommended Dietary Allowances

Recommended Dietary Allowances (RDA), Revised 1989[a]

	Weight[b]		Height[b]			Fat-Soluble Vitamins				Water-Soluble Vitamins							Minerals						
Age (Years)	(kg)	(lb)	(cm)	(inches)	Protein (g)	Vitamin A (µg RE)[c]	Vitamin D (µg)[d]	Vitamin E (mg α-TE)[e]	Vitamin K (µg)	Vitamin C (mg)	Thiamin (mg)	Riboflavin (mg)	Niacin (mg NE)[f]	Vitamin B$_6$ (mg)	Folate (µg)	Vitamin B$_{12}$ (µg)	Calcium (mg)	Phosphorus (mg)	Magnesium (mg)	Iron (mg)	Zinc (mg)	Iodine (µg)	Selenium (µg)
Infants																							
0.0–0.5	6	13	60	24	13	375	7.5	3	5	30	0.3	0.4	5	0.3	25	0.3	400	300	40	6	5	40	10
0.5–1.0	9	20	71	28	14	375	10	4	10	35	0.4	0.5	6	0.6	35	0.5	600	500	60	10	5	50	15
Children																							
1–3	13	29	90	35	16	400	10	6	15	40	0.7	0.8	9	1.0	50	0.7	800	800	80	10	10	70	20
4–6	20	44	112	44	24	500	10	7	20	45	0.9	1.1	12	1.1	75	1.0	800	800	120	10	10	90	20
7–10	28	62	132	52	28	700	10	7	30	45	1.0	1.2	13	1.4	100	1.4	800	800	170	10	10	120	30
Males																							
11–14	45	99	157	62	45	1000	10	10	45	50	1.3	1.5	17	1.7	150	2.0	1200	1200	270	12	15	150	40
15–18	66	145	176	69	59	1000	10	10	65	60	1.5	1.8	20	2.0	200	2.0	1200	1200	400	12	15	150	50
19–24	72	160	177	70	58	1000	10	10	70	60	1.5	1.7	19	2.0	200	2.0	1200	1200	350	10	15	150	70
25–50	79	174	176	70	63	1000	5	10	80	60	1.5	1.7	19	2.0	200	2.0	800	800	350	10	15	150	70
51+	77	170	173	68	63	1000	5	10	80	60	1.2	1.4	15	2.0	200	2.0	800	800	350	10	15	150	70

Females																							
11–14	46	101	157	62	46	800	10	8	45	50	1.1	1.3	15	1.4	150	2.0	1200	1200	280	15	12	150	45
15–18	55	120	163	64	44	800	10	8	55	60	1.1	1.3	15	1.5	180	2.0	1200	1200	300	15	12	150	50
19–24	58	128	164	65	46	800	10	8	60	60	1.1	1.3	15	1.6	180	2.0	1200	1200	280	15	12	150	55
25–50	63	138	163	64	50	800	5	8	65	60	1.1	1.3	15	1.6	180	2.0	800	800	280	15	12	150	55
51+	65	143	160	63	50	800	5	8	65	60	1.0	1.2	13	1.6	180	2.0	800	800	280	10	12	150	55
Pregnant					60	800	10	10	65	70	1.5	1.6	17	2.2	400	2.2	1200	1200	320	30	15	175	65
Lactating																							
1st 6 months			65		65	1300	10	12	65	95	1.6	1.8	20	2.1	280	2.6	1200	1200	355	15	19	200	75
2nd 6 months			62		62	1200	10	11	65	90	1.6	1.7	20	2.1	260	2.6	1200	1200	340	15	16	200	75

[a]The allowances, expressed as average daily intakes over time, are intended to provide for individual variations among most normal persons as they live in the United States under usual environmental stresses. Diets should be based on a variety of common foods in order to provide other nutrients for which human requirements have been less well defined.

[b]Weights and heights of Reference Adults are actual medians for the US population of the designated age, as reported by NHANES II. The use of these figures does not imply that the height-to-weight ratios are ideal.

[c]Retinol equivalents. 1 retinol equivalent = 1 µg retinol or 6 µg β-carotene. See Clinical Calculation 6–1 to convert IU of vitamin A to retinol equivalents.

[d]As cholecalciferol. 10 µg cholecalciferol = 400 IU of vitamin D. See Clinical Calculation 6–2 to convert IU of vitamin D to mg of cholecalciferol.

[e]α-Tocopherol equivalents. 1 mg d-α tocopherol = 1 α-TE.

[f]1 NE (niacin equivalent) is equal to 1 mg of niacin or 60 mg of dietary tryptophan.

Note: The Committee on Dietary Allowances has published a separate table showing energy allowances which appears as Table 8–4.

Source: From Recommended Dietary Allowances, © 1989, by the National Academy of Sciences, National Academy Press, Washington, DC, with permission.

Estimated Safe and Adequate Daily Dietary Intakes of Selected Vitamins and Minerals

Estimated Safe and Adequate Daily Dietary Intakes of Selected Vitamins and Minerals[a]

		Vitamins	
Category	Age (Years)	Biotin (μg)	Pantothenic Acid (mg)
Infants	0–0.5	10	2
	0.5–1	15	3
Children and adolescents	1–3	20	3
	4–6	25	3–4
	7–10	30	4–5
	11+	30–100	4–7
Adults		30–100	4–7

Category	Age (Years)	Copper (mg)	Manganese (mg)	Fluoride (mg)	Chromium (μg)	Molybdenum (μg)
Infants	0–0.5	0.4–0.6	0.3–0.6	0.1–0.5	10–40	15–30
	0.5–1	0.6–0.7	0.6–1.0	0.2–1.0	20–60	20–40
Children and adolescents	1–3	0.7–1.0	1.0–1.5	0.5–1.5	20–80	25–50
	4–6	1.0–1.5	1.5–2.0	1.0–2.5	30–120	30–75
	7–10	1.0–2.0	2.0–3.0	1.5–2.5	50–200	50–150
	11+	1.5–2.5	2.0–5.0	1.5–2.5	50–200	75–250
Adults		1.5–3.0	2.0–5.0	1.5–4.0	50–200	75–250

[a]Because there is less information on which to base allowances, these figures are not given in the main table of RDA and are provided here in the form of ranges of recommended intakes.

[b]Since the toxic levels for many trace elements may be only several times usual intakes, the upper levels for the trace elements given in this table should not be habitually exceeded.

Source: From Recommended Dietary Allowances, © 1989, by the National Academy of Sciences, National Academy Press, Washington, DC, with permission.

APPENDIX H

Estimated Sodium, Chloride, and Potassium Minimum Requirements of Healthy Persons

Estimated Sodium, Chloride, and Potassium Minimum Requirements of Healthy Persons[a]

Age	Weight (kg)[d]	Sodium (mg)[a,b]	Chloride (mg)[a,b]	Potassium (mg)[c]
Months				
0–5	4.5	120	180	500
6–11	8.9	200	300	700
Years				
1	11.0	225	350	1,000
2–5	16.0	300	500	1,400
6–9	25.0	400	600	1,600
10–18	50.0	500	750	2,000
>18[d]	70.0	500	750	2,000

[a]No allowance has been included for large, prolonged losses from the skin through sweat.

[b]There is no evidence that higher intakes confer any health benefit.

[c]Desirable intakes of potassium may considerably exceed these values (~3,500 mg for adults—see text).

[d]No allowance included for growth. Values for those below 18 years assume a growth rate at the 50th percentile reported by the National Center for Health Statistics (Hamill et al., 1979) and averaged for males and females. See text for information on pregnancy and lactation.

Source: From Recommended Dietary Allowances, © 1989, by the National Academy of Sciences, National Academy Press, Washington, DC, with permission.

APPENDIX I

Answers to Questions

Chapter 1

Chapter Review
1. b   2. c   3. a   4. b   5. d

Clinical Analysis
1. d   2. a   3. d

Chapter 2

Chapter Review
1. b   2. b   3. c   4. a   5. c

Clinical Analysis
1. d   2. b   3. a

Chapter 3

Chapter Review
1. b   2. b   3. b   4. d   5. c

Clinical Analysis
1. c   2. d   3. c

Chapter 4

Chapter Review
1. c   2. c   3. d   4. b   5. d

Clinical Analysis
1. d   2. b   3. c

Chapter 5

Chapter Review
1. a   2. c   3. b   4. b   5. d

Clinical Analysis
1. d   2. c   3. a

Chapter 6

Chapter Review
1. c   2. a   3. c   4. c   5. d

Clinical Analysis
1. d   2. d   3. b

Chapter 7

Chapter Review
1. c   2. d   3. c   4. a   5. b

Clinical Analysis
1. d   2. c   3. b

Chapter 8

Chapter Review
1. b   2. b   3. c   4. a   5. c

Clinical Analysis
1. b   2. a   3. b

Chapter 9

Chapter Review
1. a   2. d   3. b   4. a   5. d

Clinical Analysis
1. a   2. d   3. c

Chapter 10

Chapter Review
1. d   2. c   3. b   4. b   5. c

Clinical Analysis
1. a   2. d   3. b

Chapter 11

Chapter Review
1. b   2. a   3. c   4. b   5. d

Clinical Analysis
1. c   2. b   3. d

Chapter 12

Chapter Review
1. c   2. b   3. c   4. b   5. d

Clinical Analysis
1. d   2. c   3. a

Chapter 13

Chapter Review
1. c   2. c   3. b   4. a   5. d

Clinical Analysis
1. b   2. b   3. c

Chapter 14

Chapter Review
1. b   2. c   3. a   4. b   5. b

Clinical Analysis
1. b   2. b   3. c

Chapter 15

Chapter Review
1. c   2. a   3. c   4. b   5. a

Clinical Analysis
1. c   2. c   3. a

Chapter 16

Chapter Review
1. b   2. e   3. c   4. d   5. a

Clinical Analysis
1. c   2. c   3. a

Chapter 17

Chapter Review
1. a   2. b   3. b   4. b   5. b

Clinical Analysis
1. a   2. b   3. c

Chapter 18

Chapter Review
1. a   2. b   3. c   4. b   5. a

Clinical Analysis
1. c   2. a   3. b

Chapter 19

Chapter Review
1. a   2. c   3. d   4. b   5. d

Clinical Analysis
1. b   2. d   3. c

Chapter 20

Chapter Review
1. b   2. b   3. d   4. a   5. d

Clinical Analysis
1. c   2. b   3. a

Chapter 21

Chapter Review
1. c   2. b   3. d   4. b   5. d

Clinical Analysis
1. a   2. b   3. b

Chapter 22

Chapter Review
1. b   2. d   3. c   4. d   5. a

Clinical Analysis
1. c   2. b   3. a

Chapter 23

Chapter Review
1. c   2. c   3. b   4. d   5. c

Clinical Analysis
1. c   2. d   3. b

Chapter 24

Chapter Review
1. c   2. a   3. c   4. b   5. d

Clinical Analysis
1. b   2. b   3. c

Chapter 25

Chapter Review
1. d   2. c   3. a   4. e   5. d

Clinical Analysis
1. d   2. a   3. b

APPENDIX J

Glossary

Commonly used terms and terms that appear in boldface in the chapters can be found in this glossary. After each definition, the chapter or chapters in which the term is either introduced or discussed extensively are identified numerically in parentheses.

Abdominal circumference (girth)—Distance around the trunk at the umbilicus. (2)

Abdominal obesity—Excess body fat located between the chest and pelvis. (17)

Absorption—The movement of the end products of digestion from the gastrointestinal tract into the blood and/or lymphatic system. (10)

Accreditation—Process by which a nongovernmental agency recognizes an institution for meeting established criteria of quality. (2)

Acculturation—Process of adopting the values, attitudes, and behaviors of another culture. (2)

Acetone—A ketone body found in urine, which can be due to the excessive breakdown of stored body fat. (3)

Acetonemia (Ketonemia)—Large amounts of acetone in the blood. (16)

Acetylcholine—A chemical necessary to the transmission of nervous impulses. (7)

Acetyl CoA—Important intermediate by-product in metabolism formed from the breakdown of glucose, fatty acids, and certain amino acids. (10)

Achalasia—Failure of the gastrointestinal muscle fibers to relax where one part joins another. (21)

Achlorhydria—Absence of free hydrochloric acid in the stomach. (13)

Acidosis—Condition that results when the pH of the blood falls below 7.35; may be caused by diarrhea, uremia, diabetes mellitus, respiratory depressions and certain drug therapies. (9)

Acquired immune deficiency syndrome (AIDS)—A disease complex caused by a virus that attacks the immune system and causes neurological disease and permits opportunistic infections and malignancies. (24)

Acute illness—A sickness characterized by rapid onset, severe symptoms, and a short course. (15)

Acute renal failure—Condition that occurs suddenly, in which the kidneys are unable to perform essential functions; usually temporary. (20)

Adaptive thermogenesis—The adjustment in energy expenditure the body makes to a large increase or decrease in kilocalorie intake of several days' duration. (6)

Additive—A substance added to food to increase its flavor, shelf life, and/or characteristics such as texture, color, and aroma. (14)

Adipose cells—Cells in the human body that store fat. (4)

Adipose tissue—Tissue containing masses of fat cells. (4)

Adipose tissue mass—Fat plus its supporting cellular and extracellular structures consisting of protein and water. (2)

Adolescence—Time from the onset of puberty until full growth is reached. (12)

ADP (adenosine diphosphate)—A substance present in all cells involved in energy metabolism. Energy is released when molecules of ATP, another compound in cells, release a phosphoric acid chain and become ADP. The opposite chemical reaction of adding the third phosphoric acid group to ADP requires much energy. (8)

Adrenal glands—Small organs on the superior surface of the kidneys that secrete many hormones, including epinephrine (adrenalin) and aldosterone. (7)

Aerobic exercise—Training methods such as running or swimming that require continuous inspired oxygen. (6)

Afferent—Proceeding toward a center, as arteries, veins, lymphatic vessels, and nerves. (17)

Afferent arteriole—Small blood vessel by which blood enters the glomerulus (functional unit of the kidney). (20)

Aflatoxin—A naturally occurring food contaminant produced by some strains of *Aspergillus* molds found especially on peanuts and peanut products. (14, 22)

AIDS dementia complex (ADC)—A central nervous system disorder caused by the human immunodeficiency virus. (24)

Albumin—A plasma protein responsible for much of the colloidal osmotic pressure of the blood. (9)

Aldosterone—An adrenocorticoid hormone that increases sodium and water retention by the kidneys. (9)

Alimentary canal—The digestive tube extending from the mouth to the anus. (10)

Alkaline phosphatase—An enzyme found in highest concentration in the liver, biliary tract epithelium, and bones; enzyme levels are elevated in liver, bone, and biliary disease. (14)

Alkalosis—Condition that results when the pH of the blood rises above 7.45; may be caused by vomiting, nasogastric suctioning, or hyperventilation. (8)

Allele—One of two or more different genes containing specific inheritable characteristics that occupy corresponding positions (loci) on paired chromosomes; an individual possessing a pair of identical alleles, either dominant or recessive, is homozygous for this gene. (11)

Allergen—Substance that provokes an abnormal, individual hypersensitivity. (12)

Allergy—State of abnormal, individual hypersensitivity to a substance. (10)

Alpha-tocopherol equivalent (α-TE)—The measure of vitamin E; 1 milligram of alpha-tocopherol equivalent equals 1.5 of the older measure, International Units. (7)

Amenorrhea—Cessation of menstruation. (17)

Amino acids—Organic compounds that are the building blocks of protein; also the end products of protein digestion. (5)

Amniotic fluid—Albuminous liquid that surrounds and protects the fetus throughout pregnancy. (11)

Amylase—A class of enzymes that splits starches; for example, salivary amylase, pancreatic amylase. (10)

Anabolic phase—The third and last phase of stress; characterized by the building up of body tissue and nutrient stores; also called recovery phase. (23)

Anabolism—The building up of body compounds or tissues by the synthesis of more complex substances from simpler ones; the constructive phase of metabolism. (5, 8)

Anaerobic exercise—A form of physical activity such as weight lifting or sprinting that does not rely on continuous inspired oxygen. (6)

Anaphylaxis—Exaggerated, life-threatening hypersensitivity response to a previously encountered antigen; in severe cases, produces bronchospasm, vascular collapse, and shock. (12)

Anastomosis—The surgical connection between tubular structures. (21)

Anemia—Condition of less-than-normal values for red blood cells or hemoglobin, or both; result is decreased effectiveness in oxygen transport. (7, 8)

Angina pectoris—Severe pain and a sense of constriction about the heart caused by lack of oxygen to the heart muscle. (19)

Angiotensin II—End product of complex reaction in response to low blood pressure; effect is vasoconstriction and aldosterone secretion. (9)

Anion—An ion with a negative charge. (9)

Antagonist—A substance that counteracts the action of another substance. (7)

Anthropometry—The science of measuring the human body. (2)

Anti-insulin antibodies (AIAs)—A protein found to be elevated in persons with insulin-dependent diabetes mellitus. (18)

Anorexia nervosa—A mental disorder characterized by a 25 percent loss of usual body weight, an intense fear of becoming obese, and self-starvation. (17)

Anorexigenic—Causing loss of appetite. (17)

Anthropometric measurements—Physical measurements of the human body such as height, weight, and skinfold thickness; used to determine body composition and growth. (2)

Anthropometry—Science of measuring the body. (2)

Antibody—A specific protein developed in the body in response to a substance that the body senses to be foreign. (5)

Antidiuretic hormone (ADH)—Hormone formed in the hypothalamus and released from the posterior pituitary in response to blood that is too concentrated; effect is return of water to the bloodstream by the kidney. (9, 18)

Antineoplastic—A drug or other agent that prevents the development, growth, or proliferation of malignant cells. (16)

Antioxidant—A substance that prevents or inhibits the uptake of oxygen; in the body, antioxidants prevent tissue damage from unstable molecules; in food, antioxidants prevent deterioration; vitamins A, C, and E and selenium are antioxidants. (7, 12)

Anuria—A total lack of urine output. (20)

Apoferritin—A protein found in intestinal mucosal cells that combines with iron to form ferritin; it is always found attached to iron in the body. (8)

Appetite—A strong desire for food or for a pleasant sensation, based on previous experience, that causes one to seek food for the purpose of tasting and enjoying. (6)

Ariboflavinosis—Condition arising from a deficiency of riboflavin in the diet. (7)

Arrhythmia—Irregular heartbeat. (19)

Arteriosclerosis—A group of cardiovascular diseases characterized by the thickening, hardening, and loss of elasticity of the walls of the arteries. (19)

Arthritis—Inflammatory condition of the joints, usually accompanied by pain and swelling. (13)

Ascites—Accumulation of serous fluid in the peritoneal (abdominal) cavity. (9, 21)

Ascorbic acid—Vitamin C; ascorbic literally means "without scurvy." (7)

Ash—The residue that remains after an item is burned; usually refers to the mineral content of the human body. (1)

Aspartame—Artificial sweetener composed of aspartic acid and phenylalanine; 180 times sweeter than sucrose; brand names: Equal, Nutrasweet. (5)

Aspergillus—Genus of molds that produce aflatoxins. (14)

Aspiration—The state whereby a substance has been drawn into the nose, throat, or lungs. (15)

Assessment—An organized procedure to gather pertinent facts. (2)

Asymptomatic—Without symptoms. (24)

Atherosclerosis—A form of arteriosclerosis characterized by the deposits of fatty material inside the arteries; major factor contributing to heart disease. (19)

Atom—Smallest particle of an element that has all the properties of the element. An atom consists of the nucleus, which contains protons (positively charged particles), neutrons (particles with no electrical charge), and surrounding electrons (negatively charged particles). (3, 9)

Atopic—Pertaining to a hereditary tendency to develop allergy; the tendency is inherited but the specific clinical form (hay fever, asthma, dermatitis) is not. (12)

ATP (adenosine triphosphate)—Compound in cells, especially muscle cells, that stores energy; when needed, enzymes break off one phosphoric acid group, which releases energy for muscle contraction. (8)

Atrophy—Decrease in size of a normally developed organ or tissue. (23)

Autoimmune disease—A disorder in which the body produces an immunologic response against itself. (18)

Autonomy—Achieving independence; the psychosocial developmental task of the toddler. (12)

Autosomal recessive inheritance—Nonsex-linked pattern of inheritance in which an affected gene must be received from both parents for the individual to be affected; examples: cystic fibrosis, PKU, galactosemia. (19)

Avidin—Protein in raw egg white that inhibits the B-vitamin biotin. (7)

Bacteria—Single-celled microorganisms that lack a true nucleus; may be either harmless to humans or disease producing. (3)

Balanced diet—One that contains all the essential nutrients in required amounts. (2)

Barium enema—Series of x-ray studies of the colon used to demonstrate the presence and location of polyps, tumors, diverticula, or positional abnormalities. The client is first administered an enema containing a radio-opaque substance (barium) that enhances the visualization when the film is exposed. (15)

Beriberi—Disease caused by deficiency of vitamin B_1 (thiamin). (7)

Beta-endorphin—Chemical released in the brain during exercise that produces a state of relaxation. (6)

Bicarbonate—Any salt containing the HCO_3 anion; blood bicarbonate is a measure of alkali (base) reserve of the body; bicarbonate of soda is sodium bicarbonate ($NaHCO_3$). (9)

Bile—Yellow secretion of the liver that alkalinizes the intestine and breaks large fat globules into smaller ones to facilitate enzyme digestive action. (10)

Binging—Eating to excess; eating from 5,000 to 20,000 kilocalories per day. (17)

Bioelectric impedance—Indirect measure of body fatness based on differences in electrical conductivity of fat, muscle, and bone. (2)

Biologic value—Measure of how well food proteins can be converted into body protein. (5)

Biotin—B-complex vitamin widely available in foods. (7)

Bladder—A body organ, also called the urinary bladder, that receives urine from the kidneys and discharges it through the urethra. (10)

Blood pressure—Force exerted against the walls of blood vessels by the pumping action of the heart. (19)

Blood urea nitrogen (BUN)—The amount of nitrogen present in the blood as urea, often elevated in renal disorders; may be referred to as serum urea nitrogen (SUN). (13, 20)

Body frame size—Designation of a person's skeletal structure as small, medium, or large; used to determine healthy body weight (HBW). (2)

Body image—The mental image a person has of himself or herself. (17)

Body mass index (BMI)—Weight in kilograms divided by height in meters squared; BMIs of 20.8 to 27.7 for men and 19.2 to 27.2 for women are considered normal. (2)

Body substance isolation—A situation in which all body fluids should be considered contaminated and treated as such by all health care workers. (24)

Bolus—A mass of food that is ready to be swallowed; or a single dose of feeding or medication. (10, 15)

Bolus feeding—Giving a 4- to 6-hour volume of a tube feeding within a few minutes. (15)

Bomb calorimeter—A device used to measure the energy content of food. (6)

Botulism—An often fatal form of food intoxication caused by the ingestion of food containing poisonous toxins produced by the microorganism *Clostridium botulinum.* (14)

Bowman's capsule—The cuplike top of an individual nephron; functions as a filter in the formation of urine. (20)

Brewer's yeast—Unicellular fungus used in brewing beer and baking bread; good source of vitamin B complex. (7)

Buffer—A substance that can react to offset excess acid or excess alkali (base) in a solution; blood buffers include carbonic acid, bicarbonate, phosphates, and proteins, including hemoglobin. (9)

Bulimia—Excessive food intake followed by extreme methods, such as self-induced vomiting and the use of laxatives, to rid the body of the foods eaten. (17)

Cachexia—State of malnutrition and wasting seen in chronic conditions such as cancer, AIDS, malaria, tuberculosis, and pituitary disease. (22)

Calcidiol—Inactive form of vitamin D produced by the liver. (7)

Calcification—Process in which tissue becomes hardened with calcium deposits. (7)

Calcitonin—Hormone produced by the C cells of the thyroid gland that slows bone resorption when serum calcium levels are high. (8)

Calcitriol—The activated form of vitamin D, 1,25-dihydroxycholecalciferol. (7, 20)

Calorie—A measurement unit of energy; unit equaling the amount of heat required to raise the temperature of 1 gram of water 1 degree Celsius; laypersons' term for kilocalorie. (6)

Campylobacter—Flagellated, gram-negative bacteria; important cause of diarrheal illnesses. (14)

Candida albicans—Microscopic fungal organism normally present on skin and mucous membranes of healthy people; cause of thrush, vaginitis, opportunistic infections. (24)

Capillary—Minute vessel connecting arteriole and venule; wall acts as semipermeable membrane to exchange substances between blood and lymph and interstitial fluid. (10)

Carbohydrate—Any of a group of organic compounds, including sugar, starch, and cellulose, that contains only carbon, oxygen, and hydrogen. (3)

Carbonic acid—Aqueous solution of carbon dioxide; carbon dioxide in solution or in blood is carbonic acid. (9)

Carcinogen—Any substance or agent that causes the development of or increases the risk of cancer. (22)

Carcinoma—A malignant neoplasm that occurs in epithelial tissue. (22)

Cardiac arrhythmia—Irregular heartbeat. (17)

Cardiac output—The amount of blood discharged per minute from the left or right ventricle of the heart. (19)

Cardiac sphincter—Smooth muscle band at the lower end of the esophagus; prevents reflux of stomach contents. (10, 21)

Cardiomyopathy—Disease of heart muscle; may be primary due to unknown cause or secondary to another cardiac disorder or systemic disease. (8)

Carotene—Yellow pigment in vegetables; precursor of vitamin A. (7)

Carotenemia—Excess carotene in the blood, producing yellow skin but not discoloring the whites of the eyes. (7)

Carotenoid—Group of red, orange, or yellow pigments found in carrots, sweet potatoes, and green, leafy vegetables; includes carotene, a precursor of vitamin A and lycopene which is not. (19)

Caseinate—A derivative of casein, the principal protein in milk. (15)

Catabolism—The breaking down of body compounds or tissues into simpler substances; the destructive phase of metabolism. (5)

Catalyst—A substance that speeds up a chemical reaction without entering into or being changed by the reaction. (5)

Cataract—Clouding of the lens of the eye. (13)

Cation—An ion with a positive charge. (9)

Cecum—The first portion of the large intestine between the ileum and the ascending colon. (10)

Celiac disease (gluten-sensitive enteropathy)—An intolerance to dietary gluten, which damages the intestine and produces diarrhea and malabsorption. (10, 21)

Cell—The smallest functional unit of structure in all plants and animals. (10)

Cellular immunity—Delayed immune response produced by T-lymphocytes, which mature in the thymus gland; examples of this type of response are rejection of transplanted organs and some autoimmune diseases. (22)

Cerebrovascular accident (CVA)—An abnormal condition in which the brain's blood vessels are occluded by a thrombus, an embolus, or hemorrhage, resulting in damaged brain tissue; stroke. (19)

Chelating agent—A chemical compound that binds metallic ions into a ring structure, inactivating them; used to remove poisonous metals from the body. (8)

Chemical digestion—Digestive process that involves the splitting of complex molecules into simpler forms. (10)

Chemical reaction—The process of combining or breaking down substances to obtain different substances. (10)

Chlorophyll—The green plant pigment necessary for the manufacture of carbohydrates. (3)

Cholecalciferol—Vitamin D_3, formed when the skin is exposed to sunlight; further processed by the liver and kidneys. (7)

Cholecystitis—Inflammation of the gallbladder. (21, 24)

Cholecystokinin—A hormone secreted by the duodenum; stimulates contraction of the gallbladder (releases bile) and the secretion of pancreatic juice. (10)

Cholelithiasis—The presence of gallstones. (21)

Cholesterol—A fat-like substance made in the human body and found in foods of animal origin; associated with an increased risk of heart disease. (4, 19)

Chronic illness—A sickness persisting for a long period that shows little change or a slow progression over time. (15)

Chronic obstructive pulmonary disease (COPD)—A group of chronic diseases with a common characteristic of chronic airflow obstruction. (23)

Chronic renal failure—An irreversible condition in which the kidneys cannot perform vital functions. (20)

Chvostek's sign—Spasm of facial muscles following a tap over the facial nerve in front of the ear; indication of tetany. (8)

Chylomicron—A lipoprotein that carries triglycerides in the bloodstream after meals. (10, 19)

Chyme—The mixture of partly digested food and digestive secretions found in the stomach and small intestine during digestion of a meal. (10)

Chymotrypsin—A protein-splitting enzyme produced by the pancreas; active in the intestine. (10)

Cirrhosis—Chronic disease of the liver in which functioning cells degenerate and are replaced by fibrosed connective tissue. (21)

Client care conference—A meeting which includes all health care team members and may include the client or a significant other to review and update the client's nursing care plan. (15)

Clostridium botulinum—An anaerobic (grows without air) organism that produces a poisonous toxin; the cause of botulism. (14)

Clostridium perfringens—A bacterium that produces a poisonous toxin that causes a food intoxication; the symptoms are generally mild and of short duration and include intestinal disorders. (14)

Coenzyme—A substance that combines with an enzyme to activate it. (7)

Cognitive—Referring to or associated with the act of knowing. (17)

Colectomy—Surgical removal of part or all of the colon. (21)

Collagen—Fibrous insoluble protein found in connective tissue. (7)

Collecting tubule—The last segment of the renal tubule; follows the distal convoluted tubule. Several nephrons usually share a single collecting tubule. (20)

Colloidal osmotic pressure—Pressure produced by plasma and cellular proteins. (9)

Colon—The large intestine from the end of the small intestine to the rectum. (10)

Colostomy—Surgical procedure in which an opening to the large intestine is constructed on the abdomen. (21)

Complete protein—A protein containing all essential amino acids that humans need; usually found in animal sources such as milk, meat, eggs, and fish. (5)

Complex carbohydrate—A carbohydrate composed of many molecules of $C_6H_{12}O_6$ joined together; polysaccharide; includes starch, glycogen, and fiber. (3)

Compound—Two or more elements united chemically in specific proportions. (9)

Compound fat—Substance obtained when one of the fatty acids joined to the glycerol molecule is replaced by another molecule, such as a protein. (4)

Congestive heart failure (CHF)—Condition resulting from the failure of the heart to maintain adequate blood circulation; due to complex reactive mechanisms, fluid is retained in the body's tissues. (19)

Constipation—Infrequent passage of feces; colonic constipation is characterized by dry, hard stools, rectal constipation by delayed elimination of soft stool. (13)

Contamination iron—Iron that leaches from cookware into the food; in special circumstances, can become hazardous. (8)

Continuous ambulatory peritoneal dialysis (CAPD)—A form of self-dialysis in which the dialysate is allowed to remain in the abdominal cavity for 4 to 6 hours before replacement. (20)

Continuous feeding—On an ongoing basis. (15)

Contraindication—Any circumstance under which treatment should not be given. (15)

Coronary heart disease (CHD)—Disease resulting from the decreased flow of blood through the coronary arteries to the heart muscle. (19)

Coronary occlusion—Blockage of one or more branches of the coronary arteries, which supply the heart muscle with oxygen and nutrients. (19)

Creatinine—Nonprotein nitrogenous end product of creatinine metabolism; because creatinine is excreted by the kidneys, serum creatinine levels are used to detect and monitor renal disease and to estimate muscle protein reserves. (20)

Cretinism—A congenital condition resulting from a lack of thyroid secretions characterized by a stunted and malformed body and arrested mental development. (8)

Crohn's disease—Inflammatory disease appearing in any area of the bowel in which diseased areas can be found alternating with healthy tissue. (21)

Cross-contamination—The spreading of a disease-producing organism from one food, person, or object to another food, person, or object. (14)

Cruciferous—Belonging to a botanical mustard family; includes broccoli, brussels sprouts, cabbage, cauliflower, kale, kohlrabi, and swiss chard. (22)

Crystalluria—The presence of crystals in the urine; may be caused by the administration of sulfonamides. (16)

Culture—The learned, shared, and transmitted values, beliefs, and norms of a particular group that guides their thinking, decisions, and actions in patterned ways. (2)

Cyanocobalamin—Vitamin B_{12}; essential for proper blood formation. (7)

Cyclical variation—A recurring series of events during a specified period. (1)

Cystic fibrosis—Hereditary disease often affecting the lungs and pancreas in which glandular secretions are abnormally thick. (21)

Cystitis—Inflammation of the bladder. (20)

Daily food guide—Tool used to assist consumers in making informed food choices. (2)

Deamination—Metabolic process whereby nitrogen is removed from an amino acid. (10)

Deciliter—100 milliliters or 100 cubic centimeters. (18)

Decubitus ulcer—A pressure sore on the lower back, such as a bedsore. (15)

Delusion—False belief that is firmly maintained despite obvious proof to the contrary. (7)

Dementia—The impairment of intellectual function that usually is progressive and interferes with normal social and occupational activities. (1)

Dental caries—The gradual decay and disintegration of the teeth; a dental cavity is a hole in a tooth caused by dental caries. (3)

Dental plaque—Colorless and transparent gummy mass of microorganisms that grows on the teeth, predisposing them to decay. (3)

Deoxyribonucleic acid (DNA)—Protein substance in the cell nucleus that directs all the cell's activities, including reproduction. (5)

Desirable body weight—A person's body weight as compared with the 1959 Desirable Height/Weight Table. (17)

Desired outcome—The behavioral or physical change in a client that indicate the achievement of a nursing goal. (2)

Development—Process of changing to a mature individual; involves psychosocial and physical aspects, often including an increase in size. (12)

Dextrose—Another name for the simple sugar glucose. (3)

Diabetes incipidus—Increased water intake and increased urine output resulting from inadequate secretion of antidiuretic hormone (ADH) by the posterior pituitary or by failure of the kidney tubules to respond to ADH; underlying causes can be tumor, surgery, trauma, infection, radiation injury, or congenital anomaly. (9)

Diabetes mellitus—Disease caused by insufficient insulin secretion by the pancreas or insulin resistance by body tissues causing excess glucose in the blood and deranged carbohydrate, fat, and protein metabolism. (18)

Diabetic neuropathy—Degeneration of peripheral

nerves occurring in diabetes; possible causes are microscopic changes in blood vessels or metabolic defects in nerve tissue. (18)

Diacetic acid—A ketone body found in the urine, which can be due to the excessive breakdown of stored body fat. (3)

Diagnostic—Relating to scientific and skillful methods to establish the cause and nature of a sick person's illness. (15)

Dialysate—In renal failure, the fluid used to remove or deliver compounds or electrolytes that the failing kidney cannot excrete or retain in proper concentrations. (20)

Dialysis—The process of diffusing blood across a semipermeable membrane to remove toxic materials and to maintain fluid, electrolyte, and acid-base balances in cases of impaired kidney function or absence of the kidneys. (20)

Dialysis dementia—A neurological disturbance seen in clients who have been on dialysis for a number of years. (20)

Diastolic pressure—Pressure exerted against the arteries between heart beats; the lower number of a blood pressure reading. (9, 19)

Dietary fiber—Material in foods, mostly from plants, that the human body cannot break down or digest. (3)

Dietary recall, 24-hour—Description of what a person has eaten for the previous 24 hours. (2)

Dietary status—Description of what a person has been eating; his or her usual intake. (2)

Digestion—The process by which food is broken down mechanically and chemically in the gastrointestinal tract into forms simple enough for intestinal absorption. (10)

Diglyceride—Two fatty acids joined to a glycerol molecule. (4)

Disaccharide—A simple sugar composed of two units of $C_6H_{12}O_6$ joined together; examples include sucrose, lactose, and maltose. (3)

Disulfide linkage—Specific chemical bond joining amino acids; in hair, skin, and nails, holds amino acids in their distinct shapes. (8)

Diverticulitis—Inflammation of a diverticulum. (21)

Diverticulosis—Presence of one or more diverticula. (21)

Diverticulum—A sac or pouch in the walls of a tubular organ; pl., diverticula. (21)

Dopamine—Catecholamine synthesized by the adrenals; immediate precursor in the synthesis of norepinephrine. (16)

Double bond—A type of chemical connection in which, for example, a fatty acid has two neighboring carbon atoms, each lacking one hydrogen atom. (4)

Drink—An alcoholic beverage; one drink is usually 12 ounces of beer, 4 ounces of wine, or 1.5 ounces of liquor. (19)

Duct—A structural tube designed to allow secretions to move from one body part to another body part. (10, 18)

Dumping syndrome—A condition in which the contents of the stomach empty too rapidly into the duodenum; mostly occurs in patients who have had gastric resections. (21)

Duodenum—The first part of the small intestine between the stomach and the jejunum. (10)

Dyspnea—Difficulty breathing. (23)

Ebb phase—The first phase in the stress response; the body reduces blood pressure, cardiac output, body temperature, and oxygen consumption to meet increased demands. (23)

Eclampsia—An obstetrical emergency involving hypertension, edema, proteinuria, and convulsions appearing after the 20th week of pregnancy. (11)

Edema—The accumulation of excessive amounts of fluid in interstitial spaces. (9)

Edentulous—The state of having no teeth. (13)

Efferent—Directed away from a center; used to describe arteries, veins, lymphatic vessels, and nerves. (17)

Efferent arteriole—Small blood vessel by which blood leaves the nephron. (20)

Electrocardiogram (ECG)—A graphic record produced by an electrocardiograph that shows the electrical activity of the heart. (9)

Electroencephalogram (EEG)—The record obtained from an electroencephalograph that shows the electrical activity of the brain. (9)

Electrolyte—An element or compound that when dissolved in water separates (dissociates) into ions that are capable of conducting an electrical current; acids, bases, and salts are common electrolytes. (9)

Element—A substance that cannot be separated into simpler parts by ordinary means. (3)

Elemental or "predigested" formula—Formula that contains either partially or totally predigested nutrients. (15)

Embolus—A circulating mass of undissolved matter in a blood or lymphatic vessel; may be composed of tissues, fat globules, air bubbles, clumps of bacteria, or foreign bodies, including pieces of medical devices. (19)

Embryo—A developing infant in the prenatal period between the second and eighth weeks inclusive. (11)

Empty kilocalories—Refers to a food that contains kilocalories and almost no other nutrients. (6)

Emulsification—The physical breaking up of fat into tiny droplets. (10)

Emulsifier—A molecule that attracts both water- and fat-soluble molecules. (14)

Emulsion—One liquid evenly distributed in a second liquid with which it usually does not mix. (4)

Endogenous—Produced within or caused by factors within the organism. (16)

End-stage renal failure—A state in which the kidneys have lost most or all their ability to maintain internal homeostasis and produce urine. (20, 24)

Energy—The capacity to do work. (1)

Energy balance—A situation in which kilocaloric intake equals kilocaloric output. (6)

Energy expenditure—The amount of fuel the body uses for a specified period. (6)

Energy imbalance—Situation in which kilocalories eaten do not equal the number of kilocalories used for energy. (17)

Energy nutrients—The chemical substances in food that are able to supply fuel; refers collectively to carbohydrate, fat, and protein. (1)

Enrichment—The addition of nutrients previously present in a food but removed during food processing or lost during storage. (3)

Enteral tube feeding—The feeding of a formula by tube into the gastrointestinal tract. (15)

Enteric-coated—A type of drug preparation designed to dissolve in the intestine rather than in the stomach. (16)

Enzyme—Complex protein produced by living cells that acts as a catalyst. (5, 6)

Epidemic—Occurrence in a region of more than the expected number of cases of a communicable disease. (24)

Epinephrine—Hormone of the adrenal gland; produces the fight-or-flight response. (23)

Epithelial tissue—A type of tissue that forms the outer layer of skin and lines body surfaces opening to the outside; functions include protection, absorption, and secretion. (7)

Ergocalciferol—Vitamin D_2 formed by the action of sunlight on plants. (7)

Ergot poisoning—Poisoning resulting from excessive use of the drug ergot or from the ingestion of grain or grain products infected with the *Claviceps purpurea* fungus. (14)

Erikson, Erik—Psychologist who devised a theory of human development consisting of eight stages of life, each with a psychosocial developmental task to be mastered. (12)

Erosion—Destruction of the surface of a tissue, either on the external surface of the body or internally. (21)

Erythropoietin—Hormone released by the kidney to stimulate red blood cell production. (20)

Esophageal reflux—Regurgitation of the stomach contents into the esophagus. (21)

Esophagostomy—A surgical opening in the esophagus. (15)

Esophagus—A muscular canal extending from the mouth to the stomach. (10, 21)

Essential amino acid—One of the amino acids that cannot be manufactured by the human body; must be obtained from food or artificial feeding. (5)

Essential (primary) hypertension—Elevated blood pressure that develops without apparent cause. (19)

Essential nutrient—A substance found in food that must be present in the diet because the human body lacks the ability to manufacture it in sufficient amounts for optimal health. (1)

Estimated Safe and Adequate Daily Dietary Intake (ESADDI)—Intake of 2 vitamins and 5 minerals for which insufficient information is available to establish a Recommended Dietary Allowance (RDA). (2)

Ethanol—Grain alcohol; ounces of ethanol in beverages can be estimated with the conversion factors of 0.045 for beer, 0.121 for wine, and 0.409 for liquor. (19)

Ethnocentrism—Belief that one's own view of the world is superior to anyone else's. (2)

Evaluation—The final step in the nursing process in which the actual outcome is compared to the desired outcome. (2)

Evaporative water loss—Insensible water loss through the skin. (9)

Exchange—A defined quantity of food on the American Dietetic and Diabetes Associations' food exchange list or on another, similar, exchange list. (2)

Exchange list—A food guide developed by the American Dietetic and Diabetes Associations; often used in clinical practice to aid in meal planning. (2)

Excretion—The elimination of waste products from the body in feces, urine, exhaled air, and perspiration. (10)

Exogenous—Outside the body. (18)

External muscle layer—Muscle layer of the alimentary canal. (6)

External water loss—Water lost to the outside of the body. (9)

Extracellular fluid—Fluid found between the cells and within the blood and lymph vessels. (9)

Extrinsic factor—Vitamin B_{12}, necessary for proper red blood cell development. (7)

Failure to thrive (FTT)—Medical diagnosis for infants who fail to gain weight appropriately or who lose weight. (12)

Fasting—The state of having had no food or fluid enterally or no parenteral nutrition. (15)

Fasting blood sugar (FBS)—Blood glucose measured in the fasting state; normal values are 70 to 110 mg per deciliter. (3, 18)

Fat-free mass—Lean body mass plus nonfat components of adipose tissue. (2)

Fatty acid—Part of the structure of a fat. (4)

Fatty liver—Accumulation of lipids in the liver cells; may be reversible if the cause, of which there are many, is removed. (21)

Ferric iron—Oxidized iron, which is less absorbable from the gastrointestinal tract than ferrous iron; abbreviated Fe^{3+}. (8)

Ferritin—An iron-phosphorus-protein complex formed in the intestinal mucosa by the union of ferric iron with apoferritin; the form in which iron is stored in the tissues, mainly in liver, spleen, and bone marrow cells. (8, 20)

Ferrous iron—The more absorbable form of iron for humans; abbreviated Fe^{2+}. (8)

Fetal alcohol syndrome (FAS)—A condition characterized by mental and physical abnormalities in an infant caused by the mother's consumption of alcohol during pregnancy. (11)

Fetus—The human child in utero from the third month until birth; also applicable to the later stages of gestation of other animals. (11)

Fiber, dietary—Material in foods, mostly from plants, that the human body cannot break down or digest. (3)

Fibrin—Insoluble protein formed from fibrinogen by the action of thrombin; forms the meshwork of a blood clot. (8)

Fibrinogen—Protein in blood essential to the clotting process; also called Factor I; see fibrin. (8)

Filtration—The process of removing particles from a solution by allowing the liquid to pass through a membrane or other partial barrier. (20)

Flatus—Gas in the digestive tract, averaging 400 to 1200 milliliters per day. (21)

Flow phase—The second phase in the stress response; marked by pronounced hormonal changes. (23)

Fluorosis—Condition due to excessive prolonged intake of fluoride; tissues affected are teeth and bones. (8)

Folic acid—B-complex vitamin necessary for DNA formation and proper red blood cell formation. (7)

Food acceptance record—A checklist that indicates food items accepted or rejected by the client. (15)

Food allergy—Sensitivity to a food that does not cause a negative reaction in most people. (10)

Food frequency—A usual food intake or a description of what an individual usually eats during a typical day. (2)

Food infection—One acquired through contact with food or water contaminated with disease-producing microorganisms. (14)

Food intoxication—An illness caused by the consumption of a food in which bacteria have produced a poisonous toxin. (14)

Food Pyramid—Food guide commonly used to evaluate a person's dietary status and to educate clients about food choices; food is divided into six groups: each contains foods of similar nutritional content. (2)

Food record—A diary of a person's self-reported food intake. (2)

Free radicals—Atoms or molecules that have lost an electron and vigorously pursue its replacement; in doing so, free radicals can damage normal cell constituents. (7)

Fructose—A monosaccharide found in fruits and honey; a simple sugar. (3)

Fundus—Larger part of a hollow organ; the part of the stomach above its attachment to the esophagus. (21)

Galactose—A monosaccharide derived mainly from the breakdown of the sugar in milk, lactose; a simple sugar. (3)

Galactosemia—Lack of an enzyme needed to metabolize galactose. (12)

Gallbladder—A pear-shaped organ on the underside of the liver that concentrates and stores bile. (10,21)

Gastric bypass—A surgical procedure that routes food around the stomach. (17)

Gastric lipase—An enzyme in the stomach that aids in the digestion of fats. (10)

Gastric stapling—A surgical procedure on the stomach to induce weight loss by reducing the size of the stomach; also known as gastroplasty. (17)

Gastrin—A hormone secreted by the gastric mucosa; stimulates the secretion of gastric juice. (10)

Gastritis—Inflammation of the stomach. (21)

Gastroparesis—Partial paralysis of the stomach. (18)

Gastrostomy—A surgical opening in the stomach. (15)

Gene—Basic unit of heredity; occupies a specific location on a specific chromosome. (5)

Generativity—The seventh of Erikson's developmental stages, in which the middle-aged adult guides the next generation. (13)

Generic name—The name given to a drug by its original developer; usually the same as the official name given to it by the Food and Drug Administration. (16)

Genetic susceptibility—The likelihood of an individual developing a given trait as determined by heredity. (3)

Geriatrics—The branch of medicine involved in the study and treatment of diseases of the elderly. (13)

Gestation—The time from fertilization of the ovum until birth; in humans the length of gestation is usually 38 to 42 weeks. (11)

Gestational diabetes (GDM)—Hyperglycemia and altered carbohydrate, protein, and fat metabolism related to the increased demands of pregnancy. (11, 18)

Globin—The simple protein portion of hemoglobin. (5)

Glomerular filtrate—The fluid that has been passed through the glomerulus. (20)

Glomerular filtration rate (GFR)—An index of kidney function; the amount of filtrate formed each minute in all the nephrons of both kidneys. (20)

Glomerulonephritis—Inflammation of the glomeruli. (20)

Glomerulus—The network of capillaries inside Bowman's capsule (20)

Glucagon—A hormone secreted by the alpha cells of the pancreas; increases the concentration of glucose in the blood. (5, 18)

Gluconeogenesis—The production of glucose from noncarbohydrate sources such as amino acids and glycerol. (23)

Glucose—A monosaccharide (simple sugar) commonly called the blood sugar; the same as dextrose. (3)

Glucose tolerance factor (GTF)—Organic compound containing chromium, which enhances the action of insulin, facilitating the uptake of glucose by the body's cells. (8)

Glucose tolerance test—A test of blood and urine after the patient receives a concentrated dose of glucose; used to diagnose abnormalities of glucose metabolism. (18)

Gluteal-femoral obesity—Excess body fat centered around an individual's buttocks, hips, and thighs. (17, 19)

Gluten—A type of protein found in wheat, rye, oats, and barley. (10)

Gluten-sensitive enteropathy (celiac disease)—An intestinal disorder caused by an abnormal response following the consumption of gluten. (10)

Glycemic index—A measure of how much the blood glucose level increases following consumption of a particular food that contains a given amount of carbohydrate. (18)

Glycerol—The backbone of a fat molecule; pharmaceutical preparation is glycerin. (4)

Glycogen—The form in which carbohydrate is stored in liver and muscle. (3)

Glycogenolysis—The breakdown of glycogen. (23)

Glycosuria—Glucose in the urine. (18)

Glycosylated hemoglobin—Hemoglobin to which a glucose group is attached; in diabetes mellitus, if the blood glucose level has not been controlled over the previous 120 days, the glycosylated hemoglobin level is elevated. (18)

Goiter—Enlargement of the thyroid gland characterized by pronounced swelling in the neck. (8)

Goitrogens—Substances that block the absorption of iodine, thereby causing goiter; found in cabbage, rutabaga, and turnips, but only related to goiter in cassava. (8)

Gout—A hereditary metabolic disease that is a form of acute arthritis and is marked by inflammation of the joints. (20)

"Gut failure"—Impaired absorption due to structural damage to the small intestine; symptoms include diarrhea, malabsorption, and unsuccessful absorption of oral food. (10)

Harris-Benedict equation—A formula commonly used to estimate resting energy expenditure in a stressed client. (23, 24)

Health—A state of complete physical, mental, and social well-being, not just the absence of disease or infirmity. (1)

Healthy body weight (HBW)—Estimate of a weight suitable for an individual based on frame size and height and weight tables. (2)

Hematocrit—Percent of total blood volume that is red blood cells; normals are 40 to 54 percent for men; 37 to 47 percent for women. (8)

Hematuria—Blood in the urine. (20)

Heme—The iron-containing portion of the hemoglobin molecule. (8)

Heme iron—Iron bound to hemoglobin and myoglobin in meat, fish, and poultry; 10 to 30 percent of the iron in these foods is absorbed. (8)

Hemochromatosis—A disease of iron metabolism in which iron accumulates in the tissues. (8)

Hemodialysis—A method for cleansing the blood of wastes by circulating blood through a machine that contains tubes made of synthetic semipermeable membranes. (20)

Hemoglobin—The iron-carrying pigment of the red blood cells; carries oxygen from the lungs to the tissues. (5, 8)

Hemolysis—Rupture of red blood cells releasing hemoglobin into the plasma; causes include bacterial toxins, chemicals, inappropriate medications, vitamin E deficiency. (7)

Hemolytic anemia—An abnormal reduction in the number of red blood cells due to hemolysis. (8)

Hemosiderin—An iron oxide-protein compound derived from hemoglobin; a secondary storage form of iron. (8)

Hemosiderosis—Condition resulting from excess deposits of hemosiderin, especially in the liver and spleen; caused by destruction of red blood cells, which occurs in diseases such as hemolytic anemia, pernicious anemia, and chronic infection. (8)

Heparin—A chemical, found naturally in many tissues, that inhibits blood clotting by preventing the conversion of prothrombin to thrombin; also given as an anticoagulant medication. (7)

Hepatic portal circulation—A subdivision of the vascular system in which blood from the digestive organs and spleen circulates through the liver before returning to the heart. (10)

Hepatitis—Inflammation of the liver, caused by viruses, drugs, alcohol, or toxic substances. (21)

Hiatal hernia—A protrusion of part of the stomach into the chest cavity. (21)

High-density lipoprotein (HDL)—A plasma protein that carries fat in the bloodstream to the tissues or to the liver to be excreted; elevated blood levels are associated with a decreased risk of heart disease. (19)

High-fructose corn syrup (HFCS)—A common food additive used as a sweetener; made from fructose. (3)

Hives (urticaria)—Sudden swelling and itching of skin or mucous membranes, often caused by allergies; if the respiratory tract is involved, may be life-threatening. (12)

Homeostasis—Tendency toward balance in the internal environment of the body, achieved by automatic monitoring and regulating mechanisms. (6)

Hormone—A substance produced by cells of the body that is released into the bloodstream and carried to target sites to regulate the activity of other cells and organs. (4, 5)

Human immunodeficiency virus (HIV)—The virus that causes AIDS. (24)

Humoral immunity—Development of antibodies to specific antigens by the B-lymphocytes, some of which retain the ability to recognize the antigen if it is encountered again; basis of immunizations. (22)

Humulin—Exact duplicate of human insulin manufactured by altering bacterial DNA. (18)

Hunger—The sensation resulting from a lack of food, characterized by dull or acute pain around the lower part of the chest. (17)

Hydrochloric acid (HCl)—Strong acid secreted by the stomach that aids in protein digestion. (10)

Hydrogenation—The process of adding hydrogen to a fat to make it more highly saturated. (4)

Hydrolysis—A chemical reaction that splits a substance into simpler compounds by the addition of water. (10)

Hydrostatic pressure—The pressure created by the pumping action of the heart on the fluid in the blood vessels. (9)

Hyperalimentation—Another name for total parenteral nutrition. (15)

Hyperbilirubinemia—Excessive bilirubin in the blood; bilirubin is produced by the breakdown of red blood cells. (8)

Hypercalcemia—A serum calcium level that is too high; in adults, more than 5.5 milliequivalents per liter. (8)

Hypercholesterolemia—Excessive cholesterol in the blood. (19)

Hyperemesis gravidarum—Severe nausea and vomiting persisting after the fourteenth week of pregnancy. (11)

Hyperglycemia—An elevated level of glucose in the blood; fasting value above 110 or 120 milligrams per deciliter, depending on measuring technique used. (18)

Hyperglycemic hyperosmolar nonketotic syndrome (HHNS)—Life-threatening complication of NIDDM characterized by blood glucose levels greater than 600 milligrams per deciliter, absence of or slight ketosis, profound cellular dehydration, and electrolyte imbalances. (18)

Hyperkalemia—Excessive potassium in the blood; greater than 5.0 milliequivalents per liter of serum in adults. (8)

Hyperlipoproteinemia—Increased lipoproteins and lipids in the blood. (19)

Hypermetabolism—An abnormal increase in the rate at which fuel or kilocalories are burned. (23)

Hypernatremia—An excess of sodium in the blood; greater than 145 milliequivalents per liter of serum in adults. (8)

Hyperparathyroidism—Excessive secretion of parathyroid hormone, causing changes in the bones, kidney, and gastrointestinal tract. (8)

Hyperphosphatemia—Excessive amount of phosphates in the blood; in adults, greater than 4.7 milligrams per 100 milliliters of serum. (8)

Hypertension—Blood pressure above normal, usually more than 140/90 on three successive occasions. (10, 19)

Hypertensive kidney disease—A condition in which vascular or glomerular lesions cause hypertension but not total renal failure. (20)

Hyperthyroidism—Oversecretion of thyroid hormones, which increases the metabolic rate above normal. (8)

Hypertonic—A solution that contains more particles and exerts more osmotic pressure than the plasma. (9)

Hypervitaminosis—Condition caused by excessive intake of vitamins. (7)

Hypocalcemia—A depressed level of calcium in the blood; less than 4.5 milliequivalents per liter of serum in adults. (8)

Hypoglycemia—A depressed level of glucose in the blood; less than 70 milligrams per deciliter. (18)

Hypokalemia—Potassium depletion in the circulating blood; less than 3.5 milliequivalents per liter of serum in adults. (8, 16, 20)

Hyponatremia—Too little sodium per volume of blood; less than 135 milliequivalents per liter of serum in adults. (8)

Hypophosphatemia—Too little phosphates per volume of blood; in adults, less than 2.4 milligrams per 100 milliliters of serum. (8)

Hypothalamus—A portion of the brain that helps to regulate water balance, thirst, body temperature, carbohydrate and fat metabolism, and sleep. (9)

Hypothyroidism—Undersecretion of thyroid hormones; reduces the metabolic rate. (8)

Hypotonic—A solution that contains fewer particles and exerts less osmotic pressure than the plasma does. (9)

Iatrogenic malnutrition—Excessive or deficit intake of one or more nutrients induced by the oversight or omissions of health care workers. (15)

Ideal body weight—A person's weight as compared with the 1943 Height/Weight Tables. (17)

Identity—The fifth developmental task in Erikson's theory, in which the adolescent decides on an appropriate role. (12)

Ileocecal valve—The valve between the ileum and cecum. (10)

Ileostomy—Surgical procedure in which an opening to the small intestine (ileum) is constructed on the abdomen. (21)

Ileum—The lower portion of the small intestine. (10, 21)

Immune—Produced by, involved in, or concerned with resistance or protection against a specified disease. (22)

Immune system—The organs in the body responsible for fighting off substances interpreted as foreign. (22)

Immunity—The state of being protected from a particular disease, especially an infectious disease. (5, 24)

Immunoglobulin—Blood proteins with known antibody activity; five classes of immunoglobulins have been identified. (5)

Immunosuppressive agent—Medication that interferes with the body's ability to fight infection. (14)

Impaired glucose tolerance (IGT)—A type of classification for hyperglycemia; for persons who have a glucose intolerance but do not meet the criteria for classification as having diabetes. (18)

Implantation—Embedding of the fertilized egg in the lining of the uterus 6 or 7 days after fertilization. (11)

Incidence—The frequency of occurrence of any event or condition over a given time and in relation to the population in which it occurs. (17)

Incomplete protein—Protein lacking one or more of the essential amino acids that humans need; found primarily in plant sources such as grains and vegetables; gelatin is an animal product but is an incomplete protein. (5)

Incubation period—The time it takes to show disease symptoms after exposure to the causative organism. (14)

Indication—A circumstance that indicates when a treatment should or can be used. (15)

Indoles—Compounds found in vegetables of the cruciferous family that activate enzymes to destroy carcinogens. (22)

Industry—The fourth stage of development in Erikson's theory in which the school-age child learns to work effectively. (12)

Infection—Entry and development of parasites or entry and multiplication of microorganisms in the bodies of persons or animals; may or may not cause signs and symptoms. (24)

Initiation—The first step in the cell's becoming cancerous, when physical forces, chemicals, or biologic agents permanently alter the cell's DNA. (22)

Initiative—The third stage of development in Erikson's theory, in which the preschooler learns to set and achieve goals. (12)

Insensible water loss—Water that is lost invisibly through the lungs and skin. (9)

Insoluble—Incapable of being dissolved. (3)

Insulin—Hormone secreted by the beta cells of the pancreas in response to an elevated blood glucose level. (5)

Insulin-dependent diabetes mellitus (IDDM)—Type I diabetes; persons with this disorder must take insulin to survive. (18)

Insulin resistance—A disorder characterized by elevated levels of both glucose and insulin; thought to be related to a lack of insulin receptors. (18)

Intact feeding—A feeding consisting of nutrients that have not been predigested. (15)

Intact nutrients—Nutrients that have not been predigested. (15)

Intact or "polymeric" formula—An oral or enteral feeding that contains all the essential nutrients in a specified volume. (15)

Integrity—The final stage of Erikson's theory of psychosocial development, in which the older adult learns to look back on his or her life as worthwhile. (13)

Intermittent feeding—Giving a 4- to 6-hour volume of a tube feeding over 20 to 30 minutes. (15)

Intermittent peritoneal dialysis—Method of dialysis treatment in which the dialysate remains in a patient's abdominal cavity for about 30 minutes and then drains from the body by gravity. (20)

International Unit (IU)—Individually scaled measure of vitamins A, D, and E agreed to by a committee of scientists; largely replaced by finer measures. (7)

Interstitial fluid—Extracellular fluid located between the cells. (9)

Intimacy—The sixth stage of development in Erikson's theory, in which the young adult builds reciprocal, caring relationships. (13)

Intracellular fluid—Fluid located within the cells. (9)

Intravascular fluid—Fluid found in the blood and lymph vessels. (9)

Intravenous—Through a vein. (3)

Intrinsic factor—Specific protein-binding factor secreted by the stomach, necessary for the absorption of vitamin B_{12}. (7)

Invisible fat—Dietary fats that cannot be seen easily; hidden fats in foods such as baked goods, peanut butter, emulsified milk, and so forth. (4)

Ion—An atom or group of atoms carrying an electrical charge; an ion with a positive charge is called a cation; an ion with a negative charge is called an anion. (9)

Ionic bond—A chemical bond formed between atoms by the loss and gain of electrons. (9)

Iron-deficiency anemia—Anemia due to a greater demand on the stored iron than can be supplied; causes include inadequate iron intake, malabsorption, and chronic or acute blood loss. (8, 11)

Irrigation—Flushing a prescribed solution through a tube or cavity. (15)

Irritable bowel syndrome—Diarrhea or alternating constipation-diarrhea with no discernible organic cause. (21)

Islet cell antibody—A protein found to be elevated in a person with insulin-dependent diabetes mellitus. (18)

Islets of Langerhans—Clusters of cells in the pancreas including alpha, beta, and delta cells; alpha cells produce glucagon, beta cells produce insulin, and delta cells produce somatostatin. (18)

Isotonic—A solution that has the same osmotic pressure as blood plasma. (9, 15)

Jaundice—Yellowing of skin, whites of eyes, and mucous membranes due to excessive bilirubin in the blood; causes may be obstructed bile duct, liver disease, or hemolysis of red blood cells. (7)

Jejunoileal bypass—A surgical procedure that removes a portion of the small intestine, bypassing about 90 percent of it. (17)

Jejunostomy—A surgical opening in the jejunum. (15)

Jejunum—The second portion of the small intestine. (8, 10)

Kaposi's sarcoma—A type of cancer often related to the immunocompromised state that accompanies AIDS; characterized by multiple areas of cell proliferation, initially in the skin and eventually in other body sites. (24)

Keto acid—Amino acid residue left after deamination. (5)

Ketoacidosis—Acidosis due to an excess of ketone bodies. (18)

Ketone bodies—Compounds such as acetone and diacetic acid that are formed when fat is metabolized incompletely. (4)

Ketonuria—The presence of ketone bodies in the urine. (18)

Ketosis—The physical state of the human body with

ketones elevated in the blood and present in the urine; one example is diabetic ketoacidosis. (3, 23)

Kilocaloric density—The kilocalories contained in a given volume of a food. (6)

Kilocalorie—A measurement unit of energy; the amount of heat required to raise 1 kilogram of water 1 degree Celsius; often referred to as calories by the general public. (6)

Kilocalorie : nitrogen ratios—A mathematical relationship expressed as the number of kilocalories per gram of nitrogen provided in a feeding. (23)

Kilojoule—A measurement unit of energy; one kilocalorie equals 4.184 kilojoules. (6)

Korsakoff's psychosis—Amnesia, often seen in chronic alcoholism, caused by degeneration of the thalamus due to thiamin deficiency; characterized by loss of short-term memory and inability to learn new skills. (7)

Krebs cycle—A complicated series of reactions that results in the release of energy from carbohydrates, fats, and proteins; also known as the TCA (tricarboxylic acid) cycle. (10)

Kussmaul respirations—Pattern of rapid and deep breathing due to the body's attempt to correct metabolic acidosis by eliminating carbon dioxide through the lungs. (18)

Kwashiorkor—Severe protein deficiency in child after weaning; symptoms include edema, pigmentation changes, impaired growth and development, and liver pathology. (5, 9)

Lactase—An intestinal enzyme that converts lactose into glucose and galactose. (10)

Lacteal—The central lymph vessel in each villus. (10)

Lactose—A disaccharide found mainly in milk and milk products. (3)

Large intestine—The part of the alimentary canal that extends from the small intestine to the anus. (10)

LCAT deficiency—A lack of LCAT, an enzyme that transports cholesterol from the tissues to the liver for removal from the body. (20)

Legumes—Plants that have nitrogen-fixing bacteria in their roots; a good alternative to meat as a protein source; examples are dried beans, lentils. (5)

Lesion—Area of diseased or injured tissue. (20)

Leukopenia—Abnormal decrease in the number of white blood corpuscles; usually below 5000 per cubic millimeter. (24)

Life expectancy—The probable number of years

that persons of a given age may be expected to live. (13)

Linoleic acid—An essential fatty acid. (4)

Lipectomy—The surgical procedure in which fat tissue is removed through a vacuum hose. (17)

Lipid—Any one of a group of fats or fat-like substances that are insoluble in water; includes true fats (fatty acids and glycerol), lipoids, and sterols. (4)

Lipoid—Substances resembling fats, but containing other groups than glycerol and fatty acids that make up true fats; example: phospholipids. (4)

Lipolysis—The breakdown of adipose tissue for energy. (18, 23)

Lipoprotein—Combination of a protein with lipid components such as cholesterol, phospholipids, and triglycerides. (4)

Lipoprotein lipase—An enzyme that breaks down chylomicrons. (19)

Listeriosis—Infectious disease caused by *Listeria monocytogenes*, a soil saprophyte that causes opportunistic infections. (24)

Liver—A digestive organ that aids in the metabolism of all the energy nutrients, screens toxic substances from the blood, manufactures blood proteins, and performs many other important functions. (10)

Loop of Henle—The segment of the renal tubule that follows the proximal convoluted tubule. (20)

Low-density lipoprotein (LDL)—A plasma protein containing more cholesterol and triglycerides than protein; elevated blood levels are associated with increased risk of heart disease. (19)

Luminal effect—Drug-induced changes within the intestine that affect the absorption of nutrients and drugs without altering the intestine. (16)

Lycopene—A red pigmented carotenoid with powerful antioxidant functions but no provitamin A activity; found in tomatoes and various berries and fruits. (22)

Lymph—A body fluid collected from the interstitial fluid all over the body and returned to the bloodstream via the lymphatic vessels. (10)

Lymphatic system—All the structures involved in the transportation of lymph from the tissues to the bloodstream. (10)

Lysine—Amino acid often lacking in grains. (4)

Macrocytic anemia—Anemia in which the red blood cells are larger than normal; also found in folic acid deficiency; one characteristic of pernicious anemia. (7)

Malabsorption—Inadequate movement of digested

food from the small intestine into the blood or lymphatic system. (10)

Malnutrition—Poor nutrition; results when the body's cells receive either an excess or a deficiency of one or more nutrients. (1)

Maltase—An intestinal enzyme that converts maltose into glucose. (10)

Maltose—A disaccharide produced when starches are broken down by the body into simpler units; two units of glucose joined together. (3)

Marasmus—Malnutrition due to a protein and kilocalorie deficit. (5)

Mastication—The process of chewing. (10)

Mechanical digestion—The digestive process that involves the physical breaking down of food into smaller pieces. (10)

Megadose—Dose providing 10 times the recommended dietary allowance or more. (7)

Megaloblastic anemia—Anemia characterized by the formation of large immature red blood cells that cannot carry oxygen properly; caused by folic acid deficiency. (7)

Menadione—Synthetic, water-soluble vitamin K; also called vitamin K_3. (7)

Menaquinone—Vitamin K that is synthesized by intestinal bacteria; also called vitamin K_2. (7)

Metabolism—The sum of all physical and chemical changes that take place in the body; the two fundamental processes involved are anabolism and catabolism. (1, 6, 10)

Metastasis—The "seeding" of cancer cells to distant sites of the body; spread via blood or lymph vessels or by spilling into a body cavity. (22)

Methionine—Amino acid often lacking in legumes. (5)

Microalbuminuria—Small amounts of protein in the urine. Detected by a laboratory using methods more sensitive than traditional urinalysis. (18)

Microgram—One-millionth of a gram or one-thousandth of a milligram; abbreviated mcg or μg. (7)

Micronize—To pulverize a substance into very tiny particles. (16)

Microvilli—Microscopic, hairlike rodlets (resembling bristles on a brush) covering the edge of each villus. (10)

Midarm circumference—Measure of the distance around the middle of the upper arm; used to assess body protein stores. (2)

Mildly obese—Twenty to 40 percent overweight; 120 to 140 percent healthy body weight. (17)

Milliequivalent—Unit of measure used for determining the concentration of electrolytes in solution; expressed as milliequivalents per liter. (9)

Milling—The process of grinding grain into flour. (3)

Milliosmole—Unit of measure for osmotic activity. (9)

Mineral—An inorganic element or compound occurring in nature; in the body, minerals help regulate bodily functions and are essential to good health. (8)

Mixed malnutrition—The result of a deficiency or excess of more than one nutrient. (15)

Moderately obese—Forty-one to 100 percent overweight; 141 to 200 percent healthy body weight. (17)

Modular supplement—A nutritional supplement that contains a limited number of nutrients, usually only one. (15)

Mold—Any of a group of parasitic or other organisms living on decaying matter; fungi. (14)

Molecule—The smallest quantity into which a substance may be divided without loss of its characteristics. (3)

Monoamine oxidase inhibitor (MAO inhibitor)—A class of antidepressant drugs that may have critical interactions with foods. (16)

Monoglyceride—One fatty acid joined to a glycerol molecule. (4)

Monosaccharide—A simple sugar composed of one unit of $C_6H_{12}O_6$; examples include glucose, fructose, and galactose. (3)

Monounsaturated fat—A lipid in which the majority of fatty acids contain one carbon-to-carbon double bond. (4)

Morbidity—The state of being diseased; number of cases of disease in relation to population. (15)

Mortality—The death rate; number of deaths per unit of population. (13)

Motility—Power to move spontaneously. (13)

Mucosal effect—Drug-induced changes within the intestine that affect the absorption of drugs or nutrients by damaging the tissues. (16)

Mucus—A thick fluid secreted by the mucous membranes and glands. (10)

Mucosa—A mucous membrane that lines body cavities. (10)

Muscular dystrophy—A disease characterized by wasting away of skeletal muscle with replacement of muscle cells by fat and connective tissue; most forms are genetic but one form is associated with a vitamin E deficiency. (7)

Mycotoxin—A substance produced by mold growing in food that can cause illness or death when ingested by humans or animals. (14)

Myelin sheath—Fatty covering surrounding the long appendages of some nerves; serves to increase the transmission speed of impulses. (7)

Myocardial infarction (MI)—Area of dead heart

muscle; usually the result of coronary occlusion. (19)

Myocardium—The heart muscle. (19)

Myoglobin—A protein located in muscle tissue that contains and stores oxygen. (8)

Myxedema—A condition that occurs in older children and adults, resulting from hypofunction of the thyroid gland characterized by a drying and thickening of the skin and slowing of physical and mental activity. (8)

Narcolepsy—A chronic condition consisting of recurrent attacks of drowsiness and sleep. (17)

Nasoduodenal tube (ND tube)—A tube inserted via the nose into the duodenum. (15)

Nasogastric tube (NG tube)—A tube inserted via the nose into the stomach. (15)

Nasojejunal tube (NJ tube)—A tube inserted via the nose into the jejunum. (15)

Neoplasm—A new and abnormal formation of tissue (tumor) that grows at the expense of the healthy organism. (22)

Nephritis—General term for inflammation of the kidneys. (20)

Nephron—The structural and functional unit of the kidney. (20)

Nephropathy—A kidney disease characterized by inflammation and degenerative lesions. (18)

Nephrosclerosis—A hardening of the renal arteries; may be caused by arteriosclerosis of the kidney arteries. (20)

Nephrotic syndrome—The end result of a variety of diseases that cause the abnormal passage of plasma proteins into the urine. (20)

Neuropathy—Any disease of the nerves. (18)

Niacin—A B-vitamin that functions as a coenzyme in the production of energy from glucose; obtained from meat or produced from the amino acid tryptophan, present in milk, eggs, and meat; also called nicotinic acid. (7)

Niacin equivalent (NE)—Measure of niacin activity; equal to 1 milligram of preformed niacin or 60 milligrams of tryptophan. (7)

Night blindness—Vision that is slow to adapt to dim light; caused by vitamin A deficiency or hereditary factors, or, in the elderly, by poor circulation. (7)

Nitrogen—Colorless, odorless, tasteless gas forming about 80 percent of the earth's air. (5)

Nitrogen balance—The difference between the amount of nitrogen ingested and that excreted each day; when intake is greater, a positive balance exists; when intake is less, a negative balance exists. (5)

Nitrogen-fixing bacteria—Organisms that absorb nitrogen from the air, which, upon the death of the bacteria, is released for legume plants to use in the anabolism of protein. (5)

Nomogram—A chart that shows a relationship between numerical values. (17)

Nonessential—In nutrition, refers to a chemical substance or nutrient the body can manufacture. (1)

Nonessential amino acid—Any amino acid that can be synthesized by the body in sufficient quantities. (5)

Nonheme iron—Iron that is not bound to hemoglobin or myoglobin; all the iron in plant sources. (8)

Noninsulin-dependent diabetes mellitus (NIDDM)—Type II diabetes; insulin resistance commonly occurs; although some persons with this disorder take insulin, it is not necessary for their long-term survival. (18, 19)

North American Nursing Diagnosis Association—An organization of nurses, established in 1973, that fosters the use of standard terminology in describing client problems. (2)

Nursing action (intervention)—Specific care to be administered, including physical and psychological care, teaching, counseling, and referring. (2)

Nursing-bottle syndrome—A condition in which an infant has many dental caries caused by drinking milk or other sweet liquids during sleep. (3)

Nursing diagnosis—Statement of a client's nursing problem that the nurse is licensed to treat. (2)

Nursing process—Systematic and orderly method of delivering nursing care, composed of five steps: assessment, nursing diagnosis, planning, implementation, and evaluation. (2)

Nutrient—Chemical substance supplied by food that the body needs for growth, maintenance, and/or repair. (1)

Nutrient density—The concentration of nutrients in a given volume of food compared with the food's kilocalorie content. (6)

Nutrition—The science of food and its relationship to living beings. (1)

Nutrition support service—A team service for clients on enteral and parenteral feedings that assesses, monitors, and counsels these clients. (15)

Nutritional assessment—The evaluation of a client's nutritional status based on a physical examination, anthropometric measurements, laboratory data, and food intake information. (2)

Nutritional status—Refers to the condition of the body as it relates to the intake and use of nutrients. (1)

Obese—Body fat content greater than 24 percent in males or 33 percent in females. (17)

Obesity—Excessive amount of fat on the body; obesity for women is a fat content greater than 33 percent; obesity for men is a fat content greater than 24 percent. (17)

Objective data—Findings verifiable by another through physical assessment or diagnostic tests, also termed signs. (2)

Obligatory excretion—Minimum amount of urine production necessary to keep waste products in solution, amounting to 400 to 600 milliliters per day. (9)

Oliguria—A decreased output of urine. (20)

Odds ratio—A measure of disease occurrence in epidemiological, case-control studies; the odds in favor of a particular event occurring in an exposed group are divided by the odds in favor of the disease occurring in an unexposed group. If the condition under study is rare, the odds ratio is a close approximation to the relative risk. (19)

Oncogene—A potentially cancer-inducing gene; when altered by radiation, chemicals, or viruses, may cause cell to become malignant. (22)

Opportunistic infection—Infection caused by normally nonpathogenic organisms in a host with decreased resistance. (24)

Opsin—A protein that combines with vitamin A to form rhodopsin, a chemical in the retina necessary for vision. (7)

Optic nerve—The second cranial nerve, which transmits impulses for the sense of sight. (7)

Oral cavity—The cavity in the skull bounded by the mouth, palate, cheeks, and tongue. (10)

Organ—Somewhat independent body part having specific functions. Examples: stomach, liver. (10)

Orthostatic hypotension—A drop in blood pressure producing dizziness, fainting, or blurred vision when arising from a lying or sitting position or when standing motionless in a fixed position. (9)

Osmolality—Measure of osmotic pressure exerted by the number of dissolved particles per weight of liquid; clinically usually reported as mOsm/Kg. (9)

Osmolarity—Measure of osmotic pressure exerted by the number of dissolved particles per volume of liquid; clinically usually reported as mOsm/L. (9)

Osmosis—The movement of water across a semipermeable cell membrane from an area with fewer particles to one with more particles. (9)

Osmotic pressure—The pressure that develops when a concentrated solution is separated from a less concentrated solution by a semipermeable membrane; only water crosses the membrane. (9)

Osteoblasts—Bone cells that build bone. (8)

Osteoclasts—Bone cells that break down bone. (8)

Osteodystrophy—Defective bone formation. (20)

Osteomalacia—Adult form of rickets. (7)

Osteoporosis—A loss of bone mass. (8)

Ostomy—A surgically formed opening to permit passage of urine or bowel contents to the outside. (15)

Overnutrition—The result of an excess of one or more nutrients in the diet. (1)

Overweight—Ten to 20 percent above healthy body weight; 110 to 120 percent healthy body weight. (17)

Ovum—The egg cell that, after fertilization by a sperm cell, develops into a new individual. (11)

Oxalates—Salts of oxalic acid found in some plant foods; bind with the calcium in the plant, making it unavailable to the body. (8)

Oxidation—The process in which a substance is combined with oxygen. (7, 10)

Oxytocin—A hormone produced by the posterior pituitary gland in the brain; effects are uterine contractions and release of milk. (11)

Pancreas—An abdominal gland that secretes enzymes important in the digestion of carbohydrates, fats, and proteins; also secretes the hormones insulin and glucagon. (10, 21)

Pancreatic lipase—An enzyme produced by the pancreas; used in fat digestion. (10)

Pancreatitis—Inflammation of the pancreas. (21, 24)

Pantothenic acid—A B-complex vitamin found in almost all foods; deficiencies from lack of food have not been documented. (7)

Paralytic ileus—A temporary cessation of peristalsis that causes an intestinal obstruction. (23)

Paralytic shellfish poisoning—Disease caused by the consumption of poisonous clams, oysters, mussels, or scallops. (14)

Parasite—An organism that lives within, upon, or at the expense of a living host. (14)

Parathyroid hormone (PTH)—Hormone secreted by the parathyroid glands; regulates calcium and phosphorus metabolism in the body. (7, 8, 20)

Parenteral feeding—A feeding administered by any route other than the gastrointestinal tract. (15)

Parotid glands—One of the salivary glands of the mouth, located just below and in front of the ears; the mumps virus causes infectious parotitis. (10)

Pectin—Purified carbohydrate obtained from peel

of citrus fruits or apple pulp; gels when cooked at correct pH; used in jelly and jam. (22)

Pellagra—Deficiency disease due to lack of niacin and tryptophan; characterized by the so-called three Ds: dermatitis, diarrhea, and dementia. (7)

Pepsin—An enzyme secreted in the stomach that begins protein digestion. (10)

Pepsinogen—The antecedent of pepsin; activated by hydrochloric acid, a component of gastric juice. (10)

Peptidases—Enzymes that assist in the digestion of protein by reducing the smaller molecules to single amino acids. (10)

Peptide bond—Chemical bond that links two amino acids in a protein molecule. (5, 10)

Perforated ulcer—Condition in which an ulcer penetrates completely through the stomach or intestinal wall, spilling the organ's contents into the peritoneal cavity. (21)

Periodontal disease—Any disorder of the supporting structures of the teeth. (13)

Peripheral parenteral nutrition (PPN)—An intravenous feeding via a vein away from the center of the body. (15)

Peristalsis—A wave-like movement that propels food along the alimentary canal. (10, 23)

Peritoneal dialysis—Method of removing waste products from the blood by injecting the flushing solution into a client's abdomen and using the client's peritoneum as the semipermeable membrane. (20)

Peritoneum—The membrane that covers the internal abdominal organs and lines the abdominal cavity. (20)

Peritonitis—Inflammation of the peritoneal cavity. (21)

Pernicious anemia—Inadequate red blood cell formation due to lack of intrinsic factor from the stomach, which is required for the absorption of vitamin B_{12}; leads to neural deterioration. (7)

Pesticides—A chemical used to kill insects or rodents. (14)

Petechiae—Pinpoint, flat, round, red lesions caused by intradermal or submucosal hemorrhage. (7)

pH—A scale representing the relative acidity or alkalinity of a solution; a value of 7 is neutral, less than 7 is acidic and greater than 7 is alkaline. (9)

Pharynx—The muscular passage between the oral cavity and the esophagus. (10)

Phenylalanine—Essential amino acid, which is indigestible if a person lacks a particular enzyme. Accumulation of phenylalanine in the blood can lead to mental retardation. (5)

Phenylketonuria (PKU)—Hereditary disease caused by the body's failure to convert phenylalanine to tyrosine because of a defective enzyme. (5)

Phospholipid—An organic compound in the lipid group composed of one glycerol, two fatty acids, and one phosphate molecule; examples include lecithin and myelin. (8)

Photosynthesis—Process by which plants containing chlorophyll are able to manufacture carbohydrates from carbon dioxide and water using the sun's energy. (3)

Phylloquinone—Vitamin K_1, found in foods. (7)

Phytic acid—A substance found in grains that forms an insoluble complex with calcium; phytates. (8)

Phytochemicals—Nonnutritive food components that provide medical or health benefits including the prevention or treatment of a disease. (1)

Pica—The craving to eat nonfood substances such as clay and starch. (11)

Placenta—The organ in the uterus through which the unborn child exchanges carbon dioxide for oxygen and wastes for nourishment; lay term is afterbirth. (11)

Plasma—The liquid portion of the blood including the clotting elements. (9)

Plumbism—Lead poisoning. (8)

Pneumocystis pneumonia—A type of lung infection frequently seen in AIDS patients; caused by the organism *Pneumocystis carinii*. (24)

Polydipsia—Excessive thirst. (18)

Polymer—A natural or synthetic substance formed by combining two or more molecules of the same substance. (3)

Polypeptide—A chain of amino acids linked by peptide bonds that form proteins. (5, 10)

Polyphagia—Excessive appetite. (18)

Polysaccharide—Complex carbohydrates composed of many units of $C_6H_{12}O_6$ joined together; examples important in nutrition include starch, glycogen, and fiber. (3)

Polyunsaturated fat—A fat in which the majority of fatty acids contain more than one carbon-to-carbon double bond; intake is associated with a decreased risk of heart disease. (4)

Polyuria—Excessive urination. (18)

Positive feedback cycle—Situation in which a condition provokes a response that worsens the condition. Example: low blood pressure due to a failing heart stimulates the kidney to save sodium and water. (19)

Precursor—A substance from which another substance is derived. (7)

Preeclampsia—Hypertension, edema, and proteinuria, appearing after the 20th week of pregnancy. (11)

Preformed vitamin—A vitamin already in a complete state in ingested foods, as opposed to a provitamin, which requires conversion in the body to be in a complete state. (7)

Pregnancy-induced hypertension (PIH)—A potentially life-threatening disorder that may develop after the 20th week of pregnancy; includes preeclampsia and eclampsia. (11)

Pressure ulcer—Tissue breakdown from external force impairing circulation. (15)

Prevalence—The likelihood of an occurrence taking place within a population group. (17)

Primary malnutrition—A nutrient deficiency due to poor food choices or a lack of nutritious food to eat. (15)

Principle of complementarity—Combining incomplete-protein foods so that each supplies the amino acids lacking in the other. (5)

Prion—A proteinaceous infectious agent, extremely difficult to destroy; resistant to heat, pressure cooking, ultraviolet light, irradiation, bleach, formaldehyde, and weak acids; even autoclaving at 135° for 18 minutes does not eliminate infectivity. (14)

Prognosis—Probable outcome of an illness based on client's condition and natural course of the disease. (24)

Promotion—The second step in a cell turning cancerous, through the action of environmental substances on the altered, initiated gene. (22)

Prostaglandins—Long-chain, unsaturated fatty acids mostly synthesized in the body from arachidonic acid; have hormone-like effects. (4)

Protein—Nutrient necessary for building body tissue; composed of carbon, hydrogen, oxygen, and nitrogen (and sometimes with sulfur, phosphorus, or iron); amino acids represent the basic structure of proteins. (5)

Protein binding sites—Various sites in the body tissues to which drugs may become attached, rendering the drug temporarily inactive. (16)

Proteinuria—Protein in the urine. (20)

Protein-calorie malnutrition (PCM)—Condition in which the person's diet lacks both protein and kilocalories. (5)

Prothrombin—A protein essential to the blood-clotting process; manufactured by the liver using vitamin K. (7)

Protocol—A description of steps to be followed when performing a procedure or providing care for a particular condition. (15)

Provitamin—Inactive substance that the body converts to an active vitamin. (7)

Provitamin A—Carotene. (7)

Proximal convoluted tubule—The first segment of the renal tubule. (20)

Psychology—The science of mental processes and their effects upon behavior. (17)

Psychosis—Severe mental disturbance with personality derangement and loss of contact with reality. (7)

Psychosocial development—The maturing of an individual in relationships with others and within himself or herself. (12)

Ptyalin—A salivary enzyme that breaks down starch and glycogen to maltose and a small amount of glucose; also known as salivary amylase. (10)

Puberty—The period of life at which the physical ability to reproduce is attained. (12)

Pulmonary—Concerning or involving the lungs. (23)

Pulmonary edema—The accumulation of fluid in the lungs. (19)

Pulse pressure—The difference between systolic and diastolic blood pressure; normally 30 to 40 mmHg; narrows in fluid volume deficit and widens in fluid volume excess. (9)

Purging—The intentional clearing of food out of the human body by vomiting, and/or using enemas, laxatives, and/or diuretics. (17)

Purines—One of the end products of the digestion of some nitrogen-containing compounds. (20)

Pyelonephritis—An inflammation of the central portion of the kidney. (20)

Pyloric sphincter—The sphincter muscle guarding the opening between the stomach and small intestine. (10)

Pyridoxine—Coenzyme in the synthesis and catabolism of amino acids; also called vitamin B_6. (7)

Pyruvate—An intermediate in the metabolism of energy nutrients. (10)

Quality assurance—A planned and systematic program for evaluating the quality and appropriateness of services rendered. (15)

Radiologist—Physician with special training in diagnostic imaging and radiation treatments. (14)

Rancid—Term used to describe a deteriorated fat that has an offensive odor and taste caused by the partial breakdown of its structure. (4)

Rate—The speed or frequency of an event per unit of time. (17)

Rationale—Reason certain actions are likely to achieve a desired outcome; in nursing, ideally based on research indicating a nursing action was effective in similar circumstances. (2)

Rebound scurvy—Vitamin C deficiency produced in a person following cessation of megadosing due to a habitually lessened rate of absorption. (7)

Recessive trait—One that requires two recessive genes for the trait, one from each parent, for the trait to be expressed (to be manifested) in the individual. (21)

Recommended Dietary Allowance(s)—RDA(s); the levels of essential nutrients that, on the basis of scientific knowledge, are judged by the Food and Nutrition Board of the National Research Council to be adequate to meet the known nutrient needs of practically all healthy persons. (2)

Rectum—The lower part of the large intestine. (10)

Refeeding syndrome—A series of metabolic reactions seen in some malnourished clients when refed; characterized by congestive heart failure and respiratory failure. (23)

Regurgitate—To cause to flow backward, as with an infant "spitting up." (15)

Relative risk—In epidemiological studies, the ratio of the frequency of a certain disorder in groups exposed and groups not exposed to a particular hereditary or environmental factor. (19)

Renal—Pertaining to the kidney. (9, 20)

Renal corpuscle—Refers collectively to both Bowman's capsule and the glomerulus. (20)

Renal exchange lists—A specialized type of exchange list for clients with kidney disease who require restriction of one or more of the following: protein, sodium, phosphorus, and potassium. (20)

Renal osteodystrophy—Defective bone development caused by phosphorus retention, a low or normal serum calcium level, and increased parathyroid activity. (20)

Renal pelvis—A structure inside the kidney that receives urine from the collecting tubules. (20)

Renal threshold—The blood glucose level at which glucose begins to spill into the urine. (18)

Renal tubule—The second major portion of the nephron; appears rope-like. (20)

Renin—An enzyme produced by the kidney that catalyzes the conversion of angiotensinogen to angiotensin I. (9)

Rennin—An enzyme that coagulates milk. (10)

Residue—Trace amount of any substance in a product at the time of sale; substance remaining in the bowel after absorption. (14, 21)

Respiration—The exchange of oxygen and carbon dioxide between a living organism and the environment. (23)

Respirator—A machine used to assist respiration. (23)

Respiratory acidosis—Blood pH less than 7.35 caused by pulmonary disease, characterized by a retention of carbon dioxide. (23)

Respiratory alkalosis—Blood pH greater than 7.45 caused by pulmonary disease, characterized by a loss of carbon dioxide. (23)

Resting energy expenditure (REE)—The amount of fuel the human body uses at rest for a specified period of time; often used interchangeably with basal metabolic rate (BMR). (6)

Retina—Inner lining of eyeball that contains light-sensitive nerve cells; corresponds to film in camera. (7)

Retinol—The chemical name for preformed vitamin A. (7)

Retinol equivalents (RE)—A measure of vitamin A activity that considers both preformed vitamin A (retinol) and its precursor (carotene); 1 RE equals 3.3 International Units from animal foods and 10 International Units from plant foods; 1 RE corresponds to 1 microgram of retinol. (7)

Retinopathy—Any disorder of the retina. (18)

Retrolental fibroplasia (RLF)—A disease of the vessels of the retina present in premature infants; often caused by exposure to high postnatal oxygen concentration. (12)

Rhodopsin—Light-sensitive protein in the retina that contains vitamin A; also called visual purple. (7)

Riboflavin—Coenzyme in the metabolism of protein; also called vitamin B_2. (7)

Ribonucleic acid (RNA)—A substance in the cell nucleus that controls protein synthesis in all living cells. (5)

Rickets—Disease caused by a deficiency of vitamin D that affects the young during the period of skeletal growth, resulting in bones that are abnormally shaped and weak. (7)

Rooting reflex—The infant's natural response to a stroke on its cheek, which turns the head toward that side to nurse. (12)

Rugae—Folds of mucosa of organs such as the stomach. (10)

Salivary amylase—An enzyme that initiates the breakdown of starch in the mouth. (10)

Salivary glands—The glands that secrete saliva into the mouth. (10)

Salmonella—A genus of bacteria responsible for many cases of foodborne illness. (14)

Salmonellosis—A bacterial infection manifested by

the sudden onset of headache, abdominal pain, diarrhea, nausea, and vomiting. Fever is almost always present. Contaminated food is the predominant method of transmission. (14)

Sarcoma—A malignant neoplasm that occurs in connective tissue such as muscle or bone. (22)

Satiety—The feeling of satisfaction after eating. (4, 10, 15)

Saturated fat—A fat in which the majority of fatty acids contain no carbon-to-carbon double bonds. (4)

Scurvy—Disease due to deficiency of vitamin C marked by bleeding problems and later, by bony skeleton changes. (7)

Seasonal variation—Refers to differences during spring, summer, fall, and winter. (1)

Sebaceous gland—Oil-secreting gland of the skin; most sebaceous glands have a hair follicle associated with them. (4)

Secondary diabetes—A World Health Organization (WHO) classification for diabetes when the hyperglycemia occurs as a result of a second disorder. (18)

Secondary hypertension—High blood pressure that develops as the result of another condition. (19)

Secondary malnutrition—A nutrient deficiency due to improper absorption and distribution of nutrients. (15)

Secretin—A hormone that stimulates the production of bile by the liver and the secretion of sodium bicarbonate juice by the pancreas. (10)

Self-monitoring of blood glucose (SMBG)—A procedure that persons with diabetes follow to test their own blood glucose levels. (18)

Sensible water loss—Visible water loss through perspiration, urine, and feces. (9)

Sensitivity—A characteristic of a diagnostic test; the proportion of people correctly identified to have the condition in question. (21)

Sepsis—A condition in which disease-producing organisms are present in the blood. (23)

Serosa—A serous membrane that covers internal organs and lines body cavities. (6)

Serotonin—A body chemical that assists the transmission of nerve impulses; it produces constriction of blood vessels and is thought to be related to sleep. (7, 17)

Serum—The liquid portion of the blood minus the clotting elements. (9)

Severely obese—Greater than 100 percent overweight; also expressed as greater than 201 percent healthy body weight. (17)

Shelf life—The duration of time a product can remain in storage without deterioration. (4)

Shigella—Organisms causing intestinal disease; spread by fecal-oral transmission from a client or carrier via direct contact or indirectly by contaminated food. (14)

Signs—See objective data. (2)

Simple carbohydrate—Composed of one or two units of $C_6H_{12}O_6$; includes the monosaccharides (glucose, fructose, and galactose) and the disaccharides (sucrose, lactose, and maltose). (3)

Simple fat—Lipids that consist of fatty acids or a simple filler such as a hydroxyl (OH) molecule joined to glycerol. (4)

Small intestine—The part of the alimentary canal between the stomach and the large intestine, where most absorption of nutrients occurs. (10)

Solubility—The ability of one substance to dissolve into another in solution. (3)

Soluble—Able to be dissolved. (3)

Solute—The substance that is dissolved in a solvent. (9)

Solvent—A liquid holding another substance in solution. (9)

Somatostatin—A hormone produced by the delta cells of the islets of Langerhans that inhibits both the release of insulin and the production of glucagon. (18)

Specific gravity—The weight of a substance compared to an equal volume of a standard substance; usual standard for liquids is water, its specific gravity set at 1.000. (16)

Specificity—A characteristic of a diagnostic test; the proportion of people correctly identified as not having the condition in question. (21)

Sphincter—A circular band of muscles that constricts a passage. (10)

Spore—A form assumed by some bacteria that is highly resistant to heat, drying, and chemicals. (12)

Sprue—Chronic form of malabsorption syndrome affecting the small intestine; subcategories: tropical and nontropical. (10, 21)

Staphylococcus aureus—One of the most common species bacteria, which produces a poisonous toxin. The main reservoir is nose and throat discharge. Food can act as a vehicle for transmission, so proper hand washing is an essential means of control. (14)

Starches—Polysaccharides; many units of $C_6H_{12}O_6$ joined together; complex carbohydrates. (3)

Steatorrhea—The presence of greater than normal amounts of fat in the stool, producing foul-smelling, bulky excrement. (10, 21)

Sterol—Substance related to fats and belonging to the lipoids; for example, cholesterol. (4)

Stimulus control—The identification of cues that precede a behavior and rearranging daily activities to avoid such cues. (17)

Stoma—A surgically created opening in the abdominal wall. (21)

Stomach—The portion of the alimentary canal between the esophagus and small intestine. (10)

Stomatitis—An inflammation of the mouth. (16, 20)

Stress—The total biologic reaction to a stimulus, whether physical, mental, or emotional, that threatens to disturb the body's equilibrium. (23)

Stress factor—A number used to predict how much a client's kilocalorie need has increased as a result of a disease state. (23)

Subcutaneously—Beneath the skin. (18)

Subjective data—Experiences the client reports, also termed symptoms. (2)

Submucosa—Structural layer of the alimentary canal below the mucosa; contains tissues and blood vessels. (10)

Sucrase—An enzyme in the intestinal mucosa that splits sucrose into glucose and fructose. (10)

Sucrose—A disaccharide; one unit of glucose and one unit of fructose joined together; ordinary white table sugar. (3)

Superior vena cava—One of the largest diameter veins in the human body; used to deliver total parenteral nutrition. (15)

Symptoms—See subjective data. (2)

System—An organized grouping of related structures or parts. (10)

Systemic circulation—Refers to the blood flow from the left part of the heart through the aorta and all branches (arteries) to the capillaries of the tissues. Systemic circulation also includes the blood's return to the heart through the veins and lymph vessels. (22)

Systolic pressure—Pressure exerted against the arteries when the heart contracts; the upper number of the blood pressure reading. (9, 19)

T-lymphocytes (T-cells)—White blood cells that recognize and fight foreign cells such as cancer; thymic lymphocytes. (22)

Tapeworm—A parasitic intestinal worm that is acquired by humans through the ingestion of raw seafood or undercooked beef and pork. (14)

Target heart rate—Seventy percent of maximum heart rate (number of heartbeats per minute); a person's target heart rate can be objectively determined by a stress test. Individuals can estimate their target heart rate by subtracting their age from 220 and multiplying the difference by 70 percent. A person's target heart rate is the rate at which the pulse should be maintained for at least 20 minutes during aerobic exercise. (6)

Teratogenic—Capable of causing abnormal development of the embryo; results in a malformed fetus. (11)

Term infant—Any newborn, regardless of birth weight, born between weeks 38 and 42 of gestation inclusive. (12)

Tetany—Muscle contractions, especially of the wrists and ankles, resulting from a disorder characterized by low levels of ionized calcium in the blood; causes include parathyroid deficiency, vitamin D deficiency, and alkalosis. (7)

Thermic effect of exercise (TEE)—The number of kilocalories used above resting energy expenditure as a result of physical activity. (6)

Thermic effect of foods (diet-induced thermogenesis, specific-dynamic action)—The energy cost to extract and utilize the kilocalories and nutrients in foods; the heat produced after eating a meal. (6)

Thiamin—Coenzyme in the metabolism of carbohydrates and fats; vitamin B_1. (7)

Thiaminase—An enzyme in raw fish that destroys thiamin. (7)

Thoracic—Pertaining to the chest, or thorax. (10)

Thoracic duct—Major lymphatic vessel draining all except the right upper half of the body; empties into left internal jugular and left subclavian veins. (9)

Threonine—Essential amino acid often lacking in grains. (5)

Thrombus—A blood clot that obstructs a blood vessel; obstruction of a vessel of the brain or heart are among the most serious effects. (19)

Thrush—An infection caused by the organism *Candida albicans;* characterized by the formation of white patches and ulcers in the mouth and throat. (24)

Thymus—Gland in the chest, above and in front of the heart, which contributes to the immune response, including the maturation of T-lymphocytes. (22)

Thyroid stimulating hormone (TSH)—A hormone secreted by the pituitary gland that stimulates the thyroid gland to secrete thyroxine and triiodothyronine; thyrotropin. (8)

Thyrotropin releasing factor (TRF)—Stimulates the secretion of thyroid-stimulating hormone; produced in the hypothalamus. (8)

Thyroxine (T_4)—A hormone secreted by the thyroid gland; increases the rate of metabolism and energy production. (8)

Tissue—A group or collection of similar cells and their similar intercellular substance that acts together in the performance of a particular function. (11)

Tolerance level—The highest dose at which a residue causes no ill effects in laboratory animals. (14)

Total parenteral nutrition (TPN)—An intravenous feeding that provides all nutrients known to be required. (15)

Traction—The process of using weights to draw a part of the body into alignment. (15)

Transcellular fluid—Located in body cavities and spaces; constantly being secreted and absorbed; examples: cerebrospinal fluid, pericardial fluid, pleural fluid. (9)

Transferrin—Protein in the blood that binds and transports iron. (8)

Trauma—A physical injury or wound caused by an external force; an emotional or psychological shock that usually results in disordered behavior. (23)

Triceps skinfold—Measure of skin and subcutaneous tissue over the triceps muscle in the upper arm; used in body fat assessment. (2)

Trichinella spiralis—A worm-like parasite that becomes embedded in the muscle tissue of pork. (14)

Trichinosis—The infestation of *Trichinella spiralis;* a parasitic roundworm, transmitted by eating raw or insufficiently cooked pork. (14)

Triglyceride—Three fatty acids joined to a glycerol molecule. (4)

Triiodothyronine (T$_3$)—A hormone secreted by the thyroid gland that increases the rate of metabolism and energy production. (8)

Trousseau's sign—Spasms of the forearm and hand upon inflation of the blood pressure cuff; sign of tetany or lack of ionized calcium in the blood. (8)

Trust—First stage of Erikson's theory of psychosocial development, in which the infant learns to rely on those caring for it. (12)

Trypsin—An enzyme formed in the intestine that assists in protein digestion. (10)

Tryptophan—An essential amino acid, often lacking in legumes. (7)

Tubular reabsorption—The movement of fluid back into the blood from the renal tubule. (18)

Tubule—A small tube or canal. (20)

Turgor—Resilience of skin; when pinched quickly returns to original shape in well-hydrated young person; test for fluid volume deficit that is not reliable for elderly clients. (9)

Tyramine—A monoamine present in various foods that will provoke a hypertensive crisis in persons taking monoamine oxidase (MAO) inhibitors. (16)

Ulcer—An open sore or lesion of the skin or mucous membrane. (21)

Ulcerative colitis—Inflammatory disease of the large intestine that usually begins in the rectum and spreads upward in a continuous pattern. (21)

Uncomplicated starvation—A food deprivation without an underlying stress state. (23)

Undernutrition—The state that results from a deficiency of one or more nutrients. (1)

Underwater weighing—Most accurate measure of body fatness. (2)

Universal precautions—A list of procedures developed by the Centers for Disease Control for when blood and certain other body fluids should be considered contaminated and treated as such. (24)

Unsaturated fat—A fat in which the majority of fatty acids contain one or more carbon-to-carbon double bonds. (9)

Urea—The chief nitrogenous constituent of urine; the final product, along with CO_2, of protein metabolism. (10)

Uremia—A toxic condition produced by the retention of nitrogen-containing substances normally excreted by the kidneys. (20)

Ureter—The tube that carries urine from the kidney to the bladder. (20)

Urinary calculus—A kidney stone, or deposit of mineral salts. (20)

Urinary tract infection (UTI)—The condition in which disease-producing microorganisms invade a client's bladder, ureter, or urethra. (20)

USDA Dietary Guidelines—Seven guidelines for health promotion issued by the US Departments of Agriculture and Health and Human Services; revised in 1995. (2)

Usual food intake—A description of what a person habitually eats. (2)

Vaginitis—Inflammation of the vagina, most often caused by an infectious agent. (18)

Ventilation—Process by which gases are moved into and out of the lungs; two aspects of ventilation are inhalation and exhalation. (23)

Very low-calorie diet (VLCD)—Diet that contains less than 800 kilocalories per day. (17)

Very low-density lipoprotein (VLDL)—A plasma protein containing mostly triglycerides with small amounts of cholesterol, phospholipid, and protein; transports triglycerides from the liver to tissues. (19)

Villi—Multiple minute projections on the surface of the folds of the small intestine that absorb fluid and nutrients; plural of villus. (10)

Virus—Very small noncellular parasite that is entirely dependent on the nutrients inside host cells for its metabolic and reproductive needs. (14)

Visible fat—Dietary fat that can be easily seen, such as the fat on meat or in oil. (4)

Vitamin—Organic substance needed by the body in very small amounts; yields no energy and does not become part of the body's structure. (7)

Waist-to-Hip Ratio (WHR)—Waist measurement divided by hip measurement; if >0.85 in women or > 1.0 in men, indicates increased risk of health problems related to obesity. (2)

Warfarin sodium—Anticoagulant that interferes with the liver's synthesis of vitamin K-dependent clotting factors II, VII, IX, and X. (7)

Weight cycling—The repeated gain and loss of body weight. (17)

Wernicke-Korsakoff syndrome—A disorder of the central nervous system seen in chronic alcoholism and resulting thiamin depletion; signs and symptoms include motor, sensory, and memory deficits. (7, 21)

Wernicke's encephalopathy—Inflammatory, hemorrhagic, degenerative lesions in several areas of the brain resulting in double vision, involuntary eye movements, lack of muscle cordination, and mental deficits; caused by thiamin deficiency often in chronic alcoholism but also in gastrointestinal tract disease and hyperemesis gravidarum. (7)

Wilson's disease—Rare genetic defect of copper metabolism. (8, 16)

Xerophthalmia—Drying and thickening of the epithelial tissues of the eye; can be caused by vitamin A deficiency. (7)

Xerostomia—Dry mouth caused by decreased salivary secretions. (19)

Yo-yo effect—The repeated loss and gain of body weight. (17)

Index